THE OXFORD

Essential Guide to
Egyptian Mythology

THE OXFORD

Essential Guide to Egyptian Mythology

EDITED BY
Donald B. Redford

B

BERKLEY BOOKS, NEW YORK

THE OXFORD ESSENTIAL GUIDE TO EGYPTIAN MYTHOLOGY

A Berkley Book / published by arrangement with
Oxford University Press, Inc.

PRINTING HISTORY
Berkley edition / July 2003

Copyright © 2002 by Oxford University Press.
Published originally in 2002 under the title
The Ancient Gods Speak: A Guide to Egyptian Religion.
Oxford is a registered trademark of Oxford University Press, Inc.
All rights reserved.
This book may not be reproduced in whole or in part, by mimeograph or by any other means, without permission. The scanning, uploading, and distribution of this book via the Internet or via any other means without the permission of the publisher is illegal and punishable by law. Please purchase only authorized electronic editions, and do not participate in or encourage electronic piracy of copyrighted materials. Your support of the author's rights is appreciated.
For information address: Oxford University Press, Inc.,
198 Madison Avenue, New York, New York 10016.

ISBN: 0-425-19096-X

BERKLEY®
Berkley Books are published by
The Berkley Publishing Group, a division of Penguin Group (USA) Inc.,
375 Hudson Street, New York, New York 10014.
BERKLEY and the "B" design are trademarks
belonging to Penguin Group (USA) Inc.

PRINTED IN THE UNITED STATES OF AMERICA

10 9 8 7 6 5 4 3 2 1

CONTENTS

INTRODUCTION

The ancient riverine communities which lived along the Nile in North-east Africa experienced their world as an unrelenting manifestation of power, often creative, sometimes destructive, but always regular and predictable. Annually in the spring the melting snows in the Abyssinian highlands caused the Nile to flood and inundate the flood-plain along the lower courses of the river during the summer and early fall; and thereafter the falling waters left behind fen, marsh, and meadow teeming with life, a source of food both abundant and immediately available. During the autumn and spring the river was at its lowest, and the desert seemed to encroach upon the arable land. The two in fact seemed always to be in a "balanced tension" which was never resolved, a conflict between "Black Land" (the Nile Valley) and the "Red Land" (the desert). The former stood for life, regeneration and rectitude; the latter for death, culmination, and malevolence. The desert never represented "chaos," if by that we mean something disorderly, capricious, and unpredictable: the desert shows a very orderly configuration and takes the same, predictable toll on life at all times. It is generally "anti-life," but when that quality is directed towards sealing off the Nile Valley and Delta from interference from outside, either from demographic shifts or outright invasion, the desert functions as a reliable barrier.

Within this charmed world the Ancient Egyptian confronted the power in his environment largely in a positive experience. He knew little about it, and through most of the life of the long-lived Egyptian culture his investigation of the divine took the form of a never-ending voyage of discovery. The elements of nature seemed all to work for the good of the human community: the rich, fertile earth, the fructifying waters of the Nile, the air with its life-giving breezes and the fiery light of the sun.

Permanent and beneficent as elemental power appeared, it struck the Egyptian as multifarious and varied. The universe of power was conceptualized as a pleroma of infinite number, never as a monad (a concept which later finds a place in theological speculation and ethics). Power appeared everywhere under an infinity of guises and in constantly changing shape. The problem was to identify power, locate it, define it and learn how to placate, reduce, or thwart it.

Despite its infinity of forms, deity manifested itself essentially in a parochial context. A power had shown itself primordially in a specific spot within a community, and that locale remained for all time "sacred space." The local power, or *numen*, when it appeared was by definition in the Egyptian perception a strange but awe-inspiring apparition, *nater, in the native tongue, a term regularly translated as "god." In its parochial setting this power was often experienced as, or identified with, one of the very elements of the landscape, either animate or inanimate: the local god (or goddess) had inexplicably shown him or herself in the avatar of, or associated with, a bull, cow, lion, reptile, snake, bird, fish, insect, stick, or stone. Historically the relationship varied in nature and intensity: sometimes the deity *was* a single member of the species, chosen because of the supposed in-dwelling *numen* of the god; at other times the association loosened to the point of mere emblematic representation.

While the local or "town" god remained for all time an irreducible foundation to the Ancient Egyptian concept of deity, the political experience of Egyptian history caused an immense and universal superstructure to arise on that simple base. Shortly before 3000 B.C. Egypt experienced a quantum leap in the socio-political sphere from a simple, locally autonomous agricultural community to a highly complex, centralized state. The development was *de novo*: no one had a model for it. But now a new power had manifested itself in the form of a human, a paramount chief in process of graduation to something for which Egypt had no name, a *king*. He was great and perfect, and so the Egyptians called him the "Great God," and the "Perfect God"; he embodied and reconciled the antithetic forces, life and death, and so he was identified as "Horus," the falcon, lord of the air and the arable land, and "Seth," the misshapen pig(?) representative of the desert. A whole array of representations was created around the figure of the king, actualizing the context of his new power, but not tied to any local setting : the palace (Nephthys), the throne (Isis), the royal mother (Hathor). Side by side with these the

new royal authority co-opted local deities to represent the numinous aura within which the king moved: the jackal (Wepwawet), the falcon (Horus), the bull (Kamutef). His universal authority promoted the sun (Ra) in all its forms, and his close association with life-in-death transformed him at death into the archetypal ancestor (Osiris).

Power cannot be ignored: one must come to terms with it. The strange, awful *numen* within the community demands recognition and submission. What takes shape is a system of practices, modelled on hospitality and service extended to authority in general, in fact a cult centered upon a grand domicile, the "god's house (or mansion)," i.e. the shrine or temple. It is in the interface between cult and its divine recipient that the latter becomes intensely anthropo- or theriomorphic. For god is a real, tangible presence here: he must be fed, adorned, celebrated, entertained, and served in a variety of ways. He enjoys festivals, hymns, rowing on the river; and his festival calendar is full of performances of varied sorts. Someone has to provide the service, whether on a full- or part-time basis, and over time a priesthood takes shape, comprising "god's-servants," and "pure ones." By the halcyon days of the New Kingdom this cadre of divine servitor had become numerous and professional (full-time), and the temples large and grandiose structures given over to the spectacle and drama of cult performances and processions. A vast support staff underpinned the administration of these divine abodes, now grown into sizeable landed estates. Service was built around the offering of food and gifts to the god for which elaborate endowments of farms and orchards were required.

All this smacks of subservience, supplication, and appeasement in the presence of absolute power; but the Egyptians never conceived of the godhead in terms of absolutes. True, it was better to cultivate a good relationship with a spiritual presence of superior capabilities; but the gulf between man and god was not unbridgable. For dispersed throughout the cosmos were two informing elements which held the universe, including the gods, in a state of beneficial equilibrium. These were *ma'at*, "right-dealing, order, truth," and *ḥḳ3*, "magic." While human society was, in its best state, ordered by *ma'at*, the gods for their part were said to live on it. As for *ḥḳ3*, it encompassed a dynamic potential available to anyone who knew the appropriate incantation The gods, of course, excelled mankind in a quantitative sense in their possession of greatly superior magical knowledge; but it was not inconceivable that a "Faustian" magician of great aptitude might rival the very pantheon itself. The gods themselves could be threatened with the curtailment of temple service or the onset of cosmic calamity, if they did not do the bidding of him who controlled the magic spell. Magic of a prophylactic sort entered into every aspect of life to ward of baleful influences and ensure integrity and health.

If the Egyptian temple provided the focal point for *serving* the divine in the present, with all that this entails, Egyptian mythology provides a hermeneutic regarding the imponderables: origins, succession, structure, eschatology. While the temple confronts us with the sometimes crass reality of the godhead confined by the limiting fixity of form, the myth has the potential of liberating the creative imagination by fastening upon the metabolic aspect of deity. Nonetheless the results are mixed, ranging from the boorish to the sublime. As understood from the eighteenth century, the word "myth"—the history of the term is chequered to the point of virtual meaninglessness—may be defined as a meta-language of the community which puts ideology in narrative (less often iconic) form. In Egypt myths tend to cluster in thematic cycles. What might be termed the "Creation Cycle" fastens upon the Primordial State, the "First Occasion" as the Egyptians called it, and its components are the most ancient in terms of point and time of origin. Broadly speaking stories of creation may be grouped under three heads (although such a grouping would probably have been foreign to Egyptian thinking): 1. The primaeval ocean and mound, on which the creator effected his creation; 2. The separation of earth and heaven by air; and 3. The inauguration of order through the defeat of violent malevolence. The first type is best known in historic times through the version which became standard in the solar cult and in which the deity is in the form of a winged being. The action of the golden falcon sets in motion the elements of the cosmos through the dissemination of light. In the second type, which finds vague parallels in the cosmogonic speculation of early Mesopotamia, the life force latent in the cosmos lies within the undifferentiated whole, and is only activated through gender distinction pursuant to the insinuation of air: male earth impregnates female sky and a generational cycle informs the never-ending sequence of creation. The third type takes the form of a combat between life and anti-life, order and confusion, beneficence and malevolence: the hero successfully engages the monster and creates the cosmos from the shattered remnants of this evil one. Well known in several versions in Western Asia, this plot motif enjoyed only limited use in Egypt as a celestial or inauguration aetiology.

Other myths of origin are cult specific and smack of artifice. Plots which center upon the potter's wheel of Khnum, the loom of Neith, the tools of Ptah all betray composition within a complex society of technological accomplishment. Features of divine cults the origins of which are lost often find explanations in plays-on-words, on the basis of the assumption that homonyms reveal a common essence.

The largest corpus of myths, and the one enjoying the greatest degree of expansion and permutation, was that devoted to Osiris and his coterie of deities. The strands of this exceedingly complex web of tales defy disentanglement; and today one tends to lay stress on the *integrity* of the figure of Osiris, rather than its composite appearance. The origin of Osiris has often been sought in the concept of the "king-in-death," the archetype of the deceased royal ancestor, and insofar as the name itself is concerned, this may contain an element of truth. But Osiris also encompasses a variety of other hypostaseis, rendering this mysterious figure an approximation of an *Anthropos* extending over earth and heaven. He is life itself, and that which promotes life; he is life in death. He is the exonerated victim, the righteous one, demanding and guaranteeing rectitude and order, the prototype of the saved and blessed spirit. The story told of his murder, trial and acquittal and his translation into the Beyond could be expanded with each telling, depending upon the demands of the cult, and thus had application on many levels. It is at one and the same time the account of "regicide" which upsets the cosmos, of decay in death which ineffably creates life, the triumph over evil and the story of salvation for eternity.

Interwoven in historic times with the Osiris myth were other tales of originally independent origin. The eternal struggle of life vs. death, fertility vs. sterility, desert and sown, found expression in the unresolved struggle of Horus and Seth, now subsumed as the revenge story pursuant to Oriris's murder and the contest for the rule of Egypt. The myth of the bereaved goddess forced to flee with her infant son to the fastness of the Delta, pursued by the monster bent on destroying her seed, was likewise grafted into the Osiris story; and in one version included flight to Byblos on the coast of Lebanon. This plot motif conforms to a myth-type widely known in the Levantine cults devoted to Baal, Astarte and Yam.

It is doubtful if one should speak of a "solar cycle" of myths, as the narratives are patchy and of a disparate nature. Many center upon the destructive nature of the heat of the sun. The latter, represented as a lioness, the "suns-eye," descends to earth at Re's behest and proceeds to destroy rebellious mankind. Having wandered, appropriately, into hotter climes to the south, the lioness has to be sought and brought back to Egypt. The sun's daily progress in his barque on the celestial Nile and his passage through the Underworld at night, provide a scenario for a complex of myth-vignettes: the rising of the god from the "Island of Fire" in the east; the combat of the crew of the sun-boat with the monster Apophis who seeks to devour the sun; the passage through the hours of the night, each hour fraught with multiple dangers, and finally the union of Re and Osiris in the deepest and darkest part of the Underworld. This mystic union between the active power of the fiery sun and the latent power of life-in-death, re-invigorated the waning life force just at the moment when, in the middle of the night, it was at greatest risk, and propelled the sun upwards towards the dawn.

One of the most important mythic creations involving solar concepts was the Ennead, or cycle of Nine Gods. As a cosmogony the Ennead provided sequence to the elemental structure of the cosmos; as a theogony it fixed the kingship within thtat cosmos. Inert within the Primordial Sea (Nun) sat the All-inclusive (Atum), who contained within himself (the One) the infinity of Being. Creation assumes the form of projection: Atum exudes Air (Shu) and moisture (Tefnut), who in turn bring Earth (Geb) and Sky (Nut) into existence. From the level of the elements the pedigree proceeds to the plane of terrestrial authority: Earth and Sky produce the archetype of the royal ancestor (Osiris), the Throne (Isis), the Palace (Nephthys), and Antilife (Seth). The cosmic pedigree is now complete: the product of royal ancestor and throne, Horus, the living king, is immanent in the "Now," but ineffably incorporates within himself the universe. The mythology we have passed in review represents in its point of origin not one, but a variety of levels within Egyptian society and its body politic. If an aesthetic of mythology were to be applied, the raw ingredients of the myth of the Primaeval Ocean and Mound would be approached on the same plane as the Memphite Theology. But there is a world of difference in the intellect and creative imagination of the nameless savant who was responsible for the latter work.

For the constellation of treatises to which the Memphite Theology belongs, many known from fragments of passing allusions, takes us into the rarified heights of a remarkable speculation reminiscent of (and not unrelated to) the break-through represented by Pre-Socratic philosophy. Here hermeneutic thought centers upon two things: the identity of essence, and the problem of infinity and the monad. The Primordial Sea (Nun) with its latent power is hypostasized in "negative" concepts in the number four (totality): darkness, limitlessness, infinity and directionlessness. But the "negative" is balanced and held in tension by the "positive." The notion of the consciousness which conceptualizes and the sound which brings into being produces the metonyms of "heart" and "tongue" as the essence of the creative process, the godhead itself. And since the ability to think and articulate in speech is found throughout the animate world, god must reside within his creation: Being is in truth *his* Being, and no Being came into being before *he* came into Being.

The quest for a monadic substrate, manifest only in the infinite, draws on a model other than the natural world. The prospect of the hierarchical ordering of the human community invites the formulation of the concept of the high god working through lesser powers, creations and demiurges, who enjoy existence only in him. The resultant "king of the gods" thrusts into the celestial realm a mirror image of Pharaoh with political overtones: Amun-re, the hidden one united with the solar orb, becomes the divine reflection of the might of Egypt, guarantor of her conquests and father to the king. As Egypt's power fluctuates over the centuries, so does that of Amun-re; and it is no surprise that, in the first century B.C. the final resistance to the Hellenism of the Ptolemies should have centered in the great temple of Amun-re at Karnak. Through an essentially syncretistic process, the figure of the high god historically absorbs deity, and turns the godhead into a triune being: hiddenness (Amun), creativity (Ptah), and solar essence (Re).

Consciousness of Being and the syncretism of numinous power have nothing to do with monotheism. The concept of the "King of the Gods" arises from beneficent monarchy; the concept of the "Sole god" derives from despotism. Only once in Egypt's long history did the official dogma become monotheistic, and that was under Pharaoh Amenophis IV (Akhenaten) during the fourteenth century B.C. The Sun-god whom this king worshipped did not arrange and absorb other manifestations of deity: he excluded, demonized, and obliterated them. For monotheism is not intrinsically benign, but belligerent and uncompromising. In the Egyptian experience it deprived the worshiper of mythology, mythological symbolism and the speculative urge: all truth came from the sole god and his earthly protégé.

The notion of the "god within you" introduces a concept markedly different from the concept of "god of the community." For the latter must be served in congregation as an expression of civic religion; but the "god within you" points to a private, individual relationship to the divine world. Man's behavioral obligations under a code of ethics are spelled out in a voluminous body of instructional literature, related to similar compositions in the Levant and Mesopotamia, called "Teaching." Often set within the framework of the father-to-son "chat," this genre sets forth simply and directly a series of moral precepts that will lead people to wisdom and aid them in fitting into society and achieving goals. Through all this material runs the common admonition to act with circumspection, discretion, right-dealing, and industry. And since the immanence of god implies a one-on-one relationship

between the individual and "his" god, the former cannot seek refuge in the mass of citizenry: he will be obliged to answer directly for his deeds to the god within himself. The private relationship with god is closely linked to a self-conscious personal piety. The individual is acutely aware of a moral lack which seems to be endemic in humankind, not quite the tenet of "original sin," but certainly a generic incapacity: "god is always in his success, man is always in his failure." Sin, however unintentional, inevitably brings punishment from god, usually in the form of sickness. The penitent sinner beseeches the almighty as to the nature of his sin, and pleads for forgiveness. If healed, he or she might well compose a testimonial to the saving grace of god, and carve it on a stela for all to see.

The predestination which seems to be implicit in the Egyptian concept of sin, finds full expression in their overriding belief in fate. One's horoscope might well be cast at birth by the Seven Hathors, or it might be dictated by the very calendar date on which one came into the world. Tension between notions of free will and predestination finds expression in the Tale of the Doomed Prince, but the fact that the final pages are missing prevents us from appreciating how the author resolved the issue. The popularity of almanac-like hemerologies, however, suggests that the Egyptians viewed fate as inevitable.

In some respects the individual's link to "the god within" depended on the well-being of his own psyche. In contemplating the non-corporeal, psychological side of a human being, the Egyptians were impressed by the animating principle, the individual personality and the transfiguration of the spirit. The first of these was conceived of as, the life force (*ka*), a virtual twin of its owner, born at the same time and co-extensive with the body during life. Death sundered the *ka* from the body, and the ritual of mortuary practice was in large measure designed to re-unite the two. The personality conjured up the image of the human-headed bird (*ba*), free to wander the universe, unrestrained, supported only by the body of its owner with whom it regularly communicated. Periodically and especially at festival time, the *ba* returned to family who deposited water and food for it outside the door. While *ka* and *ba* were active during life, their potency was crucial to the long span of eternity during which their survival meant the survival of the deceased himself. If the necessary preparations were made the three would be transfigured into a glorified, luminous spirit, the *akh*.

From time immemorial—the roots undoubtedly extend into early Prehistory—the Egyptian community as a whole has laid great stock in perpetuating a strong link with the "Ancestors," "those who were aforetime," "the fathers." Whether their memorials lay in a desert cemetery or in the abode of the living, the ancestors were to be served in perpetuity. The community as a whole honored them collectively as a link to eternity, but the individual too looked forward to the continued existence of his personality, distinct from the group. His body *must* survive to maintain his individuation; his life force *must* find a means to acquire sustenance.

Out of this denial of death and affirmation of a glorious continuation of life there arose a series of practical means implemented to service the state beyond death. The need to preserve the corpse led to experimentation in increasingly artificial techniques of protection from decay: matting and skins to wrap the cadaver, linen padding to "flesh out" the shape of the body in life, coffins of wood and stone, and eventually cartonnages. The possibilities of natural dessication prompted the development of various ancillary practices such as treating the body with aromatic preservatives, removing the viscera and placing them in canopic jars, and extracting parts of the body which might promote decay. As time passed what had originally been a simple excavated pit deepened to a subterranean burial chamber approached by a shaft; and the original mound of backfill came to be interpreted as a house of the life force, expanded into a substantial rectangular superstructure and decorated as a mock-up of a domicile of the living. Here, supported by representations of the deceased in painting, relief or sculpture, the *ka* could enjoy a point of contact with posterity. The interface between the world of the living and the realm of the dead was the False Door and offering table, whereon the relative or celebrant would place food and drink for the dead. In order to entice any passer-by to enter the tomb to present an offering as an act of piety, tombowners began to increase the relief decoration of their chapels with scenes depicting activity in life, and to include a biographical statement proclaiming the worthiness of the owner to be remembered by coming generations. The evolutionary trajectory followed by the royal tomb differed somewhat from that of the nonroyal burials in that from the Third Dynasty on, the governing ideology was solar: the superstructure of the tomb was interpreted, not so much as a house of the dead, but as a means of ascent to join the sun, first by a stepped structure (the Step Pyramid) and later by the true pyramid. During most periods of Egypt's history, but especially during the Old Kingdom, the tomb of the king provided a focal point for interments of his subjects who clustered close around him in death, as they had in life.

The protection afforded by tomb, embalmment and necropolis were but initial steps in the preparation of the individual for eternal existence. The inert reliefs and statues of the deceased would have to be made ready by magical means to receive the food offerings, and so an elaborate "Opening-of-the-Mouth" ceremony was devised for mummy and sculpture. As back-ups in a "worst case" scenario, servant figurines and (later) *shawabtis* were placed in the tomb and magically activated to serve the deceased in the next life. Furniture, clothing, personal adornments, mementos, and treasured documents might also go into the next life with their owners. In particular beatification spells were to be intoned during the preparation of the body on the day of the interment to guarantee the transfiguration of the deceased into a glorious spirit (*akh*). Copies of these spells ideally would accompany the tomb-owner into the Beyond, either as texts inscribed on the walls of the inner tomb (The Pyramid Texts), or in ink copy on the inner surfaces of wooden coffins (The Coffin Texts), or yet again on papyrus roll (Book of the Going Forth by Day) secreted in the coffin for use at will in the next life.

Beyond the grave the deceased would enter not an unfamiliar twilight world, but a projection of the one he had left, cast upon a canvas of eternity. He would encounter a landscape of arable land and canals, lagoons and marshes wherein lurked dangerous beasts. The Nile of Egypt found its mirror image in the celestial Nile whereon sailed the sun-barque; and the deceased entertained the fervent hope of perhaps securing a place in this heavenly craft in order to accompany the sun-god on his daily rounds. But danger was ever present. Malevolent entities would threaten, reluctant ferrymen would refuse a fare, hunger and thirst would prove a constant threat. While the magic spell would always provide a protective antidote, the deceased might well appeal to the presiding authority for a guarantee of safety. For as in life, the *king in death*, "the Great God," presided over a court in which victims could seek redress. As time went on the concept of the purview of this heavenly court began to expand into the moral sphere: the trial before this otherworldly king, Osiris in fact, came to be construed as a "litmus" test for ethical rectitude. Everyone had to submit to it, and Osiris sent forth fierce-eyed messengers, often identified as the emissaries of death, or Death itself personified, to bring the souls of all mankind at the point of death before the judgment seat of the god. The mechanics of the trial evolved over time. At first a visual estimate based on the relative quantities of good and bad deeds, the assessment in classic form was achieved through the weighing of the heart of the deceased against the feather of *ma'at*. Those who passed the test could look forward to eternity in the *Field of Reeds*, a sort of Elysian fields, where the dead would enjoy a lifestyle similar to that which they had left behind, but enhanced beyond human belief. The damned, on the other hand, were consigned to punishment in the Underworld which now undergoes a bifurcation into a realm of the Blessed and a place of torment, a veritable *Paradise* and *Hell*. This concept, providing a fertile field for the imagination, experienced strong growth in detail and was inherited by Christianity which transformed the whole into a Heaven set over against a Dante-esque inferno.

The last judgment before the tribunal of Osiris was unavoidable; but the soul of the deceased could hope for salvation through emulation. Just as Osiris, "the First of Westerners," i.e. the archetype of the dead, had successfully conquered death, so might anyone by following in his train. Mummification, beatification, magical protection and interment had, in the first instance, been devised for Osiris himself, and through them the god had been acquitted of wrong and exonerated in his trial with Seth. By following these mortuary procedures the deceased had every expectation, of making himself *an Osiris*, of surmounting death too, and being declared "justified" before the tribunal. He had in truth died and risen with Osiris.

The Ancient Egyptian belief system, though complex, imaginative and meaningful, was relevant to Egyptians alone: it "transplanted" only with difficulty. True, beliefs regarding the Afterlife did exert a certain influence on later religious expression in the Mediterranean lands and in Europe; and during the first and second centuries C.E. the worship of Isis, Osiris, and Harpokrates spread abroad through the Roman Empire, challenging other Mystery Religions (including Christianity). But on the whole the commitment of the Egyptian himself to his ancestral beliefs diminished during the same period, thanks to the inimical attitude of the Roman authorities, the siege mentality of the dwindling numbers of priests, and the onslaught of a welter of cults and philosophies from outside Egypt. The only conduit, both geographical and spiritual, through which something of Ancient Egypt survived to enter the world of the European West, was Alexandria, that great intellectual and mystical hub of the world, wherein all beliefs, cults and philosophical systems thrived, often in a syncretistic amalgam. It is to Alexandria that we must look for the origins of two great systems of thought, Gnosticism and Hermeticism, in which a modicum of the Ancient Egyptian belief system survived the Middle Ages to re-emerge in the Renaissance. Today it survives in the guise of Masonic thought and New Ageism.

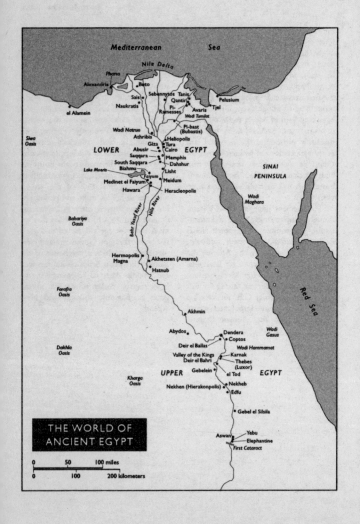

THE WORLD OF
ANCIENT EGYPT

DIRECTORY OF
CONTRIBUTORS

JAMES P. ALLEN, Curator of the Department of Egyptian Art, The Metropolitan Museum of Art, New York

CAROL A. R. ANDREWS, Assistant Keeper, Department of Egyptian Antiquities, The British Museum, London, United Kingdom

DIETER ARNOLD, Curator, Department of Egyptian Art, The Metropolitan Museum of Art, New York

ANDREY O. BOLSHAKOV, Curator of the Ancient Orient Section, Hermitage Museum, Saint Petersburg, Russia

MARIE-ANGE BONHE'ME, Paris, France

PETER BRAND, Independent Scholar, Toronto, Canada

LORELEI H. CORCORAN, Associate Professor and Director, Institute of Egyptian Art and Archaeology, The University of Memphis, Tennessee

ANN ROSALIE DAVID, Reader in Egyptology, University of Manchester, United Kingdom

ALEID DE JONG, Independent Scholar, Utrecht, The Netherlands

AIDAN DODSON, Visiting Fellow, Department of Archaeology, University of Bristol, United Kingdom

DENISE M. DOXEY, Assistant Curator, Ancient Egyptian, Nubian, and Near Eastern Art, Art of the Ancient World, Museum of Fine Arts, Boston, Massachusetts

GERTIE ENGLUND, Senior Lecturer in Egyptology, Uppsala University, Sweden

PAUL JOHN FRANDSEN, Professor of Egyptology, The Carsten Niebuhr Institute of Near Eastern Studies, Copenhagen, Denmark

FLORENCE DUNN FRIEDMAN, Curator of Ancient Art, Museum of Art, Rhode Island School of Design, Providence

CATHERINE GRAINDORGE, Lecturer in Egyptian Religion and Archaeology, Agyptoloisches Seminar der Freie Universitat, Berlin, Germany

J. GWYN GRIFFITHS, Professor Emeritus of Classics and Egyptology, University of Wales, Swansea, United Kingdom

JAMES K. HOFFMEIER, Professor of Old Testament and Near Eastern Archaeology, Trinity International University, Wheaton, Illinois

JENNIFER HOUSER-WEGNER, Keeper, The Egyptian Section, University Museum, University of Pennsylvania, Philadelphia

OLAF E. KAPER, Independent Scholar, Berlin

DIETER KESSLER, Professor of Egyptology, Institut fur Agyptologie, Ludwig-Maximilians-Universitat, Munchen, Germany

JEAN-MARIE KRUCHTEN, Senior Lecturer in Egyptian Language, Universite Libre de Bruxelles, Belgium

GÜNTHER LAPP, Arlesheim, Switzerland

RONALD J. LEPROHON, Professor of Egyptian Languages and Literature, University of Toronto, Canada

BARBARA S. LESKO, Administrative Research Assistant, Department of Egyptology, Brown University, Providence, Rhode Island

LEONARD H. LESKO, Charles Edwin Wilbour Professor of Egyptology, Brown University, Providence, Rhode Island

MICHEL MALAISE, Professor of Egyptology, University of Liege, Belgium

LISE MANNICHE, External Lecturer in Egyptology, Carsten Niebuhr Institute of Near Eastern Studies, University of Copenhagen, Denmark

DANIEL R. MCBRIDE, Cairo, Egypt

DIMITRI MEEKS, Research Director of the Centre National de la Recherche Scientifique, Paris, France

EDMUND S. MELTZER, Independent Scholar, Stevens Point, Wyoming

MAYA MULLER, Curator, Museum of Cultures, Basel, Switzerland

KAROL MYS'LIWIEC, Professor of Ancient Egyptian Archaeology, and Director of the Research Centre for Mediterranean Archaeology, Polish Academy of Science, Warsaw, Poland

ANDRZEJ NIWINSKI, Professor, Department of Egyptian Archaeology, University of Warsaw, Poland

BOYO OCKINGA, Senior Lecturer in Egyptology, Macquarie University, Sydney, Australia

STACIE L. OLSON, Independent Scholar, Sanatoga, Pennsylvania

PAUL F. O'ROURKE, Research Associate, Department of Classical and Ancient Middle Eastern Art, The Brooklyn Museum of Art, New York

STEPHEN G. J. QUIRKE, Assistant Curator, The Petrie Museum of Egyptian Archaeology, University College London, United Kingdom

JOHN D. RAY, Herbert Thompson Reader in Egyptology, Faculty of Oriental Studies, University of Cambridge, United Kingdom

ROBERT K. RITNER, Associate Professor of Egyptology, The Oriental Institute, University of Chicago, Illinois

GAY ROBINS, Professor of Ancient Egyptian Art, Emory University, Atlanta, Georgia

EUGENE ROMANOSKY, Project Editor, Oxford University Press, USA; Independent Scholar, New York

ANN MACY ROTH, Associate Professor of Egyptology, Howard University, Washington, D.C.

HERMANN A. SCHLÖGL, Professor of Egyptology, University of Fribourg, Switzerland

STEPHAN J. SEIDLMAYER, Altaegyptiches Woerterbuch, Section Director, Berlin-Brandenburg Academy of Sciences and Humanities, Berlin, Germany

DAVID P. SILVERMAN, Curator in Charge, Egyptian Section, University of Pennsylvania Museum of Archaeology and Anthropology; Chair and Professor, Department of Asian and Middle Eastern

Studies, University of Pennsylvania, Philadelphia

CATHERINE SIMON, Curator, Shelby White and Leon Lery Collection, New York

ANTHONY J. SPALINGER, Associate Professor of Egyptology, University of Auckland, New Zealand

DONALD B. SPANEL, New York

EMILY TEETER, Associate Curator, Oriental Institute Museum, University of Chicago, Illinois

STEPHEN E. THOMPSON, Independent Scholar, Coral Springs, Florida

VINCENT ARIEH TOBIN, Professor of Classics, Saint Mary's University, Halifax, Canada

ANGELA M. J. TOOLEY, Independent Scholar, Manchester, United Kingdom

CLAUDE TRAUNECKER, Strasbourg, France

JACOBUS VAN DIJK, Lecturer in Egyptology, University of Groningen, The Netherlands

HERMAN TE VELDE, Professor Emeritus of Egyptology, University of Groningen, The Netherlands

DEBORAH VISCHAK, Graduate Student, Institute of Fine Arts, New York

KENT R. WEEKS, Professor of Egyptology, American University in Cairo, Egypt

JOSEF W. WEGNER, Assistant Professor of Egyptology, Department of Asian and Middle Eastern Studies, University of Pennsylvania, Philadelphia

EDWARD F. WENTE, Professor Emeritus of Egyptology, University of Chicago, Illinois

EDWARD K. WERNER, Independent Scholar, Jupiter, Florida

RICHARD H. WILKINSON, Director of the University of Arizona Egyptian Expedition, Tucson

A

AFTERLIFE. Belief in the afterlife is among the fundamental concepts of Egyptian culture. Since late prehistoric times, the Egyptians found means to ensure eternal life in comfort after death. These practices underwent continuous development into Roman times. That the afterlife was of paramount importance for the Egyptians can be seen from the number of richly furnished tombs found in the Nile Valley, the most extensive remains preserved from ancient Egypt. In fact, the Egyptians invested a large portion of their wealth in the afterlife—more than any other culture in the world. The afterlife was a luxury commodity which only the king and the elite could afford. For the royal household and the higher officials, the highest values in life were the favor of the king and a happy afterlife. In the Egyptian conception, people were as unequal in the afterlife as in earthly life, and existing documents disclose no interest in what happened to ordinary people after death. Anyone who wanted a good afterlife had to do much during life to achieve it. First, one had to have a tomb built and had to acquire a large number of objects thought to be needed in the afterlife. In addition, it was necessary to ensure that one's heirs would mummify the body and carry out the funeral ritual. Finally, a regular schedule for offerings at the tomb had to be organized. The best way to accomplish this was to set up a mortuary foundation by designating the income from a given parcel of land for that purpose.

The sources from which we learn how the Egyptians conceived of the afterlife are extraordinarily rich and span four and one-half millennia. They include the objects the deceased took along into the tomb (from the mid-fifth millennium onward); the tomb as a building (from the Predynastic period); the images applied to the walls of tombs (from the third dynasty); and the texts that describe the afterlife (from the late fifth dynasty).

The basic conception of the afterlife held that the body must be preserved. The deceased was just as dependent on nourishment—food and drinks—as on earth. According to the Egyptians' conception, human life, whether in time or in eternity, supposed individual consciousness. The formulation that the literature of the dead found for this was that the deceased individual always wanted to remember his own name. However, it was clearly the body that was the bearer of the individual's consciousness. Besides the body, a human being had other elements which accompanied the body invisibly and represented different aspects of its vitality. The Egyptian terms for these—*ka*, *ba*, and *akh*—are not easy to translate, though often rendered as "soul." After death, this situation was reversed: the body was an immobile mummy, but the "souls" could leave it on occasion and wander around. Life in the afterworld was thus not appreciably different from a person's former life on earth, except that it was conducted in a different place. Since the late Old Kingdom, tomb inscriptions refer to the starry heaven as well as "the beautiful west," that is the mountains on the western bank of the Nile where the sun sets, as the regions of the dead. There, in the place where the gods dwelt, the deceased was very near the gods and attained a state of being like theirs. A king became an actual god upon his death, and his afterlife was entirely like that of the gods; indeed, from the time of the Middle Kingdom, nonroyal persons too could become divinities of a kind in the afterlife.

It was, however, a fundamental principle that the afterlife of a king was quite different from that of ordinary mortals, because the king descended from the gods. We must therefore consider separately the ways kings and nonroyal persons were thought to live after death.

In the last part of the prehistoric period, from the middle of the fifth millennium until the late fourth millennium BCE, a rich burial culture first developed in Egypt. From this we can conclude that a wealthy elite intended to extend into the afterlife the standard of living to which they had become accustomed on earth. The finds point to two major themes: the body had to be nourished in the afterlife, and it had to be kept fresh and beautiful by means of cosmetic objects which symbolize eternal rejuvenation. The high artistic quality of these objects reflects a strong aesthetic sense. This was the beginning of a longstanding characteristic of Egyptian culture: the beauty of the objects and images in the tomb elevated the quality of life in the afterworld.

With the beginning of dynastic times, tombs, which had previously been reinforced shafts, evolved into buildings made of mud brick. Kings and members of their households had rectangular buildings erected, which had an ever-increasing number of storerooms to accommodate furnishings and supplies: huge quantities of food in ceramic jars, luxurious stoneware dishes, tools, household furniture, and game boards. In addition, the tomb contained a stela that had the appearance of a door, in front of which the mortuary priests and family members were expected to place food and drink offerings. Already at this time there were one or more statues of the deceased, in which he could take material shape. Provisions for the afterlife now took on the definitive form that was to continue into the Roman period. The deceased was provided with a house befitting his high status, with all the accessories and provisions required by a large household with family and servants. The false door symbolized the ability of the deceased to leave the tomb at will and take up the offerings. The false door and tomb statues reflect the principle that an artfully crafted model could fulfill the same purpose as the real object; however, the model does not replace the real object but instead supplements it. In Egypt, there was no separation between material and immaterial existence; rather, they continuously and imperceptibly merged.

At the beginning of the Old Kingdom stone masonry was developed, and from this time on the tomb complexes of kings and those of high officials differ sharply. The kings of the third through sixth dynasties built huge pyramid complexes. The cult spaces contained extensive cycles of wall reliefs, and in the chamber for the coffin, from the end of the fifth dynasty, the Pyramid Texts were inscribed. Thus, for the first time, comprehensive information is available about the conception of the king's life in the afterworld. The only protagonist in the reliefs is the king. We see him seated at the table, looking over an endless abundance of food. He is also depicted as a child being nursed by a goddess; this ensures his sustenance and rejuvenation. He is shown carrying out several important official acts: he celebrates this coronation jubilee at which all the gods and courtiers pay homage to him. When he encounters the gods, he does so as an equal. A flourishing economy is depicted by the arrival of a fleet of trading ships. He slays his enemies and traitors, both real and symbolic, in that he locates dangerous animals in the desert or in the marshes of the Nile Delta. Through these symbolic acts, both his own life force and that of the whole country are regenerated, and his power over rebels and his dominance over the world are confirmed.

The Pyramid Texts ensure the difficult passage from the death of the king to his divine existence in the afterlife. A major theme is the bountiful provision of the deceased king with food and drink. In addition, the crown goddesses give birth to him anew every day, nurse him at their breasts, and never wean him; thus, the king experiences a symbolic rejuvenation for all eternity, as depicted in the reliefs. However, the Pyramid Texts also recount a story different from the reliefs: the king must be awakened from the sleep of death and ascend to heaven as a god. This he can do, because he is descended from the creator god. In the beginning, the sun god, Re, who came into being spontaneously, created Shu and Tefnut, or air and moisture. They in turn begot the sky goddess Nut and the earth god Geb, parents of the two divine pairs Osiris and

Isis and Seth and Nephthys. Seth killed his brother Osiris; however, after Re awakened him, Osiris became the lord of the realm of the dead, and his son Horus succeeded him as king on earth. In life, every pharaoh was the son of Osiris and the son of Re, and in death he became Osiris and Re themselves. The nine most ancient gods therefore represent the closest relatives of the king. Over and over again, the Pyramid Texts describe how the king is awakened and his body kept whole and incorruptible through the cultic purification; how he receives his raiment and crown; and how his Osiric family, the third generation of gods, helps him in these acts. Also essential is the idea that he descends from Re, which is always invoked to reinforce his claim to rule. When the king has risen from the dead as Osiris and the court of the gods confirms his claim to the throne, he is able to ascend into heaven. This is perilous, because he needs the aid of the heavenly ferryman, who transports to Re only a king who convinces him of his power. Therefore, the king must associate his arrival in heaven with an impressive demonstration of power. His coming is announced by earthquakes and thunder; the gods tremble when they glimpse the sword in his hand. Now he captures even the gods; he cooks and devours them in order to incorporate their cumulative power. Finally, he journeys like the sun god across the heavens or becomes a star like Orion. Like the sun, he is swallowed up every evening by the goddess of heaven, Nut, and reborn at daybreak. It is typical that the texts describe the unending existence of the king—his cyclical renewal—using a great variety of metaphors, such as the sun in its course, one of the circumpolar stars, the daily-reborn child of the goddess of heaven or of the crown goddesses.

The pyramid complexes make the statement that the deceased king is now definitively a god who must have his own temple and cult so that he, like the other major gods, may be effective in blessing the country. The texts witness his integration into his divine family. The reliefs reflect his specific role as a god: the rites of victory over enemies and those for the renewal of life are the tasks of the king who rules and regenerates the earthly world, in analogy with the sun god, who rules and regenerates the cosmos. This is the meaning of the huge investments that he mobilized for his tomb complex during life.

The reliefs in the tombs of high officials depict life in the hereafter as a mirror image of life on earth. Here too, a central idea is the provision of food and drink. But in contrast to the king, who becomes a god and enters the divine family, the entombed official lives with his actual family in the afterworld. He goes hunting in desert and marsh, but primarily he oversees economic life— agricultural and cattle-raising, the production and transport of goods, all carefully depicted in many scenes. The passage of the deceased into the afterlife is described not by texts but rather by the representations of the burial ritual. From the sparse inscriptions, we learn only that he wants to "walk on the beautiful ways of the west." The deceased official is not a god but rather an *akh*-spirit who has generative powers: he causes the work in fields and workshops to bring blessed prosperity; he keeps in motion the same segment of the world that was assigned to him in life.

The royal tomb complexes of the Middle Kingdom are so poorly preserved that we can learn nothing new from them about concepts of the afterlife in that period. By contrast, officials and local princes now had their own collec-

tion of texts that supplied them with necessary information—the so-called Coffin Texts. These are derived from the Pyramid Texts, and the deceased is now addressed as Osiris, just like the king. This thinking remained normative well into Roman times: the deceased shared the fate of the god who ruled over the dead and who died and rose again. The Egyptians had a distinctive conception of the boundaries of the individual. These boundaries were not fixed; the dead person could be transformed or permeated; he was able to transpose himself into different gods and act like them; he could borrow a divine personality while at the same time remaining himself. Existence with Re and with Osiris was desired and was described as being of equal value. Along with this, the dead person wanted to be free to leave the tomb and go into the sunlight, to be transformed into various gods, to feast in paradisiacal fields of offerings, or to be cared for by goddesses.

First, however, he had to be acquitted by the court of justice. Justification functioned according to the paradigm of Horus and Seth: Seth was the mythical rebel who went against the order established by the gods by murdering his brother with the intention of usurping Horus's place as the rightful heir. Likewise, the deceased received vindication against his enemies who seek to challenge his place in the afterworld. He mobilizes all his magical power and knowledge in order to ward off his enemies' attack. If he failed, he might end up in the fishnets cast by the demons or in their slaughterhouse. He was at particular pains to avoid being forever numbered among the damned, who had to walk upside down, eat feces, and drink urine. This is the epitome of the dreadful fate that befalls the rebel. The justification of the deceased did not involve his personal ethical behavior; rather, it was a matter of never having been disobedient and having always submitted unconditionally to the order established by the gods and the king.

Court officials of this period inscribed the Pyramid Texts in their tombs, formerly the privilege of kings. The reliefs and paintings in their tombs deal with the same themes as in the Old Kingdom, but a few new episodes from the lives of the tomb-owners—often local princes—begin to appear, such as the transport of colossal statues of themselves. Such scenes reflect their increased political autonomy.

At the beginning of the New Kingdom, a sudden development occurred with respect to conceptions of the afterlife. Everything changed, including the tomb architecture and the images and texts that were placed inside. The domain of the king and that of the officials still developed along separate paths. For the first time, the afterlife was depicted. The tombs of the kings are underground tunnels, the walls of which are decorated with the so-called Underworld Books. These contain a precise report of how the sun god, Re, traveled through the underworld during the twelve hours of the night and what took place there. Texts and pictures complement one another, somewhat like a modern comic strip. Re sails in the "bark of the millions" in which the blessed dead are seated, on a river along which Osiris dwells with innumerable gods, demons, and the dead, both blessed and damned. The sun god allows favors to be bestowed on the good dead, while the damned must endure hellish tortures. When he has sailed on, everything once again lies in darkness and the sleep of death. Every night those who rebel against the order established by the creator god lie in wait on his path, embodied in the serpent Apophis, but they are always slain. After Re has been rejuvenated in the serpent which embodies time, he rises renewed on the eastern horizon. The daily rebirth of the sun was for the Egyptians the paradigm of eternal regeneration, in which humans, kings, gods, and all of creation partook.

Most of the books of the underworld do not mention the king explicitly; only the Litany of Re portrays his fate in the afterworld. The new concept of the existence of the king in the afterworld affirms that he is one both with Re and with Osiris, and that every night Re and Osiris enter into one another. Despite this proud equating of the king with the gods, the king runs the risk of falling into the hands of demons who could slay him, tearing him limb from limb, and annihilate him. The text gives no reason for this astonishing threat; clearly some skepticism about the divine nature of the king is filtering through here, even as this belief is still being strongly asserted. In the New Kingdom, the mortuary temple became separated from the tomb and no longer served only as the place of worship of the king; instead, it was also open to other gods. Owing to this fusion of cults, the king lived there in eternity in the company of his divine family.

The *Book of Going Forth by Day* (the so-called *Book of the Dead*) is a collection of sayings that provided deceased nonroyals with all the necessary knowledge about life in the afterworld. It is composed of both texts and pictures, which can appear on papyrus or on tomb walls. The deceased wanted to be able to venture forth from the tomb and move about freely. He wanted to be able to assume any form and to be in the retinue of Osiris or Re. Another desired place was the field of offerings, where the dead live fully, move, eat, and beget. One characteristic of the *Book of Going Forth by Day* is the multiplicity of tests that the deceased must pass in order to ward off the attacks of the demons who seek to hand them over to eternal torment. What is most important is the judgment in which the deceased counts up all the conceivable evil deeds that he has not committed. Here for the first time the deceased assumes ethical responsibility for his or her conduct during life on earth. Evil deeds are subject to punishment, but people rely on the power of the litany of denial. The text is full of exacting theological considerations about Re and Osiris and their relationship to each other. Here, too, a certain skepticism can be detected as to whether the words and the images will adduce the hoped-for effect. It must be asserted with ever greater insistence and ever more words that the deceased is as unscathed and unassailable as a god.

The tomb reliefs and paintings of the early New Kingdom spread before us an abundance of scenes from life on earth. High court officials tended to depict the official actions that they carry out in the presence of the king. The tombs are also abundantly equipped with beautiful cosmetic articles, symbolizing eternal rejuvenation. In time, illustrations from the *Book of Going Forth by Day* become more common, until scenes of daily life practically disappear. This development shows that people no longer attributed any beneficial effect to pictures of life on earth, either for the deceased or for his surviving posterity.

Toward the end of the second millennium BCE, conceptions of the afterlife drastically changed once again with the Third Intermediate Period. Of royal tombs, only those of the twenty-second and twenty-third dynasties at Tanis remain, and these are much smaller than previous ones and include only a few ex-

cerpts from the royal Underworld Books. In general, what stands out is that there was no longer any difference between the afterlife of kings and that of other individuals. The royal books were now available to everyone. From the eleventh century to the eighth there are no tombs with murals; depictions and texts about life in the afterworld instead appear on painted coffins and papyri. These consist of quotations from the *Book of Going Forth by Day* and the *Book of That Which Is in the Underworld*, ever more richly illustrated until little more than pictures remains. From the late twenty-fifth dynasty (c. 700 BCE) onward, sumptuous officials' tombs with wall reliefs and inscriptions once again appear. Some of these are enormous palaces that surpass anything before them. Their owners were scholars who had significant historical knowledge and used this learning to introduce a collection of quotations from the full range of older pictorial themes and texts.

From the Persian period (fifth century BCE) we have no evidence of funerary practices. In the Ptolemaic and Roman periods, however, the tradition of tombs decorated with images was resumed, partly in Egyptian style but increasingly in a mixed Egyptian-Hellenistic style. The Underworld Books are found on stone sarcophagi, and spells from the *Book of Going Forth by Day* are painted directly onto the wrappings of mummies. Two new texts were created which opened up new prospects for life in the hereafter: the deceased had the air needed for breathing (i.e., everlasting life) supplied to him by decree of the gods; and he or she gained access to earthly life in order to partake in the feasts offered to the gods in the temples. In the second century CE, the old conceptions of the afterlife disappeared as Christianity spread.

The images and texts that the ancient Egyptians created in general present no emotion, so it is not easy to say what their attitude toward death was. From the Middle Kingdom (about 2000 BCE) on, however, in many tombs we find an inscription addressed to visitors that reads "O you who love to live and hate to die." In fact, from all periods there are sayings suggesting that a long life was seen as the highest good on earth. In the New Kingdom, there are more bitter laments over the darkness and loneliness that prevail in the afterworld. Especially starting around 1000 BCE, there is formulated the sad certainty that a deceased person loses individual consciousness and lingers on in a gloomy state of slumber. However, this notion did not lead to a new concept of life in the hereafter; rather, the old beliefs persisted. People learned to live with the conflict between skepticism and confidence in the ancient magical means which promised a conscious life in a beautiful afterworld.

Maya Muller
Translated from German by Robert E.
Shillenn and Jane McGary

AKH (Eg., *3ḫ*), a term that occurs regularly throughout ancient Egyptian secular and religious texts, represented by the crested ibis hieroglyph. The *akh*-concept appears to have no intrinsic relation to the bird, to which it might only have been related phonetically. The fundamental meaning of *akh* was "effectiveness," whether in daily affairs or during the afterlife. In the afterlife, *akh* designated a transfigured deceased who, capable of unhindered movement and full physical functioning, would be an effective deceased. Unlike *ba* and *ka* forms, the *akh* individual was often identified with light.

In the mortuary sphere, *akh* denoted the deceased who became an effective

being by virtue of having the proper offerings and knowing the efficacious spells. One was made an *akh* after burial through a mortuary ritual that "caused one to become an *akh*" (*s3ḫ*), which had been performed as early as the Early Dynastic period by a *sekhen-akh* priest (*sḫn-3ḫ*; "an *akh*-seeker"). The divine source of *akh*-transformation was unseen, reflecting what Karl Jansen-Winkeln (1996) called an invisible *akh*-effectiveness, its hidden nature being part of its power.

In the living sphere, *akh* commonly referred to "the effectiveness" of kings, officials, or townsmen who acted on behalf of their gods, kings, lords, or one another. Members of all levels of society could be *akh*-effective or perform *akhu*-effective deeds, which were not simply glorious or useful things, as often translated, but concrete acts that affected eternity. For example, in the twelfth dynasty, Senwosret I, in his filial role of Horus, built monuments for his divine father and supplied his offerings, "doing that which is *akh*-effective." Sety I, in the nineteenth dynasty, after completing a chapel at Abydos for his deceased earthly father, said, "I have performed *akhut* ['that which is *akh*'] for you [since] I built for you a temple for your *ka*." In the twenty-seventh dynasty, a nonroyal individual, Oudjahorresne, performed *akhu*-deeds on behalf of his townspeople, defending the feeble, saving the fearful, and doing all *akhu*-acts for them as a father acts for his son. The nature of *akhu*-deeds was thus closely allied to the maintenance of societal *maat* ("justice").

In virtually all the periods of ancient Egypt's religious and secular texts, the concept of *akh* operated in a reciprocal relationship between god and king, between father and son. In the Pyramid Texts, the king as Horus became *akh* through his father Osiris, just as Osiris became *akh* through his son Horus: "It is through you [Osiris] that he [Horus] has become *akh*." In a Coffin Text, the son became *akh* by the father and the father by the son. In the *Book of Going Forth by Day* (*Book of the Dead*), each embraces the other "that he might be an *akh* thereby." The same reciprocity obtained in nonmortuary literature: Senwosret I of the twelfth dynasty constructed a temple for his divine father, providing for his altars, and doing all that which was *akh*-effective; Akhenaten named himself "son of eternity who came forth from the Aten [his father], *akh* for him who is *akh* for him" (Sandman, 1938, p. 91).

Cosmic, primordial notions of luminous power were allied to the concept of *akh*. Whether the concept of *akh*-effectiveness was projected from pragmatic, daily affairs into the cosmic sphere, or the reverse, has become a point of debate. Gertie Englund (1978) opted for the latter and considered the primary meaning of *akh* to be a form of primordial creative power related to the birth of light. Indeed, *akh* often denoted forms of effective light—such as the circumpolar stars (especially in the Pyramid Texts), the solar eye, and sunbeams—which are all intensified forms of celestial effectiveness; sunlight is effectiveness *par excellence*, since light in the mortuary texts daily brings forth and maintains creation. In the Coffin Texts, Atum created Shu and Tefnut with his *akhu*-power; the deceased, the product of *akh*-creation is an *akh*, lord of *akhu*, who himself created an *akh* at his will and who is lord of *seshep* light (*sšp*). This same "lord of *seshep* light" appellation was used in the *Book of Going Forth by Day* for the sun god Re. Light, which produces creation, is by definition effective.

The luminous associations of *akh* were reflected on the understanding of the *akh*-deceased, who would be transfigured in light. In the Coffin Texts, the deceased said, "Re does it [various things] for me and his *akh* is in me" and "as for any *akh* that knows the name of the shining sun, he knows his own name." The *Book of Going Forth by Day* states that Re looks on this *akh* as himself, so the *akh*-deceased can be seen as the very beams of Re. The *akh* thus became both Re and his emanation of light, thus at once creator and creation. Yet *akh*-power can also denote nonsolar forms of effective power, as in the creative speech of the gods, or even the milk full of *akhu* that Hathor, in cow form, imparts when suckling her daughter Hatshepsut.

The ability to function as an *akh* in the netherworld depended, in part, on having material sustenance. Early Dynastic cylinder seals denoted the deceased, hieroglyphically, as an *akh*-bird with head turned back toward a table of food offerings. A number of fourth and fifth dynasty tombs at Giza show the tomb owner, probably understood as a statue, in a funerary cult ceremony labeled "the feeding of the *akh*" (*snmt 3ḫ*), in which offerings were laid down by priests, including the embalmer priest. "Feeding the *akh*" reflected a concrete view of the deceased *akh*, without notions of transfiguration or bodily transformation; this understanding was echoed in Old Kingdom autobiographical tomb inscriptions, in which the owner asserted that he or she is an *akh iker* (*3ḫ ikr;* "an able/effective *akh*") or an *akh aper* (*3ḫ ꜥpr;* "an equipped *akh*")—the effective, equipped status based on having the proper tomb goods, knowledge of magical spells, and food goods.

Letters to the dead, during the Old Kingdom and the First Intermediate Period, were often written on offering vessels and were sometimes addressed to the *akh* or *akh iker* and left at his or her offering slab, similarly reflecting an image of the *akh*-deceased as an effective being without overtones of luminosity. Those are *akh*-beings who, though dead, can still act for or against the living and exist with them in a reciprocal arrangement. A group of New Kingdom stelae were dedicated to the deceased as an *akh iker en Ra* (*ȝḥ iḳr n Rʿ*); these able or effective *akhs* of the sun god Re were depicted as seated individuals (again, probably statues), who were recently deceased ancestors of the dedicators. The purpose of the *akh iker en Ra* dead was to intercede on behalf of their worshipers. Anthropoid busts, sometimes found in conjunction with *akh iker en Ra* stelae and related offering tables, may actually be abbreviated statue forms of *akhs* in that New Kingdom ancestor worship.

Florence Dunn Friedman

AMULETS and jewelry that incorporated amuletic elements were an essential adornment worn by ancient Egyptians at every level of society, both in life and in the hereafter; even sacred animals wore them. Royalty, however, were rarely depicted wearing individual amulets; they wore amuletic forms that had been incorporated into jewelry, such as pectorals, bracelets, or bangles.

Three of the four words translated as "amulet" came from verbs meaning "to guard" or "to protect," confirming that the primary purpose of these personal ornaments was to provide magical protection, although in many instances the wearer clearly hoped to be endowed, in addition, with magical powers or capabilities. A fourth word meant essentially "well-being."

The amulet's shape, the material from which it was made, and its color were crucial to its meaning. Many types of material—precious metal, semiprecious stones, glazed composition (a sand core with a vitreous alkaline glaze), glass, and organic matter—were employed in the production of amulets, and most had an underlying symbolism. For example, lapis lazuli was the color of the dark blue, protective night sky; green turquoise and feldspar were like the life-bringing waters of the Nile River. Green jasper was the color of new vegetation, symbolizing new life; red jasper and carnelian were like blood, the basis of life. Gold represented the sun with all its inherent lifepromoting properties and connotations of daily renewal; silver was the color of the monthly reborn moon. All those materials could be imitated by like-colored glass, glazed composition, glaze, or paint. Although a particular amulet's material might have been specified in texts, almost any material, as long as its color was appropriate to the symbolism, could be substituted.

Most provenanced amulets came from burials or were found on bodies; however, the distinction between amulets for the living and funerary amulets is often problematic, since amulets worn in life for their magical properties could be taken to the tomb for use in life after death. Funerary amulets were made specifically for burials. They were placed on the corpse to give aid and protection during the perilous journey to the netherworld and to supply and supplement the requirements of the afterlife. Ancient sources provide the most information about funerary amulets. The forms of certain funerary amulets were prescribed by chapters of the *Book of Going Forth by Day* (*Book of the Dead*). In those chapters, the material to be used was stipulated, the spell to be recited was provided, the desired result was stated, and the amulet's appearance was illustrated in an accompanying vignette. The *Book of Going*

Forth by Day was placed in the tomb and functioned as a funerary amulet, since its spells were aimed at helping its deceased owner reach the netherworld and obtain a comfortable life there.

Other sources of information for funerary amulets include a list from the Ptolemaic era of 104 amulets from the temple of Hathor at Dendera. These amulets were depicted without written description on a doorway of the temple's roof in the western Osiris complex. The verso of a contemporary funerary text, the MacGregor Papyrus, contains images of seventy-five amulets, usually with names. In addition, the text of a wooden tablet of New Kingdom date (now in the Berlin Museum) specifies the materials of a select group of amulets, and a Late period sheet-gold plaque (now in the British Museum) is embossed with a selection of amuletic forms.

Funerary texts usually specified where on the corpse an amulet should be placed. From the New Kingdom until later dynastic times, the exact positioning was important. Some rare diagrams on Late period papyri provided a schematic layout for the positioning of amulets on mummies, although contemporary bodies had amulets scattered over them in a random fashion. During the nineteenth century, when many mummies were unwrapped but not recorded, information about the positioning of amulets was lost. The pioneering recording work in this field by W. M. Flinders Petrie (conveniently republished in his *Amulets*, London, 1914) was restricted to mummies that were dated to the very end of dynastic times. In the latter twentieth century, however, information provided by modern X-ray techniques on still-wrapped corpses, careful documentation of new finds, and reassessment of existing evidence, constantly add to the current state of knowledge.

Amulets were worn on the body in several ways. A means of suspension or holes for attachment were not essential for funerary amulets since they were often laid on the body, but in rare instances amulets on their original stringing have survived. From the First Intermediate Period, twisted flax fibers were knotted between widely spaced amulets. Two thousand years later, this tradition of stringing survived on the chests of Roman mummies, worn in rows of well-spaced amulets, on flax threads, attached to palm-fiber frames. In all other instances, the order of restringing was arbitrary. Depictions of strings of amulets and surviving, still-strung examples show that the living wore individual amulets combined with strings of beads on either gold chains or wire.

Recognizable amulets have been dated as early as the Predynastic Badarean period, some fifteen centuries before the first dynasty. Most take the form of a living creature or part of a living creature (with the part representing the whole). Though all came from burials, they were intended to function as a magical aid to the living and were taken to the grave subsequently. Some, such as a hobbled hippopotamus made of shell and pierced to be worn upside down, were meant to work apotropaically—to ward off an evil or dangerous force by its very representation. (Throughout Egyptian history the male hippopotamus was feared for its unpredictable savagery and became linked with the demonized form of the god Seth.) Amulets of the head of a dog, bull, panther or lioness, gazelle or antelope could also have been used apotropaically, but they might have been intended to transfer the animal's particular qualities or characteristic behavior to the wearer by sympathetic magic—to confer the wild dog's swiftness or cunning, the bull's virility or strength, leonine savagery, or the desert creature's agility and speed. W. M. Flinders Petrie, in his seminal work on amulets (1914), attempted to classify into five broad categories (homopoeic, ktematic, dynatic, theophoric, and phylactic) the 275 types of amulets known to him, based on the amulet's function. He termed such examples *homopoeic,* that is, the amulets, shaped like living creatures (or their parts) with special characteristics or capabilities that their owner wished to acquire by assimilation.

The fly amulet, which first appeared in the Predynasticperiod, had significance until the Third Intermediate Period, but whether it was worn apotropaically, to ward off Egypt's most prevalent pest, or to endow its wearer by sympathetic magic with its unrivaled powers of reproduction, is uncertain. A Predynastic amulet's specific function may, in most instances, only be surmised. When of New Kingdom date and made of precious metal, especially gold, a fly was considered representative of a royal award, originally for bravery in the field, perhaps for persistence in attacking the enemy, based on the insect's characteristic behavior. Other Predynastic amulets depict the reclining jackal and crouched falcon. (Although both animals represented a specific deity in dynastic times, the historical identities of Anubis and Horus are not attributable retrospectively to Predynastic amulets.) Natural objects, such as shells and birds' claws, were also used amuletically in Predynastic times, and their forms were retained well into the pharaonic era, imitated in other materials.

Although only a few amulets and pieces of amuletic jewelry can be securely dated to the Early Dynastic period, the expanded range of materials and manufacturing techniques used is exemplified by a bracelet that was found in the tomb of the first dynasty pharaoh Djer at Abydos. It is comprised of alternating gold and turquoise *serekh*-beads surmounted by crouched falcons that were identified with the living king—and were presumably his protector. One of three contemporary gold amulets from a woman's burial at Naga ed-Deir in Upper Egypt was shaped like an elaterid beetle, sacred to the warlike goddess Neith of Sais; its top was also inlaid with her emblem. Although, the amulet placed its wearer under Neith's protection, it might also have been the insignia of her priestess. During the succeeding period, the Old Kingdom, a woman buried at Giza wore some fifty gold elaterids around her neck.

By the end of the Old Kingdom, the range of amuletic types was expanded; many took the form of living creatures. The earliest firmly dated scarab (dung beetle) was made of ivory and the find was excavated in a sixth dynasty burial at Abydos. Its appearance marked the beginning of an amuletic form that was to become the most prevalent in ancient Egypt. Ancient misapprehensions about the insect's characteristic behavior—that baby beetles were spontaneously generated from a ball of dung rolled about by an adult—led to its consideration as a symbol of new life, regeneration, and resurrection. Other new forms, such as turtles, scorpions, and crocodiles, which appeared in numbers at that time, were apotropaic, worn to ward off the evil or danger they represented.

Within the history of ancient Egyptian mythology, the turtle remained a creature of darkness, waiting in the waters of the underworld to impede the nightly progress of the sun god's bark. The harmful powers of the scorpion, however, later came to be harnessed for good as the goddess Serket (who wore the venomous creature on her head), who—with Isis, Neith, and Nephthys—became an amuletic protectress of the dead, linked with the embalmed internal organs. Yet throughout dynastic times, scorpion-form amulets continued to be used apotropaically. Amulets of crocodiles, which predate the first dynasty, also exemplify this strangely ambiguous attitude. Throughout the pharaonic period, they were worn to ward off this most feared creature which, in eating its victim, denied a person the chance of an afterlife. At the same time, the crocodile was revered as the deity Sobek who, thus propitiated, in theory could do no harm. The amulet of a crowned crocodile, or of a man with a crocodile's head, represented Sobek and could be worn as a sign of the god's patronage and protection. As early as the Old Kingdom, amulets of a standing hippopotamus probably depicted the beneficent Taweret as the goddess of childbirth; a horned cow's head probably represented the goddess Hathor as the archetypal mother; and a vulture probably symbolized Nekhbet as the patroness of Upper Egypt. It is not certain that the frog was then associated with the goddess Heket who assisted Khnum at mankind's creation. Because of its apparent self-generation from mud in teeming numbers, the frog always had connotations of fertility and resurrection.

Other amulets of living creatures that first appeared in the late Old Kingdom pose greater problems of classification. Does the duckling represent a food offering to be a magical supplier of offerings not presented at the tomb? If this is its function, it would belong to Petrie's *ktematic* class (from Greek for "property") of amulets representing items connected with the funerary cult. Other amulets in this category functioned as substitutes for funerary goods taken to the tomb for use in the afterlife but which might be stolen or destroyed: they

take the form of various types of jewelry, clothing, and *shawabti* servant figures. Then, too, the duckling might be interpreted as a forerunner of the duck-form amulet with head turned back as though in sleep, awaiting awakening, which symbolized resurrection. A new amulet form, one shaped like a *bolti* fish, certainly had connotations of regeneration because of its habit of hiding its young in its mouth when danger threatened, spitting them out later to reappear as though reborn. The simian-shaped amulets may have represented the vervet, guarantor of its wearer's sexuality, or they were forerunners of a sacred baboon.

The couchant hare as amulet had a long history, and was especially popular in the Late period. It is unclear, however, whether it was expected to endow its wearer with the creature's legendary speed, awareness, or fecundity, or to guarantee the same victory over death that it achieved by surviving in the inhospitable desert, death's domain. Another amulet new to the Old Kingdom, which also enjoyed its greatest popularity in the Late period, represented in its developed form, two back-to-back couchant lions. The sun rose each dawn over their backs, and the amulet would afford its owner a similar daily rebirth. Uncertain, however, is whether a single couchant lion form was intended to bestow fierceness or to afford protection.

The first animal-headed human deity as amulet occurred in the Old Kingdom as a jackal-headed man, undoubtedly Anubis, the god of mummification. Perhaps the chief embalmer as early as that time donned a jackal's mask to carry out his work and thus initiated the iconography. Like the crocodile, the black jackal was a dangerous force that had to be propitiated; since its main activity was prowling desert cemeteries for bones to crunch, and since destruction of the body prevented an afterlife, the jackal was deified as the god of embalming, assigned to protect the very corpse it would by nature attack. A new amuletic form, one of a kneeling man with a palm rib in each outstretched hand, exhibits the unchanging iconography of Heh, god of millions, bestower of eternity. The significance is unknown, however, from the considerable extant examples of human-form amulets of men, women, and children; these are distinguished by various postures and children are always identified by the characteristic pose, with a finger to the mouth.

Some of the best known, in the form of inanimate objects, made a first appearance in the Old Kingdom. Most belong to Petrie's *dynatic* category: amulets that were invested with particular powers whose use could be transferred to their wearers. Although the *ankh*, the T-shaped cross with a loop handle later adopted by the Copts (representing pictorially a sandal's tie-straps) appeared early, few amuletic examples have survived from any period of pharaonic history. The hieroglyph *ankh* was used to write the words "life," "to live," "living," and "alive." The *ankh*, however, was employed far more as an element of design, in a hieroglyphic context, and as a large scepterlike emblem carried by deities and offered to the favored.

New, too, was the *djed*-pillar amulet, in the form of the hieroglyph meaning "enduring" and "stable," originally representing a stylized tree trunk with lopped-off branches. It was associated first with Sokar, funerary god of Saqqara (near Memphis), and later with Ptah, the creator god of Memphis. It was already becoming linked with Osiris, the god of the dead during that time, and henceforth represented his backbone with ribs. Once it became a prescribed funerary amulet in the early New Kingdom,

chapter 155 of the *Book of Going Forth by Day* associated it solely with Osiris. Although its specified material was gold, most examples of this form were made of green or blue materials having regenerative connotations.

The *wedjat* ("sound one") also made its first appearance in the Old Kingdom; it took the form of the eye of the falcon sky god Horus. The Eye of Horus was considered the most powerful of protective amulets. Abundant examples with many variant forms and materials have survived from all subsequent dynastic periods. Its basic shape resembles a human eye with eyebrow, but beneath the eye it has a drop and a curl, markings of the lanner falcon (*Falco biarmicus*). It is usually considered to represent the left "lunar" eye, plucked out by Seth and restored to Horus by Thoth—a reference to the moon being "injured" as it wanes and "restored" as it waxes each month. Yet the term might also apply to the right "solar" eye that was never injured; interestingly, right *wedjat* amulets also exist.

During the First Intermediate Period, the number and range of amuletic forms noticeably increased. A new category of funerary amulets that represented royal regalia and divine emblems, once only of use to royalty in the life after death, became available to everyone as a result of the democratization of funerary beliefs and practices already in evidence. Henceforth, any burial might have contained amulets of the most royal of all protective creatures, the human-headed, lion-bodied sphinx. Other examples include the Red Crown or Double Crown; the vulture and cobra, emblems of Upper and Lower Egypt respectively; and the *uraeus* (upreared cobra), solar protector of royalty, which in life was worn only by the pharaoh. Other forms of amulet that fall within Petrie's dynatic classification were not added to the repertory for commoners until the Late period. Examples include the royal beard and headdress, the White Crown, and the crook and flail; some divine emblems, such as the animal-headed *was*-scepter, bestower of dominion; the cord-formed *shen*, which granted solar protection; the tall feather plumes, emblem of divine majesty; and cosmic forms, such as the sun and moon, symbolic of a celestial afterlife to which only the pharaoh once had access.

Unique to the First Intermediate Period was a category of funerary amulet in the shape of various parts of the human anatomy. These were intended to bestow their particular functions and capabilities on their dead owner and physically substitute for those bodily parts should they be damaged or destroyed. The hand, fist, or arm with fist would endow their wearer with manual dexterity and the capability for forceful action; the leg with foot would bestow the power of movement; the eye would give sight; and the face would provide the use of the senses in general. Perhaps most of them came to be considered inessential later because improvements in mummification methods made limbs less likely to become detached or injured. Body-part amulets demonstrate the problem of attempted classification into only five broad categories; their function is essentially homopoeic, but by providing a substitution, they are ktematic.

During the Middle Kingdom, the range of amuletic types widened, although some were to prove not only characteristic of, but virtually exclusive to, the period. Curiously, most were intended for use by women. Such is the case for the protective cylinder amulet, whether solid or of hollow precious metal, and for the amulet shaped like an oyster shell, also frequently of precious metal, which guaranteed the wearer's good health—and whose name (*wedja*) came to be one of the generic words for an amulet. Although actual cowrie shells were worn amuletically far earlier, only in the Middle Kingdom were they made of precious metals or semiprecious stones and strung as girdle elements, intended to ward off harm from the female genitalia they were thought to resemble. (The New Kingdom development of the shape is so unlike the original as to be termed "wallet-bead.") The bird's claw, too, was imitated during the Middle Kingdom in inlaid precious metal or in semiprecious stone, and this amulet was attached to anklets to bestow swiftness and grace to a dancer's steps. Cloisonné-work clasps that spelled hieroglyphic good wishes to their royal wearers are found only during the Middle Kingdom. Exceptionally, a typical Middle Kingdom form, the hunched, squatting female human-headed sphinx (the proto-*ba*) of amethyst or turquoise was developed by the end of the New Kingdom into a seated cat whose human female head sported the stranded hairstyle characteristic of Nubia, which has been linked with childbirth and nursing. Virtually unique to the Middle Kingdom as an amulet, although commonplace throughout dynastic times as a protective decorative element, is the *s3* (used as hieroglyph to write the word "protection"); it is shaped like the reed protector worn as a life jacket by marsh dwellers.

Scarabs appeared in increasing numbers during the Middle Kingdom, and their amuletic properties were enhanced by texts and decorative images on their undersides, although some examples were employed as seals and were inscribed with the name and titles of their owner. Often the scarab seal acted as the bezel of a finger ring and was attached to the ring's shank so that it could revolve. During the New Kingdom, when scarabs as seals were superseded by metal signet rings, their amuletic function became all-important once more. The range of decoration on the underside of the scarab was enormous, from religious and royal scenes, texts, mottoes, and good luck signs to geometric and floral patterns and cryptography. Exactly contemporary with fully developed scarab amulets, and having an identical function were the scaraboids. Those forms have the same flat, oval, decorated underside, but instead of the insect's body, the back takes the shape of almost any living creature, often in multiples. These carved in high relief or free standing included kneeling antelopes, reclining lions, standing hedgehogs, recumbent ducks, reclining hippopotami, crocodiles back to back, *bolti* fish, baboons, and monkeys. A deviant form is the cowroid, a scaraboid with an elongated base and a back that resembles a stylized cowrie shell.

One particular form of scarab, the heart scarab, was to become the funerary amulet *par excellence*, so-called because it was made solely to be placed over the mummy's heart. Ideally shaped from a specified (but unidentified) green stone, its underside bore the heart scarab formula (chapter 30B of the *Book of Going Forth by Day*). Its function was to bind the heart to silence while it was being weighed in the underworld, so as to ascertain its deceased owner's worthiness to enter the Egyptian version of paradise. The heart was weighed and left in place during mummification (as the only internal organ to remain in the body) because it was believed to be the seat of intelligence, the originator of all feelings and actions, and the storehouse of memory. Consequently, four chapters of the *Book of Going Forth by Day* were concerned with preventing the deceased

from being deprived of the heart in the afterlife. Heart-shaped amulets (substitutes for the organ should the unthinkable occur) were occasionally inscribed with the heart scarab formula. The earliest were contemporary with their first depiction as a prescribed funerary amulet in early New Kingdom books of *Going Forth by Day* and were made only of materials with regenerative symbolism or with connotations of eternity. Their characteristic shape resembled a pot with a neck and two lug handles, rather than the organ in question, but their ability to represent the very essence of their owner was demonstrated by forms with human heads. The earliest dated heart scarab bearing chapter 30B belonged to Nebankh, a thirteenth dynasty official of Sobekhotpe IV. It predates the earliest royal example to survive, which belonged to the seventeenth dynasty pharaoh Sobkemsaf II by more than a century. Generally, such innovations appeared among nonroyalty only after an earlier introduction for royalty.

Royal heart scarabs of the New Kingdom and later were frequently incorporated into a pectoral and supplied with inlaid wings, an acknowledgment that the dung beetle could fly and a visualization of the concept of resurrection. For commoners in the Late period, the same imagery was conveyed by a large flat-based winged scarab of glazed composition used for stitching to the mummy wrappings or for incorporation into the bead netting that enveloped contemporary mummies. A less well-known type of Late period funerary scarab has relief legs clasped to a highly convex belly that was pierced or had a loop for attachment to mummy wrappings. Sometimes the insect's head was replaced by that of a ram, falcon, or bull—presumably having connotations of solar rebirth.

Another prescribed New Kingdom funerary amulet was the *tyet* or Girdle of Isis, representing an open loop of cloth with a bound lower end and a long hanging sash that is flanked by two folded loops. Its specified material was red jasper, the color of the goddess's blood, and it conferred her protection. Papyrus exemplified green vegetation (considered symbolic of new life) and as the *wadj*, or papyrus scepter, it became another example of prescribed funerary amulets. Made predominantly of green material, it occurred first in the eighteenth dynasty; some Late period examples had two plants carved side by side on a plaque.

Surprisingly few amulets of deities, whether in human, animal-headed, or sacred animal form, predate the New Kingdom. Even then, the number of examples was not great and the repertory remains restricted. By far the most popular forms were the minor household deities connected with birth who would help with rebirth in the afterlife. The goddess Taweret—a composite of a hippopotamus with fearsome teeth, always in upright posture but with the pendulous breasts and swollen stomach of a pregnant woman, and with a crocodile's tail—aided woman in childbirth. Her attendant Bes was a good-natured genie, who warded off evil influences at the moment of birth by noisy music-making or by wielding a knife. This dwarflike deity had a lion's mane surrounding leonine features, a lion's tail, and bandy legs and was usually depicted naked, except for tall plumes on his head. During the New Kingdom, the major deities as amulets were the falcon-form sun god, Isis suckling Horus, Hathor as cow, Thoth as baboon, the ram-headed creator Khnum, and a divine child (Horus or the infant sun). Unique to the Ramessid period was an amulet depicting

the god Seth with a long curved snout and tall squared-off ears. Although patron of the Ramessid pharaohs, his amuletic form would only be worn in life as a sign of devotion; in the afterlife, Osiris was king. After his demonization, in the Late period, amulets were made showing Seth in hippopotamus form being harpooned by Horus, thus protecting the owner against evil.

From the end of the New Kingdom, amulets of deities became numerous and more diverse in subject. Most of the great gods and goddesses and their animal manifestations, as well as some obscure deities were represented during this time. Examples of those in completely human form were Amun-Re, king of the gods; Ptah, the Memphite creator; the lotus god Nefertum; Shu, god of air; Maat, goddess of cosmic order; Hathor with cow's horns and disk; and Mut, Amun-Re's wife, first appeared early in the Third Intermediate Period, as did Hatmehit, the local goddess of Mendes who wears a fish on her head. Not until the twenty-sixth dynasty, however, were there amulets that depicted the ancient war goddess Neith; the Theban lunar god Khonsu; Imhotep, the deified architect of the Step Pyramid at Saqqara; and the local hunter god Inhert. Amulets of the Apis bull, Ptah's earthly animal manifestation, were, surprisingly, introduced at that late date.

Numerous falcon-headed deities first occurred as amulets during the Third Intermediate Period. Such were Horus of Edfu, Horus-the-Elder, Horus, son of Osiris, the Theban war god Montu, and a secondary form of lunar Khonsu. More obscure amuletic deities for this period were the snake-headed Nehebkau who symbolized invincible living power, and Mayhes, the only lion god who appeared as amulet. Maned, lion-headed goddesses, however, were particularly popular during the Third Intermediate Period. Those included Bastet, patroness of the Libyan dynasties; Sekhmet, symbolizing the destroying heat of the sun; Tefnut of Heliopolis; Wadjyt, protectress of Lower Egypt; and local deities, such as Mehyt and Pakhet. It was also usually a lion goddess's head which surmounted the broad collar of the protective *aegis* amulet. Amulets of Bastet as a cat were proliferate. Petrie had classified all amulets of deities as theophoric (better theomorphic), but in function most can be allotted to his phylactic (protective) category or to his homopoeic category, for the wearer wished to assimilate the deity's particular powers or characteristics.

First occuring in the Third Intermediate Period and characteristic of it, were amulets of the Four Sons of Horus, the canopic deities who guarded the embalmed internal organs. At that time, a change in mummification practices caused the canopic packages to be returned to the body cavity, each with an amulet of the relevant deity attached, shown full length and mummiform. Even when the packages were placed in canopic jars, an amuletic set containing falcon-headed Kebehsenuef, baboon-headed Hapy, human-headed Imsety, and jackal-headed Duamutef would still be supplied for stitching to the mummy wrappings or for incorporation into the bead netting that enveloped contemporary mummies.

During the Saite period, funerary amulets were used in significantly increased number and form. Types which had previously been found only in royal burials were now made available to all. The *weres*-amulet, in the shape of a headrest, the preferred support for the head during sleep and usually made from hematite, became characteristic of Late period burials. Its primary purpose was to raise the deceased's head magically in

resurrection, just as the sun was raised over the eastern horizon each dawn. The *pss-kf* amulet with a bifurcated end was used in the Opening of the Mouth ceremony, which reincorporated the spirit into the corpse on the day of burial. It reappeared in the New Kingdom form at this time. The carnelian or red jasper snake's head, which protected the dead against snake bites and gave refreshment to the throat, was manufactured only for royalty and the highest officials during the New Kingdom.

New forms were invented during the Saite period, perhaps to fill a perceived lack. The two-fingers amulet, always of a dark material (obsidian or black glass), perhaps represented the index finger and the second digit of the embalmer, and was invariably found near the embalming wound. It might have been intended to confirm the embalming process or to give protection to the most vulnerable area of the corpse. Amulets in the form of the carpenter's set, square, and plummet, which bestowed eternal rectitude and everlasting equilibrium; the writing tablet amulet, which gave access to magical formulas; and the *sma*-sign, which represented an animal's lungs and windpipe, symbolizing unification, were unique to the period. These examples belong to Petrie's *dynatic* category but are representative of a state or condition that the owner wished to enjoy in the afterlife.

The amuletic form of the triad of the Osirian holy family—comprised of Isis and Nephthys flanking the child Horus—has not been dated earlier than the Saite period. Always made of glazed composition, the figures are almost invariably shown in frontal raised relief against a plaque. The goddesses would bestow to the deceased the same protection that they afforded their dead brother Osiris and his infant son Horus. It is noteworthy that amulets of the god of the dead continued to be extremely few in number. Earlier, Osiris was depicted only as a pectoral element in the company of family deities. Most of the tiny bronzes of Late period date that characteristically depict him in mummiform not only have suspension loops but also show tangs below the feet and were not intended to be worn as a personal ornament.   *Carol A. R. Andrews*

AMUN AND AMUN-RE. The god Amun, who later became Amun-Re, was the focus of the most complex theological system of ancient Egypt. In his developed form, Amun-Re combined within himself the two opposite realities of divinity—the hidden and the revealed. The name Amun (Eg., *Imn*) indicated his essential being, for its meaning was "the hidden one" or "the secret one." According to myth, his true name was unknown, thus indicating his unknowable essence. This imperceptibility owed to the absolute otherness or holiness of the deity, and it attested that he was totally different from all other beings and transcendent of the created universe. The second element in his name, *Re,* was the common Egyptian term for "the sun." In this *Re* element, which was also the name of the sun god of Heliopolis, Amun was revealed—thus, Amun-Re.

Amun was known at an early date, since a few references in the Pyramid Texts (from the Old Kingdom) attest to his antiquity. Although those references are scanty, they show him as a primeval deity, a symbol of the creative force. Amun was also known as one of the eight Heh gods of the Ogdoad of Hermopolis, where he was paired with his original spouse, Amaunet, as a symbol of hiddenness and mystery. Since he was an element in the Hermopolitan Ogdoad, that might indicate Hermopolis as his

The Gold Amun, twenty-second dynasty. This solid gold statue of the solar god Amun is an extremely rare example of Ancient Egyptian precious statuary. Found in Karnak, it many have been a part of the royal offerings to the temple. (The Metropolitan Museum of Art, Gift of Edward S. Harkness, 1926 [26.7.1412])

place of origin, although another possibility makes him an ancient deity of the area around Thebes. It was at Thebes that Amun's power developed, although he was, at first, less important than

Montu, the war deity and the original chief god of the city. As the power of Thebes grew during the latter decades of the First Intermediate Period, Amun grew along with it. Even at that early date, Amun's nature tended toward syncretism, and the name Amun-Re appeared on a stela erected by the governor Intef of Thebes before 2000 BCE. Amun's growth was accelerated when Amenemhet I seized power in Thebes and founded the twelfth dynasty in 1991 BCE.

The hidden aspect of Amun enabled him to be easily syncretized and associated with other deities. Amun was identified with Montu and he soon replaced Montu as protector of Thebes. As the power of Thebes increased, Amun's identification with Re became more pronounced. That identification was probably encouraged by the moving of Egypt's capital from Thebes to Itjtawy, at the apex of the Nile Delta, under Amenemhet I (r.1991–1962 BCE). Amun and Re were thereby placed in closer contact, and a syncretism of the two would have been very astute, both theologically and politically. The syncretism did not imply the absorption of one deity by the other; nor did it imply the creation of yet another god. Amun and Re still remained as separate hypostatic deities, but their syncretism was an expression of the unity of divine power. Associations with other deities were also found, and Amun soon came to bear such designations as Amun-Re-Atum, Amun-Re-Montu, Amun-Re-Horakhty, and Min-Amun.

In the middle of the sixteenth century BCE, the expulsion of the Hyksos as rulers provided an impetus to Amun's growth, for that event was a vindication of both Egyptian power and Amun-Re. Temples to him were erected throughout Egypt, the two most significant being that in the heart of ancient Thebes, present-day Luxor, and the Great Temple at Karnak, the major shrine of Amun-Re, on the outskirts of the present city. The importance of those shrines is evident in the extravagant manner in which they were enlarged and enriched over the centuries by rulers of Egypt who were eager to express their devotion to Amun-Re, who had become the state god. At Thebes, the annual Opet festival was celebrated in his honor. During the Opet festival, the statue of Amun was conveyed by boat from the Karnak temple to that at Luxor. The festival was a celebration of Amun's marriage to Mut in his aspect of Ka-mut-ef (K3 mwt.f, "bull of his mother")—a recognition of his procreative function—but it was also the festival of the Egyptian state, for Amun-Re had become the protecting deity of Egypt and the monarchy. During the New Kingdom, Amun-Re received the title of "king of the gods," and the growth of the empire transformed him into a universal deity. By the twenty-fifth (Nubian) dynasty, Amun-Re was even chief god of the Nubian kingdom of Napata.

The might of Amun-Re and the strength of the royal throne were not seen as competing powers. Essentially, they were two sides of the same coin: the monarchy supporting Amun-Re, and the god being the mainstay of royal power. Such interdependence of state and religion was underscored by the official mythology that made Amun-Re the physical father of the pharaoh. According to myth, Amun-Re could take the form of the ruling monarch to impregnate the chief royal wife with his successor—a tradition first recorded in New Kingdom times, under Hatshepsut, but most probably was more ancient. Furthermore, according to official state theology, Egypt was ruled by Amun-Re through the pharaoh, with the god revealing his will through oracles. Amun-Re was concerned with the maintenance of *maat* (*mзʿt*; "truth," "justice," "goodness"), not only on the wider scale but even at the level of the individual. He became the champion of the poor and a focus of personal piety. The magnitude of Amun-Re's spiritual and political power helped transform ancient Egypt into a theocracy, and his priesthood became one of the largest and most influential. That situation was beneficial both to the political powers and to the spiritual power for as long as each supported the other. At times, however, conflict arose, as happened during the eighteenth dynasty reign of Amenhotpe IV (Akhenaten). The most obvious proof of the political power of Amun-Re and his temple was the emergence of the Theban priest-kings during the twenty-first dynasty.

Amun-Re was the Egyptian creator deity *par excellence*. His association with the air as an invisible force facilitated his development as supreme creator. According to Egyptian myth and theology, he was self-created, thus without mother or father. His creative role, stressed during the Middle Kingdom (and even as early as the Pyramid Texts of the Old Kingdom), developed fully during the New Kingdom, when he became the greatest expression of a transcendent creator ever known in Egyptian theology. He was not immanent within creation, and creation was not an extension of himself. He remained apart from his creation, totally different from it, and fully independent of it. As with the creator deity of the Hebrew scriptures, Amun-Re carried out his creative action in virtue of his supreme power; he did not physically engender the universe, as had happened in the creation myth of Re-Atum at Heliopolis.

During the New Kingdom, the theology of Amun-Re at Thebes became very complex. His position as king of the gods increased to a point that approached monotheism. In Amun-Re's most advanced theological expressions, the other gods became symbols of his power or manifestations of him—he himself being the one and only supreme divine power. This absolute supremacy of Amun-Re was eloquently expressed in the sun hymns found in the eighteenth dynasty tombs at Thebes. As Amun, he was secret, hidden, and mysterious; but as Re, he was visible and revealed. Although for centuries Egyptian religion had been flexible and open to contradictory mythological expressions, the Theban theology of Amun-Re came close to establishing a standard of orthodoxy in doctrine.

Although the daily ritual in the temple of Amun-Re was essential for the maintenance of political and universal order, elaborate public rituals occurred only at the great festivals, when the focus was on the revelation of the god in the cult statue. His temple was not the gathering place for common worship but, rather, the abode of the god and the point of contact between the divine realm and this world. The daily cult was celebrated as a mystery, within the temple, although this did not imply that its rituals were totally unknown. The performance of the daily ritual was a necessity, for by means of it the deity was imbued with new life, purified, anointed, clothed, and presented with the figure of the goddess Maat as a symbol of universal order; the performance of those rituals constituted an assurance that the cosmic and political orders would endure. An essential component of the ritual was the chanting of hymns to Amun-Re, for not only did they express the theology of the deity but their articulation was also an actualization of their content. Theoretically, it was the pharaoh who conducted the rituals, but for practical reasons their performance was delegated to the priesthood.

Like many gods, Amun was frequently expressed in association with a triad. The triad at Thebes was Amun, his spouse Mut, and their son Khonsu, a moon god. (Mut was originally a vulture goddess of Thebes, who replaced Amun's first spouse, Amaunet, after Amun came to power.) The sacred animal of Amun had originally been the goose and, like Geb, he was sometimes known as the "Great Cackler." The ram, as a symbol of fertility, later became the major theriomorphic symbol of Amun, and the goose symbol was suppressed. Yet Amun was always portrayed in anthropomorphic form, never as a ram or as a man with a ram's head. His association with fertility was symbolized by statues of him with an erect penis. When depicted as king of the gods, Amun-Re was usually shown as wearing a crown of two plumes, a symbol borrowed from Min of Coptos.

With the possible exception of Osiris, Amun-Re is the most widely documented of all Egyptian deities. His textual materials and iconography are too numerous to list, and the wide variety of sun hymns and theological texts have provided ample material for the exposition of his nature and function.

Vincent Arieh Tobin

ANUBIS. The most important of Egypt's canine gods, Anubis (*Inpw*) was the patron of embalmers and protector of the necropolis, who guided the deceased and participated in the divine judgment. During the embalming and Opening of the Mouth rituals, priests wore masks representing Anubis.

Anubis's role as god of the cemetery probably originated from the observation of animals scavenging among burials. Al-

Anubis, god of the dead, leaning over Sennutem's mummy. A religious painting in the vaulted tomb of Sennutem, a necropolis official of the early Ramessid Period (18th Dynasty, 16th–14th BCE) in the cemetery of Deir el-Medina. (Art Resource/© Photograph by Erich Lessing)

though he has features of a wild dog, he was probably intended to be a jackal, as indicated by his long, drooping, club-shaped tail. He is usually shown lying on his stomach on a shrine-shaped chest, sometimes wearing a collar, with a flail upright on his back. From the New Kingdom on, he is depicted as a jackal-headed human, rarely appearing in fully human form. Like Wepwawet and Khentyamentiu, the other canine gods of the necropolis, Anubis is black, a color symbolic of the afterlife and fertility. Anubis is represented by the *imy-wt* fetish, a headless animal skin hanging from a pole.

The etymology of the name *Inpw* is unclear; Kurt Sethe (1930, sec. 17) and others derive it from the Egyptian word for "puppy," although previous scholars have suggested a derivation from the terms for "to putrefy" or "prince." Anubis's most common epithets relate to his funerary role, including "He Who Is upon His Mountain"; "Lord of the Sacred Land"; "He Who Is before the Divine Booth"; "He Who Is in the Mummy Wrappings"; and "Undertaker."

Anubis originated as Egypt's principal funerary god. Old Kingdom offering prayers invoke primarily him. The Pyramid Texts portray him as the judge of the dead, and the deceased king is said to have the body of Atum and the face of Anubis. When Osiris supplanted him in the Middle Kingdom, Anubis was credited with aiding Isis and embalming Osiris, while remaining a guide, protector, and judge of the dead. He appears in the vignettes accompanying chapter 125 of the *Book of Going Forth by Day* (*Book of the Dead*), where he weighs the heart of the deceased against *maat*. Tombs of the New Kingdom and later show him attending the mummy and holding it upright during the Opening of the Mouth ceremony. In the Ptolemaic period, Anubis was transformed into a cosmic deity, and in his funerary role was identified with that of Hermes Psychopompos. In Roman times, he gained popularity as Isis's companion and protector.

Originally the local god of the seventeenth Upper Egyptian nome, the Greek Cynopolis, Anubis was eventually worshipped throughout Egypt. As Anubis-Horus, he had a sanctuary at the site of Hut-nesut, probably Sharuna, in the eighteenth nome. At Memphis, he presided over the cemeteries with Sokar, and he had a sanctuary at Tura. At Heliopolis, where extensive dog cemeteries of the Late and Ptolemaic periods have been excavated, he was identified with Horus. The predominance of Anubis in the embalmers' area at Saqqara has given it the name "the Anubeion."

Anubis's parentage is uncertain. The Pyramid Texts call both the cow-goddess Hesat and the cat-goddess Bastet his mother. Later sources call him the son of Nephthys by Re, Osiris, or Seth. According to Plutarch, his birth resulted from an extramarital liaison between Nephthys and Osiris, but Isis then raised him as her own son. A Demotic magical papyrus calls Osiris and Isis-Sekhmet his parents. The Pyramid Texts identify Anubis as the father of the serpent goddess Kebehut, who assisted him in the purification of the dead.

Denise M. Doxey

ATEN. The word *Aten,* which signifies the disk of the sun, is a term that first appears in the Middle Kingdom. In texts of the New Kingdom's eighteenth dynasty, *Aten* is frequently used to mean "throne" or "place" of the sun god. Because the Egyptians tended to personify certain expressions, the word *Aten* was written with the hieroglyphic sign for "god." Through metonymy, Aten was

Akhenaten, accompanied by his wife Nefertiti and his six daughters, making offerings to the Aten. In the Amarna period, the god is typically represented by an image of the sun's disk, from which extend life-giving rays ending in human hands.

eventually conceived as a direct manifestation of the sun god, as Jan Assmann (1975) has pointed out.

Aten was particularly favored during the New Kingdom reigns of Thutmose IV (1419–1410 BCE) and Amenhotpe III (1410–1382 BCE). Nevertheless, for the actual origin of the deity Aten, sole credit must be given to Amenhotpe IV (later Akhenaten, 1382–1365 BCE), who initiated the first historic appearance of that god by formulating a didactic name for him. In the early years of Amenhotpe IV's reign, the sun god Re-Horakhty, traditionally pictured with a hawk's head, was identical with Aten and was worshipped as a deity. The ruler's pronounced affinity with the newly created god revealed itself in the construction of an enormous temple east of the Great Temple of Amun at Karnak in the third year of his reign. The structure was adorned in a novel "expressionistic" style that broke with previous tradition and soon influenced the representation of all figures. This new style of art introduced by Amenhotpe IV reflected a concomitant religious upheaval. First he replaced the state god Amun with the god Aten, who was newly interpreted in iconography and nomenclature. The hawk-headed figure of Re-Horakhty-Aten was abandoned in favor of the solar disk, now pictured as an orb emitting rays that ended in human hands giving "life" to the nose of both the king and the great royal wife, Nefertiti. Now interpreted as a sole ruler, the Aten received a royal titulary, inscribed like royal names in two oval cartouches. The Aten's didactic name meant "the living One, Re-Harakhty who rejoices on the horizon, in his name (identity) which is Illumination ('Shu, god of the space between earth and sky and of the light that fills that space') which is from the solar

orb." This designation reflects radically new theological positions. Contrary to the traditional concept of a god, these names meant that Re and the sun gods Khepri, Horakhty, and Atum should no longer be accepted as manifestations of the sun. The perception of the new deity was not so much the sun disk, but rather the light radiating from the sun; to make this distinction, his name should be more correctly pronounced "Yati(n)."

In addition to possessing royal names, the Aten now celebrated his own royal jubilees, as described by Jocelyn Gohary in *Akhenaten's Sed-Festival*, London, 1990. Thus, the ideology of kingship and the realm of religious cult were blurred, as noted by Silverman (1995). Aten was the king of kings: he needed no goddess as a companion like other Egyptian deities; no enemy existed that could be of danger to him; he was the light that permeated the world, giving life everywhere.

Although it was customary for gods to commune verbally with the pharaoh, Aten remained silent. He had Amenhotpe IV to function as his herald and his prophet. Even though Aten had ascended to the top of the pantheon, most of the old gods retained their positions at first. This situation soon changed, however, and the gods of the dead, like Osiris and Sokar, were the first to vanish from religious life.

Step by step, the king pursued his reformation. At the beginning of the sixth year of his reign, Amenhotpe IV founded a new capital city in the desert valley of Tell el-Amarna in Middle Egypt. Fourteen unique stelae cut out of rocks in the manner of holy shrines marked the boundaries of the new residence he called Akhetaten ("horizon of Aten"). On these stelae the king explained why he chose this site: on this virgin ground to which no one could lay claim, the new city of Aten was to be erected. Here Aten could be worshiped without consideration of other deities.

Two major temples were built for Aten at Akhetaten. The great temple was an open, unroofed structure covering an area of about 800 by 300 meters (2500 by 950 feet) at the northern end of the city. The other temple was a smaller building of similar design. Both were strewn with offering tables. The first court of the small temple contained a massive mud-brick altar; these monuments may have been the first structures erected in the new city. Around the time of the founding of Akhetaten, Amenhotpe IV changed his royal titulary to reflect the Aten's reign. More remarkably, he altered his birth name from Amenhotpe, which may be translated "Amun is content," to Akhenaten, meaning "he who is beneficial to the Aten" or "illuminated manifestation of Aten." The king then proceeded to emphasize Aten's singular status above all other gods through excessively preferential treatment. In a continuing attempt to redefine and consolidate his doctrine of Aten, he ultimately suppressed all other deities. The new creed could indeed be summed up by the formula "There is no god but Aten, and Akhenaten is his prophet," as Erik Hornung has stated in *Conception of God: The One and the Many*, London, 1982, p. 248. Even though this belief was not born of the people, the king forced it on his subjects. Formerly polytheistic Egypt had always tolerated foreign gods and religions, but now the king would allow no rivals to Aten.

A hymn, the "Sun Hymn of Akhenaten," offers some theological insight into the newly evolved image of the god. This literary masterpiece, perhaps composed by the king himself, is in-scribed in thirteen long lines on the walls of the tomb of the courtier Ay, who later succeeded King Tutankhamun on the throne. The essential part of the poem is a hymn of praise for Aten as the creator and preserver of the world. Parts of the text recur in *Psalm* 104 of Hebrew scriptures. Since the names of other gods are not mentioned, there are no allusions to mythical concepts. The themes of night and death, elaborated with allusions to godlike beings in all other religious texts of Egypt, are cited only briefly in this hymn, as signifying the absence of Aten. The great hymn to Aten abounds with descriptions of nature. It indicates the position of the king in the new religion. It is to him alone that the god has revealed itself: "There is no other who knows you." Only the ruler knew the demands and commandments of his god. In this setting, be became the sole intermediary between the people and Aten, a deity who remained distant and incomprehensible to the populace.

The king's family shared this exclusive privilege. The dearth of myths in the new religion was filled with the ruler's family history. The great royal wife Nefertiti, almost an equal to the king, claimed her position in cult and state. It is therefore not surprising that the faithful of the Amarna period prayed in front of private cult stelae that contained a representation of the royal "holy" family. Surely no home in Akhetaten would be without such a monument as an official place of worship.

In about the regnal Year 9, the name of the god Aten was changed once more. All mention of Horakhty and Shu disappeared. The divine name Horakhty was replaced by the more neutral one "Ruler of the Horizon." With this change, the ancient and venerable manifestation of the sun god, the hawk form, was replaced definitively, and a purer form of monotheism was introduced. The god was henceforth named "the Living One, Sun, Ruler of the Horizon, who rejoices on the horizon in his name, which is Sunlight, which comes from the disk."

The essence of the Amarna religion, which inaugurated theocracy and systematic monotheism, revolves around two central themes: the light and the king. Probably after the final alteration of Aten's name, the ruler ordered that all the other god's temples in the country be closed. To extinguish the memory of them completely, a veritable persecution commenced. Armies of stonemasons swarmed all over the land as far as Nubia, above all to hack away the image and name of the despised Amun.

Other gods were persecuted as well; even the plural "gods" was avoided. When this persecution started, the Amarna period was already at the beginning of its end, and just before or soon after the king's death, the worship of the old gods was restored. Akhetaten was abandoned as a capital, and Aten disappeared from the Egyptian pantheon. In the aftermath of the Amarna period, there was an attempt to expunge the memory of the king, his queen Nefertiti, and all those associated with this heresy—by erasing references to them and destroying their monuments.

Hermann A. Schlögl

ATUM is one of the main creator and sun gods, with Re, Horakhty, and Khepri. His name, derived from the verb *tem*, has either a positive meaning, "the accomplished one"—or a negative one, "the one who did not come to being yet." He is known from numerous textual and iconographic sources. Atum is considered to be the primeval, self-made god of the Heliopolitan cosmogony; he then created, by masturbating, the first

couplet of gods, Shu and Tefnut. This act associates Atum's hand with various goddesses responsible for sexual pleasure and fertility, such as Hathor and Nebet-Hetepet.

Memphite theology (as recorded on the stela of Shabaqa of the twenty-fifth dynasty) holds that the creation occurred differently: the gods came out of Atum's mouth, and humans from his eyes. In another cosmogony, the Hermopolitan theology, Atum appears to have been created by the Eight Gods (Ogdoad). The *Book of Going Forth by Day* (*Book of the Dead*) presents Atum as the god who would continue to exist after the destruction of the world.

Atum's most frequent epithets are "Lord of Heliopolis" and "Lord of the Two Lands." The first refers to the main center of his cult, and the second stresses the king's association with him. In the Pyramid Texts, the body of Atum is literally identified with that of the ruler, an association that Egyptian artists also made when they represented Atum, in two dimensions, as a male wearing the royal double crown of Lower and Upper Egypt. The only iconographic detail that distinguishes god from king is the shape of his beard. Representations of Atum in the round are far less numerous than those of any other god of similar importance, and we may speculate that statues showing a king as "Lord of the Two Lands" may also have been viewed as incarnations of Atum. The largest of the rare statues to show Atum himself is a group depicting King Horemheb of the eighteenth dynasty kneeling in front of the seated god; it was found in the "cache" of the Luxor temple in 1989.

Atum's solar associations are with the sunset and the nightly journey of the sun, when he appears with a ram's head or, sometimes, as a tired old man walking with a stick. His solar aspect also has royal associations as "Lord of Heliopolis." From the New Kingdom onward, he is often depicted on temple walls as the god inscribing royal names on the leaves of the sacred tree (*ished*). In some reliefs, mostly of Lower Egyptian origin—for example, on the shrine of Ramesses II from Pithom—Atum is the god crowning the king. Another episode of the mythicized "coronation cycle" portrays Atum as a representative of Lower Egypt and a counterpart of an Upper Egyptian god, leading the king toward the main deity. The importance of Atum in the new year feast confirming the king's rule is described in the Brooklyn Papyrus, which dates from the Late period.

Atum has anthropomorphic, zoomorphic, and composite forms. In the first, he most frequently wears the royal double crown; other attributes, either alone or in combination, include the solar disk and a long tripartite wig. Various animals are associated with Atum, and some of them also functioned as hieroglyphic signs used in the notation of his name. For example, the beetle (or scarab) appears in the god's name from the late New Kingdom until the Roman period, and the ape hieroglyph functions simi-larly in inscriptions of the Greco-Roman period. In these periods, particularly in the region of Heliopolis, Atum as a solar god was identified with an ape-bowman shooting at his enemies. The ichneumon, devourer of snakes, was associated with Atum in a similar way; benign snakes were, however, another holy animal of the solar god. Numerous small bronze coffins containing mummified eels, bearing a figure of the fish on the top of the box and an inscription incised on it, attest to yet another zoomorphic incarnation of Atum.

Although the cult of Atum existed throughout Egypt, its principal centers were in the Nile Delta. Atum was the god of Heliopolis, where he had a special sanctuary, and he was the main deity of Per-Tem ("house of Atum"), the biblical Pithom in the eastern Delta. He was associated with a number of other gods, especially other forms of the solar deity. Various syncretistic versions that combine the names, epithets, functions, and iconography of Re, Horakhty, Khepri, and Atum (and sometimes other solar and nonsolar gods) became popular after the Amarna period, particularly during the Third Intermediate Period.

Karol Mysliwiec

B

BA. Along with the body, the ka (k3; "life force"), the shadow, and the name, the ba (Eg., b3) was one of the major components in the Egyptian concept of an individual. Its closest analog in Western thought is the "soul"—a term with which ba is often translated—although the two concepts are not fully comparable.

In some respects the ba seems to have been understood from the point of view of an observer rather than that of the individual with whom it was associated, personifying the impression that individuals make on the world around them or their effect on others. This aspect of the ba is embodied in an abstract term, bau (b3w), meaning something like "impressiveness," "effect," or even "reputation." The *Instructions for Merikare* summarizes its advice to the pharaoh on the proper conduct of kingship with the words "A man should do the things that are effective for his bau"—that which enhances his image in the eyes of others and the gods. Similarly, the king's actions against Egypt's enemies or the gods' intervention in human affairs are often called the bau of their agents. The ba itself seems to have been a property only of human beings or the gods, but the notion of bau is also associated with objects that would otherwise be considered inanimate. Warning against the misappropriation of grain, for example, the *Instructions of Amenemope* admonishes that "the

threshing-floor of barley is greater of bau [i.e., has a greater effect] than an oath sworn by the throne."

Like the soul, the ba seems to have been essentially nonphysical. Unlike the soul, however, the ba could be viewed as a separate physical mode of existence of its owner, even before death. Any phenomenon in which the presence or action of a god could be detected could be viewed as the ba of that deity: for example, the sun as the ba of Re, or the Apis bull as the ba of Osiris. In the Late period, sacred writings are frequently called "the bas of Re." One god could also be viewed as the ba of another. This is particularly true of Re and Osiris, who coalesced each night in the depths of the Duat (netherworld), a union through which Re received the power of rebirth and Osiris was resurrected in Re; the combined deity was occasionally called "He of two bas." Like the gods, the king, too, could be present as a ba in another mode of existence: Old Kingdom pyramids were often called the bas of their owners (for example, "The ba of [King] Neferirkare") and officials sometimes bore names that identified them as a ba of the king, such as "Izezi is His ba" (commemorating a pharaoh of the fifth dynasty).

Texts rarely refer to the ba of ordinary human beings during their lifetime. This silence has been interpreted as evidence that such individuals did not possess a ba before death, but the Middle Kingdom literary text known as the *Dialogue of a Man with His Ba* presents a major obstacle to that view. In this unique composition, a man living in difficult times argues with his *ba* the merits of life, even in misery, versus the uncertain nature of life after death. The text concludes with the *ba*'s advice to "Desire me here [in life] and reject the West [land of the dead], but also desire that you reach the West when your body is interred and that I alight after your death: then we will make harbor together." This passage demonstrates the existence of an individual's *ba* during life and reflects the view of the *ba* as a separate mode of existence—in this case, an alter ego with whom its owner could hold a dialogue.

The *ba* appears most often in texts that deal with life after death. In these sources it is both a mode of the deceased's new existence and a component of the deceased as in life. The Pyramid Texts of the Old Kingdom, the earliest textual source for the concept of the *ba*, inform the gods that the deceased "is a *ba* among you" and assure the deceased that "your *ba* is within you." In the Coffin Texts of the First Intermediate Period and Middle Kingdom, the deceased appears as the *ba* of various gods but also as his own *ba*, with the physical powers of a living body. The latter view is also reflected in the destiny described in the eighteenth dynasty tomb of Paheri at Elkab: "Becoming a living *ba* having control of bread, water, and air."

At the same time, however, Paheri's text also states that "your *ba* will not abandon your corpse," echoing the Coffin Texts: "my *ba* cannot be kept from my corpse." This relationship is reflected in vignettes of the New Kingdom *Book of Going Forth by Day* (*Book of the Dead*), which show the *ba* not only returning to the mummy and hovering over it but

also participating in activities outside the tomb. This vision of the afterlife, which appeared in the earlier Pyramid Texts, is based on the daily solar cycle. Like the sun, the *ba* reunites each night with Osiris—embodied, in this case, in the mummy—and through that union is enabled to be reborn again each day among the living in a new, noncorporeal form of existence.

No depictions of the *ba* earlier than the New Kingdom have been identified with certainty, although some funerary statues of the Old Kingdom have been interpreted as showing the *ba* in fully human form. The illustrations that first appear in the *Book of the Dead* depict the *ba* as a bird with a human head and occasionally other human attributes, symbolizing both its human nature and its mobility. This image was adopted by the Meroitic civilization of Sudan in statues of the deceased—essentially as human figures with the wings of a bird. Whether the angels or birds of Coptic art can be traced to the same motif is doubtful. Coptic texts adopted the Greek word *psyche* in place of the native *bai* (from *b3*) as the term for "soul," demonstrating an essential difference between the Christian concept and that of the earlier *ba*.　　　　James P. Allen

BES. The image of the deity Bes is both comic and appalling, to disarm malevolent spirits. Often represented full-faced under the more or less composite aspect of a bandy-legged gnome with a grotesque lionlike face, he might be winged, with protruding tongue, wearing a headdress of high feathers. His apotropaic (protective) power was strengthened by the musical instruments and weapons he brandished. His iconography and the very name of Bes are, respectively, attested in the New Kingdom and the twenty-first dynasty. Moreover, not until the Ptolemaic period is this iconography unambiguously linked in inscriptions, to the name of Bes.

Possibly, Bes was but an avatar of an ancient deity called Aha, "the fighter," who was represented on the magical ivory wands of the Middle Kingdom. Made for the protection of children, those objects often included images with an attitude and features similar to that of Bes. Even in Greco-Roman inscriptions, Bes still had names that seem derived from Aha. Several similar lionlike genii may have originally existed, but they were later confused with one another. Alternatively, this diversity reflects local or functional differences of a unique type.

The name Bes may be connected with *bs3* ("to guard," "protect"), reflecting an obvious function of the god, or it might correspond to a rare ancient word that denoted a premature child, a weak and stunted being, perhaps related to an image of the sun or moon as it comes into being; the figure of Bes would then be the apotropaic transfiguration. The functions of Bes ranged from those of a familiar protecting genius to that of a divinity integrated in the solar cycle. A popular deity, he protected during birth, childhood, sleep, and eroticism, and his image, therefore, was put on numerous amulets and objects of everyday life, such as beds, mirrors, and toilet articles. His figure was painted on the walls of the royal palace of Amenhotpe III, as well as on those of craftsmen's houses.

Bes has been linked with Egypt's far South, not because of a Nubian origin but because of his role in the myth of the distant goddess, in which his dancing and music must convince the rebellious divinity to return to Egypt. Bes also participated in the Hathor myth as part of her entourage. There, Bes could protect the solar child, young Horus (i.e., Hor-

pakhered, Harpocrates), thus moving from the familiar genius of popular beliefs to a guardian of the divine heir in the solar theology. That role, first clearly attested in the decoration of lotiform chalices of the twenty-second dynasty, later appeared in reliefs in the *mammisi*s (birth-houses). References to it are seen on some statuettes showing Harpokrates and his tutor together or in the presence of Bes' mask, at the top of the *cippi* (stela) of Horus standing on the crocodiles.

Associated with the child Horus, Bes gradually assumed that god's aspect and nature—as Isis' son and as an incarnation of the renewed sun—under the name of Horbes. If Bes was indeed the incarnation of a premature child, that syncretism was made possible by the myth in which Horus himself was a premature and weak newborn; that relationship was illustrated in the representations of Bes-Harpokrates, as well as in scenes where Bes appeared in the company of animals linked to the solar cycle (lions, apes, oryx, and falcons). Sharing intimately, then, in the nature of Horus, Bes sealed new alliances with several gods that have been interpreted as hypostases of Horus, such as Soped, Nefertum, Horus-Min, and Hormerty. Furthermore, the head of Bes appeared atop a series of composite figures (usually called pantheistic Bes), which incarnated the omnipotence of the solar gods. The metamorphosis of Bes to the young solar Horus may also explain the birth of Beset, who was thought to be the mother of that exceptional child.

Michel Malaise
Translated from French by
Paule Mertens-Fonck

BULL GODS. The ancient Egyptian pantheon included bull, cow, and calf divinities. Alongside the forms of higher gods—human figures with bovine heads—representations of naturalistic forms show a corresponding variety, from cult figures shaped like bulls, cows, and calves to small sculptures and amulets. Bovine shapes and cult figures of bulls with changing attributes have been found on processional and district standards, on the finials of staffs, in reliefs and paintings on temple walls, on stelae, coffins, and other surfaces. The figures reflect the theological role of the bull-shaped god as a form of the sun god and the events of creation at the beginning of time.

Origins. Various origins have been suggested for the bull gods of Egypt. Generally, they are thought to have originated in Late Paleolithic to Neolithic times. Four categories have been distinguished: the wild bull; the herd bull; the threshing animal; and the heavenly bull, in a star group. Eberhard Otto (1923) had assumed that bulls and bull cults emerged out of the locally venerated bull gods of the Nile Delta. They were thought to be connected with Egypt's royal cattle, raised on the western edge of the Delta. Through those herds, the Apis bull became the sacred bull of the western district, where it was later venerated in a sanctuary, alongside the Sechathor cow goddess, its mother figure. From there, it may have gone to the royal city of Memphis. Similar prehistoric origins have been claimed for the bull on the district standard of the eleventh Lower Egyptian nome (province), the "black bull." There is, however, reason to posit an Upper Egyptian milieu for the wild bull—the Buchis bull of Armant, first attested in the New Kingdom; its theological name means something like "who makes the ba dwell within the body." There was also the Merhu bull ("the anointed one") who was identified with a daughter of an Old Kingdom queen.

Very early in dynastic times, the aggressive wild bull became the manifestation of the Egyptian king. Its subsequent butchering; the selection of the choicest parts (front shank); the sacrifice of the flesh with presentation to the god; and the eating of the flesh, whereby the bull's strength was assimilated—all were certainly very ancient components of hunting activity that were ritualized as a chief's or king's duty. On late prehistoric rock drawings near Hierakonpolis and on dynastic ceremonial palettes, the "charging bull" depicts the chief or king. In Hierakonpolis, some tombs of bovine groups were found. There is early documentation, under Horus Aha, of the royal ritual of capturing and spearing the wild bull. Since the wild bull was encountered in the mid-Delta (Chois and Buto), however, Wolfgang Helck (1987) prefers to assume a different kind of prehistoric world of eastern Mediterranean cultures—all with a common veneration of the "storm bull." At the harvest feast of the god Min, a "white bull" was used. The bull called Tjai-sepf ("the manliest of his threshing floor") is part of the title used by queens of the Old Kingdom. Both bulls must have been connected to the threshing of grain.

The heavenly bull was associated with a star group that had rows of bull heads. Their horns encompassed a star. One of the signs of the Egyptian zodiac was the front part of a bull.

Most bull gods of dynastic Egypt were initially connected with the king or queen. A bull cult that came from Egypt's own regional prehistory cannot yet be demonstrated. Perhaps the bull gods of the Delta came to the settlements of the Delta only in dynastic times, via the royal seat of Memphis, as divine protection figures for the new royal administration (in the standards and bull statues of the temple court). From the first dynasty, the "manifestation of the king" was firmly connected with the "course of the Apis bull." During the royal residence feasts in Memphis, a holy bull was led to the Nile or to its herd of cows; this yearly procession played a roll in the official cattle count (which at first took place every two years). For the Memphis court, it represented a guarantee for the annual Nile flooding and the fertility of the cattle herds, as well as a reaffirmation of the power of the kingdom.

According to the Late period Greek historian Manetho, only in the second dynasty was the Apis bull installed as a god in Memphis—with its own shrine or an external stone image of a bull in stride. The Apis god of Memphis that protected the king and the residence, however, must be sharply distinguished from the holy Apis bull of the Memphite festival procession. Like every Egyptian god, the new tutelary god of the royal seat of Memphis needed a yearly renewal process to make him effective at the enthroning of the high gods. From the Old Kingdom, the recording of the "capture of the (wild bull) Apis," the "drowning of Apis" in the Nile, or the "eating of the flesh of Apis" appears to contradict the original task of the bull of the royal seat of Memphis—ensuring the fertility of the herds. The renewal ritual of the bull god included the royal sacrifice of the bull, his ritual killing, and his transformation into Osiris, god of the dead. In the feast of Apis at Memphis, there may have been an increasing use of substitute animals. The yearly festival was repeated at Egypt's sacred places, in reduced ritualized forms, but with the help of Apis standards, staffs, and sacrificial bulls. Formal scenes of the royal Apis hunt were later added to many temples. The royal military and administrative seat at Heliopolis had its own holy bull for annual festival processions, and a protective cultic image of a bull was in-

stalled. Theologically, the Mnevis bull god of Heliopolis had many parallels with Apis as a royal god—both turned over the goddess Maat to the heavenly sun god (Atum and Re) at the first creation. Perhaps the origin for the Mnevis bull of Heliopolis was an archer with the head of a bull, derived from comparable later archers with the head of a bull, which were erected at the royal *sed*-festival.

Theology. In texts, the bull of the Egyptian festival procession was designated as a "holy animal," an "animal belonging to a god." From the New Kingdom, increasing theologizing of the bull gods occurred, which previous theory had considered of secondary importance. Earthly bull gods that protected the temple and the city were minor filial forms of the cosmic creator gods. In the texts, they can be the "*ba* of a high divinity"; however, if the high god wished to manifest himself in a permanent manner in a living bull, he could do so. Thus the living Memphite Apis bull became a form of the son and representative of the god Ptah; the living Mnevis bull became the son and representative of the god Re. In fact, all the bull gods could have *ba*-forms of the various primeval and high gods (the gods of the Great Ennead; the Nine Great Gods). Depending on the text, Apis was Ptah, Ptah-Sokar-Osiris, Geb-Shu, Osiris, Re, Atum, and/or Horus—or, as later texts say, "all in one." That the living holy bull is something like a "*ba* of Osiris, the god of the dead" is not stated anywhere.

The changing *ba* of the bull gods may describe various identity phases that are not possessed by the living bull but only by the bull god made manifest in the visible statue. These identities with the gods of the Great Ennead are possessed by a bull god during his yearly cyclical renewal (or the reduced cultic form repeated daily)—for example, at the annual civil new year feast, after the bull god has first become Osiris during the procession into the necropolis. The form in which the bull god was first carried to the tomb during the procession was that of the resting bull, and from the Saqqara cemetery, a portable, wooden processional bull survives. After its resurrection as Osiris, during the Osiris feast some days before the new year's festival, the god that reigned and sat upon the throne as Osiris held such syncretic names as Osiris-Apis, Osiris-Mnevis, Osiris-bull of Pharbaithos, and the like. The Osiris bull god was made visible outside the necropolis temple, in the stone cultic image of the resting bull. On new year's day, the bull was then once again presented as a "revived god," in the cultic image of the pacing bull. As a youthful god resembling Horus, it could effectively act as the tutelary (guardian) god of the city. During the procession, it accompanied Horus the king, and in a standing image it assisted in the enthronement of Horus. Only during the enthronement of the youthful city god on new year's day, however, was the holy processional bull similar to Horus in the role of the royal "city god." Only then were the Horus king and Horus-like bull god identical in phase, like "twins" at the enthronement of the bull god in Memphis. Official name-taking by several Ptolemaic kings reflects this.

The very ancient fusion of Egypt's king with the bull—with both the aggressive wild bull and the bull of fertility—allowed the bull's characteristics, his strength and sexual potency, to become part of the essence of royalty. The bull's primeval strength became an essential element of kingship. During the *sed*-festival the king became a bull as part of his own physical and bodily renewal. The king's Horus-name is "the strong bull," from the time of the eighteenth dynasty, and the king is also the "bull of his mother." With the incorporation of the bull's strengths through the sacrifice, the king attains all the various identities. The burning of the sacrificed bull's flesh led the deities Atum and Re through his smoke in the morning and evening rituals.

Eventually, the royal characteristics from the primeval bull and their related phase identities were transferred to the gods. Since every Egyptian high god functioned as a king, theoretically the bull form could be attributed to all of them: Amun, Atum, Re, Ptah, Thoth, Shu, Osiris, Min, Seth, and others. There were cow forms, as well, for the corresponding female deities. The high gods transformed themselves during mysterious primeval divine processes (in the events of the creation of the world, as repeated in the ongoing cult), for example, on the feast days before the new year. Among the most significant original forms—alongside the bull—were the lion, crocodile, falcon, and ram. The essential characteristics of the primeval bulls were then needed for subsequent transfer to the god of heaven: the entire group of bulls were again found with this high god—the heavenly sun god Re, Amun-Re, the high Ptah-south-of his wall, and others. The earthly bull image, as youthful divinity, was in turn visible every morning, as the son of this high god, who then dwelled in the form of the bull. Thus in the cosmogony of Memphis, eight primeval bulls were used and attributed to the creator god Ptah (-Tatennen).

What relevance the numerous bull gods had for the Egyptian population is in dispute. Were the bull gods derived from early agricultural beliefs or was their origin in the renewal ritual of the king and his administration at the royal temple? Entering into the temples of Egypt by way of the royal administration, the bull gods might have been associated with the people, as perhaps is the case in Saqqara. As a rule, where bull gods were venerated, only that local population could erect its own stela, to which they became administratively and personally bound, as partakers in that feast and the ensuing cultic event. The people had no free access to the bull gods, and they could not present them with personal petitions. Priests, however, were entitled to such access, as were officials who visited the necropolis shrines on the days of processions out of the city. Despite the popularity of the Apis bull processional among the common people, even into Roman times, and its status as a tourist attraction, the people had no real emotional attachment to or faith in the individual Apis god. The Memphis Apieion was insignificant, and the court god Apis was only one of innumerable animal-shaped gods representing royalty in all the temples.

Historical Development. During the Old Kingdom, the bull gods, aside from the Apis bull, are mentioned mainly in titles, but they occur also in inscriptions in pyramids and coffins. During the New Kingdom, under Thutmose III, the sacred herd of Mnevis bulls of Heliopolis was mentioned for the first time. From the time of Amenhotpe III, animal tutelary gods were increasingly placed into the courts of the royal temples, and the Amun-bull-of-Egypt may have been among them. Under Amenhotpe III, the Apis bulls of Memphis were interred in sumptuous individual tombs in the necropolis of Saqqara. The entombment of the Apis bulls should not be ascribed to or confused with any popularity of the Memphis bull. The Apis god, to whom the processional bull belonged, was essential for the king's bodily

renewal and his *sed*-festival; through that cyclical renewal, the king and the bull divinity were brought together. Akhenaten (Amenhotpe IV) abandoned the many royal tutelary gods, keeping only one god, Aten, in his new theology; however, in his early boundary stelae as his new capital, Akhetaten (Tell el-Amarna), he mentions a tomb to be erected for the Mnevis. Whether this was ever carried out is not known, but what was involved was not the entombment of a bull but a planned processional cult, as was customary for the monarchy, between the royal temple and the necropolis that ensured the ongoingness of *maat* ("order"). The bullshaped tutelary gods were returned to the temple court alongside the image of the king after Akhenaten's death.

For the first time, under Ramesses II of the nineteenth dynasty, the cultic image of the Buchis bull of Armant was encountered on a stela. Not until the thirtieth dynasty was the processional bull entombed for the first time in its own tomb complex, the Bucheion near Armant. When the Buchis bull processions began to visit the places where bull images were venerated—Medinet Habu, Tod, and Medamud—is not known. Eighteenth dynasty tomb images for Thutmose, which show a bull statue, cannot be unequivocally ascribed to Buchis. Nineteenth dynasty kings had the royal temples in the necropolis expanded, including in Saqqara, at which the king entered into a phase identity with Apis; a place was also made for Osiris-Apis and, underneath that, chambers for the Apis bulls. The bulls that became gods only after death were then accessible through the cult.

In the necropolis of Heliopolis, the complex for the Osiris-Mnevis bull must have been a new building, since there the calves of the Mnevis were entombed.

In Elephantine, a priest violated sacred law, using royal cattle (showing their precisely defined coloration) for prosaic tasks. Beginning in the New Kingdom, a royal necropolis temple, the Osiris shrines, and the tomb chambers of the bull required their own caretaker organization. The *sḏm-ꜥš* group ("those that hear the call") comprised the organization's working staff; they cared for the living sacred animal and recorded the vital data in its stall in the city or in its area of the necropolis. They also carved out the underground vaults for the bulls. Their superiors, often royal scribes and officials, exercised mainly temporary priestly service. The caretaking organization was controlled by the clergy of the Ptah temple, and its theological requirements were set by its elders.

The cult leaders belonged to the distinguished Pastophoren group, which regularly gathered to offer burnt sacrifices at the *dromos* access, between the royal temple and the Osiris shrine. On a feast day, the replies of the god were proclaimed. The oracle god Osiris-Apis in Saqqara, personally accessible only to the Egyptian mystery bearers, became increasingly the giver of authoritative decisions for the population of Memphis. In time, the mysterious "incorporeal" oracle god of the nightly invocation was separated—even by name—from Osiris-Apis (Gr., Osoroapis). Ptolemaic rulers finally give the oracle the Greek name Sarapis.

The stelae of the initiated partakers in the burial and its personnel help explain the Apis organization. The access of non-Egyptian soldiers and merchants to the royal feasts had been restructured. In the temple handbooks, the standards of Apis, Mnevis, and Buchis appear, and they may have been carried by the army, long responsible for such insignia. The military was important in the Apis en-

tourage and the ceremonies on mourning the deceased Apis bull. Under Amassis, the Memphis shrine of Apis (the Apieion, theologically the "birthplace" of the god) was rebuilt along with the bull's stall, and he had the mother cows ("mothers of the Apis bull"), which were equated with Isis, entombed in their own complex in Saqqara-North (they are still undiscovered as of the 1990s). The cattle skeletons known from that vicinity may belong to the many substitute bulls of the great yearly festivals. The youthful divinity, which was numbered among the children of Apis, was Kem (Gem). Statues of the young bull god Gem were found at several sites, probably in the vicinity of the cattle herds from which the sacrificial animals were taken.

The Ptolemies followed ancient Egyptian tradition, maintaining the sacred animals as well as their sumptuous funerals. Alexander the Great had set precedent for the Greek Ptolemies with his sacrifice to the Apis, not to the living bull. In the fourth century CE, the non-Christian populations of Egypt's cities still had processions of their sacred bulls, which remained economically lucrative although the imperial subsidies had long since been discontinued. The Buchis entombments were stopped under the Roman emperor Diocletian, but the date of discontinuation of the sumptuous Apis funeral ceremonies is unknown. An attempt to revive the Memphis Apis processions, under the Roman emperor Julian, was unsuccessful.   *Dieter Kessler*

BURIAL PRACTICES. Numerous tombs of various dates and styles, many containing carefully prepared bodies as well as a variety of funerary goods, reveal an ancient Egyptian belief in life after death. The decoration in some tombs, in paint or relief, includes representations of burial rites and rituals. Some texts from the body of ancient Egyptian literature relate the views of the afterlife and emphasize the need for offerings made in perpetuity. Such archaeological, artistic, and textual evidence show that the burial practices centered around three events: the construction of the tomb; the burial of the body; and the performance of cultic rituals to permit the deceased to attain the afterlife and remain there for eternity.

Tomb Construction. With the exception of the cenotaph (an empty, honorary monument), such as those built during the Middle Kingdom at Abydos, ancient Egyptian tombs were designed to contain at least one body. Tombs were usually built during an owner's lifetime, to be ready upon his or her death. Tombs were usually built in groups, with others of similar date and similar class, within cemeteries located in the desert. Most of the cemeteries are on the western bank of the Nile River. Tomb structures can generally be divided into three components: the superstructure; the substructure, which often includes the burial chamber; and the shaft or passage that connects the above- and below-ground structures. Originally, not all tombs had all three components, and some tombs have been partly destroyed in the centuries since they were built. Enough well-preserved tombs remain, however, to demonstrate that tomb styles change with time; tomb size and degree of embellishment also often reflect the relative wealth and status of a tomb's owner. Since the king was the most powerful member of society, royal tombs are the most elaborate known from ancient Egypt, and they often show forms different from those of nonroyal tombs.

The earliest Predynastic tombs, such as those in the Nile Delta cemetery of Merimda, consist of simple oval or round pits hollowed out of the sand, wherein the body was placed in a contracted position; sometimes mounds of sand (*tumuli*) marked the placement of those graves. More elaborate tombs, presumably owned by wealthy and high-status individuals, were developed as early as the late Predynastic; a tomb of that date at the site of Hierakonpolis included a large mud-brick chamber; its western wall was painted with scenes of ships and hunters.

Abydos, site of the burials of the first dynasty kings and those of the last two kings of the second dynasty, provides clear evidence for the elaboration of royal tomb types during the Early Dynastic period. The Early Dynastic royal tombs at Abydos consist of two structures, located some distance from each other; near the cliffs at Umm el-Gaab, where the kings' bodies were placed, lie large mud-brick underground chambers, which are supported and roofed with wooden beams. The superstructures of those tombs had offering niches in their eastern sides, with stelae placed in them. Surrounding the royal burials at Umm el-Gaab were small mud-brick tombs built for the servants of the king, some of whom were sacrificed at the death of their ruler; the Egyptians abandoned such practices before the end of the second dynasty. Closer to the Nile at Abydos, large mud-brick enclosures were built, which contained cultic buildings. Near one were buried twelve boats.

During the Old Kingdom, the elaboration of royal tomb types continued, with the construction of the most famous royal tomb type in Egypt—the pyramid. If modern visitors have attributed many other functions to them, pyramids at the simplest level represent the most visible component of an Old or Middle Kingdom royal tomb complex. The large-scale stone pyramid complexes at Giza of the fourth dynasty kings

Khufu, Khafre, and Menkaure are the most well known; the main pyramid of these complexes contained the burial chamber for the king and smaller pyramids near the main pyramid contained the burials of royal wives. Elements of such pyramid complexes that emphasized the importance of cultic rituals in royal burials included a chapel built next to one side of the main pyramid, a valley temple built close to the river's edge, and a causeway that connected them. The precursors of many such pyramid-complex elements can be seen in the third dynasty Step Pyramid complex of King Djoser at Saqqara and, to some extent, even earlier at Abydos.

Around the pyramid complexes were clustered many tombs of Old Kingdom officials. These are *mastaba* tombs (from the Arabic word for "bench") and are known as early as the Early Dynastic (Archaic) cemeteries, like Saqqara; they have free-standing rectangular superstructures, constructed of mud-brick or stone, which contain one or more rooms. The burial chamber lies below ground. One interior wall of a chamber in the *mastaba* bears a false door—a carved depiction of a niched doorway. An offering table would have been placed on the floor of the *mastaba* in front of that doorway; the ka (*k3*), a spiritual aspect of the deceased important for his or her nourishment, would come to the false door to partake of the offerings. Some *mastaba* tombs have very ornate superstructures—the Saqqara *mastaba* of Mereruka, a vizier under the sixth dynasty king Teti, is justly famous for its large size and complex relief decoration. Texts within such *mastaba* tombs often state that they or parts of them were given to officials as gifts from the king. *Mastaba* tombs continued to be built into the twelfth dynasty, yet by the First Intermediate Period, most private tombs were of the rock-cut type.

The main chambers of many officials' tombs of the Middle and New Kingdoms are carved in the cliffs bordering the Nile Valley. The New Kingdom necropolises at Thebes include numerous rock-cut tombs with burial chambers below ground, connected by a vertical or stepped shaft. In front of some of them were courtyards that once contained trees or shrubs. Although many rockcut tombs have no built superstructures today, the Ramessid tombs of the artisans at Deir el-Medina often included very small pyramidal superstructures. Theban superstructures were sometimes decorated with rows of funerary cones—cone-shaped objects of baked clay whose flat end was often stamped with the name and title(s) of the tomb owner. [*See* Funerary Cones.]

New Kingdom rulers had rock-cut tombs, excavated on the western bank of the Nile at Thebes, in the Valley of the Kings, where the surrounding cliffs effect a naturally occurring pyramidal peak. The tombs in the Valley of the Kings were often extended deep into the cliff face, to include numerous corridors and chambers. The lack of a man-made superstructure may reflect architects' attempts to make such royal tombs less conspicuous than the earlier royal tomb complexes, and so safer from tomb robbers. (Nevertheless, only the relatively small eighteenth dynasty tomb of Tutankhamun was discovered with most of its burial goods still inside.) Since the tomb locations in the Valley of the Kings were supposed to be unknown, funerary cult offerings had to be performed elsewhere; often, they took place in separate royal mortuary temples, also built on the western bank at Thebes but close to the river's edge.

A few architectural components appeared consistently in ancient Egyptian tombs despite regional, chronological, and socioeconomic differences. All tombs contained at least one chamber for the body of the deceased, which might also contain the funerary goods, though a wealthier or more ornate tomb might have extra chambers for burial equipment. A place in the tomb or in an associated structure provided access for the living to place offerings for the deceased. The consistent inclusion of those structural elements makes clear the importance of placing the body in a protective burial chamber, surrounding the body with objects, and making offerings to the deceased.

After a tomb was constructed, it was often decorated. Tombs were decorated with flat painted scenes, with scenes carved in either raised or sunken relief, or with scenes carved in relief and then painted. In the Old and Middle Kingdoms, tomb scenes included activities of the tomb owner and his family. For example, they were shown hunting or fowling in the marshes (which might have had symbolic meaning as well). Some Old and Middle Kingdom tombs included models, small clay or wooden figures engaged in activities similar to those on the walls. By the Ramessid period, in the later New Kingdom, only scenes depicting aspects of the afterlife were used, such as tomb owners adoring various deities. Most earlier decorated tombs showed the deceased receiving offerings: in numerous Old Kingdom tombs, the tomb owner is shown seated on a chair before a small table. Upon and around the table appear all types of food offerings—bread, jars containing liquids, and cuts of meat. Processions of people carrying similar offerings also appear in many tombs.

Sometimes tomb decoration included scenes of the burial itself. The eighteenth dynasty Theban tomb of Kamose, for example, bears on one wall a painting of the funerary procession carrying the tomb owner's funerary goods to his tomb; it included weeping women throwing sand on their heads, in a gesture of mourning, and men carrying chests and pieces of furniture. Scenes in tombs also depicted rites that would have been carried out there, such as the Opening of the Mouth ceremony.

The texts that accompanied the decorative scenes in tombs ranged from short inscriptions identifying individuals and/or their actions and speech to long autobiographical texts describing the tomb owner's life. Many tomb texts pertained to offerings, with the deceased's name and a list of items following an introductory phrase that emphasized the offerings (in theory) coming from the king or a deity. Offerings were also itemized in a list, and they appeared on a wall of the tomb, frequently near the false door. Such lists itemized the names of the goods desired by the deceased, including materials for the tomb and food items, sometimes in numbers indicating the amount, in hundreds or thousands.

Burial. The process began with the death of the owner and the preparation of the body. In Predynastic burials, bodies were not artificially preserved; the desiccating action of the hot sand in which they were placed was often sufficient to ensure some degree of preservation. Predynastic bodies were usually placed on their left sides, with their faces looking toward the west. In ancient times, the finding of some naturally preserved bodies, caused by shifting desert sands, may have strengthened the Egyptian belief that preservation of the body was necessary for life after death. During the Early Dynastic period, the development of more ornate tomb structures and the use of coffins resulted in the separation of the body from the surrounding sand. Thus, artificial preservation of the body—mummification—became necessary.

From the Old Kingdom, a second

dynasty body is known with evidence of rudimentary mummification techniques. The process was perfected in the embalmers' workshop (*w'bt; wabet*), and by the New Kingdom, the steps in mummification included removal of the brain through the nose; evisceration of the body (except for the heart, which was left in place); drying of the body with a natron (salt) mixture; and the separate drying of the internal organs. After the fourth dynasty, the lungs, liver, stomach, and intestines were each placed in a container; such canopic jars were sometimes held within a canopic chest. By the early Middle Kingdom, the four canopic jars were believed to be under the protection of the four demigods called the Sons of Horus: Imsety, Hapy, Duamutef, and Kebehsenuef. After the body was sufficiently dried, it was wrapped in yards of linen. During Greco-Roman times, the wrappings on mummies showed very ornate patterns, yet the bodies within were often poorly preserved. Amulets were sometimes included among the wrappings, to help protect the deceased. The entire mummification process lasted about seventy days. When completed, the mummy was usually placed inside a coffin, which might be rectangular or anthropomorphic (human-shaped), and might, especially in the cases of royal burials, be enclosed within a sarcophagus. Coffin styles have often provided information about the date of a burial. For example, Middle Kingdom rectangular coffins may bear simple bands of painted hieroglyphs; early New Kingdom anthropomorphic coffins from Thebes were often decorated with painted multicolored feathers, called a *rishi* pattern.

Scenes and inscriptions from various tombs of pharaonic times illustrate rituals (only some of which may have been performed for most burials) that took place after the preparation of the body. The mummy received food offerings in the *wabet weskhet* (*w'bt wsht*; "purification hall") and was then carried in procession to ritual places named for the sites of Sais and Buto. The *tekenu* (*tknw*; a priest crouched on a bier) was then pulled to the tomb; the *tekenu* procession included the canopic chest. At the tomb, offerings were presented and a bull was slaughtered. Then priests recited words of protection for the deceased, whose mummy was placed in the burial chamber.

Along with the mummy, burial goods were usually placed within tombs, and some could have been used by the owner while alive, while some were designed solely for use in the tomb and afterlife. Just as analysis of mummies provides information about nutrition and health in ancient Egypt, analysis of grave goods provides glimpses into the Egyptian view of the afterlife. The most basic burial goods found within the tombs of all the pharaonic periods were the ceramic containers for such foodstuffs as bread and beer or wine. Other containers, such as vessels of stone and, especially in the New Kingdom, faience, might also be included among funerary goods. Some tombs included clothing and objects for personal adornment, such as *kohl*-jars for eye makeup and jewelry of gold and/or silver and semiprecious stones. Wooden furniture, such as chairs and the headrests used for sleeping, might be placed in a tomb. Weapons (such as daggers) and tools (such as chisels and axes) were also placed in tombs. All such objects were similar to or identical with those the deceased would have possessed while alive and suggest that in death the basic necessities of life on earth were required.

Other types of funerary equipment were manufactured solely for use in the tomb. First Intermediate Period tombs and sometimes those of later times contained small-scale statuettes, often depicted holding agricultural implements, such as picks and hoes, and sometimes inscribed with a text describing their duties. The text written on them (chapter 6 of the *Book of Going Forth by Day*) tells us that funerary figurines, or *ushabtis*, were designed to work on behalf of their owner in the afterlife. Offering tables, often inscribed with texts, were also manufactured for placement in the tomb. The presence in the tomb of many images of the deceased, which could be used as substitute bodies should the mummy be destroyed, implies the importance of the body's preservation. Although much of the funerary equipment recovered by excavation has been adversely affected by tomb robbery and decay, the types of objects that remain reflect the wealth and status of the tomb owner. For example, meat and metal were limited to high-ranking burials.

Cultic Rituals. Although archaeological and artistic evidence from Egyptian tombs provide some information about burial practices, knowledge remains incomplete without reference to the texts, including the inscriptions that accompany scenes of cultic activity, the funerary literature, and the autobiographical inscriptions in tombs. Such texts provide a rationale for the construction of tombs. In the most simple terms, before the New Kingdom, tombs were modeled after houses of the living; after the New Kingdom, tombs were constructed to mirror aspects of the afterlife. Texts are particularly useful for delineating the steps involved in the *funerary cult*, defined here as the ritual activities that centered around the tomb and the deceased.

The Opening of the Mouth ceremony was a burial ritual that accompanied the placement of funerary goods in a tomb—and was a necessary step in the deceased's rebirth. A few New Kingdom tombs (e.g., the Theban tomb of the eighteenth dynasty vizier under Thutmose III, Rekhmire) provided detailed texts and pictures of the rites that formed this ceremony, most components of which probably occurred at the tomb. Served by this ritual were statues, scarabs, sacred animals, temples, and, most importantly, the mummy. New Kingdom scenes show statues being dressed in various materials, purified with water, and offered sacrificed animals. Priests touched the mouth of the object undergoing the ritual with a number of items, to "open" it. A recitation of spells accompanied the actions, to render them effective. When completed, the ceremony supplied inanimate objects with the ability to perform all the functions of a living being.

Most aspects of the funerary cult were designed to continue in perpetuity, for to exist, the deceased's spirit required daily offerings of food, incense, and libations. The deceased's oldest son was responsible for making the daily offerings, and he is often shown doing so on tomb walls; by performing the rituals, the oldest son took on the mythical role of Osiris' son, Horus. Usually, however, a priest hired by the family performed the cultic activity on behalf of the eldest son, and the priest's wages included the use of the offerings after the spirit of the deceased had taken what was wanted. In the early Old Kingdom, three types of funerary priests were identified in tomb representations: the *wedpu* (*wdpw*), the *wety* (*wtj*), and the *kherywedjeb* (*ḫrj-wdb*). During the fifth dynasty, the *hery-khebet* (*ḥry-ḥbt*; lector-priest) appeared in texts; he was responsible for the recitation of the necessary spells for the deceased. The title *hem-ka* (*ḥm kꜣ*; "servant of the *ka*") first appeared in the Middle Kingdom;

that priest, whose Old Kingdom counterpart was called the *hem-sekhen* (ḥm shn), offered the deceased such items as incense and water.

Ritual activities like the festivals of the dead provide evidence for ancient Egyptian ancestor worship, although it usually extended back only a generation or two. Festivals of the dead were held at the new year, among other days, and involved celebrating in the courtyard of the tomb with music, dance, and food. Some other evidence for ancestor worship includes letters written to the dead, which suggest that the deceased spirit could aid—or hurt—the living, and the later so-called ancestor busts that were found in the houses at Deir el-Medina. There were not, it seems, any formal rituals in the funerary cult that centered around the worship of ancestors.

Egyptian funerary literature provides information about the afterlife as the society understood it and helps to illuminate many aspects of the burial process and the funerary cult. The Pyramid Texts, called that because they were found first in an Old Kingdom royal tomb, are the oldest examples of Egyptian funerary texts. Although the earliest Pyramid Texts were discovered in the pyramid of Unas, last king of the fifth dynasty, and some were also found in queens' burials of the late sixth dynasty, their language and images seem to reflect an even older tradition, one perhaps first preserved orally. The restriction of the Pyramid Texts to royal burials emphasizes the differences between royal and nonroyal interment during the Old Kingdom—already visible in the monumental scale of the royal pyramid tomb versus the comparatively small nonroyal *mastaba*. The Pyramid Texts describe in part the dead king's ascension to the heavens as a god, to join the other deities. Biographical inscriptions reveal that

during the Old Kingdom, nonroyal individuals did not attain an afterworld but continued to "live" in their tombs; they did not become gods, but their *ka* lived in proximity to the divine dead king. That religious belief was also represented physically, by the rows of officials' *mastaba* tombs built near and around the royal pyramids. Prior to the Middle Kingdom, however, nonroyal individuals acquired some access to texts for the afterlife. Certain Pyramid Texts and Coffin Texts began to appear in private tombs. By the eleventh dynasty, and later in the Middle Kingdom, versions of the Pyramid Texts appeared frequently on the walls of tombs of nonroyal officials and on the walls of their coffins. In addition, the Coffin Texts—the later, private version of funerary literature derived in part and edited from the Pyramid Texts—also appeared regularly. These new texts contained knowledge that the deceased required to attain the afterlife, where he or she wished to be in the company of the underworld god Osiris and to travel in the bark of the solar deity Re. Osiris' underworld, which now accompanied the heavenly afterworld seen earlier in the Pyramid Texts, was inhabited by demons and other dangers that the deceased must recognize and be able to circumvent by means of the knowledge contained in this body of information.

By the New Kingdom, another development in funerary literature took place. That set of spells, called the *Book of Going Forth by Day* (modern editors call it the *Book of the Dead*) has about two hundred spells. Some individual spells or a set are found inscribed on tomb objects, on jewelry, amulets, and architectural elements—but the largest group are found on rolls of papyrus. In the *Book of the Dead*, the deceased continued to want to see the gods Osiris and Re in the afterlife (though during the Amarna period, when the ruler Akhenaten worshiped only the solar disk called the Aten, the *Book of the Dead* spells did not refer to the underworld of Osiris, but instead contained wishes that the deceased receive offerings in the tomb and see the Aten). The afterlife that the deceased hoped to attain was, in many respects, identical to the world of the living. The afterworld was believed to contain a river, like the Nile; there were fields on either side of the river, wherein food was produced; the sun traveled through the sky of the underworld at night after it had set in the west, just as it traveled from east to west through the sky of the physical world during the day. This daily "death" of the sun lead to the placement of most cemeteries on the western bank of the Nile, as well as the placement of some burials with the heads or faces toward the west.

To reach the underworld, the deceased had to be judged free of sin. The *Book of the Dead* Spell 125 described the judgment of the dead that allowed each one to become an Osiris. The vignette accompanying that spell showed the deceased, dressed in white robes, entering before the god Osiris and the forty-two deities who served as judges. Believed to be the seat of an individual's character (and thus important enough to be left inside the mummy), his or her heart appeared on one pan of a balance-scale, with the feather of Maat, goddess of righteousness, on the other pan. A creature with the head of a crocodile waited nearby, to eat the heart if judged unworthy, and so condemned the unfortunate deceased to a permanent, second death. If the deceased was judged worthy *ma'a-kheru* (*m3' ḥrw*; "true of voice"), he or she was allowed to enter the presence of Osiris for eternity.

When studying ancient Egyptian burial practices, the limits of the available evidence must be respected. Most Egyptians could not afford to pay for the construction of a tomb, to outfit it with funereal goods, to maintain the cult after the funeral, or to hire priests to conduct the necessary rituals; they may have been buried in simple shafts dug into the desert sand. To some degree, then, the burial practices described above were those of the wealthy and highranking. Women, too, remain underrepresented; most often, females appear within tombs only as wives, mothers, or daughters of the male tomb owners. High-ranking women, were, however, sometimes accorded the same or similar burial practices as men (see Erik Hornung, *Valley of the Kings*, translated by David Warburton [New York: 1990], for a discussion of royal burial practices from the Valley of the Queens tomb of Nofretari).

Within limits, the evidence shows all elements of ancient Egyptian burial practices were designed to work together, to permit the deceased to achieve spiritual immortality. The body was carefully mummified and placed in the burial chamber; should it somehow be destroyed, substitute bodies were available there in the statues and the two-dimensional depictions of the tomb owner. The priests made offerings of food, drink, and recitations for the spirit of the deceased; should the offerings not be made, they were also available in representations on tomb walls and among the burial goods. Rituals needed to be performed for the spirit of the deceased on a regular basis; if they were not, representations of the rituals on tomb walls, and written versions of the necessary spells on tomb goods and papyri, would serve as substitutes. *Stacie L. Olson*

C

CANOPIC JARS AND CHESTS.
Items intended as containers for the internal organs removed during the process of mummification are generally termed *canopic*. They principally comprise jars and chests but also miniature coffins and masks. The actual term *canopic* derives from a case of mistaken identity: one form of visceral container was a human-headed jar. According to writers of the Classical period, the Greek hero, Kanopos, helmsman for Menelaus, was worshiped at Canopus in the form of just such a jar. Early Egyptologists saw a connection between that object and the quite separate visceral jars and began calling them "canopic." The name has stuck and has been extended by scholars to refer to all kinds of receptacles intended to hold viscera removed for mummification in ancient Egypt.

From the end of the Old Kingdom, the four basic organs removed became associated with a specific deity, (each called a *genius*): (1) the liver was identified with the genius Imsety, one of the four sons of Horus, who could claim protection from the goddess Isis; (2) for the lungs, the pairing was the genius Hapy and the goddess Nephthys; (3) for the stomach, the third son Duamutef and the goddess Neith; (4) for the intestines, the fourth son Kebehsenuef and Selket. These genii are usually identifiable from the middle of the New Kingdom by their heads: Imsety having a human visage; Hapy that of a baboon; Duamutef that of a jackal; and Kebehsenuef that of a hawk.

The earliest canopic installations placed the desiccated and wrapped visceral bundles directly into a chest or a specially built cavity in the wall. Although such potential canopic niches have been alleged to occur at the cemetery of Saqqara in tombs of the second dynasty, the first clear examples are dated to the fourth dynasty reign of Sneferu (c. 2649–2609 BCE), where a number of tombs at Meidum contain niches whose size and position (corresponding to later canopic usage) point to their being canopic. An actual chest was provided for Sneferu's wife, Hetepheres, carved from a block of translucent calcite (Egyptian alabaster) and divided into four square compartments, each of which contained a mass that almost certainly was part of her internal organs, immersed in a weak solution of natron.

During the fourth dynasty, it became firmly established that canopic receptacles should be placed at the southern (foot) end of the corpse, most often slightly offset to the southeast. Normally, such receptacles were cubical niches in the chamber wall or cuttings in the floor. The earliest identifiable kingly example was constructed in the paving blocks to the southeast of the sarcophagus of Khafre, in the second pyramid of Giza. (Suggestions that the South Tomb of

Set of limestone Canopic jars from Giza, twenty-sixth dynasty. (University of Pennsylvania Museum, Philadelphia, Neg. #S4-143069)

Djoser and later subsidiary pyramids had canopic roles were shown to be wrong.) The niches and rock-cuttings within burial chambers may have held wooden boxes; by the end of the dynasty, the organs were sometimes placed inside simple stone or pottery jars, with flat or domed lids. The earliest such canopic jars came from the fourth dynasty tomb of Queen Meresankh III at Giza, during the reign of Menkaure (c. 2551–2523).

Early chests were normally cut from soft stones or into the fabric of the wall or floor of the burial chamber. From the beginning of the sixth dynasty, however, granite examples begin to be found in royal tombs, sunk in floor pits southeast of the foot of the sarcophagus. Fragments of a canopic jar and its complete contents were recovered from the tomb of Pepy I (r. 2354–2310 BCE). The wrapped viscera had been soaked in resin and had

solidified in the shape of the interior of the jar.

During the First Intermediate Period, a number of innovations appeared; most important, canopic jars started to have human-headed lids instead of flat or domed lids. In parallel, the wrapped bundles of viscera were adorned occasionally, with cartonnage masks, again with human faces. During that period, human heads and faces seem to represent the dead, rather than the genius who was invoked on the jar and/or the chest. Previously, any inscriptions had been restricted to the name and title of the deceased, but wooden canopic jars now followed the design of contemporary coffins: strings of text were run around the upper part and on occasion displayed vertical complements. The close link between the design of the canopic chest and either the coffin or the sarcophagus was maintained in most cases until the latter part of the New Kingdom.

By the end of the Middle Kingdom, a basic ideal pattern for canopic equipment had been achieved. A stone outer chest would reflect the design of the stone sarcophagus; the inner, of wood, that of the coffin. The texts of the wooden chest would call on each of the four tutelary goddesses to wrap her protective arms about her particular genius, and would proclaim the deceased's honor before her and the genius. Within the wooden chest would be four human-lidded jars, one per genius, with texts repeating the sentiments expressed on the chest. A typical example of such a text, from the Imsety (liver) canopic jar of the thirteenth dynasty king Awibre Hor, ran as follows:

Isis, extend your protection about Imsety who is in you, O honoured before Imsety, the King of Upper and Lower Egypt, Awibre [Hor].

Not all burials could conform to that ideal, but the existence of the pattern for canopic jars and chests was confirmed by the appearance of painted representations of the jars, complete with texts, on the inner lid of one chest whose size showed that it had contained only simple bundles of viscera—the chest of King Sobkemsaf (II).

During the seventeenth dynasty, the period that saw the definitive replacement of the traditional rectangular coffin by one of human form, a new decoration was initiated for the canopic chest, centering on a recumbent figure of the jackal god Anubis. Early examples imitated the latest group of rectangular coffins, with a background painted in black varnish; later ones were decorated on a ground of plain or yellowish gesso. Those chests also have exaggerated

vaulted lids, with raised end pieces which were characteristic of late rectangular coffins.

Early in the eighteenth dynasty, canopic chest decoration was changed again, to focus on images of the four goddesses and their genii. The form of the chests also evolved from simple boxes with flat or vaulted lids to those that imitated the form of naos shrines. Usually mounted on a sledge, the upper part of the box had a flaring cavetto cornice, while the lid was rounded at the front and sloped down to the rear. The color schemes followed those on contemporary wooden coffins and sarcophagi: beginning with a white background, shifting to yellow/gold on black, and then to polychrome on yellow at the very end of the eighteenth dynasty.

Initially, canopic jars followed Middle Kingdom patterns, but as the New Kingdom progressed, more and more sets of lids included animal and bird heads, replacing the uniformly human faces used on earlier jars. That change resulted from New Kingdom modification of the iconography of three of the four canopic genii. That also marked a definitive shift from the jar embodying the dead person to embodying the relevant genius. (The distinction had been blurred for some considerable time, but the change in the mode of representing the genii resolved this confusion.) Various materials were used to make canopic jars during the eighteenth dynasty, including calcite, limestone, pottery, wood, and cartonnage.

Until the late eighteenth dynasty, the placing of masks on visceral bundles was a cheap alternative to using jars; however, some particularly rich eighteenth dynasty burials have both—a fine example being the canopic material from the burial of Tjuiu, the mother-in-law of Amenhotpe III (r. 1410–1372 BCE). She was equipped with a *naos* form chest, black varnished, with texts and divine images richly gilded on raised gesso. Within the chest lay four human-lidded calcite jars, having long texts filled with black pigment. Inside, the visceral bundles had been shaped into mummies; over the "head" of each was placed a gilded cartonnage mask; in all those cases, human heads were used.

Before the New Kingdom, royal canopic equipment had broadly followed contemporary private practices in their basic forms, but from the reign of Amenhotpe II (r. 1454–1419 BCE) there was a marked divergence. The earliest royal chests of the eighteenth dynasty, that of Queen Hatshepsut (r. 1502–1482 BCE) and that made for Thutmose I by Thutmose III (r. 1504–1452 BCE) were simple *naos*-form boxes, ornamented with simple texts and distinguished from private examples only by being made of stone (quartzite) rather than wood. Amenhotpe II, however, had an elaborate calcite confection prepared for himself, with the jars carved within the matrix of the box and raised figures of the protective goddesses enfolding each of the corners; the jar stoppers represented the king. Such a pattern, further elaborated, was followed by the kings until the early part of the nineteenth dynasty.

The Amarna interlude toward the end of the eighteenth dynasty, when Aten was worshiped, is but little represented in the canopic record. The most impressive items are the four jars found accompanying the mummy in the Valley of the Kings, tomb 55. Their fine human heads seem to have been made for one of Akhenaten's daughters; the jars once belonged to the king's junior wife, Kiya. Although erased before final use, their texts were successfully read as giving the names and titles of the king, those of the

Aten, and those of the deceased. The traditional gods and goddesses of burial had no place in Akhenaten's religion. Akhenaten (r. 1372–1355 BCE) used a chest in the general pattern of his predecessors, but with the hawk, the earliest embodiment of his god, replacing the protective goddesses at the corners. Those divine ladies reappear in the equipment of Tutankhamun (r. 1355–1346 BCE), where they not only enfold the corners of the stone chest but also, as gilded wooden statuettes, stand guard around a great gilded wooden shrine that enclosed it. Within the chest—a solid block bored with four cylindrical compartments and topped with carved heads of the king—lay four solid gold miniature coffins, each holding a package of viscera. The later (fragmentary) calcite chests of Horemheb (r. 1343–1315 BCE), Sety I (r. 1314– 1304 BCE), and Ramesses II (r. 1304–1237 BCE)—the last two from the nineteenth dynasty—are similar in pattern, but added wings to the arms of the goddesses and, for Ramesses II, glass inlay. By the end of the nineteenth dynasty reign of Ramesses II, uniformly human lids seem to have been replaced definitively by the faunal forms of the genii. Private jars showed considerable variation, some being made of faience; and some were replaced altogether by wooden or stone miniature coffins, which usually showed the faunal heads of the genii.

Royal calcite chests were changed under Merenptah (r.1237–1226 BCE), in that they no longer displayed corner goddesses; they were then replaced by four separate jars early in the twentieth dynasty. How the jars were housed is unclear, but they do not seem to have been put in a stone chest. The one extant royal example, that of Ramesses IV (r. 1166–1160 BCE), is very large. Large canopic jars are also found in the Ramessid burials of the sacred Apis and Mnevis bulls at Saqqara and Heliopolis.

From the beginning of the twenty-first dynasty, if not somewhat earlier, most mummies had their viscera returned to the body cavity after embalmment. The canopic jar had become so fundamental to the funerary outfit, however, that high status individuals still used them, even though they were empty. By the twenty-second dynasty, they were superseded by solid dummies—an extreme example of that triumph of form over function was reached when dummy packets of viscera were placed inside the silver canopic coffinettes of Sheshonq II (c. 910 BCE). Twenty-first dynasty jars broadly followed Middle and New Kingdom prototypes in their texts, with the exception of some unique examples belonging to Smendes (r. 1081–1055 BCE). In contrast, the texts on jars of the twenty-second to twenty-third dynasties tended to be rather simple, frequently resorting to the minimalist approach of merely naming the dead person and the genius. Form varied considerably, as did decoration, which was often in bright polychrome during the twenty-third dynasty. Although not uncommon, canopic equipment is found in a minority of Third Intermediate Period burials. The dummy jars were often placed within chests of the *naos* form, although decorated in ways different from those of the New Kingdom; about the beginning of the Third Intermediate Period, a recumbent jackal of Anubis was affixed to the lid of the chest. Kings generally had wooden canopic chests, with the exception of Sheshonq I, who had a calcite box, the design of which was derived directly from those of the eighteenth dynasty kings.

The number of canopic jars increased considerably at the end of the twenty-fifth dynasty and during the following Saite period. Also, formulations were used in the texts. Rather than merely differing in the deities invoked, the actual wording on each was somewhat distinctive. The two jars of Apries of the twenty-sixth dynasty (r. 589–570 BCE) are interesting in that neither seems to have been used in his burial. (One was used a century or so later to contain a mummified hawk; the other found its way into an Etruscan tomb in Italy.) Jar shapes were also changed in Saite times becoming somewhat rotund. Earlier jars usually had their widest points at their shoulders; with Saite jars, the greatest width tended to be lower. Such jars all bear the usual faunal genius heads. There appears to have been a brief reversion to uniformly human heads during the early twenty-seventh dynasty (First Persian Occupation), to judge from the tomb of Iufa (found at Abusir in 1996); his jars also have a nonstandard textual decoration. Unfortunately, there is insufficient material to judge properly the trends of that epoch.

Canopic material from the end of the Late period is rare, but it seems to follow Saite practice. A few Ptolemaic jars are known, yet they were superseded by small but tall shrinelike chests, brightly painted, including images of the genii, and topped by a three-dimensional hawk figure squatting on its haunches in the "Archaic" pose. In shape, the boxes were very similar to some *ushabti* boxes of the same time span.

The point at which canopic equipment disappeared is unclear, but it seems to have been well before the end of Ptolemaic times in Egypt.   *Aidan Dodson*

COFFINS, SARCOPHAGI, AND CARTONNAGES. The distinction between the three terms for containers to protect a mummified corpse is conventional. Coffins may be made of

Inner lid to a coffin from the twenty-first dynasty. It is now in the Egyptian Museum, Cairo. (Photo by Andrzej Niwinski)

wood, metal, or pottery; sarcophagi are usually understood to be objects made of stone; and cartonnages are made of several layers of linen pasted together and covered by a thin layer of plaster.

The most important cemeteries of the ancient Egyptians lie on the western side of the Nile, the side of sunset and of the world of the dead; this explains several characteristics of the Egyptian tomb and its decoration. The deceased lies on the left side, with the head facing north so that it may look toward the east, where the bereaved approach bearing offerings. The eastern face of the coffin and the coffin chamber is therefore reserved primarily for the offering motif, while the western face displays scenes showing the burial and the tomb equipment. A pair of eyes is painted on the eastern side of the coffin, through which the deceased

can watch the offerings, gaze on the rising sun, and participate in the diurnal journal of the sun god. The desire of the deceased to leave the coffin chamber freely and return at any time is made possible with the help of the false door façade which is often used to decorate the long, narrow sides of the coffin; this can be reduced to a simple false door on the eastern face alone, near the pair of eyes. Another essential idea is that of protection, ensured by the coffin itself and the preservation of the corpse; the repulsion of dark forces is guaranteed through apotropaic gods, which are listed in vertical lines on the coffin.

The Egyptian word for coffin is $krsw$; the same root, whose meaning is unclear, forms the basis for the words for "tomb" and "tomb equipment." The coffin is also sometimes euphemistically called "Master of Life." Inner coffins are distinguished as wt $šri$ or $wsht$, and outer ones as $wt'3$ or $db3$.

Old Kingdom and Middle Kingdom. The question of whether the royal tombs of the Old Kingdom were situated in Saqqara or in Abydos is still unanswered. Therefore, the first clearly established royal coffins date from the third dynasty. Stone coffins (sarcophagi) of kings from the Old Kingdom and the Middle Kingdom have been preserved. Some are very plain in form—a simple rectangular coffin with a flat cover—and some are more elaborate in design, with vaulted lids and crosspieces. The royal sarcophagi are sparsely decorated, the main motif being the false-door façade along the perimeter of the coffin. Bands of hieroglyphs are rare. These sarcophagi are notable for their precious materials, such as calcite (Egyptian alabaster), granite, or quartzite. They seem to have had little influence on the decoration of the coffins and coffin chambers of nonroyal individuals, perhaps because the king was able to equip his tomb with all the objects necessary in the underworld. Private people were more limited, for financial reasons and no doubt by decorum, so they sought other ways of ensuring access to these desired objects, which were then painted on the coffin and on the interior walls of the tomb. By Predynastic times, the Egyptians enshrouded corpses in mats or furs and enclosed them in pots, baskets, or clay coffins. In some areas a wooden scaffold was constructed around the body; this may be considered a precursor to the later coffins. At this time, the dead were usually buried in a crouching position—a practice clearly maintained in the first wooden coffins, which are only long enough to accommodate a flexed body. By the second and third dynasties, however, coffins display some of the typical characteristics of the later stone and wooden coffins—they have vaulted lids with crosspieces and are decorated with false doors.

Coffins and coffin walls are decorated from an early date. The main motifs are initially the false door and false-door façade, which first appear on wooden coffins of the second and third dynasties, and later on royal and private sarcophagi of the Old Kingdom. A new phase in development took place in the transition from the fifth to the sixth dynasty, when Unas was the first king to decorate the interior walls of the tomb chamber in his pyramid with Pyramid Texts and false-door façades. As a consequence of this innovation, private individuals of that period also began to decorate the interiors of their subterranean tomb chambers, but they developed their own elements of decoration. In Giza, the walls were decorated with scenes of offering, agriculture, boating, music, and other activities, similar to the decorations in the aboveground tombs. During the Old

Kingdom, typical friezes show containers and vessels, first on the walls of the tomb, while the coffins remain relatively plain and devoid of decoration. At most, coffins have a pair of eyes and a horizontal band of hieroglyphs on the outside; and on the inside, a false door, list of offerings, and bands of hieroglyphs.

During the Middle Kingdom, the traditions of Giza and Saqqara developed into the Upper and Lower Egyptian styles. The Lower Egyptian style extends from the Nile Delta to Thebes, while the Upper Egyptian reaches south from Asyut. Development of burial practices among private individuals during the Old Kingdom was led by the highest officials of the kingdom, and at the beginning of the Middle Kingdom we find decorated tomb walls exclusively in the tombs of the highest officials of the Theban eleventh dynasty. During the subsequent period, mostly wooden coffins were decorated. Because the tombs of nobles were conspicuous, they were often prey to tomb thieves, so very few of their wooden coffins remain. The few preserved examples show, however, that while the decoration of these coffins is elaborate, they are in other respects basically the same as those of lower officials.

Lower Egyptian and Upper Egyptian styles. The Lower Egyptian style, also known as "standard class coffins," is relatively homogeneous compared to the variable Upper Egyptian style. In the eleventh dynasty, the coffin is positioned in a north/south direction, allowing the deceased within to observe ceremonies at the offering site above ground. The interior eastern wall of the coffin is often decorated with a painted false door through which the dead can step out to the offering site. The pair of eyes painted on the outside is intended to enable him to see the activities at the offering site.

Osiris is mentioned in the offering spell on the outer eastern side, followed by a plea for offerings to the dead. On the inside are painted offerings and a list of offerings, in lieu of a depiction of the offering ceremony. The western side of the coffin is decorated with the burial scene, where the god Anubis is included in horizontal bands of hieroglyphs, followed by a plea in which the dead expresses desire for a beautiful burial. During the eleventh dynasty, the frieze of objects is shown on the western side and on the narrow sides of the coffin. The objects shown are mostly those which the dead person carried in life, such as jewelry, rods, weapons, and clothing. Coffin Text spells, originally written on papyri, were copied onto the interior sides of the Lower Egyptian style coffins and are generally not restricted to a specific side of the coffin. Such specific references, however, do occur, for example in a group of coffins from Asyut with Coffin Text Spells 589–606. The most significant innovation of the twelfth dynasty is the transfer of friezes of objects onto the east side of the coffin and the addition of vertical lines on the exterior sides. During this period more objects are shown in the friezes, and even entirely new classes of objects, such as amulets or royal attributes.

The Upper Egyptian style exhibits strong local characteristics, although they are more difficult to date. All coffins of this style are decorated mostly on the exterior sides and have freely rendered representations of the human figures, in contrast to the Lower Egyptian style. Cities and towns such as Asyut, Akhmim, Thebes, and Gebelein develop their own distinctive styles. The coffins from Akhmim are decorated in a very simple fashion: the main motif is the food offering; below the offering spell on the east side, which asks for the habitual offering to the dead, a pair of eyes is shown to the right and a list of offerings to the left.

In Asyut, almost all coffins have vertical as well as horizontal bands of hieroglyphs on the exterior sides. In general, bands of hieroglyphs from this period consist of a single line; in Asyut, however, we find two or three lines. In addition to the offering spell, the lines often contain Coffin Text Spells 30, 31, 32, 345, and 609. Coffins from Asyut are easily recognized by these characteristics. Salve containers, offerings, weapons, fabrics, and other objects are painted in the rectangles between the vertical and the horizontal lines. On each narrow side of the coffin appear images of two children of Horus.

Sarcophagi in Thebes from the eleventh dynasty are decorated in an especially beautiful and careful manner. Most notable is a scene showing a cow being milked while the calf next to it receives no milk; this scene is sometimes also set in a papyrus thicket. Often a female tomb owner is shown holding a mirror while being attended by her maids. On Gebelein coffins, the most noticeable difference is the representation of scenes from the burial ritual. The deceased is shown resting on a stretcher surrounded by maids. Scenes depicting the brewing of beer also seem to be popular in this location.

Other styles. In addition to the Upper and Lower Egyptian styles, there exist two other Middle Kingdom types, both richly decorated. One of these appears only in Asyut. It is characterized by interior paintings whose arrangement is in contrast to the standard style. Here we find a theme of food offerings on the western side, while the frieze of objects is on the eastern side. The objects of the frieze are usually arranged in horizontal registers, but in Asyut the longitudinal side of the coffin is divided into laterally arranged rectangles within which the objects are painted. The second type is represented only by four coffins originating from Thebes, Gebelein, and Aswan. They too are decorated on the inside and are exceptional because they all contain the same group of Coffin Text spells, whose significance—and this is rare for this period—is emphasized with ornamental designs.

Aside from the types and styles described above, there is the court style, which was reserved primarily for members of the royal family. Court coffins are decorated exclusively with bands of hieroglyphs, in a very simple style. On some coffins the corners and bands of hieroglyphs are embellished with gold leaf. The thirteenth dynasty coffins from Thebes whose outer sides are painted in black constitute another separate group. Horizontal and vertical bands of hieroglyphs are painted on the black ground; these hieroglyphs are mutilated in a characteristic fashion, in which only the upper bodies of all birds and snakes are shown.

Anthropomorphic forms. The main coffin shapes used in Egypt are rectangular and anthropomorphic. In the Old and Middle Kingdoms, the body is usually placed in a rectangular coffin; there are, however, attempts to wrap the body itself and to imitate its outline. This development leads to the anthropomorphic (or "anthropoid") coffin. Early on, the body is wrapped in strips of linen soaked in various solutions for preservation. Representations of the face and other body parts are then painted onto these strips. Another technique is modeling of the body—or in some cases, only the head—in gypsum. This may have been the origin of the custom of creating separate cartonnage masks which were then placed on the corpse. The next phase in

development occurs in the twelfth dynasty, when we find the first indications of separate anthropomorphic coffins into which the body is laid. These become more frequent during the transition to the thirteenth dynasty. They are placed, like the mummy, into a rectangular coffin, lying on the left side so that the dead can look through the pair of eyes painted onto the outer coffin. In the seventeenth dynasty the anthropomorphic coffin is separated from the rectangular coffin and becomes the sole container for the body. The lids of these coffins are decorated with a feather pattern and are called *rishi,* from the Arabic word for "feather." They mostly originate from Thebes and are also used for kings.

Eighteenth Dynasty through Greco-Roman Times. The elaboration of coffin styles continued during the New Kingdom. Single coffins, particularly those made of cheap materials like pottery or reeds, indicate the low social status of the owner, although exceptions—richly equipped mummies buried in single cartonnage or wooden coffins—are known. Double, triple, or quadruple sets of coffins, one placed inside the next, are typical of middle-class and upper-class burials. These coffin ensembles utilize various combinations of materials and shapes: one cartonnage and two anthropomorphic wooden coffins, anthropoid coffins in rectangular sarcophagi; or cartonnages in stone sarcophagi. The materials for stone sarcophagi include quartzite, used in most royal sarcophagi of the eighteenth dynasty; red granite, typical in the Ramessid era; gray or black granite and basalt, from the twenty-sixth dynasty to Ptolemaic times; Egyptian alabaster (calcite), employed in the sarcophagus of Sety I; green serpentine; and limestone. The finest wooden coffins are made of cedar, and others of sycamore or acacia. Solid gold and silver were reserved for kings, while gilding or silvering of a coffin or its parts may indicate the owner's relationship with the king's or high priest's family. In all periods, coffins vary in quality of execution, having originated from various workshops. Even the best of these produced both custom-made coffins, on which the name and titles of the owner were inscribed during the making, and less expensive anonymous coffins.

Many wooden coffins, and some stone sarcophagi as well, bear evidence of usurpation. In some cases the coffin of an earlier pharoah was usurped as a powerful amulet; for example, the coffin of Thutmose I was reused for Pinudjem I, and the sarcophagus of Merenptah for Psusennes I. In most instances, however, usurpation was clandestine, perhaps because wood was in short supply; craftsmen employed in the coffin workshops arranged the changes. To adapt a coffin for a new possessor, craftsmen had to alter the names and titles of the first owner, and sometimes the general appearance of the anthropoid lid; for example, the characteristic traits of a twenty-first dynasty man's coffin (striped wig, ears, beard, and clenched hands) could easily be changed into those typical for a woman's coffin (monochrome wig, earrings instead of ears, lack of beard, and open hands). Gilded coffins were tempting to robbers, and the surface of many has been chipped off. The coffins belonging to King Pinudjem I, his sister, and his wife were damaged in this way, but some gilded figures and texts were left untouched, perhaps for religious reasons.

Theological meaning. Cartonnages or inner mummiform coffins represented the deceased person during the burial ceremony of the Opening of the Mouth, often depicted in tomb paintings and funerary papyri. In these the coffin is shown in a vertical position, which explains the solid foot-boards of anthropomorphic coffins and cartonnages. When positioned horizontally, the mummyshaped container resembles the dead Osiris awaiting resurrection. The figures of Isis and Nephthys are often represented on both extremities of the coffin, behind the head and under the feet, evoking the ritual of the Lamentations of Isis and Nephthys over their dead brother. These figures also recall a vignette in chapter 151 of the *Book of Going Forth by Day* (*Book of the Dead*), entitled "Spell for the mysterious head" (i.e., the mummy mask). The iconography and text of Spell 151 relate to the burial assemblage, and the mask accompanied by wig and collar is the most representative decorative element of anthropomorphic mummy containers.

The frieze of cobras and the feathers of justice of the goddess Maat on the upper edges of some coffin-cases, squatting divine figures (often armed with knives), and the judgment scene are typical elements of the figural decoration of coffins and sarcophagi. They evoke the Hall of Maat—the Double Truth—where the fate of the deceased in eternity is decided: the coffin thus plays the role of the Hall of Maat. After the judgment, the deceased took on the role of Osiris, the king of the underworld. Royal coffin lids reflect this idea in portraying the deceased as Osiris, with his typical scepters held in crossed hands. On private coffins, carved or painted representations of hands crossed on the breast have the same function. The coffin or sarcophagus, being a "residence" of the deceased identified with Osiris, was a theological counterpart of the Osirian kingdom.

The iconographic repertoire painted on the interior of mummy containers is also to be understood in cosmological

Drawing of a krsw-type coffin from the Third Intermediate Period. It is now in the Ashmolean Museum, Oxford. (Courtesy Günther Lapp and Andrzej Niwiński)

terms. The deceased is placed between the figure of *a*-pillar (often painted on the bottom of the case, inside or outside) and that of the goddess Nut, represented on the lid, and thus between earth/underworld and sky, a position corresponding to that of Shu in the scene of creation. The coffin is thus cast in the role of the universe. In the twenty-first dynasty, this is corroborated by cosmological compositions placed on both shoulders of the coffin cases, representing the lower, Osirian part and the upper, solar part of the created world. The fourth dimension is alluded to by numerous scenes of the eternal solar circuit, scenes from the *Book of That Which Is in the Underworld* (*Amduat*), figures of the "goddesses of hours," or the Uroboros—the serpent biting its own tail. Numerous cosmogonic symbols (scarabs, *bnw*-birds, lotus flowers, etc.) made the coffin a symbol of the primeval hill on which the Creation took place; the deceased was identified with the solar creator god. The word for the inner coffin; *wst*, means "egg," which evokes associations with the Creation myth of the cosmic egg.

Finally, according to another theological conception, the mummy container decorated with the principal figure of Nut and inscribed with a prayer to her played the role of the sky, which swallowed the sun every evening, became pregnant, and gave birth to it at the next dawn; this created a mythic model of the future rebirth of the deceased.

Historical development. The different workshops undoubtedly varied in their respect for tradition and interest in novelty, so various forms of mummy containers often existed contemporaneously. This is particularly true for the intermediate periods of Egyptian history; by contrast, periods of political stability are characterized by more standardized shapes, colors, and iconography of coffins throughout the country.

Eighteenth dynasty. The rishi-coffins and rectangular chest-coffins, still decorated with the motifs of the Middle Kingdom tradition, were used sporadically until the reign of Thutmose III, but meanwhile a new type of anthropoid coffin spread in Thebes to become the most characteristic form of the early eighteenth dynasty. These wooden coffins—called "white" because of their predominant ground color—reproduce, in a sense, the mummy that in previous periods had been provided with a cartonnage mask and collar. An inscribed vertical band is painted in the middle of the lid and descends to the edge of the feet, and four transverse bands are painted on both sides of the lid and case of the coffin, in imitation of mummy bandages. Texts on these bands contain the common formulae *ḥtp-dl-nsw* ("a gift that the king gives"), *dd-mdw-in* ("words said by the king"), and *imȝhy ḫr* ("revered before"), evoking the names of Osiris, Anubis, and the Sons of Horus. Figures of these mythical protectors of embalming and burial are sometimes painted in the panels between the texts, but the most typical iconography of the "white" coffins shows various burial motifs: the transport of a mummy, mourners, offering rituals, and so on. On the lid, at breast level, a figure of a protecting goddess (Nekhbet or Nut) is usually painted.

Once political conditions stabilized, Theban carpenters quickly mastered the technique of constructing and shaping mummiform coffins. The finest examples of their craftsmanship are the atypically large (over 3 meters/10 feet high) cedarwood coffins made for the queens Ahmose-Nefertari, Ahhotep, and Meritamun. These coffins accurately render the shape of the upper body, with portrait mask and arms crossed on the breast, while the gilded pattern of feathers covering the lower mummiform part reveals a link with the *rishi*-coffins. This type of adornment was in use for royal tomb equipment until the end of the eighteenth dynasty, including Tutankhamun's coffins, and probably also in the Ramessid era and twenty-first dynasty (e.g., the silver inner coffin of Psusennes I).

The complete nested set of Tutankhamun's coffins suggests what other royal burial equipment in the New Kingdom probably comprised. The mummy, provided with a golden mask and golden inscribed bands imitating bandages lay in three mummiform coffins; the innermost is made of solid gold, and the other two of wood covered with sheet gold. Figures and hieroglyphs impressed in the gold are inlaid with colored paste, glass, and semiprecious stones such as lapis lazuli and carnelian. In the New Kingdom, a set of anthropomorphic coffins was laid into a rectangular or cartouche-shaped stone sarcophagus, which in turn was surrounded by several chapel-like wooden structures, gilded and covered with religious texts and motifs. Of these funerary ensembles, only that of Tutankhamun survives intact; only the stone sarcophagi remain of others. Their icon-

ographic repertoire comprises figures of Nut on the top and under the lid, Nephthys and Isis at the head and foot ends, and Anubis and the Sons of Horus on the walls of the case. Inscribed bands envelope the lid and case. Sarcophagi after the Amarna period also have figures of four winged goddesses carved at the corners of the case.

In the nonroyal sphere, from the reign of Thutmose III a new color scheme predominates in wooden coffins: figures and texts are gilded or painted in yellow on a black ground. The iconographic repertoire of these "black" coffins is constant: a winged figure on the lid, the Four Sons of Horus, and Thoth and Anubis on the walls of the case. This type of coffin is also attested outside Thebes, in Memphis and the Faiyum. The richest ensembles of "black" coffins—such as those of Yuya and Tuyu, Amenhotpe III's parents-in-law—comprised several objects: the cartonnage mask and collar; the "network" of bandage imitations lying on the mummy; two or three anthropomorphic coffins; and an outer rectangular coffin, shaped like a chapel and set on runners, which served for transport during burial.

Nineteenth and twentieth dynasties. In the post-Amarna period, there developed a new type influenced by the coloring of royal coffins. These "yellow" wooden coffins are attested from Thebes and Memphis. Figures and texts are painted in red and light and dark blues on a yellow ground; the yellow varnish that covers the exterior makes the blue appear green. In the coffin ensembles (e.g., that belonging to Sennedjem), the outer receptacle is still a chapel-like rectangular case on runners; the one or two inner coffins are anthropoid, with carved forearms crossed on the breast. On men's coffins, the hands are clenched and hold sculpted amulets, while those of women are open and lie flat on the breast. The mummy is covered with a wooden or cartonnage "false lid" or "mummy board," usually imitating the shape of the lid. These mummy covers consist of two pieces: the upper one represents the face, collar, and the crossed arms, while the lower piece, often made in openwork technique, imitates the network of mummy bandages, with figural scenes filling the panels between the bands.

In the early nineteenth dynasty a new type of mummy cover and lid was used. It represents the deceased as a living person, dressed in festive garments, with the hands either placed on the thighs (men's coffins) or pressed to the breast and holding a decorative plant (women); the naked feet are also sculpted below the costume. The wigs of men are of either the Ramessid duplex type or of the traditional tripartite, vertically striped type; women's wigs are richly ornamented with curls and plaits. Both the male "Osirian" lid and the "living effigy" lid were also fashioned in stone for the anthropomorphic sarcophagi of high officials. The innermost coffins of some royal sarcophagi are anthropomorphic (e.g., the alabaster case of Sety I), but others are cartouche-shaped.

In the twentieth dynasty, the royal sarcophagi were buried in crypts cut into the floor of the burial chamber and were covered with massive granite lids. Osirian effigies of the kings sculpted in high relief decorate the exterior of the lid, while the goddess Nut is sculpted on the lid's underside. Besides the traditional repertory, there appear scenes and texts from royal funerary books. The repertory of nonroyal coffins is enriched with vignettes and texts from the *Book of Going Forth by Day* (e.g., chapter 17) and with solar motifs (bark of Re, scarab, etc.). In most instances, however, only the traditional scheme is used, continu-

ing the repertory of the "black" coffins. This pattern is repeated on pottery coffins of the lower classes discovered in the eastern Nile Delta, at Tanis and Tell el-Yehudiyya.

Twenty-first dynasty. Only anthropomorphic coffins are known from this period, mostly from Thebes, similar in form and coloring to Ramessid examples. Only wooden mummy covers are yet attested; these are made in one piece and are usually of the "Osirian" type. The last decade of Ramesses XI's reign brought revolutionary changes in iconography. The old motifs (e.g., the Four Sons of Horus, Isis and Nephthys as mourners, or the Nut figure on the lid) are never entirely abandoned, but a great number of new scenes are introduced. New motifs derive from the *Book of Going Forth by Day* (e.g., the vignettes from chapters 30, 59/63, 81, 87, 125–126, 148, 186), as well as from newly created compositions. The latter focus on cosmological deities such as Geb and Nut or the Serpent on *tn3t* scenes that illustrate the god's activities during the journey through the underworld, the revivication of a mummy, the triumph over the Apophis serpent, the Osirian myth, and the eternal circuit of the sun. Each scene includes both solar and Osirian elements, illustrating the solar-Osirian unity as the theological principle of the period. This extensive repertoire is supplemented by numerous offering scenes covering every surface of the coffin except the exterior of the bottom. Texts comprising rather simple formulae are of secondary importance. Most of the figures are represented in small scale in an attempt to fill all empty spaces.

In the late twenty-first dynasty new iconography appeared on coffins as a consequence of the royal status gained by the high priest Menkheperre. This includes excerpts from the *Book of That*

Which is in the Underworld and some other elements of royal iconography (e.g., scenes of the *sed*-festival). The pattern for an ensemble of royal mummy containers is furnished by the tomb of Psusennes I at Tanis. A two-piece golden mummy cover lay on the king's mummy, deposited in the innermost anthropomorphic coffin made of silver. This was placed in a reused Ramessid anthropomorphic granite sarcophagus, which was enclosed in another sarcophagus, rectangular in form, that had belonged to King Merenptah.

Third intermediate period (twenty-second to twenty-fifth dynasties). The early years of Libyan rule in Egypt exerted no visible impact on coffins, and the "yellow" type persisted in Thebes until the reign of Osorkon I. The frequent usurpation of these wooden coffins suggests illicit dealings. This may have influenced the introduction, under Osorkon I, of one-piece anthropomorphic cartonnage mummy containers. The multicolored, varnished decoration on a white or yellow ground utilizes such motifs as a winged, ram-headed vulture, a falcon with spread wings (both surmounted with solar disks), the sacred emblem of Abydos, and the Apis bull with a mummy on its back (painted on the only wooden piece, the foot-board).

The political chaos of the middle and late Libyan period generated multilineal development of forms and decoration schemes. Richly painted one-or two-piece cartonnages (the latter also decorated inside) coexisted with variously shaped and decorated wooden coffins, originating from different workshops. First, there are coffins of traditional anthropoid form, with a case deep enough for the mummy, and covered with a flat or convex lid. Second, there are mummy-shaped coffins consisting of two equal parts, a shallow lower case and an upper

lid, joined at the level of the mummy lying inside; a rectangular pedestal under the feet served as a base for the coffin in vertical position; and the back of the lower part projects slightly (the so-called dorsal pillar). A third type is the rectangular coffin reproducing the *ḳrsw* form, with vaulted roof and four posts in the corners. A richly varied iconography accompanies this plurality of forms.

This complexity increased in the turbulent times of the eighth and seventh centuries BCE, when a trend toward archaizing revived motifs of the Middle and New Kingdoms. In this troubled period, a scarcity of skilled craftsmen resulted in the widespread production of crude coffins, particularly in Middle Egypt and the Memphite region.

During the period of stability in the reign of Taharqa, however, coffins became more uniform. The inner coffin of a typical ensemble of this time is of the mummiform type with a pedestal; the "dorsal pillar" has a large *ḏd*-column depicted on it. On the lid, below the winged Nut figure on the breast, appear scenes of the judgment and the mummy on its bier. On both sides of the lid are small figures of protective deities. The inside of the coffin contains excerpts from the *Book of Going Forth by Day*, often accompanied by the figure of Nut. The outer coffin of the typical twenty-fifth dynasty ensemble is of *ḳrsw* form, decorated with solar scenes on its vaulted roof and the Four Sons of Horus on the side walls. A sculpture of a recumbent Anubis is placed on the roof, while small figures of falcons surmount the posts. Little royal material of the period is known; kings in Tanis were buried in usurped stone sarcophagi, but the falcon-headed silver coffin of Sheshonq is remarkable.

Late period (twenty-sixth dynasty and later). During the Saite period, the highest officials used rectangular and anthropomorphic stone sarcophagi. The former resemble the royal sarcophagi of the New Kingdom, with effigies of the deceased sculpted in high relief on the lids. The latter, usually of gray granite or basalt, are in general form and decoration replicas of the wooden "pedestal" coffins, though with a preponderant lid. Wooden coffins of this period have similar shapes. The flat lower part of the coffin serves merely as a support, not a container, for the mummy, because it is now covered with much more convex lid. Figural representations become less numerous, replaced partly or totally by long texts—excerpts from the "Saite version" of the *Book of Going Forth by Day*—written on the lid in vertical columns. Some wooden coffins of the Saite or post-Saite periods have carved decoration.

Innovations include the gilded cartonnage mask and painted coverings, consisting of several pieces, regularly laid on mummies. Figures of bound enemies now appear under the feet of the mummy on a separate cartonnage piece. The "bulging" coffin was prevalent in the Late period, alongside other types. The stone sarcophagi of the archaizing twenty-ninth and thirtieth dynasties used for inspiration not only royal compositions of the New Kingdom but even the much earlier Pyramid Texts. Types of coffins and a "new generation" of complete cartonnages appeared, reproducing very old patterns.

At the present stage of research, exact dating of this late funerary material is risky. On the other hand, welldated burials of the Roman period have been excavated in various spots in Egypt, including Thebes, the Faiyum, and Marina el-Alamein. These discoveries reveal the variety of mummy containers then in use: wooden coffins resembling the old

krsw form, with vaulted roof and corner posts; wooden anthropoid coffins with hands and portrait masks made of plaster and attached to the lid (these first two types of coffins have painted decoration with traditional iconography and hieroglyphic inscriptions); cartonnages "living effigies" of the deceased, in Roman dress; and mummies, bandaged in characteristic manner following a rhomboid pattern, and provided with portraits painted in encaustic on wooden panels (the so-called Faiyum portraits).

Günther Lapp and Andrzej Niwinski

COLOR SYMBOLISM. The use of color in art and its symbolic value depended on the range of pigments available; for example, a blue pigment was introduced in ancient Egypt about 2550 BCE. Much color use—whether in visual or written materials—was ultimately based on natural colors, but it was schematic, used to indicate the class of object depicted rather than its relationship to a specific object at a specific time. In addition to natural coloring, there were nonrealistic uses of color, as, for example, the skin color of some gods. Color choices were also, in many instances, governed by systems of patterning. Both the realistic and the nonrealistic uses of color carried symbolic meaning.

In Old Egyptian, basic color terminology was more restricted than the range of colors actually used in art: Old Egyptian had four basic color terms—*km*, *ḥd*, *dšr*, and *w3d* Other terms were secondary. Although color terms rarely translate exactly from one language to another, the general range of those terms is not in doubt. *Km* corresponds to "black" and had been used as a pigment from prehistoric times. In dynastic times, it was considered the color of the fertile soil of *kmt* ("the Black Land"), one of the names for Egypt; it therefore carried connotations of fertility and regeneration. It was also the color of the underworld, where the sun was regenerated each night. The deity Osiris, ruler of the underworld, was referred to in texts as *kmjj* ("the black one"), which not only alluded to his role in the underworld but also to his resurrection after he was murdered. Black stones were used in statuary to evoke the regenerative qualities of Osiris and the underworld. During some periods, coffins were given a black ground as a reference to the underworld, to Osiris, and to the renewal of the deceased.

The term for "white" was *ḥḏ*. Like black, it was also a pigment from prehistoric times. White was associated with purity, so it was the color of the clothes worn by ritual specialists. The notion of purity may have underlain the use of white calcite for temple floors. The word *ḥḏ* also meant the metal "silver," and it could incorporate the notion of "light"; thus the sun was said to "whiten" the land at dawn.

The term *wꜣḏ* seems to have had its focus in "green" (as the term for "malachite," a green mineral), but it may also have included "blue." Green had been used as a pigment from prehistoric times. The term *wꜣḏ* was written with a hieroglyph that represented a green papyrus stem and umbel; it also carried connotations of fresh vegetation, vigor, and regeneration—giving it very positive and beneficial symbolism. For example, the deity Osiris was frequently shown with green skin, to signify his resurrection, and in the twenty-sixth dynasty, coffin faces were often painted green to identify the deceased with Osiris and to guarantee rebirth. In the *Book of Going Forth by Day* (*Book of the Dead*), chapters 159 and 160 are for making a *wꜣḏ*-amulet of green feldspar, although the known amulets show that a variety of materials

were used, ranging in color from green to light blue. Such amulets were included in funerary furnishings to ensure the regeneration of the deceased.

The most valued of the green stones was *mfkꜣt* ("turquoise"), which was mined in the Sinai. This stone was connected to the deity Hathor, who was called "Lady of Turquoise," as well as to the sun at dawn, whose disk or rays might be described as turquoise and whose rising was said "to flood the land with turquoise." Because the color turquoise was associated with the rebirth of the sun, it promised rebirth in a funerary context, so turquoisecolored faience wares were often used as items of funerary equipment.

There was no basic color term in Old Egyptian for "blue," and there was no blue pigment until about 2550 BCE, with the introduction of one, based on grinding lapis lazuli (Lat., "azure stone"), a deep blue stone flecked with golden impurities. Blue was therefore not part of the original system of color symbolism found in texts, although it became the most prestigious paint color, owing in part to its initial rarity. Because lapis lazuli had to be imported, it was a very prestigious material, which may provide one of the reasons for the high value placed on the color blue in art. In Old Egyptian, "lapis lazuli" was called *ḥsbḏ*, and the term was then extended to mean, secondarily, the color "blue." The stone, and by extension its rich blue color, was associated with the night sky—often rendered in dark blue paint with yellow stars—and with the primordial waters, out of which the new sun was born each day; the rising sun was sometimes called the "child of lapis lazuli." From the post-Amarna period, the deity Amun-Re was normally given blue skin, to symbolize both his role as the creator god who came out of the primordial waters and his nightly regeneration as he passed through the primordial waters in the underworld. Items of funerary equipment made of blue faience were to harness the regenerative properties of the color.

The last basic color term was *dšr*, written with a hieroglyph that represented a flamingo; it is a warm color, with its focus in red, but for which there were no basic terms. Red was a pigment used from the earliest prehistoric times. It was considered a very potent color, hot and dangerous, but also life-giving and protective. It is both the color of blood, a substance that relates to life and death, and of fire, which may be beneficial or destructive. It is also a color frequently given to the sun, which may be red at its rising or at its setting, and which can overwhelm with its heat or warm to bring life. In contrast to *kmt* (the fertile "Black Land"), the term *dšrt* ("the red land") referred to the desert, which was inimical to human life and agriculture; it was the domain of the god Seth, who represented chaos, who both threatened the order of the world and helped maintain it by protecting the sun god in his nightly passage through the underworld. The dangerous, uncontrolled aspects of red connected the color to notions of anger, as in the expression *dšr jb* ("red of heart"), meaning "furious" or "raging."

In texts, rubrics (Lat., "red pigments") were often used to emphasize headings, but red ink was also sometimes used to write the names of dangerous entities. For example, in calendars of lucky and unlucky days, the lucky days were written in black and the unlucky ones in red. In execration rituals, red ink was used for the names and figures of enemies, and in many religious and magical texts, the names of dangerous beings, such as Seth and Apophis, were written

in red. By contrast, the name of Re is written in black, even in rubrics.

Stones such as rosey or golden quartzite and red granite had solar significance, because of their colors, and they could be used to invoke the regenerative properties of the solar cycle. Royal statuary made of such stones stressed the solar aspect of the kingship. In jewelry, the most frequently occurring red stones were *ḥnmt* ("red jasper"), mostly used for beads and amulets, and *ḥrst* ("carnelian"), mostly used for inlay. Chapter 156 of the *Book of Going Forth by Day* contains the recitation and instructions for activating an Isis-knot amulet of red jasper. The recitation begins: "You have your blood, O Isis. You have your power," showing the connection between blood, power, and the color red. In Greco-Roman times, *ḥrst* acquired the meaning of "sadness" or "sorrow," perhaps because of an increasing emphasis on the negative aspects of red. The stone is unlikely to have carried such negative connotations earlier, because of its popularity as a jewelry component. In the Middle and New Kingdoms, the most frequent combination of stones in inlaid jewelry consisted of lapis lazuli, turquoise, and carnelian. By analogy with the positive symbolism attached to the first two, it seems reasonable to assume that the red carnelian was then valued for its life-giving potential and for its apotropaic (safeguarding) properties. Wearers thereby might harness the potentially dangerous powers of red for their own protection and benefit.

Although yellow occurred as a pigment from prehistoric times, there was no basic color term for it in Old Egyptian, unless it was included in *dšr*. Like red, it was used as a color for the sun disk and so carries solar significance. In art, yellow pigment was often used to represent the metal "gold" (*nbw*), and gold, too, was closely associated with the sun god, who was said "to be made of gold" and "to flood the Two Lands with gold." In the eighteenth dynasty, black-ground coffins were decorated in yellow or gold, symbolizing the nightly renewal of the sun in the underworld, from which it rose each morning.

According to texts, gold was not only associated with the sun but also was the flesh of the gods. Re's bones were said to be of silver, his flesh of gold, and his hair of true lapis lazuli. The divine snake (in the *Story of the Shipwrecked Sailor*) had a body covered with gold and eyebrows of true lapis lazuli. Descriptions of divine cult statues indicate that they were fashioned from precious metals and stones. One of the very few surviving cult statues is made of solid silver, originally overlaid with gold; the hair is inlaid with lapis lazuli. Those three minerals were considered to be solidified celestial light, and they were fitted to form the bodies of deities.

Although the painted images of deities in temple reliefs and elsewhere were often shown with blue hair, their skin color seldom indicated gold flesh. Most male deities were represented with reddish-brown skin; most female deities with yellow skin, similar to the colors used to differentiate human figures. Nevertheless, other colors, such as the green skin of Osiris, also occurred. Osiris was occasionally shown with black skin, to refer to the renewing properties of Egypt's black soil and the underworld. The jackal that represented the deities Wepwawet and Anubis was also shown in black (although the majority of jackals are sandy-colored), to signify the funerary role of those gods and their connection with the underworld. The reference of black to fertility also makes it a suitable color for the ithyphallic figures of Min and Amun-Re (-Kamutef).

Black skin was given to some royal images, to signify the king's renewal and transformation. Although throughout his funerary temple at Deir el-Bahri, the eleventh dynasty king Nebhepetre Montuhotep I was regularly shown in relief and in statuary with reddish-brown skin, one statue found ritually buried shows the king with black skin, to symbolize his renewal in the afterlife and possibly his identification with Osiris. A fragment of relief, on which the king is suckled by the Hathor cow, shows him with black skin, to portray the transformation caused by the divine milk. The eighteenth dynasty king, Amenhotpe II, erected a statue group at Deir el-Bahri to illustrate the same theme. There, however, the image of the king being suckled had the normal reddish-brown skin—but in a second royal image, the transformation of the king was symbolized by his black skin, as he stood beneath the head of the Hathor cow.

The association of black with the underworld and its transformatory powers explains the black statues of the king that were buried in the royal tomb of Tutankhamun and in other New Kingdom royal tombs. For similar reasons, the faces on nonroyal coffins were, during some periods, also painted black. The most common color for coffin faces, however, apart from "natural" red (male) and yellow (female) was gold, which both showed the owner of the coffin as successfully transformed into a divine being and also linked the deceased with the sun god, whose endless cycle he or she hoped to join.

From the eighteenth dynasty onward, figures of Amun-Re were depicted as blue. The color referred both to the primordial waters of lapis lazuli and to the blue of the sky across which the sun travels. The lapis lazuli blue skin set the god apart from the other deities, emphasizing his status as "king of the gods": the most important god was given a body of the most precious stone. Perhaps a lapis lazuli cult statue of the god once existed.

Goddesses show far less variation in skin color than gods, usually being depicted with the yellow skin also given to human women. When male deities are shown with a reddish-brown skin, they have the color normally given to human men. Thus, the gender distinction encoded for human figures was transferred at times to the divine world. The symbolism inherent in the skin colors used for some deities and royal figures suggest that the colors given to human skin—although initially seeming to be naturalistic—might also be symbolic. Male and female skin colors were most probably not uniform among the entire population of Egypt, with pigmentation being darker in the South (closer to sub-Saharan Africans) and lighter in the North (closer to Mediterranean Near Easterners). A woman from the South would probably have had darker skin than a man from the North. Thus, the colorations used for skin tones in the art must have been schematic (or symbolic) rather than realistic; the clear gender distinction encoded in that scheme may have been based on elite ideals relating to male and female roles, in which women's responsibilities kept them indoors, so that they spent less time in the sun than men. Nevertheless, the significance of the two colors may be even deeper, marking some as yet unknown but fundamental difference between men and women in the Egyptian worldview.

The choice of the single red-brown color to represent the Egyptian man, rather than a more realistic range of shades, should also be considered within a wider symbolic scheme that included the representation of foreigners. The foreign men to the north and west of Egypt were depicted by yellow skin (similar to that of traditional Egyptian women); men to the south of Egypt were given black skin. Although undoubtedly some Egyptians' skin pigmentation differed little from that of Egypt's neighbors, in the Egyptian worldview foreigners had to be plainly distinguished. Thus Egyptian men had to be marked by a common skin color that contrasted with images of non-Egyptian men. That Egyptian women shared their skin color with some foreign men scarcely mattered, since the Egyptian male is primary and formed the reference point in these two color schemes—contrasting in one with non-Egyptian males and in the other with Egyptian females. Within the scheme of Egyptian/non-Egyptian skin color, black was not desirable for ordinary humans, because it marked out figures as foreign, as enemies of Egypt, and ultimately as representatives of chaos; black thereby contrasted with its positive meaning elsewhere. This example helps demonstrate the importance of context for reading color symbolism.

The color that regularly embodied both positive and negative meanings was red. While the potency of red undoubtedly derived from the power inherent in its dangerous aspects, again it was the context that determined, in any given case, whether the color had a positive or a negative significance.   *Gay Robins*

CULTS. *This entry surveys various types of cults in ancient Egypt, with reference to their organization, and to the types of priests, services, prayers, offerings, and sources of documentation associated with them. It comprises five articles:*

> *An Overview*
> *Royal Cults*
> *Private Cults*

Late period aegis, most likely of Mut, Isis, or Hathor. An aegis was a cult object usually featuring the head of a female deity over a large collar. It was associated with protection, and, as such, was often placed on temple equipment. This one is bronze, with glass inlays. (University of Pennsylvania Museum, Philadelphia. Neg. #S8-134396)

Divine Cults
Animal Cults

An Overview

For the ancient Egyptians, religion did not consist of a set of theological prin-

ciples to which they gave assent, nor was it based on the content of particular writings deemed canonical. Religion consisted rather in what people did to interact with their gods. These actions are termed "cult," and when used in this fashion, "cult" is roughly synonymous with "ritual." There is no specific word for "ritual" in the Egyptian language; they variously referred to it as *irt ḥt* "doing things," *irw*, "things done," or *nt-ꜥ*, "regular procedure (lit. that pertaining to prescription)."

The focus of Egyptian ritual was entities referred to with the substantive *nṯr*. Since the Ptolemaic period, *nṯr* has been translated as "god" (*theos*). While entities labeled as *nṯr* and "god" share several characteristics, the Egyptians applied the term to people and things which we would hesitate to call gods. In a recent article, Dimitri Meeks has suggested that the common feature shared by all entities called *nṯr* by the Egyptians is that they are the beneficiaries of ritual. These beings can be divided into several classes. First are those beings who existed originally as gods; ritual serves to preserve their existence as gods through providing them with sustenance. Second are entities who become *nṯr* through undergoing a ritual. This category can be further subdivided into those who undergo ritual, and hence become *nṯr*, during their lifetimes, and those who become *nṯr* after death. Examples of the former include the king and special animals who were thought to be manifestations of the gods. Individuals who become *nṯr* after death include common people, special "heroized" individuals, and mummified animals. While this definition of *nṯr* may be overly reductionistic, it provides a useful framework.

To conduct the cult of the gods, the Egyptians constructed temples, which they called *ḥwt-nṯr*, "the house of the god." Frequently several gods were worshipped in a single temple. In order to conduct the rituals, a temple needed to control an extensive network of land, livestock, and personnel; all the elements necessary for the business of the temple were referred to as *r-pr*, or "temple estate." The earliest Egyptian temples seem to have been built of perishable materials. Only temples dedicated to the funerary needs of the dead kings survive from the Old Kingdom, but a few nonroyal temples from the Middle Kingdom remain. Beginning with the New Kingdom, and continuing until the end of the Greco-Roman period, the enormous stone temples and their reliefs are our main source of evidence for the cult which went on within their walls.

An Egyptian temple employed a large number of priests and servants. Technically, only the king, the only living person in Egypt who possessed the status of *nṯr*, could officiate in the cult before the gods. He was considered to be the high priest of all the gods and goddesses of Egypt. In actual practice, the king delegated this responsibility to the priesthoods of the various gods throughout Egypt. Many priestly appointments came directly from the king, but some could be made by local administrators. Frequently, priestly offices could be inherited.

There were two main classes of priests. The higher class was the *ḥm-nṯr* ("god's servant"), who functioned in the cult before the god's statue. The Greeks translated *ḥm-nṯr* as "prophet," an equation which derived from the priests' role in interpreting oracles. The lower class was the *wꜥbw*, or "pure ones." They served as carriers of the god's bark, pourers of water for libations during the temple service, as overseers of craftsmen, artisans, or scribes, or as craftsmen themselves, making such sacred objects as the gods' sandals. There was also a third title, the *it-nṯr* or "god's father." It has been suggested that the title "god's father" was given to senior *wꜥb*-priests who had reached the level of prophet but were not yet formally inducted into that office. One of their functions seems to have been to walk in front of the god's image in processions and sprinkle water to purify the path.

Priests were divided into four groups, called *s3w wnwt* ("gangs of the service"), to which the Greeks gave the name *phyles*. Each phyle served one lunar month in rotation, so that during the year each gang served for a total of three months, with three months off between months of service. This free time allowed individuals to hold priesthoods in several temples. The chief priests of a temple were designated by ordinal numbers, and the high priest of the temple was called the *ḥm-nṯr tpy*, or "first prophet"; the next senior priest was the second prophet, followed by third and fourth prophets. The high priests of some gods bore special titles: the high priest of Ptah was called "he who is great at directing the crafts," that of Re was "he who is great at seeing," that of Thoth was "the arbitrator between the two," and that of Khnum was "the modeler of limbs." These titles derive from the various spheres of influence or mythological roles of these gods.

In addition to these classes of priests, there were also priestly specialists. The *ḥry-ḥb* ("he who carries the festival roll") was responsible for reading the hymns and spells which accompanied many rituals. The *sš n pr'nḥ* ("scribe of the house of life") was responsible for copying the papyri used in temple and funerary ritual. Women also participated in the temple priesthood. During the Old Kingdom, women of high social station could hold the office of priestess (*ḥmt-nṯr*) of Hathor, or of Neith. Women rarely served as priestesses in the cult of a god. Prior to the New Kingdom, the priesthood was not viewed as a full-time occupation, but with introduction of a professional class of priests, women no longer were able to hold priestly titles. They then served mainly as musicians, singers, and dancers in the temple. Later, however, they could hold titles associated with deities: at Thebes the "Divine Adoratress" held a prominent position from the Middle Kingdom.

The main purpose of the temple and its priests was to carry out the cult for the gods. The successful performance of the cult was thought to be absolutely vital to Egypt's continued existence and prosperity. At the time of creation, the Egyptians believed, a small space of order had appeared in the midst of chaos. It is within this space of order that life was possible. In order to keep chaos from encroaching on the created world, it was necessary to perform the cult of the gods. This cult took two main forms: those rituals conducted on a daily basis, and rituals carried out during particular festivals.

The focus of temple ritual was the statue of the god, called *'ḥm* ("image"). This was usually a small (one estimate is that they averaged about 50 centimeters/ 22 inches tall) statue of the divinity, kept in a *naos* or bark shrine in the chapel of the temple. Since most temples housed more than one god, they also contained more than one cult statue. These statues could be made of wood, stone, or precious metals. After a cult statue had been completed by the craftsman, it underwent a ritual called the "Opening of the Mouth" which transformed it into a vehicle through which the god could manifest itself and in which the divine *b3* and *k3* could take up residence. The statues themselves were not the object of worship; they were simply one means through which the gods received worship and offerings and made themselves manifest in the world.

The daily temple ritual took essentially the same form in every temple in

Egypt. It derived from the ritual for the sun god Re at Heliopolis, and represented the rebirth of the sun each morning. Later, elements of Osirian belief were incorporated into the ritual, and it also came to symbolize the restoration and revivification of the dismembered body of Osiris. For the purposes of the ritual, the cult-statue was identified as both Re and Osiris. Our information regarding the sequence of events of the daily temple ritual comes from two main sources: temple reliefs depicting the king performing the various rituals of the ceremony, and papyri listing the rituals and the hymns which accompany them. Analysis of these various sources has allowed scholars to reconstruct the likely sequence of events of this ritual. Because the sources do not agree as to the order of events, scholarly reconstructions differ.

Before dawn, two priests filled containers with water from the sacred well of the temple and replenished all the libation vessels. Priests were busy in the temple kitchens preparing offerings for the gods. The main officiating priest, a *ḥm-nṭr*, went to the *pr-dw3t* ("house of the morning") where he was ceremonially purified, dressed, given a light meal, and prepared to conduct the morning ceremony. The priest approached the shrine containing the god's image, and as the sun rose the bolt was drawn back and the door opened. Since only the king was able to confront the god, the officiating priest declared that "it is the king who has sent me to see the god." Once the doors to the shrine had been opened, the priest prostrated himself before the image, and a ritual purification of the chapel with water and incense took place in preparation for removing the image from its shrine. At this point, the statue was presented a small figure of the goddess Maat, which sym-

bolized the proper order established for the world at creation. The image was then removed from its shrine, and the clothing and ointment that had been placed on it the previous day were removed. The image was then placed on a pile of clean sand and the shrine was purified with water and incense. Next, green and black eye paint were applied to the image and it was anointed with several oils. The god was dressed in four colored cloths: white, green, blue, and red. The white and red cloths protected the god against his enemies, the blue hid his face, and the green ensured his health. The god was presented with various objects, such as his crowns, scepter, crook, flail, and *wsḫ*-collar. Next the god's face was anointed, sand was scattered around the chapel, the cult image was replaced in the shrine, and the door bolt was thrown and sealed. Finally, the priest performed the final purifications and exited the sanctuary, dragging a broom behind him to obliterate his footprints.

At some point during the morning ritual, the offering ritual would take place. The purpose of this ritual was to provide the god with his "breakfast." Some reconstructions of the ritual have it occurring before the final purification of the chapel in preparation for replacing the statue in the shrine, while others would have the offering ritual take place before the undressing and dressing of the statue. In this ritual, the offerings prepared that morning by the priests were presented to the god. Although an enormous meal was prepared for the god, consisting of meat, bread, cakes, beer, milk, honey, vegetables, and fruit, only a small part of this repast was actually placed before the statue. An offering formula listing the various items of the offering was recited by the priest, and incense was burned and libations made to purify and sanctify the offerings. Since the god did not actually consume the offerings, but simply partook of their essence, they could be shared with the other deities in the temple. The offerings were also used in the ritual of the royal ancestors, in which the king made offerings to all his predecessors in office, often depicted in the form of a list of their names. After this ritual, the offerings could then be made to the statues of other individuals found in the temple; finally, they became the property of the priests, who received a share based on their rank in the priestly hierarchy. This reuse of the offerings until they were finally consumed by the priests, called the "reversion of offerings" (*wdb ht*), was one way in which the priests were compensated.

This morning ritual was the main one of the day, but less elaborate ceremonies were also held at noon and in the evening. During these rituals, the doors of the sanctuary housing the god's statue were not opened. These rituals consisted primarily of pouring water libations and burning incense before the shrines of the gods. In addition to these offering rituals, certain apotropaic dramatic rituals were conducted in the temples throughout the day and night in order to repel the threats to existence, frequently thought of in terms of Seth, the murderer of Osiris, or Apophis, the serpent who tried to stop the daily voyage of Re and thereby bring an end to creation. Hymns were sung during the twelve hours of the day and night to protect Re from Apophis and to keep the solar bark moving along on its voyage. Images of enemies were created from wax or clay and then destroyed, thereby bringing about their destruction through magic.

In addition to their daily rituals, temples also celebrated a number of festivals (*hbw*) throughout the year. For example,

during the reign of Thutmose III, the temple of Amun-Re at Karnak celebrated fifty-four festival days, and Ramesses III's temple at Medinet Habu celebrated sixty festival days. Festivals could last from one to twenty-seven days, and involved large expenditures of food and drink for those participating in or observing the festival. Records from the village of Deir el-Medina indicate that workers were frequently given days off for festivals. During one festival of Sokar, 3,694 loaves of bread, 410 cakes, and 905 jars of beer were distributed. Important festivals included New Year's Day, the festival of Osiris at Abydos—during which the "mysteries" of this god were celebrated [*m*]; the festival of Hathor, during which the goddess would visit the royal cult complex (as did Sokar during his festival), and the festival of the Coronation of the Sacred Falcon at Edfu. The Beautiful Festival of the Valley was an important occasion during which Amun-Re traveled from Karnak to the temple at Deir el-Bahri and visited the royal cult complexes on the west bank of the Nile, particularly that of the reigning king. This was also an occasion for people to visit the tombs of their relatives, where they observed an all-night vigil and shared a feast with their deceased relatives.

The focus of a festival was the gods in their bark shrines. Egyptian gods always traveled in boats—in real boats when traveling by water, or in bark shrines carried over land on the shoulders of priests. Festivals could involve the procession of the god in his boat within the temple, or the god could leave the temple to visit another deity. These shrines were carried along processional avenues, often lined with sphinxes. At intervals, small altars were built which were essentially open-ended buildings containing a station on which the priests could rest the bark. When the porters rested, priests performed fumigations and libations and sang hymns to the god in its boat.

Such festivals and processions provided the general population with access to the gods, since the farthest most people were admitted into the temples was the open forecourt. It is usually thought that the shrine in the bark containing the god's image was closed during the procession, hiding the image from onlookers. Dirk van der Plaas (1989) has argued otherwise, suggesting that the doors of the bark shrine were open during such travels, since numerous texts describe the desire of people to see the image of a god. It was believed that beholding the image during a procession could heal an individual of illness.

It was also during festival processions that people could approach the gods seeking an oracle. The first clear evidence for oracles occurs in the New Kingdom. John Baines (1987), however, has argued that evidence for the existence of oracles occurs much earlier, perhaps as early as the First Intermediate Period, and earlier examples may exist. During processions, people could approach the god with a yes-or-no question written on small flakes of limestone or on ostraca, which would be placed before the god. Surviving examples of such questions include "Is it he who has stolen this mat?" "Shall Seti be appointed as priest?" and "Is this calf good so that I may accept it?" The movement of the bark-shrine as it was carried on the shoulders of the priests indicated the answer: forward for affirmative, backward for negative.

Private Cults. The temple was not the only place where the Egyptians worshipped their gods. The New Kingdom sites of Amarna and Deir el-Medina preserve evidence of public chapels which would have contained either a small cult statue or, more commonly, a stela with an image of the god. Here private individuals served as lay priests. Some homes were also equipped with areas set aside for worship. Domestic shrines at Amarna had domestic shrines containing statues of Akhenaten and his family, or stelae showing the royal family venerating the Aten. Many houses of the workmen at Deir el-Medina contained household shrines, which consisted of a wall niche which could be accompanied by an offering table or libation trough. These niches can be found in any room, including the kitchen. Deities particularly popular in such shrines were Meretseger, Renenutet, Sobek, Amun, Taweret, and Hathor. Deceased relatives were frequently worshipped in the home, in the form of $3h$ ikr n r^c ("able spirit of Re") stelae or small anthropoid busts ranging in height between 10 and 25 centimeters. We are ill informed about the nature of the cult practiced at such public and domestic chapels and private shrines, but the worship of the gods undoubtedly involved making offerings of food, libations, and incense. Such shrines would have served as places where people could make specific requests of their gods in prayer.

Royal Cults. The king, by virtue of his status as ntr, received a cult both while living and after his death. The study of ancient Egyptian kingship has been beset with confusion: on the one hand, the king of Egypt was labeled a god, but on the other hand, numerous texts describe the king in a very ungodlike fashion. A further confusion may arise from applying Western notions about the characteristics of a god to the Egyptian king. In ancient Egypt, the king acquired and maintained his "divinity" as a result of specific kingship rituals.

The primary kingship ritual was the coronation, which transformed the king into a *ntr* by means of his union with the royal *k3*. According to Lanny Bell (1997, p. 140), the *k3* personified "inherited life force," and the royal *k3* was "the immortal creative spirit of divine kingship." All previous kings of Egypt had possessed the royal *k3*, and at his coronation the king became divine when he became "one with the royal *ka*[*k3*], when his human form [was] overtaken by this immortal element, which flows through his whole being and dwells in it" (Bell 1985, p. 258). Since his status as *ntr* depended on his union with the royal *k3*, there were rituals intended to reinforce this relationship during the king's reign. Every year, the Opet festival was held at the temple of Amun-Re at Karnak during the fourth month of the inundation season, during which the king had his union with the royal *k3* renewed and his right to rule reconfirmed. After roughly thirty years of rule, the king celebrated his first *sed*-festival, which served both to reconfirm his relationship to the royal *k3* and to restore his flagging vitality.

Just as the cult statue was the receptacle of the divine *b3*, the king, as the receptacle of the royal *k3*, could also receive a cult. This practice became especially prominent in the New Kingdom, beginning with the reign of Amenhotpe III. The cult was patterned after the daily temple ritual of the gods. Kings erected statues of themselves, sometimes colossal, for the purpose of receiving offerings; perhaps the most famous monument dedicated to the cult of the living king is the temple of Ramesses II at Abu Simbel. The image of the living king, representing the royal *k3*, could be shown traveling in a bark carried on the shoulders of priests, just as the gods traveled during their festivals. There are even depictions of a king making offerings to his deified self. The king is worshipping not himself, but the concept of deified kingship as represented in the royal *k3*, which he embodies.

The worship of the divine king continued after his death. From the beginning of Egyptian history, royal burials included a place where the dead ruler's spirit could receive offerings of food and drink. The royal pyramid establishments introduced by the fourth dynasty kings included a temple complex situated on the east side of the pyramid for the cult for the deceased king, represented by a statue. Beginning with the pyramid of King Userkaf of the fifth dynasty, a false door stela became the focal point for offerings to the spirit of the deceased king. The kings of the eighteenth dynasty instituted a new form of royal burial, building rock-cut tombs in the Valley of the Kings at Thebes. Nearby, along the west bank of the Nile across the river from Karnak, the kings built structures which Egyptologists have called "mortuary temples," although the propriety of the term has recently been called into question by Gerhard Haeny. Here the spirit of the deceased king continued to receive offerings, frequently in the company of Amun and Re-Horakhty. Temples known as "houses of millions of years" were built by the New Kingdom kings as places where a royal cult could be carried out both before and after their deaths. Worship of deceased kings was not limited to state-run temples: the tomb builders at Deir el-Medina built shrines to the deified Amenhotpe I and his mother Ahmose Nefertari, who were revered as the founders and patrons of the city, and during the Middle Kingdom, Egyptian miners in the Sinai carried out a cult for the long-deceased Sneferu.

Funerary Cults. Not only kings attained divine status after death. A deceased person was transformed into a *nṯr* through the rituals of mummification and interment, which included the Opening of the Mouth ceremony. This ritual could be performed on the mummy or on a statue of the deceased, and through the use of spells and gestures it served to animate the image and enable the *k3* of the deceased to consume the offerings brought to it. The dead, like the gods, needed daily sustenance, provided by means of the offering ritual. Egyptian tombs were equipped with an area in which offerings could be made for the deceased. In Old Kingdom *mastaba*s, this area began as an offering niche on the south end of the east side of the *mastaba* and later evolved into an elaborate offering chapel inside the *mastaba*. A chamber inside the *mastaba* enclosed a *k3*-statue of the deceased and served as another focal point of offerings. After the Old Kingdom, *k3*-statues could be set up in separate *k3*-chapels near the temples of the gods. Rock-cut tombs included an aboveground chapel, which contained a stela of the deceased, giving his name and titles and showing him either before a table of offerings or receiving offerings from family members. Offerings were deposited on offering tables before these stelae.

The Offering ritual included the recitation of the offering formula, known as the *ḥtp-dỉ-nswt* ("an offering which the king gives"). Since in Egyptian theology only the king was able to make offerings to the gods, every time an offering was made, the offerer claimed that it had been made by the king to a god and was then passed along to the deceased, or that the king and a god were jointly making an offering to the deceased. This formula listed the typical items of a funerary offering. The offering itself was called *prt-r-ḥrw* ("going forth at the voice"), referring to the role of recitation

in providing the deceased with sustenance. Even if no offerings had been brought to the tomb, simply by reciting the formula a visitor was able magically to provide the dead with food and drink. A typical example of the offering formula from the Middle Kingdom is the following: "An offering which the king gives (and) Osiris, Lord of Busiris, the great god, lord of Abydos, so that he may make invocation offerings (consisting of) oxen, fowl, bread, clothing, alabaster, (and) every good and pure thing which a god lives on, (including) offerings, provisions, and divine offerings for all the gods, to the *k3* of the revered one, the overseer of the house, Montu-hotep, deceased" (Papyrus Berlin 9). The offering formula frequently stressed that the deceased was to receive the same offerings as the gods did in their daily cult. In order to ensure a continual supply of offerings at the tomb, an Egyptian would establish a funerary foundation prior to his death in which an individual (or individuals) was given land in exchange for an agreement to carry out faithfully the cult of the deceased. These individuals, the *ka*-priests (*ḥm-k3*), were responsible for providing for the funeral, burial, and continued offering cult. Frequently the eldest son of the deceased fulfilled this role. The establishment of funerary foundations was common during the Old and Middle Kingdoms, but was replaced during the New Kingdom by the statue foundation, in which a statue of the deceased would be dedicated to a temple, and the deceased through his statue would participate in the daily offerings and festivals there.

For the vast majority of Egyptians, offerings to the dead were made largely by family members, or by those under contract to carry out such offerings. For a few individuals who had been particularly prominent during life, their funerary cults took on a wider currency and began to resemble those of gods. People would visit their shrines to make offerings in hope of receiving blessings or favors. The cult at the tomb of Isi, a nomarch of Edfu during the early sixth dynasty, continued for six centuries after his death. A large temple was built at Elephantine during the Middle Kingdom to honor the sixth dynasty nomarch Hekaib. The worship of these divinized individuals was primarily a local affair, but some expanded and became national. Imhotep, the chief architect of the third dynasty king Djoser, was worshipped as a healing god of wisdom during the Greco-Roman period, and even provided with a divine lineage—he was said to have been the son of Khereduankh, his real mother, and the god Ptah. Amenhotep, son of Hapu, a prominent official under the eighteenth dynasty king Amenhotpe III, was also worshipped during the Ptolemaic period as a god of wisdom and healing.

Animal Cults. No other aspect of Egyptian religion elicited more derision from Classical-era authors than did the worship of animals, for which evidence dates back to the fourth millennium BCE. Predynastic burials of animals such as gazelles, dogs, cattle, monkeys, and rams have been found at such sites as Badari, Naqada, Maadi, and Heliopolis. Erik Hornung has observed that "the care with which these animals were buried and provided with grave goods is evidence for a cult of sacred animals" (1982, p. 101). The earliest mention of the Apis bull dates from the reign of King Aha of the first dynasty. The cult of animals received particular emphasis beginning with the twenty-sixth dynasty, perhaps as part of a resurgence of Egyptian nationalism.

The complexity of Egyptian animal cults escaped the Greco-Roman critics.

The Egyptians rarely (if ever) worshipped animals *as* gods, but rather as *manifestations* of the gods. Animals functioned much as did cult statues, and were simply one vehicle through which the gods could make their will manifest, and through which the faithful could demonstrate their devotion to the gods. There were three types of sacred animal honored in ancient Egypt. One type is the temple animals, which performed the same function as the cult statues in the temples; they could visit other deities in their temples and could give oracles. These animals lived in or near a temple and were distinguished by special markings. For example, the Apis bull, who lived at Memphis, had to be a black bull with a white triangle on its forehead, a crescent moon on its chest and another on its flanks, and double hairs (black and white) in its tail. The Apis bull was thought to be the $b3$ (manifestation) of Ptah. At certain times of day the bull was released into a courtyard where worshippers would gather to see him and receive oracles. Apparently, people could put yes-or-no questions to the bull, and the answer was received when the bull entered into one of two stables. When the bull died, there was a time of general mourning and elaborate embalming. The Apis bull was buried in an enormous stone sarcophagus in the Serapeum at Saqqara, and then the search for the next bull began. Other examples of this type of temple animal are the Mnevis bull at Heliopolis, which was the manifestation of Atum-Re; the Buchis bull at Hermonthis, who represented Montu and was especially important during the reign of Nektanebo II; the ram of Mendes (Osiris-Re); and the ram of Elephantine (Khnum).

The second category was animals of the same species as the temple animal. Large numbers of these animals could be kept near a temple. For example, at Saq-qara there was an extensive complex of buildings dedicated to the priestly care of large flocks of ibises (who represented Thoth) and falcons (Horus). It is from such flocks and herds that the enormous number of animal burials found in Egypt derive. Sacred animal necropolises throughout Egypt contain literally millions of mummified animal burials. In addition to the ibis necropolis at Saqqara, there are necropolises for cats at Bubastis; rams at Elephantine; crocodiles, snakes, falcons, and ibises at Kom Ombo; and ibises and falcons at Abydos. These burials were frequently paid for by pilgrims during visits to the temples at festivals or when seeking divine blessings. The mummified animal corpse served as a votive offering for the god, and the devotee hoped to earn the goodwill of the deity by providing for the burial of one of its sacred animals; an inscription on a jar containing an ibis mummy preserved a prayer asking Thoth to be benevolent toward the woman who had embalmed his sacred animal. Major differences between the temple animal and the animals kept in large numbers are that there was only one temple animal at a time; the temple animal received a cult, while these animals did not; and the mortuary services for the temple animals were much more elaborate. The third type of sacred animal comprises members of the same species as the temple animal which were kept in private homes as representatives of the gods. For example, snakes, cats, or dogs were often kept in cages and buried at their death. This practice is analogous to the construction of household shrines to allow for domestic worship.   *Stephen E. Thompson*

Royal Cults

The cult of the king is one of the most prominent features of ancient Egyptian society. Physically, the importance of royal cult is visible in the numerous great monuments still standing today, such as the great pyramid complexes of the Old and Middle Kingdoms or the mortuary temples on the west bank of the Nile at Thebes. The characteristics of royal cult, as attested by the buildings themselves and evidence for associated cult practices, derived from the central religious and political role of the king. The Egyptian pharaoh was a sacred individual. Although mortal, he was understood to be related to the gods through a multilayered mythology which is articulated in scenes and texts on royal cult buildings and in the decoration of royal tombs. The king was the son of Re, the sun god. He was a manifestation of Horus, the falcon god and son of Osiris. From the time of the Middle Kingdom, increasing emphasis was placed on his relationship with the syncretic deity Amun-Re, and the king was described as the son of Amun, king of the gods. The king was the intermediary between mankind and the divine, responsible for sustaining the balance of the universe through maintaining *maat*, or divine order, in his earthly functions. In death, the king was held to become a fully divine being. Central to the royal afterlife was the king's assimilation with Osiris and the sun god Re. These divine associations provided the basis for the development of cults of both living and deceased kings.

Royal Funerary Cults. Early evidence for the development of the royal funerary cult occurs in the mortuary buildings of Early Dynastic kings at Abydos. Burial places of the kings of the first and second dynasties have associated "valley enclosures." The full repertory of functions of these structures remains a matter of debate; however, evidence for long-term presentation of offerings in the enclosures of Khasekhemwy and Peribsen suggests the existence of a mortuary cult for the deceased king. The third dynasty Step Pyramid of Djoser at Saqqara is the first fully articulated funerary monument where concepts of the king's divinity and the associated funerary cult can be analyzed in detail. The Step Pyramid includes numerous architectural elements designed to perpetuate the role of the king in the afterlife. Symbolic components of the royal palace, both above ground and below the pyramid itself, provide a palace complex from which the king could rule for eternity. Elements associated with celebration of the *heb-sed* (festival of rejuvenation of the kingship) express the desire to maintain the king's rulership in the netherworld. Integrated into this architectural setting was a full offering cult, which was housed in a mortuary temple positioned on the north side of the Step Pyramid. This assemblage of architectural elements alongside a sustained offering cult for the king presents a concrete statement on the importance of kingship and its divine associations in both living world and afterlife.

With the fourth dynasty, the royal pyramid complex increased in size. The tremendous scale and physical investment required for the pyramid complexes of Sneferu, Khufu, and Khafre is testimony to the central importance of the pharaoh and his cult during this period. It has been suggested that a significant proportion of the activities of the central government during the Old Kingdom were focused on the construction of the royal funerary complex. Thus, royal cult became a driving force in the political and economic growth of the Old Kingdom state.

Royal pyramid complexes from the fourth, fifth, and sixth dynasties typically are situated on an east–west axis and include two main cult buildings: the mortuary temple, situated on the east side of the pyramid, and a valley temple at the edge of the Nile floodplain. The mortuary temple was the location of the funerary offering cult, which was maintained by rotating teams of priests. The valley temple was decorated with scenes and statuary expressing the king's association with a wide variety of deities; it appears to have been a building used especially in linking the royal cult with other temples through periodic festivals and processions. Beginning with the reign of Unas in the late fifth dynasty, a major source of information on royal funerary cult is the Pyramid Texts, which are inscribed on the walls of the burial compartments of kings. The Pyramid Texts present a complex series of spells and religious statements intended to aid in the king's entrance into the netherworld: his transfiguration in the image of Osiris and his association with Re. Parts of the Pyramid Texts record embalming and burial rituals; other parts are written versions of the offering formulae and records of the offering ritual itself.

During the Middle Kingdom the tradition of royal pyramid construction continued, but with changes in emphasis. The first royal mortuary complex of the period, the eleventh dynasty burial complex of Montuhotpe I, represents a departure from the pyramid complexes of the Old Kingdom in its emphasis on veneration of the newly important state god of Thebes, Amun-Re. The cult of the king is given legitimacy through the king's association with that deity. The sanctuary of the Montuhotpe I complex focuses principally on the Theban triad (Amun, Mut, and Khonsu) but integrates a statue cult for the king. The link between king and god was emphasized in ritual form by the annual Valley festival, called the "Beautiful Festival of the

Valley," in which the image of Amun was borne on his traveling bark to the west and visited the king's funerary temple.

Although later royal funerary complexes of the Middle Kingdom attempted to return to the Old Kingdom model, there were significant changes in conceptions of kingship which had restructured ideas on the nature of the king's role. These changes are reflected in the design and decoration of royal cult buildings. Royal funerary temples of the later Middle Kingdom appear to place increasing emphasis on veneration of the gods, with the king's cult appended and legitimized through his association with the gods. Late in the twelfth dynasty, the term "mansion of millions of years" appears in reference to the funerary temple of Amenemhet III at Hawara. This term can be understood to denote royal cult buildings in which the king's cult was important but subordinated to the cult of major deities.

Trends in royal cult structures of the Middle Kingdom set the stage for the New Kingdom, when the mansion of millions of years became the standard type of royal cult building. On the west bank of Thebes, the rulers of the eighteenth, nineteenth, and twentieth dynasties erected a series of great temples, of which the best preserved today are the Ramesseum (Ramesses II) and Medinet Habu (Ramesses III). These New Kingdom royal cult buildings were associated with the burial places of the rulers in the Valley of the Kings. They were surrounded by precincts which included storerooms and housing for priests and officials who ran the economic foundations that sustained the temple cult. Although many of these royal cults were supported by economic foundations set up at the time of the temples' construction, they were also considered part of the domain of Amun and were connected administratively with the great temple of Amun at Karnak. The temples were constructed first as buildings dedicated to Amun-Re, and the cult of the king was mediated by his divine associations with that deity. The Beautiful Festival of the Valley, which had emerged in the Middle Kingdom, continued as the most important ritual link between the royal funerary temples and the main cult place of Amun.

The construction of mansions of millions of years was not limited to Thebes. The temple of Sety I at Abydos is one in which royal cult is linked with Egypt's principal gods, especially Osiris. Insofar as Osiris was understood to be a deceased king of Egypt reborn to rulership in the netherworld, the Sety temple was also a temple to the institution of kingship itself as embodied in Osiris.

Cult of Royal Ancestors. In addition to incorporating the cult of the king, Osiris, and other gods, the Sety temple at Abydos illustrates a royal cult of another nature: veneration of royal ancestors through cult activity mandated by a living king. This practice is attested during the Old and Middle Kingdoms but becomes especially visible during the New Kingdom. Veneration of royal predecessors could be established through patronage of existing temples, as is illustrated by activity at Karnak, or the dedications of Senwosret III within the funerary temple of Montuhotpe I. It might also be articulated within a newly founded cult building, as occurred in that of Sety I at Abydos.

Royal Cult in Gods' Temples. In addition to monuments specifically created for the cult of a king, provisions for royal cult were regularly made in gods' temples throughout Egypt. Kings of all periods would have expressed their association with the gods by dedicating statuary and votive objects. In many of the large state temples, the cults of god and king became inextricably linked. Sites such as the temple of Horus at Hierakonpolis or the temple of Montu at Medamud include considerable remains of royal dedicatory material, and many gods' temples no doubt maintained subsidiary royal cults. Provisions for royal cult in a god's temple may have been as simple as a king's statue which received a portion of the daily offerings. In many of the larger state temples, however, entire ancillary buildings were created linking royal cult with god's cult. Sites such as Bubastis, Dendera, Hierakonpolis, Abydos, and Tell ed-Dab'a preserve remains of structures that can be identified as royal "*ka*-chapels"—buildings in which a royal offering cult was maintained and the link between the king and local god was expressed. Other royal structures within gods' temples were intended to emphasize overtly the king's divine connections. From the New Kingdom on, chapels decorated with scenes of the divine birth of the pharaoh were erected in the temple precinct of Amun at Karnak. This type of structure is a precursor to the large and complex *mammisi*, or divine birth houses, at sites such as the Hathor temple at Dendera.

Cult of the Living King. The fact that the king was a sacred being engendered by the gods provided the basis for the development of the cult of living kings. This type of royal cult was more significant in certain periods, and emphasis on the divine associations of the living pharaoh may have been linked with political and economic as well as religious trends. One context in which the cult of living kings may have been emphasized was periods of coregency. During the Middle and New Kingdoms, evidence suggests that the coronation of

a king's successor could occur before the death of the elder ruler. In this case, the senior ruler may have been projected into a fully divine role, perhaps conceptualized as a living Osiris and venerated as a god before death.

The most important development in the cult of the living king, however, occurred during the New Kingdom, when there is evidence for greater emphasis on the divine birth of the ruler. The key concept in the divine birth is that a pharaoh was engendered by the seed of the god Amun himself. Cult activity focused on the divinity of the ruling monarch may possibly have been linked to a need to legitimize claims to the throne by such rulers as Hatshepsut in the early eighteenth dynasty. It continued to be expressed, however, through the remainder of the New Kingdom and may be understood partially as a means of contributing to royal power and legitimacy over an increasingly complex governmental system. The Luxor temple is the greatest surviving monument dedicated to this concept. The building had roots in the Middle Kingdom but underwent its major construction during the reign of Amenhotpe III, with significant additions during the Ramessid period. The building can best be understood as a cult place of the living king and his divine associations with the Theban triad. The Luxor temple was the focal point of the great Opet festival, in which the image of Amun journeyed from his sanctuary at Karnak and the living king participated in rituals celebrating his divine origins.

The period characterized by the greatest emphasis on the divine authority of the pharaoh was the Amarna period of the late eighteenth dynasty. The reign of Akhenaten (successor of Amenhotpe III) witnessed the emergence of a royal religion focused on the supreme power of the sun disk or Aten. The religious program of Akhenaten emphasized the indispensable role of the king as the sole intermediary between mankind and the life-giving force of the Aten. Direct worship of the Aten was limited to Akhenaten himself, while the king and royal family were the intended object of worship by the populace at large. Household cults at Amarna included offering stelae depicting the royal family. Such veneration of the king within the domestic sphere represents an emphasis on divinity of the living king not seen in other periods. Following the Amarna period, royal cult buildings—such as the temples of Ramesses II at Abu Simbel—were erected during the ruler's lifetime and presented the royal cult as an inseparable part of the divine order.

Royal Cult at the Popular Level. Aside from royal cult within the established context of mortuary buildings and gods' temples, the veneration of deceased kings could develop in a more spontaneous fashion in the framework of popular cult. In such cases, the royal cult displays many similarities with the cult of local deities. An example of such a popular royal cult is the veneration of Amenhotpe I by the community of royal tomb builders at Deir el-Medina. During the eighteenth through twentieth dynasties, Amenhotpe I was venerated for his role in the early establishment of the community. He became a patron deity of the town, and his cult was celebrated at the popular level during periodic festivals and processions. During such events the populace was able to interact with a statue of the king carried by priests, particularly through the mechanism of oracles. Similar royal cults are attested in the Sinai, where Sneferu emerged as a local patron deity, and in the Second Cataract region, where Senwosret III was venerated locally as a god.

This type of popular royal cult contrasts with the more formal structure of royal worship maintained in state-established temples, which were generally off limits to the community at large. Formal royal cult temples could, however, conduct similar processions in which royal images were carried in procession and were subject to popular veneration. The mortuary temple of King Ahmose at Abydos is one documented example of a royal cult building where a statue of the king was carried by priests during festivals and gave oracles.

Cult and Ritual. Like other cults in temples throughout Egypt, the most important element of ritual in royal cult buildings was the daily offering ritual. This was essentially a statue cult in which the priests were responsible for ritual interaction with a cult image, which thereby was imbued with the elements necessary to make it a suitable abode for the *ka* of the king. Elements of the offering cult are presented in the Pyramid Texts. The most detailed records are those that document in scenes and texts the steps involved in the daily temple ritual. These are recorded in detail in the nineteenth dynasty temple of Sety I at Abydos and in the Ptolemaic period temple of Horus and Edfu. The daily temple ritual involved a series of ritual acts accompanied by spells and offering formulae uttered by the priests. These rituals included the awakening, cleansing, anointing, and dressing of the cult image. The spirit of the king would be invited through the burning of incense before the face of the cult image. Following the summoning of the spirit, libations and food offerings would be presented. After completion of the offering presentation, the shrine would be closed and the floor swept clean. The daily temple ritual was repeated three times daily, and in large royal cult temples it was certainly enacted for multiple images and subsidiary cults within the temple. The daily cycle of the offering ritual was punctuated by periodic festivals and statue processions in which a royal cult image was taken to nearby gods' temples. This type of activity provided for interaction between surrounding community and royal cult.

Cult Personnel. Royal cults from the time of the Old Kingdom were maintained by large, complex organizations of priests and officials. Old Kingdom papyri excavated in the pyramid complexes at Abusir are an important source of information on the administrative and economic aspects of royal cults in the late Old Kingdom. These documents record a system of five phyles (groups of priestly personnel responsible for running the cult) which rotated on a monthly basis. Temple personnel were organized into priests (principally *ḥmw-nṯr*, "god's servants") and a group of royal cult officials (termed *hntyw-s*). Also detailed in the Abusir records are the complex arrangements for supply of the mortuary cult, which depended on income from estates owned by the temple as well as on material distributed from other major temples in the Memphis region. For the Middle Kingdom, temple archives of the valley temple of Senwosret II at Illahun provide evidence on cult organization in a twelfth dynasty royal funerary temple. For the New Kingdom, extensive scenes and texts in the Theban royal temples are important evidence on the organization of the royal cult. The temple of Ramesses III at Medinet Habu is decorated with an extensive list detailing the festivals and offerings. Material from administrative records as well as scenes and texts in private tombs provide detail on the complex organization that surrounded royal funerary temples during the New Kingdom. The "reversion of offerings" was an important aspect of the royal cult, as it was in temples throughout Egypt. The offerings presented in the king's temple were redistributed to the priesthood and their dependents, and in many cases to secondary cults such as nonroyal chapels. The reversion of offerings was administered through contracts which defined the amount of offerings due to various people.

Josef W. Wegner

Private Cults

It is obvious from discoveries in prehistoric cemeteries that belief in magic, life after death, and the presence of sacred power in animals (clan divinities) existed long before political unification and the arts of civilization flourished in Egypt. The large female figures and numerous images of hills, fields, water, and herds in the early pot paintings suggest, to prehistorians like Fekri Hassan, the veneration of a goddess associated with the cycles of nature, including death and resurrection. Private cults that focused on sacred trees, on impressive places (like the Peak of the West at Thebes) believed to be inhabited by divine force, or on deities helpful with plentiful harvests and human fertility continued to flourish throughout the country after prehistoric times, but it is the funerary rituals that are the best documented over the long history of ancient Egypt.

Funerary Rituals of the Historic Period. Euphemisms in texts and lack of portrayal in art show the Egyptians' distaste for death. To mitigate death they established elaborate procedures. The wrapping of the body, resembling the reassembling of Osiris's corpse, symbolized the overcoming of death, a transfiguration to a new body. Placement in the coffin was putting the deceased into the arms of the sky goddess Nut, to be born anew. Pouring of water, for its life-giving as well as purification qualities, was part of every ritual. The corpse, whether first desiccated or not, would have been washed (in the Tent of Purification) and then anointed and wrapped in the embalmer's shop. Seven sacred oils used for anointing the body are known already in the first dynasty. Last rites before interment were performed by the officiating *sem*priest, who libated and burned incense and then carried out the Opening of the Mouth ritual to renew faculties: "opening" the mouth, nose, eyes, and ears by ritually presenting tools such as the adz to the orifices (originally on the statue of the deceased, and later on the mummy itself), while an ox was slaughtered and its foreleg and heart presented to the image as part of the revivification process. Offerings were also presented to the deceased, and then the body and the statue were transported to the burial site. An accompanying liturgy of prayers or spells was read by the lector-priest (*hry-hb*), who was distinguished by wearing a leopard-skin across one shoulder. At the funeral and afterward, the invocation of offerings, known as "the boon which the king gives," called for the sustenance of the dead. Music and acrobatic—perhaps ecstatic—dancing were as much a part of the funeral at the tomb door as was the shrieking of mourners. The *hnr* or musical troop of the goddess Hathor perhaps both announced the goddess who would receive the deceased in the netherworld and also reawakened the dead, or even sexually charged the atmosphere, since the deceased needed to be reborn in the afterlife. Incense was burned and floral tributes, as well as furniture and foodstuffs, were deposited in the tomb, which was seen as a dwelling for the dead. A wealthy funeral might include a pilgrimage to Abydos and the great shrine of Osiris, lord of the dead, where many people left cenotaphs or stelae

commemorating themselves, understanding that they could hope for eternal life in the god's realm. The judgment rendered by his divine tribunal, with the heart of the deceased weighed against the feather of truth, seems to be a development of the eighteenth dynasty.

The maintenance of the identity and personality of the deceased required a funerary cult at the tomb, which was ensured by endowments for mortuary priests. Such *ka*-servants would bring bread and beer regularly to the tomb; illumination and prayers were probably also part of their duties. However, the supplies of early burials in time were replaced by models and then just lists of commodities needed by the deceased. This menu became a sacred text itself. Survival was possible for the worthy dead in two destinations: the sun's boat in the original solar cult, and the fields of the Osirian cult. Both demanded justification, which involved wisdom (knowing secret names of many entities of the netherworld) and passing an examination before forty-two judges in Osiris's tribunal. For this, magical spells, such as the religious literature on Middle Kingdom coffins and the later funerary papyri, were furnished in the burial.

Religion and the Commoner in the Old and Middle Kingdoms. With the establishment of the Egyptian state (c. 3050 BCE), the theology was organized to support the king, giving him a divine genealogy and making him identical with the great falcon god Horus. Only the king was represented in literature and art as having direct access to the gods. The idea of the king as sole worshipper must lie behind the *htpdinsw* formulas on commoners' monuments, on which a person's fortune in life and death depended: "a boon which the king gives of a thousand of bread, a thousand of beer, of oxen and fowl, of ointments and cloth." Although the dead king (and later also queen) of the Old Kingdom was laid in the pyramid accompanied by the power of sacred texts containing very old hymns and rituals, the Old Kingdom nobles had nothing comparable and were able to have an afterlife only as a dependent *akh*.

Not until after the fourth dynasty, when the royal power began to decline, are commoners found holding divine offices in major cults; the goddess Hathor's is best documented, with hundreds of priestesses and numerous male overseers of priests. The collapse of the centralized government in the First Intermediate Period allowed for the stealing and divulging of magic spells (as Ipuwer describes in horror) that were once the exclusive knowledge of royalty. Texts on Middle Kingdom coffins utilize much of the Pyramid Texts, giving their nonroyal owners divine status once deceased and promising an eternity spent with the gods. At least two autobiographical texts of elite commoners describe their participation in the pageants and rites of Osiris at Abydos, and the *Instructions for Merikare* speaks of the sun god's sympathy for humans in distress. In a literary tale, the nobleman Sinuhe credits the mercy of a god for his survival and prosperity in Syria after his flight from Egypt. Thus, Middle Kingdom people interacted with deities as never before.

Developments in New Kingdom Religion. Nonroyal Egyptians continued to borrow what were once prerogatives of royalty, and the eighteenth dynasty tombs of the elite contain paintings of the once-royal hippo hunt rite, a metaphor for the victory of Osiris's avenging son Horus over Seth. Also beginning in the eighteenth dynasty, scenes depict the deceased worshipping a god directly, showing no royal intermediary. Now almost everyone had access to the

divine. The cheaper papyrus scrolls containing the *Book of Going Forth by Day*, the so-called *Book of the Dead*, put immortality even closer at hand for larger numbers of people. This was the principal collection of funerary literature used by commoners in the New Kingdom and continuing into the early Roman period. While copies vary in length, some being quite short, there are 192 spells presently associated with the work which provided a deceased person with an aid to gaining eternal life. In the twenty-first dynasty, another text, the *Book of That Which Is in the Underworld* (*Amduat*) was added, and toward the end of Egypt's history, the *Book of Breathings* was also deposited with the dead.

Temples and Votives. There is more evidence for the laity's access to temples in the New Kingdom than has been generally realized: the spacious open courtyards of Luxor Temple, and even the hypostyle hall at Karnak, bear inscriptions which indicate that members of the public were able to assemble and praise pharaoh and experience the manifestation of the king of the gods himself. A shrine built under Sety II (nineteenth dynasty) just outside the hypostyle hall was a "place of honoring and praying to all the gods." A chapel of the Hearing Ear was built against the north exterior wall of Karnak under Ramesses II, where people could come to pray to listening deities. Indeed, engravings of ears are found on many exterior temple walls, and an image of Ptah Who Hears Prayers exists in the passage of Ramesses III's High Gate at the Medinet Habu temple, which facilitated people's access to the great gods within.

The Egyptians' desire for progeny motivated many votives offered to helpful deities. Pottery fertility figurines have been found in private houses of the Middle Kingdom and, by the New Kingdom, at shrines within many temples and at local community shrines. Excavations at the eighteenth dynasty royal temples of Deir el-Bahri (which included major chapels of Hathor, a promoter of sex and fertility) reveal votive items so uniform as to suggest mass production. Visitors to temples would pray, offer perishables like food, flowers, and beverages as their sacrifice, and then leave a purchased nonperishable votive in the form of a pottery cow, miniature Hathor-mask pillar, jewelry, or a painted cloth showing the goddess and containing a brief text into which the donor's name could be inserted. Such votives suggest female devotees, but men also made appeals for progeny and dedicated wooden and stone phalli to ensure their virility and fertility.

Deification of Mortals. Even with their huge pantheon, the Egyptians embraced foreign deities and also elevated mortals to divine status when warranted. Probably no one could have a statue of himself placed within the great temples of the land without royal favor. Imhotep, the architect who served King Djoser of the third dynasty (c. 2687–2668) and designed for him the first pyramid, was revered by later generations as a sage; by the New Kingdom he was being called "the son of Ptah" and had become something of a patron saint of artisans. During the last dynasties, he became known as a healer—an attribute of a number of major deities—and was identified by the Greeks with Asclepios. Ptolemaic temples in Egypt often had sanatoriums on their premises where the afflicted in mind or body could come to spend the night and, in dreaming, be approached and helped by the resident deity of the temple. Other early sages became divinities, as did certain famous kings. Amenemhet III (1843–1797) was worshiped in the Faiyum two thousand

years after his death, and scarabs bearing the name of Thutmose III, the great empire-builder, were made for centuries after his death, showing that the power of his name really was potent magic. Great queens like Ahmose Nefertari, and her son, Amenhotpe I, enjoyed cults for centuries after their deaths.

A royal scribe who served Amenhotpe III of the eighteenth dynasty as counselor and architect was Amenhotep, son of Hapu, born in the Delta town of Athribis during the reign of Thutmose III. This courtier was so highly regarded by the king that he was allowed to set up statues in Karnak near the Tenth Pylon, where he exhorts people to come to him for the transmission of their requests both to the king of the gods and to the living king. Thus, during his lifetime Amenhotep was introduced to the Egyptian public as someone in direct communication with the divinities, and something of a saint. Five hundred years after his death, his cult still flourished at Karnak, and by the twenty-sixth dynasty he was being credited as a divine physician. Under the reign of Ptolemy VI, Amenhotep, son of Hapu, was referred to as "the great god" and had an oracle at Deir el-Bahri. Both he and Imhotep were given cults at the temple Ptolemy VIII built at Qasr el-Aguz, attracting large numbers of votive statues, offering tables, and texts on ostraca. Seen as a healer and the granter of progeny, Amenhotep's original identity as a wise man was not forgotten either. A colossal statue in front of the magnificent First Pylon at Karnak temple commemorates him a millennium later as a great scholar of Amenhotpe III's reign. In the Hellenistic period, moral didactic texts were attributed to him.

Oracles. New Kingdom Egyptians generally saw their gods' interest extending to them as individuals, and this encouraged the use of oracles. Direct appeals to the opinion of the deity for a decision in a matter were utilized by ordinary people, sometimes when the findings of the local tribunal did not please the claimant. At the tomb-builders' community of Deir el-Medina, the oracle of prominence was the deified king Amenhotpe I, who had many feasts during the year when his statue was carried in procession. He might then be called on to resolve disputes concerning property rights and the guilt or innocence of accused persons in matters of theft. Questions could be put orally or in writing and were presented before the image of the god when it was carried by his priests. An affirmative response seems to have been expressed by a downward movement of the front carriers, and a negative by a withdrawal away from the petitioner. The findings of the local tribunal could be overturned at such occasions.

Interactions with the Dead. Similarly, the Egyptians believed that the dead were still part of the population and could be of assistance or cause problems. Thus, families looked after the tombs of their relatives, and at home a statue bust of an ancestor of the family received prayers and oblations from the lady of the house, judging from artistic portrayals in the New Kingdom. Such busts are also found in shrines and tombs, and a rectangular stone stela showing a deceased person seated and holding a lotus before a table of offerings identifies the portrayed as an Able Spirit of Re (*akh iqr n R'*). These were dedicated by living relatives and apparently also used for imploring the deceased by those who also brought offerings to seek cooperation. Such stelae are found throughout Egypt but seem to be a phenomenon of the late eighteenth through twentieth dynasties; letters to the dead are found from all pe-

riods, often written on a bowl that had contained an offering at the tomb. Many are attempts to inform a deceased relative about a family crisis for which intercession is sought. In other cases, the dead person is suspected of causing the problems of the living and is asked to desist from this malign intervention.

Personal Religious Practice and Private Cults. The royal artisans' community unearthed at Deir el-Medina, dating to the New Kingdom, reveals many signs of personal religious practice and private cults. Numerous chapels to various deities are scattered about the outskirts of the community. Artisans naturally responded to the god Ptah, patron of craftsmen, and he had a small temple here, but so did foreign gods from Canaan and deities associated with the southern boundary of Egypt, at the First Cataract of the Nile. Local deities—such as Meretseger, a cobra goddess who inhabited the thousand-foot peak overlooking the village, and the alleged founder of the village, Amenhotpe I, and his mother, Ahmose Nefertari—were popular here too.

Thus both national and local deities were worshipped by ordinary people who built their own chapels, carved the cult statues, and filled the roles of clergy. Mostly *wab*-priests are attested, with only certain families being eligible to fill the role. A few men held the superior office of a *ḥm-nṯr* (prophet) in the local cult, carrying fans rather than the poles of the divine bark shrine. Some literate men could easily have served as lectors, reading a liturgy; women participated by singing hymns and playing musical accompaniment. Were daily services maintained here, or only festivals celebrated? The nature of the community makes the latter seem more likely. Some chapels had benches that seated twelve: seven seats on one side, five on the other. Ash from cooking as well as libation basins and animal pens suggest that here were gathering places for family groups or guilds to assemble to mark special events. There would have been numerous holy days when everyone was freed of work duty, and a joyous festival replete with eating, drinking, and dancing was enjoyed by all. But personal celebrations of one's own god were also observed: "Pray by yourself with a loving heart, whose every word is hidden" (*Instructions of Anii* [*Any*]). At home, certain deities protective of women, childbirth, and the young were given homage (Taweret and Bes in particular). Deities were not regarded as remote from ordinary people, at least not after the First Intermediate Period.

So religious were the workers on the royal tombs that fifty small shrines to various deities were maintained near the encampment where they spent the nights of their workweek at the royal tomb. Stelae of the Ramessid period reflect expressions of faith, gratitude for divine favor, and petitions in adversity. Some workmen have left pious testimonials to the power of the gods to affect a person's life for good and evil. Afflictions were understood as divine punishment meted out to those who had transgressed. Mercy is attributed to the god who is omnipresent and caring and may be called on in distress. Even the greatest gods were inclined to aid the deserving, as the painter Neb-Re recorded in a hymn of thanksgiving that Amun himself had saved the draftsman Nakht-Amun. A votive stela of Nefer-abu contains a long penitential hymn to the patron god of craftsmen, Ptah, which describes a failing and eventual salvation. Universalism is another feature of the hymns beginning in the reign of Amenhotpe III and continuing into the following dynasty.

It is not known how people were selected to serve in temples. That the vast majority of the clergy were the *wab*-priests who were lay people is obvious. The intermittent one-month service of these people, who were organized in phyles, demanded that they observe rituals of cleanliness and abstinence. Shaven bodies, including the head, were required during the time of temple service. Washing of the body and chewing natron to cleanse the mouth were also demanded before one could come in contact with the deity. Women also did such temple service, as is clear from a letter dated to the twelfth dynasty in which a woman explains her absence from her job as due to her month of temple service as a *wab*-priestess.

A vast proportion of personal names in ancient Egypt were theophorous and expressed faith: Amun is Strong, My God is a Mountain for Me. Herodotus described the Egyptians of the Late period whom he encountered as the most pious of all nations.   *Barbara S. Lesko*

Divine Cults

The gods of ancient Egypt were considered to have much in common with humans: they needed food, clothing, entertainment, and recreation. These basic requirements were met by a series of performative actions and utterances that were formalized into cult actions and liturgy. These preestablished actions served the needs of the gods, and their special repetitive nature established a routine through which humans and the divine routinely and predictably interacted.

Documentation for divine cult comes from many different types of sources. These include representations of deities and brief references to gods and their festivals, recorded on ivory labels and carvings from the first dynasty and the annals on the Palermo Stone. Later and more complete information is given by the reliefs that adorn the walls of temples (especially the eastern interior wall of the hypostyle hall of the temple of Amun at Karnak, the chapels of the temple of Sety I at Abydos, and the sanctuaries of the temples of Horus at Edfu and of Hathor at Dendera). These are especially rich sources because they depict the individual acts that made up the divine service. Types and amounts of offerings employed in the cult are listed in calendars and so-called menus carved on temple walls. Biographical inscriptions record the duties that priests and priestesses performed for the god. Papyri, such as the Papyrus Berlin 3055, contain lengthy records of the liturgies and actions that were performed before the god. Although these records date to the New Kingdom or later, there is little reason to assume that the basic services performed for the god were significantly different in earlier, less well-documented eras.

A conventional anthropological model suggests that divine cults originated in the worship of local deities whose veneration eventually spread throughout the country, but this does not fit the Egyptian situation. Textual evidence indicates that the cult centers of many Egyptian deities were unrelated to a god's earliest attested place of origin. For example, Khnum, whose main cult center developed at Elephantine, first had a cult in Memphis and Abydos; Amun, who was so closely associated with Thebes, gained that geographic association only in the early New Kingdom after he supplanted and eclipsed the veneration of Montu, who had previously been associated with Thebes. Alongside these gods who gained their cult centers secondarily are purely local gods whose cult centers are in the same location as their first attestation.

Divine cults can be traced well back into the Early Dynastic period. The cult of Neith, perhaps at Sais, is mentioned on an ivory label of the first dynasty, and that of a baboon deity called Hedjwer, to whom votive offerings were left, is attested from a label of Semerkhet of the first dynasty. The Palermo Stone records festivals of the second dynasty that may be associated with early divine cults. Among the deities for whom early cults can be documented are Satet at Elephantine, Khentyamentiu at Abydos, Ptah at Memphis, and Horus at Nekhen (Hierakonpolis). The cults of certain gods were, for unknown reasons, subject to fluctuation in popularity. For example, the cult of Hathor was especially prevalent during the Old Kingdom, the cult of Amun became important only during the New Kingdom, and that devoted to Isis was not significant until the Ptolemaic period.

There were innumerable divine cults celebrated throughout Egypt, Nubia, and Egypt's foreign outposts. Although specific areas were associated with certain gods (Amun with Thebes, Re with Heliopolis, Satet and Khnum with Elephantine), the cult of a single god was not restricted to a particular area, and there were multiple cult centers for a single god throughout Egypt. For example, Hathor had temples in Dendera, Thebes, Nubia, Sinai, and elsewhere. In addition, a deity might have several temples in one area, as documented by the many shrines of Amun in his various aspects in Eastern and Western Thebes. These cult centers could be linked by divine ritual; for example, during the annual festival of the marriage of Hathor and Horus, the goddess of Dendera traveled to Edfu. In similar way, Amun of Karnak traveled to the Luxor temple, and Amun of the Luxor temple on the eastern bank of the Nile traveled to cult centers at Deir el-Bahri and Medinet Habu on the western bank.

Divine cults played an important role in the Egyptian economy. Great numbers of people were involved in the fulfillment of ritual, from those who served as priests, to those who built and maintained the shrines, wove the fabric offerings, and grew and prepared the food offerings. The economic structure of the divine cult paralleled that of the state's, in that the offerings given to the divine image during the thrice-daily offering service (see below) reverted to the temple workers as a part of their compensation.

The cult actions were executed by men and women of various ranks who were arranged in a hierarchical structure. These posts include the wab (wˁb; the "pure one"), a part-time priest who served in the temple on a rotational basis one month a season, hence three months a year. There were innumerable wab-priests, and the majority of workers in the divine cult were probably these low-estlevel priests. They permeated the entire society, since they held other, non-priestly positions outside the period of their rotation. The lector-priest (ḥry-ḥbt) was responsible for the recitation of prayers during the rituals and thus had to be literate. The "prophets" (ḥm-nṯr) were, at least in Thebes, divided into four ranks, the fourth prophet of Amun being the equivalent of the high priest. These men, whose range of duties is not entirely clear, evidently also served as the administrators of the vast temple domains of the divine cult. Other ranks of lesser priests, known from later period texts, include the stoalists (a Greek term), perhaps to be equated with the ranks of the ḥm-nṯr (the "pastophores"), who carried sacred objects in the divine cult, and the ranks of water-carriers (wȝḥ mw).

The method and means of priestly appointment is not entirely understood. It is unclear, for example, whether the highest-ranking priests of a regional temple were appointed by a central administration (perhaps located at the largest or most influential cult center), or whether appointments were handled on a purely local level, or through a combination of the two means. Clearly inheritance was a major factor, since genealogies indicate that a son often held the same priestly title as his father. The appointment of Nebwenenef as high priest of Amun was, according to his autobiography, made directly by Ramesses II, and in the Restoration Decree of Tutankhamun, that king claims that he personally appointed both wab-priests and prophets. Other priests were confirmed by oracles. Our imperfect understanding stems in part from the facts that few regional records have survived, and that most of the records extant come from Thebes, one of the greatest metropolitan centers.

Activities. The divine cult enacted in temples consisted of adoration of the god and making offerings to the divine being. In theory, the divine cult actions were performed by the king, who was the highest priest of all the cults and who bore the title "Lord of [ritual] Action" (nb írt ḫt). In actual terms, a priest acted on behalf of the king, declaring to the god "It is the king who sends me." The god, in the form of a statue, dwelled in a shrine (or naos) within the temple sanctuary. Our best description of what a cult statue looked like is preserved in the Restoration Decree of Tutankhamun: "his holy image being of electrum, lapis lazuli, turquoise and every precious stone." As attested by the well-preserved example at Edfu, the shrine in which the god dwelled had a pyramidal roofline and its base was carved with lotus and papyrus plants, thereby equating it with the place of creation. The shrine was equipped with double wooden doors and was closed with a sealed cord.

The daily cult was enacted three times a day, roughly coinciding with the interval of meals, in each of the numerous temples, large and small, throughout the Nile Valley. The cult actions were closely patterned on the established rhythms of human needs transferred to the world of the gods. Various versions and sequences of the cult activities are attested, and often the exact sequence is not clear because of the ambiguous order in which the scenes on temple walls can be read. Generally, the offerant first purified the *naos* and the surroundings of the god with incense. The seals of the divine shrine were broken, an act likened to "opening the doors of heaven to see the god." The priest then prostrated himself, "kissing the earth" before the face of the god. Praises of the god were recited as the priest began the ritual purification of the cult image. In some temples, a pile of clean sand was poured on the ground in imitation of the mound of creation. After the priest intoned prayers for "laying hands upon the god," the statue of the god was removed from the shrine and placed on the mound of sand, symbolizing the rebirth of the god. The unguents and garments that had been applied in the previous service were removed and the statue was cleansed with incense and ointments. Pieces of red, green, blue, and white fabric were purified with natron and presented to the god. A broad collar was placed on the statue and again purified with incense and libations. A crown, scepters, and amulets in the form of an Eye of Horus and the goddess Maat were arrayed on the statue. Food offerings were presented to the god and a prayer intoned to encourage the god to partake

of the meal. The statue was clothed in special *nms*-cloth, adored four times, and finally wrapped in a length of pure linen. The priest then closed the doors of the shrine and backed from the room, wiping away his footprints with a broom.

The temple-based divine cults probably showed little variation in cult activity from deity to deity; all gods were served by forms of the daily offering service. Yet there was more diversity in cult practice in the smaller localized cults, which, though possibly supported by state patronage, were outside the formalized context of the temple. The type of worship enacted by the nonelite tended to focus either on simple adoration of the god or on establishing an understanding under which the worshiper prayed and sacrificed or left food, drink, or votive offerings to the god; this was a means of obtaining divine intercession against sickness or infertility, or to secure wealth or guidance. Such worship may not have been executed on a regular basis, but only when an individual required divine intercession.

The best documentation for such informal divine cults are shrines to various deities, votive objects made of clay, wood, or bronze, and graffiti and more formal texts. Divine cult rituals performed outside the temple context can be traced to the Early Dynastic period by means of ivory, stone, and faience figurines of men, women, and animals excavated at the temple of Satet at Elephantine. These offerings were found in the temple precinct, where they had apparently been left by those who came to worship and, presumably, to petition the goddess for her help.

This practice is well attested by the New Kingdom cult of Hathor at Deir el-Bahri. That cult demonstrates the permeability of classification in Egyptian religion. Although it was dedicated to

Hathor and hence is classified as a divine cult, it had decidedly funerary overtones; not only was Hathor associated with the Western Hills (the cemetery), but in addition, life after death was a constant concern of the Egyptians. Their veneration of gods during their lifetime was often in association with the hope for a happy afterlife.

The cult of Hathor at Deir el-Bahri indicates that there was considerable variety of type in cult activities. A series of shrines dedicated to the goddess date from the eleventh dynasty into the Ptolemaic period. The center of her worship was at the Montuhotep temple and also at the eighteenth dynasty chapel of the mortuary temple of Thutmose III. There, recovered from the ruins, were Hathor masks, faience figurines of eyes and ears, *menat*s, sistra, plaques molded with the image of a cow, and linen shirts or pieces of fabric painted with scenes of Hathor.

These small-scale cults, like the more formalized ones, appear to have employed priests. The biography of a certain Ameniminet relates that "I am the *is*-priest of the goddess [Hathor]. Anyone with petitions, speak . . . to my ear, then I will repeat them to my mistress in exchange for offerings [consisting of beer and oil]." These offerings were given directly to the priest, circumventing the official practice of presenting the offering to god briefly before it reverted to the temple staff.

Nothing is known about the rituals that may have been enacted in conjunction with the manufacture and deposition of the votive objects; nor is it known if the votives were somehow consecrated by a priest before they were left in the shrine, nor whether priests were employed by the shrines to maintain the offerings.

Cults of Deified Kings. Although in theory all kings were venerated after their deaths through their mortuary cults, a few kings were worshiped in a deified state during their own lifetime. The king was venerated in his form of the royal *ka* or in his association with an aspect of Amun or Re. The cult of the living king focused on a statue of the pharaoh. Sacred boats that bore these images of the deified king in ritual processions are attested from Nubian and Egyptian temples.

Stelae and temple reliefs show the king and members of the community offering and adoring the statue of the deified king. Among the statues that have been identified as the focus of the divine cult of a king are those before the first and second pylons of the Luxor temple, the four colossal statues of Ramesses II on the facade of Abu Simbel, and the statue of Ramesses II within the sanctuary of that temple. Some stelae, such as that of Rahotep, a contemporary of Ramesses II, have the depiction of ears alongside an image of the divine statue, suggesting that the royal cult could involve the hearing of petitions. So too, the temple of "Ramesses II Who Hears Petitions," situated to the east of the temple of Amun at Karnak, was a place of public supplication based on worship of the divine king. Although little is known about the staff of such cults, the base of the cult statue of Ramesses II at the Luxor temple depicts *iwenmutef*-priests who officiated in the divine cult.

Few kings were honored with a cult during their lifetime; the cults of Sneferu, Senwosret III, Amenemhet III, Amenhotpe III, Tutankhamun, Sety I, Ramesses II, and Ramesses III are the best documented. Little is known about the rituals that were enacted in their honor, but certainly the creation of such a cult bolstered the prestige of the king during his lifetime. Ironically, most of the kings who created a divine cult for themselves were all longreigning, powerful kings, rather than ephemeral rulers who might have profited more from such artificial status.

Other royal cults were activated only long after the death of the king, such as the cult of Amenhotpe I in Western Thebes. Most of our information about this cult involves the role of the king as a community oracle. As attested by paintings from private tombs and from petitions, a statue of the god-king, often in the company of his mother Ahmose-Nefertari, was dragged on a sledge in community processions. In the course of the procession, questions were put to the statue for adjudication. A similar role was played by Montuhotep and by Amenhotpe III and Tiye. Such attestations suggest that a major focus of the royal divine cults was to make the king more approachable to the populace.

Cults of Deified Individuals. A few private individuals elevated to the status of gods were the recipients of cults after their death. The best attested are the architects Imhotep (designer of the Step Pyramid, third dynasty) and Amenhotep, son of Hapu (architect of Amenhotpe III, eighteenth dynasty). Temples or shrines to both those men, or to them together, were situated throughout Thebes, as well as at Aswan, Dendera, Armant, Aswan, Saqqara, and Memphis. Other individuals so honored include Hekaib (governor of Aswan, sixth dynasty) and Isi, a sixth dynasty vizier who, as late as the thirteenth dynasty was referred to as a "living god." As with the divine cults, the object of these cults was also viewed as an intercessor who could make the needs of an individual known to the gods. An inscription on the base of a statue of Amenhotep, son of Hapu, is particularly explicit about the function of the cult:

O people of Karnak who wish to see Amun, come to me! I will transmit your request because I am the herald of this god. . . . I will transmit your word to Amun in Karnak. Give me an offering and pour a libation for me, because I am an intermediary nominated by the king to hear requests of the suppliant, to report to him the desires of Egypt.

As indicated by the text, the cult of these deified individuals apparently consisted of offerings to the memory and honor of the deceased in hope that the cult figure would obtain assistance from the gods.

The cult of deceased individuals became more common in the Late and Ptolemaic periods. Examples include Djedhor (thirtieth dynasty), who was deified as a form of Thoth, and Petosiris of Tuna el-Gebel, who was closely associated with Imhotep and Amenhotpe. From the thirtieth dynasty, individuals who drowned were accorded cults and were the subject of popular veneration. The divinity of such people was apparently based on the analogy of their drowning with the dispersal in the Nile of the body parts of Osiris. Among the best-known recipients of this cult are Pedesi and Pihor, who were buried at the Temple of Dendur and who are shown in that temple receiving offerings from the Roman emperor Augustus.

Emily Teeter

Animal Cults

Like all early societies, the Egyptians lived their lives surrounded by animals. They depended on them for their livelihood, and they could not afford to be sentimental about them. At the same time, they were aware that animals possessed some qualities that were similar to those of humans and others that differed in important ways. This ambiguity aroused their curiosity. In addition, the

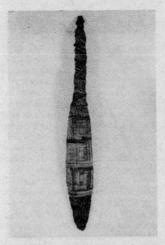

Crocodile mummy. (University of Pennsylvania Museum, Philadelphia, Neg. #S4-141201)

Egyptians were often averse to making hard-and-fast distinctions in their view of reality. The living and the dead, for example, were often thought of as part of the same continuum, and the same to an extent was true of gods and human beings. It was therefore natural that the Egyptians would regard animals as part of a seamless world in which clues to the divine nature could be found.

Not all animals fell into the category of the potentially sacred. Most beasts of burden were regarded as unsuitable, though the donkey can be given religious associations that were disruptive or hostile to divine order. The ant was not recognized as sacred and seems to be absent from the hieroglyphic script. The horse, which in many societies was given heroic status, was highly valued, but it

arrived too late in Egyptian history, when the canon of the sacred was already fixed. (It is true that the Syrian goddess Astarte could be shown riding a horse, but she too was borrowed.) The same is true of exotic animals such as elephants. Another late arrival was the camel, which also had the misfortune to be a beast of burden. However, most other animals were considered to reflect the world of the gods in some way. Occasionally they appear as divine mascots; for example, the gazelle accompanies the goddess Anoukis. But normally it is the animal itself that is thought of as conveying the divinity to which it is assigned; hence the falcon can be an image of Horus and in late texts can even be described as his soul (*b3*), while the cat and the ichneumon are seen as embodiments of the gods Bastet and Atum, respectively. An interesting offshoot of this association is the use of animal heads on top of human figures to represent gods. Some gods can be shown this way as an option—for example, the occasional representation of Osiris with the head of a hare, which may be a lunar symbol. Other gods, such as Thoth and Sokar, are invariably shown as hybrids of this type. It is possible that the Egyptians conceived of such a head as a mask that served to hide the true form of the god, which was inexpressible. Whatever the explanation, the prominence of animals in the iconography is beyond doubt.

Since the animal and human worlds were thought to be parallel, it is not surprising to find the animal equivalent of the pharaoh. This is the Apis bull of Memphis, which is attested as early as the first dynasty. The principal titles of the Apis are of significance: he is *nswt n iw'nb ntry* ("king of every divine animal"), which emphasizes his preeminence; he is also *whm n Pth* ("repetition (?) of Ptah"). The word *whm* refers to the particular incarnation of the god that was thought to be present in his animal, and in some respects it is close to the Hindu concept of the avatar. It may also convey the notion of a herald or mouthpiece. On death, the Apis was thought to merge into the god Osiris, and the compound *Wsir-Hp* (Osiris-Apis or Osorapis) was used to signify the entire procession of historical animals that had gone to their divine destiny. The worst crime that could be ascribed to the Persian conqueror Cambyses was the (untrue) allegation that he had murdered the Apis. At Memphis, the theologians of the later period provided the bull with a mother: Isis, mother of the Apis, who had her own sacred cow. There was even a cult of children of the Apis, known from papyrus contracts of Ptolemaic date.

The complexity of Egyptian religion combined with the facts of geographical rivalry to make sure that the Apis was not unique. At Heliopolis there was the Mnevis (*Mr-wr*), a jet-black bull that was the *whm* of Atum; at Armant in the South, there was Buchis, a white bull with a black head, which was taken to be the *whm* of various solar deities. The splendor of the Buchis bull's temple and catacomb shows that, at least in the Late period, the Buchis was a serious rival to the Apis. There were other sacred bulls, notably in the Delta, and there was also the ram of Mendes. Edfu had the cult of a royal falcon. All these animals were singular and were succeeded by another only when they died. Most of them had elaborate rituals of enthronement and public display which were adapted from royal ceremonial. Many of them were thought to have oracular powers, doubtless because of their close associations with the divine.

Below this stage in the hierarchy were animals that functioned in small groups, like faunal aristocracies. The best known example is the sacred baboons of Memphis; Ptolemaic texts from the Sacred Animal Necropolis at Saqqara confirm that a colony of these animals was kept in the temple of Ptah "under his *moringa*-tree" in the valley. From time to time this colony was replenished with monkeys brought either from Ethiopia or from the royal zoo in Alexandria. There may have been a dozen or more in the colony at any one time. They had their own names, and the dates of their births were recorded when possible. One of the baboons would be singled out as oracular, and *d-h* was given the name *Dd-hr-p3-"n* ("the face of the baboon has spoken"). When an animal died, it was mummified and placed in a special catacomb hewn out of the rock at North Saqqara. A short obituary was written across the front of the niche where it was buried. A similar colony sacred to Thoth seems to have existed at Hermopolis in Middle Egypt, but it is uncertain how far back this practice extended. The lions of Leontopolis, in the Nile Delta, may have been a similar group.

The next step was to extend the concept of divinity to animals *en masse*, and there are signs even in the New Kingdom that this was beginning to happen. In the Cairo Museum there is a sarcophagus of a cat that may have belonged to Prince Thutmose, the short-lived elder brother of Akhenaten. The cat is depicted as a mummy and is termed *Wsir t3mit* ("Osiris the she-cat"). There is a jar in Munich with a Hieratic inscription recording that it contained the body of an ibis, which the dedicator had found in a canal of Ramesses I. It had presumably drowned and therefore had been claimed by the gods. In later times, the custom of burying animals found by chance may have become the norm, as suggested by the fifth-century BCE Greek historian Herodotus. This is confirmed by a Demotic text from Saqqara that records the burial of a falcon found dead at the entrance to some temple outbuildings; it was still sacred, whether in its right place or out of it.

By the Late period, reverence for cats and ibises, which could be kept in hundreds or even thousands, became commonplace. The true situation can be seen from the lists compiled by Dieter Kessler of sites and their associated animal cults. There were several major centers of worship for ibises, falcons, crocodiles, monkeys, ichneumons, cats, and most other animals, and there were many lesser centers as well. Theologically, these represent a straightforward extension of the notion of divinity resident within an animal, but there are several interesting ramifications. At Saqqara, the lunar and solar connotations of falcons and ibises were developed into a contrasting system, and the ibis god Thoth also acquired the epithet "Three Times Great."

In general, however, these extended cults were treated in a more reticent way. Ibises, for example, were not named individually, and on death were merely thought to merge into a collective entity known as Osiris the Ibis (*Wsir p3 hb*). Nevertheless, when dead and awaiting burial, they might be referred to openly as "gods" (*ntrw*). With a few exceptions, their burials are uninscribed, and no obituaries survive. The underground catacombs, however, are extensive, as they needed to be. One figure suggests an ibis population at North Saqqara of sixty thousand, and the late Ptolemaic-era Prinz-Joachim Ostraca from Kom Ombo reveal a burial rate of several hundred a month. Ibis mummies could be stacked in chapels known as "houses of waiting" (*'wy.w n ḥrr*), since the catacombs would be opened only on ceremonial occasions for mass burials. In the case of ibises, the final total could run into millions, as at Saqqara and at Tuna el-Gebel, west of Hermopolis.

The driving force behind these enormous cults was that they paid. They were expensive to run, but they attracted worshipers and pilgrims in the thousands, in some cases from outside Egypt, as can be seen from hieroglyphic dedications on bronze votive statues. This mass appeal is evident in the large numbers of oracular questions and responses that survive. Oracles were a mechanism for decision-making, important or otherwise, and in a sense they occupied the niche nowadays filled by personal therapists and professional advisors. In addition, they were tangible and accessible in the way that conventional cults were not. They could interpret pilgrims' dreams. The same was true of the cults of the deified men Imhotep and Amenhotep, son of Hapu, which developed along similar lines. These gods listened: one of the epithets of the baboons at Saqqara was "The Hearing Ear." A worshiping prayer to the deified Buchis, inscribed on a pebble from his temple at Armant, shows this well: "Come to me Osiris-Buchis, my great lord. . . . I am your servant, and call upon you. I never weary of calling. Cares are heavy upon me, and I am small against them all. . . . Do not weary of calling upon [a] god. Has he his hour of dying, when he will not hear?"

The care offered by animal cults could be more than psychological. George Hughes has published a Demotic papyrus of Ptolemaic date, probably from the principal ibis cult at Hermopolis. This is a plea to the god of the temple by two children who have been thrown out of their home by a cruel father or stepfather. They are reduced to sleeping in holes in walls and begging for food. This plea is essentially a request to be taken into care, and in practice the various animal cults offered a variety of solutions to social problems, such as asylum for political refugees, self-sale (in which a person would do menial work for the temple in exchange for maintenance), and forms of refuge for debtors and persons in similar difficulties. Perhaps the founding of Alexandria and the removal of the court from Egypt proper increased feelings of alienation among the native Egyptians; whatever the explanation, these cults filled a social need.

Another interesting discovery has come from the dedications on the temple furniture found in the falcon galleries at Saqqara. Some of these items were extremely costly, and most were offered to the cult of a young ibis deity, otherwise unknown, named Thutmose. (Whether this is linked to the earlier prince of the same name is still unknown.) Many of these dedications were by women from the nearby township of Abusir, and in one case the occasion was a personal festival, perhaps a marriage. The cult of Thutmose was clearly a favorite with these women, some of whom had considerable wealth to spare. Perhaps they too felt excluded from more conventional worship.

We know something about the organization of these cults. There were the usual *wab*-priests and prophets (*ḥmw-ntr*), but the more menial caretakers or animal feeders were known as servants (*sḏmw-ʿš* or *sḏmw*). Jobs of this sort ran in families, and a similar arrangement can be found among the masons (*byw* or *byw mnḫ*) who excavated and maintained the catacombs. These operated in teams, and it was not uncommon for such teams to be seconded from one cult to another. A similar, but probably more important, body was the stonecutters, workmen who made and installed the huge sarcophagi of the Serapeum and the nearby Mothers of the Apis. Some of the former at least had minor priestly titles, and all were attached to the cult of the appropriately named Ptah "great of strength" (*ʿ3 pḥty*). From the mid-Ptolemaic period's Archive of H. or, all the animal cults at Saqqara were known to be subordinate to the Serapeum; however, in a major crisis, authority could be referred to the temple of Ptah in Memphis, which had the power to enforce reforms and punish abuse.

Self-regulation had its limits. In the Ptolemaic period, animal cults received an annual subsidy from the crown, known in Greek as *syntaxis*. In return for this, each cult had to accept a royal inspector (*epistates*), whose job it was to keep an eye on the administrative head of the temple, the *mr-šn* or *lesonis*, who was normally an Egyptian. In addition, rights such as asylum were rigorously controlled, and major building projects seem to have been subject to the royal purse-strings.

Proving a negative is difficult, but the sudden collapse of most animal cults after the Roman conquest in 30 BCE makes it likely that the new conquerors abolished the subsidy. The notion of animal worship was anathema to the Romans, especially when it was conducted by people whom they regarded as Hellenes, and they would not have been interested to know that Hermes Trismegistos was originally an ibis. However, traditional cults such as the Buchis were allowed to continue in reduced form. One of the last stelae from the Bucheum at Armant was dedicated by the Roman Emperor Constantius II (r. 337–361 CE), who was a declared Christian. Animal worship dwindled along the Nile, although the occasional Coptic icon showing a saint such as Christopher with a dog's head shows that vague folk memories persisted for centuries.   *John D. Ray*

CURSES. In modern times, popular myths about pharaonic Egypt often focus on the use of curses. During the twentieth century, the press and entertainment media have concentrated on supposed curses against individuals who seek hidden burial places in the land of the pharaohs, disturb them, and desecrate the tombs. In these recent interpretations, such blasphemous activities inevitably lead to a dire fate for the defilers and can often haunt their families and friends as well. The most famous of these updated maledictions is "The Curse of King Tutankhamun." It surfaced shortly after the death of Lord Carnarvon on 6 May 1923, and was reported throughout the world. Carnarvon was the financial supporter of the expedition led by the discoverer of the tomb, Howard Carter. This tragic incident occurred less than one year after the tomb of that pharaoh had been opened. Although the tomb contained no hieroglyphic text that resembled the supposed curse that the media issued, the public apparently preferred to accept what they read about the curse in the newspapers and journals, rather than to listen to scholars. In the beginning, only one death was attributed to the curse, but soon the death of anyone even remotely connected with the tomb was ascribed to the same cause. Books focused on it; films were made about it, and interest in it surfaces every so often, despite frequent published refutations. Although Howard Carter lived more than seventeen years after discovering the tomb, his longevity is never referred to. What should be perhaps of more interest is that the ancient Egyptians did in fact employ various types of curses and threats, and some of them

were specifically aimed at trespassers who attempted to violate the tomb.

The presumed efficacy of these curses derived in part from a belief in the power of the written and spoken word, and this form of magic (*ḥkꜣ*) was a divine property accessible to the pharaoh as well as to humankind. Traditionally, the antagonist could take the form of a being, either human or spiritual, living or dead. Fear of the known or the unknown could be controlled through the use of this *ḥkꜣ*. The first step was to identify the foe, an act that exerted some power over it, and this was often accompanied by a description of any potential or actual action. Then the consequence for such deeds could follow. Some times a statement of protection against a hostile act would accompany the identification of it.

Though recorded in both hieroglyphs and Hieratic, curses clearly also had a spoken aspect, and occasionally a spell included directions for its recitation. Certain spells in mortuary literature (for example, BD 151 regarding magical bricks) and some inked on other types of papyri (for example, a letter to the dead) could function as curses, and texts on tomb façades or clay figurines could also have the same role. The execration texts, which represent extensions of this practice, are lists of the names of hostile individuals and foreign enemies that appear on figures or pottery. The ritual destruction of these items was thought to render such antagonists harmless. This practice, a form of sympathetic magic, took place at various levels of Egyptian society.

To deal with potential or actual afflictions, the Egyptians also made use of spoken and written incantations. These would address the entity that they thought was responsible for such ills and threaten it with destruction. "The Magical Spells for Mother and Child," for instance, warn that any foe intending to take an action against the child would be met with resistance and repelled. Though not always explicitly expressed, similar intentions can be inferred by the existence of amuletic objects such as magical wands. These artifacts, which were used especially for newborn children, could carry the same protection, even if their surfaces omitted the traditional text and had only the associated iconography. Both royal and nonroyal individuals used magical bricks in their tombs to safeguard them against demons that might come against the deceased from each of the four cardinal points. These inscribed objects generally occur with accompanying images and were meant to be apotropaic devices to threaten potential antagonists. Such objects were also part of the funerary equipment of Tutankhamun, and might be identified more properly as the real curse in the tomb of that pharaoh.

Slightly different were the letters to the dead, entreaties to the *akh*s, residents of the netherworld who often were deceased relatives of the sender. Those who were still among the living would write to these spirits requesting aid in time of need. The *akh*s were assumed to have some control over events that were taking place (or would occur) in this world, and, in order to ensure that they responded positively, the sender would often threaten to deprive them of their offerings and thus jeopardize their eternal existence.

The ancient Egyptians spent considerable time and effort preparing for their afterlife. Since the tomb was an essential element in the plans for their eternal survival, they considered it important to protect it in the best manner possible. One of the means that they used to secure their final resting places was a curse. They believed that a threat could safeguard the structure from a variety of attacks against the construction itself, its purity, its contents, the mummy, and the accompanying imagery, iconography, and texts. Among the many types of hostility that the ancient Egyptians specified were any sort of damage to the tomb, theft, disrespect or vilification of the owner, and sacrilege. Old Kingdom tomb owners were especially preoccupied with fears that an impure individual might enter the chapel and thereby defile the sacred area. Traditionally, such blasphemers are referred to as those who had not purified themselves, or those who had eaten a forbidden food before entering the chapel. At least one example, however, also places adulterers in this category. Negative connotations regarding sexual activities before entering a holy place such as a temple are documented later in the mortuary literature.

Many messages to potential enemies were carved on stone and inscribed as part of the tomb owner's biographical statement, such as those referred to above. Examples can be found from most periods of Egyptian history, although those from the earlier times are more common. Inscriptions with similar communications can occur in the form of graffiti at quarries, but they can also be inscribed on stelae, offering tables, temple walls, and papyri. During different time periods, there were certain preferences in terms of the style of the curse, the type of individual addressed, the reaction to the hostility, or the medium on which the message was placed. For example, it appears that biographical maledictions in private tombs were more popular in the Old and Middle Kingdoms than in the New Kingdom. The Egyptians also incorporated threats in their legacies. Often, especially in the Third Intermediate Period and later, wills inscribed on papyri would contain a malediction to ensure the desired distribution of willed property to the appropriate beneficiary.

Curses inscribed on the walls of temples date primarily from the New Kingdom and later, but even in earlier times royalty had threats inscribed as punishments to violators (see, for example, the temple inscription of Senwosret I at Tod). The pharaohs used not only the walls of temples but also stelae and other types of inscriptions (see, for example,

the Nauri Decree of Sety I) to record their warnings.

The terminology in the first part of the curse often appears to have parallels in legal or juridical texts, and the same observation seems to be even more valid in the statements that follow. Some of the threats against the hostility are expressed in terms of judgment, sentencing, or punishment; in the later periods, the offender can be exposed to sexual penalties, some including bestiality.

David P. Silverman

D

DEITIES. Mankind began settling in the Nile Valley long before the dawn of our era and well before the beginning of the pharaonic society that the modern public associates with ancient Egypt. The seeds of the civilization that was to develop and many of the concepts that appeared in the time of the pharaohs, therefore, clearly came into being well into the distant past. Some of the ideas were generated before the establishment of any settlements along the banks of the river Nile. Archaeological evidence from the earliest periods suggests that the environment in which mankind lived played a very influential role in the religious ideology that would be recorded much later. At first, these beliefs were private and focused only on the personal level, but as people became more settled in particular areas and oriented more toward structured groups, they adapted doctrines to reflect the requirements of a larger society. The doctrines of an earlier era did not necessarily disappear; in fact, some clearly survived the initial transition to the society and can be seen in the development of local cults and such practices as ancestor worship. Eventually these succumbed to change and adaptation when the even more settled organization of the state emerged. Once the country became united under a single ruler, it eventually favored the establishment of a national religion to which the local beliefs would have to become sec-

ondary. A king could, however, bring to national prominence a deity known primarily in the area from which the pharaoh came, but even when that did not happen, the local cults could persist. For example, the god Ptah had national significance during the pharaonic period and was especially prominent in the creation texts, but his original connection with Memphis never ceased to be recognized, and his status as a god in that region was maintained.

The Environment and Early Beliefs. Some traditions can be traced back to the early stages of the development of the state such as the falcon god Horus, whose image appears along with the names of the earliest kings on early dynastic monuments, and then it becomes a standard element in the royal titulary. He also maintains an important role in several creation myths. Other animals, such as cattle, also figure prominently in pharaonic religion, and they appear to have an even longer history. Artisans created sculptures, reliefs, and paintings of cowgoddesses such as Hathor, who was known on a national level throughout dynastic times and was an important deity to whom the Egyptians built and dedicated temples. Other goddesses whom they associated with cattle, such as Bat and Mehetweret, were perhaps less well known, and their popularity did not remain constant. Images of these goddesses could take the form of a complete bovine or composite human/bovine. The latter type, occasionally accompanied by stars, appears during the Early Dynastic period. The head of a human female with bovine ears and horns in frontal view appears in raised relief, two times at the top of each side of the Narmer Palette. The repetition of the image four times, as well as its placement at the pinnacle of the composition, imply that this deity was particularly influential. Reinforcement for this conclusion might be seen in the inclusion of the image on a work whose main scenes appear to commemorate perhaps Egypt's earliest king uniting the legendary two lands of Upper and Lower Egypt.

The prominence of the human/bovine divine emblem at the beginning stages of recorded Egyptian history suggests that it may have been a focus of reverence and veneration even earlier. Archaeological evidence indicates that cattle were apparently quite important as a source of milk, blood, and perhaps also meat in pre-pharaonic cultures that developed in the southern part of Egypt, near modern Sudan. These benefits, as well as certain characteristics of cattle, may have led early mankind to hold these animals in high esteem. The recent excavations by the American and Polish expeditions in the Sahara Desert, about 100 kilometers (60 miles) west of Abu Simbel, have unearthed sacrificial burials of cattle bones as early as five thousand years before any pharaoh walked the earth. Such findings, as well as their recent discovery of the burial of a completely intact cow, suggest that practices originating in earlier African cultures may well represent the root of the later ideology that appears in the historic periods of the riverine society out of which pharaonic culture emerges.

While the flora and fauna in the environment helped shape the form that their deities took, the varying elements of the physical world were the significant factors affecting the underlying concepts of the gods and goddesses. The world around early mankind provided memorable experiences that shaped the beliefs of these individuals. Their universe could sometimes be most hostile, yet at other times quite gentle and beneficent, and they had to find ways of coping with and surviving in it. Certain elements of nature such as the sky brought forth the crop-supporting rain and the warm, life-sustaining rays of the sun, but from it also emanated chaotic windstorms, damaging torrential downpours, and lethal, parching heat. Likewise, later, when the Egyptians settled along the Nile, the river became to them a source of sustenance in the form of its life-giving water and the fertile soil it left after its yearly flooding. It too, however, could become the bearer of disaster in the form of an inundation that was either too high, resulting in devastating floods, or too low, leading to droughts.

Early individuals certainly observed and experienced the effects of these phenomena, but their struggles for survival took precedence over their contemplation of the causes and results of such forces of nature. As time progressed these peoples accumulated both knowledge and experience, and they soon acquired the necessary skills to thrive in their environment. Only then did they have the opportunity to contemplate their own role within their physical world and how they related to it. In other words, they no longer simply reacted to the elements of their environment, but stepped back to observe them and recognize the dynamics occurring before them. At these early stages of cultural development, however, the cognitive processes functioned primarily on a personal level. It is possible to suggest a simple model of how these events might have happened. An early human might one day notice that the light of the new day also brought warmth as well as a renewal of energy. Repetition of these feelings day after day might cause the individual to associate the initial perceptions of security with elements of the physical environment. In a subsequent move, he or she might then attribute the consequences to the disk of the sun as it reappeared at the eastern horizon. Some people might respond similarly to the same stimuli, while others react differently. Whatever their sentiments, they may have communicated them among each other as they came together once society came into being. Through these processes, they developed the basic concepts underlying the inner workings of the universe. That these very elements were critical at this point in history seems to be suggested by the many deities, appearing later in the recorded Egyptian pantheon, that focus on the environment.

Explicating the "behavior" of the universe was in a way a means of controlling it. Attributing some logic to the manner in which all of the physical elements functioned allowed early man to begin to predict what would or could happen rather than to react after it happened. In time, increased observations would result not only in refined knowledge of the world, but also in more elaborate explanations for its existence and interactions among its components. A theoretical universe was envisioned, and its relationship to the real world and mankind's role in both were explained through the use of myth. It is likely that attributing animal imagery, characteristics, and traits to the elements of the physical world was also part of this process. Such associations may well have happened through the ancient Egyptians'

keen sense of observation. An often-cited example is the falcon, an animal that the Egyptians associated early on with the sun. It has been suggested that this creature's ability to fly so high that it appears to merge into the disk of the sun may well underlie its relationship to the solar deity Re.

Such a correlation allowed the Egyptians to link a conceptual element, heat and light, with a less abstract one, the solar disk, and then a concrete one, the falcon. By making further attributions with human traits, the mystical, enigmatic, and indefinable became recognizable, approachable, and tangible. This transcendence was facilitated through the allocation of special space for communing with the conceptualized deity. These specialized areas, which would later give rise to temples, were places where some form of the divinity could be approached, venerated, supplicated to, or worshiped. To visualize it in concrete form, the Egyptians used a fetish, a statue, or other type of related symbol or image, and in these locations appropriate ritual could take place. Eventually the structures became quite elaborate and were understood as residences for the god. The Egyptians used particular decorative programs of carvings and paintings and employed architectural elements of specific forms to reflect cosmic symbolism.

Gods, Goddesses, and the Stories of Creation. Most of the deities that comprise the pantheon of ancient Egypt can be thought of as relating to the environment in some way. The question has often been asked whether the Egyptians viewed each god as a distinct element of the cosmos, or as integral components held together by a single universal force. Scholars have debated such questions over the last century and have proposed many arguments to support their conclusions. It is clear that a hierarchy among the deities existed and that it reflected societal divisions among mankind. For example, just as there was a king on earth, there was a king of the gods. For much of the historical period Re, or his composite form Amun-Re, had this role. Another divine king was Osiris, whose realm was limited to the afterlife, but the two were connected in many ways, some of which are reflected in the funerary texts written on papyri and recorded on coffins, tombs, vessels, and amulets. Osiris's son Horus resembles the crown prince, and the relationship between the two—as well as the events of their lives—mirror the transfer of power involved with inherited kingship. Some gods had bureaucratic positions, such as Thoth, the scribe and messenger of the gods, while others, such as Montu, were related to the military.

To be sure, associations such as these came well after the early beliefs that focused on the forces of the universe confronting early man. Cosmic powers, however, continued as part of Egyptian ideology into the historical period. The Egyptian concept of primeval gods appears to reflect these doctrines. This group would consist either of several gods or a series of divine couples that represent the aspects of the universe prior to creation. The Egyptians associated creator gods with different geographic areas, and separate myths and creation theologies were set around the major religious centers such as Heliopolis, Hermopolis, and Memphis. In Heliopolis, which was linked with the center of the solar cult in the North, Atum functioned as the primary deity, and the Ennead was completed by his eight children: Shu, Tefnut, Geb, Nut, Osiris, Isis, Seth, and Nephthys. Atum is the progenitor, and he singlehandedly creates the elemental components of the uni-

verse. He begets air and moisture, as a matched pair, and this couple in turn creates earth and sky, the chthonic and celestial elements, who in turn are responsible for the last two pairs. Further elaboration of this mythology involves the conflict between the two brothers, Horus and Seth, and the battles between Horus, the son of Isis and Osiris, and his uncle Seth. The relationship of this doctrine and ancient Egyptian kingship is clear, and the derivation of it rests, at least in part, on the ostensible need for the legitimization of the royal genealogy.

Hermopolis, the local association of another version of creation, is a site in Middle Egypt. There prevailed the god Thoth, who was associated with wisdom, writing, and the moon. Eight gods grouped into four couples comprise the Hermopolitan mythology, which focuses on the ordering of the chaotic universe at the time of creation. Traditionally, Amun and his female counterpart Amaunet refer to hiddenness, and they are called in early texts the source of the other gods. They are paired with primeval waters, Nun and Naunet. Kuk and Kauket, representing darkness, and Heh and Hauhet, endlessness, make up the last two pairs. These in turn generate other divinities, and already in the Coffin Texts, passages relate that the deities of this cosmogony are associated with that of Heliopolis.

Memphis in the North is one of the earliest religious centers, and it retains its importance throughout most of Egyptian history. Its story of creation, however, derives from an ancient inscription, recorded in the eighth century BCE under the reign of King Shabaqa, that purports to be a copy of a much earlier original. Recent scholarship, however, disputes that attestation in the text and dates the document to the Late period, thereby suggesting that it represents the latest of the theologies of this type. Ptah, a deity associated with Memphis from early times, is the primary focus in this version. He is a god who is capable of creating with his heart and tongue, and this ability refers to the concepts of intellectual activity (thought) and its result (speech). Ptah also creates Atum in this myth, and through this action the Memphite theology is linked to that from Heliopolis. Many of the deities involved in these ideologies were of national renown during historic times, but their associations with a particular area may reflect their role as local deities at an earlier period.

Other gods and goddesses also became prominent figures or featured players in the stories of creation, as well as in the related narratives that became associated with them. For instance, the deity Nefertum, known both in the funerary texts as well in the local cult of Memphis, is symbolized as the lotus blossom, the first form of life that appears from the primeval mound after waters of chaos recede.

In all levels of the divine hierarchy and throughout Egyptian society there existed the unifying concept of balance and harmony. The creation myths describe the earliest periods in the memory of humankind as pure chaos. Out of it derived some form of harmony, and this calmed state made possible the existence of the world as the Egyptians knew it. The gods are responsible for maintaining the order and presenting it to the king who in turn reinforces the system. Humankind must live according to its rules and regulations; no one is exempt. So important was the concept of order and balance in the universe that it was deified as a goddess, Maat.

Divine Unions. It is not unusual for a deity to be amalgamated, that is to say, syncretized, with one or more divinities, such as Re-Atum, Khnum-Re, Ptah-Sokar-Osiris, and Amun-Re-Horakhty. In these divine links, one god was combined with another, or became an extension of another, and the elements of each would become unified in the composite without the loss of their original identity. Other less bound associations would include the series of couplets generally made up of a god and a goddess. Often the two divinities are a reflection of the elements of the environment, perceived as dual opposing components, such as light and darkness, air and moisture, and other "dualities" that figure prominently in the creation myths referred to above. Although not as common, same-sex pairs exist, as with the sisters Isis and Nephthys. The Egyptians also formed triads of deities, which groupings consist generally of two elemental gods and goddesses along with their offspring. Often these sets of divinities become associated with specific geographic areas. Ptah and Sekhmet, long linked with Memphis, add a son, Nefertum, in the New Kingdom, but other kinship groups, such as Osiris, Isis, and Horus, are attested as a group much earlier. Three deities also form a trinity, and this phenomenon, derived perhaps because of political considerations, was more common after the eighteenth dynasty. Such associations linked not only primary deities like Amun, Re, and Ptah, but also their cult places, Thebes, Heliopolis, and Memphis.

Categories of Egyptian Deities. Several different terms for the classification of Egyptian gods have been used in the sections above, such as creator, local, and national. While some of these designations and others are of modern derivation, it is not unreasonable to assume that the Egyptians themselves would have sought some means of differentiating among the hundreds of deities that comprised their pantheon. In fact, the phrases "local gods" and "district gods" are referred to in both the Pyramid Texts and biographical inscriptions. In addition, the names of several gods derive directly from the city of their provenance, as with the goddess Nekhbet of Nekehb.

Modern publications often refer to the gods of the afterlife, and in fact the ancient Egyptians understood that many of the supreme beings they venerated functioned primarily in that domain. Such a reference could be made iconographically in statuary or relief, in which case the representation would situate the deity within an environment, clearly not that of the contemporaneous world. The Judgment of the Dead scene would be a good illustration of this process. There the god Osiris, whose visible body parts appear either green or black, presides over a court composed of animals as well as composite and fantastical creatures. The genre of text in which the god would appear, or the accompanying descriptive phrases might also help to categorize him or her. Funerary literature like the Pyramid Texts, the Coffin Texts, and the *Book of Going Forth by Day* (*Book of the Dead*) focus on these deities. Phrases such as "who is in the netherworld" might designate a specific god, perhaps Horus, in one text, or it might refer to a group of demons to be avoided in a particular area of the underworld in another inscription. This category of deities was perhaps the most populated of all, and because so much funerary material has survived into modern times, we are aware of the many gods and goddesses who played a role in this environment. The mortuary temples of the pharaoh and the tombs focus on Osiris, the king of the underworld, but Isis, Horus, Re, Anubis, and Thoth figure prominently as well. Those associated

with embalming, in addition to Anubis—i.e., Nephthys, Selket, Neith; and the four sons of Horus: Imsety, Hapy, Duamutef, and Kebehsenuef—also belong to this classification. Other spirits of the netherworld included demons, demigods, and personifications of the underworld. In addition, major deities like Ptah and Hathor also took part in the afterlife, but their role was not as significant as that of others. Their presence, however, indicates that the Egyptians imagined their gods as functioning in more than one capacity, and they assigned many roles to them. Re, for example, was instrumental not only as a funerary deity, but as a national one as well; likewise, Hathor appears in the context of the afterlife, was a state deity, had an international role, and also was the focus of local cults.

The Egyptians did not treat each god in the same way throughout the country. With the local, district, or domestic deities the relationship was more personal, and access was more direct and less formal. Other divinities that maintained more prominent positions in the pantheon, however, were worshiped at more of a distance. The formalized rituals were more uniform, since these gods and goddesses were worshiped all over Egypt. Temples were dedicated to these national divinities, and services, rituals, and festivals were held in their honor on a statewide basis. The temples of Luxor and Karnak were built in honor of Amun-Re, the king of the gods, and during certain holidays the image of the god would be brought forth from the shrine for view and worship by the people. Further access occurred when the priests transported the image to other temples along a prescribed route. Hathor, Isis, and Ptah are among other state deities to have been held in such repute.

The type of temple, the texts and decoration therein, as well as the associated documents help to distinguish the roles of the major gods and allow us to identify the many categories into which they were classified. A sense of the popularity of a divinity, the manner in which it was approached, and the type of group to which it belonged can also be seen by looking carefully at figurines, hymns, and prayers. Amulets represented a sign of devotion to and respect for a particular god, but they could also become a means of protection, benefit, and advantage. Deities associated with the more personal aspects of the individual are often rendered in the form of an amulet to be worn or carried. In amulets to be used in the afterlife, funerary deities predominate. Amulets used by the living with their magical properties were frequently used as personal adornments, and their use can be traced back to the earliest periods. Most of the early amulets took the form of animals, and these can be seen as symbols of particular deities. Particularly popular were the frog and hippopotamus, associated with fertility, over which, along with childbirth, the goddesses Heket and Taweret would later have influence. Another of the minor deities, Bes, also important at birth, was particularly popular in the New Kingdom. Not much later, the repertoire of deities would increase and include many of the major figures, such as Sekhmet, Isis, Sobek, or Khnum, as well as minor ones like Heh, Horpakhered, and Imhotep. These tiny figures were thought to offer the wearer the protection or power of the divinity represented. It is clear from the great variety of deities depicted in amulets, from the many different forms of votive figurines, and the numerous deities addressed in prayers that the Egyptians eventually considered most of their gods and goddesses as capable of performing the role of a personal god.

Certain members of the pantheon had roles beyond the borders of Egypt, for during different periods, the pharaohs had extended the country's influence over foreign areas. Moreover, settlements outside Egypt would require access to native deities. Hathor was worshiped in the Sinai and at Byblos, and she along with Horus, Amun, Re, and others had cults in Nubia. Certain of Egypt's gods were assigned to border areas, like Ash, who is associated with the Western Desert and sometimes Libya. Especially in the New Kingdom and later, foreign deities made appearances on Egyptian monuments and were mentioned in texts. Reshef, Ba'al, Hauron, Astarte, and Anat are some of those from western Asia who figure prominently in the iconography and inscriptions; Dedwen appears to derive from Nubia.

Part of the concept of kingship included the doctrine of the pharaoh's deification after death, but this process was extended occasionally to lesser members of society as well. Perhaps the most famous of nonroyal individuals to receive such status was Imhotep, the high priest of Re during the third dynasty. Reputed to be the architect of the Step Pyramid, this vizier of King Djoser was, according to later sources, a great sage and the author of some of the earliest Wisdom Literature. Although he achieved cult status, as did other writers of similar works, such as Ptahhotep, Hordjedef, and Kagemni, only Imhotep was worshiped as a god, but not until the Late period. A cult for the deified late Old Kingdom official Hekaib was established after his death, and several centuries later people still visited the sanctuary. Amenhotep, son of Hapu, the director of works for Amenhotpe III, was accorded the honor of having a funerary temple dedicated to him in Western Thebes in an area reserved for pharaonic mortuary temples. Apparently a cult to him, especially in regard to medicine, developed later.

A king, however, was thought to achieve divinity routinely after death, and worship was in theory expected to occur through the mortuary cult in the funerary temple forever. Just how long the cult would actually last was determined by the length and quality of a particular ruler's reign, as well as political, sociological, and economic conditions during the king's life and after. Some officials of the Middle Kingdom held titles in the priesthood of kings who died in the Old Kingdom, a situation that indicates that cults could survive several centuries. Some cults, for example that of Amenhotpe I, existed beyond the mortuary temple. He became known as a personal god and often, along with his mother Ahmose-Nefertari, was accepted as a patron deity of Western Thebes and the village of Deir el-Medina. He could be approached for aid with other deities, and an oracle associated with him helped resolve legal issues.

While earlier evidence exists for the concept of the deification of a pharaoh prior to his death, it is not displayed so obviously until the eighteenth-dynasty reign of Hatshepsut. The reliefs depicting her divine birth occur, however, in her mortuary temple. Later, those of Amenhotpe III were carved on the walls of the state temple built for Amun at Luxor. He promoted the concept further by establishing cults at several locations dedicated to his living divine form. This idea promoted the conception of the king less as a superhuman hero whose divinity after death was assured than as a divine living being. His son and successor, Amenhotpe IV, was iconoclastic in both his conception of the divinity of the

king and the manner in which he expressed it. This enigmatic figure changed his name to Akhenaten, abolished the many gods of the ancient pantheon in favor of a single preeminent one, the Aten, and moved the capital to Amarna, an area with no preexisting deity. Many scholars see in these and other moves a major step in the evolution toward monotheism, but others recognize rather a radical sociopolitical experiment to raise the level of kingship to a status more equal with the godhead. Other interpretations exist as well, but whichever is correct, to the Egyptians the concept was not acceptable. The changes were short-lived, and the orthodoxy was quickly reestablished. Eventually, with traditional religious ideas restored, Ramesses II of the nineteenth dynasty adapted the concepts of divine kingship developed in the preceding dynasty. He had many representations of his divine living image created, and in several inscriptions referred to his own deified state. The people, however, probably had at all times both an official and a personal view in regard to these ideas, and they expressed them for example in letters where the monarch is described in very human rather than divine terms.

David P. Silverman

DEMONS. From an ancient Egyptian point of view, any being, whether supernatural, human, or material, which was involved in a ritual at some time, whether occasional or incidental, was a "god." The performance of a ritual did not necessarily require a temple, and thus demons were part of the "god" category. There is no Egyptian term, however, that corresponds even approximately to our word "demon." Demons are usually classified by Egyptologists as "minor divinities," a category that is hard to define. A temple reveals the theological and political importance of a deity but it does not show the real degree of the god's popularity. The importance of a divinity is a matter of subjective interpretation. For example, the hippopotamus goddess Taweret began her career anonymously during the Middle Kingdom among the fantastic animals figured on magic wands. During the New Kingdom, she acquired a name and became a renowned and revered goddess in temples and with priests. The lionmasked dwarf Bes had a similar origin and destiny. He also became an important god, although there is little evidence of his temples and priests. Many demons were not associated with temples or priests but were nonetheless greatly feared and respected.

The fact that demons were subordinates to a superior authority defined them most appropriately. They were not autonomous and performed tasks on command, usually in a specific sphere, while the greater gods were more universal in character. The specificity of demons concerned their actions, their behavior, and their location. Some demons were attached to a person, place, or building, and these demons remained there. When a demon was freed from his specific bonds of subordination, he became a greater god. This "promotion" was not the result of a conscious decision by an authority; rather, it evolved over centuries from a historical process that involved Egyptian society as a whole.

Demons had a protective-aggressive role: they were aggressive and hostile because they had to protect something or someone. Even evil, cosmic enemies had something to protect. In their passive role, demons repelled whatever threatened the object of their protection; in their dynamic role, they were sent to punish those who transgressed the principles that organized the created world,

which had been established by the gods themselves. The dual nature of demons made them either dangerous or beneficial to humans. Demons were distinguished from genies through this aggressive-protective aspect. Though assigned to specific tasks and usually subordinated to another deity, genies were not, by their very nature, involved in protective-aggressive activity. This was true, for example, of numerous genies concerned with economic production. Other deities, either subordinate or dangerous, were assistants to the creator god; they personified different aspects of his creative power and his comprehensive, divine authority. As assistants, they were incorporated in the insignia of royal power on crowns and scepters. They were considered "auxiliaries" to creative power and divine or royal authority outside the categories of "demon" or "genie."

Demons in the ancient world were also differentiated by their origins or the type of their subordination. Some demons were emanations of human beings, either dead or alive; they were evoked for an individual by divine decision, either permanently or occasionally. Divine subordinates, though used by gods for their personal purposes, were sometimes invoked by humans for their own protection. Cosmic enemies represented a specific case of "subordination" which involved the survival of the created world.

From the beginning of life, the ancient Egyptian was surrounded or assisted by powers which affected his destiny in many ways. Demons of fate were present at his side all his life and accompanied him after death, as witnesses before the Tribunal of Osiris. Such is the case of Shai ("Destiny") and his female companion Renenet ("Nurse"), or the spirit of the birth-stool, Meskhenet. Shai and Renenet represented a given span of life that could be lengthened or shortened by good or bad deeds. Meskhenet was the personal share or stock of capabilities given to each person at his birth, a kind of life-program to be respected. The righteous man came before Osiris without having modified his personal Meskhenet. These demons were not passive attendants who simply executed a god's will or checked human actions. They were generally positive protectors who acted like "guardian angels" to repel what threatened their charges. Demons of fate also dispensed advice. Unfortunately, protector demons were not always able to shield the ancient Egyptian from bad demons. A child who died was usually not considered the victim of a decision carried out by Shai and Renenet. A demon called Shepeset ("Noble Lady") seems to have had a more personal relationship with those she was supposed to assist. Each month of the year had its Shepeset, who was a kind of fairy godmother for all born in the month under her protection. The Seven Hathors, also known as the "old ladies," played a role akin to that of European witches. They were supposed to state, at the moment of birth, all the events (usually bad ones) that one would have to face during life. Once their words had been pronounced, it was impossible to avoid the bad fortune they promised. Magic spells were recited to close the mouths of these Hathors and prevent them from foretelling the future. Other spells, however, ask for their help in desperate situations.

Protective personal demons probably belong to ancient traditions. Fantastic animals represented on magic wands of the Middle Kingdom were the ancestors of some of the above-mentioned creatures. The hippopotamus holding a knife with its feet later became the major god-

dess Taweret. She was the patroness of childbirth and motherhood, chasing away demons dangerous to the vulnerable mother and her child. Many of these features were shared by Bes. Both Taweret and Bes—or, at least, hippopotami and Bes-like demons—recur later on in birth scenes. They protected not only human children but also the young Horus and his mother Isis when they were hidden in the Nile Delta marshes. There the young Horus was subject to sickness, stung by scorpions, and hunted by demons sent by Seth, the murderer of his father; that is why his image is represented on stelae from the end of the New Kingdom, the so-called Horus *cippi*, which are engraved with magic spells against fever, crocodiles, and venomous animals.

People were also surrounded by petty domestic demons that resided practically everywhere: in water, doors, bolts, pots, and so on. Some of these had very little power and could be used, after divine approval, by humans themselves for their own purposes. Incubi that "sat" inside a person were also known. Some demons teased humans, apparently just for fun. Peasants usually attributed to them all kinds of mishaps—bad weather, sick cattle, or domestic conflicts.

Once dead, a human could trouble those still alive, so surviving relatives occasionally wrote letters to complain to the dead and try to calm them. A deceased human might even become a dangerous demonic power, not only as an evil soul escaped from the tomb but also as a physical entity. It could attack sinners or those disturbing the tomb, but also any other person without apparent reason. As a ghost, it could haunt homes, perhaps to obtain the reconstruction of the ruined tomb. Little tablets inscribed with the names of supposedly demonic dead persons were buried to prevent them from coming back from the grave. A tale tells how a dead man, wishing to have news about his survivors, asked Osiris to sculpt for him an earth-man, a kind of semi-live "golem." This human-like being was sent out to the world of the living to report on the situation and punish those behaving badly to the dead one's family.

Gangs of demons were responsible for many troubles and misfortunes. Most of the main deities had such troops at their service. They could be used against both men and other gods, though the latter had demon bodyguards. These demon troops bear names like *khatyu* ("fighters"), *habyu* ("emissaries"), *wepwetyu* ("messengers"), or *shemayu* ("wanderers"), which reveal a good deal about their basic nature. They are very anciently known: the *khatyu* were mentioned in the Pyramid Texts from the Old Kingdom, the first known Egyptian corpus of religious texts. There is no important religious or magical text that does not mention them in some way, to invoke them or to avert them. All these troops are known under the more generic term *sheseru* ("arrows"). Because the groups usually have seven members, or a multiple of seven, they were also called the "seven arrows." Their superiors were often dangerous goddesses like Sekhmet, Bastet, and Nekhbet, or the sphinx god Totoes. *Sheseru* is also the name of the seven Decan stars that are closest to the sun. Emissary demons, arrows, and Decans were identified. All these demons could punish sinners, but they could act simply out of malice to strike any person they found in their path. They occasioned inexplicable illness. Magic spells written on a papyrus strip, simply folded or wrapped inside a little container and worn on a necklace, were considered effectual in keeping them at a distance. In medical documents, spells may be added to recipes to improve the treatment or to protect the patient from demonic influence.

The relationship of demons with astronomic cycles made them most active during specific periods: for instance, when the Decan they belonged to culminated, or at a time corresponding to a baleful mythological event. The last five days of the year—those which were "over the year" because they did not fit in the ideal year of 360 (30 . 12) days—were considered especially dangerous because their departure from the ideal pattern introduced chaotic elements in the organized world. During that period, demons, unbound and uncontrolled, spread over the earth. In all the temples of Egypt, priests recited litanies to dangerous goddesses and their demonic servants, to appease them and calm their wrath.

Demons that protected a person or a place were similar to the emissaries, but their behavior was more static and defensive. The arrow demons were related to the Decans of the southern sky, where the new year star (Sirius) rose and whence came the Nile flood. In contrast, the troop of demons protecting Osiris was connected with the northern sky, the realm of the dead. The underworld was full of evil demons, especially in the spaces between the living world and the Hall of Osiris, which gave access to the green fields of paradise. They guarded the gates, channels, crossings, and so on, which the dead had to pass to reach the hall. Unable to avoid them, the deceased had to persuade them to let him pass. He usually had to answer questions posed by the demons, who only let pass those who could prove that during life they had learned enough about the underworld to be allowed to travel in it. Living persons might meet these demons, too, at least in pictures, but even these images were dangerous. In pharaonic times, visitors to the Osireion of Abydos were frightened by the underworld demons painted on the walls and left inscriptions asking the sun god to protect them from these *khatyu*.

The demons created to protect the sun god against cosmic enemies might be invoked to protect Osiris, the dead, or even a temple. Emissaries and guardian demons were depicted as having human bodies with animal heads. What usually distinguished them from other deities were the long knives they bear in each hand, hence the name "knife-bearers" or "butchers" sometimes given to them.

Each temple was supposed to be an ordering of the world, and the same held true for Egypt. Once the world was created, the original unorganized and chaotic element was cast out to its margin. A demon called Apophis was supposed to dwell in this element, endlessly fighting to reconquer the space of which the chaotic element was deprived. Every day he attacked the sun in his bark, and after every defeat he returned, a permanent threat to the world. Many rituals were performed to protect the sun bark, to prevent the victory of the chaos demon, or to destroy his evil eye. Similarly, the territories around Egypt were supposed to shelter Seth and his allied demons, who were striving to reconquer Egypt. Here again rituals were used to keep them at a distance. The world, Egypt, gods, and men were bound to be threatened or attacked by demons wanting to gain power over them. Other demons were invoked to repel them, keeping the world in order and people and gods at peace.

Dimitri Meeks

DIVINITY. In considering the confrontation between the two opposing concepts of the "unity" and "multiplicity" of the divine in ancient Egypt, we must begin with some of the intellectual modes of thought in that culture. To begin with, Egyptian religious philosophy did not employ abstraction but used a concrete vocabulary. It defined from the external and the global a reality—here, a divinity—with the aid of images that complete and correct each other. As a consequence, this mode of thinking is a stranger to the principle of contradiction and postulates simple identities. In ancient Egypt, the principle of "identity" had far wider application than in our culture, resulting in what Henri Frankfort called a "multiplicity of approaches." Facts do not exclude one another, but are added in layers, doing justice to the multiple facets of reality. This art of combining rests on the capacity of an entity to manifest itself in different forms: one divinity may be taken for the manifestation of another. Finally, thought and utterance are seen as creative. In the Memphite doctrine, the operative mode of the creator god is thought, which resides in the heart, which in turn is informed by the senses—and thought is executed in language. This results in a creation, through the word of the elements of the world, which the god Ptah named after having perceived and thought them—an intellectual concept without precedent, completed by the creative value of the image. The image of the gods is an extension of reality that goes beyond representation. On the one hand, there is a plurality of meanings of images and objects; on the other, the performative character of word and image.

Concept of God. The hieroglyph for "god" has been described as a "staff wrapped in cloth"—"whose extremity projects like a flap or a streamer." Hornung (1986) specified that the "cult drape or curtain" is doubtless a secondary form, and that the original model was rather a stick wrapped in bands or ribbons and thus charged with strength or power. This hieroglyph then suggests the veneration of inanimate objects or a representation of a cult object whose derivatives were drapes and other streamers. At the same time, there is evidence of the veneration of divinities in the form of animal figures perched on a staff. Several centuries later, the anthropomorphic forms of gods appear in depictions.

The application of etymology to comprehend the Egyptian notion of "god" (*ntr*) produces hypotheses that are sometimes seductive but rarely convincing. It is more interesting to study the use of the word *ntr*. The plural may refer to a limited group of gods at a specific location or region, or gathered into a particular theology, or to the totality of all Egyptian gods. The dual form was applied exclusively to divine pairs, such as Horus and Seth, "the two masters," or to "the two ladies"—Isis and Nephthys or Nekhbet and Ouadjet—to designate the titular divinities of Upper and Lower Egypt. Important to an understanding of divinity is the use of the singular without reference to a particular god. The absolute form is found in the names of persons, in titles, and in Wisdom texts. Names including the word *ntr* indicate a relationship between a person and a particular individual divinity to which the person giving the name to his child alludes. In the ecclesiastic title "servant of god," the use of the word *ntr* is so generic that it can also be applied to a goddess; it is used in a vague sense to designate certain specific divinities. In the Wisdom texts, we find a preference for the indefinite word *ntr* instead of the names of individual gods. The reason for this is that the Wisdom texts were written for professional purposes, usually to instruct a son or a successor; far from being treatises that pose axioms and definitions, these texts are meant as practical advice for students. They contain descriptions of specific situations and detail the preparations necessary for entering into contact with a god, whose identity will depend on the locality where the apprentice official finds himself established. Thus, the word *ntr* in the Wisdom texts is by no means to be interpreted as the unique God of monotheism; rather, this is the god that the student will encounter in his professional life.

Aside from this pragmatic polytheism, from the middle of the second millennium BCE onward the priestly elite made a genuine attempt to define *divinity*. The god Amun could be described both in his immanence as "prodigious in transformations" and also in his transcendence in a manner that recalls great monotheisms: unknown, distant, and unapproachable, Amun is "he who hides from the gods, his appearance is unknown, he is farther than the highest heaven" (Leyde Papyrus, end of the eighteenth dynasty). Derchain (1981) has shown that the sun hymns studied by Assmann, according to whom a "crisis in the polytheistic philosophy of life" occurred in the Ramessid era, were written according to a body of century-old archival texts. They did not constitute an "intangible canon" and became a reservoir from which the theologians drew to transform the initial concepts, by correlating and modifying expressions. The text engenders knowledge and allows one to move from familiar expressions to the formulation of a new conceptual apparatus in relation with history. Every divine quality remains open to new interpretation, which retroactively redefines the known qualities, making more severe the uncertainty with regard to the ultimate nature of the god.

Transcendent in his demi-urgic pre-existence, Amun is immanent in his manifestations. The paradox is important: it expresses the passage from non-time to time.

Multiplicity of the Divine. Are the gods alone at the heart of the divine sphere? More precisely, is there a diversity of the divine—and what kinds of divinities are encountered among the Egyptian gods, the god-king, and the sacred animals?

From the first dynasties onward a cult developed based on the images of living kings and their predecessors. Ancestry and the veneration of the reigning king were used to reinforce the monarchy. In the Sinai during the twelfth dynasty, Senwosret II surrounded his statue with those of Montuhotep I, Montuhotep II, and Amenemhet I; in another depiction, an expedition leader offers pieces of turquoise to Amenemhet II wearing the crown of Soped, the god of the Arabian borderlands. These are revealing instances of commemorating royal deeds—note the divine nature which the turquoise confers on the king.

In the New Kingdom, the Akhmenu at Karnak is the building with the most complete ensemble of ancestral kings ever assembled by a living king: sixty-one. Thutmose III brings to them "the offering given by the king," and they participate in processions inside the building as do the statues of the gods. The Great Sphinx at Giza, probably sculpted in the image of Khafre and restored by Thutmose IV, is given the name Harmakhis ("Horus-in-the-horizon") Khepre-Re-Atum, a manifestation of its divine character and of the influence of the clergy of Heliopolis. The solar aspect of the sovereign, beginning with Amenhotpe III, leads to the veneration of the living king in colossi

erected at either side of the temple entrance, in which the spirits that inhabit the king are incarnated; they carry the name of the king linked to that of Re: "Amenhotpe-sun-of-sovereigns," "Ramesses-beloved-of-Atum." Ramesses II, who established a cult to his own likeness, becomes of necessity a servant of his own image for the perpetual cult, thus engendering a functional dislocation in the person of the king. During the reign of Ramesses II, the image of the sovereign wearing the *atef*-crown merged with the dyads consisting of the principal Egyptian gods. The statue sometimes carries a name: "Living-image-of-Ramesses-beloved-of-Amun" —that is to say, image of himself. He is even identified (by osmosis, as it were) with Re-Horakhty in a relief above the entrance door to the temple of Abu Simbel, showing a falcon-headed figure crowned with the sun disk and holding a scepter (*wsr*) in one hand and the feather of Maat in the other, a rebus of the crown name of the king: User-Maat-Re (*Wsr-m3ʿt-rʿ.*). On the one hand, the efficacy expected of the king is comparable to that of Re, the luminous god who repels the enemies of Egypt into the shadows; the king and Re collaborate in the magical protection of the lands of Nubia. On the other hand, the king, who is not the god, is the sign of the efficacy of the god's power, which requires royal intermediation to be actualized.

It must be understood that the "divinized" kings who created a cult of their deified images differ from the gods, in whom this dislocation between being and image does not exist. In this respect, kings can be likened to the sacred animals—not the species protected by a taboo, but the unique animals, chosen for veneration, which succeed their deceased predecessors in the same manner as royalty does. Enthroned, sometimes given grand funerals and rituals of passage like kings, they are equally depositories of the divine presence: the animal's body is the receptacle of divinity. In the end, however, the divinity of kings and animals alike derived from the gods and is therefore not original. If kings and sacred animals can be compared to gods, the resemblance lies only in the identity of their situations: both preside over the destinies of a world, but the worlds in question are not the same. Mortal kings and sacred animals are not confused with a god who is perpetually present, despite intermittency.

The representations of Egyptian gods and their names confirm the multiplicity of the divine nature. Anthropomorphic, zoomorphic, composite, the gods change form among many bodies, heads, and attributes; there is no canon of divine representation. With the exception of the iconography of Anubis as a dog and that of Taweret in a body composite of hippopotamus, lion, and crocodile, Egyptian divinities are "rich in manifestations" and "of numerous faces," so the inscribed name frequently provides the only means of recognizing Isis or Hathor. The numerous forms of the gods are limited, though: Thoth never takes the form of a tree or a snake. The boundaries of the individuality of gods prevents infinite actualization and forbids certain manifestations so as to prevent a progression toward complete pantheism. This process of creating divine representations correlates with an "anthropomorphization of powers" (Hornung 1986) during the first dynasties, contemporaneous with the end of the practice of forming kings' names from animal names. Man passes from a world in which he does not live in opposition to nature—a universe that shares power

with the animal, which was the highest referent of strength—into a world where man submits the universe to his capacity for organization.

The multiplicity of names for a divinity is another fundamental characteristic. Litanies are sung to Osiris under all his names. On the architraves of the first hypostyle hall at Edfu, the "Powerful Ones" taking the form of Hathor receive as many epithets as there are days in the year and, the astronomical calendar being divided in two parts, each epithet has two variants. The gods are "rich in names" and these are innumerable, as in the case of Amun, "whose number [of names] is unknown." The names of the gods are open repertories, even if certain names—such as the "secret name"—enjoy an exceptional status, which protects one who retains it from any annexation of his power; by contrast, the formula "I know you, knowing your name," protects the traveler in the underworld from demons. The multiple epithets of a god whom one invokes, far from being exclusive to that god, are transferable to other gods. The notion of identity is not limited by strict outlines and reveals itself as an expandable concept. A god may even leave his own "body" and temporarily inhabit that of another god.

Finally, a major question of the history of religion, and one not limited to ancient Egypt, is that of why and how a god from one location moves from his place of origin to other places. How do the specific attributes of an ancient god from one place change, allowing the accretion of new attributes and a new ubiquity for the god?

In local theologies surrounding the god of Athribis in the Nile Delta, a double effort at synthesis is made; this effort aims to unify the multiple local traditions in the sphere of the principal gods of the nome (province) and to give to the cult of these gods a sense of belonging to the mainstream of the "national" religion. The goal is to inform the idiosyncrasy and thought spread throughout Egypt. With time, this reveals itself not as the irreducible expression of a single proto-historic cult, but rather as a continuous speculative effort to express the power of local divinities, across temporal evolution and alongside other local divinities. In the act of adoration, power is concentrated in the chosen god whom one addresses, and any other gods become insignificant. In this sense, the god to whom one speaks is the "first"—hence the term "henotheism," to describe the veneration of one god at a time, who is nevertheless not unique.

Ancient Egyptian theologians utilized the legend of the dismembered god Osiris to unify Egypt. Through the expedient word plays conflating geographic terms and parts of the human body, any nome might become a place where the divine body of Osiris, torn apart by Seth, and dispersed across Egypt, might be restored. This egalitarian and unifying point of view undoubtedly explains the extraordinary prevalence of Osirian mythology in Ptolemaic temples, one characteristic of which is to manifest Egyptian "nationalism."

In addition to these pan-Egyptian theological reflections, an anthropomorphic concept of the structure of the world led the Egyptians to assimilate deceased persons with deities responsible for cows, milk, grain, or clothing, or otherwise connected to production. The domains of human activity are also personified; the spirit of fishing in a duck-headed body; Renenutet, the harvest goddess; or Hedjhotep and Tait, the spirits of weaving. There are gods of the administrative regions of Egypt, the forty-two nomes, as well as of other as-

pects of the physical world: Heb and Sekhet, the spirits of the marshes; Hapy, the spirit of water for agriculture; Ou, the arable soil of the nome; Mer, the canal or the portion of the Nile that crosses it; Pehu, the fringes or green parts of the marsh, refuge for fish and birds; Wadjur, the "Very-green," that is the ocean; and the four spirits of the winds. These geographical personifications, derived from a taxonomy of the physical world, frequently appear on the base of temples, close to the fertile soil. This peopling of the invisible enabled Egyptians to enter into dialogue with the forces of nature and to tame them. Guilty of abusing nature, they asked for its consent to take from it what it contains.

Nontranscendence of the Divine. The immanence of gods is especially noticeable in *The Contendings of Horus and Seth*, a long account of the succession conflict between Horus, son and rightful successor of Osiris, and Seth, Osiris' brother and a counter-claimant. Their rivalry for the royal role of Osiris is fought out in front of the tribunal of the Ennead, which, in its enlarged form, consists of some thirty divine members who are lazy, fickle, and prone to human frailties. This anthropomorphism also characterizes the gods as having an appetite for power and all its attendant vices, a viewpoint that extends to their physical aspect. The gods of this account are equipped with human bodies, although free of human weaknesses and limitations. The visibility of these bodies is the first hint that they lack complete transcendence: Thoth places on his head a disk of gold taken from the forehead of Seth. The battle equipment—Seth's "scepter of four thousand five hundred *nemes*," Horus's "knife of sixteen *debens*"—demonstrates that the use of arms is an expression of the energy of the gods. The abilities of the gods, while exceptional, once again bring them closer to mankind, since they are described in terms of a human body: longevity, in a process that has lasted eighty years; the ubiquity of their adventures on Earth, from fields, woods, and mountains to the depths of the oceans and the sky; reversible wounds, without bleeding or scars, and short-lived amputations; tirelessness; and even triumph over death (the decapitated Isis reappears intact in a subsequent episode)—with the exception of Osiris. Finally, the appearance of the gods is a finely drawn evocation of human bodies that are not directly described. Horus and Seth are "mysterious in form," and Horus appears in his veil of light on the day of coronation. Yet this heroic attenuation still makes reference to the human body: hands, semen, eyes, head, and the infirmity of Horus are mentioned. It makes reference to human behaviors and reactions: speech and tears, the greediness and brutality of Seth, the fury and weariness of Horus, the subtle intelligence of Isis, and the inertia of the creator god. The human body of a god is at times replaced by that of an animal—the hippopotamus for Seth, and the kite for Isis—as the god attempts to be elusive. The human body is also liable to metamorphosis through aging, as when Isis, "young girl of beautiful body," changes into "a bent old woman" to aid the just cause of her son Horus through her deceptions; or through transsubstantiation, when Isis turns into a statue of flint, or when the dead god Osiris "feeds on gold and precious stones."

The immanence expressed in the likening of gods to man is revealing, with regard to the divisions of the divine that is to say, its fragmentation. The ontological approach to the problem of the one and the many in the cosmogony texts that elaborate on the Pyramid Texts provides a good insight into the struggles attendant on the hereditary transfer of the royal function. The "enemy brothers" Horus and Seth, in reality nephew and uncle embroiled in eternal conflict, reflect the "complementary duality of the world and the necessity for constant confrontation" (Hornung 1986). Ancient Egyptians held a negative view with regard to the natural course of human life, which took place in a world that was originally uninhabitable and could be made harmonious only through tireless efforts. There is no doubt that hereditary monarchy was the order intended by the gods, in order to establish maat, the correct order of the world. This myth was therefore a meditation on the relationships between force and right through the medium of the divine antagonists, Horus and Seth.

Two aspects of divine fragmentation include (1) the ancient formulation of the trinity of gods and (2) the underlying proto-arithmetic thought in constituting the Ennead of Heliopolis. The triad of Amun-Re-Ptah appears on the trumpets of the funeral equipment of Tutankhamun, but the *Hymn of Leyde* to Amun (end of the eighteenth dynasty) is the first known textual formulation of the trinity of these three gods: "All gods are three . . . His name is hidden as Amon. He is Re (before men). His body is Ptah. Their cities on Earth remain for ever: Thebes, Heliopolis and Memphis, for all eternity." The plural "all gods" is followed by a singular pronoun that carries a specific name, and the cult sites remain distinct. Yet the text does not say that "god reveals himself in three forms," as is emphasized by Hornung (1986). In effect, there is no text in which the unique god is designated by the name of "god." Undoubtedly, Egyptian thinkers came close to remaking the traditional religion, but they were not yet ready to unify that which appeared irreconcilable—the various manifestations of a unique sun god—in order to go beyond the models inherited from ancient times.

The Heliopolitan cosmogony, behind its genealogical presentation composed of three generations, contains the elements of a proto-arithmetic. When the autogenous demi-urge forms Shu and Tefnut, each of the gods becomes one-third of the universe: "When he (Atum) begat Shu and Tefnut, when he was One and became Three." This reasoning by means of dividing the unity applies to subsequent generations, when Geb and Nut, the issue of Shu and Tefnut, and then their four children, Osiris, Isis, Seth, and Nephthys, each become one-fifth and one-ninth part of the world, respectively. The mathematical sequence 1–3–5–9 governs the first increments of the world. The multiplicity is seen, by giving preference to fractions with a numerator of one, as the decomposition of a sum, and thus the choice is made for an arithmetic of identity. The Egyptians were surely aware of the exponential sequence 1–2–4–8, etc., as the unlimited incremental law of the universe. After the demi-urge, Shu and Tefnut, Geb and Nut, and their four children, "it was their children who created the crowd of forms existing in this world in the shape of children and grandchildren" (Bremner Rhind Papyrus). This sequence that doubles at each stage is an instrument indicative of the dynamic future, that of a universe in expansion. And yet, the ancient Egyptians preferred [m] in order to verify that their national state conformed to the initial intentions of the creator god—to use their knowledge of fractions to imagine the following result: Atum, uncreated and without beginning, takes Osiris with him into a distant future where nothing changes (Book of Going Forth by Day [Book of the Dead], chapter 125), that is, to the original point of departure.

All these are indications that the religious universe of Egypt is unlike the Cartesian system, wherein God is uniquely transcendent. The "absolute" was not a necessary attribute of the divine, even though Egyptian thinkers were able to perceive their gods as transcendent and to express this at certain stages of their history.

Marie-Ange Bohême
Translated from French by
Elizabeth Schwaiger

DRAMA. The topic of drama in ancient Egypt is a complex and somewhat controversial one. Many have categorically claimed either its existence or its nonexistence. A judicious assessment of the evidence, or lack thereof, indicates that a more qualified position allows greater insight into this question.

There is no archeological or textual evidence for theaters as we know them in pharaonic Egypt. There do not appear to be specific words in the Egyptian language for technical terms like "drama," "play," or "actor." Thus, the claim for the presence in Egypt of secular drama, as we know it, seems to have no supporting evidence to date.

There are a number of religious texts from papyri and temples that have been labeled "dramatic texts" by some modern scholars in their search for drama in religious rituals. These texts, for the most part, focus on certain acts performed by the god(s) at the beginning of time, at "the first occasion," and are believed to contain material for commemorative reenactments of incipient cosmic events for the purpose of maintaining life and the order of the cosmos. Their content is based on myth, and their purpose is to reenact, not to instruct or to reflect. In no way do they attempt to explain human behavior, good or bad.

Studies of such texts by modern scholars have provoked some interesting discussions, most of which founder on the rocks of semantics. The majority of those who have looked into the question of the origins of drama in ancient Egypt have begun their discussions with somewhat subjective and personal definitions of drama and its essential elements; they have then proceeded to manipulate the details of the so-called Egyptian dramatic texts to prove their points. Many of these studies led to the coining of terms like "dramatic ritual," "liturgical drama," "sacred drama," and the like—rhetorical niceties that offer nothing by way of an answer to the question. Furthermore, in the case of most specific "dramatic" rituals, even in the so-called Osirian mysteries celebrated at Abydos and the rituals conducted in the Edfu temple in which Horus triumphs over Seth/Apophis and the forces of chaos, what we encounter is fundamentally different from anything that we today would regard as drama. Additionally, the majority of the texts identified as "dramatic texts" are hopelessly fragmentary and often abbreviated—perhaps intentionally so. Therefore, what one can say about such texts as drama is usually limited to conjecture.

These objections, however, can best serve as caveats to underscore the difficulties encountered in attempting to address the question of drama in ancient Egypt. There is no denying that a number of Egyptian rituals can be viewed as dramatizations of certain events in the lives of the Egyptian gods. To what degree these dramatizations were "staged" is difficult to say.

Many of the texts identified as "dramatic" contain elements that point to their oral components. The oral nature of Egyptian religious texts is well known. Many texts and sections of texts are framed by labels like $r3$ or $dd\ mdw\ in$ . . . , "Utterance," and "Words to be recited by . . . ," respectively. Do such oral markers indicate that texts so labeled are to be dramatically enacted as well as recited? If one simply answers yes, as a number of Egyptologists have done, then one may well argue that virtually all religious texts are dramatic texts by definition, an all-inclusive definition that seems to beg the question.

It has generally been argued by the proponents of Egyptian drama that the actors in these plays were members of the priesthood under the direction of a lectorpriest. They have postulated dramatic reenactments both inside and outside the temple proper. In certain rituals depicted on the walls of Egyptian temples, scholars have claimed to find not only dramatic texts but reliefs as well that depict various stages of what they perceive as drama; one of these rituals belongs to the Osirian Khoiak festival. Unfortunately, the evidence for the ritual is found piecemeal in a number of temples and papyri, and the sources for the evidence are also scattered over a broad time span. An assessment of the dramatic elements of this ritual, thus, relies on the reconstruction of the ritual from its various components and their locations, a process that is largely hypothetical. A second ritual is that of the socalled Triumph of Horus over his enemies, found in the Ptolemaic temple at Edfu. The texts and reliefs of this ritual, found on a single wall, form a connected series that has been seen by some as a play. The texts and reliefs involve a number of different deities, and the sequence of the texts does move forward in storyline form. One editor has even argued that certain elements within the texts comprise stage directions. Despite the fact that this ritual is self-contained within a single temple, in order to see it as drama, primitive or otherwise, we are faced with the problem of a hypothetical reconstruction and evaluation of what may only possibly be dramatic elements.

An examination of two texts, both of which form part of the so-called mysteries of Osiris celebrated at Abydos, reveals several important pieces of information and may serve as better evidence for dramatic elements in Egyptian rituals. Both papyri have been dated to the Ptolemaic period. The first text, from a papyrus in Berlin, contains a ritual to be performed in the Abydos temple on the twenty-fifth day of the fourth month of Akhet, or Inundation. The ritual involves strophic addresses to the god Osiris by the goddesses Isis and Nephthys. The colophon states that at the completion of the ritual, the temple where it was read is to be "made holy, not seen [and] not heard by anyone except the chief lector-priest and a *sem*-priest." It then states that "two women beautiful in body are to be brought and made to sit on the ground in the first doorway of the Hall of Appearances, the names of Isis and Nephthys written on their upper arms." After receiving certain offerings, they are required to sit with "their faces bowed down." The reading of the text is to be conducted twice on that day, at the third hour and at the eighth hour, apparently by the lector-priest.

In the second text, the Bremner-Rhind Papyrus in the British Museum, similar but expanded instructions are given at the beginning of the text. The text is said to contain the ritual of the Two Kites—i.e., Isis and Nephthys—which is celebrated in the temple of Osiris Kentyamentiu in the fourth month of Akhet, from the twenty-second to the

twenty-sixth day. The instructions then state that "the entire temple shall be made holy [and] there shall be brought in two women pure in body, virgins, the hair of their bodies removed, their heads adorned with wigs . . . tambourines in their hands, their names inscribed on their upper arms, namely Isis and Nephthys. They shall sing from the stanzas of this book in the presence of this god." The alternations between first person singular and plural in the text seem to indicate shifts between solos sung by Isis and duets sung by the two goddesses.

The instructions in these two texts contain important differences. The two women mentioned in the first text are required to possess physical beauty, to sit in a specific place in the temple, to have the names of the goddesses Isis and Nephthys written on their arms, and to sit with their faces bowed down. These are their only requirements, and no further specific roles are assigned to them. The text specifically states that it is to be read, apparently by the lector-priest despite the fact that the title of the text is "The evocation of ritual recitations which is made by the Two sisters." In the second text, the women are required to be ritually pure and virgins, to undergo depilation, to wear wigs, and to have the names of Isis and Nephthys written on their upper arms. The text also explicitly states that it is they who are to sing the ritual. Thus, the women in the second text take on active roles as the sisters of Osiris, whereas in the first text their role appears to be passive, almost that of players in a tableau. These differences in instructions may simply indicate variant forms of the same ritual.

Beyond the descriptions and instructions encountered in texts like the two discussed above, we have little other information about the nature of the reenactment of these rituals. They both contain clear elements that we would associate with dramatic performance, namely song and role-playing. Despite the presence of such elements of dramatic expression in Egyptian ritual, at this point we can discuss them only as such. The question of the existence of an independent genre of drama in ancient Egypt, and what its individual components may have been, remains to be answered. *Paul F. O'Rourke*

F

FANTASTIC ANIMALS. A fantastic animal refers to a creature not found in nature—but a product of human imagination. Generally, the parts that form the animal's body are borrowed from various species and fitted together. The composite character of the body gives an approximate, though useful, way to define the category; yet the families observed in it are based on our modern sense of classification. For example, a sphinx, which is in most cases a human-headed lion, though fantastic in the very sense of the term, does not fit exactly in the so-called animal category, since it includes a part of the human body. If we consider only those beings with nonhuman animal parts, we still have a classification problem. Composite animals, from an Egyptological point of view, represent fantastic animals—but also demons or even gods, since no clear-cut border existed between those categories. A duck with four wings, legs, and a serpent's tail represented a constellation based on late Egyptian zodiacs; it was out of human reach, not only physically but also intellectually. The composite animal body was, in many cases, only the tentative representation of a divine, supernatural power. From an ancient Egyptian point of view, fantastic animals could be considered real, since they were often depicted as living in the wild, among antelopes and lions, in the deserts surrounding the Nile Valley. There, hunters supposedly caught a glimpse of them in the distance, though they were never supposed to have captured one.

Origins and History. Fantastic animals mingling in the wild with "natural" animals were pictured for the first time during the late Predynastic period (c. 3100 BCE). Carved on luxury objects, and probably of royal origin, such scenes appeared on ceremonial slate palettes, ivory plaques, and ivory knife handles. Many such objects were unearthed at Hierakonpolis or from the neighborhood of Naqada, in Upper Egypt; both were among the main centers that developed the small kingdoms from which the Egyptian civilization originated. The winged, falconheaded griffin—the "serpopard," a leopard with a long, winding neck—and most of the accompanying animals were depicted on objects in a style usually considered to be inspired indirectly from Mesopotamian models. During the Middle Kingdom, fantastic animals appeared again on the walls of tombs of some high officials of Beni Hasan and Bersheh, in Middle Egypt. A little farther south, in Meir, also during the Middle Kingdom, the capital city, el-Kusiyeh, when written in hieroglyphs, had two serpopards back to back, their necks held by a man. Beni Hasan and el-Kusiyeh were only about 65 kilometers (40 miles) from each other. Bersheh and Beni Hasan were the starting points for the desert roads that led to the Red Sea coast, to the Sinai peninsula, and to Nubia. Beni Hasan nomarchs, who were in charge of controlling and inspecting those roads, were in contact with the nomadic populations living east of the Nile Valley. Their special interest in fantastic animals was, in all probability, motivated by their contacts with the peoples of the Eastern Desert and their beliefs about curious desert animals, beliefs that had come from a long desert tradition. Moreover, hunting in the desert was the preferred pursuit of those nomarchs. Some were very proud of their zoological knowledge. On a wall of his tomb, Baqet III of Beni Hasan had a detailed hunting scene in which there were fantastic animals, although they were not hunted as the other animals were. On the same wall was a whole catalog of real birds, represented in color, with their names—indicating the extent and accuracy of Baqet's knowledge of the fauna. There, as in all contexts already mentioned, fantastic animals were perceived as an integral part of the natural environment.

During the Middle Kingdom, fantastic animals were also represented on so-called magic wands. Made from hippopotamus ivory (tooth) reworked into a simple curved blade, these wands include fantastic animals in a scene of a procession of demons. These figures and the few accompanying texts show plainly that the animals were considered as beings having magical and protective powers. Apparently, these objects were used mainly by the elite, many of whom came from Thebes or el-Lisht, the two prominent political centers of that time. Some were also found in Naqada, Hierakonpolis, and other cities of Middle and Upper Egypt. All those demons—and not only the fantastic animals—were connected with religious and mythological beliefs that had their origins in Middle

Egypt, more or less in the same area as the tombs of the nomarchs mentioned above. Since some of the wands were also found in Palestine (at Gaza and Megiddo) and in Nubia (at Kuban and Kerma), the inhabitants of those regions also had a special attraction for the very same demons and fantastic animals. During the Middle Kingdom, in Nubia (at Kerma), animals and demons (among which were winged giraffes), strikingly similar to those depicted on magic wands, were used as inlay motifs. A study of the material shows that the Egyptian wands and the Nubian inlays are related, on both historical and mythological grounds.

The frequency of use of fantastic animals during both the late Predynastic to Early Dynastic period and the Middle Kingdom might best be explained by the strong local powers that were probably in contact with nomadic populations of the Eastern Desert. Originating in Mesopotamia in the fourth millennium BCE, fantastic animals were probably part of the local folklore and beliefs, which then influenced the Egyptians who traveled the desert to control its roads.

Later, fantastic animals were less frequently represented in Egypt. The winged griffin alone appeared again, during the New Kingdom, at a time when Egypt was in close contact with Near Eastern populations and borrowed some religious features from them. Despite long chronological gaps in our documentation, fantastic animals were probably present during all of Egyptian history. Their images were still used as hieroglyphs even in Roman times, in the inscriptions of the temple of Esna (in Upper Egypt, second century CE).

Role and Significance. The oldest representations of fantastic animals were clearly, like dogs and lions, hunting animals. Hunting on the edges of the Nile

Valley had, from the very beginning of Egyptian history, a religious connotation. To kill or capture wild animals beyond the valley and its civilization was, symbolically, to subdue and tame the hostile forces that threatened fertile and organized Egypt. The fantastic animals became actors in this protective hunt for the benefit of Egypt.

In the Beni Hasan and Bersheh tombs, such animals apparently played the same role, but they were not represented in hunting scenes alone. On three occasions, at least, they appeared in a daily-life context, in the company of tamed animals, like monkeys and dogs. In one scene, a winged griffin is portrayed as so similar to the dogs playing nearby that it can be distinguished only because of the wings on its back. In Beni Hasan, a lavishly colored griffin with bitch's teats bears a collar and what seems to be a leash; it accompanies a man with a dog. Its term, *sgt*, also appears in a Bersheh tomb, associated with another griffin, this one shown in the company of monkeys. This word, *saget*, was probably not the name of the animal but might have been a designation for the so-called domesticated griffin. It has been supposed that those griffins were, in fact, dogs that were disguised to look like griffins. The purpose of such a masquerade was, perhaps, to transform an ordinary hunting dog into a ferocious, ceremonial or legendary hunter. At the same time, the possession of such an animal, be it only created by magical disguise, might have enhanced the prestige of the owner. During the New Kingdom, the griffin appeared again in hunting scenes. Often it hauled the chariot in which there was a young god, whose task was to chase the desert animals that were dangerous to Egyptians.

The inclusion of fantastic animals among the demons on magic wands indicates that they probably had the same purpose. All were protective beings supposed to frighten, by their strange aspect, any kind of malevolent beings. The wands were offered to women, especially to young mothers, to protect them and their children against demons bearing sickness. Since some of those objects were also found in tombs, fantastic animals probably exerted their magic protective power in the world beyond. Before reaching the felicities of a new life, in the netherworld, the dead had to cross a border zones guarded by dangerous beings. The fantastic animals portrayed on palettes, tomb paintings, and magic wands helped in this task.

Fantastic animals retained beneficial powers until pagan religion in Egypt was eclipsed by Christianity in the Roman era. Even then, their silhouettes were still used in hieroglyphic script, to write the sacred name of Osiris, an impossibility if they were representations of evil.

Serpopard. With a feline body, a very long neck, and a leopard head, only the serpopard among fantastic animals attacked other animals. When depicted in pairs, the two were shown with intertwined necks, as on the celebrated Narmer Palette. On magic wands, the serpopard usually has a serpent in its mouth (and infrequently wears a collar). This animal is not known to be on other documents, except in the hieroglyphs described above and in writing the name of the town of el-Kusiyeh. The term for the serpopard, in Old Egyptian, is unknown, unless the ancient name of el-Kusiyeh, *Qis*, which possibly derives from a verb meaning "to tie, to form a ligature," has some etymological connection with the supposed name of the pair of serpopards with intertwined necks. Mesopotamian serpopards also had interwoven necks. In some tombs at Beni Hasan and at Bersheh, another form, perhaps a subspecies of serpopard, was depicted. It had a feline body, but its neck and head were portrayed as a snake. This variety is termed *sedja*, which possibly means "one who travels afar."

Griffin. The winged specimen was the most common form of griffin in ancient Egypt; the stout feline body has a falcon head on a short neck. On early monuments, the wings are horizontal and parallel to the back of the animal, in accordance with Mesopotamian models. This species survives in the Beni Hasan tomb of Khnumhotep II, where a new one was also found, with V-shaped wings, a slender and speckled body, and a longer neck; the beak of the falcon is less apparent. Between the wings is a human head. This variant is common on magic wands, where it is frequently depicted wearing a collar and occasionally shown wearing a leash. This type is not found after this period. The stout variant reappears sporadically as an image of the war god Montu (unwinged) or as a hieroglyph in texts of the temple of Esna (winged). The Egyptian term *srf* or *sfrr* (possibly borrowed from a foreign language) was used to label figures of the animal in Beni Hasan; it also appeared in texts of different periods, once in a Middle Kingdom religious spell in the Coffin Texts. Another term, *tštš*, "one who tears to pieces," was used in the Coffin Texts and in Bersheh, to name a griffin with a stout body, short neck, and what looks like a feather crown. From the New Kingdom onward, a new winged type appeared, with a slender canine body and a vulture's or eagle's beak. It originated in a particular form of griffin, one with a Seth-animal (see next column) head, depicted once on a Middle Kingdom toilet object. The relationship between the two seems established in that the New Kingdom griffin sometimes

had a Seth-animal head too. The term for this creature, "the swift one," stressed its capability to run swiftly, while hauling a chariot in which the young savior god Shed, an Egyptian aspect of the Semitic god Reshef, pursued and killed dangerous animals.

Seth animal. Among the fantastic animals of the Beni Hasan tombs, one of them was, in all respects, identical to the animal that usually embodied the god Seth. Called *šꜥ*, it was also represented on magic wands, on which it wore a collar, a feature known from carefully engraved hieroglyphic examples of the Seth animal in Old Kingdom inscriptions. Its general stance was that of a dog or other canine animal, but it had triangular ears, an elongated snout, and an arrow in the guise of a tail. The *šꜥ* was known as a desert dweller, and a gang of *šꜥ* animals was supposed to haul the solar bark.

Related animals. The double-headed bull, which was pictured once on both a palette and a magic wand, could be added to this group of creatures. Other composite animals became associated with the human species; if originally part of the same family, they had a different destiny. A hippopotamus with a crocodile back and tail, Taweret, though represented on magic wands, became from the New Kingdom onward a great goddess; she was worshiped in temples and was highly renowned. The same was true of the lion-masked dwarf, Bes.

Dimitri Meeks

FATE. The principal Egyptian word for fate was *šꜣy/šꜣw*, which derives from the word *šꜣ*, meaning "ordain" or "fix," generally the action of a deity. Divine predetermination is found in the *Story of Sinuhe*. The protagonist describes his flight to western Asia as a "fateful flight." Earlier in the story, Sinuhe refers to his journey in a slightly different manner: "I do not know what brought me to this country; it is as if planned (*shr*) by god" (Lichtheim 1975, p. 225). Clearly the ideas of a divine plan and that which has been fated are synonymous.

š3w is first attested toward the end of the Old Kingdom and continues to be used down to the Late period. It appears with some regularity in texts, especially in the Wisdom Literature. From the sixth dynasty occurrence in the *Instruction of Ptahhotep*, it seems that *š3w* has to do with death, and that it is inescapable: "His time does not fail to come; one does not escape what is fated" (Lichtheim, 1975, p. 72). "Death is a kindly fate" (Lichtheim, 1975, p. 196) well reflects the pessimism of the *Admonitions of Ipuwer*, but it clearly connects *š3w* with one's demise. In fact, the writing of *š3w* is at times determined by the Hieratic sign for "death." There is textual evidence that fate was also believed to govern non-Egyptians, even enemies. Concerning the Nubian enemy Aata, Ahmose son of Ibana reports: "His fate brought on his doom. The gods of Upper Egypt grasped him" (Lichtheim 1976, p. 13).

Apparently various aspects of one's fate, such as time and manner of death, were ordained at birth. In the *Story of Two Brothers*, Re-Horakhty, king of the gods, directs Khnum to create a wife for Bata. The seven Hathors are present, and together they proclaim, "She will die by the knife" (Lichtheim 1976, p. 207). In the story of the birth of the three children of Ruddedet in the Westcar Papyrus, Re sends Isis, Nephthys, Meshkhenet, Heket, and Khnum to assist in the birth of the triplets. The sun god announces, "Please go, deliver Ruddedet of the three children who are in her womb, who will assume this beneficent office in this whole land. They will build your temples. They will supply your al-

tars. They will furnish your libations. They will make your offerings abundant" (Lichtheim 1976, p. 220). No indication is given here of the time and manner of death, but Re does disclose that these three will become kings, build temples, and provide for their offerings. After their delivery, it is actually Meshkhenet who declares of each one; "A King who will assume the kingship in this whole land" (Lichtheim 1976, p. 220). This latter text demonstrates that the other deities are acting on Re's behalf, and that the idea of fate goes beyond lifespan to include foretelling the kingly office they will hold. The statement in *Story of Two Brothers*, on the other hand, discloses the instrument by which death will come. A third aspect of fate is associated with the goddess Renenet. Because of her association with fertility and harvest, Renenet appears to be responsible for endowing individuals with material possessions (Miosi 1982, p. 76).

This would mean that there were three forces (or deities) associated with one's fate in the thought of the New Kingdom: *Š3w*, who is closely associated with the seven Hathors and is responsible for one's lifespan and manner of death; Meshkhenet, who decides one's status or work; and Renenet, who settles one's material fortune or misfortune. By the New Kingdom, the word for "fate" could be written with a deity determinative, as if *š3w* were personified or deified, perhaps because of its association with particular deities.

A number of critical questions regarding the Egyptian understanding of fate must be asked. Was it absolutely fixed? Could it be altered or manipulated? If so, how could it be changed? In the *Report of Wenamun*, the prince of Byblos refers to sending Egyptian envoys back to Egypt with timber "so as to beg for me from Amun fifty years of life over and above my allotted fate" (Lichtheim 1976, p. 228). This statement suggests that the Egyptians believed in a divinely ordained lifespan, and that they thought (or hoped) that Amun could extend it.

The *Story of the Doomed Prince* offers the most notable instance of altering one's fate. At the time of his birth, the Hathors announce, "He will die through the crocodile, or the snake, or the dog." The time of death is not announced, and, untypically, three possible instruments of death are introduced. The ill-fated prince thus spends much of his life not knowing which of these entities will bring his demise. Nevertheless, he asks for a pet puppy, which his father reluctantly gives him. After years of living reclusively in hope of avoiding his fate, the prince announces: "To what purpose is my sitting here? I am committed to Fate (*šȝw*). Let me go, that I may act according to my heart, until the god does what is in his heart" (Lichtheim 1976, p. 200). So he sets off on his chariot, believing that he cannot alter his fate, and arrives in Naharin. It is not clear whether the prince thinks that by leaving Egypt he may prolong his life, but he takes his dog with him.

In Naharin he marries a princess, to whom he discloses his three deadly fates. The horrified wife wants the pet dog killed, but the prince feels this dog could not cause his death because he has raised it. A crocodile has followed him from Egypt to Naharin, but it is prevented from killing the prince by a demon or water spirit (*nḫt*). On another occasion, the wife kills a snake, which has entered the prince's bedroom. She then announces: "Look, your god has given one of your fates into your hand. He will protect [you from the others also]" (Lichtheim 1976, p. 202). This fate being averted, the prince made an offering

to Pre, who has delivered him from this fate, but two fates remain.

One day while strolling with his dog, it discloses that it is his fate. The prince tries to escape by running down to the lake, only to have the crocodile snatch the dog and carry it off "to where the demon was" (Lichtheim 1976, p. 202). The crocodile returns to tell the prince that it is his fate, but offers to release him if he will help kill its nemesis, the water spirit. Unfortunately, the end of the papyrus is missing, but it is generally thought that the prince manages to avoid this final fate and lives happily ever after. The *Story of the Doomed Prince* certainly shows that one could not avoid one's fate by leaving Egypt; however, with divine intervention, life could be extended and the fated means of death perhaps changed.

It is unclear whether the calendar of lucky and unlucky days relates to one's fate. F. T. Miosi concludes, "There is no convincing grounds for positing an 'astrological' basis to the Egyptian concept of fate, destiny or whatever other term one wishes to use" (1982, p. 73). There is certainly nothing in the literature to suggest that amulets and other forms of magic had a role in altering one's fate. However, amulets may have been used in connection with unlucky days. Similarly, prophetic name formulae (e.g., *djed ʿnḫ.f/s* = "deity X says he/she will live") may have been used when a baby was born on an unlucky day. It is unlikely that the use of such names was an attempt to negate one's *šȝw*, because people did not know their fate. On the other hand, a parent would know if the birthday had a bad omen and might select a name that expressed the hope that the child would live.

Thus, one's fate appears in a sense to have operated on two tracks: the *šȝw* was set by the sun god and announced at birth by the Hathors (at least in folkloristic tales); and the lucky or unlucky days were determined by mythological precedent. How these two were interrelated is uncertain, but people would not have known their ordained fate unless it was divinely revealed in some manner, whereas they would have known if they faced an ill-fated mythological omen. Prophylactic steps could be taken in the latter case, but a person could apparently do little to alter *šꜣw*, as a statement in the *Story of Sinuhe* suggests: "Is there a god who does not know what he has ordained, a man who knows how it will be?" (Lichtheim 1975, p. 227).

James K. Hoffmeier

FELINE DEITIES. The oldest and best known of the Egyptian feline deities is the cat goddess Bastet, who is attested since the Old Kingdom. Although Bubastis was obviously the town of her origin, evidence exists to suggest that she was worshiped in various other places and associated with a number of different deities. In Memphis, Bastet was identified with the lion goddess Sekhmet.

During the Middle Kingdom Sekhmet was known primarily for her wild and warlike qualities and was generally feared, like the ferocious lioness, and Bastet came to be considered the milder, appeasing aspect of the same divinity. Likewise, Bastet was considered the mild eye of Re, as opposed to the scorching Sekhmet-eye. This position of Sekhmet and Bastet as simultaneous complements and opposites is also reflected in the association of the first with war, pestilence, and illness, and that of the second with female fertility, sexuality, and the protection of pregnant women and infants. In Heliopolis, Bastet was equated to Tefnut; she was thus acknowledged as the daughter of Atum and consequently integrated into the Heliopolitan pantheon. From Old Kingdom times, Bastet was associated with Hathor, and during the Middle Kingdom with Mut. There are also references to an association with Isis, who is occasionally pictured as a cat; in Edfu, Bastet is referred to as "the *bꜣ* of Isis."

It is not always easy to distinguish the strictly feline traits from leonine traits in the representations of deities. A current suggestion is that Bastet had originally been a wild lioness, whose features in the course of time lost their ferocity and softened into those of a benevolent cat. This alleged change of character has often been ascribed to ecological and societal developments, including the gradual migration of lions from north to south and finally out of Egypt, and the increasing presence and growing popularity of the cat there. However, the proposition that mythology and religion followed zoological developments is one

Bronze figurine of Bastet, from Merenptah's palace at Memphis, Late period. (University of Pennsylvania, Philadelphia. Neg. #S8-68303 [detail])

that cannot be confirmed. Furthermore, since in the Late period Bastet appears to have regained her lioness features, it is more likely that she alternatively represents both aspects.

To a certain extent, this ambivalence of character may also be attributed to the other goddesses that are sometimes, completely or partially, pictured as felines, such as Mut, Hathor, Wadjit, Pakhet, and Tefnut. As Dale Osborn points out, the goddess Mafdet, who is often included in this list, does not belong there: she must be identified as a lynx rather than a cat.

Although feline deities are predominantly female, there is one divine male cat that is often encountered in religious texts (for example, in the *Book of Going Forth by Day* [*Book of the Dead*]); he is pictured cutting off the head of a snake. This scene represents the traditional theme of the sun god in the act of destroying the evil power of Apep; the tomcat is but one of the many manifestations of Re.   *Aleid De Jong*

FESTIVAL CALENDARS. Egyptian temple walls or doorways were inscribed with a series of detailed accounts connected with the religious activity of the residing deity or deities. These texts are called "festival calendars." Being a requisite element of the inscriptional setup, they were put into place shortly before the temple was fully operational. Usually they consist of a terse, nonnarrative rendering of the key events of the Egyptian civil year as they affected the particular temple: religious celebrations, sacerdotal duties, and lists of offerings that had to be made. These texts are often crucial for reconstructing the calendrical outlook of a single priesthood and for understanding the complex economic subsistence of the priests and workers.

The most ancient festival calendar that is preserved dates from the Old Kingdom. It is written on two sides of the doorway in King Newoserre Any's funerary sun temple. Although fragments from Sahure's mortuary temple, situated in his valley complex, may be an earlier fifth dynasty example, it is Newoserre Any's lengthy account that provides us with the basic arrangement of these calendars. Generally, there is a preamble covering the construction of the temple or additions made to an existing one, the donations made by the pharaoh, often with dates, and the purpose of these offerings. Newoserre Any's text then details the festival celebrations themselves. Exact dates within the civil year are listed in conjunction with precisely described foods—for example, one haunch of beef or five bundles of vegetables. Even when the celebration is related to the moon, the calendrical organization is that of the 365-day civil year. For a lunar-based feast, such as the full moon, additional data are presented. In certain of these calendars, but not all, the estates providing the temple equipment and foods are credited. Ramesses III's extensive Medinet Habu festival calendar is the most highly itemized in this way.

Festival calendars were a continuous and characteristic aspect of most religious institutions from the Old Kingdom onward. For instance, we can reconstruct what occurred at the twelfth dynasty site of Illahun from the fragmentary temple accounts there; unfortunately, the scarcity of royal hieroglyphic records limits us in interpreting any changes over time.

These lists of religious events attempted to cover all the standard celebrations. The lunar-based "feasts of heaven" were expressly separated from the "seasonal festivals" that occurred only once a year. Thutmose III of the eighteenth dynasty left us a long but fragmentary account of additions made to his endowments at Karnak. This composition, posted in his festival temple

Akhmenu, is archetypical of the more exact yet simplified approach taken by later kings. The entire calendar is drawn up as a grid, with the left-hand column containing only dates and the righthand columns having numbers referring to headings describing foods such as oxen, bulls, and ibexes. The almost mathematical regularity of this system of horizontally and vertically ruled boxes distinguishes the New Kingdom festival calendar arrangement from that of the Old. In fact, from this king's reign there remain five other separate festival calendars: at Buto in the Nile Delta (see below); at Karnak, south of the granite sanctuary; Karnak, Pylon VI, north wing; Karnak, south wall of the temple of Akhmenu; and at Elephantine. In the latter calendar there occurs one of the few references to the key ideal New Year's Day of the helical rising of Sirius (Egyptian Sothis) set on a specific day within the Egyptian civil year. In addition, Thutmose III's Buto text, this time recorded on a freestanding stela instead on a temple wall, presents a calendar that can only be dated to an earlier time period.

It must be kept in mind that kings could often renew the offerings of past monarchs without altering the earlier or original calendar. On the other hand, they might expand or revise old calendars; and it is only from internal evidence that we can judge between these two possibilities. To take an example, the fragmentary Amenhotpe I festival calendar seems to have been recopied from the Middle Kingdom, yet some of the celebrations appear to have been current rather than anachronistic. The same may be said with regard to a very late calendar, at Esna, where the composer has added some New Kingdom references to his up-to-date calendar.

From the late New Kingdom we have a contemporary calendar of Ra-

messes II at Abydos, as well as the great Medinet Habu exemplar dated to the reign of Ramesses III. The latter is known to be a copy of Ramesses II's with minor additions, such as the basic daily offerings; indeed, one key festival of victory has been added later as a palimpsest over the original account. These two calendars are the most detailed cases from the New Kingdom. Others—of Thutmose IV at Karnak, Akhenaten at Thebes, or even Ramesses III and IV— do not present the awesome size of that at Medinet Habu.

By the Late period in Greco-Roman Egypt, the purpose of such calendars had changed. No longer do they mention the provisioning of the temple, and the endowments of the feasts are ignored. Instead, there is a detailed list of the official processional, but not the daily, feasts. These calendars could take either a fulsome or an abbreviated form, with only the day and number of celebrations cited. Dendera, Edfu, and Kom Ombu provide both versions of their calendars; Esna appears otherwise. Always the overriding emphasis is on the religious activity, not the economic substructure of the provisioning, since the entries of specific days refer solely to the travels of a local deity, his or her individual rituals, and so forth. Such festival calendars are no longer concerned with the establishment of a cult center, nor do they refer to the surplus that the priests would receive from the unused food offerings.

Anthony J. Spalinger

FESTIVALS. Ancient Egyptian festivals were part of the official cultic religion of the Nile Valley. Many religious celebrations are known from pictorial as well as textual evidence. We possess a number of the liturgies of such events— hymns and prayers that allow us to reconstruct the arrangement and settings of the services.

It is often easy to categorize the festivals from a simple calendrical point of view. Most of them were fixed within the civil calendar so that they took place either on one set day within the year or on many. These events, labeled "annual festivals" by scholars, began with the opening of the year, New Year's Day (*Wep-renpet*), which heralded both the first day in the civil calendar and the idea/time when rejuvenation and rebirth took place. Seventeen days after this event, but still during the first month of the year, was the more somber feast of Wagy. Eventually associated with the festival of Thoth on day nineteen, Wagy was connected with the ingrained mortuary rituals of pharaonic Egypt. This event was celebrated by private individuals outside an official cultic setting as well as within the precincts of the major temples in Egypt. We see it as early as the fourth dynasty in the brief private feast lists that every tomb owner eventually felt it necessary to inscribe in his funerary monument. Interestingly, its original lunar basis was not discarded: in historical times, there were actually two separate Wagy feasts, one set according to the cycle of the moon and a later one firmly placed at day eighteen of the first civil month.

In the second civil month, the great New Kingdom celebration of Opet predominated. It was a rite expressly connected with the pharaoh and his father Amun(-Re). This extensive festival, also set by the moon, saw the pharaoh-to-be traveling to the temple of Luxor at Thebes in order for his father Amun to give him the powers of kingship as the living Horus falcon. By the New Kingdom, the intimate connection between Amun and pharaoh was solidified in official state religion by this festival, and its twenty-seven-day duration in the twentieth dynasty indicates how significant it had become. Before the eighteenth dynasty, however, we know nothing about this celebration, and there is little doubt that the rise of Thebes to national importance brought with it the predominance of the deity Amun, who became a state deity. The might and power of Amun were ritually bequeathed to his living son, the king. Hence, this celebration belonged to the official royal ideology of the state and, not surprisingly, witnessed the personal involvement of pharaoh, especially on his official visit to Luxor in order to be crowned.

Equal in importance to the Opet feast, but far older, was that of Choiak or Sokar, celebrated in civil month four. This event reveals the age-old importance of the god of the afterworld, Osiris, and his link with the archaic powers of Memphis, especially Sokar. Known during the Old Kingdom (unlike Opet), Sokar grew in importance owing to the early move of the capital of Egypt from the south to Memphis. It is first found in the private feast lists of the Old Kingdom, indicating that Sokar belonged to one of the oldest cult centers of the land. However, there is little doubt that the funerary deity Sokar himself predates the unification of Egypt at the beginning of the first dynasty and the foundation of Memphis as its first capital.

By the Late period, the number of days that Sokar encompassed had grown considerably beyond the original interval of six (days 25 to 30 of the fourth month). In many ways, the festival of Sokar served the duty of completing the first season of the Egyptian year (Inundation), if only because the first day of the following month was considered to open a new era. The last days of the fourth month, observed with much agony and sadness, were soon associated with the god Osiris, who was considered to be dead by the central date of the Sokar feast, day 26 in month four.

Not surprisingly, day 1 of month five had its own New Year's day of rebirth, Nehebkau, occurring just five days after the death of Osiris. The intervening days were left for the eventual rebirth of the god and later connected to the rebirth of the king as the living Horus. Nehebkau, then, paralleled the calendrical New Year of the first day of month one, and virtually the same rituals and performances took place on the two occasions.

Two other key yearly events should be mentioned. The first, the festival of the fertility god Min, not surprisingly also opened a new season; it was enacted in the ninth civil month, although set according to the moon. This is also an archaic celebration, the nature of which can be gleaned mainly from New Kingdom and later sources. The king's role was to cut the first sheaf of grain (see p. 128), and the four corners of the universe took on significance. The Min feast saw the ritual performance of the pharaoh as life-sustainer of his people, a role that certainly reflects his original one, and the association of Min clearly indicates the fecundity and virility of rebirth. Hence, this event can be considered a third festival originally focused on birth, with the agricultural aspect predominating.

Month ten saw the famous Valley Feast, a second Theban celebration that can be traced back to the Middle Kingdom and also became quite important during the New Kingdom. From Karnak, the statues of Amun, his consort Mut, and their son Khonsu were carried across the Nile to Deir el-Bahri on the western bank. Significantly, inscriptions in the private tombs at Thebes reveal that the Feast of the Valley was an occasion for families to visit the tombs of their relatives and to venerate their dead ancestors. In many ways these private affairs parallel the present customs of modern Egypt and other cultures in which people celebrate a holiday on the grass of cemeteries in which their dead ancestors are buried.

Within the Nile Valley there were innumerable local religious sites separate from the main centers of the nation. From the extant data we can reconstruct a cultic calendar for the major deities of Egypt, such as Amun of Thebes, Hathor of Dendera, Horus of Edfu, and others. Often inscribed on the walls of the associated temples are detailed lists of the feasts, all presented in a regularized and programmatic fashion. These festival calendars were copied from the official liturgical rolls kept in the temples' archives. From these calendars we can determine whether a feast was set only within the civil calendar or according to the moon. Moreover, there were the regular lunar celebrations, one for each lunar day. The latter, the so-called seasonal festivals, were explicitly separated from the annual ones mentioned earlier.

Very rarely do we have information about a festival for a secular event; usually the data pertain to feasts within a purely cultic setting. One exception is the annual celebration established by Ramesses III to honor his victory over the Libyans (Meshwesh), who had unsuccessfully invaded Egypt during his reign. A second one was the king's coronation, the date of which would normally be included in a religious calendar. Perhaps the Heliacal Rising of Sothis (the star Sirius) can be added, insofar as there was no specific cult of the deity Sothis. This event was recognized as all-important one because the reappearance of Sothis after a period of seventy days' invisibility originally marked the emergence of the New Year and later was thought of as the ideal rebirth of the land.

One celebration that was observed over a long time span but does not appear in the festival calendars is that of the king's rejuvenation after the first thirty years of his reign. This event, the *heb-sed* festival, was a truly secular one, directly concerned with the vitality and virility of the pharaoh. The origins of the event are lost to us, although it must have been celebrated in Predynastic times. Known from extensive pictorial and inscriptional evidence, the *heb-sed* was probably originally established on a lunar basis: consider the coincidence of thirty years with the length of a month (thirty days). But it is the series of complicated events recorded that allows us to determine the exact arrangement of this key festival. The Rising of the *Djed*-Pillar, for example, symbolizes the king's role in rebirth (the pillar is an archaic symbol of Osiris). It is significant that there is a separate feast connected with the same fetish, timed to the second season, soon after the death of Osiris during the Choiak feast.

A large number of scenes depicting this event have been preserved. Key ones found in the sun temple of Newoserre Any, the tomb of Kheruef at Thebes, the temple of Amenhotpe III at Soleb in Nubia, Akhenaten's East Karnak Temple, and from later Saite times (twenty-sixth dynasty) allow us to reconstruct some of the program of events and to identify the large number of important individuals involved. Ceremonial palaces appear to have been built expressly for its duration, and the garb of the participants, including the king, reveals its age-old nature.

Behind the mere mention of a feast's name and duration were the exhaustive records connected to the celebration. Ordinarily, we possess only a fraction of the original texts that were connected to the processions, chanting, and readings, and the exact timing of the separate rituals. From the Greco-Roman period, however, the walls of the temples of Dendera, Edfu, Esna, Kom Ombo, and Philae provide additional information not included in the festival calendars, and so allow us to reconstruct the events in greater detail. Moreover, papyri rolls and fragmentary biographical texts reveal the intricate and often hidden details such as processions; morning, noon, and evening ablutions of the deity; chants; and speeches. For example, at the Min festival, the detailed program at Ramesses III's mortuary temple of Medinet Habu casts welcome light on the interesting performance of the cutting of the first sheaf of barley. Festival calendars, on the other hand, merely list in a terse fashion the date, deity, and perhaps a sentence concerning the involvement of a specific priest.

Behind these enormous records was the endowment required for the performance of the feasts. From the Old Kingdom to the New, the festival calendars contain explicit references to the offerings required by the deity or deities. This information was not trivial; the official endowment as established or renewed by a king demanded that the economic support of a feast be indicated. Once more, it is the temple of Medinet Habu that provides the most information concerning these seemingly mundane activities culminating in the religious events. The details are remarkable: exact number of bread loaves, cakes, beer containers, meat, fowl, incense, cultic charcoal, and the like are listed beside each event. The amount of grain that went into making a certain type of loaf or a specific type of beer can be determined by a specific integer that refers to the cooking or brewing undertaken (called the "cooking ratio").

Often, the introductory segments of the temple calendar include details of the provenance of such foods, although these additions might be placed next to the respective religious celebration. By listing the amount of grain (barley or emmer) that went into producing a certain number of beer jugs or loaves in conjunction with the cooking ratio, we can easily determine the exact amount of grain that was needed for these feasts. Therefore, it is relatively easy to add up the total amount of grain that was needed for the subsistence of the cult, if only for the major ceremonies celebrated in the civil year.

By means of these calculations, scholars have been able to evaluate quantitatively exactly how wealthy a temple was and approximately how many priests were necessary for the preservation of the cult. Major festivals such as Sokar (Choiak) and Opet, not surprisingly, required a greater outlay of foods than lesser ones; the number of days each festival lasted is given in these calendars, and the duration was not brief. With regard to the anniversary of a king's accession, we learn from some of these lists that separate and additional supplies were distributed to the temple priesthood, who celebrated a holiday in recognition of this important event. Once more, by means of simple calculation, it is relatively easy to determine the approximate number of officiating personnel in a given temple such as Medinet Habu.

In addition to the almost voluminous New Kingdom data that can be gleaned from the various festival calendars, the account papyri from the Middle Kingdom temple site of Illahun help us to no small degree. In this case, although the hieroglyphic inscriptions containing such economic details are absent, the workaday records are noteworthy. Dated to the reigns of Senwosret III and Amenemhet III, the papyri from Illahun reveal the actual procedures of a middle-sized religious institution of that time. In this case, the wealth of the mortuary temple of Senwosret II is easy to calculate. As

befits the era, such temples were not major land-owning corporations like Karnak in the New Kingdom. The total number of personnel probably never exceeded fifty, and their normal incomes, which can be calculated from the daily records, were relatively modest. Some of the papyri list the monthly rotas in which certain sections of the priests worked. The entire priesthood was divided into phyles, a system known from the Old Kingdom as well. Lists of festivals and the exact amount of food offered are given, with the time of delivery specified and, of course, the precise time for the ceremony noted.

From accounts such as these, it is easy to see the extent of a temple's wealth and who contributed to its upkeep. The maintenance of the cult required offerings, and since those items had to be produced, land especially was required in order to support a temple on a purely economic basis. New Kingdom festival calendars, for example, sometimes (but not always) specify the origins of foods and refer to the tenant farmers and gardeners who had to grow these supplies. Additional surveys of land-owning institutions in Egypt allow us to reconstruct the extent of agricultural territory that a certain temple owned and the revenues due to it from the agricultural laborers who leased the land from the religious corporation. It is clear that the wealth of a few key temples, such as Karnak, had increased dramatically from the Middle Kingdom. Indeed, the simple act of reversion of offerings—whereby the foods offered to the gods were subsequently redistributed (in unequal portions) to the temple hierarchy—reveals the importance of the various festivities, as well as the benefits the clergy gained from their roles within a specific temple.

One major problem associated with these celebrations remains as an outstanding question about ancient Egyptian religious thought. On the one hand, it is relatively easy to reconstruct the importance of such major celebrations as Opet or the Valley festival. The festival calendars and associated textual and pictorial evidence reveal the participation of key nonroyal figures and officials of the land as well as the officiating priests. From the Greco-Roman period, the walls of temples such as Edfu, Dendera, and the others publicly describe in detail the voyages the local gods made. The complicated myth of Horus of Edfu and his association with Hathor of Dendera indicates a more public aspect to these religious events than the terse, programmatic lists of the calendars. Such evidence is paralleled by separate descriptions and reliefs recounting the celebrations of Opet, the Valley festival, and even the *heb-sed* rites.

In many cases—and Opet is a key example—individuals not associated with the cult were involved. This can be clearly seen from data about the processions during these feasts. Such visible manifestations of the deity were rare; however, they occurred outside the temple precincts. This more public revelation of the god (or gods) frequently had further implications for the ensuing religious fervor. For example, oracles could take place with more than a few priests present. Many of these prognostications happened during the procession of the deity, and records of such decisions—auspicious or otherwise—remain to indicate how frequent these questions to the gods were. Private individuals consulted their local or regional god for a revelation. Such oracles also took place when important public decisions had to be made, such as the elevation of a private individual to the position of high priest of Amun, and in this case hieroglyphic records were publicly written on

temple walls or on stone stelae. More perishable or private means, such as ostraca or papyri, were used to record a god's decision concerning private matters, such as theft. The local chapel of the deified Amenhotpe I on the west bank of Thebes, for example was often consulted by the workmen of this area to render a judgment on a contested point. Oracles usually took place on important feast days, especially those in which the god was borne outside his temple walls.

This public versus private aspect of the cult cannot be downplayed. Commencing with the mortuary temples of the first dynasties, the Old Kingdom saw an accumulation of wealth and importance of such cults. Whether associated with the king (mortuary temple) or a god (sun temple for the solar deity Re), religious entities possessed economic and social importance. Generally, however, such institutions appear to be self-centered and more for-bidding to the public than actual centers of religious fervor. The same can be said for the Middle Kingdom, and the account papyri from Illahun indicate just how separate the life of a temple was from that of the town.

By the New Kingdom, the evidence indicates otherwise. Major celebrations took place that were viewed by outsiders, who looked on while the god Amun proceeded from Karnak to Luxor or crossed the Nile westward to visit Deir el-Bahri (for the Valley festival) or Medinet Habu (for the Opet festival). Oracles could be granted at these times, and the occasions were times for public and private celebrations. Similarly, when Hathor of Dendera visited Horus of Edfu, entire towns filled the streets in a carnival atmosphere.

Although this overt extramural aspect of official cults cannot be ignored, inside the temple walls more private and secret performances took place. The daily morning, noon, and evening rituals were not seen by the public. Even important nonroyal personages could rarely proceed beyond the first court. The inner chambers of the temple, roofed and dark, were kept distinct from the more sunlit public areas. Furthermore, even when the king was reinvigorated at Luxor, the mass of the townspeople had to remain outside the edifice. Permission to enter a temple and to participate in a religious ceremony was rare.

For these reasons, scholars speak of "official" or "cultic" religion in contrast to "popular" religion. The former is amply represented by the temples and their extant inscriptions and reliefs. In addition, various liturgies on papyri and other mythological tractates are preserved which enable us to imagine what the official hieroglyphic texts narrate. Thus, our material concerning ancient Egyptian festivals has a very biased point of view. Most of what remains concerns the religious celebrations connected to the major gods and goddesses of Egypt, including the pharaoh. Hence, the highest level of ancient Egyptian society, down to the major nonroyal bureaucrats, is what is reflected by these sources, among them the monumental buildings themselves. Yet the daily religious life of the average Egyptian is not revealed. The private cults did not intrude on the massive temples, nor were the somewhat tawdry and relatively inexpensive private shrines connected with the state gods.

Archaeological finds have revealed that side by side with the official cults there existed numerous personal ones. Small offering tables and votive stelae which honor a particular deity have been found in houses and courtyards. Nevertheless, we know little about the festival practices of the private Egyptian. Various records, mainly on ostraca or papyri and datable to the late New Kingdom (nineteenth and twentieth dynasties), indicate that there was a strong feeling of personal piety within pharaonic Egypt, an attitude that is not shared, for the most part, in the official records. Even the justly famous Middle Egyptian literary masterpiece, the *Story of Sinuhe*, emphasizes the protagonist's personal god, who is never named. Yet among this plethora of information, only the records of the private oracles indicate a connection to a festival.

The main temples of the land operated quite apart from the average Egyptian. Mortuary temples, which by the New Kingdom were situated on the west side of Thebes, were erected to honor the pharaoh as a god both in his lifetime and after death. This practice goes back as far as the Early Dynastic period, and there is little doubt that a separate cult for the pharaoh existed earlier. The activities of these temples were established by the king soon after he was crowned. In the Old Kingdom such temples played the predominant role within official cultic religion: witness, for example, the massive pyramids of the third through sixth dynasties. Other temples were for the most part local and small—e.g., the temple for Min or even various chapels at Abydos. With the exception of the temple of Osiris at Abydos, from the first dynasty onward, few major religious edifices were erected in the Nile Valley. Only in the fifth dynasty did a change occur, and even then it was limited to one royal lineage. Because the pharaohs of the fifth dynasty placed great emphasis upon the cult of the sun god Re, the theological father of the pharaoh at that time, they chose to honor their allegiance in a grandiose and explicit manner: each monarch attempted to erect a sun temple for Re. This practice ceased at the close of the fifth dynasty, and until the fall of the Old Kingdom, the major temple-building reverted to that of the king's own mortuary complex.

By the Middle Kingdom, minor temples were still present but somewhat greater in size than previously. This can be seen most clearly from the expansion of the temple of Satet at Elephantine. Nonetheless, although mortuary temples continued to be built, these edifices were small, self-contained economic units. Only with the rise of Thebes, and especially with the expansion of the cult of Amun during the late Second Intermediate Period, did a decided change occur. By the early eighteenth dynasty, the pharaohs reconstructed the mainly wooden temple of Amun at Karnak in stone, began to add sizable pylons to the building, and started to utilize the available free space on the temple walls for historical and religious texts and pictures. By the middle of that dynasty the burgeoning state of Egypt had at its fingertips enough resources to be able to enact a series of temple-building projects in Egypt and in Nubia as well. By the end of the Amarna period, this practice was in full swing. Therefore, it is not surprising that we find the enormous temple of Soleb in Nubia, built by Amenhotpe III, and the later numerous grotto temples of Ramesses II in the same southern region.

Karnak, Luxor, and various temples at Memphis were maintained by the pharaoh. Additions to the key centers of Thebes, Memphis, and even Heliopolis were effected by the nineteenth and twentieth dynasties. In Western Thebes, the mortuary temples continued to be placed along a north–south axis, but by the end of the New Kingdom alterations in the importance of the cults had evidently occurred. In the Third Intermediate Period, except at Karnak, there was

a cessation of this cultic expansion. As Amun-Re had come to predominate in the south, with his high priest running this region, the other Middle and Upper Egyptian cults had diminished even further in importance. Only with a powerful dynasty such as that of the Kushite (twenty-fifth) or the Saite (twenty-sixth) was there the growth in importance of these religious corporations once more. By the twenty-sixth dynasty the major thrust of the religious cults was in the north, as befits the seat of power of that lineage, Sais.

When the Greeks and Macedonians came to dominate the Nile Valley, the local cults were left to operate their own religious ceremonies. The Ptolemaic kings, recognized as pharaohs, were worshiped as rulers and actors within edifices such as Edfu and Esna. Nevertheless, the wealth of these temples was considerably limited, especially in comparison with that of Amun-Re of Karnak many centuries earlier. Perhaps for this reason, the festival calendars avoid listing the foods and other offerings brought to the deity at specific times. In fact, they do not mention the tenant farmers or specific lands that were under the jurisdiction of the temple and which supplied their revenues to the god.

Our knowledge of religious festivals during the Ptolemaic period comes mainly from private papyrus rolls of a religious nature. They, and some funerary stelae, indicate that many of the old religious celebrations had declined, if not disappeared. Opet still remained, though considerably weakened; but the cult of Osiris was practiced throughout the land, as the famous tractate of Plutarch on Isis and Osiris bears witness.

Anthony J. Spalinger

FOUR SONS OF HORUS, the funerary deities, or genii (sing., genius), named Imsety (*Imsti*), Hapy (*hpy*), Duamutef (*dw3-mwt.f*), and Kebehsenuef (*kbḥ-snw.f*), who are attested from the Old Kingdom to Greco-Roman times. They appear fourteen times in the Pyramid Texts, the earliest extensive set of Egyptian religious texts. In Spell 2078 and 2079, they are described as:

friends of the King, (who) attend on this King . . . , the children of Horus of Khem (Letopolis); they tie the rope-ladder for this King, they make firm the wooden ladder for this King, they cause the King to ascend to Khepri when he comes into being in the eastern side of the sky.

In Spell 1333, they "spread protection of life over your father the Osiris King, since he was restored by the gods." In Spell 552, they eliminate hunger and thirst: "I will not be thirsty by reason of Shu, I will not be hungry by reason of Tefnut; Hapy, Duamutef, Kebehsenuef, and Imsety will expell this hunger which is in my belly and this thirst which is on my lips."

In the New Kingdom *Book of the Going Forth by Day* (*Book of the Dead*), the roles of the four genii in the afterlife are further elaborated, as in Spell 137:

O sons of Horus, Imsety, Hapy, Duamutef, Kebehsenuef: as you spread your protection over your father Osiris-Khentimentiu, so spread your protection over [the deceased], as you removed the impediment from Osiris-Khentimentiu, so he might live with the gods and drive Seth from him.

Spell 17 states:

As for the tribunal that is behind Osiris, Imsety, Hapy, Duamutef, Kebehsenuef; it is these who are behind the Great Bear in the northern sky. . . . As for these seven spirits, Imsety, Hapy, Duamutef, Kebehsenuef, Maayotef, He-Who-is-under-his-Moringa-Tree, and Horus-the-Eyeless, it is they who were set by Anubis as a protection for the burial of Osiris.

Finally, in the tenth division of the *Book of Gates*, Imsety, Hapy, Duametef, and

Kebehsenuef appear restraining the *ummti* (*wmmtí*) snakes with chains. These snakes were allies of Re's enemy, the serpent Apophis. The four genii are also depicted on the western part of the astronomical ceilings found in Ramessid royal tombs.

Clearly stated to be the sons of Horus in a number of texts, their precise familial affiliations are not definitive. Apart from the aforementioned Horus of Khem, Harsiese and Horus the Elder are also cited as being their father in various texts. Isis was their mother, although a view of their having sprung from a lotus flower can be seen in the vignette that accompanies the *Book of the Going Forth by Day* judgment scene (Spell 125).

Dating from their earliest appearances in the Pyramid Texts, the Four Sons of Horus are found exclusively in mortuary contexts, and seem not to have had any cult as such; they are thus generally referred to as "genii." From the Middle Kingdom onward, however, they are ubiquitous within the tomb, invoked upon almost all coffins and canopic containers. In the earlier Pyramid Texts they were among the deities before whom the deceased was stated to possess "reverence" (*ỉm3ḫ*); such texts are normally found on the coffins' lateral textbands, with actual depictions added during the eighteenth dynasty. The later representations occurred on the sides of the coffin trough, with Anubis-Imywet and Anubis-Khenty-seh-netjer standing between the genii. This type of depiction recalls Spell 1092 of the Pyramid Texts, where "they flank the dead king when on the ferry to the Field of Rushes." The Four Sons likewise appear on New Kingdom sarcophagi in stone and wood, which featured less common textformulations.

On canopic containers, where their heads functioned as lids, the Four Sons were regarded as guardians or reincarnations in the specific organs removed during the mummification process: Imsety—the liver, Hapy—the lungs, Duamutef—the stomach, and Kebehsenuef—the intestines. There is evidence for the responsibilities of Hapy and Duamutef being switched in some cases. Other anatomical relationships existed, as is attested by Pyramid Text Spell 149. Hapy and Duamutef were associated with the hands; Imsety and Kebehsenuef with the feet.

The Four Sons of Horus had various other relationships. Geographically, Imsety was linked with the South, Hapy with the North, Duamutef the East, and Kebehsenuef the West. In addition, Hapy and Duamutef were linked to the Delta city of Buto; Imsety and Kebehsenuef with the Upper Egyptian city of Hierakonpolis. These two ancient cities are the earliest of all Egyptian settlements. An association can be made between Imsety and the herb dill, owing to the similarity in Old Egyptian between their names. Upon both coffins and canopic containers, Imsety, Hapy, Duamutef, and Kebehsenuef are shown under the individual tutelage of the goddesses Isis, Nephthys, Neith, and Selket, respectively. These pairings are generally fixed, although variations can be found.

Until the eighteenth dynasty, the Four Sons were usually depicted with human heads, although a few canopic chests of the Middle Kingdom contain images of all four gods with the heads of falcons. They were normally shown wearing the usual divine tripartite wig, but in the tomb of King Ay (tomb 23 of the West branch of the Valley of the Kings), Imsety and Hapy are each depicted with the Red Crown, Duamutef and Kebehsenuef each with the White Crown, which derived from the respective pairs' association with Egypt's North and South. Between the early eighteenth and mid-nineteenth dynasties, how-

ever, each genius gained a distinctive head: Imsety—human, Hapy—ape, Duamutef—jackal, and Kebehsenuef—falcon. These henceforth remained standard, except during the twenty-second and twenty-third dynasties, when at least six different combinations can be found, the most common showing Duamutef and Kebehsenuef swapping heads.

From the late Third Intermediate Period onward, the presence of the four genii in mortuary contexts expanded. In addition to their presence on coffins and canopic containers, faience amulets of the four were attached to shrouds or incorporated into the bead nets that came into use as body-covers. Images of the genii, often of wax, were placed in the deceased's body cavity from the time of Ramesses III (r. 1198–1166 BCE) onward. In the latter part of the twentieth dynasty, this practice was instituted in conjunction with the return of the internal organs to the abdomen, following separate mummification.

The Four Sons of Horus continued to be depicted on items of funerary equipment into Ptolemaic and Roman times; the last instances are found on stucco mummy casings of the fourth century CE.   *Aidan Dodson*

FUNERARY CONES, the cone-shaped objects of baked clay inserted as a frieze, with the circular face exposed, above the doors of Middle and New Kingdom private tombs, mainly in the Theban necropolis. During the New Kingdom, the cone's visible face bore a stamp of the owner's name and title(s), sometimes including those of a relative, or had a short supplementary text. Any number of cones belonging to one person might therefore be in existence, so the cones constitute a proof of the presence of a tomb, either extant or now lost.

The cones have been interpreted in several ways: as a means of identification of the owner of the tomb; as an ornamental memorial; as a boundary marker for the territory of the tomb; as dummy offering loaves; or as symbolic pieces of meat. The circular surface has also been interpreted in several ways: as the ends of roofing poles; as a form of visitors' cards; as a decorative element; or, most recently, as reflecting the shape of the sun disc—to thus become one vehicle for the deceased tomb owner's attainment of eternal life, by following the circuit of the sun. Possibly, the Egyptians were themselves in doubt as to the nature of the object, for they painted the cones in several colors (red, blue, white). In Egypt, colors indicated materials, and the colors mentioned encompassed substances as different as bread, meat, pottery, and the sun's red glow. As some of the texts accompanying the burial refer to solar matters, this was likely to have been one reason for the cones' existence.

The earliest known funerary cones were dated to the eleventh dynasty. Although they have no inscriptions, they have been found in context. Some are 53 centimeters (20 inches) long, but they decreased in size as the New Kingdom progressed. In the eighteenth dynasty they abounded from the reign of Thutmose I onward. In the Ramessid period, they were quite scarce compared to the number of tombs known from that time.

Funerary cones were mainly used at Thebes, although the Egyptian style tomb of the official Anu at Aniba also included cones. Yet the tomb of his more famous colleague, Penne, in the same location did not. Cones have also been found at Naga ed-Deir and at el-Deir north of Esna; the latter, in a Middle Kingdom context, but presumably intrusive, are particularly interesting in that they give the name of the locality near which they were found. It is thus unlikely that they should have been taken

there from Thebes. They probably came from a tomb in the vicinity of Esna, now lost. Middle Kingdom tombs at Rizeiqat, Armant, Naqada, and Abydos have yielded uninscribed cones.

No cones have come from the Memphis area, but some of those found at Thebes contained evidence of a Memphite connection. One belongs to Kenamun, steward of the dockyard of Memphis—but he had a tomb cut at Thebes, where the cones were found—so the reference to Memphis was purely verbal. Two seal impressions that mentioned the dockyard probably also derived from Thebes. Some other cone users had occupations that took them to various towns in Egypt, such as Heliopolis and Dendera; this distribution is also apparent from titles found in the tombs at Thebes, and there is nothing to suggest that these persons were buried elsewhere. No cones have been recovered from Tell el-Amarna (where their presumed solar symbolism might have fit in well), nor are any known from the few Theban tombs of the late eighteenth dynasty.

Funerary cones were thus largely restricted to the Theban area, and they conformed to the tradition in that part of the country. They may have been thought of as particularly suited to rock-cut tombs, and in fact most of the cones related to existing tombs have come from those with painted, not sculpted, decoration. Actually, the majority of tombs from that period were painted, so there are too many unprovenanced cones to provide significant statistics.

The Theban necropolis covers a large area, and within its various sections a pattern of distribution may be distinguished. The majority of the eighteenth dynasty tombs are at Sheik Abd-el-Qurna, so this is where most of the attributable cones would belong. In contrast, at Deir el-Medina, only one tomb has yielded a funerary cone; this is interesting, for in that locality, the solar cycle was more frequently referred to in the wall decoration than elsewhere in the necropolis. Bernard Bruye're, who excavated Deir el-Medina, suggested that *shawabti* figures somehow took over the function of the funerary cones, and he did not include the cones in his reconstruction of the Deir el-Medina tombs. Yet some tombs certainly had both cones and *shawabti* figures, so it is difficult to see a connection.

The corpus of known funerary cones is a valuable source of information on the prosopography of New Kingdom Thebes, to be compared with such objects as scarabs and seals. Cones can also be used as an indication of the number of tombs that existed in the Theban area, which far exceeded those known at present. The number of funerary cones not immediately assignable to a known tomb is more than four hundred, a figure that may be compared to the number of New Kingdom tombs in the area, about 406. The number of New Kingdom tombs for which funerary cones exist is seventy-nine, with fifty-two of these being at Sheikh Abd-el-Qurna and forty-eight dating to the eighteenth dynasty. As with other funerary items produced for the elite of ancient Egypt, funerary cones were used by both men and women.   *Lise Manniche*

FUNERARY FIGURINES. Known as *shabti*s, *shawabti*s, and *ushebti*s, funerary figurines were small statuettes fashioned either as mummies or as living persons dressed in fine linen garb. They served as proxies for ancient Egyptian deceased by magically performing various obligatory agricultural tasks in the underworld. Over time, so many funerary figurines were produced that apart from scarabs and amulets, they are the most numerous

of all ancient Egyptian antiquities. Over time they became one of the characteristic components of a proper burial.

The three terms for funerary figurines are indiscriminately and incorrectly used as synonyms. Each designation has historical limits to its usage, and the term *shawabti* is restricted geographically as well—to Deir el-Medina and other Theban areas. The appropriate spelling is found in the version of chapter 6 of the *Book of Going Forth by Day* (*Book of the Dead*) that was painted or inscribed on the figurines at some point before the eighteenth dynasty. However, because many of these statuettes lack chapter 6 and have simply the title and name of the deceased, none of the three terms applies. Hence, the designation "funerary figurines," despite its antiquarian ring, is at least accurate for all types in all periods.

Small wax prototypes appeared at Saqqara during the Herakleopolitan period and in the eleventh dynasty mortuary complex of Nebhepetre Montuhotep I at Deir el Bahri in Thebes. Shaped as humans, wrapped in linen, and deposited in coffins, these little wax figurines were miniature mummies. These earliest examples do not have chapter 6 or any other specific word for funerary figurine; however, they continue the tradition of work done on behalf of the deceased, which appears in the Old Kingdom in the form of both servant statuettes and tomb paintings or reliefs of laborers.

Throughout the Middle Kingdom, funerary figurines appeared in small numbers per burial. Usually made of stone, they were consistently mummiform and uninscribed or labeled only with the title and name of the deceased. Either in the thirteenth or the seventeenth dynasty, a simple form of chapter 6 of the *Book of the Dead* appears on spo-

Painted wooden *shawabti* figure of Maya, a New Kingdom official, in the coffin, nineteenth dynasty. (University of Pennsylvania Museum, Philadelphia, Neg. #S4-143062)

Two *shawabtis*. (*Left*) Blue-glazed faience *sha-wabti* of Queen Henutawy, probably from the Deir el-Bahri royal cache at Thebes, twenty-first dynasty. (*Right*) *Shawabti* of Paw(y) Khonsu, from Dra Abul Naga, Third Intermediate Period. (University of Pennsylvania Museum, Philadelphia, Neg. #S4-143070)

radic examples. This text enumerates the agricultural labors to be performed—irrigation, cultivation, and sand removal. In the early version, both the spellings *shabti* and *shawabti* appear, but the latter is restricted to the strange stick figures from the Theban area. *Shawabti* does not recur until the nineteenth dynasty on no more than a few dozen figurines from Deir el-Medina and elsewhere in the Theban necropolis; hence, it is probably a dialectical variant and is the least preferable of the three spellings for general reference. The etymology of *shabti* and *shawabti* is not clear.

The eighteenth dynasty was a time of great innovation, not only in the development of funerary figurines but also in all other Egyptian art. No longer made primarily of stone, funerary figurines appeared in wood, faience, terracotta, metal, and even glass, in rare examples.

An expanded version of chapter 6 occurs regularly on the figurines, and *shabti* is the routine spelling. The numbers of *shabtis* per burial increase from a few to dozens and even hundreds. Still made only in mummy form, *shabtis* from the first half of the eighteenth dynasty are large and bulky. Although some terracotta and faience *shabtis* are mold made and mass produced, most figurines are hand fashioned and are of high quality.

The great innovation in funerary figurines, not only in the eighteenth dynasty but also in their entire history, happened during the reign of Thutmose IV, when craftsmen reinforced their agricultural nature—fashioning them with baskets, sacks and hoes, or mattocks held in their hands on the chest or waist. Some *shabtis* have separate models of the agricultural tools, and still others are unadorned. Once established, however, the decorative scheme of the agricultural tools became a standard feature of funerary figurines. Either at the end of the eighteenth or early in the nineteenth dynasty, figurines in the garments of the living first appeared. Finely rendered with loose folds and tight pleats, the clothing resembles the dress of the elite classes often seen elsewhere in Egyptian art. Because these raiments were inappropriate for hard labor in the fields, they perhaps had a religious significance, indicating that the deceased were reborn in the underworld and dressed in their best for all eternity.

Although many *shabtis* and most *shawabtis* of the nineteenth dynasty were carefully rendered, the majority of funerary figurines were roughly fashioned. Mold-made *shabtis* of faience or terracotta became increasingly popular, and the numbers per burial increased appreciably. Chapter 6 of the *Book of the Dead* also became elaborated; however, uninscribed figurines or those with only the title and name of the deceased are also numerous. In the twenty-first dynasty, the spelling *ushebti* occurs and is the standard word that appears in chapter 6 throughout the Ptolemaic period, when the last figurines were made. The etymology of this spelling is again uncertain; perhaps it derives from the verb *wšb* ("to answer"). The *ushebtis* of the twenty-first dynasty and the rest of the Third Intermediate Period are consistently fashioned of blue-colored faience, with details in black. In the Late period and thereafter, *ushebtis* are again rendered in faience, in pastel tones of green or blue. In the Late and Ptolemaic periods, *ushebtis* are consistently mummiform; examples in the dress of the living are exceedingly rare, if at all existent. So numerous were the figurines in each burial that in many instances there are "overseer" figurines designed to control the gangs of workers. *Donald B. Spanel*

FUNERARY LITERATURE. The funerary literature of the ancient Egyptians includes various collections of texts associated with elite burials from almost all of Egypt's historic periods. These texts were copied in many ways on the walls of tombs, and occasionally on temple

Page from the book of the Dead. Deceased before Osiris. Aegyptisches Museum, Staaliche Museen, Berlin, Germany (Art Resource, NY)

walls, as well as on various objects placed inside tombs—principally coffins and papyri. The term does not cover the biographical texts, formulaic offering texts, and texts that are essentially hymns to various deities, which may also be found in tombs. Some ritual texts are included, but others—such as the Opening of the Mouth ritual, often found in tombs—are not generally included. Some mythological and cosmogonic texts found in tombs, such as the *Book of the Heavenly Cow* or the *Birth of the Solar Disk*, are included, but the Jumilhac Papyrus and Bremner-Rhind Papyrus, which are largely mythological, are not. The emphasis of funerary literature is on eschatological works, principally those that deal with life after death in the company of the gods—that is, guidebooks to the beyond. Despite the narrowness of the topic, such works were popular in all periods of Egyptian history and represent the largest genre of texts that survive, and also the group that is represented by the largest number of copies.

The Old Kingdom's Pyramid Texts, the Middle Kingdom's Coffin Texts, and the New Kingdom's *Book of Going Forth by Day* (*Book of the Dead*), as well as certain guidebooks to the beyond, such as the *Book of That Which Is in the Underworld* (*Amduat*), the *Book of Gates,* and the *Book of Caverns,* are the principal works of this genre, and there is a certain amount of overlap among them. The Old Kingdom's Pyramid Texts include some variants found on Middle Kingdom coffins as well as on the walls of a few Saite period priests' and priestesses' tomb-chapels at Thebes that date from almost two thousand years later. The Middle Kingdom's Coffin Texts include some variants of Pyramid Texts as well as other Old Kingdom material and early versions of chapters of the *Book of Going Forth by Day.* Copies of the *Book of Going*

Forth by Day are essentially papyrus documents, but many individual chapters are found on tomb walls and even on the walls of at least one royal mortuary temple; since this is the New Kingdom mortuary temple of Ramesses III at Medinet Habu, the last large and the only well-preserved pharaonic temple, such texts could also have occurred on others now lost. Some of its chapters are also found on scarabs, *shawabtis*, linen strips, and hypocephali, and in many forms these continued to be very popular well into Roman times.

In the case of the Pyramid Texts, there is a clear chronological order to the surviving documents; the burial chamber of Unas, last king of the fifth dynasty, held the earliest known copy. Earlier examples might have been on perishable materials placed in tombs that were later robbed and despoiled. Most of the funerary literature has in common the reconciliation of the two principal cults involved with death and the afterlife, and both are related to the myth of divine kingship. They come down to us first and foremost in the royal context: the Pyramid Texts within the kings' burial chambers. Considered a living king from earliest times was the divine Horus—son and avenger of his father, Osiris—who at death became Osiris, with all the mythological connections involved. In the fifth dynasty's Pyramid Texts, the king has also become the "son of Re," who at death joins his father on the sun's bark in his daytime and nighttime voyages through the sky. The cyclical nature of these cults, as well as their death and rebirth motifs, makes it possible for them to be assimilated together even if not always entirely reconciled. All three collections of texts have certain sections that show total separation, others showing some syncretism, and still others that show complete assimilation of the two deities, their cults, and their descriptions

of the afterlife. What is remarkable is that these kings' texts were almost immediately used in queens' tombs, and thereafter were quickly taken over by nonroyals, then eventually made available to almost anyone.

The earliest examples of funerary literature in Old Kingdom pyramids were not all created specifically for the purpose of accompanying those royal burials. Judging from their contents, which refer to both pyramids and desert burials, and both royal and nonroyal owners, these texts indicate that they were composed from various sources dealing with death and the afterlife and were compiled by priests, generally of the Heliopolitan persuasion. The language and orthography of the texts also seem to indicate that the texts came from different time periods and perhaps from different places as well.

One interesting feature is that many if not all of the Pyramid Texts (and the Coffin Texts, too) were written originally in the first person, and an attempt (not always successful) was made to change the pronoun references to the actual names of the intended owners. This personalization or customizing of the texts was deemed essential to ensure that the owner was fully incorporated into the texts, but the effort involved hundreds of substitutions for each document. Coffins were occasionally reused with incomplete substitution of names, which seems to indicate that some individuals were more interested in the convenience or attractiveness of a second-hand coffin than in personalized textual content.

Manuscripts of the *Book of Going Forth by Day* include not only the name of the deceased with the title of Osiris prefixed to it but also, often, his or her official title in the bureaucracy, with filiation as well. Perhaps because of individual preferences, but also to keep the books' customized appearance, they were generally written to order from beginning to end rather than produced as anonymous shelf copies with spaces left for names to be filled in later. The few drawings or paintings of the deceased in the books can hardly be considered portraits, but with the names and titles of the deceased appended, and their correct gender and proper dress for the time depicted, the purchasers would probably have been satisfied. The cost of the books probably varied considerably, based on the length and height of the scrolls and on the details of workmanship, but the proliferation of short versions, especially from the Late period, suggests that some such guide was available to almost anyone who could afford any burial expenses at all.

The *Book of Going Forth by Day* is perhaps best known for the vignettes that accompany many of its chapters. Some of these drawings, such as the judgment scene of chapter 125, are very elaborate and provide the focal point of the book even when they are not the logical heart of the work. (This vignette, without accompanying text, survives alone on a very late papyrus.) The number of vignettes is far from uniform from copy to copy. In the case of the high priest Pinedjem of the twenty-first dynasty, there is no vignette for any of the chapters following the single introductory depiction of him at the beginning of the book, while in the book of his daughter Nesitanebetisheru, almost every chapter has a rather large though sketchy drawing.

Some manuscripts seem to show that artist and scribe worked separately (even if these tasks were done by the same person), and most frequently the layout of the whole with drawings was done before the texts were added. This, of course, resulted in some dislocation of drawings, and also in the omission or abbreviation of some texts because of lack of available space. There probably were manuscripts that were carefully collated, but there were also texts that had duplications and misreadings or were otherwise garbled; presumably the latter were provided by scribes who knew that the appearance of the document was enough to satisfy a buyer who either would not or could not read it.

It is reasonably clear that some of the utterances in the Pyramid Texts contain labels that were not intended to be complete sentences or part of the text proper. Some of these may have been titles or filing entries to identify the texts, and others were there to label the deities or objects in plans or vignettes that were not depicted in these pyramid sources. It is, of course, possible that the sources (perhaps on papyri) of the Pyramid Texts had rubrics or some vignettes or both, but the Coffin Texts provide the earliest examples of real rubrics written in red; they also have the earliest vignettes, some of which continued into the *Book of Going Forth by Day*.

Today, there are editions and translations of these bodies of texts available for study, but there are problems with each of the publications of the edited versions. For the Pyramid Texts, Kurt Sethe (1908–1922) first collected the utterances from the sarcophagus and burial chamber, then worked out toward the antechamber and entrance. Since it is now clear that the texts were originally set forth to follow the funeral procession into the tomb, Sethe's numbering of the spells essentially goes backwards. The pyramid of Unas (being the earliest to have these texts) was taken as a starting point, but it had only about a third of the known texts, and the new texts found in succeeding pyramids were tacked onto the first lot with little regard to where they belonged logically. R. O. Faulkner's translation in this numerical order, though fairly literal, makes no real sense of the whole. A. Piankoff's translation of the Unas texts is closer to the proper order in proceeding from the entrance inward, but he followed the texts around each room, rather than taking the texts of opposite walls to complement each other, and his translations are in some cases a bit free.

One interesting characteristic of some of the Pyramid Texts, which also survived on some coffins, is the mutilation of most of the hieroglyphic signs representing animate objects. In some cases, these individual hieroglyphs are actually carved as two separate pieces divided by blank space, and in others, the snakes, animals, and other creatures have knives in their backs. These were two practices intended to ensure that the intact animal representations would be unable to offer any threat to the deceased person buried in proximity to them.

In editing the Coffin Texts, A. de Buck and his team had neither an established chronological order to help them, nor beginnings or endings that were consistent from one place to another, or even from one coffin to another from the same place. De Buck logically started with one fairly long sequence of spells that occurred on a comparatively large number of manuscripts. He followed this with succeeding sequences that had the best representation, until eventually he had picked up all the loose ends. Exceptions to this method were the texts on papyri included with the corpus, which were quite logically taken in order, and also the *Book of the Ways of Rosetau* (modernly known as the *Book of Two Ways*), which was recognized as a complete unit regardless of where it occurred on the coffins, though it was generally on the inside bottoms of the coffins from Bersheh. These two lots were numbered and included at the end of the whole collection, though clearly the latter at

least should not have been relegated to this position, and a few spells that belonged with this group had earlier been mistakenly edited separately. Again, a reading or translation of these Coffin Text spells in numerical order has no relation to the arrangement or order of the spells on any manuscript from any of the many places where they were found. Admittedly, it is no easy task to establish an order to these spells: they occur on all six inner faces of the coffins, and in some cases they can be shown to proceed from one side to its opposite parallel wall, and in other cases from one to another contingent sides, while the tops and bottoms generally seem independent.

Among the most difficult problems to resolve in dealing with the Coffin Texts is to establish the precise chronological order of the actual manuscripts, which would probably help in producing stemmata of the texts themselves which would help us better understand the differences among them. Although much development could have taken place in papyrus versions before the texts reached what are essentially definitive versions on the coffins, until the stemmata are worked out, any changes, major or minor, can be seen as going in either direction. Of special interest in the Coffin Texts is the diversity of the texts and their layout in documents from different places, especially since they were found at so many sites throughout Egypt. The coffins from Bersheh have been studied most, but the large number from Meir, and the huge size of the coffins from Siut, make these two sites particularly attractive for further research.

It would seem that the *Book of Going Forth by Day* would have been the easiest of these collections to edit properly; however, the very early publication of one Late period papyrus established an order for the chapters that was not relevant at all to earlier manuscripts. When E. Naville published a number of parallel versions of the much earlier eighteenth dynasty manuscripts, his desire was to establish the best early text of each chapter, but when he numbered them following Richard Lepsius's publication of the Turin Papyrus, he succeeded in destroying the logical arrangement of all the early documents. When newly discovered chapters are merely tacked onto the end of a growing collection, it is clear that translations of the chapters in numerical order keep getting further from any logical order; indeed, modern translators are in no agreement on where to end the *Book of Going Forth by Day*.

Division of the texts into units of varying size was indicated in the original manuscripts in several ways. The vertical columns of hieroglyphs that are the Pyramid Texts generally have horizontal line breaks with small squares atop and to one side of these dividing lines to turn them into "houses" (*hwt*) and thus to indicate textual units, which in this collection are usually termed "utterances." For the Coffin Texts written in cursive hieroglyphs without lines to divide the vertical columns, the unit (known as a "spell") could be indicated either by a bent arm in red or black, or by single or double horizontal strokes. These are often accompanied by rubrics (headings in red) which can either name a spell at its conclusion or otherwise introduce a spell in some form at its beginning. In the *Book of Going Forth by Day*, the units are likewise spells, though commonly termed "chapters" by Egyptologists and these are regularly headed by their assigned rubrics.

Of the three major collections of funerary literature, it is generally clear that these were not separate books in the Egyptian sense, though each could contain books or portions thereof. Many would say that the modern names given to these collections of funerary literature are inaccurate and should be discarded in favor of the ancient names, which survive at least in some cases. The old designation the *Book of the Dead* derives from a label in Arabic that refers to the fact that the books were commonly found with mummies. "The Beginning of the Spells for Going Forth by Day" is the way this "book" starts chapter 1 (and also chapter 17), and even though it is not clear that this describes all the spells rather than merely those at the beginning of the book, it is clear that the ancient Egyptians thought that it applied to the bulk of the work. Because chapter 163 is preceded by "Spells taken from another papyrus as additions to Going Forth by Day," it is fairly clear that in the Late period the original book of that name included the spells through chapter 161. Chapter 162 regularly follows 165 and should be considered part of that added group. It is also clear, then, that this ancient name should not properly be applied to the present entire corpus of 192 chapters.

With respect to the numbering of chapters, it can only be said that any total can be quite misleading. Many chapters have variants that are labeled "A," "B," and so on, but sometimes the variants were actually additional, newly discovered chapters given the number of the preceding identifiable chapter (e.g., chapter 41B). Sometimes the same chapter was given two different numbers, as in the case of 52B and 189; but totally different chapters can have the same numbers as well. The whole series of W. Pleyte's chapters 166–174 have no relationship to the standard chapters with those numbers. It is also clear that many of these supposed additions actually had the titles of other works. Similarly, the rubric title of Spell I, found on perhaps three coffins of the entire Coffin Texts corpus, labels this as the "beginning of the Book of justifying a man in the necropolis." If this were indeed the title for the bulk of the texts, it is strange that no form of "judgment scene" is to be found anywhere in that corpus. It can also be pointed out that there are other books in the Coffin Texts, including the *Book of the Ways of Rosetau* (otherwise known as the *Book of Two Ways*), which is both labeled as a book and has a typical colophon at its conclusion. A similar colophon is found on one coffin after Spell 467, indicating that this *Field of Ḥetep* spell or spells may also have been considered a book.

The book of the *Field of Ḥetep* is one of the more interesting units included in both the Coffin Texts (Spells 464– 468) and the *Book of Going Forth by Day* (chapter 110). Ḥetep can be singular or plural and determined by either a deity or a bookroll or offerings, which means that it can refer to the god named Ḥetep, who presides over this field, or it can mean "peace" or "offerings." There are references to the field in the Pyramid Texts, and the earliest description of the place, which seems to have been located in the western sky, presents it as a place where the deceased person lives and works for the god Osiris. The field has an abundance of water and is very productive, and in the Coffin Texts it was a sort of Elysian fields, or a paradise, where the deceased can enjoy a pleasant existence in the hereafter. The spells in the Coffin Texts that deal with the *Field of Ḥetep* are essentially different versions of the same text and vignette. On some coffins from Bersheh, the plan of the field seems to mark the starting point for the whole collection of texts. The *Book of Going Forth by Day* version, which can be much more elaborate than any version of the Coffin Texts, is for some reason found preceding the judgment scene (chapter 125) in the standard order of chapters on Late period manuscripts.

Some chapters in the *Book of Going Forth by Day* had a life of their own. One example is chapter 30, the heart spell, which is carved on stone amulets placed within the mummy's thoracic cavity before wrapping. Another is chapter 6, found on countless *shawabtis*, which were mummiform statuettes intended to act for the deceased with respect to any task that he might be called on to perform in the afterlife. In the Late period, chapter 162 was used separately under the head of the mummy to provide warmth.

Chapter 17 of the *Book of Going Forth by Day* has one of that work's most unique and interesting features—glosses. The development of these glosses can be traced fairly clearly in a large number of Middle Kingdom coffins with essentially the same material (i.e., Coffin Texts, Spell 335). This particular text has a number of rubrics, with questions about the meaning of each phrase, and it includes two or three quite different interpretations as answers to each question. These glosses indicate the difficulty that the Egyptians would have had in understanding some of the mythological and theological allusions in these texts; they also show how the proponents of different temples, gods, or religions could read and understand the same words entirely differently, entirely from their own perspectives. Some answers are strictly solar and others are Osirian, and some are less clear, but all these interpretive glosses, which may originally have been marginal notations, became part of the standard text and remained with it for the next two thousand years of Egyptian history.

Clearly, the fact that the standard text had occasionally become unintelligible would have been recognized by some scribes who could have corrected it— but apparently they did not dare to change it. For the really intractable sections of the *Book of Going Forth by Day*, most modern translators have opted to translate any available earlier parallels in the Coffin Texts, which generally make much better sense; but these were, of course, not the actual words copied for so many centuries.

The *Book of That Which Is in the Underworld* (*Amduat*) is generally a New Kingdom guidebook to the beyond that takes on significance as the principal such work in the royal tombs of the eighteenth dynasty. A portion of the work was included in the *Book of Two Ways*, which is dated at least to the early Middle Kingdom and probably earlier; and its inclusion of Sokar, the funerary god of Saqqara, the necropolis at Memphis, would seem to point to an Old Kingdom origin. Novelty, antiquity, and the illustrative nature of the work may all have helped bring it to the fore. The work itself is not a unity but has at least two and probably three or more versions. Two versions appear first in Thutmose III's tomb in the Valley of the Kings: one is the well-known painting of an enlarged papyrus roll surrounding the walls of the burial chamber, and the other comprises individually named deities in more than seven hundred boxes drawn on the walls of the antechamber to the tomb. The King's "papyrus roll" version has a cosmological plan that depicts the voyage and daily rebirth of the sun, with registers, passages with doors and keepers, and Sokar's mound—all to illustrate what was to be encountered in the afterlife journey. Shorter versions of this plan on actual papyri in different sizes belonging to the elite became fairly

commonplace, especially in the twenty-first dynasty, and there are also a number of what are termed the "real" *Amduat* papyri, which have long rows of standing anthropomorphic deities.

The *Book of Gates* is the principal guidebook found in nineteenth dynasty royal tombs. The emphasis is on the gates with guardian deities, whose names must be known in order to pass them. This is an elaborate representation of what was a very old tradition, dating at least to the *Book of Two Ways* in the Coffin Texts, where there are seven gates with three keepers each, which became two different lists that survived separately as chapters 144 and 147 of the *Book of Going Forth by Day*. The Ramessid versions have twelve gates corresponding to the twelve hours of the night, which are also depicted in the star-clocks on the ceilings of the burial chambers.

The *Book of Caverns* is a later Ramessid (twentieth dynasty) underworld book that shows people in holes or caves, as well as some drowning in water or bound to stakes. As if everything before had been too easy and all the worthy deceased had succeeded in attaining their goals, this guidebook seems to be trying to show that not everyone makes it. It is certainly more threatening, and perhaps it is appropriate that it appears in very elaborate tombs just before the end of pharaonic Egypt.

The *Book of the Heavenly Cow* (its earliest version coming from Tutankhamun's tomb) begins as a mythological text, which relates how the aging sun god Re, distressed by the plotting of humans against him, takes counsel with the eldest gods and sends his eye, Hathor, to diminish the number of people on earth. Hathor was enjoying her task too much, but Re had a change of heart and provided beer as a substitute for blood to bring an end to her slaughtering. This is an etiology for the feast of Hathor and the concomitant beer-drinking, the propitiation for evildoing, and the sacrifice to ward off suffering—all are involved in this part of the text. In the next episode, Nut is the cow on whose back Re goes forth to overthrow his enemies. Riding high in the sky, Re makes Nut a multitude, and stars come into being, along with the Fields of H. etep and Iarru ("reeds"). Re gets Shu ("air") and the Hdeh gods to support the wobbly sky goddess, providing a picturesque cosmological description. The next scene brings in Geb the earth god, snakes, and the need for magic spells as protection against them. When eventually it is said that he who knows these divine words and spells will go forth and come down from the sky, it is clear that like the other funerary books, this is a guidebook for the deceased who joins Re and who must know the heavenly topography, names, spells, and so on, as magical means for "going forth by day." The book has clear ties to the Pyramid Texts, Coffin Texts, and the *Book of Going Forth by Day*; what sets it apart is its unity, its humanized deities, and its picturesque literary style. There is also the aspect of divine punishment for the evil that people do.

Stelae are generally much better sources for information on personal piety than for funerary literature, and even instructional literature such as the *Instructions for Merikare* can provide much better ethical material. The one section of the funerary literature that provides the closest thing we have to a code of ethics or morality is the so-called Negative Confession, which is really a protestation of innocence (*Book of the Dead*, 125). As part of the judgment scene, where the heart of the deceased is weighed against the Feather of the goddess Maat (truth

personified), these claims of innocence are addressed to forty-two judges—the number is presumably related to the number of nomes or districts of Upper and Lower Egypt. Of the divine judges from perhaps two dozen identifiable places, however, the vast majority are from the northern half of the country, with several locations mentioned twice. In addition to Heliopolis and Memphis as sites of major importance for the creation and compilation of funerary literature, Hermopolis and Herakleopolis may also have been particularly important for several of the books found in the Coffin Texts, and also for the *Book of Going Forth by Day*, chapters such as 64 and 175. The evils that the deceased says were not done by him or her in the Negative Confession include several generalizations such as "evil" or "wrongdoing"; many evils, such as robbery, killing, lying, cheating, stealing, doing violence, reviling the king or "god," or committing adultery; some less serious crimes, such as being ill-tempered, eavesdropping, being garrulous, inspiring terror, dissembling, gossiping, being puffed up or being loud-voiced; and some we cannot clearly understand as evils, such as wading in the water or washing the god. The practicing of homosexuality was a specified evil, though nothing was said about the mistreatment of either parents or children. Certain of the evils were specifically excepted when done in self-defense.

Of course, much of what has been said about the individuality of these collections of texts and their association with different periods is based on what has survived and how this material was published. Thus, the Pyramid Texts on Middle Kingdom coffins were omitted from the Coffin Texts publications—even when in some cases these were predominant—and these and almost all other later occurrences of the Pyramid Texts still remain unpublished.

It is clear that new discoveries could considerably change our thinking about the origins and applications of the various texts. The discovery of the tomb of Tutankhamun revealed no papyri and comparatively little of a documentary nature, but the four golden shrines that were nested to encase his sarcophagus and coffins contain excerpts from a whole cross-section of the funerary literature. Texts that we identify specifically as Pyramid Texts, Coffin Texts, and *Book of Going Forth by Day*, as well as the *Book of That Which Is in the Underworld* and the *Book of the Heavenly Cow*, all occur together on these shrines. The distinction between royal and nonroyal texts was probably not strictly maintained at any time, although it appears to us that certain texts first used for royalty later became more proletarian and that this led the priests serving the royals to seek out and in, some cases, produce new and different texts for their patrons.

All in all, ancient Egyptian funerary literature is far from being exhaustively studied. Many documents have not been published, and most have still not been studied as logical entities. Only after these basic first steps have been taken can the interrelationships of the various texts be analyzed and perhaps understood, at least a little better.　*Leonard H. Lesko*

FUNERARY RITUAL. Rituals performed by the living for the dead were one of the principal ways that the ancient Egyptians insured their immortality after death. We know of these rituals through their depiction (or partial depiction) on tomb-chapel walls, and through ritual scripts preserved in underground portions of tombs (for example, in the Pyramid Texts) or on papyrus. Other aspects of the rituals must be deduced from administrative accounts and from references in nonmortuary texts or from the architecture of the spaces in which the rituals were performed and the placement of the texts that decorate those spaces. There are two sets of funerary rituals, which overlap and are often difficult for Egyptologists to distinguish. "Funeral rituals" were performed only once, at the funeral of the deceased; these rituals included any ceremonies connected with the process of embalming and interment and any other rituals that required access to the sealed part of the tomb. They probably also included the processional journeys with the mummy (or a statue substitute) and various farewell gestures by the family of the deceased. The second type of rituals were performed after the funeral, either by cult functionaries maintained by a perpetual mortuary endowment or by family members or others visiting the deceased at the tomb-chapel. Ideally, many of these "mortuary cult rituals" would have been performed daily, as they were in the mortuary temples of dead kings of the Old Kingdom period. (In a royal context, the rituals may have been begun before the death of the king, to maintain his cult statues.) Other rituals seem to have been offered more rarely, on special occasions, such as festivals and on other regularly recurring dates, as given in the lists of festivals that were sometimes recorded in tomb-chapel decoration. The full set of mortuary cult rituals was probably performed for the first time at the funeral itself, although possibly some cult rituals were performed only on particular occasions or festivals and not at the funeral. Some dates may have required full repetitions of the cult ritual, while other performances may have been perfunctory. Such variations in performance are impossible to demonstrate.

It is also often difficult to determine which of the rituals depicted in funerals were repeated as part of the mortuary cult. Moreover, the types of rituals used under various circumstances probably changed with time. One funerary ritual that is particularly well attested, the Opening of the Mouth ceremony, seems constantly to have been augmented by reinterpretations and borrowings from other realms of ritual; probably, the developmental evolution of other, less well-attested, rituals was similarly complex. Our limited sources have left us with a set of rituals that is undoubtedly incomplete. Some rituals may have had a secret or particularly sacred character that prohibited their representation, whereas others may have been omitted from tomb-chapel depictions for other reasons.

In most periods, a distinction must be drawn between the rituals performed for kings and those performed for other Egyptians. The general pattern seems to be that rituals appeared first in a royal context, were then adopted by the elite, and eventually by the rest of the population. This "democratization of the afterlife," though well attested archaeologically, may not reflect actual practice; the general population possibly performed rituals that decorum forbade them to record. Given that the king and his people shared a system of beliefs about the afterlife (however those beliefs varied from period to period), the rituals performed for the king probably shared many fundamental elements with the less elaborate rituals performed for his subjects.

Old Kingdom. The most fundamental mortuary cult ritual is the earliest attested; this is the *ḥtp di nswt* offering

formula, which begins "an offering that the king gives." (The formula is not limited to nonroyal contexts, since the king it mentions is presumably the living king, who may be asked to make offerings to his royal predecessors.) The earliest examples, from the fourth dynasty at Meidum, do not mention the king, but only the mortuary god Anubis (*ḥtp dj Jnpw*); however, the king appears very soon thereafter, although he is often joined in his gift by various gods (normally Anubis and, after the middle of the fifth dynasty, Osiris). The gifts are not limited to food offerings but extend to a good burial and admission to the realm of the spirits. The formula recorded on tomb walls often includes a list of festivals at which the offerings are to be provided. An example of such an offering formula would be that of Ankhhaf (see *British Museum Hieroglyphic Texts l2*, London, 1961, pl. 15), which reads, *ḥtp dj nswt ḥtp dj Jnpw ḫnt t3 ḏsr qrst.f m smyt jmntt prt-ḫrw n.f t ḥnqt k3w 3pdw m wp rmpt, ḏḥwtj, tp rmpt, w3g m ḥb nb rˁ nb, n rḥ nswt zš pr-ḥḏ ˁnḫ ḫ3f*, and which translates, "An offering that the king gives and an offering that Anubis, foremost of the sacred land, gives: his burial in the Western Desert and invocation offerings of bread, beer, cattle, and fowl, on the opening of the year feast, the feast of Thoth, the first of the year feast, the *wag* feast and on every festival and every day, to the king's acquaintance and scribe of the treasury Ankhhaf." This formula seems to imply that only the king and the gods can give offerings to the dead, and that the wish that they do so is likely to benefit the deceased person for whom it is made.

The recitation of the offering formula is illustrated in tombs by a man standing with his right arm outstretched. In Old Kingdom scenes depicting the entire offering ritual, he is often accompanied by men who are offering poured water, burning incense, kneeling at an offering table, and reading the ritual from a scroll. Men reciting the formula are occasionally identified as lector-priests (ẖrjw-ḥb), and the men reading from the scroll are invariably so identified. Three men are shown kneeling, beating their breasts with clenched fists; the fourth dynasty representations clearly show the arms in motion, while later renderings are more static, showing the men with one fist held against the chest and another raised behind the head, with the arm bent at a right angle. These men are usually identified as embalmers (wtw) but may also be called lector-priests. Several of these actions may be captioned sꜣḥt ("causing to be a spirit"), which indicates that these rituals were responsible for transforming the dead person into an akh (ꜣḥ), a glorified, ghostlike spirit. Another part of the ritual, not depicted but often mentioned in the caption, is the "breaking of the red jars," presumably to keep away bad influences. At the end of the ritual, a man is often depicted walking away from the cult place, dragging a broom behind him (although the caption says he is "bringing the leg"). This action removed any footprints or other traces of the ritual activity and left the offering place pristine and ready for the next repetition of the ritual. The sixth dynasty tomb-chapel of Qar shows two additional parts of the ritual, as illustrated in William Kelly Simpson's *Mastabas of Qar and Idu* (Boston, 1976, plate 25). First, a priest with little fingers outstretched in front of him is followed by a man carrying three jars on a little table. The caption tells us that he is anointing with oil, but it is unclear what is being anointed. Another man brings two strips of cloth, labelled wnḥw.

A fuller complement of mortuary rituals from the Old Kingdom period is the corpus of Pyramid Texts, which are first attested in the pyramid of Unas at the end of the fifth dynasty. While many of the rituals recorded there may have been considerably older, the many spells incorporating the deities Osiris and Isis had, presumably, been recently composed or adapted from older texts, since Osiris is first attested only a few decades before the reign of Unas. (Indeed, it was probably his growing ascendance and the consequent increased emphasis on the underground parts of the tomb that led to the recording of the texts on the walls of the burial chambers.) The Pyramid Texts seem to consist of both magical spells to be used by the deceased and two rituals that were probably performed at the funeral. The spells include those for the protection of the deceased and those for the transportation of the king to the realm of the gods and his rebirth in the afterlife; they are recorded in the third person, but they seem to have been adapted from spells written in the first person. The king is identified throughout as the god Osiris, and the speaker acts as his son Horus. There are two rituals carved on the walls of the burial chamber that address the king in the second person, thereby suggesting that they were performed before his mummy or a statue surrogate. The sequence on the northern wall is an offering ritual that presents the king with offerings, after first magically enabling him to partake of them by means of the Opening of the Mouth ceremony. Each ritual act (including the Opening of the Mouth sequence) was accompanied by an offering, usually of food but sometimes of ritual equipment. The southern wall shows a ritual for bringing about the dead king's resurrection. The offering ritual, at least, was also performed as part of the mortuary cult. The offerings that accompany the addresses to the king are identical with the compartmental offering list, which dates back to the fourth dynasty, although the Opening of the Mouth sequence was omitted until the reign of Sahure. The shorter versions of such compartmental offering lists (Barta's [1963] Type A list) also found in nonroyal tombs of the Old Kingdom, suggesting that a version of the same ritual was performed in nonroyal cults. The administrative papyri found at the mortuary temple of King Neferirkare at Abusir also list the nonperishable equipment for the offering ritual in monthly inventories, including notations of damage and wear, which demonstrate that the equipment was in regular use. Such equipment also occurs archeologically, in both royal and private contexts.

At about the same time that the Pyramid Texts began to appear in royal tombs, nonroyal tombs began to depict aspects of the funeral more extensively. These scenes usually begin with one of mourning at the home of the deceased (men and women mourned separately). The coffin is then carried to a special funerary boat, called the *wrt*-boat, which was towed by an ordinary boat. Throughout these travels, the coffin was accompanied by two women called *drt* (one of whom was probably the wife of the deceased), as well as the embalmer (who sometimes clapped sticks together as he walked) and the lector-priest. The boat was towed to a riverside building, with two entrances, where offerings are depicted. This building is in some sources called *tp-jbw*, which has been translated "purification tent." It may be here that the mummification of the body took place. Afterward, the coffin was carried to the desert in the hands of the mourners, with supporting poles held by formally dressed pallbearers. In some cases, this scene includes a row of vaulted shrines and palm trees that are usually associated with the Nile Delta city of Buto. The goal of this procession was the shrinelike building called the *w'bt*, where an offering ritual was performed. *Muvu*-dancers perform outside the enclosure, often wearing tall openwork headdresses; and the wife, lector-priest, and embalmer make offerings on the altar of the *w'bt*, often slaughtering bulls and oryxes for the occasion. Some scenes label this building not *w'bt* but *z3w*, identifying it (symbolically) with a shrine in another Delta city, Sais. The *w'bt* is usually the last element in these scenes. The funeral presumably moved on to the tomb after the completion of the rituals (if indeed the *w'bt* is not itself the tomb). Scenes of the rituals at the tomb (not usually attached to the preceding processions) suggest that the last stages of the ritual took place on the roof of the *mastaba*, before the body and the *serdab* statues were lowered into the burial shaft and the *serdab* chambers.

Middle Kingdom. Middle Kingdom funerary texts offer fewer clues to the nature of funeral and mortuary cult rituals than do those of the previous period. The Coffin Texts consist largely of a greatly expanded number of the transportation spells of the Pyramid Texts; neither the incantations nor the ritual texts were recorded. The compartmental offering list, derived from the offering ritual, continues to appear, including the implements used in the Opening of the Mouth ceremony. In at least one Middle Kingdom tomb, the offerings were accompanied by depictions of the men who were offering them. The *Book of Two Ways*, found on coffins from Bersheh, depicts the journey to the underworld by the deceased—a journey that may have been acted out in the course of the funeral.

Although it may have taken place earlier, it has been suggested that there was a major change in the offering formula (ḥtp dj nswt) during this period. Whereas previously the king and various gods were jointly desired to give offerings to the deceased, the Middle Kingdom version suggests that the king was asked to make an offering to the gods, so that they might in turn supply offerings to the deceased. The funeral itself was less often depicted in the Middle Kingdom tombs than it was in late Old Kingdom tombs; however, the scenes resemble those known from the Old Kingdom, with the addition of some new elements, such as the figure known as the *tekenu* (*tknw*). In the Middle Kingdom, the *tekenu* appears to be a crouching figure with its limbs and torso wrapped in a striped material, which may represent an animal skin, but its head is left free. Later, in the New Kingdom, the head is sometimes also wrapped, resulting in a pear-shaped bundle; at other times, an arm as well as the head is free, or it is simply a nude human figure. All these depictions presumably represent the same thing: a human figure wrapped in a skin. In later depictions of the period, the *tekenu* can be attended by a priest of the scorpion goddess Serket, and this, together with other textual indications, seems to connect the *tekenu* with the Delta region. Its function in the funerary ritual is unknown, but it has often been suggested that it functioned as a symbolic human sacrifice. Its fetal position and its proximity in some scenes to the basin of the birth goddess Heket has also led some to suggest a connection with birth and rebirth.

The coffin was also carried differently in Middle Kingdom depictions. Rather than traveling at waist height, held on carrying poles, it was dragged on a sledge by oxen and men or, in one case, placed on a wagon. Another addition to the Middle Kingdom offering scenes is the reproduction of some of the ritual speeches spoken by the participants in the funeral. A textual account of a Middle Kingdom private funeral is to be found in the *Story of Sinhue*. It mentions an ox-drawn procession accompanied by musicians, and *muw* dancers at the door of the tomb. An offering ritual is read aloud, and then animals are sacrificed. Although brief, the text agrees with the depictions.

Royal funerary ritual during the Middle Kingdom period is less well attested than private funerals. Nevertheless, the tortuous routes of many of the pyramid entrances of the period have been connected with the complicated maps of the underworld found in nonroyal Coffin Texts; passing through the barriers may have been part of the rites. Overall, royal ritual was probably not unlike the private rituals, particularly since private individuals became identified with Osiris in the Middle Kingdom in the same way that kings and queens had been in the late Old Kingdom.

New Kingdom. Funerals and mortuary cult rituals of the New Kingdom are often depicted in the wall scenes of painted tombs, both in Memphis and Thebes. Episodes from the funeral are also sometimes depicted on anthropoid (human-shaped) coffins, particularly in the early New Kingdom and the Third Intermediate period. In addition, there is a new, more extensive depiction of the Opening of the Mouth ceremony, which is sometimes used in tomb-chapel decoration.

In this later period, the funeral seems to have become more elaborate, or perhaps it was just more fully represented. The order of the elements of the funeral is uncertain and may have varied. The departure of the coffin from the house and its journey across the river to the cemetery and the place of mummification were presumably among the earlier parts of the ceremony. The coffin was placed on a canopied sledge, often pulled by both oxen and male mourners; it was accompanied by a group of priests, including a *stm*-priest, wearing a leopard skin, and the *jmj-ḫnt* priest, wearing a short white robe that resembled the royal *sed*-festival (Jubilee) garment. Two women were often part of the procession. Interestingly, scenes do not include depictions of the bringing of the food and sacrificial animals that must have been part of the actual procession.

The wall scenes of the procession include the four canopic jars that held the four internal organs removed from the body (lungs, liver, stomach, and intestines). The jars were generally shown placed in a small shrine that was dragged on a sledge some distance behind the coffin; some of the men who accompanied this sledge are depicted carrying papyrus stalks. Also dragged on a sledge was the *tekenu* figure. The final (though not necessarily the last) elements of the procession were the women who wept and wailed in mourning and the men who carried the furniture and other grave goods of the deceased. The furniture-bearers were sometimes preceded by four men, each carrying a small statue (two of the statues were mummiform and wore the red crown).

After leaving the house of the deceased, the procession went aboard a special boat, which was towed by another boat or by people on a riverside towpath. The boat carried the procession to the *sḥ ntr Jnpw*, the divine booth of Anubis—probably to be equated with the purification tent of earlier representations. Since Anubis was the god responsible for overseeing mummification, it was probably there that the body was embalmed. Afterward, the procession continued to the *jˁbt wsḫt*, the broad hall

of purification, which can probably be equated with the *wˁbt* of the Old Kingdom. Unlike the procession to the *wˁbt*, however, the procession to the *jˁbt wsḫt* seems to have traveled by boat. The rituals performed there were less clearly shown than those in Old Kingdom scenes, and the building no longer seems connected with the city of Sais, which was accorded its own separate ritual. While the Old Kingdom ritual had hinted at associations with both Buto and Sais, the New Kingdom depictions included explicit ritual visits to those Delta cities, as well as to Heliopolis and the Upper Egyptian city of Abydos. Such pilgrimages may in actuality have been carried out separately, before death or afterward, using statues as substitutes for the mummy; or they may have been made symbolically to places that had been designated to represent those cities. (In the case of kings, such voyages may actually have been made, to demonstrate the death of the king and legitimize his successor's assumption of the kingship.) The voyage to the site designated as Sais was made on a boat. There, oxen joined the procession to pull the coffin on its sledge and to be sacrificed. The procession continued by land to the place designated Buto, probably within the cemetery. The coffin was either dragged on a sledge or, in the later New Kingdom, placed in a model boat and carried on the shoulders of the bearers. At the Buto site, they were received by *muwu*-dancers who were only rarely depicted wearing the tall headdresses of earlier periods. The visit to Heliopolis took place by boat, and it may represent a real pilgrimage, one undertaken separately and merely added to the funeral scenes. The pilgrimage to Abydos was also undertaken separately, perhaps by a statue of the deceased. (Neither of these voyages is attested in the Old Kingdom.)

On arriving at the tomb, the mummy (or perhaps the anthropoid coffin) was removed from its box coffin and set upright to receive the blessings of the ritual. Ritual actions shown here include censing, libations, and selected episodes from the Opening of the Mouth. (The fuller sequence of the Opening of the Mouth ceremony is usually depicted separately from the funeral scenes, but it may have been carried out at this time.) Women belonging to the family of the deceased are often shown weeping and embracing the coffin during these ceremonies. Other rituals followed. These included the pulling of the (empty) sarcophagus back and forth by a *ka*-priest, who pulled it to the north, and the embalmer, who pulled it to the south. The *tekenu* on its sledge was also pulled back and forth, accompanied by some enigmatic ritual statements by the *s3-Srḳt* priest or the *jmj-ḥnt* priest. The mummy, sarcophagus, *tekenu*, and canopic chest (which held the four canopic jars) were then presented with offerings, including the sacrificed animals. The sarcophagus, mummy, and canopic chest were then probably introduced into the tomb, along with the funerary furniture. The ceremony closed with protective ritual recitations. At the same time, in other parts of the necropolis, animals were sacrificed to ensure the safety of the deceased—sacrifices that involved the mysterious *tekenu*.

Although during the New Kingdom, private funerals and mortuary cult rituals were comparatively well documented, there is very little evidence for these rituals in the royal context. The tomb of Tutankhamun contains a rare depiction of the king's funeral cortege on the eastern wall of the burial chamber. There, the king's coffin lies on a bier, covered by an open canopy decorated with garlands, banners, and royal *uraeus* snakes;

the whole rests on a boat dragged on a sledge pulled by twelve men, including two shaven-headed priests. The caption tells us that the priests are chanting "Nebkheperure, come in peace! O god, may the earth protect (him)!" Adjacent to this, on the northern wall of the chamber, Tutankhamun's successor, King Ay, is shown with an adze, performing the Opening of the Mouth ceremony. These scenes, which are almost identical to those found in private tombs, suggest that Tutankhamun's funeral was not too unlike those of his wealthier subjects.

Royal mortuary cult rituals may have differed more significantly from those in the private realm. They were carried out far from the royal tombs in the Valley of the Kings, in temples built for the purpose. In such temples, the principal shrine belonged to the god Amun, while Re was worshiped in an open courtyard to the north and the king shared a cult place to the south with his ancestors. This southern shrine contained a traditional false door to serve as a cult place, but the overall architecture and decoration of the temples suggest that the rituals were less mortuary and more divine.

Late Period. The depiction of the funeral became rare in the Late period, although decorated tombs such as that of Petosiris at Tuna el-Gebel still contain such scenes. They differ from the New Kingdom examples only in that they often incorporated motifs from earlier periods, combining them with the later. It is not certain whether these scenes reflect the actual practices of the period or are just copied from older prototypes. One part of the funerary ritual that was not attested in the earlier periods is the embalming ritual. Two texts of this ritual have survived, both dating from the first or early second century CE. The ritual contains both practical and religious instructions for mummification. It begins with the perfuming of the head and the body, with spells referring to the divine scent of the gods and the body's receipt of ten sacred oils. The canopic organs are removed, and again the ten oils are mentioned. The body is again anointed and partially wrapped, while spells mention the unguents and the amulets that are placed on it. While the nails of the hands and feet are gilded, spells are recited to ensure the freedom of action of the hands and feet. After a last anointing, the wrapping of the head is begun. Accompanying spells guarantee the functioning of the eyes, mouth, ears, and nose, as the oil from the anointing soaks into them.

The final anointing of the head accompanies spells to ensure that the deceased will appear triumphant in the netherworld and will not be deprived of his head. The hands are then wrapped, with spells protecting the entire mummy of the deceased and assuring that the deities Isis and Nephthys are mourning and helping him. Finally, the legs and feet are anointed, perfumed, and wrapped, while spells are recited rendering them effective and allowing the deceased to walk. Concluding spells ensure the resurrection and rejuvenation of the deceased.

Ann Macy Roth

G

GEB. As god of the Earth, Geb plays a crucial role in the Egyptian cosmogony; he is the planet personified. On his back, which forms the globe, vegetation is cultivated. He has been likened to the god Chronus in classical mythology.

Geb is the product of the divine alliance of Shu, the god of the air, and Tefnut, the goddess of moisture; both were created by the sun god Atum-Re. Geb has been referred to as the "father of the gods"; his union with his twin sister, Nut, goddess of the sky, spawned some of the most prominent deities in Egyptian mythology—Osiris, Isis, Seth, and Nephthys. He is a member of the Ennead of Heliopolis, a group composed of the nine most important divinities venerated by the priests of the city. The others are his four sons, as well as Nut, Tefnut, Shu, and Atum-Re. This cult was closely connected to the religious interests of the pharaoh.

Geb's father, Shu, disapproved of Geb's relationship with Nut. He set out to split the two. Geb was deeply saddened by this loss and his many tears formed the oceans. Above the earth, there was the sky, and below, the underworld. This is represented by a figural composition in which Shu (the air, the void) is supported by the goddess Nut (the sky) and beneath her lies Geb, the earth.

Geb's two sons Osiris, the god of order, and Seth, the god of chaos, are involved in the greatest Egyptian mythological conflict: the power-hungry Seth brutally murders Osiris. Their father judges the case when it is tried before the Heliopolitan gods. Geb's mythological rule was fraught with other problems. A tale involving the god Re illustrates these troubles. Geb finds a gilded chest containing the uraeus of Re, which has been placed with Re's hair and staff at the country's border to ward off evil forces. When the case is opened, a snake lunges out. Its breath kills all Geb's friends. Although Geb survives, he is seriously harmed. His injuries can only be repaired by the magic strands of Re's hair—so powerful that they cure him on contact. Upon recovery, the god of the earth is again a prudent ruler and administrator.

Geb is involved in the cult of the dead. He is said to travel through the sky with Atum-Re as a member of the crew in his solar boat. In representations, Geb wears the crown of Lower Egypt. He is also seen with a goose on his head. He is sometimes referred to as "the Great Cackler"; according to myth, he laid the egg that hatched into the Sun. As a "divine pharaoh," Geb was succeeded by his son, Osiris, and then by Horus. All the mortal rulers of dynastic Egypt viewed him as their noble ancestor. His image appears on the walls of the third dynasty temple of the pharaoh Djoser in Heliopolis, among others.

Catherine Simon

H

HATHOR. The goddess Hathor was one of the most important and popular members of the Egyptian pantheon. She was most commonly represented as a cow goddess. Her manifestations and associated activities were numerous and diverse, and complementary aspects such as love and hate, or creation and destruction, characterized her from the earliest stages of her worship. Because she was a prehistoric goddess, the origins of her nature and her cult are difficult to discern, but her existence is evident from prehistoric times continuously through the period of Roman domination. Her aspects incorporated animals, vegetation, the sky, the sun, trees, and minerals, and she governed over the realms of love, sex, and fertility, while also maintaining a vengeful aspect capable of the destruction of humanity.

Hathor's name in Egyptian, *Ḥwt Ḥr*, means "House of Horus" and is written in hieroglyphs with the rectangular sign for a building, with the falcon symbol of Horus inside. The imagery of Hathor emphasizes her primary manifestation as a cow goddess. She most often appears as a female figure wearing a headdress comprised of a sun disk with an appended *uraeus* set between two tall cows' horns. In later times this headdress often incorporates two tall feathers standing between the horns; or she may wear a vulture cap or the hieroglyph for "west," depending on the context of her depiction. She very often wears a *menat*, a necklace made of many strings of beads counterbalanced by a heavy pendant at the back. Hathor is also frequently depicted as a cow; the Hathor cow usually bears the sun disk between its horns and wears the menat necklace. A third type of image of Hathor is a female face seen from the front, with the ears of a cow and a curling or tripartite wig. This face appears on certain types of votive objects and can form the capitals of columns in temples to the goddess. The back-to-back version may have originated from the cult object of another cow goddess, Bat, whose similar iconography was absorbed by Hathor by the eleventh dynasty.

The roots of Hathor's cult may be found in the predynastic cow cults, in which wild cows were venerated as embodiments of nature and fertility. Even in early images of her, the multiplicity of Hathor's aspects is apparent. For example, the rim of a stone urn from Hierakonpolis, dated to the first dynasty, is decorated with the face of a cow goddess with stars at the tips of its horns and ears, a reference to her role (or that of Bat) as a sky-goddess (compare also the Narmer Palette). This role may be linked to her relationship to Horus: since he was a sun and sky god, she, as his "house," resided in the sky as well. Evidence for this belief appears in the funerary texts: as early as the Pyramid Texts, the pharaoh is said

Diorite head of a statue of Hathor, depicted with a cow head, eighteenth dynasty, reign of Amenhotpe III. Between her horns is the sun disk (which may refer to her roles as both the daughter and the eyes of the sun god Re). (The Metropolitan Museum of Art, Rogers Fund, 1919 [19.2.5])

to ascend to Hathor in the sky, and later, in the Coffin Texts, the nonroyal deceased also engage her there.

An ivory engraving from the first dynasty shows a recumbent cow and is inscribed "Hathor in the Marshes of King Djer's city of Dep (Buto)," reflecting Hathor's association with the papyrus marsh and vegetation in general. Hathor was also a tree goddess, and from the Old Kingdom was called "Mistress of the Sycamore." Her role as tree goddess complemented her aspect as cow goddess, allowing her to embody all the creative and fertile qualities of the natural world. The tree goddess was also important to the deceased, to whom she offered shade and a drink from her branches. Hathor's aspect as tree goddess originated in the Nile Delta, and in this role she had a close relationship with Ptah, a creator god from Memphis. A procession in the New Kingdom brought Ptah to visit Hathor, then referred to as his daughter.

Hathor was also a goddess associated with love, sex, and fertility. On another ivory engraving from the first dynasty, a front-facing Hathor is flanked by signs for the god Min, a god identified with fertility, indicating their affiliation. The Greeks likened her to Aphrodite, their own goddess of love and beauty. Numerous hymns praise her and the joy and love for which she was responsible, and in these she is often addressed as *Nb.(t)*. "the Golden One," a name whose origins and intent are uncertain. Throughout the history of her cult, Hathor received as offerings a variety of fertility figurines, as well as votive phalli, and she was viewed as a source of assistance in conception and birth. One of her epithets was "Lady of the Vulva," and she appears in medical texts as well as prayers in relation to pregnancy and childbirth.

Hathor was an important funerary goddess. In Thebes she was called "Mistress of the West" or the "Western Mountain," referring to the mortuary area on the west bank of the Nile. Her prominent role in funerary imagery and ritual was strongly connected with her role in promoting fertility. It was believed that Hathor, as the night sky, received Re each night on the western horizon and protected him within her body so that he could be safely reborn each morning. Based on this divine paradigm, Hathor was seen as a source for rebirth and regeneration of all the deceased, royal and nonroyal, and they all hoped for similar protection from her.

Hathor was also associated with the mountains in the Sinai, where the Egyptians mined for turquoise and copper. The "cave of Hathor" formed the core of her temple at Serabit el-Khadim, where she was worshipped as "Mistress of Turquoise." She was also worshipped at the copper mines at Timna, a site on the eastern edge of the Sinai Peninsula. Hathor's popularity extended out of Egypt to foreign cities; she was worshipped as "Mistress of Byblos" at that city on the eastern coast of the Mediterranean Sea. Because the prehistoric cow cults from which Hathor's cult emerged existed throughout the country, her original cult center is difficult to determine. Her cult may have originated in the Delta region, where her son Horus also had an important role, and she is known from the site of Kom el-Hisn. Dendera in Upper Egypt was an important early site of Hathor, where she was worshipped as "Mistress of Dendera (*Iunt*)." Meir and Kusae were also important cult sites from the Old Kingdom and later. Based on the distribution of titles within her cult, it appears that the Giza–Saqqara area was the focus of the cult in the Old Kingdom. By the First Intermediate Period, however, that focus had shifted southward, and from then on Dendera served as the cult center of Hathor. Evidence indicates that a temple existed there from the Old Kingdom, and a temple structure of some sort was maintained continuously through the time of the major Greco–Roman temple that still stands today. At Dendera, Hathor had a close relationship with Horus of Edfu, a nearby site. In this case she was not mother but consort to Horus, and had with him two children, Ihy and Harsomtus.

Deir el-Bahri, on the western bank of Thebes, was also an important cult site of Hathor. The area was the site of a popular cow cult prior to the Middle Kingdom. This cow goddess was specified as Hathor in the eleventh dynasty when the pharaoh Nebheptre-Montuhotpe built his mortuary temple there. He closely identified himself with the falcon god Horus and took the title "Son of Hathor, Lady of Dendera"; he also built temples to Hathor at Dendera and Gebelein. In the New Kingdom, both Hatshepsut and Thutmose III built their mortuary temples at Deir el-Bahri, and both temples incorporated Hathor shrines. Hathor was worshipped as a cow at this site, and the mortuary temples were decorated with reliefs of the king being suckled by Hathor as a cow.

Hathor's appearances in narrative mythology equally reflect her varied and often obscure nature. One unusual myth, the meaning of which is uncertain, nonetheless clearly implies her sexual aspect. In the *Contendings of Horus and Seth*, a troubled Re is approached by Hathor, who then exposes her self to him, causing the god to laugh. Two more fully understood myths that involve Hathor and Re reveal the duality of Hathor's nature, veering between joyful and destructive. In the *Destruction of Humanity*, the elderly Re, ruling on Earth, sends Hathor as his eye to punish his wayward subjects. Upon witnessing the destruction wreaked by Hathor, Re repents his decision, and to stop her from continuing, floods the land with beer dyed to resemble blood, to which Hathor is drawn. She becomes harmlessly drunk, and the people are saved. Based on this myth, Hathor was also worshipped as the goddess of drunkenness. In a second myth, Hathor is described as a lioness in the Nubian desert. Re sends Thoth to bring her to him for protection and companionship. On their return, Thoth immerses the lioness in the cool waters of the Nile in order to quell her fierceness, rendering her calm and joyful. These myths illustrate the aggressive and destructive aspects of Hathor which were integral to her complete character. In this mode she was linked to Sakhmet, the destructive lioness, and Tefnet, the angry lioness in the Nubian desert. This transformation of the goddess from a destructive aspect to a calm and joyful one was essential for the Egyptians in the maintenance of their cosmos, and thus festivals devoted to Hathor incorporated excessive drinking along with music and dance with the intent of pacifying the great goddess.

These myths also illustrate Hathor's complicated relationship with Re. In the myth in which Hathor is the eye of Re, she is interpreted as his daughter, as is also the case in the *Contendings of Horus and Seth*. Yet Hathor is commonly perceived as the mother of Re, based on several factors. Hathor was understood to be the mother of Horus, based on a metaphorical reading of *Ḥwt* as "womb," and as Re overtook Horus in the mythology, especially as related to kingship, Hathor was described as the mother of Re as well. She also absorbed this role from another cow goddess, *Mḥt Wrt*, the great flood, who in the creation myth was the mother of Re; she gave birth to the sun god and carried him between her horns, an iconographical element later adopted by, and essential to, Hathor. Hathor's role as Re's mode of successful rebirth each day made her both wife (whom he impregnates with himself) and mother (who gives birth to him on the eastern horizon).

In her role as mother, Hathor's importance in the institution of kingship was established from its earliest stages. Because Horus was the first royal god, Hathor became symbolically the divine mother of the pharaoh. She is often depicted in this role as a cow, linked to a myth in which the infant Horus is hidden from his murderous uncle Seth in the marshes of Chemmis, and there suckled by the divine cow. The image of Hathor as a cow suckling the pharaoh is common from the New Kingdom, emphasizing the divine aspect of the king, and it was as a cow that Hathor was worshipped at Deir el-Bahri, site of several royal mortuary complexes. The cow goddess is integral to the concept of kingship from its first appearance, exemplified on the Narmer Palette, which depicts the original unification of Egypt and presents the canonical image of the Egyptian king. The top of the palette shows the name of the king flanked by two cow heads—perhaps of Bat, in this case, but because of Bat's close relationship and eventual submission to Hathor, this can be seen as basic to Hathor's character as well.

Hathor also appears in relation to the king in the Pyramid Texts, in which the king is said to perform ritual dancing and shaking in the Hathor cult. Sculptures of the king with Hathor appear as early as the reign of Menkaure and are common through the late periods. In addition, Hathor played a significant part in the *sed*-festival, the royal ritual devoted to the symbolic rebirth of the king, as is illustrated by the reliefs in the tomb of Kheruef depicting the *sed*-festival of Amenhotpe III.

Rituals in Hathor's honor often incorporated music and dance. Beginning in the Old Kingdom, we find numerous tomb scenes showing dancers performing with musicians in her honor. In Thebes, the music and dancing integral to the Valley Festival, a celebration that brought relatives to the tombs of their deceased family members on the western bank, were performed under the patronage of Hathor. The two objects most characteristic of and sacred to Hathor were the sistrum, a type of rattle, and the *menat* necklace, which could be shaken like the sistrum; both were utilized in these dance and music rituals. A related ritual was the *zšš w3ḏ*, or Shaking of the Papyrus, which is said to be performed by the king in the Pyramid Texts and is portrayed in the tombs of many private individuals as well. The shaking of the papyrus plants sacred to Hathor is linked to the shaking of the sistrum, which in its earliest form was called *zššt* ("shaker"). The king also danced for Hathor during his *sed*-festival, as written in the reliefs from the tomb of Kheruef.

The calendar in the temple at Dendera lists more than twenty-five festivals in which Hathor was celebrated. Many occurred only under her aegis, while others were specifically celebrated for her. On New Year's Day her cult statue was brought to the roof of her temple so that she could be united with Re in the form of the sun rays, an act which occurred on other festival days as well. On the twentieth day of the first month, the Egyptians celebrated the Festival of Drunkenness in her honor, and in the spring there was another festival in her honor that related to the myth of her return from the Nubian desert. The most prominent and elaborate festival of Hathor was her sacred marriage as Mistress of Dendera to Horus of Edfu. In this summer festival, Hathor's cult statue was taken by boat from Dendera to Edfu, stopping along the way at several cult sites and arriving at Edfu at the new moon. She stayed at Edfu with Horus for thirteen days before returning to her temple. This union produced two sons, Ihy and Horus-Sematawy.

Hathor was one of the most complex and mysterious of the Egyptian gods, and also one of the most enduring. Her status as a prehistoric goddess makes determining her origins nearly impossible, and it is also difficult to untangle the myriad aspects and myths which together form her character. Nonetheless, it is clear that she played a vital role in Egyptian society from its highest levels to its lowest, essential to the identity and characterization of the king and a favorite goddess of the general population, who flooded her local cults with offerings and prayers.

Deborah Vischak

HELL. The principal sources for our knowledge of the Egyptian conception of hell are the so-called Books of the Underworld which are found inscribed on the walls of the royal tombs of the New Kingdom (eighteenth to twentieth dynasties) in the Valley of the Kings at Thebes, then later also on papyri and other funerary objects belonging to nonroyal persons. The chief subject of these richly illustrated books—the most important of which are the *Book of That Which Is in the Underworld* (*Book of the Hidden Room*, commonly known as the *Amduat*), the *Book of Gates*, and the *Book of Caverns*—is the nightly voyage of the sun god Re through the underworld. During this journey the sun god temporarily unites with the body of Osiris, the god of the dead, which is resting there, and this enables him to regenerate and to be reborn in the morning. Since the underworld also harbors the abode where the damned are punished and annihilated, these books contain vivid descriptions and depictions of this terrifying place.

The nocturnal journey of the sun god through the underworld is not yet a prominent theme in the oldest corpus of royal mortuary literature, the Pyramid Texts, and descriptions of hell are therefore absent from these spells. By contrast, the picture that emerges from the Books of the Underworld is reflected in the nonroyal funerary spells found in the Coffin Texts and the *Book of Going Forth by Day* (the *Book of the Dead*), even though these do not contain elaborate descriptions of hell either. This is not surprising, as these spells take it for granted that their owners have successfully passed the judgment of the dead and are therefore numbered among the blessed who follow the sun god Re on his eternal journey along the sky and through the underworld. Spells mentioning the dangers of the world of the damned which the blessed dead pass on this journey are plentiful, but these spells are aimed principally at steering clear of such dangers, and the subject of the fate of the damned is therefore usually avoided as well. The role of the divine pharaoh is different, however. During his life he had been the earthly incarnation and representative of the sun god; his principal task had been to maintain the cosmic and social order (*maat*) established by the god at creation and to repel the forces of chaos which constantly threaten the ordered world. This he did either symbolically, by means of the daily temple ritual, or more literally, for example by hunting dangerous animals in the desert or fighting battles against Egypt's enemies, or by administering justice and punishing criminals. After his death the king "unites with the sun disk and his divine body merges with him who made him"; that is, he is identified with the sun god, and in this new existence he continues to perform the task of subduing the powers of chaos. This active role of king and sun god necessitates a detailed description of the punishment of the damned, who represent the forces of evil. Their fate is therefore described in terms similar to those used for earthly

adversaries of the king and of Egypt: they are "enemies" who are "reckoned with," "overthrown," "repelled," "felled"; they are "under the feet of" the king or, the god. The exact nature of their misdeeds is never spelled out, nor is there a direct relationship between their punishment and the crime they committed. There are no separate areas in hell for different categories of evildoers, nor is there any sort of Purgatory, where sinners can repent so that they can be admitted to the company of the followers of Re at a later stage. The crimes of those who are condemned to hell consist of nothing more and nothing less than having acted against the divine world order (*maat*) established at the beginning of creation; by doing so they have excluded themselves from *maat* and revealed themselves as representatives of chaos. After death they are forever reduced to the state of "nonbeing" [*m*] the chaotic state of the world before creation, for which they have shown themselves to be predestined by their behavior in life. For them there is no renewal of life, but only a second, definitive death. In mythological terms, they are the "gang of Seth," the god who brought death into the world by murdering Osiris, or the "children of Nut" (the mother of Seth), the first generation of mankind, who rebelled against Re.

The fate of the damned is in every respect the opposite of that of the blessed (*ȝḥw*). When the righteous die and are mummified and buried with the proper rites, they successfully pass the judgment of the dead and start a new life in the company of Re and Osiris. Their limbs are "tied together" again, and the ritual of the Opening of the Mouth ensures that they regain control over their senses. Their bodies rest in their tombs, and at sunrise, when Re is reborn from the underworld in the east, their *ba*-souls leave the tomb unhindered and join the sun god. They spend a happy time in the Fields of Rushes (paradise), where they have plenty of cool air, food, drink, and sexual pleasures. At night, when Re once more enters the underworld in the west and unites with Osiris, they too return to their mummified bodies. When the damned (mtw) end their earthly lives, however, demons tear away their mummy wrappings and uncover their bodies, which are left to decompose. In the place to which they are condemned, the normal order of things is reversed, even to the extent that the damned have to walk upside down, eat their own excrement, and drink their own urine. Their hands are tied behind their backs, often around stakes; their heads and limbs are severed from their bodies and their flesh is cut off their bones; their hearts are taken out; their ba-souls are separated from their bodies, forever unable to return to them; and even their shadows are wiped out. They have no air and suffer from hunger and thirst, for they receive no funerary offerings. Worst of all, they are denied the revivifying light of the sun god, who ignores them, even though they cry out loud and wail when he passes them in the underworld at night. Thus, they are excluded from the eternal cosmic cycle of the renewal of life. Instead, they are assigned to the "outer darkness" (kkw sm3w), the primeval darkness of the chaotic world before creation, which is situated in the deepest recesses of the underworld, outside the created world. There they are punished by demons, the representatives of chaos, who are often recruited from the ranks of the damned dead (mtw) themselves, so that they torture and kill one another. They are subjected to knives and swords and to the fire of hell, often kindled by fire-spitting snakes.

These terrible punishments are carried out in the "slaughtering place" (nmt) or "place of destruction" (ḥtmyt), presided over by the fierce goddess Sakhmet, whose butchers (nmtyw) hack their victims to pieces and burn them with inextinguishable fire, sometimes in deep pits (h3dw) or in cauldrons (wḥ3wt) in which they are scorched, cooked, and reduced to ashes; demons feed on their entrails and drink their blood. Another location is the Lake of Fire (š n sḍt), which is already mentioned in the so-called Book of Two Ways in the Coffin Texts (Spell 1054/1166) and illustrated in the Book of Going Forth by Day (chapter 126). Like the "outer darkness," it is a place of regeneration for the sun god and his blessed followers, to whom it provides nourishment and cool water, but a place of destruction for the damned. Birds fly away from it when they see its burning, bloody water and smell the stench of putrefaction which rises up from it. In the vignette of chapter 126, its shores are guarded by "the four baboons who sit at the bow of the bark of Re," and who are usually associated with sunrise. Here they figure as the judges of the divine tribunal "who judge the poor as well as the rich" and who decide who is going to be granted access through "the secret portals of the West" and who will be delivered to the hellhound, who, according to another spell (CT 335 BD 17), is in charge of this place, the "Swallower of Millions" who "devours corpses (or shadows), snatches hearts and inflicts injury without being seen."

At the end of the eighteenth dynasty, a similar monster appears in the well-known vignette of chapter 125 of the Book of Going Forth by Day that shows the judgment of the deceased before the divine tribunal. In this scene, the heart of the deceased is weighed in the balance against a feather, the symbol of *maat*. In many cases, the Lake of Fire of chapter 126 is also shown in this vignette. A late (Demotic) text explains that "if his evil deeds outnumber his good deeds he is delivered to the Swallower . . . ; his soul as well as his body are destroyed and never will he breathe again." In the vignette this monster is called "Swallower of the Damned" ('*mt mtw*); she is depicted with the head of a crocodile, the forelegs and body of a lion, and the hindquarters of a hippopotamus. Another name for her is *šзyt* ("beast of destiny"). She is usually sitting close to the balance, ready to devour her victim, but since the owner of the *Book of Going Forth by Day* in question is naturally supposed to survive the judgment, the Swallower is almost never shown grabbing her prey. Only a few very late instances dating to Roman times depict this; in one case, the monster is sitting beside a fiery cauldron into which the emaciated bodies of the damned, stripped of their mummy wrappings, are thrown.

In these late times, Egyptian conceptions began to be influenced by images from elsewhere in the Hellenistic world, as is shown by a representation of the Swallower that is very reminiscent of the Greek Sphinx, who was also a demon of fate and death. In their turn, later Egyptian representations of the Christian Hell, from Coptic and other early Christian texts, may well have influenced medieval European descriptions and depictions of the Inferno.   *Jacobus Van Dijk*

HORUS, the name of the deity generally written with the falcon hieroglyph and transliterated fully *Ḥrw*, commonly *Ḥr*. The generally accepted etymology is "the distant one," which seems to be supported by Pyramid Text orthographies, as well as an implied pun in the

Coffin Texts, Section 148. The ancient Egyptians also seem to have connected it to *ḥry* ("one who is above/over"). The name occurs in many compounds, notably *Ḥr-smꝫ-tꝫwy* (Gk., Harsomtus, "Horus Uniter of the Two Lands"). The name of Horus has been widespread in theophorous personal names throughout Egyptian history. As a personal name, Hor has outlived the native Egyptian religious tradition, often the case with theophores (e.g., Thor, Isadora, Onnofrio, Diana, etc.).

The roles, local cult foundations, and titles or epithets of Horus are sometimes correlated with distinct or preferred forms in iconography; for example, the

Basalt statue of Horus in the form of a hawk, from Heliopolis, thirtieth dynasty. The god is shown protecting Nektanebo II, the last native king of Egypt. (The Metropolitan Museum of Art, Rogers Fund, 1934 [34.2.1])

falcon, the falcon-headed man, the winged disk, and the child with a side-lock (sometimes in his mother's arms). Egyptologists therefore often speak of distinct, sometimes originally distinct, Horuses or Horus-gods. Combinations, identifications, and differentiations were, however, possible for Horus, and they are complementary rather than antithetical. A judicious examination of the various Horuses and the sources relating to them supports the possibility that the roles in question are closely interrelated, and so they may be understood as different aspects, or facets, of the same divine persona.

Horus is one of the earliest attested of the major ancient Egyptian deities, becoming known to us at least as early as the late Predynastic period (Naqada III/Dynasty 0); he was still prominent in the latest temples of the Greco-Roman period, especially at Philae and Edfu, as well as in the Old Coptic and Greco-Egyptian ritual-power, or magical, texts. The earliest documented chapter in the career of Horus was as Horus the falcon, god of Nekhen (Hierakonpolis) in southern Upper Egypt. In this capacity, Horus was the patron deity of the Hierakonpolis monarchy that grew into the historical pharaonic state, hence the first known national god, the god of kingship. Both his sponsorship of the monarchy and, probably, his identification with the king were shown on early decorated monuments from Hierakonpolis and by his appearance in the king's Horus-name, which came from the same period. Horus became the patron of several Egyptian military colonies in Nubia, Buhen, Miam (Aniba), and Baki (Kuban).

With the rise of the full-blown Horus-Osiris-Isis mythological complex (visible in the Pyramid Texts during the late Old Kingdom), the living king was identified as an earthly Horus and the dead king (his father/predecessor) as Osiris. When the king died, he became Osiris (or, as I have suggested, joined the sphere of identity of Osiris, in *NAOS, Notes and Materials for the Linguistic Study of the Sacred* 12.1–3 [1996], pp. 2–5). Horus is the royal heir/successor *par excellence*, the epitome of legitimate succession. In the expanded Osiris mythological complex, Horus vindicates and avenges his father Osiris, thus bringing us to a consideration of the vital relationship between Horus and the god Seth.

Seth, the embodiment of disorder, was predominantly seen as a rival of Horus, a would-be usurper who assassinated Osiris and was defeated; Seth was also portrayed in a balanced complementarity with Horus, so that the pair of them represented a bipolar, balanced embodiment of kingship. Thus, on the side of the throne, Horus and Seth—symmetrical and equal—tie the papyrus and lotus around the *sema*-sign (*smȝ*; "unity"): *see also*, the end of the Thutmose III Poetical Stela. When the full Osiris complex became visible, Seth appeared as the murderer of Osiris and the would-be killer of the child Horus. Since about the turn of the twentieth century in Egyptological research, much debate has ensued about whether the struggle of Horus and Seth was primarily historical/geopolitical or cosmic/symbolic; the answer depends partially on the researcher's choice of myth interpretation theories. In addition, this question has been complicated by the ambivalent geographical polarities of the two gods' cult centers. For Horus, Hierakonpolis (Nekhen) and Edfu (Djeba, Mesen) in Upper Egypt are complemented by Hermopolis Parva I, Letopolis (Khem, Ausim) and Behdet (Tell el-Balamun) in the Nile Delta (Behdet is also identified with Edfu). Another Delta site important in connection with Horus is Khemmis (Akhbit), regarded as his birthplace. For Seth, Ombos (Nubt, near Naqada), in Upper Egypt, was balanced by his center in the Sethroite nome of the Delta, ostensibly established by the Hyksos at Avaris. Other relevant deities also show both Southern and Northern centers, for example, Osiris at Abydos and at Busiris/ Djedu. A crucial observation is that Ombos, although in Upper Egypt, is north of Hierakonpolis and that the so-called Lower Egyptian Red Crown was first attested on a sherd from Naqada. This suggests the possibility that one source at least of the conflict is in the early expansion of the proto-kingdom of Hierakonpolis and its absorption of the proto-kingdom of Naqada. A Horus–Seth conflict occurred in the second dynasty and was resolved under Khasekhemwy, presumably setting the stage for the subsequent equilibrium. The nature of this conflict is not entirely clear, but it was reflected in the following: the use of a Seth-name instead of the usual Horus-name by King Peribsen; the combining of Horus and Seth above the *serekh* (*srḫ*; palace-façade design) of Khasekhemwy; and the indications of warfare, as well as some limited geographical ranges, for some rulers. During the Old Kingdom, the Horus-name was joined in the royal titulary by the so-called name of "Golden Horus" or "Horus of Gold" (the interpretation of which is highly debated). Some regard it as signifying "Horus and the Ombite (Seth)" or "Horus over the Ombite," the latter allegedly supported by both the Demotic and Greek translations: "He who is over his enemy/superior to his foes."

The most common genealogy of Horus is as the son of Osiris and Isis, making a tenth on the family tree of the Heliopolitan Ennead. The full picture is more complex: Hathor (herself identified with Isis) also appears as the mother of Horus; Horus the Elder (Haroeris) can appear in the Heliopolitan family tree as a brother of Osiris and son of Geb and Nut, thus an uncle of Horus in his more usual manifestations; Osiris can also be equated with Haroeris, who in that scenario is the murdered victim of Seth. Analogously, at Edfu, Horus appears as the consort of Hathor and the father of another form of himself, Harsomtus ("Horus Uniter of the Two Lands"). Horus and Seth are sometimes described as nephew and uncle, sometimes as brothers.

Horus the falcon was predominantly a sky god and a sun god; as the former, his eyes are the sun and moon; as the latter, he has a sun disk on his head and is syncretized with the deity Re, most often as Re-Harakhty. He also appeared frequently as a hawk-headed man. Horus of Behdet/the Behdetite was normally shown as a winged disk with pendant *uraei* (snakes) and, as such, often appeared on the upper border or lunette of stelae. Horus the falcon/disk had the epithets *ntr ʿ3 nb pt s3b šwt*, "Great God, Lord of Heaven, Dappled of Plumage." Horus the child/Horus son of Isis and Osiris was often portrayed as a boy wearing the sidelock and frequently appeared in the arms of his mother Isis. Bronzes representing him, with or without Isis, were ubiquitous in Late and Greco-Roman times. Horus as a boy with the sidelock also appears dominating crocodiles, serpents, and other noxious animals on *cippi* of Horus or apotropaic stelae of "Horus-on-the-Crocodiles," which were the common manifestation of the importance of Horus in healing ritual and popular ritual practice. Horus the successor was also referred to as Iunmutef ("Pillar of His

Mother"), which was used as a funerary priestly title (often the deceased's eldest son). The Great Sphinx at Giza was identified during the New Kingdom as Harmakhis (Hr-m-$3ht$, "Horus in the Horizon"). In the person of the Sphinx and elsewhere, Horus was identified in the New Kingdom with the Syrian-Canaanite deity Hauron (an identification regarded by some as contributing to the choice of the Arabic name of the Sphinx, Abu-'l-Hul, "Father of Terror"). Aside from the sun disk already mentioned, Horus in various forms often wore the Double Crown, as befitted his status as king of Egypt; the *atef* ($3tf$; a type of crown), triple *atef*, and disk with two plumes were also used. On *cippi*, the head of the child Horus was often surmounted by a fullfaced Bes-head (or mask?).

The iconography of Horus either influenced or was appropriated in early Christian art. Isis and the baby Horus may often be seen as the precursor for Mary and the infant Jesus; Horus dominating the beasts may have a counterpart in Christ Pantokrator doing the same; and Horus spearing a serpent may survive in the iconography of Saint George defeating the dragon.

The textual and mythological materials relating to Horus are extremely rich, comprising hymns, mortuary texts, ritual texts, dramatic/theological texts, stories, the Old Coptic and Greek so-called magical papyri, and the most complete ancient exposition of the Osiris narrative, Plutarch's *De Iside et Osiride* (in Latin translation). In characteristic Egyptian fashion, many of the hymns and the mortuary and ritual texts incorporated substantial narrative material or were taken from narrative, though they are not comprehensive, consecutive myths per se. In addition to Plutarch's account

in Greek, the most substantive sources for the Osiris-Isis-Horus cycle include the following: the Memphite Theology or Shabaqo Stone (now generally placed at least as late as the New Kingdom); the *Mystery Play of the Succession*; Coffin Texts, Spell 148; the "Great" Osiris hymn in the Louvre; the Late Egyptian *Contendings of Horus and Seth* (and perhaps, in allegorical form, *Truth and False-hood*); the Metternich Stela and other *cippus* texts; and the Ptolemaic *Myth of Horus at Edfu* (also known as the *Triumph of Horus*). These texts take the reader or audience, with a number of variations and contrasting perspectives, from the conception and birth of Horus, through his childhood hidden in the marshes, his protection by Isis, his conflict with Seth and his followers, and his succession as legitimate king. The healing of Horus from scorpion stings by Isis provided the reason for the production of the *cippi* of Horus and his role in healing. The blinding of one of Horus' eyes by Seth and its restoration by Thoth was the mythological basis for the popularity of the Eye of Horus (the $wd3t$ or "whole or sound [eye]") amulet and its significance in offerings and sacrifice (as found in Pyramid Texts offering liturgies). The roles of Horus and Seth are interesting for folkloric analysis. Seth is often considered the "trickster" figure of ancient Egyptian religion, but it has been noted that in the *Contendings of Horus and Seth*, Horus had elements of the "trickster" and Seth acted the fool.

Horus was combined, syncretized, and closely associated with deities other than the sun god Re, notably (but not exclusively) Min, Sopdu, Khonsu, and Montu. The Greeks' association of Horus with Apollo gave rise to the name of the author of the *Hieroglyphica*, Horapollo. The deities of the canopic jars,

protectors of the four internal organs removed during mummification, were
known as the "Four Sons of Horus."
Throughout the Roman Empire, Horus
became popular, along with his fellow
deities of the Osirian family and others,
such as Anubis. That and his prominence
in the Isis temple of Philae, the last functioning center of the traditional Egyptian
religion, made Horus one of the ancient
Egyptian deities who survived longest, as
Christianity slowly gained its ascendancy
over the Roman world.

Edmund S. Meltzer

I

ISIS. The goddess Isis (or *Aset; 3st*) is well attested in the early sources and eventually became the best known of all Egyptian goddesses. It was the theology of kingship that assigned to Isis a special significance. In the Pyramid Texts (1655 a–b), she was viewed as a member of the Ennead of Heliopolis, and other allusions in the Pyramid Texts show that she was constantly linked to the pharaoh in both life and death. Her name, meaning "seat" or "throne," firmly points to her association with sovereignty. An interpretation implying "seat" or "dwelling" with reference to a bond between Isis and the sun god Re is less likely than one that alludes to a link with Osiris, although a precise exegesis is still debated. The throne is certainly a basic symbol of the goddess, being present both in her hieroglyphic name and in her iconography.

Role in the Myth and Ritual of Osiris. Presented as the wife and sister of Osiris, Isis is prominent in his myth and also in the rites associated with his death. In the Pyramid Texts, Osiris is said to have been smitten by his brother Seth in a place called Nedyet or Gehestey; the episode should perhaps be connected with the tradition that Osiris was then drowned by Seth. In a later era, there are allusions to a belief that death by drowning was a blessed fate because it recalled the death of Osiris. In a related legend, Seth is presented as the enemy of Horus;

the two figure as hostile brothers, rather like Cain and Abel, and in their feud Seth is said to have torn out the eye of Horus, whereas Seth's testicles were removed by Horus. The pair are also involved in a homosexual episode in which Horus is violated by his brother, but a text recently restored by Leclant shows that Horus too is said to violate Seth. What is clear is that the Horus-Seth myth was conflated with that of Osiris and Seth, with a revision of the family links; Seth as the brother of Osiris became the uncle of Horus. Isis appears in these texts as the mother of Horus, and she is said to give birth to him at Khemmis, a place apparently in the Nile Delta. Her role as the mother of Horus becomes increasingly evident with time, although Hathor figures occasionally in early allusions to this function. At the same time, Isis protects Osiris against the threats of Seth, and both these functions emphasize her basic significance vis-a-vis the pharaonic divine kingship. The living pharaoh was equated with Horus; he was also regarded as the son of Re. When the king died, he was identified with Osiris, and this illumines the supreme importance of Isis in the funerary ceremonies. With her sister Nephthys, she fulfills the part of the mourning falcons and also aids the rites of purification and mummification. To these rites and that of the Opening of the Mouth ceremony was assigned the power of renewing life, and eventually the role of Isis in the myth was specifically to ensure the revival of life in the dead Osiris, including his sexual and procreative potency. This power is alluded to in the New Kingdom *Hymn of Amenmose* and is sculpturally figured in tombs of the same era (see Otto 1968, plates 16 ff.).

It is the close nexus with kingship that distinguishes Isis from the paramours of the Near Eastern deities who are associated with renewed life after death, such as Ishtar, Cybele, and Aphrodite, with the beloved ones of Tammuz (Dumuzi), Attis, and Adonis. This is not to claim that the role of Isis was consistently prominent in Egyptian royal rites. A funerary framework usually attaches to both Isis and Osiris. In the coronation rites, attention is naturally focused on the new king, who is equated with Horus, but since Isis is the mother of Horus (in his forms as Horus the Child and Horus the Elder), she figures in the retrospective aspect of such rites, as indeed does Osiris as his father. Within the mythic pattern, Isis holds a conspicuous lead role in the story of her quest for the lost and slain Osiris. Texts often refer to the anxiety of the search, followed by the relief of the finding. Nephthys joins Isis in the task, while Horus and Geb are also mentioned. The seeking and finding mirror the fear that the body of the king may be lost in the Nile or in the desert and may thus be deprived of the solace and assurance of due burial rites. The society in which the concept had its origin was probably one of nomads and hunters who feared the dismemberment and dispersion of the body.

Relationship to Other Deities. Isis and her sister Nephthys are closely grouped in funerary rites, not only as the chief mourners but also as sacred performers in roles to which priestesses were assigned. Ambivalence marks the role of Nephthys. She is named as the consort of Seth, in a pair parallel to Isis and Osiris as offspring of Geb and Nut, yet her close relation to Isis brings her to a shared sexual link to Osiris. This is especially clear in two groups of songs assigned to Isis and Nephthys in the Ptolemaic era: the Festival Songs and the Lamentations. In one of these texts Osiris is called the "Bull of the Two Sisters." Plutarch in *De Iside et Osiride* takes this further in an allusion to the adultery of Osiris with Nephthys, albeit through mistaken identity; and he names Anubis as the fruit of their illicit union. Some Egyptian texts also refer to Anubis as the son of Osiris, yet Isis is portrayed as a consistently loyal spouse to Osiris. Hathor, in contrast, has a basic significance of her own, and a close affinity to Isis. Her name means "House of Horus"; perhaps "house" here refers to the celestial domain of the falcon god (Meeks and Favard-Meeks 1997, p. 236). But her early claim to be the mother of Horus may more probably be implied. A kind of rivalry with Isis emerges here, and also a medium of influence, since the cow-form of Hathor is sometimes transferred in part to Isis. Hathor, like Isis, is a goddess of love, but in a less inhibited form; she is a goddess too of the dance, music, and drunken abandon. An antithesis results, since Isis is a goddess of love in its socially acceptable form, with motherhood as its dominant theme. There are episodes, however, in which Horus and his mother Isis appear in dire conflict: after a violent assault by Horus on his mother, she is said to have cut off his two hands (Spell 113, *Book of Going Forth by Day*, and other texts). A piece of etiology emerges here: the writing of Nekhen (Hierakonpolis) showed two signs interpreted as the hands of Horus, who had an early cult center there. Another story (the *Contendings of Horus and*

Seth, 8, 9 ff.) tells how Horus, because his mother favored Seth, cut off her head, whereupon Thoth (according to Papyrus Sallier 4) restored the head of Isis as a cow head—another piece of etiology explaining the bovine headdress of Isis, derived from Hathor.

Nut, the goddess of heaven, was bound to come into contact with Isis, if only through her ubiquity in the funerary domain. Nut gives birth to the sun and stars and swallows them at sunset; this led to her being called "the Sow" with allusion to the sow as a devourer of her offspring. In the Hellenistic era, the connection of Isis and Nut is conveyed in art by depictions of Isis riding on a sow (see Bergman 1974). In the astral world, Isis was at times identified with the bright star Sirius, or Sothis (Sepedet), in the constellation Orion, the latter being equated with Osiris; and their sexual union is said to produce Horus Sopd (Pyramid Texts 632 a ff.).

Attributes. While the throne-sign is a constant feature in the depiction of Isis, her association with Hathor often endows her head with cow horns and sun disk. In a Middle Kingdom text, Isis identifies herself with the *nat*-serpent, the *uraeus* of the royal diadem (Münster 1968, p. 106); and in the *Book of Gates*, the twelfth gate, both Isis and Nephthys appear as *uraei* (Hornung 1992, pp. 306–307). Isis is at times figured as a serpent in the Roman era, together with a serpentine Sarapis. A combined form, Isis-Bat, connects her with the goddess Bat, but Hathor supplies the link, since Bat is a Hathor look-alike, with curling horns and sun disc (see Fischer 1961, p. 7 ff.). From Hathor, too, Isis derives the sistrum, the shaker or rattle used to accompany music in sacred rites; it was probably of African origin. In the Greco-Roman era, Isis was often figured carrying both sistrum and situla (on the latter vessel, see Griffiths 1975 pp. 208–210); it was often shaped like a nippled breast, and some examples relate to the New Kingdom. The same objects were often carried by priestly servants of the goddess (Witt 1997, plates 31–32).

A popular amulet used in a funerary context was explained as "the blood of Isis." It represents the *ankh*-sign, that of life, in a form that suggests a girdle. Spell 156 of the *Book of Going Forth by Day* shows the amulet with the words, "Thou hast thy blood, O Isis, thou hast thy magical power." Perhaps the object is a bandage for use in menstruation. Magical power was often ascribed to the goddess, particularly in the sphere of healing. In the *Story of Re and Isis*, she heals even the god Re by eliciting from him the truth about his name; in the Metternich Stela, she saves Horus.

Several cult centers were assigned to Isis, including Behbet el-Hagar in the Nile Delta, Akhmim, Coptos, and Philae. Where the cult began is uncertain. Her celebrated temple in Philae had its origins only in the last pharaonic dynasties (see Žabkar 1988). Some of these hymns dwell on her warlike power, doubtless in relation to the hazards of the region.

The Universal Goddess. During post-pharaonic eras, the cult of Isis witnessed a remarkable expansion in two ways: spatially, it spread to most parts of the known world; and its spiritual content was much widened in that Isis became a universal goddess who subsumed the functions of many other deities. The spatial expansion was achieved in the Ptolemaic era, not through political pressure by the rulers but by merchants, priests, and private devotees. By that time, the god Sarapis had to some extent replaced Osiris as the consort of Isis. Yet other deities of the Isiac-Osirian circle were still prominent, especially Anubis and Harpocrates, who are among those mentioned in the *Aretalogies* or *Praises of Isis*, in works by Plutarch and Apuleius, and in a massive corpus of inscriptions. In the Isis-Book of Apuleius, Isis claims to be "mother of the universe" and "mistress of all the elements."

A part of this process of expansion was an influx of Greek religious ideas. In particular, Demeter was equated with Isis, a tangible result being the depiction of Isis with sheaves of grain as part of her headdress. The "Isis-knot," however, was a feature of Isiac dress derived from an Egyptian fashion. Whereas the Isiac mysteries were partly based on the Greek model of Eleusis, their elements of initiation and secrecy had Egyptian antecedents. The Hellenistic Isis offers a deeper human approach in the paradigm of the loyal wife and mother; she retains an element of chastisement and validates, on the pattern of Osiris, a faith in immortality.

J. Gwyn Griffiths

J

JUDGMENT OF THE DEAD. Two kinds of judgment of the dead are attested in Egyptian documents: tribunals operating in the underworld in the same continuous manner as tribunals on earth; and in a later version, a single moment for each person after death when a divine tribunal determines whether that individual is worthy of eternal life.

The first version is attested first in late Old Kingdom hieroglyphic tomb-chapel inscriptions with threats to would-be vandals of tombs, and in Hieratic "Letters to the Dead"; references continue in the early Middle Kingdom funerary literature (Coffin Texts). Here the afterlife is a continuation of life on earth; plaintiffs can bring cases to the authorities, who execute justice. The texts do not name the "great god" of the tribunal; he may be the deceased king or the god Osiris, though this is a matter of expression rather than of substance.

In the later version, death marks discontinuity, as a moment determining the immortality of the individual. Here people are either pure or evil; the evil die a second death to become *mut* "dead" (*mt*; "damned"), whereas the good achieve the status of *akh* (*ȝḫ*; "transfigured spirit"). Unerring divine judgment is expressed figuratively by the scales used to weigh precious metals with mathematical objectivity in treasury accounts. This judgment conflates two episodes in the myth of the god Osiris: his resuscitation

by his sister-wife Isis after his murder by Seth, and the declaration by the gods that his son Horus was telling the truth in his physical and legal battles with Seth over the inheritance of Osiris. At death, each individual becomes Osiris if declared "true of voice" like Horus; "Osiris (name) true of voice" comes to be the commonest formula for referring to the deceased. In some periods, a word such as "to" before the word "Osiris" can be repeated before the title and name of the deceased, as if to separate the divine and human aspects of the identity surviving death. The very retention of the personal name and official titles marks a limit to the assimilation of the individual to the deity. In early Roman times, identification as Osiris for both men and women was superseded by a system assigning Osiris for men and Hathor for women.

The new judgment appears first in the Middle Kingdom. The term "calculation of differences" later denotes assessment of the individual after death; it occurs already in the phrase "his voice is true in the calculation of differences" on the Abydos stela of an eleventh dynasty general, Intef (Copenhagen Ny Carlsberg Glyptothek AE.I'N.963, lower, line 6). The First Intermediate Period stela of Merer may include a reference to the scales of reckoning but is of uncertain interpretation. Unambiguous references to scales occur in the Coffin Texts (CT) on early to mid-twelfth dynasty coffins

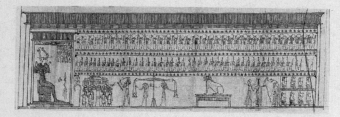

Detail of a papyrus of the *Book of Going Forth by Day* (*Book of the Dead*). This is a section of what was originally a continuous roll about 23 meters (72 feet) long. Here, the heart of the deceased is being weighed before Osiris, who is enthroned on the left. The papyrus is from the late dynastic to early Ptolemaic period. (The Metropolitan Museum of Art, gift of Edward S. Harkness, 1935. [35.9.20.(7)])

(CT 335, "whose eyebrows are the arms of the balance"; CT 452, "that balance of Ra on which Maat is raised"); four coffins of that date bear a text in which the dead are polarized as good and evil (CT 338, "the tribunal which is in Abydos on that night of distinguishing the damned and reckoning the blessed dead"). However, none of these sources attests certainly to "death as judgment time" rather than an afterlife court of appeal. In the *Instructions for Merikare*, a Middle Egyptian literary discourse dated perhaps to the twelfth dynasty, one section (P53–7) warns against wrongdoing with reference to the afterlife: "Do not trust in length of years—they see a lifetime as an hour; when a man is left over after mourning, his deeds are piled up beside him." This might indicate simply a better hearing for the good than for the evil, on the legal principle that those of good character are trustworthy. However, there follows: "As for the man who reaches them without doing evil, he will abide there like a god, roaming (free) like the lords of time." Here the good person undergoes transformation. The classic exposition of judgment at death comes in the *Book of Going Forth by Day*

(the *Book of the Dead*) texts numbered BD 30 and BD 125 by the nineteenth-century Egyptologist Karl Richard Lepsius, and the associated illustration in which the heart of the deceased is weighed against the goddess Maat ("what is right"). The two chapters and the weighing illustration are among the most frequently attested elements of the Egyptian funerary corpus, though not every manuscript or burial includes an example. Of the three elements, BD 30 is first attested, on four late Middle Kingdom human-faced heart scarabs (Neferuptah, Nebankh, Dedtu, and one erased), on a late Middle Kingdom or Second Intermediate Period gold plaque, and in both later versions (BD30A and B) among the *Book of Going Forth by Day* coffins of the seventeenth dynasty queen Montuhotpe. In this, the deceased appeals to the heart not to weigh down the balance or testify in a hostile manner before the keeper of the balance. The longer chapter, BD 125, is first attested in the mid-eighteenth dynasty, from the joint reign of Hatshepsut with Thutmose III, in connection with a new burial custom of placing a funerary papyrus with the dead (*Book of the Dead*). In editing earlier *Books of the Dead*, Naville used as the main manuscript the papyrus of Nebseny, dated stylistically to the reign of Thutmose IV (British Museum EA 9900). In the first part, the deceased is led into the "broad court of the Two Maats," to declare innocence of wrongs before the great god (List A), and before the full tribunal of forty-two divine assessors, including Osiris and Ra (List B). The texts conclude with announcements by the deceased of purity and initiation into the afterlife. The declarations of innocence (often called "negative confession" in Egyptology) form the most explicit statement in Egyptian texts of *maat* (*m3ˁt*; "what is right"), by delineating its opposite, wrongdoing. However, there is a culturally specific setting for both series: some denials reflect the precepts of the literary tradition of *Instructions* or *Teachings*, a genre in which a father or master instructs a son or apprentice in the correct way to behave in life; others are related to the priestly oaths of purity taken at the moment of entering priestly service, a genre attested only in later copies but probably in existence earlier. The sequence of declarations varies between manuscripts. In List A, in the *Book of the Dead* of Nebseny, thirty-six declarations of innocence are given, opening with "I have not done evil to anyone" and "I have not slain the sacred herd" (interpreted in some manuscripts as humankind). Other declarations of List A include the religious norms "I have not blasphemed," "I have not harmed the offering-loaves of the gods," "I have not removed the offerings of the blessed dead," and, related, the affirmation of sexual rules "I have not copulated" (in some versions "with a male") and "I have not ejaculated" (in some versions "in the sanctuary of my city god"). Other rules concern probity in administrative measurement: "I have not re-duced the aroura land-measure"; "I have not tampered with the counterpoise of the scales."

In List B, the forty-two declarations are tabulated graphically, divided into on the model "O broad of strides, he who comes forth from Iunu, I have not committed evil." The deities before whom List B was to be recited are thus identified not by their primary names but by epithets, sometimes not attested elsewhere, with the addition of a cult center or other place of origin (e.g., cavern, twilight, darkness). All named towns are in Lower or Middle Egypt, a feature that might identify the period and place of redaction as being the Herakleopolitan kingdom of the First Intermediate Period but, perhaps, more simply reflecting compilation at an unknown date in a northern scribal school, such as Iunu/Heliopolis. The date of composition of BD 125 remains uncertain; there is no precise parallel from the Middle Kingdom, though a positive series of declarations of good character is graphically tabulated on one early twelfth dynasty stela in a manner reminiscent of the List B tabulation. This is the period in which the royal cult complex gained "Osirian" features. The pyramid of Senwosret II at Illahun had a rectangular tree border, with underground chambers on a pattern later echoed by the cenotaph of Sety I at Abydos, while Senwosret III had a major royal cult complex constructed at Abydos South. However, the few sources for funerary literature of the royal family attest to BD 30 but not to BD 125 (heart scarabs, coffin of queen Montuhotpe). It remains possible, then, that the textual edition dates, with the vignette, to the eighteenth dynasty.

The texts and vignettes of BD 30 and 125 may seem to encapsulate an explicit code of ethics, but they are intended to establish a purity analogous to the purity of the priest entering a period of temple service. Therefore, this afterlife codification does not include every precept of didactic literature; some, such as respect for seniors and parents, were evidently not deemed relevant to the aim of entering the underworld. Modern agnostic reading might suggest that, by including declarations of innocence in their burials, the elite may have hoped to secure automatic entry to a good afterlife; when such a question becomes widespread, the questioners already stand outside the particular system of belief. There is no evidence that inclusion of texts exempted anyone from judgment; the texts affirm the desired outcome but insist on judgment. The ethics of providing religious texts for those who could afford them, whatever their biography, seems to receive no explicit treatment in Egyptian sources until the comparison of the damned rich man and the blessed poor man in the Demotic tale of *Setna and his Son*, in which Hellenistic influence may be involved.

The principal vignette to BD 30 and 125 illustrates "truth of voice" in declaring innocence as a weighing of the heart on scales against Maat, before Osiris. Throughout the history of its use, the scene often includes the four sons of Horus as protectors of the internal organs of the deceased after mummification. Weighing vignettes vary in number and role of figures, and in scale within a compositional field, occupying on a papyrus the full height of the roll or only a part. Eighteenth dynasty depictions on papyrus occupy only part of the full height of a roll, and they present the scales as managed by Thoth in baboon form, beside the god Osiris on his throne. In the *Book of the Dead* of Nebseny, this scene is provided as illustration to BD 30; the text of BD 125 occurs farther on in the sequence of the roll,

where the "Hall of the Two Maats" becomes a full-height vignette enclosing the tabulated declarations of innocence. Other small-scale weighing scenes of this period and later place Horus in charge of weighing, while Thoth is shown as a scribe declaring or recording the result of the weighing to Osiris. Later eighteenth dynasty versions sometimes make Anubis, god of embalming, the deity in charge of weighing, and they may add nearby a monster called variously Amemet ("Swallower") or Am-mut ("Swallower of the Damned"). The earliest manuscript with Anubis and Amemet is the *Book of the Dead* of Nebqed (Louvre N 3068, reign of Thutmose IV or Amenhotpe III). Here the monster is already the hybrid specified in a caption on the Papyrus of Hunefer (British Museum EA 9901, early nineteenth dynasty): "Its fore as a lion, its rear as a hippopotamus, its middle as a lion." After the Amarna era, the weighing scene tends to occupy the full height of manuscripts, offering opportunities for increasing detail. Ramessid depictions begin to shift the emphasis from the weighing to the declaration of innocence; in the version for Hunefer just cited, Anubis leads the deceased to the scales, which he then oversees alongside Amemet, following which Horus leads the justified deceased to the throned Osiris. This focus on justification recurs in Third Intermediate Period papyri, while in the standard version of the Late to Roman periods (first attested in the tomb of Sheshonq III at Tanis), weighing and justification are given equal importance as an interwoven scene in front of Osiris.

Supplementary figures in more complex vignettes include the goddesses Isis and Nephthys supporting Osiris, and, particularly in the standard Late period version, one or two figures of the goddess Maat. After the Amarna era, features of individuality are added: Shai (allotted life), Meskhenet (birth-brick), and Renenet (nurturing of the deceased). Later vignettes generally include a secondary human figure beside the scales: from the Ramessid era, the *ba*-soul of the deceased; from the Third Intermediate Period, a crouching figure; and from the Late period, evoking Horus and/or Re, a divine child on a scepter. Besides these full-height vignettes, other versions include narrower compositions of stacked horizontal registers, or single excerpts such as the weighing. On coffins of the twenty-fifth and twenty-sixth dynasties, a single band extends over the coffin breast, with the weighing scene over the heart, and, toward the center, the deceased before a line of deities.

The judgment motif continues to be used into Roman times. For example, the weighing and the arrival before Osiris are depicted in a single scene on the papyrus of Kerasher (British Museum EA 9995), and as separate scenes on the coffin of Teuris (weighing along mummy's left side, introduction before Osiris on right side). Texts in Roman period manuscripts come mainly not from the *Book of the Dead* but from the *Books of Breathing*, including sections of BD 125. In versions of this period (or perhaps slightly earlier), the vignette is often reduced to select elements, and the dead souls are sometimes shown as black shadows or skeletal creatures.

Sometimes the weighing scene (e.g., *Book of of the Dead* of Nebqed) or a part of the text of BD 125 (e.g., *Book of the Dead* of Nebseny, concluding text of BD 125) attracts a vignette of the Lake of Fire. This underworld lake actually judged the dead by scorching the evil but sustaining the good. The vignette shows a rectangle of water with red flaming-torch hieroglyphs and a baboon at each corner. It is more often attached to the separate text BD 126, the appeal to the four baboons (Thoth as justice, at each of the four cardinal points).

Illustrations of a hall for divine judgment also occur in other contexts. The royal Underworld Books of the New Kingdom describe in varying details the fate of the evil and of the blessed dead in the underworld, but they are less often explicit on the place or moment of judgment. In the *Book of Gates*, a version of the night journey of the sun god first attested on the walls of the tomb of Horemheb as king, the central scene of the composition presents Osiris enthroned at the top of a stepped platform with a scales, in part as a mummiform deity; on each of the nine steps is a human figure beneath the collective caption "Ennead of the retinue of Osiris." Beneath Osiris appears a text damning the "enemies," and above him are four inverted gazelle heads labeled *hmhmyw* ("the roarers"). The inscriptions of this scene are distinguished by unusual extension in selection and meaning of signs (cryptography). Above the Ennead, beside the scales, a boat bears a monkey wielding a curved stick to drive off a pig, and the monkey and stick are repeated outside the boat without the pig; this employs the force of ridicule to overpower enemies. This vignette recurs on later sources, sometimes combined with the *Book of the Dead* version (as on the Third Intermediate Period cartonnage Harvard 2230). Sarcophagi of the thirtieth dynasty attest to another version of the hall of Osiris, in which the enthroned god is offered life by his son Horus.

Stephen G. J. Quirke

K

KA. The complex of ideas concerning the *ka* is one of the most important in Egyptian religion. Since these ideas have no exact analogues in European cultures, it is impossible to translate adequately the word *k3* and to identify the *ka* with more familiar concepts. Interpretations of the *ka* are numerous, ambiguous, and usually unsatisfactory, and they range from its identification with the Latin *genius* to analogy with "mana."

The word *ka* was expressed by the hieroglyph of two upraised arms, usually considered a symbol of the embrace (or protection) of a man by his *ka*, although other interpretations are possible. A distinction should be made between the internal and external *ka*, as well as between the royal and the human *ka*, since these concepts were qualitatively different.

The idea that there was something securing the physical and mental activities of man arose in Egypt and elsewhere in prehistory. The *ka* (internal *ka*) was one of those entities. Its nature is reflected in numerous words going back to the same root: *k3j* ("think about," "intend"), *k3.t* ("thought"), *nk3j* ("think about"), *k3j* ("speak"), *k3.t* ("vagina"), *bk3.tj* ("testicles"), *nkj* ("copulate"), *nkjkj* ("fertilize"), *bk3* ("be pregnant," "impregnate"), *nk3k3* ("good condition of flesh"). Such words as *ḥk3*, *ḥk3.w* ("magic," "magic spells"), *ḥk3* ("enchant," "be enchanted"), *ḥk3j* ("sorcerer"), and *ḥk3(w)* ("god Heqa, person-

ification of magic") reflect the supernatural essence of the *ka*. The reproductive role of the *ka* is obvious, but its connection to thought processes is less clear. The mind was usually related to the *ba* (as in the *Dispute of a Man with his Ba*, where confusion of thought is described as a dialogue with that entity), but the word *ḥmt* ("think" or "to act three together") leads one to suppose that there was also an idea of thinking as a trilateral process, with the *ka* playing some obscure role, along with the *ba*. Owing to the role of the *ka* in thinking, *k3* could designate human individuality as a whole, and in different contexts it could be translated as "character," "nature," "temperament," or "disposition." Since character to a great extent preordains the life of an individual, *k3* also means "destiny," or "providence." This use of the word engendered a tradition of interpreting the *ka* as a kind of universal vital force, but this idea is too abstract, and even the examples cited above show that the meaning of *k3* was far more concrete in each context.

The ancient mind adopted personifications readily. It transformed this "inner motor" into a certain being. It seems that this being (the external *ka*) was primarily associated with the placenta (the twin of a man), and was born with him. Supernatural associations of the placenta and the umbilical cord are reported by ethnographers in central Africa, but in Egypt such

Statue of King Auibra Hor, with gilt collar and inlaid eyes. The figure stands naked and bears on his head the *ka* hieroglyph, a pair of oustretched arms. It also has the long beard indicating divine status. (Werner Forman Archive, Egyptian Museum, Cairo/Art Resource/NY)

notions were forced out early by more elaborate ideas, and only allusions to them can be traced in dynastic times.

The scenes of the king's birth depict Khnum forming the baby king and his *ka* on a potter's wheel. In Old Kingdom pyramid temples, New Kingdom royal tombs, and the temples of the gods, there are many representations of the *ka* accompanying the king, either as a personified *k3* sign or as a human form with the *k3* sign on its head. The *k3 hieroglyph holds the serekh* with the Horus name of the king, while the *ka* itself bears an ostrich feather (the symbol of the world harmony, or *maat*) in one hand, and a long staff with a finial shaped like the ing's head (*mdw-špsj*) in the other hand. Thus, the royal *ka* is related to the Horus name describing the presence of the sky-god in the king. This portrays the dualism of the king's nature, which combines divine and mortal components: divinity is realized

through the *ka*. In a number of cases (especially in the Old Kingdom), the finial is arranged at the level of the head of the falcon on the *serekh*, thus forming a composition structurally and semantically similar to the statues depicting the king with his head embraced by the falcon's wings, and demonstrating his double nature. The relation between the royal *ka* and Horus is apparent in its identification with Harsiese in the New Kingdom (although it could hardly be originally associated with Osirian ideas).

Another, qualitatively different aspect of the *ka* can be seen mainly on the monuments of private persons. The Egyptians were amazed by the fact that depiction can evoke in consciousness an image of the represented. These images were objectified, turned from a part of the psyche into a part of the medium, and identified with the external *ka*. As a result, these representations (at first statues, but also murals) became the main cult objects in tombs and temples. This is further supported by the words *n k3 n NN* ("for the *ka* of NN"), which were almost obligatory in the adjacent offering formulas. The most common translation of the word *k3* as "double" is applicable mainly to this external human *ka*.

Unlike the royal *ka*, the human *ka* was never represented as a separate figure, because any representation itself is the *ka*. This explains the indifference of Egyptian artists to rendering individual features. They did not reproduce the portrait of an individual, but that of his *ka*, who was eternally youthful and in perfect shape.

In an Old Kingdom private tomb, the pictures created an entire world for the *ka*. It is an exact although incomplete copy of the earthly world: only people and objects essential for the owner are depicted. Being a reproduction of everyday life, this "doubleworld" is surprisingly realistic; nothing supernatural, the gods included, is represented. Every tomb formed its own Doubleworld, and their total did not merge into an aggregate next world.

The notion of the *ka* was a dominating concept of the next life in the Old Kingdom. In a less pure form, it lived into the Middle Kingdom, and lost much of its importance in the New Kingdom, although the *ka* always remained the recipient of offerings.

Andrey O. Bolshakov

KA-CHAPEL. As far as one can judge from incomplete archaeological data, humans never produced burials without monuments marking their location or without cult places. This may not be considered axiomatic only because open cult monuments decay and so disappear much more easily than hidden burials. In Egypt, the functional dualism of the tomb and its division into burial and cult parts (usually substructure and superstructure, although other variants are also possible) is most obvious, owing to the hypertrophy of the latter.

The term "*ka*-chapel" is used mainly in American writing on ancient Egypt and has two meanings. In the narrowest sense, it was the chamber for the bringing of offerings, which contained the false door and the offering stone; in the widest sense, it was the whole complex of chambers in the superstructure open to priests, relatives of the deceased, and passers-by (multiple-roomed chapels). The term is misleading and conceals to some degree the true meaning of the phenomenon, for the notion of the *ka* as related to figurative tomb decoration was later than the earliest chapels and existed in its pure form only in the Old Kingdom. In the Middle Kingdom, the *ka* concept was somewhat profaned and, in the New Kingdom, it was mixed with

qualitatively different concepts (see p. 183–84). Thus, *tomb-chapel* or *cult chamber* (*Kultkammer, Opferkammer*) may be more appropriate terms for this type of architectural structure. The Egyptians designated "*ka*-chapel" by the word *ḥz*, which they also used for the "whole tomb" and for rooms of varying functions (e.g., offices and workshops), and they never developed more specific terms.

The time when the first *ka*-chapels were built is hard to establish. The earliest *mastabas* seem to have no chapels; their false doors were arranged openly on the façade. Some light (e.g., reed) structures, however, might have been erected in front of the false doors to vanish without any trace. *Ka*-chapels appeared in order to fulfill both ideological and purely practical requirements. The cult place was sacred, owing to its very function, and had to be separated from the surroundings; moreover, offering rituals had to be concealed from strangers. With that, a closed chapel was the best possible means to protect the false door and ritual equipment from vandalism and weathering (this became imperative when vulnerable murals were added).

Ka-chapels of the first dynasties were shaped either as a small court (sometimes roofed) in front of the false door, as a narrow roofed corridor along the eastern façade of the *mastaba* (exterior corridor chapel), or as a similar corridor penetrating into the body of the *mastaba* (interior corridor chapel). The only *ka*-chapel of the third type belonged to Hesyre (third dynasty) and was the first to house numerous mural decorations. From this time, murals were the main factor determining the architecture and appearance of the *ka*-chapels. Narrow corridor chapels with no adequate field of vision vanished, while those resulting from the deepening of the niche where the false door was placed predominated.

The only exceptions to this new type were the tombs of the "style of Khufu" at fourth dynasty Giza, with exterior brick ka-chapels attached to stone *mastaba*s (they were combined frequently with interior chapels).

The structure of the ka-chapel was influenced by both its genesis and ideology. Special attention was always paid to the east–west axis because of the association of the west with the next world. The false door was arranged in the western wall, while the entrance to the ka-chapel was placed in the opposite, eastern wall or in the eastern part of the northern or southern wall. In multiple-roomed tombs, the ka-chapel was the westernmost chamber of the whole complex. The arrangement of murals conformed to strict rules, which depended on the opposition of the west and the east (e.g., ritual topics were treated on the western wall, while everyday scenes were usually located on the eastern wall). In the second half of the fifth dynasty, multiple-roomed *mastaba*s became numerous; their decoration followed the same rules, although less extensively.

The tightly closed statue chamber, the *serdab,* is usually regarded as an independent component of the tomb, but the cult of statues is identical to that in front of the false door and murals of the ka-chapels. There are several Old Kingdom *serdab*s shaped as chapels with statue chambers behind their walls (*mastaba*s of Baefba, Seshemnefer II and III at Giza). The similarity in function of these *serdab*s to those of the ka-chapels is proven by the fact that the term $hw.t-k_3$ applied to them both, as well as to other chambers in the superstructure.

The spatial organization of rock tombs was somewhat different. Because of the technical difficulties of hewing stone, their cult chambers could not be numerous, and rarely exceeded one or two rooms. Such rooms combined the functions of the ka-chapels, *serdab*s, and other tomb chambers. Orientation of rock-cut ka-chapels was determined by the orientation of the cliff in which they were hewn, and often it differed dramatically from the traditional rules. The false door need not be arranged in the western wall, the entrance need not be opposed to it; moreover, both might be located in the same wall. The rules of the arrangement of murals were similarly modified. In the chapels of Old Kingdom rock tombs, the tradition of carving statues in the wall was developed; later, those engaged statues were adopted in the mastaba chapels.

The ka-chapel had two main functions. First, it was the offering place where everyday and festive priestly services were celebrated, where offerings where left on the offering stone, and where they were accepted by the tomb owner going forth from the false door. Second, when the first representations appeared, the ka-chapel acquired another function—its decorations started to create the world where the ka, the "double" of the owner, existed—in the Doubleworld. Decoration of the ka-chapel with realistic murals created the Doubleworld, reproducing earthly life and assuring it forever. That idea so elated the Egyptians that during the initial development of murals, they constructed several immured ka-chapels, which were isolated and independent from the cult (*mastaba*s of Nefermaat and Rahotep at Meidum). That experiment had no aftermath, and the next life was always regarded as secured both by cult and representations.

Although representations in the ka-chapel created the Doubleworld, it would be wrong to suppose that it was regarded as located within that chamber—

it existed in another dimension and only touched the earthly world wherever images were placed. Contact of the two worlds in the chapel was reflected in the ritual of Cleaning the Footprints; leaving the tomb, priests wiped up their footsteps to eliminate traces of the earthly in the realm of the Double. (For another interpretation, see H. Altenmü ller, "Eine Neue Deutung der Zeremonie des INIT RD," *Journal of Egyptian Archaeology* 57 (1971), 146–153.)

From the first half of the Old Kingdom, exceptional Memphite *ka*-chapels are known for the highest nobility and king's relatives (at Saqqara, Giza, Abusir, Dahshur, Meidum, and Abu Rowash); in the second half of the Old Kingdom, monuments of the lower strata of officialdom and those of nomarchs were also built in the homes (provinces). There were several standard sizes of cult chambers corresponding to the places of their owners in the official hierarchy; however, since decoration of the *ka*-chapels was practically identical, their Double-worlds were also almost indistinguishable, thus leveling inequality within the ruling class in the next life. Previously, it was supposed that even high-ranking craftsmen could not erect monuments of any significance during the Old Kingdom, but the 1990s discovery of a cemetery of necropolis artisans at Giza alters this perception.

After a century-long decay of the First Intermediate Period, *mastabas* of the old types were revived in the Faiyum and near Memphis. Regrettably, they are badly deteriorated, but several well-preserved chapels may be easily mistaken for Old Kingdom monuments (e.g., those of Ihy and Hetep at Saqqara). The main trend of development of the *ka*-chapels, however—beginning from the First Intermediate Period and Middle Kingdom—is represented by rock-cut

tombs. Scattered throughout Upper Egypt, rockcut tombs of those periods are a provincial phenomenon and, thus, several local tendencies coexist in the development of architecture and the decoration of their chapels. Such important necropolises as Hawawish (Akhmim), Meir, Bersheh, and Beni Hasan generally followed traditions of the Old Kingdom, although they deviated from a standard style, owing to provincialism and long independent development. In Thebes (at Tarif, Asasif, Gurna), Armant, and Dendera, the new type of *saff*-tomb appeared, with their chapels cut deeply into the rock and joined to the pillared façade by a narrow corridor. At Qubbet el-Hawa (Aswan) the corridor is longer and the chapel placed in the heart of the cliff seems to be separated further from the world of the living. In addition to rock-cut chapels, the tomb complexes of Qau el-Kebir (Antaeopolis) had free-standing chapels in the valley, which were analogous to the lower temples of royal burial edifices.

From the New Kingdom, the greatest number of rockcut tombs are known, with the Theban region having the most examples. Among other types of tombs, there was the extensive complex constructed at Thebes for Amenhotep, son of Hapu; like royal monuments, it contained a widely separated cult structure (temple) and hidden burial component (rock-cut chamber). A number of temple-shaped tombs of high officials from later decades was discovered at Saqqara. The most important among them is the complex of General Horemheb, built and decorated prior to his enthronement as last king of the eighteenth dynasty. The increased well-being of the lower classes was reflected in numerous tombs of necropolis craftsmen at Deir el-Medina; the decoration of their chapels was sometimes innovative and less restricted by tradition than decoration in the tombs of high officials.

In spite of the increased number, size, and splendor of New Kingdom tombs, their development marked the end of the *ka*-chapel. The number of religious motifs increased in the decoration of cult chambers during the eighteenth dynasty. Such scenes as funeral processions, which had been of limited importance in the previous epochs, were turned into detailed pictorial narrations. In Ramessid times, everyday scenes disappeared and representations and texts going back to the *Book of Going Forth by Day* (*Book of the Dead*) prevailed. Thus, the Doubleworld of Old Kingdom tradition declined in use and, accordingly, the term "*ka*-chapel" should not be applied to cult chambers of most tombs after that time.

Egypt's Late period was characterized by a general decline in tomb construction. The widespread use of family vaults and the usurpation of old tombs by new generations made traditional cult chambers useless and nonsensical. Degradation of chapels was mostly a result of the economic difficulty in sustaining a cult. The most remarkable exceptions to that rule were the Theban tombs of the twenty-fifth through twenty-sixth dynasties, which contained superstructures and cult quarters more extensive than any in the history of ancient Egypt. The greatest among them is that of Petamenophis at Asasif.

Of particular interest in the late history of tombchapels was the archaizing tendency of the twenty-fifth through twenty-sixth dynasties, which revived traditions of the Old Kingdom. Carved reliefs in those chapels mimicked decoration of ancient tombs almost exactly, but their owners did not understand the ancient ideology; realistic everyday topics were reinterpreted symbolically, and

the resurrection of the Doubleworld in the archaized chapels was suggested only with serious reservations. The last attempt to revitalize old chapel decorations was made in the late fourth century BCE, in the tomb of Petosiris at Tuna el-Gebel (Hermopolis), with its eclectic mix of everyday scenes in the Greco-Egyptian style and religious texts from early Egyptian times.   *Andrey O. Bolshakov*

KAMUTEF, literally, "bull of his mother," is not exactly the name of a deity, but rather is a functional epithet associated with the name of a deity—usually Amun-Re, or less frequently the combination Min-Amun-Re, or even Min alone. It makes Amun his own father, Amun-Re-Kamutef. Kamutef is represented under the appearance of Min, a figure bound up (like a mummy), having an erect penis. Amun-Re-Kamutef is attested at Karnak during the time of Senwosret I, and its ithyphallic depiction dates to the eleventh dynasty. At Coptos during the Middle Kingdom, Min-Kamutef was considered as the son of Isis. The Osirian terminology was thereby introduced into the Coptite theology, and Min-the-son was able to assume the functional name of Horus, and even of Horus-Isis. Kamutef appears in the Hermetic texts under the Greek name "Kamephis." To impregnate one's own mother was considered incest, a practice attested in the Pyramid Texts. Such an act allowed Geb, who raped his mother Tefnut, to appropriate the royalty of Shu, who was Tefnut's brother and husband and Kamutef's father. Yet to be "Kamutef" is also a way of denying linear time and inverting the succession of generations by uniting the past and the present in one personage. This personage, being both father and son of itself, possesses a legitimacy that is not questionable. Helmuth Jacobssohn (1939,

1955) sees in Kamutef a concept employed by the Egyptians to express the continuity of the regeneration of the gods and of the royal dynasties.

Probably, the historical circumstances of the appearance of Amun-Re-Kamutef clarify the significance of this theological construction. Around 2000 BCE, Montuhotep I reestablished the pharaonic power over the entire country. Parallel to his military and political actions, he established his power by means of a new theology whose central figure was Amun, the Theban god who appeared during the reign of his father Antef II. The unifier Montuhotep I is depicted on certain reliefs as adding the feathers of Amun to his crown of Upper Egypt. Amun is not a vague and weak local god; in his first attestations he is a divine and solar king, and an immanent entity, hidden in all things. He presents himself under two forms, a normal and an ithyphallic one, the latter being an appearance borrowed from his companion Min. During the reign of Senwosret I, even the nonithyphallic form of Amun could be described as "Kamutef." The two forms were equally important. Later, they alternated systematically on the walls of the Theban temples.

In the new theocracy, Amun-Re-Kamutef was an expression of the idea of legitimate descent without ancestry, and it kept the royal function safe from dynastic contestation. Although a divinity without ancestors, Amun-Re-Kamutef was not really one of the primordial deities, those solitary and unique gods present at the beginning of the world. Amun-Re-Kamutef is practically absent from the great funerary texts and cosmogonic stories.

The processional image of Min-Amun-Re-Kamutef, a ceremonial object used in the festival of Min, was conserved at Karnak. Following Herbert Ricke (1954), it is customary to attribute to Amun-Re-Kamutef the building constructed by Thutmose III in front of Temple of Mut at Karnak, but this interpretation can be questioned. We know of several priestly titles relating to the cult of the Kamutef-forms of Amun or of Min, but there was no clergy specifically dedicated to this divine aspect.

Claude Traunecker
Translated from French
by Susan Romanosky

KHNUM. The god Khnum is well attested, from the earliest period of Egyptian religion to the latest. He played a major role in the Egyptian pantheon. His numerous cult sites are located in the South, for the most part, near the cataract region, with Esna as his cult center. His name seems to be related to a Semitic root meaning "sheep."

Khnum appears some half-dozen times in the Pyramid Texts of the later Old Kingdom (c. 2400–2200 BCE), where he is portrayed primarily as a builder—five times of ferryboats and once of a ladder that ascends to heaven. One other passage, quite obscure, depicts him as a deity who "refashions," perhaps the first allusion to his role of creator god, familiar from texts of later periods.

In the Middle Kingdom Coffin Texts (1991–1786 BCE), Khnum is depicted as a creator of men and animals but not yet as a universal creator, a status that he later achieves. In the New Kingdom reigns of Hatshepsut and Thutmose III, he is first portrayed as a fashioner of gods, men, and animals, enacting creation on a potter's wheel, a motif that becomes prevalent in texts and reliefs from the New Kingdom through Roman times and is associated with the divine birth of the pharaoh.

The iconography of Khnum is, for the most part, consistent throughout

Egyptian history. He is invariably shown as a ram or a ram-headed anthropomorphic deity. The Egyptians drew this iconography from the now extinct sheep *Ovis longipes*, subspecies *palaeoaegypticus;* it differed from subspecies *palaeoatlanticus*, which did not make its appearance in Egypt until the Middle Kingdom. At that time, the new subspecies came to be used in the iconography of the god Amun. In ovine representations of these two gods, Egyptian artists seem to have kept their iconographic programs separate, with neither exerting influence on the other.   *Paul F. O'Rourke*

KHONSU. The primary function of Khonsu in Egyptian religion was as a lunar deity, and so he was portrayed with the symbols of the moon's disk and crescent on his head. Khonsu's name means "the traveler" (*Ḥnsw*) and most likely refers to his nightly journey across the sky in a boat. In his role as a moon god, Khonsu assisted the god Thoth, also a lunar deity, in marking the passage of time. Khonsu was also influential in effecting the creation of new life in both animals and humans.

Khonsu was the son of Amun and Mut. Together with them, he formed the family triad worshiped in the area of Thebes in southern Egypt. He was depicted as a mummified youth wearing the sidelock, characteristic of childhood; he is also shown holding the royal symbols of the crook and flail and, like the god Ptah, he frequently wears a *menat*-necklace.

As a divine child of Amun and Mut, Khonsu had close connections with two other divine children: the god of air, Shu; and the falcon-headed sun god, Horus. Because of this association with Horus, Khonsu is sometimes shown with a falcon's head, wearing a headdress with a sun disk and a moon crescent. He was

also linked to Horus in his role as a protector and healer.

Khonsu is described in early Egyptian religious texts as a rather bloodthirsty deity. He was mentioned only once in the Pyramid Texts, in the spell known as the "Cannibal Hymn," where he was described as "Khonsu who slew the lords, who strangles them for the King, and extracts for him what is in their bodies." He was mentioned a number of times in the Coffin Texts, where his violent nature was again noted: in Spell 258, he is "Khonsu who lives on hearts"; in Spell 994, he lives on heads; and in Spell 310, he is capable of sending out "the rage which burns hearts."

Although he was mentioned in these earlier texts, Khonsu did not rise to prominence in the Egyptian pantheon until the New Kingdom. During its later days, one of his divine epithets was "the Greatest God of the Great Gods," and he was worshiped at Thebes as "Khonsu-in-Thebes-Neferhotpe." During late Ramessid times, most of the construction at Karnak temple focused on the temple of Khonsu, begun under Ramesses III, which is situated near the *temenos* wall of the temple of the god Amun. One of the ancient Egyptian creation myths is known as the "Khonsu Cosmogony." It is preserved in a Ptolemaic text recorded on the walls at the Khonsu temple at Karnak and explains the connection of the Theban Khonsu to the creation myths of Memphis and Hermopolis.

In his role as a healing deity, however, Khonsu became well known beyond the boundaries of Egypt. A stela, possibly dating to the twenty-first dynasty, records the sending of a statue of Khonsu to Bekhten to cure an ill princess; upon its arrival, the princess was immediately cured. The ruler of the country tried to hold the image hostage, but after experiencing a nightmare in which the god appeared as a golden hawk, he allowed Khonsu to return to his temple in Thebes, where his arrival was met with great rejoicing.

Khonsu's fame as a healer continued into the Ptolemaic period. King Ptolemy IV was healed of an unknown illness though the intervention of Khonsu, and he was so impressed that he called himself "Beloved of Khonsu Who Protects His Majesty and Drives Away Evil Spirits."

Khonsu also had cults at the sites of Memphis, Edfu, and Hibis. At Kom Ombo he was worshiped as part of a different triad, in which he was the child of the crocodile deity Sobek and the divine cow Hathor.

Jennifer Houser-Wegner

M

MAAT. The ethical conceptions of "truth," "order," and "cosmic balance" are encompassed in the Egyptian term *maat*, and the personification of those principles is the goddess Maat (*M3ꜥt*). The goddess represented the divine harmony and balance of the universe, including the unending cycles of the rising and setting of the sun, the inundation of the Nile River, the resulting fertility of the land, and the enduring office of kingship; she was considered to be the force that kept chaos (*Isft*), the antithesis of order, from overwhelming the world. Hence *maat* was a complex, intertwined, and interdependent sense of ethics that tied personal behavior—such as speaking truthfully, dealing fairly in the market place, and especially sustaining obedience to parents, the king, and his agents—to the maintenance of universal order. To transgress one aspect of *maat* threatened to encourage chaos and overwhelm order. To live according to *maat* was also fundamental to personal existence. The *Instruction of Ptahhotep* (sixth dynasty) vowed: "There is punishment for him who passes over its [*maat's*] laws." The *Instructions for Merikare* (ninth dynasty) said: "Do *maat* so that you may endure upon Earth."

Maat and the King. One of the primary duties of the king was to maintain the order of the cosmos, effected by upholding the principle of *maat* through correct and just rule and through service to the gods. In turn, the people of Egypt had an obligation to uphold *maat*, through obedience to the king, who served as the intermediary between the divine and profane spheres. The *Instructions of Kagemni* record "do *maat* for the king, for *maat* is what the king loves"; the negative confession that was recited by the deceased, as his or her soul was judged against *maat*, included the profession "I have not disputed the king." The sense of fealty to the king and its association with personal responsibility for the balance of the universe may help explain why there are so few periods of social unrest in Egypt—for to act against the king was to risk the stability of the cosmos. The association of government and *maat* reached even the lower levels of government. Viziers who dispensed justice in the name of the king wore a pendant in the form of the goddess Maat, which both alluded to their association with the goddess and their inspiration to act justly. One of the clearest indications of the association of the king and the goddess Maat was the ritual of her presentation to the other gods. This ritual, which symbolized the dedication of the king to uphold the principles inherent in *maat* is first attested in the New Kingdom reign of Thutmose III (r. 1504–1452 BCE), although textual references suggest that it may be traced to Hatshepsut. The greatest number of examples from the eighteenth dynasty come from the early reign of Amenhotpe IV (r. 1372–1355 BCE), who assumed the poorly understood epithet ʿnḫ mmꜣʿt "Living as truth." The presentation of Maat was commonly depicted on the walls of Ramessid-era temples, especially in areas that were accessible to the public, which suggests that the ritual served as a symbol of royal legitimacy. This sense of the ritual being a royal prerogative has been verified in that only kings, one queen (Nefertiti), and a few others of quasi-royal status (Prince Osorkon and the "Gods' Wives of Amun" of the twenty-fifth dynasty and the twenty-sixth) have been depicted presenting Maat to a god in nonfunerary contexts (a few tomb scenes, however, show non-royal individuals presenting the image of the goddess).

Kings were considered to be imbued with *maat*. From the Old Kingdom reign of Sneferu (fourth dynasty) onward, the concept of *maat* was a common part of the royal titulary; many kings claimed the epithets nb mꜣʿt, "Possessor of *maat*," and ḫ m Mꜣʿt, "who arises in *maat*." Most of the Ramessid kings compounded their prenomen or nomen with *maat*. From the time of Sety I onward, many kings were depicted presenting a rebus of their prenomen to the gods thereby directly equating themselves with *maat*. The deity Maat pervaded the world of the gods. She was considered to be the daughter of the sun god Re and she was the Eye of Re, so parts of her body were equated with Re's body. She was also the "food of the gods," and the gods claimed to have "gulped down Maat." Maat served as the archtypical food offering for the gods, as suggested by offering scenes in the tombs of Merenptah, Sety II, Twosret, Sethnakhte, and Ramesses III, as well as at the Small Temple at Medinet Habu where *nw* vessels (normally associated with wine or other liquid offerings) are shown presented to the god—yet the offering scene is labeled as presenting Maat. Thoth had an especially close association with Maat, and the two deities are often shown paired.

The Goddess Maat. Representations of the goddess Maat are attested as early as the middle of the Old Kingdom, initially in theophoric names. She is shown in the form of an idealized female, wearing a sheath dress and her characteristic emblem—an ostrich plume (phonogram *mꜣʿ*)—on her head. The symbolism of the emblem is uncertain, although the same emblem is shared by the god Shu, who in some cosmologies is her brother.

Temples and Cult of Maat. Despite the great importance placed on Maat, there is no evidence for a temple dedicated to her that predates the New Kingdom construction of the temple to Maat at Karnak North by Amenhotpe III. Textual references suggest that other temples of Maat were located at Memphis and at Deir el-Medina. The Karnak structure was used for the coronation of Queen Hatshepsut and, perhaps, for the investiture of some kings. The Tomb Robbery Papyri indicate that the court that met to investigate the robberies of the royal tombs during the reign of Ramesses IX convened at the Maat temple. Although texts refer to priests of Maat in the ranks *wʿb*, *ḥry-ḥbt*, *ḥm-nṯr* nothing is known about a cult specific to the goddess. The title i, "overseer of the domain of Maat," suggests that lands and resources were held by the Maat temple, but nothing more is known of their extent or administration. In temple cult-offering scenes, Maat usually stands behind the king or behind the recipient. She rarely acts as the recipient of offerings.

Maat and Funerary Beliefs. Both the goddess Maat and the conception of ethics inherent in *maat* are most closely associated in the funerary realm—for correct behavior during life was a requisite for eternal life after death. Spell 816 of the Coffin Texts relates that Maat was associated with the Opening of the Mouth ceremony. By the New Kingdom, Maat was credited with being able to grant a good burial, and she is invoked in *ḥtp di nsw* offering formulas. Her association with rebirth is most clearly illustrated by Chapter 125 of the *Book of Going Forth by Day* (*Book of the Dead*), first attested in the reign of Amenhotpe II, which shows the weighing of the heart against a small figure of Maat (or the feather emblem) to evaluate the worthiness of the deceased. In the New Kingdom and onward, Maat was increasingly associated with sun hymns and solar imagery, in reference to the deceased's union with the cycle of the sun and, hence, eternal rebirth. Maat, or a dual form (Maaty), was pictured in the solar bark with her father Re. Sun hymns on the portals of private Theban tombs, such as that of Neferhotep (tomb 49), refer to the deceased presenting Maat to the sun god. By the twentieth dynasty, Maat acquired distinctively funerary associations, particularly in Thebes, through her fusion with Imntt, the goddess of the west. The Theban necropolis was referred to as *st Mꜣꜥt*, "the place of Truth," and "the place for those who have done Maat." The peak over the Theban necropolis was referred to as "the great peak of the West in this its name of Maat." Ramessid epithets of Maat included "Mistress of the necropolis"; "Mistress of the West"; and "Mistress of the West who resides in the necropolis." By the Ramessid period, the association of the deceased with Maat was so strong that the transfigured *akhs* (souls) were, like the god themselves, considered to consume and live upon *maat*.   *Emily Teter*

MAGIC. [*This entry comprises four articles:* An Overview; Magic in Medicine; Magic in Daily Life; *and* Magic in the Afterlife.]

An Overview

The concept of "magic" has proved to be a most difficult category for modern Egyptology, with little agreement regarding the definition or scope of supposedly magical practices. The designation of "magic" has been applied subjectively to any actions or recitations deemed "nonreligious" by individual authors. Following the early anthropological theories of James G. Frazer (*The Golden Bough*, 1910) and Bronislaw Malinowski (*Magic, Science and Religion and Other Essays*, 1948), "magic" is most fre-

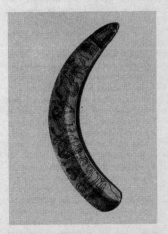

A twelfth dynasty magic "wand" made of ivory. Such amulets, inscribed with magical symbols, served to ward off snakes, poisonous insects, and other hidden dangers. (The Metropolitan Museum of Art, Theodore M. Davis Collection. Bequest of Theodore M. Davis, 1915. [30.8.218])

quently distinguished from "religion" on the basis of the former's "blasphemous," threatening attitude (as opposed to "proper" humility) and its immediate, limited, and personal goals (contrasted with rites and prayers for general well-being). Unfortunately, such distinctions are inadequate for ancient Egypt, where a threatening attitude may be adopted in orthodox public rituals for general benefit, and identical texts and rites may serve either personal or general ends. Seeking to avoid this problem, many scholars have adopted the term "magico-religious," while others have urged the abandonment of any category of magic. A working definition of *magic* as "any activity which seeks to obtain its goal by methods outside the simple laws of cause and effect" has been proposed by Ritner (1993, p. 69) and adopted in subsequent reference works (M. Depauw, *A Companion to Demotic Studies,* Brussels, 1997, p. 109).

Justification for the retention of the concept derives not from modern Egyptology but from indigenous terminology. In the Christian period, the Coptic term *hik* was equated explicitly with Greek *mageia* and Latin *magia* as a designation for impious and illegal sorcery. Coptic *hik* is the descendant of pharaonic (*ḥꜣ3*), whose pre-Christian associations were, however, neither impious nor illegal. Attested from the Old Kingdom through the Roman era, *heka* represented a primary cosmic force and, personified as Heka, the eldest son of the universal creator. In this capacity of child deity, Heka was venerated as the junior member of local triads at Heliopolis in the Old Kingdom, the Memphite necropolis in the New Kingdom, the western Delta in the Third Intermediate Period, and Esna in Hellenistic times. His pivotal theological significance, substantially formulated

before the Middle Kingdom, was recognized well beyond these local cult sites.

As detailed in the recitation "To Become the God Heka" (Coffin Text Spell 261), Heka was believed to have been formed "before duality had yet come into being" as the force that at once animated, compelled, and protected the gods and subsequent creation. Antecedent to the Creative Word (*Hu*), Heka infuses the creator's projected images, or *ka*-spirits, with his "magical" vitality, in keeping with the likely meaning of his name as "He who consecrates the *ka*-spirit." Representing the principle of consecrated imagery, Heka is styled "Lord of *ka*-spirits" in Coffin Text Spell 261, and the association recurs in Spell 648, where the "millions of *ka*-spirits within his mouth" serve as "powers" which instill fear in the gods, create the mountains, and knit the firmament together. The description of Heka's empowered imagery "within his mouth" reflects the close link between Egyptian magic and the word, whether spoken or written. His fundamental association with cosmic dynamics is indicated by the emblematic spelling of his name, from the twentieth dynasty onward, with the hieroglyph for "power." At the Roman temple of Esna, his primacy was stressed by a folk etymology explaining his name as "the First Work." In Greco-Egyptian magical papyri of late Roman date, *heka* is translated by both *hiera mageia,* signifying "holy magic," and *hiera* or *theia energeia,* meaning "holy" or "divine power." Ironically, these last mentions are contemporary with the Coptic Christian denigration of *hik/heka* as irreligious, demonic sorcery. In marked contrast to Western and orthodox Coptic notions of magic, Egyptian *heka* was considered neither supernatural nor unholy, representing instead the divinely sanctioned force that initiated, permeated, and sustained nature itself.

Heka's creative role is repeated daily, for he accompanies the sun god Re on his cyclical voyage, protects the enthroned Osiris in the netherworld, and by prayer invokes the continued separation of heaven and earth. His protective duties entail a corresponding destructive role, and Heka's power to frighten even the gods is an invariable feature of his theological descriptions. Heka's threatening character has been noted above in connection with the Coffin Texts and was already evident in the earlier Pyramid Texts, where the appearance of the deity causes the sky to tremble and the earth to quake (Spell 472). In the first example of a recitation technique that would be continued into Coptic times, a formal curse against recalcitrant spirits is said to be uttered not by the human speaker, but by a higher authority: "It is not I who says this against you, O gods; it is Heka who says this against you, O gods" (Pyramid Text Spell 539).

With similar orthodoxy, the hostile power of *heka* might be tapped for cosmic, state or even personal cursing rites. The legitimacy of such practice is specified in the literary *Instructions for Merikare*, which lists magic among the fundamental benefactions allotted by the creator to humanity, in company with the creation of heaven, earth, air, food, and proper government: "It was in order to be weapons to ward off the blow of events that he made *heka* for them (humanity)." The "Execration Texts," attested from the Old Kingdom through the Late period, illustrate the unity of state and private cursing practice. Anticipating the use of the so-called voodoo doll, these texts comprise lists of names

of foreign rulers, Egyptian enemies, and hostile forces inscribed on red pottery or on figures of bound prisoners, rendered harmless by ritual torture and burial. While the updated lists of foreign rulers certainly derived from the state chancellery, the names of condemned Egyptians may have been influenced by private sponsorship, as was surely the case with isolated figures designed to curse individuals and families. Addressing the practitioner, a late cursing ritual pairs state and divine enemies with "all foes male and female whom your heart fears" (Papyrus British Museum 10188, col. 28/17–18). In response to such techniques, "Oracular Amuletic Decrees" offered divine protection against any potential male or female magician (*hekay*). Closely related to such execration rituals are "love" spells, which are first attested in Ramessid times and become particularly common in Demotic and derivative Greek papyri. Borrowing the imagery and mechanics of cursing magic, "love" spells are equally spells of domination, ensuring that the victim can neither eat nor sleep, but only follow the magician's client "like an ox after grass" (Ostracon Deir el-Medina 1057).

The force of *heka* is thus morally neutral, and even foreign enemies and demons might be said to possess or utilize *heka*. Unlike the classical and later Christian use of *mageia* or *magia*, the Egyptian term does not serve primarily as a term of disparagement to mark cultural boundaries, distinguishing inferior, foreign "witchcraft" from positive, local "religion." Individual cases of *heka* might be described as "bad" or "evil" from the perspective of the intended victim, but no general categories of "white" or "black" magic are documented in Egyptian sources. Attempts to isolate such distinctions have proved unsuccessful (see

Ritner 1993, pp. 20–21, 30–35). In the reign of Ramesses III (c. 1198–1166 BCE), a harem conspiracy made use of standard execration techniques with manipulated wax figurines in a failed attempt to replace the monarch with a prince Pentaweret, but the surviving interrogation records constitute a trial for treason, not sorcery. The manuals of magic used by the conspirators were orthodox compositions taken from the royal archives, and the practitioner was a priest, the customary magician in Egyptian society.

As made evident by the previous references to the Pyramid Texts, Coffin Texts, Execration Texts, and Oracular Amuletic Decrees, the practice of magic in Egypt was closely associated with written manuals detailing recitations, obligatory ingredients, and ritual performance—corresponding to a tripartite categorization of magic as speech, inherent property, and rite. Spell collections, whether designed for state or royal ritual, medical healing, exorcism, cursing, or even agricultural security, were accorded sacred status as "emanations (b3w) of Re" and were products of the "House of Life" (pr-'nḫ), or temple scriptorium. Composed, compiled, and stored in the scriptorium, such magical texts were exclusive temple property, jealously guarded to prevent misuse by outsiders, whether foreign or native. Restrictions applied to simple fording spells, as indicated by the Harris Magical Papyrus (Papyrus British Museum 10042, col. 6/10): "First spell of enchanting all that is in the water, concerning which the Chief Lector Priests say: 'Do not reveal it to others.' A veritable secret of the House of Life."

The strong emphasis in Egyptian magic on written texts necessarily restricted the range of professional practitioners to members of the literate, temple-affiliated elite, who are currently estimated as comprising no more than 1 percent of the population. Old Kingdom tomb scenes may indicate that simple charms were memorized and recited by illiterate farmers and herdsmen, though representations and the Harris Magical Papyrus suggest the presence of a specialist, with the herdsmen performing only protective gestures. Rare mentions of a prophetic "wise woman" (rḫt) are found in private records from the cloistered and highly literate New Kingdom artists' colony at Deir el-Medina, which substituted community participation for professional priests in typically restricted ritual roles. Otherwise, magicians are explicitly designated as members of the priestly hierarchy, including the "Prophet of Heka" (ḥm-nṯr Ḥq3), the "Chief of Secrets" (ḥrỉ-sst3), ḥ h and especially the "Chief Lector Priest" (ḥrỉ-ḥb ḥrỉ-tp), who was entrusted with the sacred scrolls and who recited hymns and incantations during formal temple ceremonies as well as during private apotropaic and funerary rites. In abbreviated form (ḥrỉ-tp), the title becomes the standard term for "magician" from the New Kingdom onward and appears in transcription in both Akkadian (as khartibi) and Hebrew records (cf. Genesis 41.8: hartumim) to designate Egyptian magicians.

As the imagistic principle represented by heka underlies all ritual, whether conducted in a temple or private setting, so the same ritual specialist could serve either public or private interests. This dual role would have created no professional difficulty. With the exception of the very highest ranks, Egyptian priests were not on duty throughout the year, but served in groups or "phyles" in rotation. With four and, after year 9 of Ptolemy III (238

BCE), five such phyles serving in rotation, priests will have had at least three-quarters of the year off duty, with opportunity and incentive to create a lucrative "private" practice. The classical and medieval conception of magicians as itinerant and unaffiliated practitioners on the social fringe has no validity in pharaonic Egypt, where groups of off-duty priests had the training, temple access, authority, and established clientele requisite for the role of community magician. As authors, editors, and custodians of ritual texts, their monopoly on the profession was unassailable.

The best evidence for the accouterments of the professional magician derives from the find of an intact "magician's box" in a twelfth dynasty tomb shaft beneath the northern storerooms of the Ramesseum. Measuring eighteen by twelve by twelve inches, the chest was labeled on its cover as belonging to a "Chief of Secrets" and contained twenty-three fragmentary papyri, a bundle of reed pens, four broken ivory apotropaic wands, and an assortment of beads, amulets, and figurines. The papyri and writing instruments are again indicative of the importance of literacy in Egyptian magic, and the subjects of the Ramesseum Papyri (P. Ram.) reveal the range of the specialist's concerns: medico-magical treatments for eye *h* disease, stomach complaints, and constricted urination (P. Ram. III); recipes for procreation, pregnancy, and newborns (P. Ram. IV); remedies for muscular pains and stiffness (P. Ram. V); formal hymns to the crocodile deity Sobek (P. Ram. VI); incantations for protective amulets (P. Ram. VII); exorcisms of afflicting ghosts (P. Ram. C); a dramatic ritual text concerning the cult of Osiris (P. Ram B); an archaic funerary liturgy (P. Ram. E); as well as spells against

headache (P. Ram VIII), serpents (P. Ram IX-X), and for general protection (P. Ram XVI-XVII). The further inclusion of literary texts (P. Ram. I, II, A, and D) suggested to Gardiner that "the tomb-owner combined with the sterner purposes of his profession the function of a local story-teller and entertainer" (*The Ramesseum Papyri* [Oxford, 1955], p. 1).

The prominence of medical spells within the Ramesseum corpus reveals the close association between magician and physician (*swnw*), whose training was also tied to the temple scriptorium and whose methodology combined both "rational" and "magical" treatment strategies, with charged substances (magic by property), incantations (magic by speech), and ritual actions (magic by rite). From the introductory sections of Papyrus Ebers (c.1550 BCE), it is evident that even prescriptions with no specified magical component were routinely accompanied by standardized spells for applying remedies, loosening bandages, and drinking potions (cols. 1/1–2/6). A century later, Papyrus Hearst provides similar generic spells for measuring ingredients (cols. 13/17–14/4) or applying oil (col. 14/4–7). Medical compendia might also include spells seemingly more appropriate for the community magician. Papyrus Ebers contains an incantation "to prevent a kite from robbing" (col. 98/2–6), though this may have been collected to protect the pharmacist's herb garden. Physicians with distinctly theological backgrounds included the "priest of Sakhmet" (*w'b Shmt*), the goddess of plague and disease, and the "controller of Selqet" (*hrp-Srqt*), goddess of scorpions and snakes. The class of healer known as the "amulet-man" (*s3w*) was perhaps illiterate, though in company with the priests of Sakhmet and regular physicians they were trained to take the pulse and are attested at court. It was a priest of the destructive deity Sakhmet who gained access to state execration rituals and attempted the overthrow of Ramesses III.

The Ramesseum spells for childbirth and neonates are paralleled in the "Magical Spells for Mother and Child" (Papyrus Berlin 3027) of early New Kingdom date; they were recited not by anxious mothers but by lector-priests (ẖrỉ-ḥb) or "magicians of the nursery" (ḥꜣꜣy n kꜣp) related to such spells are the apotrapaic wands recovered from the magician's box, which are formed from hippopotamus tusks and engraved with a series of animal spirits. While determined by the material, the shape of these pieces is probably intended to represent a knife, comparable to those typically held by the engraved figures. Similar magical knives are well attested from the Middle Kingdom, and inscribed examples state that the figures offer protection from all evil forces. Signs of wear suggest that they may have been used to delineate defensive circles around a child's bed. As the protectress of children, mothers, and the bedroom, the leonine goddess Beset served similar ends, and her image is found both on these knives and as an individual bronze figure within the Ramesseum cache. The remaining items from the box illustrate the varied functions of magic in daily life. Female figurines probably served to enhance fertility; beads and a bronze uraeus (wrapped in hair) formed protective amulets; an ivory herdsman recalls the early scenes of fording rites noted previously and is further evidence for the participation of trained magicians in agricultural contexts.

As noted by John Barns in his edition of Papyrus Ramesseum IV (*Five Ramesseum Papyri* [Oxford, 1956], p. 25), the high incidence of magical treatments in this early corpus refutes the still common notion that magic increased over time, "corrupting" Egyptian religion and medicine. In the form of amulets and manipulated figurines, the use of magic continued with no *qualitative* change from Predynastic through Coptic times. Innovative forms and the demands of an expanding wealthy class did produce a *quantitative* increase in magical texts and objects, but the orthodox position of magic within religion and medicine remained constant. The invention of magical knives in the Middle Kingdom represents a new application of customary magical mechanics, not a new significance for the concept of magic itself. Late predilection for love spells does not signal "a spirit that is strikingly different" from earlier times, but rather a continuation of traditional execration practice, following Ramessid and earlier precedent (*contra* Borghouts, 1974, p. 17). Examples of the techniques of coercive spell, charged substance, and rite are found in all extant medical texts, and similar features pervade the funerary literature of all periods. As "practical theology" designed to compel individual salvation, the Pyramid Texts, Coffin Texts, and *Book of Going Forth by Day* (*Book of the Dead*) are inherently magical, as are the attendant grave figures, *shawabtis*, protective bricks, amuletic images, and other tomb accessories.

In addition to apotropaic knives and love spells, magical innovations include the oracular procedure termed pḥ-nṯr, meaning literally "to reach" or "to petition" a god. Although this term is often applied to private and even hostile conjurations, it serves to designate any oracular consultation of a divine image, even the temple-sponsored statue processions that functioned as formal tribunals, fully equivalent to a court of law. Temple oracles were a typical feature of New

Kingdom religious practice, and they assumed additional prestige with the subsequent decline of royal authority. The manifestation of the god was addressed directly, and by appropriate signs or documents a response was granted. Ascribed to the patronage of Heka, the "Lord of oracles, Lord of revelations," such procedures were not simply legal, but the source of local legality. Private adaptations are first attested in the Ramessid period. In the harem conspiracy against Ramesses III, the plotters "began to petition god (*ph-ntr*) for the derangement of the people." In a less hostile context from the reign of Ramesses IX, the necropolis worker Qenna from Deir el-Medina was granted an excused absence "in order to petition god" with the assistance of a lamp allotted from the village storehouse. Qenna's use of a lamp to evoke divine visions is paralleled by numerous revelatory spells in the magical papyri of Hellenistic Egypt, whether surviving in Demotic or in Greek adaptations. Like their native antecedents, the Demotic rituals are termed *ph-ntr* and are evidence of direct continuity with earlier practice. Hostile use of the *ph-ntr* was countered in post-Ramessid times by the extensive Oracular Amuletic Decrees, descendants of "royal decrees" of protection issued by individual gods against detailed lists of ills (cf. Papyrus Turin 1993, 7/6–10). From the Amuletic Decrees derive the similarly detailed "Self-Dedication Texts" of the Ptolemaic era.

Also extending from the New Kingdom through Hellenistic times are the healing stelae known as "*cippi* of Horus," which combine traditional ritual techniques with newly standardized imagery and spells to prevent or allay the effect of snakebite and scorpion sting. Produced for general distribution, or in larger scale as public benefactions, the healing stelae were not read, but placed in contact with water that was drunk by the sufferer. The notion that magical power can be consumed is found as early as the Pyramid Texts (Spells 273–274), while Coffin Text Spell 341 records the transfer of the power of inscribed imagery to ingested fluids: "This spell is to be spoken over seven sketched eyes of Horus, washed off in beer and natron and drunk by the man." In similar fashion, incantations are drawn on the hand and licked off by the practitioner (Coffin Text Spell 81), so that standard descriptions of magicians include any "who shall lick off his spell" (Coffin Text Spell 277; *Book of Going Forth by Day* Spell 149e). On the basis of such magical mechanics, the term for "swallow" acquires the nuance "to know" by the New Kingdom. The licking or drinking of charged fluids remains a basic technique for subsequent Late Egyptian, Demotic, Greco-Egyptian, and Coptic magical rites.

The techniques of Egyptian magic have been noted frequently above, with reference both to ritual mechanics such as licking, swallowing, or image manipulation and to recitation devices like threats and blame-shifting ("It is not I who says . . ."). Perhaps the most common ritual technique is circumambulation (*phr*), used to enclose and defend sacred space or to ensnare hostile forces. Circular processions accompany funerary rites and a wide variety of temple rituals and are performed by private homeowners armed with sticks to avert the "plague of the year" at the dangerous calendrical cusp. Similarly protective are the circles scratched into the earth with apotropaic knives. In contrast, an execration ritual to protect the temple scriptorium (Papyrus Salt 825) confines wax figures of enemies within a jar encircled by the practitioner. So basic is the association of "encircling" with magic that the term *phr* comes to mean "enchant" in Demotic and Coptic. Other common ritual techniques include knots, numerological and color symbolism, necromantic intercessions, and the bivalent action of spitting or the purely hostile acts of breaking, trampling, burning, reversal, and burial.

Of recitation techniques, none is so basic as the explicit identification of the practitioner with one or more deities ("I am deity NN"). By recasting the speaker, and often the client, as a god, such equations confer divine authority on the incantation and link the fate of the client with that of a divine prototype. In medical texts, the patient is almost invariably identified with the youthful Horus, whose recovery from assaults by Seth and his confederates serves as the pattern for all healing. From the Pyramid Texts onward, identifications often take the form of lists, associating each of the client's body parts with that of a deity so that "no limb of his is lacking a god" (Socle Behague h14). Direct identification with a deity is integral to Egyptian magical recitations into Coptic times, and it permeates Greco-Egyptian spells by means of the untranslated native phrase *anok* ("I am"). Similar in purpose is the abbreviated mythological episode, or "historiola," which provides a divine precedent for the desired result: as the deity triumphs in the tale, so the client will triumph likewise. The link between client and god may be either implicit or expressed by direct identification. As the spell's beneficiary is qualified by divine associations, so the opponent is equated with demonic forces. To ensure efficacy, all parties are identified as specifically as possible. For humans, the pattern is typically "NN whom the woman NN bore." Nonhuman entities may also be given filiation: "cold, son of a cold" (Papyrus Ebers, col. 90/16). Hostile spirits are listed as inclusively as possible, with strings of male and female pairs often concluded by the term *et cetera* (*hmt-r3*). The language of the spell constitutes "performative speech," often using the past tense to declare that the desired result has been accomplished.

As early as the Pyramid Texts (Spell 281), incantations may include unintelligible vocables, to be understood as either "magical words" or as transcriptions of foreign recitations (cf. Harris Magical Papyrus, cols. 7/12 and 12/1–5). Syncretistic by nature, Egyptian conjurations readily assimilated Semitic, Cretan, Nubian, and ultimately Greek elements, which were incorporated within canonical manuals at all periods. Later collections may display a higher percentage of such borrowings, but even in these compendia the underlying methodology of recitation and praxis remains primarily Egyptian. As demonstrated above, the Demotic and Greek language spells of Roman date are the direct inheritors of traditional Egyptian magic. Old Coptic spells continue the tradition, and the development of the Coptic script in part derived from the magicians' desire to specify vowels within exotic incantations. Despite a shift of deity, native techniques continue within Coptic and medieval Islamic magical practices, though the practitioner is now suspect, and his practice at variance with official theology.   *Robert K. Ritner*

Magic in Medicine

Standard discussions of medical practice in ancient Egypt typically distinguish between rational therapy ("medicine") and the use of incantations and rites ("magic"). On the basis of this modern categorical bias, rational treatments have been the focus of detailed study, while magical aspects are often marginalized and their significance to the ancient audience is undervalued. The prevailing attitude is exemplified by the primary edition of Papyrus Edwin Smith, which isolates Case 9, in which the physician recommends a comforting spell for a terminal skull fracture, as a "characteristic product of the recipehawking physician (as contrasted with the surgeon) . . . our surgeon's sole relapse into the superstition of his age (Breasted 1930, p. 217)." Despite this harsh judgment, the features of the case are not aberrant in composition and include a preliminary physical examination and (rational) treatment with a compress and bandaging. In this as in other instances, "magical" and "rational" treatments are paired, and the two methodologies are complementary, not in conflict.

The physician's use of ritual and spell is in keeping with ancient medical education, which was affiliated with the temple scriptorium (pr-ʿnḫ), a repository for medical and other sacred texts. Medicine, like all sciences, fell under the patronage of the god Thoth, although other deities might be seen as healers, including Amun, Isis, and Horus, as well as the deified sages Imhotep and Amenhotep son of Hapu. Priesthoods of these benign gods might be expected to include religious healers, but the most notable physician-priests are associated with potentially threatening goddesses: Sakhmet, goddess of disease, and Selqet, goddess of scorpions and snakes. The priest of Sakhmet is mentioned explicitly in both the Edwin Smith (col. 1/6) and Ebers (col. 99/2–3) papyri as a medical practitioner likely to take a measurement of the pulse, in common with the standard physician (swnw) and even the amulet-seller (z3w). This "amulet-man" noted in Papyrus Ebers might find state service as well, and amulet-men of the king of Upper and Lower Egypt are attested at court. The "controller of Selqet" treated scorpion sting and snakebite, and groups of these professionals were enlisted by the state to accompany mining expeditions, where noxious animals posed a constant danger. The handbook of such a specialist is now preserved in the Brooklyn Museum (47.218.48 and 47.218.85). Dating to the thirtieth dynasty or early Ptolemaic period, the manual provides not only a "rational" analysis of snakes by name, description, and relative toxicity, but also a "magical" analysis of the reptiles' divine associations. As expected, treatment incorporates both strategies, with incisions, emetics, topical applications, and recited spells. Magical spells against snakebite are the oldest medical remedies known from Egypt, preserved in large number within the Pyramid Texts (spells 226–244, 276–299, 314, 375–399, 499–500, 501, 538, etc.) and subsequent literature adapted from daily life for funerary purposes. These incantations include the first examples of unintelligible glossolalia, or "abracadabra" words, presumably representing foreign or divine speech (Pyramid Text Spell 281).

Within the more narrowly defined medical literature, spells are a regular and undifferentiated feature. The earliest preserved medical treatise, the Kahun Papyrus of the twelfth dynasty (c.1850 BCE), deals with both gynecology and veterinary medicine. A series of six prescriptions (nos. XXVI–XXXI) to determine whether a woman will conceive includes physical examinations, anointing, fumigation and, in prescription XXX, a fragmentary spell. Nothing formally distinguishes this manner of treatment, which is labeled simply "another instance" like those that precede and follow it. The Ramesseum Papyri III–V (c.1786–1665 BCE) are poorly preserved, but the combination of "rational" and "magical" therapy is again evident, with ingested recipes charged by spells recited over stems of onions (III, 5), flax knots placed at a child's throat (III, 33–34, and cf. IV, iii/5), fumigations and recitations over an image of a child (IV, 23–24), recitations over ointment at childbirth (IV, 30), and incantations over beer (IV, iii/4 and iv/1). Papyrus Ramesseum V preserves no spells, but its reliance on oil of hippopotamus, crocodile, lion, mouse, donkey, and lizard seems motivated by magical associations, rather than by purely physical properties. Medical spells appear also in contemporary Middle Kingdom magical manuals, with Papyrus Turin 54003 offering spells against snakebite, eye problems, and swallowed fishbones.

The use of magic in Case 9 of the Edwin Smith Papyrus (copied c.1550 BCE) has been discussed above. Further incantations against the "plague of the year" were added by the original scribe on the verso of the papyrus. As noted in a perceptive study by Wilson (1952), the relative paucity of magic in this "Surgical Papyrus" is likely due to the nature of the injuries under consideration. Most are simple fractures of obvious origin and straightforward treatment. Had the text dealt with the more mysterious problem of internal disease, magic would have been more prominent, as is the case in the corresponding Ebers Papyrus, copied by the identical scribe. In both papyri, infection is attributed to "something entering from the outside," depicted as a demonic figure with antennae.

The Ebers Papyrus (also c.1550 BCE) is a compilation of remedies and theoretical discussions, and it freely joins "rational" and "magical" methodology. The magical component of the papyrus is evident from the very beginning, as the first three sections detail the "First spell for applying remedies on any limb of a

man" (col. 1/1–11), "Another spell for loosening any bandage" (col. 1/12–2/1), and a "Spell for drinking a remedy" (col. 2/1–6). Each spell contains a brief mythological episode, known as a "historiola," which assimilates the patient and his fate to the successful healing of a deity and offers protection against "the stroke of a god, the stroke of a goddess, from a dead man, a dead woman, from a male adversary, a female adversary," etc. All spells are recommended as "truly effective—(proved) millions of times." The introductory position of these generic spells indicates that their use is to be understood in all subsequent remedies without any further specification. By implication, even recipes lacking explicit magical features would still have been accompanied by standard healing incantations. Thus, the absence of spells from individual sections of the Edwin Smith, Ebers or other medical papyri should not be used as evidence of an exclusively rational approach, and the supposed contrast between the "recipe-hawking" and rational physician is fallacious.

The Ebers Papyrus contains seventeen incantations and two birth prognostications generally treated as magical. In addition to the three introductory spells, the papyrus prescribes incantations coupled with potions for treatment of diarrhea (§ 48, col. 15/16–16/6) and roundworm (§ 61, col. 18/21–19/10). An exorcism of *whdw* conjures the principle of corruption believed responsible for natural aging and decay (§ 131, col. 30/6–17). The *whdw* or unexpelled residue of bodily waste, is commanded to leave the body as spittle or vomit and thus "perish just as you came into being." Further exorcisms expel bewitchment (§ 733, col. 88/13–16), bald patches (§ 776, col. 92/13–16), illness in the female breast (§ 811, col. 95/7–14), and prevent a kite from robbing (§ 848, col. 98/2–6). Paralleling the use of magic as a last resort in Case 9 of the Smith Papyrus, the "instructions for the swelling of the vessels" caution the physician against physical treatment, but provide a recitation for enchanting the fatal illness (§ 873, col. 108/9–17).

Several incantations are recommended for ophthalmological treatments. For blindness, the principle of substitution underlies a topical treatment with fluid extracted from pig's eyes accompanied by a statement "as magic" that the practitioner has "brought these which are put in the place of those" (§ 356, col. 57/17–21). The selection of pig's eyes evokes (and counteracts) the myth of the blinding by Horus by a black pig (Coffin Text Spell 157 and *Book of Going Forth by Day* [Book of the Dead] 112). A spell against "white spots" in the eyes recounts a historiola of the floundering of the solar bark recited over the gall bladder of a tortoise, an enemy of Re and his ship (§ 360, col. 58/6–15; cf. *Book of Going Forth by Day* Spell 161). Word association (paranomasia) forms the crux of a spell to "expel the collecting of water in the eyes (cataracts)," which invokes the presence of vigor (*w3dd*) by the application of malachite (*w3d*, § 385, col. 60/16–61/1; cf. *Book of Going Forth by Day* 160). In most spells, cures are effected by means of direct identification between patient and deity, either completely ("I am Horus"; "It is not I who recites but the goddess Isis") or in part ("My head is the head of Anubis, . . . my nose is the nose of Thoth . . . , there is no limb of mine lacking a god").

Representative examples of the pairing of rational and magical procedures are afforded by the three treatments offered for the common cold (cols. 90/14–91/1). The first remedy is simply date wine to be drunk by the patient, and the second involves ground plant material inserted into the nostrils. The third (§ 763), "Another exorcism of a cold," consists of a spell against the personified "cold, son of a cold, who breaks bones, throws down the skull, who hacks in the bone-marrow, who places illness in the seven holes in the head." Using performative speech, the cold is urged to flow out of the patient by means of a recitation over a mixture of the milk of a woman who has borne a male child and fragrant gum, placed in the nose. While a rational basis is easily found for the insertion of soothing gum into sore nostrils, the spell itself and the use of mother's milk derive from magicoreligious concepts. The "milk of a woman who has borne a male child" is symbolic of the curative milk of the goddess Isis, who healed her infant son Horus by this divine liquid. Healing spells generally associate the sufferer with Horus, the prototypical patient, and episodes of his mythical healing are often recited as historiolae within the body of an incantation. The need for this mother's milk probably inspired the creation in the New Kingdom of specialized vases in the shape of females suckling an infant son. By the magical principle of images, milk poured from these vessels derived from the body of "a woman who has borne a male child."

The same fluid is used in two exorcisms for burns (§§ 499–500, col. 69/3–7), which comprise variants of a common historiola relating the burning of Horus on the desert. Additional variants of the spell appear in Papyrus British Museum 10059 (§§ 47–48, cols. 14/14–15/4) of the eighteenth dynasty, and in Papyrus Leiden I 348 (§§ 37–38 vo. 3/1–3/5) from the nineteenth dynasty. The use of such mother's milk is found throughout the medical papyri in treatments for burns, the eyes, nose, muscles, swellings, *whdw,* and pediatrics, surviving even in the Coptic Chassinat Papyrus (ninth century) in a cure for the ear. The substance passed into the Greek Hippocratic corpus, the works of Dioscorides and Pliny the Elder, and European medical manuals from the twelfth to fifteenth centuries, with its last attestation in an English herbal of 1671.

The blend of medical and magical treatments characteristic of Papyrus Ebers is equally evident in the related Hearst Papyrus (c.1450 BCE), which duplicates almost one hundred sections of the older text and adds further generic spells to be used when measuring medicines (§§ 212–213, cols. 13/17–14/4) or applying oil (§ 214, col. 14/4–7). Later papyri maintain a similar admixture, with spells prominent in Papyrus British Museum 10059 (c.1350 BCE), Berlin Papyrus 3038 and the Chester Beatty Papyri V–VIII and XV (all c.1300 BCE), and Papyrus Carlsberg VIII (c.1200 BCE). Spells treat the full range of human ills, including headache, eye disease, scorpion sting, internal disease, and rectal problems. As in the Middle Kingdom, medical treatments also appear in the purely magical papyri of Ramessid date. Papyrus Leiden I 348 includes incantations for head and stomach aches, accelerating childbirth, dispelling bad dreams, and healing burns. The cosmopolitan nature of New Kingdom and Ramessid society favored the incorporation of foreign elements within Egyptian magical treatments, and spells in Northwest Semitic dialects and even Cretan speech (Linear A) are recorded in Papyrus British Museum 10059 (§§ 27–33, cols. 10/6–11/7).

Magical and medical techniques continue to be joined in the latest medical papyri. Like its ancient predecessor from Kahun, the Roman-era Papyrus Berlin 13602 treats gynecological matters with physical therapy and spells. Reflecting the broader international influence during the Greco-Roman eras, the many medicinal spells of the London and Leiden Magical Papyrus (third century CE) combine Greek terminology for ingredients with native and even Nubian (*verso* col. XX) incantations. As is evident from this survey, medical texts of all periods utilize magical elements, and there is no justification for suggestions of an increase of magic in later times.

Textual material is accompanied at all periods by healing amulets, and, as noted previously, the amulet seller might also perform a limited physical examination. Since most patients will have been illiterate, written texts were commonly adapted as unread phylacteries, tied as a small packet suspended from the client's neck. Other amuletic forms were generated by evolving medico-magical needs. In the Middle Kingdom, ivory wands carved from hippopotamus tusks served as "magical knives," decorated with apotropaic figures and used to delineate a protective circle about mothers and newborn infants. Secondarily, the knives appear in funerary contexts, where they ensure the rebirth of their deceased owner. The New Kingdom mother and child vases have been discussed above, and a further anthropomorphic vessel type was created for unguents associated with pregnancy. Combining the physical attributes of a human female and a hippopotamus, the vases represent the body of the goddess Taweret, whose fluids could be used to ensure elasticity of the skin. A funerary adaptation of this sort is found among the alabaster vessels of Tutankhamun, where an unguent jug provided with the head and breasts of Hathor guaranteed that the reborn king would be nourished by the goddess herself. So-called "Besjugs" of the Late period represent a similar adaptation for divinely charged contents.

A further innovation of the New Kingdom is the roundtopped healing stela, or "*cippus* of Horus." Designed to avert or heal the wounds of snakes, scorpions, or other dangerous animals, the stelae may be traced from the eighteenth dynasty to the Roman era. Typical examples depict a central image of the youthful Horus trampling multiple crocodiles beneath his feet while grasping in both hands wild animals of the desert: snakes, scorpions, lions, and gazelles. A protective head of Bes appears above Horus, and rows of additional divine figures fill subsidiary vignettes. Depending on the size of the stela, two or more standardized texts cover all remaining surfaces. Such stelae were erected for both public and private benefit, and smaller, portable examples were carried on caravans, with examples attested from Nippur, Byblos, Hama, Meroe, Auxum, and Rome. *Cippus* spells appear on a large-scale statue of Ramesses III, placed by royal beneficence at a caravansary at Almazah in the Delta east of modern Cairo. Like the spells of the phylacteries, the texts of the *cippi* were unread; their power was acquired instead by pouring water over the words and images and ingesting the charged fluid. Larger stelae were erected above basins intended to collect the curative water. The most famous large-scale *cippus* is the Metternich Stela, now in the Metropolitan Museum of Art in New York (MMA 50.85), commissioned in the reign of Nectanebo II (c.360–343 BCE) by the priest Nes-Atum to replace texts taken from the temple of the Mnevis bull in Heliopolis. This collection of fourteen incantations gleaned from temple scriptoria provides several new historiolae but follows standard spell techniques. One celebrated spell (§ 3, ll. 9–35) uses the traditional

identification of deities with the patient's bodily members to heal an injured cat ("You cat here, your head is the head of Re . . . there is no limb of yours lacking a god"). In the thirtieth dynasty and the Ptolemaic period, the *cippus* was incorporated within public healing statues, which represent a priestly donor covered by carved incantations presenting a stela of Horus. The bases of such statues also feature basins for the reception of water offerings, which in turn became a healing drink for the supplicant.

In later Hellenistic times, *cippus* imagery also appears on carved gems, popular healing or protective amulets that were distributed throughout the Greco-Roman world. Such gems mingle native imagery with contemporary foreign elements to produce an "international style" of occult iconography once attributed to syncretistic Gnostics. Even in these late products, ancient Egyptian magical and medical concepts may be preserved, and the uterine amulets in particular reflect older gynecological practices.

The long association of the temple with the science of medicine produced new forms of sacred healing. By the later New Kingdom, rear walls of major temples had become popular shrines for divine petitions, and penitential hymns proclaimed the deity's role in inflicting and curing maladies. In the Hellenistic eras, temples and sanctuaries of sacred animals became pilgrimage sites where clients practiced incubation to receive curative visions. A sanatorium was constructed at the temple of Dendera; Deir el-Bahri became an incubation center for Imhotep and Amenhotep son of Hapu; and the ibis catacombs of Tuna el-Gebel received donations in return for miraculous cures. The technique of incubation, or ritual sleep, need not represent Hellenistic influence, since texts from the First Intermediate period onward already signal the existence of oracular dreams. The association of temple and healing shrine is perhaps clearest at Kom Ombo, focus of the popular cult of "Horus the good doctor." On the Antonine enclosure behind the rear wall of the sanctuary, a relief combines contemporary medical instruments with the ancient Eye of Horus ($wd3t$), at once the amuletic symbol for curing, the hieroglyphic representation for medical measurements, and the purported origin of the pharmaceutical symbol dR. The healing powers of the ancient temples are still invoked in modern folk rituals for fertility, entailing baths in the sacred lakes and ingested powder scraped in large gouges from temple walls.

Robert K. Ritner

Magic in Daily Life

Beyond the enclosed precincts of formal temple ritual, private individuals often had recourse to an array of religious practices now deemed "magical." Especially at times of personal crisis, "magic" served to cure disease, ease childbirth, and defend against attack by enemies, beasts, or demons. More generally, such methods might be employed at any time for a variety of purposes: to ensure the fertility of husbands, wives, fields, or livestock; to safeguard the continued health of family members and animals; to curse opponents; to compel love and respect from sexual partners or supervisors; to empower the corpse in funerary ceremonies; or to send and receive messages from deceased ancestors. The use of magic in these circumstances was legal, normative, and by no means in opposition to state religion.

Utilizing the coercive yet orthodox religious principle of $hq3$, these private rites parallel official temple cult in both mythology and manipulation of "con-

secrated imagery," and for good reason. The community magician was typically a member of the literate priesthood, whose temple obligations claimed no more than a quarter of the year. Serving in groups or "phyles" in rotation, the priest when off duty might supplement his income by offering his ritual skills to private clients. With literacy restricted to an estimated one percent of the population, it was the same close-knit community of temple-affiliated scribes who composed, edited, and guarded the rituals and recitations of temple magic, and who in the formal role of "lector-priest" ($hry-hb$) might perform such rites for state, temple, or private purposes.

Known exceptions to this rule are few and confined to the otherwise atypical workmen's village of Deir el-Medina, which lacked any resident priesthood. Living apart from the Nile community at government expense, the literate artisans served as their own priests. Dockets on the *verso* of Papyrus Geneva MAH 15274 record their communal use of magical manuals for daily concerns: "Today (came) the scribe Panetcher giving the spell for extracting the poison to the scribe of the royal tomb Paneferemdjedet" (*verso* II/1–6). A further docket (*verso V*) may record the specific antivenom spell employed by the scribes. Even these manuals probably derived from a temple source and were simply copied, not composed, by the scribes at Deir el-Medina. Evidence of a temple origin is clear in Papyrus Chester Beatty VIII, which became the property of the scribe of the royal tomb Kenherkhepeshef, and which states that "this writing was found in the library, (in) a room of the temple" (col. 4/3), and that the spell "is to be recited by the chief lector-priest" (*verso7/7*). As skilled craftsmen, the artisans of this village were quite capable of fashioning amuletic images for magical purposes, and one letter preserves the request to "make for me a *wrt*-demon, since the one that you made for me has been stolen and thus works a manifestation of Seth against me" (Ostracon Deir el-Medina 251).

A few ostraca from the same site reveal the existence of local "wise women" (*rht*), who are unattested elsewhere in Egypt. Functioning as a medium or diviner, the "wise woman" is consulted on matters of curses and possession: "I have gone to the wise woman and she told me: 'The wrath of Ptah is with you . . . because of an oath by his wife'" (Ostracon Gardiner 149). The scribe Kenherkhepeshef writes to a woman of the village: "Why did you fail to go to the wise woman on account of the two infants who died while in your care? Inquire of the wise woman about the death of the two infants, whether it was their fate or their destiny" (Ostracon Letellier).

The records of such consultations contain no reference to the practitioner's apparatus or literacy. In contrast, most evidence of magic in daily life indicates a reliance on recited spells, precise ritual, and charged, amuletic substances. The discovery of a Middle Kingdom "magician's box" from a tomb beneath the Ramesseum has provided an example of the range of materials and textual sources used by a typical practitioner. In addition to twenty-three papyri comprising hymns, detailed exorcisms, funerary rites, and spells to promote fertility and cure a variety of illnesses, the box contained writing materials, dolls, divine and serpent figures, human hair, amulets, and beads.

The interdependence of public and private magic is well illustrated by rites to protect agricultural and residential property. In Roman-era Esna, a statue of the deity Heka was carried from the temple and made to circumambulate the local fields to ensure their productivity. In Theban tomb paintings of the New Kingdom, depictions of harvest rites show comparable bark processions among the fields under the patronage of Amun, Mut, Khonsu, and the harvest goddess Renenutet, whose image is erected beside both state and private granaries. These agricultural ceremonies for public and private benefit are descendants of the ancient royal jubilee rite of "encircling a field" (*phrr sh.t*), enacted to confirm the protection and possession of the land by the royal celebrant.

Similar rites of protective encircling are performed by homeowners at the critical juncture of the new year. On the verso of Papyrus Edwin Smith, the second incantation against the annual threat of disease stipulates that the spell is to be recited "by a man with a stick of *ds*-wood in his hand while he goes outside, going around his house. He cannot die by the plague of the year" (col. 18/15–16). This private ritual, appended to a formal treatise on medicine, is paralleled not only by the agricultural and jubilee processions, but also by a wide variety of official circumambulation rites intended to maintain the sacred space of cities, temples, and burial grounds. In the Greco-Egyptian magical papyri of Roman date, such magical circles are made even about individual plants that the magician harvests for his spells, and the basic term for "encirclement" (*phr*) acquires the nuance "to enchant" in both Demotic and Coptic. From the Archaic era to the Roman era, the methodology and purpose of the "magical circle" remain constant, whether enacted for royal, temple, or private property.

Other instances of agricultural magic include a "spell to prevent a kite from robbing" added to the collection of medical recipes in Papyrus Ebers (§ 848, col. 98/2–6) and exorcisms of noxious animals from the fields in the Harris Magical Papyrus (British Museum 10042 § X, col. 10/1– 11/1). The former rite diverts the attention of plundering birds by a spell invoking the falcon deity Horus that is recited over a cake atop a branch of acacia wood. Horus reappears in the latter "spell of the herdsman" to protect his cattle from "lions, hyenas and all manner of wild animals with long tails, who eat flesh and drink blood." The protection of valuable cattle was a matter of great concern, as indicated by numerous fording spells which guard against the crocodiles that infested marshes and canals. Old Kingdom tombs often depict such a fording scene: a reluctant herd is enticed into crossing the water by a herdsman who carries a calf on his back, while a spell is recited on boats or ashore by others who make protective gestures. Though it has often been assumed that the herdsmen themselves recite the spell, the find of an ivory figurine of a herdsman carrying a calf among the objects of the Ramesseum "magician's box" suggests that even in such mundane circumstances the recitation was done by professionals. Closer examination of the Old Kingdom scenes reveals a distinctly dressed figure who acts as speaker and supervisor.

Temple authority over anti-crocodile spells is explicit in the Ramessid Harris Magical Papyrus (British Museum 10042), the first text of Egyptian practical magic published after the decipherment of hieroglyphs (1860). Entitled "Good Spells to Chant Which Drive Away the Swimming One," the collection includes twenty-three incantations of varying character, including formal hymns attested on temple walls, brief invocations, and seeming rigmaroles in glossolalia or foreign language. Such spells represent restricted knowledge, "concerning which the Chief Lector Priests say: 'Do not reveal it to others.' A veritable secret of the House of Life" (§ K, col. 6/10). In the cited passage, a secret recitation imbues an egg of clay with the cosmic force of the egg of the primordial Ogdoad. Placed "in the hand of a man in the prow of a ship," the charged egg is thrown if a crocodile should surface. As in the Old Kingdom fording scenes, there is a distinction between professional reciter and gesticulating actor. If recitation might be limited, however, apotropaic gestures certainly were made by all individuals, being perhaps the most common feature of popular magical practice. Even the depictions of Egypt's enemies show such gestures, with the *mano cornuta* raised in vain against the crushing blow of Ramesses III at Medinet Habu.

Images of defeated enemies are a staple of Egyptian magic. In royal and sacerdotal contexts, prisoner figures are incorporated into door sockets, paving stones, footstools, throne bases, sandal bottoms, coffin bottoms, canes, jar handles, linch pins, and even oar stops, so that the most mundane acts of walking, sitting, or riding are ritualized, rendering the image seized, crushed, or throttled. State and private interests intersect in the more formal execration ceremonies performed with prisoner images, which extend from elaborate assemblages inscribed with the codified "Execration Texts" to smaller groups and individual figurines. Made of stone, wood, clay, wax, or dough, prisoner figurines are typically inscribed with the personal name of the intended victim and are then misused by binding, piercing, spitting, burning, and most importantly, by premature burial. In the systematic state assemblages, enemies are represented by red pots or figures on which are inscribed the five sections of the "rebellion formula" that enumerates the potentially hostile rulers of Nubia, Asia, and Libya, as well as outcast Egyptians and generally destructive forces (evil speech, plots, dreams, etc.). The presence of personal names on jars enclosing deposits of these rituals suggests that private donors may have played a role, perhaps influencing the selection of outcast Egyptians. Just such a mixture of state and private vendetta is recorded in the late ritual against Apophis (Papyrus British Museum 10188), in which the practitioner is instructed to abuse figures of the enemies of Re, pharaoh and "all foes male and female whom your heart fears" (col. 28/17–18). Personal enemies are surely represented by often crudely produced individual figures and by smaller groups portraying cursed families. From Ramessid to Hellenistic times, execration methodology was adapted for so-called love spells, which simply constitute compulsion spells for a different goal. In such spells, the victim is made helpless, unable to eat, drink, or rest, while compelled to follow the magician "like an ox after grass" (Ostracon Deir el-Medina 1057).

Prisoner imagery may also be adapted for nonroyal clients on objects directed against demons and disease. During the Middle and New Kingdoms, protective circles were sketched around a child's bed with so-called apotropaic wands or knives, whose efficacy is enhanced by representations of defensive spirits said to offer "protection by day and protection by night." Typical examples, like those from the Ramesseum box, display files of knifewielding animals in company with Taweret and Beset, but examples now in the Metropolitan Museum of Art, New York and Paris (MMA 15.3.197; Louvre 3614. MMA 26.7.1288) add scenes of prisoners de-

voured by a lion, Taweret, and a cat. In funerary contexts, hostile forces are averted from the deceased by the image of a divine prisoner named *Nklw-mn.t*, "The Vanquished One at the Stake," used as a vignette in New Kingdom papyri; in Hellenistic times, subjugated prisoners are painted on the cartonnage beneath the feet of individual mummies.

Whether in sleep or in death, the resting body was considered particularly vulnerable, and extant spells to protect the bedchamber are varied and elaborate. From the early New Kingdom, a Berlin papyrus (Papyrus Berlin 3027) published as "Magical Spells for Mother and Child" preserves rituals of the "magician of the nursery" against childhood diseases inflicted by possessing spirits. The most famous of these spells (Text C) banishes any vampiric male or female demon "who comes in the darkness and enters in furtively" with face reversed, intent on kissing, quieting, and stealing the child. Protection is made with onions and honey, "which is sweet to mankind but bitter to the dead."

From Ramessid Deir el-Medina, Ostracon Gardiner 363 contains a ritual against ghosts "recited over four *uraei* made of pure [. . .] clay, with flames in their mouths. One is placed in [each] corner [of any bedroom] in which there is a man or woman sleeping with a man [or woman]." Similar fire-spitting *uraei* are depicted as protectors of the cardinal directions in temple reliefs and papyri, "shooting fire . . . in the darkness" (Papyrus Salt 825, col. XIX). Probably associated with such spells are two artifacts in the British Museum, one a rearing clay serpent from a house at Amarna (EA 55594) and the other a pair of gilt *uraei* entwined about the leg of a bed (EA 21574).

A Brooklyn Papyrus (47.218.156) of early Ptolemaic date contains two rituals to save the sleeper "from anything bad and evil, any fear, any terror, any dead man or any dead woman" who, as an incubus, would inject poison-laden semen into the ears. Originally designed for a pharaoh, the texts are adapted for commoners. A similar spell intended for a King Psamtek survives only in a Ptolemaic copy (Brooklyn Papyrus 47.217.49), but it signals the existence of a Saite original. Such defensive rituals were further elaborated in Ptolemaic times to safeguard the rest of the sacred falcon at Edfu, who was the beneficiary of both a "Protection of the Bedroom" (s3ḥnk.t) and an annual "Protection of the House" (s3pr), performed just before the New Year like the private ritual of P. Edwin Smith, noted above.

Much as disgruntled ghosts were thought to represent a threat to the living, so the blessed dead might bestow protection and fertility. Contacted directly by "Letters to the Dead," inscribed figurines, or by "necromantic" divinatory rituals with lamps and cups (cf. *Book of Going Forth by Day* Spells 134, 148, and 190), the dead are implored to fight on behalf of the living, with the results revealed in dreams. Belief in the continued sexual potency of the deceased is explicit in Coffin Texts Spells 576 and 619 and underlies the fear of incubus assault. When placated, departed ancestors can ensure the fertility and health of their descendants: "Let a healthy son be born to me, for you are an able spirit" (Chicago Jar Stand).

Health maintenance certainly entailed the most common applications of magic in daily life. From the simple wearing of amulets to complex rituals, medicine employed a wide variety of magical treatments. Drugs were chosen for their mythological correspondences as well as for perceived biological properties. Occasionally administered in specialized

containers representing curative deities (Isis, Taweret, Bes), they were invariably accompanied by standardized spells when measured or applied to bandages. Many treatments combined "rational" and "magical" strategies, with plant and mineral substances "charged" by spell and rite. In most such cases, the patient is equated with the youthful Horus, whose cure is sanctioned by the gods.

Magical techniques predominate in remedies for expelling the venom of snakes and scorpions, the affliction most frequently noted in healing texts. Antivenom spells are attested from the Pyramid Texts through modern times, and the ancient specialist was a trained priest, the "controller of (the scorpion goddess) Selqet." A popular innovation of the later New Kingdom was the antivenom stela or "*cippus* of Horus," used well into Roman times. Engraved with divine figures and spells, the stelae were brought in contact with water subsequently drunk by the patient.

Emphasis on deity as the ultimate source of salvation from illness led to a new development in the Third Intermediate Period. Ramessid protective spells might be headed "A Royal Decree of Osiris, Foremost of the Westerners" (Papyrus Turin 1993, vo. 7/6–10), but during the theocratic Libyan era (twenty-first to twenty-third dynasties) divine sponsorship was formalized. By petitioning the cult statue during official processions, clients received "oracular amuletic decrees" issued by the local god(s) that promised security from a detailed list of illnesses, gods, *weret* and *wrt* and other demons, as well as magicians, snakes, and ill-intentioned oracles. Written on long, thin strips of papyrus, the decrees were rolled and inserted into tubular amulet cases suspended from a cord worn about the petitioner's neck. Probable descendants of this practice are the

Ptolemaic documents from Memphis and the Faiyum known as "Self-Dedication Texts," in which the suppliant vows perpetual servitude to the deity in exchange for protection from itemized ills.

The temple setting for these late practices underscores the continued role of magic within sanctioned daily religion. Thus it is perhaps fitting that the final documents of traditional religion, preserved in Demotic and Greek translations, comprise manuals of practical magic, with rituals for oracles, healing, love and cursing.   *Robert K. Ritner*

Magic in the Afterlife

From earliest prehistoric times until the very end of indigenous Egyptian religion, burial customs provide unmistakable evidence of conscious efforts by survivors to influence the fortunes of the deceased, whether by deposited artifacts, associated texts, or ritual performance. The most pervasive feature of such magic for the afterlife is the inclusion of grave offerings within the tomb. Designed to sustain the corpse physically, spiritually, and socially, funerary offerings exhibit a wide variety of forms, extending from simple deposits of food to elaborate tomb assemblages such as that of Tutankhamun, which comprises objects of daily life and of ritual. By transferring tangible artifacts of the earthly world to the spiritual realm of the dead, all such offerings represent magical practice. Early Dynastic (Archaic) burial customs underscored this functional transition by ritually breaking or "killing" deposited objects in order to assimilate them to their deceased owner (Ritner 1993, p. 148).

In what is perhaps the single unifying "scriptural" text from Egypt, the standard funerary prayer focuses primarily on the offering process. Attested from the Old Kingdom through Hellenistic times, the prayer provides a theoretical basis for funerary offerings, in which "an offering which the king gives" to (or in the company of) attendant deities is in turn transmitted to the cult and *ka*-spirit of the deceased. While actual objects may be physically presented via this system of "reversion of offerings," the funerary prayer represents a magical supplement. By the act of reciting a common list of invocation offerings (literally, "the going forth of the voice"), the ritual performer ensures that the deceased beneficiary is provided with the underworld equivalent or intangible essence of the object named: "a thousand loaves of bread, a thousand jugs of beer, a thousand oxen, a thousand fowl, a thousand vessels of alabaster, a thousand bolts of cloth, and everything good and pure on which a god lives." Uttered both by official *ka*-priests, formally contracted to provide the service, and by pious visitors to the tomb chapel ("O you who pass by this tomb"), the invocation is characterized as a simple "breath of the mouth" without hardship for the speaker, but with enduring benefit for the dead (tomb of Pahery). Such an understanding is in accord with the basic, imagistic principle of Egyptian magic (*ḥk3*), which postulates a manipulable link between any given object and its representation in word or image.

The spoken offering prayer is typically supplemented by yet other images, including engraved texts of the prayer itself and menus of desired products, as well as depictions of such goods produced and borne by attendants or piled on stands or tables. The offering slab alone may contain a series of supplemental images, being at once provided with physical offerings, carved in the shape of the word for "offering" (*ḥtp*), inscribed with the funerary prayer, and decorated with relief images of flowing jugs, bread loaves, haunches of beef, fowl, or flowers. In any individual tomb, the series of deposited offerings, relief depictions, and textual recitation constitutes an intricate system of magical reinforcements serving the religious goal of a beatified afterlife. One must reject the common assumption that "decorative" scenes of daily life in tombs of the Old through New Kingdoms are in some sense less religious or magical than later tomb depictions of deities and underworld scenes. Egyptian tomb art is primarily functional, not decorative, and scenes of estates and crop production are intended not merely as testimonials to earthly wealth, but as objects—and status—to be transferred to the next life. Like the common banquet scenes that depict the deceased partaking of his offerings in the hereafter, the so-called scenes of daily life have their true functional locus in the afterworld. The later preference for underworld scenes is discussed below.

As food offerings are complemented by an array of consecrated imagery to maintain the nourishment of the deceased, so deposited staves, scepters, jewelry, and other insignia of status are complemented not only by tomb depictions of estates, personal triumphs, and servants, but also by an evolving set of three-dimensional servant figures. In the first and second dynasties, tombs of royalty and high officials are surrounded by numerous subsidiary (*sati*) burials of retainers, who were slain to accompany their masters. In conformity with the less destructive principle of imagistic substitution, actual sacrifices are replaced in the Old Kingdom by individual stone sculptures which represent servant figures performing a variety of activities: grinding grain, baking, brewing, butchering, playing harps, or dancing. By the

First Intermediate Period, the collapse of royal sculptural workshops led to the substitution of often crude wooden figures, typically arranged in complex group settings depicting granaries, breweries, slaughterhouses, households, or boats. Such figures were simplified in the New Kingdom into allpurpose servant images, known initially as *shawabtis* (*šwbty*), or "persea-wood figures." By simple phonetic metathesis, the term was later transformed to *ushabtis* (*wšbty*), or "answerers" associated with Spell 472 of the Coffin Texts and Spells 6 and 151h of the *Book of Going Forth by Day* (*Book of the Dead*). Should the deceased be called upon to perform any work in the necropolis, whether cultivation, irrigation, or corvée, the figure is to answer on behalf of its owner: "I shall act; here I am." Made of wood, stone, faience, or even mud, such figures multiply in number, often with one *ushabti* for each day of the year and an additional set of figures representing foremen. In keeping with the general democratization of Egyptian funerary customs, the wider availability of servant *ushabtis* allowed not merely maintenance but improvement of social status for the deceased. A reminiscence of these servant figures by the Greek satirist Lucian in his tale "The Lover of Lies" (*Philopseudes*) served as the inspiration for "The Sorcerer's Apprentice," recounted in a poem by Goethe and a symphonic piece by Paul Dukas, which was featured in a section of Walt Disney's animated film *Fantasia* (1940).

The distinguishing feature of Egyptian mortuary practice was the physical preservation of the corpse itself. With the elaboration of funerary structures and equipment, natural desiccation in the arid sands was necessarily replaced by artificial techniques of mummification. The complex process of mummification is at once a form of "medical" intervention to arrest the decay believed to be engendered by the corruptive agent *whdw*, and a "magical" process to ensure a primary repository for the *ka*-spirit, otherwise resident in supplementary *ka*-statues, in relief or painted depictions of the tomb owner, or even in simple spellings of his name. Mummification techniques are correspondingly a mixture of rational treatment (the draining of bodily fluids and application of drying natron salts) and magical incantations, amulets, and rites.

The spells and rituals associated with mummification are preserved in a series of mortuary texts successively inscribed on tomb walls, coffins, deposited papyri, or directly on the mummy bandages themselves: the Old Kingdom Pyramid Texts, the First Intermediate Period and Middle Kingdom Coffin Texts, the New Kingdom *Book of Going Forth by Day*, and the Late period *Books of Glorifications* (*s3h.w*) and *Books of Breathings* (or *Breathing Permits*). Although this funerary literature contains general theological expositions and insights into the broader religious concerns of society, the explicit purpose of these texts is one of practical theology, with coercive ritual and incantations for the benefit of the individual tomb owner. Early scholarly classifications notwithstanding, Egyptian funerary texts are hardly separable from other ritual texts commonly designated as magical, and both groups make use of identical methodology in spell and praxis. Particularly common in the recitations of both are the "historiola," or brief mythological precedent for the desired result, and the use of lists equating the spell's beneficiary or his body parts with a series of deities. Starting in the New Kingdom, underworld literature returns to the tomb walls, with elaborate, illustrated guides to the underworld (*Book of That Which Is in the Underworld* [*Amduat*], *Book of Caverns*, *Book of Gates*, for example) in royal tombs and in vignettes derived from funerary papyri in private tombs. Such depictions have often been linked to the rise of a new sense of popular piety, but as in earlier wall scenes, the purpose of these tomb illustrations is to reinforce the status of the deceased in the underworld. While the format may be new, the sentiment is traditional, and the textual sources for the representations may well extend back to the Middle Kingdom or First Intermediate Period. Insofar as the wall scenes are charged images supplemental to funerary texts and offering ritual, they are as magical as their predecessors.

The numerous spells against snakes and scorpions in mortuary literature represent an obvious link to magical practices in daily life. On occasion, the transmission of older funerary spells into later collections is accompanied by greater detail, so that the terse Spell 260 of Pyramid Texts is recast as a resurrection spell as Spell 1 of the Coffin Texts, and, as Spell 169 of the *Book of Going Forth by Day*, it is further designated as the recitation that accompanies the installation of the funerary bier. The pivotal role of magical efficacy underlying all funerary recitations is emphasized by common incantations to secure *heka* for the deceased (Coffin Texts, Spells 342, 350, 392, 402, 426, 491–492, 495, 499–500, 572–573, 705, and 1017, and *Book of Going Forth by Day*, Spell 24) and to prevent him from garbling a spell (Coffin Texts, Spell 657, and *Book of Going Forth by Day*, Spells 90, 110a3S1 and a4S).

Amulets and other charged substances are often prescribed by the ritual associated with individual mortuary spells, and tangible examples of such items are typically interred with the corpse as magical protection. The use of *ushabtis* in conjunction with *Book of Going Forth by Day*, Spells 6 and 151h has been noted above. The most important funerary amulet was certainly that of the heart, associated with *Book of Going Forth by Day*, Spells 29B and 30. Fashioned as a heart or scarab (symbol of becoming and transformation) and bearing the text of the relevant spell, such amulets served as substitute hearts. Considered the central organ of the physical body and the seat of thought, memory, and emotion, the heart was not removed during mummification. Supplementary amulets, spells, and vignettes both preserved the heart's vitality and coerced it to remain silent regarding past misdeeds when it was weighed against *maat* ("truth") in the judgment hall of Osiris (*Book of Going Forth by Day*, Spell 125).

By virtue of its form, the burial mask assimilates the corpse to Osiris, and the companion "Spell for a Secret Head" (*Book of Going Forth by Day*, Spell 151a–c) equates individual body parts with a list of gods. Other amulets associate the deceased with the protection of a particular deity, such as the *djed*-column of Osiris (*Book of Going Forth by Day*, Spell 155), the red jasper knot (*Book of Going Forth by Day*, Spell 156) and gold vulture (*Book of Going Forth by Day*, Spell 156) of Isis, and the Heliopolitan broad collar with falcon-headed terminals (*Book of Going Forth by Day*, Spell 158). Green (*w3ḏ*) feldspar amulets of papyrus columns (*Book of Going Forth by Day*, Spells 159–160) confer the quality of raw vigor (*w3ḏ*.), while the single most common funerary amulet, the Eye of Horus (*wḏ3.t*), guarantees general health and soundness (*wḏ3*). More specific assistance is offered by the headrest amulet that aids the deceased in his ascent to the sky (*Book of Going Forth by Day*, Spell 166), the snakehead amulet that offers coolness against the inflammation of snakebite (*Book of Going Forth by Day*, Spells 33–

35), the *ba*-amulet that ensures the safe return of the spirit to the corpse (*Book of Going Forth by Day*, Spell 89), and the later hypocephalus that restores bodily warmth (*Book of Going Forth by Day*, Spell 162).

If the amuletic sections of the *Book of Going Forth by Day* contain protections placed directly within the wrappings of the corpse, Spell 151d–g records spells and instructions for creating a larger defensive perimeter of the tomb interior, with four "magical bricks" surmounted by protective images placed in niches at the four cardinal directions. An extra exemplar of Spell 151f found in the doorway of the "treasury" of Tutankhamun's tomb is designed to repel the enemy of the deceased king, and is probably the source of the fictional "Curse of King Tut," supposedly promising "death on swift wings" for any desecrator of the tomb. Although Tutankhamun's curse is a fabrication of the press, genuine tomb curses are attested from other sites and eras. Such curses are typically from private tombs and are largely confined to the Old Kingdom.

Thus, in the tomb of Nikaankh at Tihna, the owner threatens violators with a complaint before the underworld tribunal: "As for any man who will make disturbance, I shall be judged with him." The door support of the steward Meni adds an immediate, earthly punishment: "A crocodile be against him in the water; a snake be against him on land, he who would do anything against this [tomb]. Never did I do a thing against him. It is the god who will judge." In the tomb curse of Ankhmahor from Saqqara, notions of retribution and ghostly manifestation are combined in the closest approximation to the vengeful mummy of Hollywood films.

As for anything that you might do against this tomb of mine of the West, the like shall be done against your property. I am an excellent lector-priest, exceedingly knowledgeable in secret spells and all magic. As for any person who will enter into this tomb of mine in their impurity, having eaten the abominations that excellent *akh*-spirits abominate, or who do not purify themselves as they should purify themselves for an excellent *akh*-spirit who does what his lord praises, I shall seize him like a goose, placing fear in him at seeing ghosts (*akhs*) upon earth, that they might be fearful of an excellent *akh*-spirit. I shall be judged with him in that noble court of the great god. But as for anyone who will enter into this tomb of mine being pure and peaceful regarding it, I shall be his protective backer in the West in the court of the great god.

The most extensive tomb curse is found in a proclamation of the twenty-first dynasty for the funerary estate of the deified eighteenth dynasty architect, Amenhotep, son of Hapu. Desecrators are warned that they will lose all earthly positions and honors, be incinerated in execration rituals as enemies of the gods, capsize, drown, and decay at sea without heirs, tomb, or offerings. Lacking a proper funerary cult, they will die a second death and lose all hope of immortality: "They will starve without sustenance and their bodies will perish."

As implied by the curse of Amenhotep, the rituals of embalming and burial are critical for the beatification of the deceased. Divine associations are conferred both by the spells recited by funerary priests and by the utensils and apparatus employed. A calcite vase from the tomb of Tutankhamun is sculpted with the head and breasts of the nurturing cow goddess Hathor, so that its unguents constitute the restorative fluids of the goddess herself. Similarly representative vessels depicting Isis, Taweret, and Bes are used in curative magic. Imagery of the sky goddess Hathor reappears on one of Tutankhamun's three funerary biers. As the mummy was placed atop this couch designed as the celestial cow, it was ritually elevated into the heavens with the sun god Re in a reenactment of *The Myth of the Heavenly Cow.* The double lion bed served a similar purpose. Representing the paired horizon deity Aker or Ruty or the twins Shu and Tefnut, the bed positions the corpse as the central sun disk in the hieroglyphic symbol for "horizon," thereby linking the deceased with the solar circuit. The remaining bed, shaped like the hippopotamus goddess, Taweret, assured the rebirth of the corpse as it was passed in ceremony through the body of this goddess of pregnancy.

The burial reenacts a mythic prototype as well, with masked "Anubis men" carrying the corpse, now transformed into Osiris by invocations, ritual masking and offerings symbolic of the defeated Seth. The Opening of the Mouth ceremony restores the senses to the body and is effected with both an adze and a ram-headed wand named, appropriately, "Great of Magic."

Even after burial, interaction with the deceased employed a variety of "magical mechanics." In addition to the continuing offering cult, necromantic consultations were possible, and instructions for such rituals are contained in the *Book of Going Forth by Day,* Spells 148 and 190, designed to ensure that the deceased is received by the gods "so that it can make known to you what fate befalls it." Visualization of the dead could be accomplished by the technique of scrying, using a bowl painted with figures viewed through a volume of oil. Direct assistance for the deceased is promised in the rubrics of many spells in the *Book of Going Forth by Day* that might be performed by the living on behalf of dead relatives. Conversely, the custom of "letters to the dead" comprises petitions from the living for assistance from the underworld. Inscribed on ostraca, linen, papyri, and on bowls once containing propitiatory offerings, the "letters to the dead" echo the phraseology of personal correspondence among the living, with a mixture of casual pleasantries, complaints, and requests. The numinous position of the beatified dead gave them authority and influence in matters of divine petitions and tribunals, demonic possessions, healing, and fertility. Thus, writers request that the dead litigate against personal enemies, intervene on behalf of suffering descendants, and ensure the pregnancy of surviving daughters. Other notes contain reproaches: "Will you remain calm about this?" "What have I done against you?" As indicated by a text from the First Intermediate Period, the response to such letters could be expected in a dream: "Please become a spirit for me [before] my eyes so that I may see you in a dream fighting on my behalf."

In exceptional cases, necromantic consultations were institutionalized, as in the cults of the saintly healers Imhotep and Amenhotep son of Hapu. At Deir el-Medina, the deceased ruler Amenhotpe I was worshipped as patron of the village and consulted in regular processional oracles. By the reign of Ramesses II, an oracle of Ahmose, founder of the eighteenth dynasty, was functioning in Abydos, and subsequent to his own death Ramesses II became the presiding spirit of oracular procedures in both Egypt and Nubia. In literature, deceased rulers are often loquacious, as in the *Instructions of Amenemhet*, and in the autobiographical Harris Papyrus and the Turin Indictment Papyrus, related by the deceased Ramesses III. Necromantic consultations were extended in later times to nonroyal spirits as well, including those drowned in the Nile, and thus especially linked to the fate and numinosity of Osiris, and the mummified remains of sacred animals, for whom "letters to deities" now replaced the older "letters to the dead."

Even the depredations of tomb robbers may attest to the pervasive character of traditional magical practices, for the willful destruction of the name, image, or mummy of the tomb owner conforms to old execration ritual. Perhaps motivated by fear of "an excellent *akh*-spirit," such injuries crippled the deceased spirit by removing his magical system of empowered supplemental imagery.

Robert K. Ritner

MASKS. The ancient Egyptian worldview was characterized by an abiding sense of liminality. A philosophical and physical engagement with permeable boundaries—with respect to finite and infinite time or space, life and death, or the human and divine spheres—is discernible in their religious texts and rituals. Living persons in ancient Egypt might have employed transformational (so-called mortuary) spells to assume nonhuman forms on earth. Masked priests, priestesses, or magicians, in the physical disguise of divine beings, such as Anubis or Beset, assumed such identities to exert the powers associated with those deities and thereby to ensure the success of dramatic cultic reenactments. The construction and use of masks and other facial coverings for mummies emphasized the ancient Egyptian belief in the fragile state of transition that the dead would successfully transcend in their physical and spiritual transfer from this world to their divine transformation in the next. In their use by both the living and the dead, therefore, masks would have played a similar role in ancient Egypt, by effecting the magical transformation of an individual from the mortal to the divine state.

Although there are numerous examples in art, dating from the Predynastic palettes (such as the Two–Dog Palette in the collection of the Ashmolean Museum, Oxford) and onward, of depictions of anthropomorphic beings with the heads of animals, birds, or fantastic creatures, which might represent humans dressed as deities, such figures were more probably understood as images of the gods themselves. This interpretation is especially true for any three-dimensional figure or statue (such as the Middle Kingdom female figure from Western Thebes, now in the collection of the Manchester Museum, sometimes referred to in earlier literature as a leonine-masked human but which must certainly have been regarded as an image of the demoness Beset). Two-dimensional representations are more difficult to interpret with such certainty, however, because they may have been designed as intentionally ambiguous. For example, one of the most commonly rendered mortuary scenes depicts the mummification of a body by a jackal-headed being. The scene may document the actual mummification rites performed upon the individual for whom the funerary scene was commissioned, or it could be interpreted as commemorating that episode of the embalmment by the jackal god Anubis in the mythic account of the death and resurrection of the god of the dead, Osiris, whom the deceased wished to emulate. That such two-dimensional scenes were encoded with dual meaning (because they could refer to specific or mythic events) also accounts for ambivalence in the interpretation of the depictions of ceremonies that were presumably carried out by priests on behalf of the king as part of royal or temple rituals. An example of one such ritual is the procession of composite animal/human figures, identified in the accompanying texts as the souls of Nekhen and Pe, who carry the sacred bark in a procession detailed on the southwestern interior wall of the Hypostyle Hall at Karnak Temple.

Such scenes can be interpreted either as literal records of the historic celebrations performed by masked or costumed priests or as a visual actualization of faith in the royal dogma, which claimed categorically that the mythic ancestors of the god-king legitimized and supported his reign.

Examples of ritual masks from the archaeological record are rare, perhaps owing to the fragile and perishable materials of which they may have been constructed. Although a fragmentary Aha or Bes-like face of cartonnage was recovered by W. M. Flinders Petrie at the Middle Kingdom town site of Kahun, incontrovertible evidence for use by the Egyptians of masks in rituals conducted by the living has been preserved only from the Late period. A unique, ceramic mask of the head of the jackal-headed god, Anubis, dated to after 600 BCE (now in the collection of the Roemer Pelizaeus-Museum, Hildesheim), was evidently manufactured to serve as a head covering. There are indentations at each of the sides of the object, which would have allowed for it to be supported atop the shoulders, lifting the snout and upraised ears of the jackal head above the actual head of the wearer. Whereas two holes cut out at the jackal's neckline would have allowed the wearer to view straight ahead, peripheral vision would have been limited, necessitating assistance, as explicitly depicted in a temple relief at Dendera. This scene from the Ptolemaic temple of Hathor presents an "X-ray" view of the head of a processing priest, who wears just such a jackal mask that covers his head and projects above his shoulders and who is accompanied and assisted by a companion priest. A description of a festival procession of Isis, which was led by the god Anubis (presumably a similarly masked priest), that took place not in Egypt but rather in Kenchreai, is provided by the second-century CE author Apuleius in *The Golden Ass*, although no textual evidence is preserved from any period in Egypt that explicitly corroborates this custom.

Among the elaborate precautions taken by the ancient Egyptians for the preservation of the body after death, the protection of the head was of primary concern. The equipment of the deceased with a face-covering fabricated of sturdy material not only provided a permanent substitute for the head in case of physical damage but preserved that countenance in an idealized form, which presented the deceased in the likeness of an immortal being. Gilt flesh tones and blue wigs associated the dead with the glittering flesh and the (semiprecious gemstone) lapis lazuli hair of the sun god; specific features of a mask—eyes, eyebrows, forehead, and the like—were directly identified with individual divinities as is explained in the *Book of Going Forth by Day* (*Book of the Dead*), Spell 151B, so that the deceased would arrive safely in the beyond and gain acceptance among the other divine immortals in the council of the great god of the dead, Osiris. Initially, the prerogative of royalty, masks used to cover the dead were manufactured henceforth throughout Egyptian history for the elite class without respect to sex.

As early as the fourth dynasty, attempts were made to stiffen and mold the outer layer of linen bandages that covered the faces of mummies and to emphasize prominent facial features in paint. The earliest masks, which were manufactured experimentally as independent sculptural works, have been dated to the Herakleopolitan period (late First Intermediate Period). Those early, hollow masks were of wood, fashioned

in two pieces held together with pegs, or of cartonnage (layers of linen or papyrus stiffened with plaster) that had been molded over a wooden model or core. The faces of both men and women, with their overexaggerated eyes and enigmatic half-smiles, were framed by long, narrow, tripartite wigs, kept secure by a decorated headband. The masks' "bibs" extended to cover the chest as well, and both male and female examples were supplied in paint with elaborate beaded and floral-motif necklaces or broad collars that served not only an aesthetic function but also satisfied an apotropaic requirement as elucidated in funerary spells. The elongated masks evolved into anthropoid inner coffins, first appearing in the twelfth dynasty. Hollow or solid masks (sometimes diminutive in size) were also created by pouring clay or plaster into a generic, often unisex, mold to which ears and gender-specific details were added. Masks became increasingly more sophisticated during the New Kingdom and Third Intermediate Period, when royalty were equipped with masks of beaten precious metal (like the solid gold mask of Tutankhamun or the series of gold and silver masks excavated at the necropolis of Tanis). Masks of all types were embellished with paint (generally, red flesh tones for males and yellow, pale tones for females) or gilt, as well as by the addition of composite, inlaid eyes or eyebrows, details that elevated the cost of the finished product. Indicators of social status—hairstyles, jewelry, and costume (depicted on body-length head covers)—are often helpful in dating masks but the idealized image of transfigured divinity, which was the objective of the mask-covering, precluded the individualization of masks to the point of portraiture, which resulted in a formal sameness or hieroglyphic quality in the anonymous facial features of mummy masks from all periods of Egyptian history.

The use of permanent face coverings for the dead continued as long as mummification rites were practiced in Egypt. With regional preferences, cartonnage and plaster masks were equally popular in the Ptolemaic period; the cartonnage masks became only one element of a complete suit of separate cartonnage pieces that covered the wrapped body, a set that included a separate cartonnage breastplate and separate cartonnage footcase. Roman-period plaster masks exhibit Greco-Roman influence only in their coiffures, patterned on styles current at the imperial court. Both beards and mustaches on the males and elaborate coiffures on the women were highly modeled in relief.

An alternative to the cartonnage or plaster mask, introduced in the Roman era, was the so-called Faiyum portrait. Such portraits were initially chiefly recovered from cemeteries in the Faiyum and first archaeologically excavated in 1888 and 1910–1911 by Flinders Petrie at Hawara but have since been found at sites throughout Egypt, from Marina el-Alemain in the North to Aswan in the South. These paintings in encaustic (colored beeswax) or tempera (watercolor) on wooden panels or linen shrouds were executed in a painterly technique adopted from the Hellenistic artistic milieu, with results stylistically comparable to contemporary frescoes at Pompeii and Herculaneum in Italy. Nevertheless, such two-dimensional paintings occupied the same position on a decorated mummy and served the same ideological function as traditional three-dimensional masks.

The immediate appeal of the portraits to late nineteenth- and early twentieth-century collectors, however, encouraged a tendency to isolate the paintings from their funerary contexts. The paintings were initially studied by classicists and art historians who, basing their conclusions on details in the paintings alone (hairstyles, jewelry, and costume), identified the portraits as being those of Greek or Roman settlers who had adopted Egyptian burial customs. Although the portraits appear, at first, to capture the unique features of specific individuals, perhaps only the earliest examples of the genre (dating from the first half of the first century CE) were painted from live models, whereas the same generic quality that permeates the visages of the cartonnage and plaster masks persists, upon closer study, within the corpus of Faiyum portraits that have been preserved. Successful attempts have been made, however, based on the analysis of brush strokes and tool marks and the distinctive rendering of anatomical features, to group the portraits according to schools and to identify some individual artistic hands.

A link might nevertheless be traceable between the ultimate funerary function of the Faiyum portraits and a cultic use for the paintings while their owners were yet alive. Evidence from the portraits themselves—that the upper corners of panels were lopped at an angle to secure a better fit before being positioned over the mummy, that there are signs of wear on paintings in areas that would have been covered by the mummy wrappings, and that at least one portrait (now in the British Museum) was discovered by Flinders Petrie at Hawara still within a wooden Oxford-type frame—indicates that the paintings had a domestic use prior to inclusion within the mummy wrappings, that they were probably hung within the home.

The cultic and funerary functions of the Faiyum portraits and the inclusion of iconographic elements (such as the gilding of lips, in accordance with funerary Spells 21 to 23 of the *Book of Going Forth by Day*, to ensure the power of speech in the afterlife), as well as the iconographic allusions to traditional deities (such as the sidelock of Horus worn by adolescents, the pointed-star diadem of Serapis worn by men, and the horned solar crown of Isis worn by adult females), in addition to the fact that these portraits, like all masks, were but one component of the overall design of the complete mummy decoration, emphasize a continuity of native Egyptian tradition. Although these two-dimensional painted faces were the products of the Hellenized cultural world of Roman Egypt, they fall toward the end of a continuum of a desire to permanently preserve the faces of the dead in an idealized and transfigured form that began in the Old Kingdom and continued to the end of paganism in Egypt.

The very latest examples of funerary masks are actually painted linen shrouds, the tops of which were pressed into a mold to produce the effect of a three-dimensional plaster mask. Examples of that type, which may date as late as the third or fourth centuries CE, were first excavated in 1894–1895 by Edouard Naville, within the sacred precinct of the mortuary chapel of Queen Hatshepsut, and were initially incorrectly identified by him as the mummies of Christians, probably for the Coptic (Christian) monastery for which the modern site, Deir el-Bahri, is named. Eventually, H. E. Winlock correctly identified the iconography—particularly the ubiquitous representation of the bark of the Egyptian funerary god Sokar—on further examples of that type to be consistent with pagan Egyptian funerary traditions, although certain motifs, such as the cup held in one hand, seem to presage the final transition from pagan mask to Coptic icon painting and the portraits of Byzantine saints.   *Lorelei H. Corcoran*

MIN, the Greek form of the name of the god whom the Egyptians called Menu. One of the oldest of the Egyptian deities, he was associated with fertility, and specifically, male sexual potency. He was also the god of the desert, especially the wastelands to the east of Coptos and Akhmim, his chief centers of worship. His protection was sought by those who traveled through those inhospitable regions in search of gold, perfumes, and incense in the lands toward Arabia, and he was specially revered by laborers who worked the Eastern Desert mines.

Min is one of the few Egyptian gods whose iconography can be traced into the Predynastic period. At that time, he was represented by an enigmatic emblem—a horizontal line with a disk in the center, flanked by two hemispherical projections. This symbol has been variously identified as a meteorite, a bolt of lightning, an arrow with barbs, the bolt of a door, or two fossilized shells. It appears on palettes, earthenware vessels, and mace heads, as well as on standards. Later, it was incorporated into the hieroglyph for Min's name and the symbol for the fifth nome of Upper Egypt, whose capital was Coptos. Among the earliest anthropomorphic representations of the god are three pillar-like colossal limestone statues excavated at the temple of Min at Coptos by W. M. Flinders Petrie, which date from the late fourth millennium BCE. Now in the British Museum, they are among the few examples of divine sculpture from the beginning of the Early Dynastic period. These damaged statues, executed in a strikingly minimalist manner, depict a male figure whose left hand grasps at a space formerly occupied by a stone phallus. The fifth dynasty Palermo Stone records that in the first dynasty a royal decree commanded a statue of Min to be carved; the sculpture was probably similar to the ones at Coptos. Much later, a Ptolemaic temple of Min and Isis (still extant) was built at Coptos by an official named Sennuu for Ptolemy II, and the Roman emperor Claudius constructed a small temple to Min, Isis, and Horus at el-Qal'a, to the north of Coptos.

The other chief center for the cult of Min was Akhmim, in the ninth nome, on the eastern bank of the Nile. There is a rock chapel dedicated to him at el-Salamuni, to the northeast of Akhmim, which was most likely the creation of the eighteenth dynasty king Thutmose III; it was decorated by Nakhtmin, the "First Prophet of Min." West of Akhmim were two companion temples dedicated to Min and Repyt (Triphis), the goddess who was considered to be his consort. Both temples probably date from the Greco-Roman period, but might possibly be older. There was also a temple of Isis and Min at Buhen in Upper Nubia, built by Thutmose's successor Amenhotpe II (the "North Temple"); it is now removed to Khartoum.

In pharaonic art, Min appears as a human figure, standing upright and wrapped as a mummy, holding his erect penis in his left hand. The earliest known example of this ithyphallic depiction is most likely an ink drawing on a stone bowl found in the tomb of Khasekhemy (died c. 2687 BCE). The other iconographic characteristics of Min are the flail that he holds in his upraised right hand, and the distinctive crown that he wears; the crown is tall and double-plumed, with a long ribbon in the back. Later, Min's crown was taken over by Amun. Lettuce (*Lactuca sativa*) was associated with Min, possibly because it was be-

lieved to be an aphrodisiac or, perhaps, because of the resemblance that its milky sap bears to human semen. Lettuces are sometimes depicted on an offering table adjacent to the god, which stands between him and his sanctuary. Depictions of Min's sanctuary resemble the tents that desert-dwellers used, and New Kingdom reliefs on temple walls illustrate the ceremony of raising the tentpoles for Min. As lord of the Eastern Desert, Min was sometimes depicted in the company of gods of foreign origin, such as Reshep, Qedeshet, and Anat. Some scholars have identified him with the being described by the Pyramid Texts as "the one who raises his arm in the East." As an embodiment of male sexuality, Min was complemented by the goddess Hathor, who was associated with the libidinous aspects of the feminine.

During the Middle Kingdom, Min was assimilated into the Horus-myth. Sometimes he was identified as the son of Isis; at Abydos he was called "Min-Horus-the-victorious," the powerful conqueror of Seth. Alternately, Isis was pictured as his wife, with Horus as their child. By New Kingdom times, however, Min was equated with Amun, especially with the primordial creative aspect of the latter deity. Min-Amun-Re was given the appellation Kamutef, which literally means "bull of his mother"—that is, one who impregnates his own mother so that she gives birth to himself. This aspect of the supreme deity Amun, depicted exactly like the mummiform, ithyphallic Min, emphasized the eternal and self-subsistent character of divine and pharaonic power. A ceremony honoring Min, featuring a procession of a statue of the god, sometimes took place during the royal coronation as a means of ensuring the king's potency. Similar rituals occurred during *sed*-festivals (royal jubilees); a twelfth dynasty limestone relief now in the Petrie Museum in London shows Senwosret I celebrating his *sed*-festival, holding an oar, and (the inscription reads) "hastening by boat to Min, the god in the midst of the city." At Medinet Habu, the second court of the temple of Ramesses II (nineteenth dynasty) shows a similar festival, during which the pharaoh worships this agricultural divinity by harvesting a sheaf of wheat. Another ritual involved annointing a statue of the god with a life-giving mixture of bitumen and various burnt ingredients. Popular worship of Min was of a riotous nature. The Greeks associated him with Pan, their own rustic god of unbridled male *eros*, and during Ptolemaic times they renamed Akhmim as Panopolis ("Pan's city"). *Eugene Romanosky*

MODELS. Ancient Egyptian models, small-scale representations of objects and people from everyday life, may be miniature tools and vessels left in foundation deposits at temples. They may be votive or trial pieces, or scale models representing architectural elements of temples, such as column capitals or monumental gateways. The term *model* is more usually used in Egyptology to refer to figures of household servants performing cooking tasks; farm laborers tending animals and crops; and men involved in manufacturing processes. They can also represent individual items of food or offering vessels substituting for real offerings, as well as tools and weapons. There are models of religious paraphernalia for ensuring the safe passage from death to rebirth, such as the *pzš-kзf* set (originally a flint knife used in the Opening of the Month ceremony), the seven sacred oils tablet, or sets of miniature libation jars and bowls. Through their outward appearance, imitating objects from life and offerings of food and drink, as well as substituting for

depictions of these in tomb decoration, these models were believed to sustain the dead in their afterlife within the tomb magically, providing the food, drink, clothing, shelter, and transport that would be needed for continued existence. The most important categories of models, offering bearers and boats, are discussed separately below.

Predynastic and Early Dynastic (Naqada II to Third Dynasty, 3500–2632 BCE). Models from the Predynastic period are rare. Their function within burials, in the absence of other evidence, is assumed to be the same as that of later models. Made from pottery, they comprise figures carrying offerings, figures within large vats perhaps intended as brewers, boats which may or may not have a crew, houses, and beds. Surviving Early Dynastic period models include large pottery jars modeled to imitate dome granaries, and ivory or bone boats.

Old Kingdom (Fourth to Sixth Dynasties, 2632–2206 BCE). Limestone statuettes of servants appeared in the mastaba tombs of the elite at Giza during the late fourth dynasty, but became more common at Saqqara and Giza in the fifth and sixth dynasties. Models of that date are of single figures, most frequently engaged in the tasks of preparing foodstuffs; the most common is a female miller kneeling to grind grain on a quern stone. Other activities include sifting, forming dough cakes, attending a bread oven, straining beer mash, preparing beer jars, cooking or stewing meat, butchering a cow, and carrying pots or sacks. Manufacturing activities include throwing pots on a slow wheel and heating a forge through a pipe. Domestic life is represented by figures of wet-nurses and harpists. Structural models are of granaries comprising rows of tall conical silos, made either of stone or, more frequently, of pottery. Boat models are of wood. Usually, only two or three servant figures were placed in a single tomb, but the tomb of Djasha at Giza contained sixteen figures, while a group of more than twenty figures is said to have come from the tomb of Nykau-Inpu at Giza.

The diffusion of models into more and more elite burials during the long reign of Pepy II at the end of the sixth dynasty resulted in stone servant figures becoming smaller and degenerate in form, and in the appearance of the use of wood for either single figures or pairs of figures. The best preserved and largest collection of such wooden models came from the tomb of Nyankh-Pepi-kem at Meir. It comprised seventeen scenes of millers, bakers, oven attendants, beer mashers, jar cleaners, duck roasters, offering bearers, cattle carrying sacks, and a man with a hoe; there were also eight boats. Contemporary with models entirely of wood are those that incorporate certain elements, such as jars or quern stones, which were made of stone and set into the wooden models.

First Intermediate Period (Seventh to Tenth Dynasties, c. 2206–2040 BCE). First Intermediate Period models are distinguished from their predecessors by being entirely of wood, and, for the first time, they comprise small groups of figures engaged in allied processes on the same wooden base, such as milling and baking, or brewing and bottling. Also at this time the square granary appears, usually with peaked corners and an internal courtyard in front of a row of flat-roofed silos. The intact tomb of Ini at Gebelein (eighth dynasty) contained a food preparation model, a granary, miniature granary sacks, and two boats.

Middle Kingdom (Eleventh to Twelfth Dynasties, 2134–1786 BCE). Most extant models of wood are from the Middle Kingdom, a time of wealth

and prosperity for the provincial elite. The period spanning the end of the eleventh dynasty and the beginning of the twelfth saw an increase in the power of provincial nobles. A reflection of this trend is seen in the number and diversity of models from all the major provincial cemeteries. A typical elite burial of the Middle Kingdom would have included at least two boats, a granary, a pair of offering bearers, a bread and beer preparation scene, and a butchering scene. Often these models were duplicated, probably to ensure a plentiful supply of offerings. Perhaps the largest collection of Middle Kingdom models came from the tomb of Djehutinakht at Bersheh, which contained thirty-three scenes, twelve offering bearers, and fifty-five boats. Paralleling this tomb is that of Karenen at Saqqara, which contained fourteen scenes, a procession of offering bearers, and eight boats. Similarly, the tomb of Tjawy at Beni Hasan contained eleven scenes, an offering bearer, and two boats.

The activities represented by Middle Kingdom models fall into five categories: agriculture and animal husbandry; food preparation; industrial processes; offering bearers; and boats. Models of men hoeing the soil, ploughing with cattle, raising calves, herding and forcefeeding cattle have been found most frequently at Asyut, Bersheh, Meir, and Beni Hasan, perhaps reflecting the agricultural wealth of this region in Middle Egypt. Industrial processes comprise spinning and weaving, woodworking and metalworking, and the manufacture of pottery and stone jars. Workshop models of this type come most frequently from Saqqara.

By the reign of Senwosret II, fourth king of the twelfth dynasty, the influence of the provincial elite began to decline because of royal intervention, and there was a concomitant decline in the number and diversity of models. However, the materials from which they were made in-creased, so that models from the twelfth dynasty Faiyum sites are of wood, faience, and various stones. Alongside the traditional wooden models of kitchen and cooking scenes, granaries, offering bearers, and boats are models of foodstuffs—fruit, vegetables, cuts of meat, cereal grains, and various types of bread—made of blue or green faience or painted cartonnage.

Second Intermediate Period, New Kingdom and Later (1786–931 BCE). With the demise of models came the rise of the *shawabti* figure, perhaps developed from mummiform figures commonly found on twelfth dynasty funerary boats. Inscribed with chapter 6 of the *Book of Going Forth by Day* (*Book of the Dead*), these figures took over many of the functions of models. An eighteenth dynasty variation of the *shawabti* is in the form of a miller. Isolated models continued to be used into the Late period, most notably boat models and figures of mourners.

The Meketre Models. Theban tomb 281 belonged to Meketre, chancellor to Montuhotep I, reunifier of Egypt in the eleventh dynasty. A niche in the entrance corridor of the tomb contained the finest collection of models ever found. These models are unique for their size, quality of craftsmanship, and attention to detail. The Meketre models are probably the product of a northern workshop, perhaps at Lisht, and probably date to the reign of Amenemhet I—hence their notable differences from other late eleventh and twelfth dynasty models from the Theban necropolis. There are nine scenes, each contained within a walled room, as well as two offering bearers and thirteen boats. Unique to this group are the two walled gardens and the inspection of a herd of cattle by Meketre and his officials. The gardens

contain model sycamore fig trees surrounding a copper-lined pond, overlooked by a colonnade and windows. The roofs have copper rain spouts. The group also includes a spinning and weaving shed and a carpentry shop. The quality of the figures in these models allows the identification of tasks depicted in other, less accomplished models.

Offering Bearers. Offering bearers are the largest models, in terms of height, of all model types and are among the earliest to be found. Predynastic period offering bearers are simple pottery figures with hollowed heads, or figures carrying hollowed receptacles. Usually these are single figures, but a rare example is known of a row of bearers, possibly from Naqada. Later bearers tend to be more carefully made than other model types, and some are on a par with figures of the tomb-owner. This implies that offering bearers were regarded by the Egyptians as more important than the generic producers of food and drink. During the Old Kingdom, depictions in relief of women carrying baskets on their heads are found on royal mortuary monuments and later in private tombs. These women are given hieroglyphic labels identifying them as mortuary estates, or land and servants assigned by the dead person as the producers of the funerary offerings. Models of offering bearers, women carrying baskets on their heads and holding flowers or fowl, may have been substitutes for the relief and painted mortuary estates or the servants of those estates.

Offering bearers are usually female, but male porters are found. Indeed, Old Kingdom stone bearers are all male; often they are dwarfs carrying sacks or jars. Male bearers tend to carry religious items such as sensors and libation jars, or scribal equipment, in contrast to the females, who carry food items.

Generally, female offering bearers are single figures, but they can be found in pairs, either two single figures or two figures sharing a single base. This pairing may represent the concept of Upper and Lower Egypt or their titular goddesses, or the two staples of Egyptian diet, bread and beer. Other offering bearers are found in processions, in single or double file, comprising a mixture of both sexes. The finest of this genre is the so-called Bersheh Procession from the Middle Kingdom tomb of Djehutinakht at Bersheh, consisting of three female bearers led by a shaven-headed priest. A similar though smaller procession was among the Meketre models, complementing the two larger offering bearers from that tomb. The largest procession is of (originally) twenty figures, from the tomb of Karenen at Saqqara.

Model Boats. Boat models were believed to provide transport along the river Nile, Egypt's main artery of communication. George A. Reisner in *Models of Ships and Boats* (Cairo, 1913) organized model boats into seven categories:

1. Square-cut craft with two rudders (Old Kingdom)
2. Craft with curling stern and one rudder (Middle Kingdom)
3. Papyrus raft/skiff (Predynastic period onward)
4. Papyriform wooden craft (Old to Middle Kingdom)
5. Papyriform wooden craft with raised finials (Early Dynastic onward)
6. Solar barks (twelfth dynasty)
7. Divine barks (New Kingdom onward)

Five further categories of New Kingdom vessels, from Dilwyn Jones's *Model Boats from the Tomb of Tut'ankhamun* (Oxford, 1990) have a deeply curved hull profile. Each type of boat had a different purpose: types 1–3 were used for transport, fishing, and leisure; types 4, 5, 7,

and sometimes 2 were used for funerals or on symbolic pilgrimages to sacred sites, such as Abydos; and types 6 and 7 represented highly specialized religious craft, used to traverse the heavens and underworld in the company of the gods.

Two models were usually placed in the tomb, one rigged for sailing south with the prevailing wind and placed facing south, the other equipped for rowing north with the current of the river and placed facing north. In some tombs, flotillas of from four to more than fifty models have been found, consisting of pairs of different types of boats.

The earliest boat models are from the Predynastic period, and are made of pottery, ivory, and bone. All are hollow canoe forms, some with raised finials closely resembling the depictions of boats on painted pottery and in tomb 100 at Hierakonpolis; others are similar to Reisner's types 3 and 5. Wooden boats appeared in the fourth and fifth dynasties at sites in Upper and Lower Egypt, becoming common at the end of the sixth dynasty. These models are carved from a single piece of wood, with masts, spars, rudders, oars, and cabins made separately and attached with pegs. Additional details are shown in paint: red and yellow for planking, white for deck details, and black for cordage. Old Kingdom boats have a more or less hollow hull, while First Intermediate period and Middle Kingdom boats tend to have solid hulls with a flat base to facilitate standing upright in the tomb.

Three important sixth dynasty groups of boats consist of eleven models from the tomb of Kaemsenu and sixteen boats from the pyramid of Queen Neith, both at Saqqara. Both these groups comprise types 1, 3, 4, and 5. The third group of eight boats, from the tomb of Nyankh-Pepi-kem at Meir, differs only in the inclusion of model sailors to crew the vessels, a feature common from the end of the sixth dynasty.

Thirteen boats came from the Middle Kingdom tomb of Meketre at Thebes. Two of the seven type 2 boats were kitchen tender boats for the preparation of meals on long journeys. Fishing and hunting in the papyrus swamps was done from a pair of type 3 skiffs, and for deeper water a small type 2 boat was provided. Meketre's type 5 ritual boats differ from most others in the provision of paddles and sails. Painted tomb scenes of the funeral and pilgrimage journeys indicate that ritual craft were usually towed to their destination.

From twelfth dynasty burials at Bersheh and el-Lisht have come the peculiar type 6 boat models. Devoid of crew, they carry instead the standards and emblems of solar deities, and were probably intended to allow the deceased to travel in the company of those gods.

A unique pair of early New Kingdom boats from the burial of Queen Ahhotep, mother of Ahmose, at Dra Abu Naga (Thebes), is of gold and silver and resemble type 7 craft. One of the boats was found resting on a model wheeled carriage. Such carriages, it is known from tomb paintings, were used to transport boats around impassable sections of the Nile.

Fragments and whole boat models have come from the eighteenth dynasty tombs of Amenhotpe II and Thutmose III in the Valley of the Kings, but it was not until the discovery of the tomb of Tutankhamun that a complete collection of New Kingdom boats was found. Comprising thirty-five boats, they form three flotillas of twenty-four traveling craft based around three larger state vessels. There are also types 3, 5, and 7 craft in the collection. The latest wooden boat model from a burial context is the type 7 craft from the twenty-first dynasty

tomb of the priests of Amun at Deir el-Bahri (Bab el-Gasus).

Boats can be helpful as a dating tool. Type 1 models are not found after the end of the sixth dynasty, when they are replaced by type 2. Type 4 boats with elongated finials and bipod masts are found during the late sixth dynasty to First Intermediate Period. Type 2 models with a high stern angle are generally of the First Intermediate Period or early Middle Kingdom, while a curled rudder fork on a low-angled stern indicates a twelfth dynasty date.

Geographical and Social Distribution. Models have been found at sites from Aswan in the south to Abusir in the north. It is probably only the damp conditions of the Nile Delta that prevents the placing of models farther north, since models, albeit of pottery, have been found at the Dakhla Oasis site of Qilâel-Daba, indicating how widespread the practice was. Predynastic models have come from such sites as Abadiya, el-Adaima, and Naqada, while Old Kingdom stone servant figures have come from the *mastaba* fields of Giza and Saqqara. Late Old Kingdom models of both stone and wood have been found at Saqqara, Dahshur, Meidum, Sedment, Dara, and Qubbet el-Hawa (Aswan). First Intermediate Period and Middle Kingdom models come from both capital and provincial cemeteries the length of the Nile, such as Saqqara, Sedment, el-Lisht, Riqqeh, Beni Hasan, Bersheh, Meir, Rifeh, Asyut, Hawawish, Sheikh Farag, Gebelein, Qubbet el-Hawa, and the Theban necropolis, to name but a few.

Only the elite in Egyptian society, those in the secular and religious professions, had models in their tombs. This elite group were buried in *mastaba* tombs, in rock-cut tombs with a decorated superstructure, and in shaft tombs with one or more subterranean chambers at the bottom. Characteristic of provincial cemeteries is the arrangement of the high-status rock-cut tombs in a good stratum of rock with the shaft tombs of provincial court members below in the foothills. It is from this latter tomb type that most models have survived. Rarely do models occur in pit tombs, a form of simple shaft, except for pottery miniature agricultural implements and tools.

Excavation of these different tomb types indicates that models were placed in a variety of locations: pits outside the tomb enclosure or shaft mouth; niches cut in the floor of the entrance corridor to the superstructure; *serdabs* (statue chambers) within the *mastaba* superstructure, tomb shaft, or burial chamber; and the burial chamber proper. Some intact tombs, such as that of Nakht at Asyut (Middle Kingdom) had some models placed in the tomb chapel, the area accessible to the living and most vulnerable to the attentions of tomb robbers. It is the discovery of such intact deposits that is most instructive, but sadly most tombs have been robbed and their contents stolen, scattered, or smashed, leaving archaeologists the task of putting the pieces together again.   *Angela M. J. Tooley*

MONOTHEISM. Attention has been given to the issue of monotheism in ancient Egyptian religion since the early days of Egyptology. One idea proposed was that Egyptian religion was originally monotheistic and only secondarily developed into a polytheistic system, following the principle of nineteenth-century anthropology that the simple precedes the complex in cultures. According to this view, intellectuals and initiates were thought to have retained a belief in a primitive monotheistic deity while accepting the multiplicity of gods and goddesses as mere personifications of divine attributes; that is, there was one

god for the wise and many for the common folk. Theologically, the solitude of the primeval god Nun before the Creation was adduced in support of an underlying primitive monotheism.

This interpretation was challenged by discoveries in the Early Dynastic royal cemeteries at Abydos and by the publication of the Old Kingdom Pyramid Texts, and it was alternatively proposed that monotheism developed from a preexistent polytheism. Some scholars have maintained that even as early as the Old Kingdom there was a nameless divine being behind the multiplicity of gods, whereas others have regarded Egyptian religion as only gradually moving toward monotheism. Since Egyptian religion was a historically developed rather than a revealed religion, polytheism has been seen by some as surviving along with the emergence in the New Kingdom of a transcendent deity who could be manifest in many forms.

The Term "God." The situations in which the Egyptian word for "god" was used in a way suggestive of a monotheistic deity are basically two: personal names and the Wisdom Literature. In the Early Dynastic period and during the Old Kingdom, there existed personal names containing the word "god." Being given to a child at birth, theophoric personal names were spontaneous expressions of joy and devotion to the god of whom the parents had asked the gift of a healthy child. In some of these names the Egyptian term for "god" appears to be used in an abstract way—for example, "god is gracious," "whom god loves," "whom god fashioned," or "god lives." But paralleling such names are others that mention a specific god, such as "Khnum is gracious," "beloved of Re," or "Ptah lives"; this suggests that when the term "god" was used in naming a child, the parents were thinking not of an abstract divinity but rather of a specific local deity to whom they had prayed. There are, in fact, personal names that instead of using the masculine word "god," employ the feminine word "goddess," as in "may the *ka* of the goddess exist," or "great is the goddess." Nowhere does evidence exist to suggest that "goddess" was ever employed as an abstract term in Egypt. So, by analogy, it is probable that when "god" appears in personal names, the speaker was thinking of the deity closest to him—one embodying all divine attributes, but not the sole divinity. In interpreting these early names, it is also possible that "my god" rather than "god" is the proper translation, owing to the fact that in Old Egyptian the first person singular pronoun was regularly omitted in writing.

Monotheism has also been held by some scholars to be present in the Wisdom Literature, where as early as the *Instruction of Ptahhotep*, the term "god" seems to be used in an abstract sense. Some have supposed that the authors of Wisdom texts, being of the elite, were acquainted with the concept of a transcendent monotheistic deity. It should be stressed, however, that in all Wisdom texts the polytheistic element is also present: use is made of the word "gods" in the plural, and specific deities are also named. Since Wisdom Literature was composed for the benefit of the elite scribal class and not intended for broad public dissemination, its polytheistic element was hardly a concession on the part of the sages to appeal to a polytheistic public. Moreover, later Wisdom texts actually mention specific deities even more frequently than earlier Wisdom texts, casting doubt on any supposed trend toward monotheism. It is most unlikely that references to various deities or to gods in the plural were mere

turns of phrase. In both the *Instructions for Merikare* and the *Instructions of Ani* there are references to caring for the cultic needs of the gods; these must be concrete deities who possessed temples and priests.

In composing a Wisdom text, the writer desired to make his work comprehensible to bureaucrats through-out the land, not just at the royal residence in Memphis or at Thebes. Along the Nile there were many towns, villages, and districts, each with its primary local deities; and in any given community a person would tend to invest the local deity with the highest attributes possible. One must also reckon with mobility as bureaucrats moved from one part of Egypt to another. Because it would have been inappropriate to name a specific god as dominant throughout the text, recourse was had to the vaguer, less precise word "god" instead. Circumstances would change in place and time, so it was best for the author of a Wisdom text to use the neutral "god" in generalizing for the reader's benefit.

Henotheism. The approach to the divine in the Wisdom Literature is related to the concept of henotheism, whereby a writer, speaker, or devotee selects a god as his or her own single almighty deity, without, however, denying the existence of other gods and goddesses, any of whom might be seen by someone else as the principal deity. Superficially, this might look like monotheism, but it is not; the Egyptians did not impose a universally exclusive god except during the Amarna period, when Akhenaten selected the Aten and curbed the cults of traditional deities. Of the terms that have been utilized to describe Egyptian religion, "henotheism" seems to be the most appropriate. It implies that when an Egyptian honored a god or goddess in hymn or in prayer, he or she treated that deity, at that moment, as though the deity possessed the characteristics of a sole divinity, with all other gods and goddesses—even the mighty ones—paling into insignificance. The deity who is being addressed at the moment stands out as all-important. The fact that more than one god could be called "king," or "lord," of the gods does not reflect a stage between polytheism and monotheism.

A nice illustration of the way a devout Egyptian might single out even a goddess as the object of his devotion occurs in the tomb inscription of the Ramessid scribe Simut. Although initially Simut speaks of the god who guided him early in life as an unnamed male deity, the bulk of the text describes his selection of the goddess Mut to be his patron (to whom he bequeaths all his property), because he found Mut to be at the head of the gods, greater than any other deity, with all that transpires at her command (Wilson, 1970).

It can be argued that the very existence of the god depended on differentiation, such as took place initially at Creation, and that it was therefore impossible to have a deity who was totally one and absolute to the exclusion of others once the existential realm had come to be. Only at the very beginning of Creation was there exclusive unity, which became lost in the differentiating process, when even the Creator became distinguished from the many other deities of the pantheon. A return to the primal monistic state would have meant the very negation of existence. Thus, the Egyptian view of Creation and of the existential realm presented a serious impediment to the development of monotheism from polytheism.

A god could be a unity, as revealed in theophany or epiphany, or when honored by an individual in prayer or hymn, but he/she was also manifold in nature, capable of appearing in numerous forms. A typically Egyptian thought structure involved thinking in pairs. Within this structure, a deity could be both the one and the many. This concept has been termed "complementary thinking," whereby opposites, instead of contradicting each other logically, complement each other in expressing reality. For monotheism to have developed would have required a radical change in this complementary thought pattern, which permitted the divine, on the one hand, to be a unity in the individual encounter, and, on the other hand, to possess many forms of appearance and attributes.

Summodeism. During the New Kingdom, particularly in the Ramessid period, hymns were composed that describe a divinity who is a kind of universal supertranscendent god, of whom all other deities are merely secondary emanations. This kind of theology, with its notion of an abstract transcendent god who stands above all other deities and whose true nature cannot even be fathomed by either gods or humans, has been regarded as reflecting a crisis in the traditional polytheism; however, it certainly is not monotheism, since the existence of many deities—even though of lesser quality—is still not denied. Here the term "summodeism" best describes the situation in which there is a supreme god heading a polytheistic pantheon, whose multitude of deities exist as hypostases of the high god by virtue of his transforming himself into the many.

Although Ramessid theologians may have been thinking about divinity along such lines, henotheism with its implicit polytheism nevertheless prevailed in the practice of religion. There is a letter written by the high priest of Amun during the reign of Ramesses IX (translation in Wente, 1990, pp. 38–39) that illustrates how even the top ecclesiastical figure adheres to polytheism when he invokes the blessing of Montu as well as of Amun-Re, king of the gods, for recipients of his letter. In correspondences penned by the elite during the late Ramessid age, there is constant mention of numerous deities. The fact that in these letters one finds the writer saying, "I'm all right today; tomorrow is in god's hands," might suggest a belief in the existence of a monotheistic deity because the term "god" is modified by the definite article just as in Coptic biblical literature, where it is used in reference to the monotheistic god of the Bible. However, the Ramessid-era expression about tomorrow's being in god's hands occurs in letters that also regularly contain invocations to numerous named deities. Such a collocation in letters written by officials at the end of the New Kingdom does not suggest monotheism, let alone summodeism—which, unlike henotheism, was largely confined to the realm of theology without seriously altering traditional religious beliefs and practices.

Akhenaten's Monotheism. Although the Aten is attested as a god prior to Akhenaten's reign, Akhenaten's institution of the cult of the Aten as sole deity is unique in the history of Egyptian religion. What he did was to single out this god—who was manifest in the sun disk and its radiating rays of sunlight—from among the others, to be the object of veneration. The Aten was the sun god, and the solar disk was the form in which this divinity appeared. In fact, over the course of Akhenaten's reign one can trace a development that reflects the king's role in implementing a radical new theology. Although other deities were initially still recognized, Akhenaten soon ordered the abrogation of their cults; the persecution of traditional deities, particularly those of Thebes, intensified, as the name and representation of the god Amun were expunged from monuments throughout the land. Even the plural word for "gods" was frequently erased. The king, who had earlier dropped the name Amenhotpe in favor of Akhenaten, had the didactic name of the Aten revised so that it no longer contained elements suggestive of polytheism.

The Amarna theology, as revealed in texts and scenes from tombs and temples, supports the idea that it constituted a form of monotheism. The Aten was about as close to an absolute god as the Egyptians got. He was a jealous god who did not tolerate other deities. Texts speak of the living Aten beside whom there is no other; he was the sole god. The Amarna religion can be described as monotheistic in the sense that it was an established religion whose theology was articulated by Akhenaten, who alone comprehended the true nature of the Aten. In effect, his theology became the religion. By proclaiming the universality and unity of Aten and rejecting the traditional pantheon, Akhenaten was negating the old polytheistic religion.

There are some qualifications to Akhenaten's monotheism. The king, for example, was himself a god and had his own high priest. Whereas Akhenaten in his inscriptions never called himself "god," but only "son of god," there are clear cases in which he is referred to as "god" by his subjects, in such expression as "my god who made me" or "the god who fashions people and makes the Two Lands to live." Akhenaten was not directly identified with the Aten, but since Aten was Re, therefore his son (who was the son of Re and also occasionally identified as Re) was of the same essence as his father, the Aten. The monotheism of Amarna comprised a father–son relationship, in which the son was the incarnation and image of the sun god, daily reborn as the Aten was reborn. In fact, the dual process of the Aten's daily self-creation and his simultaneous regeneration of Akhenaten constituted the focal point of Amarna theology, according to Žakbar (1954).

What is more, Akhenaten's queen Nefertiti also received divine attributes. At Amarna she appears as a deity along with the Aten and Akhenaten in funerary offering formulae, and there are praises and prayers to the king that are paralleled by ones directed to his queen. Hymns to the Aten can be introduced by the words, "Adoration of the Aten, Akhenaten, and Nefertiti." There thus seems to have been a triadic relationship among the Aten and his children, Akhenaten and Nefertiti. It is quite possible that in developing his religion, Akhenaten was familiar with a much older theology surrounding the creator god Atum and his two offspring, the god Shu and the goddess Tefnut, who were consubstantial emanations of the creator god, providing life and order as energizers at Creation. Thus the Aten filled the role of Atum, while Akhenaten was Shu, the god of air, light, and life, and Nefertiti was equivalent to Tefnut, who symbolized the correct order of the world. The Shu-aspect of Akhenaten is iconographically evident in the four-feathered crowns sometimes worn by the king; and Nefertiti's name, which means "the beautiful one has returned," possibly equates her with Shu's twin sister Tefnut, who according to mythology returned to Egypt as a charming woman after going south as a ferocious lioness.

The king and queen worshiped the Aten directly, whereas commoners generally approached the Aten only through the intermediation of the king. Absent from the Amarna scene were those processions of portable barks containing images of the gods that had traditionally been adored by the populace. Instead, the king and queen were the objects of popular veneration as they moved about the city of Akhetaten in procession. Evidence from two letters found at Amarna, however, indicates that a commoner could directly implore the Aten in prayer to bestow benefits, so that it would be wrong to suggest that Akhenaten had a monopoly on piety.

There are a few minor points that have been adduced as qualifications to Akhenaten's monotheism. In his boundary stelae of Year 5 of his reign, the king mentions that he found the site of Akhetaten belonging to no god or goddess—a tacit admission of the existence of other deities besides Aten. The early date of this proclamation may, however, not yet reflect the fully developed Aten theology with its exclusion of polytheism. In Amarna texts, the concepts of "fate," "fortune," and *maat* ($m3^ct$, "justice") tend to be personified as goddesses, but such deifications are of a different order than deities of cosmic nature and hardly constitute a serious objection to the characterization of the Aten as a monotheistic divinity. Although some inhabitants of Amarna bore theophoric names that contained the names of traditional deities, this phenomenon has its analogy in the persistence of old theophoric names among Coptic Christians. It has also been pointed out that in private homes and chapels at Amarna, documents have been unearthed that attest to the retention of traditional gods and goddesses as household deities. It is possible, however, that such evidence should be assigned to the reign of one of Akhenaten's successors, Smenkhkare and Tutankhamun.

All in all, Amarna theology can be considered monotheism because it proclaims "the unity of god" and excludes the constellations of older polytheistic deities. Like Judaism, Christianity, and Islam, it was an established religion, founded on the revelation of the Aten to Akhenaten, who alone knew the Aten and anathematized the old polytheistic tradition. The degree to which Amarna theology influenced Israelite monotheism has been much debated. Although there is some similarity between the Great Aten Hymn and Psalm 104 in the negative evaluation of nighttime and in the treatment of nature as nondivine, responding to the life-giving activity of the divinity who constantly nurtures creation, the peculiar theocracy inherent in the triadic relationship of the Aten, Akhenaten, and Nefertiti bears absolutely no resemblance to the god of the Hebrew scriptures.   *Edward F. Wente*

MONTU (*Mnṯw*), a local Upper Egyptian solar deity who became state god. This came about because of his association with the victorious King Nebhepetre Montuhotep I of the eleventh dynasty (r. 2061–2011 BCE), who had successfully reunified Egypt, bringing an end to the instability of the First Intermediate Period. The king's name means "Montu-is-satisfied." During the twelfth dynasty, the deity Montu became subordinated to another Upper Egyptian deity, Amun, to assume the role of war god. Cult centers were maintained for the worship of Montu at four sites within the Theban region, the fourth Upper Egyptian nome (province): Armant, southwest of modern Luxor on the western bank of the Nile; Medamud, northeast of Luxor, inland from the eastern bank; Tod, southwest of Luxor on the eastern bank; and Karnak, northnortheast of Luxor, adjacent to the northern side of the great temple of Amun. The temples date from the Middle Kingdom at all these sites, except for

Karnak, where the earliest structure is New Kingdom and is securely attributed to Amenhotpe III (r. 1410–1372 BCE).

Montu is most commonly represented as a falconheaded man, whose wig is surmounted by a solar disk, with a double *uraeus* (royal cobra crown) behind which two tall plumes extend vertically. In later periods, Montu also appears with a bull's head and a plumed solar headdress, as a manifestation of the Buchis bull of Armant. A bull sacred to Montu was also revered at Medamud.

In addition to iconography, in temple reliefs the inherent solar aspect of Montu (as the composite sun deity Montu-Re) is shown by his symmetrical pairing with the sun god Atum of Lower Egypt, frequently escorting the king into the presence of Amun. The name of Montu's chief city, Armant n Iuny (Old Eg., *Iwny*), and Atum's Heliopolis Iunu (Old Eg., *Iwnw*), or On, sounded so similar to the Egyptians that the former was referred to as On-of-Montu or Iunu-Mentu (*Iwnw Mnṯw*), for clarification.

Montu's veneration as war god began during the Middle Kingdom. In the *Story of Sinuhe*, Montu was praised by the tale's hero after he defeated the "strong man" of Retjenu. During the New Kingdom, the warrior pharaohs of the eighteenth dynasty, in particular, sought to emulate Montu. The Gebel Barkal stela of Thutmose III (r. 1504–1452 BCE) describes the king as "a valiant Montu on the battlefield." Royal warships were adorned with striding Montus, brandishing maces or spears, each figure styled as lord of one of his four cult centers. There is a mythological basis for the use of the god's image in defense of the king, the earthly son of the sun god Re. A hymn on the Armant stela of Usermontu, from that era, described Montu as "the raging one who prevails over the serpent-demon Nik," and the one "who causes Re to sail in his bark and who overthrows his serpent enemy." Later in the New Kingdom, Ramesses II's personal identification with Montu was so strong that a cult statue—using his throne name Usermaare Setepenre, compounded with the epithet "Montu-in-the-Two-Lands"—was venerated in the king's honor during his lifetime.

Montu has been depicted in the company of three consorts: Tjenenet, Iunyt, and Rettawy. He has also been paired in texts with another "raging" god, Seth, perhaps as a contrast between controlled and uncontrolled divine aggressiveness.

Edward K. Werner

MUMMIFICATION. Naturally or artificially preserved bodies, in which desiccation (drying, dehydration) of the tissues has prevented putrefaction, have been discovered in several countries. They are generally called "mummies," although originally this term was applied only to the artificially preserved bodies of the ancient Egyptians. The word *mummy* is derived from the Persian or Arabic word *mumia*, which means "pitch" or "bitumen"; this originally referred to a black, asphalt-like substance that oozed from the "Mummy Mountain" in Persia. This material, credited in the region with medicinal properties, was eagerly sought as a cure for many ailments. The demand eventually led to a quest for an alternative source, and, because the preserved bodies of the ancient Egyptians often have a blackened appearance, these were believed to possess similar properties to *mumia*; consequently, they were used as a medicinal ingredient in medieval and later times (after the mid-seventh-century Arab conquest of Egypt). The term *mumia* or "mummy" was extended to these bodies and has continued in use until now.

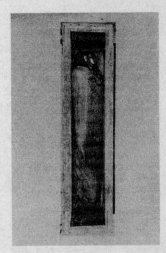

Twelfth-dynasty coffin and mummy of Khnumhotep from Meir. (The Metropolitan Museum of Art, Rogers Fund, 1912 [12.182.131])

Techniques. Human remains (consisting of the skeleton and body tissues) can be preserved indefinitely as a result of environmental and other factors. The dryness of the sand in which the body is buried, the heat or coldness of the climate, or the absence of air in the burial all help to produce unintentional or "natural" mummies. These factors, occurring either singly or in combination, have produced naturally preserved bodies in Egypt, South America, Mexico, the Alps, Central Asia, the Canary Islands, the Aleutian Islands, and Alaska; a different type of preservation also occurs in northwestern Europe, where bodies have been preserved when buried in peat bogs or fens containing lime. There is considerable variation in the extent to which these different environments have been successful in producing "natural mummies." In some areas, this natural process of preservation was intentionally developed by enhancing the existing environmental conditions. Sun, fire, or candle heat were sometimes used to desiccate the bodies thoroughly; other bodies were smoked or cured. Sometimes dry grass and natural materials were used to surround the body and to stuff its cavities, or the burial place provided a sealed environment for the corpse which, by excluding air, prevented decomposition and further deterioration.

The most advanced method of intentional preservation (to which the term "true mummification" is sometimes applied) involved various sophisticated techniques that had been developed throughout a period of experimentation. Ancient Egyptian mummification, which provides the best examples of this method, involved the use of chemical and other agents. In Egypt, a combination of climate and environment, as well as the people's religious beliefs and practices, led first to unintentional preservation of the body and then to true mummification. Because of the scarcity of available cultivatable land, the earliest Egyptians chose to bury their dead in shallow pit-graves on the edges of the desert, where the heat of the sun and the dryness of the sand desiccated the body tissues before decomposition occurred. These natural conditions produced remarkably well-preserved bodies; the skin tissue and hair have often survived, and the corpse retains some likeness of the person's appearance when alive.

History of Mummification in Egypt. Before about 3400 BCE, all Egyptians were buried in pit-graves, regardless of their status or wealth; later, increased prosperity and advances in building techniques led to the introduction of more elaborate tombs for the leaders of the society. These tombs had brick-lined underground burial chambers, which no longer provided the environmental conditions of the pit-graves that had created the natural mummies. Religious beliefs however, required that the body should be preserved as completely as possible so that the deceased owner's *ka* ("spirit") could return to the tomb and recognize it, reenter it, and thus gain spiritual sustenance from the food offerings placed at the tomb.

Although most of the population continued to be buried in pit-graves, the Egyptians now sought other means to preserve the bodies of the highest classes. There followed a period of experimentation that probably lasted several hundred years. There is some evidence to suggest that these experiments were undertaken as early as the second dynasty (c. 2850–c. 2687 BCE): the archaeologist J. E. Quibell found a large mass of corroded linen between the bandages and bones of a body interred in a cemetery at Saqqara, perhaps evidence of an attempt to use natron or another agent as a preservative by applying it to the surface of the skin. Another technique involved the production of "stucco mummies," bodies that were covered in fine linen and then coated with plaster, to carefully preserve the owner's body shape and features, particularly the head. In 1891, W. M. Flinders Petrie discovered a body at Meidum dating to the fifth dynasty (c. 2513–c. 2374 BCE), in which there had been some attempt to preserve the body tissues as well as to recreate the body form. Close-fitting bandages were molded to reproduce the shape of the torso; the limbs were separately wrapped, and the breasts and genitals were modeled in resin-soaked linen. Despite these attempts, however, the actual body had decomposed beneath the bandages, and only the skeleton remained within the elaborately wrapped outer case.

The first convincing evidence of successful intentional mummification occurs in the fourth dynasty (c. 2649–c. 2513 BCE). In the Giza tomb of Queen Hetepheres, the mother of Khufu, builder of the nearby Great Pyramid, archaeologists discovered a chest containing intentionally preserved viscera which can probably be attributed to the queen, although the previously undisturbed tomb did not contain the owner's body. When these viscera packets were analyzed, it was found that the organs had been treated with natron, the agent successfully used in later times to dehydrate the body tissues. This evidence seems to indicate that the two most important stages of Egyptian mummification—evisceration of the body and the dehydration of the tissues by means of natron—were already in use for royalty. Mummification continued to be practiced in Egypt for some three thousand years, until the end of the Christian era and the arrival of Islam in the country.

The technique gradually became available to the upper and middle classes, and in the Greco-Roman period (c. 332 BCE–third century CE) it became increasingly widespread. It was never universally available to the poorer classes, however, and most of the population continued to be interred in simple desert graves, where their bodies were naturally preserved.

According to the Greek historian Herodotus, three main types of mummification were available, and the client chose the method he could afford. The most expensive included elaborate funerary rites as well as a lengthy and complicated procedure to preserve the body. Although this involved many stages, the two steps crucial to arrest the decomposition of the body were evisceration

and dehydration of the tissues. The viscera (internal organs) were usually removed from the thoracic and abdominal cavities through an abdominal incision in the left flank; in some cases, the viscera were not extracted at all, and in others they were removed through the anus. The removed viscera were then dehydrated with natron, and either placed in canopic jars or made into four packages and reinserted in the body cavities; some were wrapped in one large packet that was placed on the legs of the mummy. The heart was usually left *in situ*, probably because it was considered to be the location of the individual owner's intelligence and life force. The brain, considered nonessential, was removed and discarded.

After evisceration, the body cavities were washed out with spiced palm wine, then filled with a mixture of dry natron, gum resin, and vegetable matter. The corpse was then left to dehydrate for a period of up to forty days. Natron (hydrated sodium carbonate, $Na_2.CO_3.10 H_2.O$), the main substance used to pack the body, is found in a dry desert valley called the Wadi Natrun; it is composed of sodium carbonate and sodium bicarbonate and includes some natural impurities. There have been different opinions regarding the use of natron, salt (sodium chloride), or lime (calcium carbonate) as the main dehydrating agent in Egyptian mummification, and there has also been discussion as to whether natron was used in solution (in water) or in a solid state. Assessment of the Greek text that describes the process, along with modern experiments on mummified tissues, has now confirmed that dry natron, which provides the most satisfactory results, would almost certainly have been used to pack the bodies.

After dehydration was complete, the temporary stuffing was removed from the body cavities and replaced with the permanent stuffing and sometimes also the viscera packages. The abdominal incision was then closed, the nostrils were plugged with resin or wax, and the body was anointed with a variety of oils and gum resins, which may have played some part in preventing or delaying insect attack and in masking the odors of decomposition that would have accompanied the mummification process. These stages were, however, essentially cosmetic and had little effect in preventing putrefaction of the tissues. The embalmers then wrapped the mummy in layers of linen bandages, between which they inserted amulets (sacred charms) to ward off evil and danger. A liquid or semiliquid resinous substance was then poured over the mummy and coffin. Finally, the embalmer returned these to the family of the deceased so that the preparations for the funeral and the burial could be made.

The two less expensive methods of mummification that Herodotus mentions did not include complete evisceration. In the second method (which was also used for animal mummification), oil of cedar was injected into the anus, which was plugged to prevent the escape of the liquid, and the body was then treated with natron. Once this was complete, the oil was drained off and the intestines and the stomach, liquefied by the natron, came away with the oil; the flesh had also been liquefied, so only the skin and the skeleton remained. The body was returned to the family in this state. In the third and cheapest method, the body was purged so that the intestines came away, and the body was then treated with natron.

In the long history of mummification in Egypt, there were only two major additions to the basic procedure. From at least as early as the Middle Kingdom

(c. 2134–1786 BCE), excerebration (brain removal) was practiced on some mummies, and by the New Kingdom (c. 1569–c. 1076 BCE), this procedure had become widespread. The embalmer inserted a metal hook into the cranial cavity through the nostril and ethmoid bone, and the brain was pulverized to fragments so that it could be removed with a spatula. In some cases, access to the cranial cavity was gained either through the base of the skull or a trepanned orbit (eye socket). Usually, it was impossible to remove the brain completely and so some tissue remained *in situ*. Before mummification was complete, the emptied cranial cavity was packed with strips of linen impregnated with resin, and molten resin was sometimes poured into the skull.

The second innovation was introduced in the twenty-first dynasty (1081–931 BCE), when the embalmers sought to develop a technique that had first been used in the eighteenth dynasty (1382 BCE) in the preparation of the mummy of King Amenhotpe III. Then, the embalmers had attempted to re-create the plumpness of the king's appearance by introducing packing under the skin of his mummy, through incisions made in his legs, neck, and arms. Later, in the twenty-first dynasty, the priests began to use subcutaneous packing not just for the mummies of royalty but for all who could afford this time-consuming procedure. The body cavities were packed through a flank incision with sawdust, butter, linen, and mud, and the four individually wrapped packages of viscera were also inserted into these cavities rather than being placed in canopic jars. Subcutaneous material was also introduced through small incisions in the skin, and the neck and face were packed through the mouth. In this way, the embalmers tried to retain the original bodily contours to some degree, to make the mummy's appearance more lifelike. Artificial eyes were often placed in the orbits; the skin was painted with red ocher (for men) or yellow ocher (for women), and false plaits and curls were woven into the natural hair. These expensive and time-consuming preparations were not retained beyond the twenty-third dynasty (813–711 BCE).

In the Middle Kingdom, the political and economic growth of the middle classes and the consequently increased importance of religious beliefs and practices among all classes of Egyptian society resulted in the spread of mummification to new sections of the population. More mummies have survived from that period than from the Old Kingdom, but it is evident that less care was taken in their preparation.

In the Greco-Roman period (332 BCE–395 CE), when foreign immigrants who settled in Egypt sometimes adopted Egyptian funerary beliefs and customs, mummification again became more widespread. It also became an increasingly commercial venture, and it tended to indicate the deceased owner's social status rather than his religious conviction, with the result that the standards of mummification declined rapidly. Although the bodies were elaborately bandaged and encased in covers made of cartonnage (a mixture of plaster and papyrus or linen), modern radiographic analysis confirms that they were frequently poorly preserved inside the wrappings.

Sources. Our knowledge of mummification is based on the archaeological evidence provided by the mummies, paleopathological studies of the bodies, painted and carved representations in tomb scenes and elsewhere on some stages of the mummification procedure, and textual references in Egyptian and classical-era accounts. There is no extant Egyptian description of the technical processes involved in mummification. The earliest available accounts occur in the writings of two Greek historians, Herodotus (fifth century BCE) and Diodorus Siculus (first century BCE). Yet, in Egyptian literature, there are scattered references to mummification and the associated religious rituals. One of these, the *Ritual of Embalming*, provides a set of instructions to the officiant who performs the rites that accompany the mummification process, as well as a collection of prayers and incantations to be intoned after each rite. This ritual is preserved in two papyri, probably copied from a common source and both dated to the Roman period (31 BCE–395 CE): Papyrus Boulaq 3 (in the Cairo Museum) and Papyrus 5158 (in the Louvre). References to embalming ceremonies also occur in the Rhind Papyri (discovered by A. H. Rhind in an eighteenth dynasty tomb at Thebes) and in other literary sources, including inscriptions on stelae; however, Herodotus's account remains the most complete literary source.

No paintings or carvings provide an extant, complete record of mummification. Wall scenes in the tombs of Thoy and Amenemope (tombs 23 and 41, respectively, at Thebes) and vignettes painted on some coffins and canopic jars show some stages in the mummification procedure, and in a papyrus that once belonged to Any (nineteenth dynasty, 1315–1201 BCE), a vignette illustrating the *Book of Going Forth by Day*(*Book of the Dead*) shows Anubis, the god of embalming, attending a mummified body inside an embalming booth.

Rituals and Accessories. The mummification procedure was carried out in the embalmer's workshop, known as *wbt* ("place of purification"). Some workshops would have been put up near the individual tombs, but because of the "impure" nature of mummification and its associated dangers, these would have been situated outside the actual tomb enclosure. Other workshops, where larger numbers of bodies were prepared, were located near burial grounds or temple sites.

Although many rites accompanying the mummification process were performed in the embalmer's workshop, one of the most important rituals—the Opening of the Mouth ceremony—was carried out at the tomb. These final rites, which sought to ensure the eternal life of the deceased owner, were an important part of the funeral; with an adze, the priest touched the mouth, hands, and feet of the mummy and of all the representations of the tomb-owner appearing in the tomb, including wall scenes, models, and statues. This action was believed to restore life to the mummy so that the spirit of the deceased could enter and use it; similarly, all the inanimate figures in the tomb would be able to act on behalf of the deceased owner. Modern experiments have shown that optimum results in mummification are achieved after a maximum period of forty days for evisceration and dehydration; however, Herodotus and other sources quote a period of seventy days for mummification, and undoubtedly much of that time would have been occupied with religious and magical rituals. A single ancient Egyptian text, however, records a much longer period, but this undoubtedly included associated rituals and ceremonies.

The embalmers and priests used a range of accessories in the mummification process and associated rites. They placed amulets between the layers of bandages and placed a cartonnage mask, chest, and foot covers over the mummy to give it the necessary physical support.

In the actual preparation of the body, the embalmers and their assistants employed a blade of obsidian to make the incision in the flank of the mummy, and they stored the viscera in a set of canopic jars. The body was also treated with plant remains and resins, and the priests used special jars and vessels when they anointed and lustrated the mummy.

Embalmers. Within the distinct group of practitioners who were concerned with the mummification process, Diodorus Siculus stated that there were three main classes who prepared the body for burial. These included the cutter (Gr., *paraschistos*) who made the incision in the flank of the mummy; the scribe who supervised this work; and the embalmer, who belonged to a special guild or organization and was responsible for leading the mummification ceremonies and for wrapping the mummy in bandages. In fact, the embalmer supervised all the stages of the mummification process. He wore a jackal-headed mask to impersonate Anubis, god of embalming, when he performed the rituals. As highly skilled professionals, the embalmers were a special class of priests who probably had close associations with doctors. Their office was hereditary, and they also employed others, such as the coffinmakers who produced coffins and wooden figurines and other items for the tomb.

In contrast, the cutters, because of the ritual "impurity" (and possible health hazards) associated with making the incision in the corpse and removing the viscera, had the lowest status in society; this group may have included convicted criminals. Other people involved in the mummification procedure and the funeral included the priests of Osiris who performed the rituals, lector-priests who recited the chants and the ritual instructions, and the men who washed and cleansed the mummy and the viscera, prepared the natron and resin, and wrapped the body with layers of linen bandages. The whole process associated with death and burial was a major industry that employed many workers.

Scientific Studies. In recent years, multidisciplinary studies of mummified remains have supplied new information about the process of mummification itself and also about disease, diet, living conditions, and familial relationships in ancient Egypt. It has been shown that natron was used in a dry rather than a liquid state, and that the composition and method of application of the natron could affect the final result. Use of the scanning electron microscope (SEM) to identify insects has provided information about insect attack on the mummies; histology and electron microscopy have supplied evidence about the success or failure of individual mummification techniques; and thin layer and gas liquid chromatography have isolated and characterized the substances that were applied to the mummy bandages.

Several techniques have contributed to the study of disease in mummies. In the 1970s, radiography—a totally nondestructive method—became a major investigative procedure, and later the additional use of computerized tomography (CT) became standard in most radiological investigations of mummies. In addition, dental studies of mummies have provided evidence about age determination, diet, oral health, and disease. Paleohistology, involving the rehydration, fixing, and selective staining of sections of mummified tissue, and paleopathology, the study of disease in ancient people, have developed considerably since the techniques were pioneered in Cairo earlier in the twentieth century by M. A. Ruffer. Endoscopy has now almost entirely replaced the need to autopsy a mummy, since this technique allows the researcher to gain firsthand evidence about embalming methods, and to obtain tissue samples for further study, without destroying the mummy. Histology, transmission electron microscopy (TEM), immunohistochemistry, and immunocytochemistry can then be used to search for evidence of disease in the tissue samples.

Although there have been several studies of bloodgroups in ancient human remains, DNA identification has now largely superseded paleoserology as a technique to examine individual familial relationships; future studies may consider the origins and migrations of ancient populations, and they may be able to identify bacterial, fungal, viral, and parasite DNA as causative agents of disease. Finally, studies have been undertaken to determine the processes of deterioration that occur in mummies so that methods of treatment can be developed to assist curators and conservators in preserving these collections; however, it is essential to ensure that such treatments do not destroy or contaminate any evidence that is yet to be susceptible to future identification and other investigative procedures.

Ann Rosalie David

MUT. The goddess Mut is known primarily as the spouse of Amun-Re, king of the gods; she forms with him and Khonsu the child the Theban triad, from about 1500 BCE until the end of Egyptian religious history. She is, however, not just a vague mother goddess, though she is often represented with the child Khonsu on her lap. She is a stately royal lady, wearing the Double Crown, the two royal crowns of Upper and Lower Egypt, as do some masculine gods. She is the divine queen mother and even queen regnant, a divine female pharaoh who represents kingship with her Double Crown. Beginning in the time of the female pharaoh Hatshepsut, the pharaoh may be called "son of Amun and Mut."

The name of Mut was written with the vulture hieroglyph, but she was not a vulture goddess like Nekhbet, as is often suggested in older literature. She was also represented as an anthropomorphic being with a human head or a lion head. Only very seldom, and evidently secondarily, was she given a vulture head next to a human or lion head. The vulture headdress that she often wears together with the Double Crown is common to many other goddesses and royal women. This vulture headdress, as well as the vulture hieroglyph with which her name was written, is a symbol and ideogram of motherhood, as Horapollo knew: the Egyptian word for "mother" is written with the vulture hieroglyph and is to be read *mut*. The name of the goddess Mut thus means "mother." (For particulars and problems, see the article by Wolfgang Brunsch in *Enchoria* 8 [1978], pp. 123–128.)

In comparison with other divinities, Mut makes a late appearance in the history of Egyptian religion, or at least in the material that is preserved. So far, no definite proof exists that she played a part in the religion of Predynastic and Early Dynastic times, or even of the Old Kingdom, First Intermediate Period, and Middle Kingdom. The oldest certain attestations date from the Second Intermediate Period and come from Middle Egypt, for example, from Megeb in the tenth Upper Egyptian nome and from Karnak. Whether, when, or how Mut was introduced in this cult center of Amun is not known, but she replaced Amaunet, the "grammatical" female companion of Amun, in the Middle Kingdom in some aspects. Mut is known from the seventeenth dynasty on as "the Great One, Mistress of Isheru."

The precise meaning of the word *išrw* is unknown. Isheru is not only the place and temple where Mut was worshiped in South Karnak, but it is also a term for a lake that surrounds a temple of lion goddesses on three of its four sides. Mythologically, Isheru is the place where these feline deities were appeased, so that their burning wrath was cooled. Leonine goddesses were considered to be representations of the Eye of Re, or the daughter of Re, or the original first feminine being; they had a dual or ambivalent nature in which pacific and creative elements coexisted with fiery, anarchic, destructive, dangerous characteristics. These goddesses had to be pacified with specific prayers or litanies and rituals (see Yoyotte 1980). The festival of the navigation of Mut, together with some other leonine goddesses, on the *išrw*-lake was famous in Thebes and all Egypt.

In Amun's train, Mut was worshiped in many places in the Nile Valley, the Delta, Nubia, and the Western Desert oases. By herself or together with other gods, such as Ptah or Re, she was worshiped near Antinoöpolis as mistress of Megeb; in Memphis, as Mut in the house of Ptah; in Giza, as Mut-Khenty-Abu-Neteru; and in Heliopolis, as Mut-Her-Senutes, the cruel goddess to whom human victims were offered, as Jean Yoyotte (1980–1981) has shown.

In a late Wisdom text (Papyrus Insinger 8, 18–19) one can read: "The work of Mut and Hathor is that what takes place among women, for there are good and bad women among those upon earth." Although Mut is not without malevolent and dissipated traits and remains a leonine goddess who is not always a peaceful cat, she is not, like Hathor, a symbol of sexual excitation. Mut is the matron, the divine mistress of the house. She is the female compassion man meets in his mother, sister, daughter, and—to a certain extent—in his wife; she is not so much the sexual attraction man finds in strange and dangerous women outside the family. Mut was venerated by women and men, and she had both priests and priestesses. The important priestesses called "God's Wives of Amun" had names mostly composed with the name of Mut and were regarded as earthly incarnations of Mut. The femininity of Mut with her royal crowns was authoritative and sometimes also aggressive and terrifying: unlike any other Egyptian goddess, she could be depicted as an aggressive woman with a penis, who frightens off her opponents.   *Herman te Velde*

MYTHS.

An Overview

Although the term "myth" is often used to signify any type of traditional story or legend, for scholars it is highly specific: a myth is a spoken word, statement, or narrative that is used, frequently within a cultic setting, to articulate realities that cannot be defined in a totally rational manner. Myth is a means of sacred revelation, a method of communication that functions through symbolic expression and has its own inner logic—a logic belonging to the realm of the mystical and metaphysical rather than to that of reason and rationality. Although this definition implies that myth has a spiritual purpose, it can encompass a wide variety of topics. There are myths of creation, myths of the gods, historical or semi-historical myths, heroic myths, political myths, myths of national identity, and psychological myths, among others. In all myth the oral aspect is essential, because to the ancient mind the spoken word was a creative force that evoked the reality of the entity or event named. The term "myth" is thus an appropriate one for

denoting the statements that the Egyptians made concerning their gods and their environment, since it reflects their consciousness of the reality and the mystery of the divine. Because of its revelatory function, authentic myth does not adapt well to written form. Myths can be recorded in writing, but they then run the risk of becoming dogmatic and unable properly to articulate the continuing revelation of the living world of the divine.

The Western mind often thinks of myth in terms of the Greco-Roman mythic tradition. The latter, however, lost much of its mysterious character under the influence of Homeric and Classical Greek rationalism. Hence, Greco-Roman myths tended to evolve into narrative accounts that provided virtually a universal history but did little to reveal the inner mysteries of existence. Egyptian myth, however, was less concerned with extended narration and was not bound to recount events in an orderly manner; thus, it retained the ability to function as a flexible, symbolic mode of revelation. The Egyptian gods, unlike the anthropomorphic gods of the Greeks, were not understood to be limited to the forms in which iconography portrayed them. Horus was shown with a falcon's head, and Anubis with that of a jackal, but these theriomorphic representations were symbolic means of articulating the sacredness and otherness of the gods. Such iconography was an essential expression of myth, especially within a cultic context. As for the problem of the relationship between myth and cult, some writers suggest that the myth evolved from the cult, while others maintain that the cult grew out of the myth. It is, however, most likely that myths and their cults evolved simultaneously, myth being primary in some cases and cult in others. Once established, myth and cult remained integral to one another and functioned in a complementary manner: the cult dramatized the myth, and the myth verbalized the cultic ritual.

Even before its conjunction with cult, myth had two main sources. One was the natural world, which humans perceived and interpreted by personalizing the natural forces so as to relate to them. The other was historical individuals and incidents, which were idealized and incorporated into myth as heroes or gods and their deeds. It is relatively easy to detect the natural sources of myth, but identifying specific historical elements is often a matter of interpretation. The ultimate sources of myth are highly complex, but in the final analysis, all myths reflect the reaction of the intellect to its background and environment.

Out of the Egyptian corpus of myth one can isolate a number of mythic cycles of primary importance. The earliest of these were the cosmogonic cycles associated with Heliopolis and Hermopolis, both of which evolved out of the observation of nature. The antiquity of these cycles is evident in that they both take their beginning from a fundamental entity, Nun (the primeval waters), the chaos from which creation emerged. The symbol of Nun was derived at an early (probably prehistoric) date from the flooding of the Nile; the primeval mound reflects the emergence of the isolated hillocks that appeared as the waters subsided.

In the Heliopolitan tradition, the god Atum (later Re-Atum) emerged out of Nun, sat on the primeval mound, and performed his creative activity through a combination of masturbation and spitting. From this action there came into being Shu and Tefnut, twin deities of the air, and from their union sprang Geb and Nut, personifications of earth and sky. In

these gods, the natural structure of the universe was complete. Geb and Nut then begat the twin couples—Isis and Osiris, and Seth and Nephthys. Through Osiris the Egyptian monarchy became an integral part of the Heliopolitan cycle, and with the defeat of Seth, the god of disorder, by Horus the son of Osiris, the Horus kingship was sacralized by mythological tradition. Both natural and historical sources contributed to this tradition: the cosmogonic elements derived from the natural world, and the political elements from the wars during the Predynastic and Early Dynastic periods. In the murder of Osiris by Seth and the defeat of Seth by Horus one can see reflections of early struggles for the throne, while figures such as Isis, Nephthys, and Hathor have frequently been interpreted as aspects of royal power. This Heliopolitan cycle, with its Ennead of nine gods, developed over an extended period, reaching completion during the fourth or fifth dynasty.

The Hermopolitan cosmogony was less complex than that of Heliopolis, but more pristine in that it was less political. The Hermopolitan cosmogony also began with Nun, but within Nun lived the Ogdoad, eight primal creator deities who later died and went to the underworld. Even after this, however, they retained their power, for it was they who caused the sun to rise and the Nile to flow. This Hermopolitan cosmogony developed in four variations. Two of them stressed the emergence of the world from the cosmic egg, which had been laid either by the celestial goose or by the ibis, the sacred bird identified with Thoth. The two other variations based the creation of the world on the symbol of the lotus from which emerged the sun god Re, either as a child or as a scarab beetle. The major development in the Hermopolitan system was the later grafting on of the god Thoth, who by tradition was self-created, like certain others of the greater gods. In the tradition of Thoth at Hermopolis, the gods of the Ogdoad were his souls. In yet other statements from Hermopolis, the sun god Re was the creator of all things. These different versions within the Hermopolitan cycle illustrate the flexibility of Egyptian myth, which was able to permit contradicting symbols within one tradition.

Among cosmogonic myths, mention must be made of the Memphite tradition preserved in a text known as the Memphite Theology, on the Shabaka stone from the twenty-fifth (Nubian) dynasty. For decades this text was regarded as an Old Kingdom composition, but general opinion now dates it to the twenty-fifth dynasty. The theory of creation that it sets forth is the most abstract and intellectual of all Egyptian cosmogonies, in that it ascribes creation to the divine mind and the utterance of the divine word. In this Memphite tradition, it was Ptah Tatenen ("Ptah of the primeval mound"), the ancient earth god of Memphis, who was the supreme deity and creator, and the gods of the Heliopolitan Ennead were manifestations of him. Ptah was also the founder of ethical order *(maat; m3ˁt)* and of the Horus kingship. This tradition is significant in that it illustrates the ability of the Egyptians to think in quasi-philosophical terms. The basic ideas of the Memphite tradition may have been based on earlier concepts, but its formulation during the Nubian dynasty suggests that the new rulers of Egypt were intent on using it to secure the reestablished unity of the Two Lands.

There were other creation myths and creator deities known to the Egyptians. Very prominent was Amun-Re of Thebes, and during the rule of the heretic pharaoh Amenhotpe IV (Akhenaten), the Aten was recognized as sole creator. At a very early stage, Neith of Sais, often known as "the mother of the gods," may have been a creator mother goddess; at Elephantine at the First Cataract of the Nile, the potter god Khnum was said to have fashioned humanity on the potter's wheel out of Nile mud. The wide variations in cosmogonic myths among the Egyptians do not reflect mythological confusion but are rather a sign of the genius of the Egyptian mythopoeic mind. In the final analysis, all these traditions attempted to articulate the basic truth that the created universe was in some manner dependent on the divine power.

The most enduring of the mythic cycles was that of Osiris, the god of immortality. The origins of Osiris are obscure, and the meaning of his name uncertain, but he was probably known at an early period, although the first mention of his name occurs only in the fifth dynasty. His origin was probably at the city of Djedu (Busiris) in the Nile Delta, but because of his association with the dead king, his chief shrine came to be at Abydos, the earliest dynastic necropolis. Osiris was attached to the Heliopolitan Ennead no later than the fifth dynasty and possibly before, a move which may have been to a great extent political. Certain references in the Pyramid Texts indicate that Osiris may originally have had a demonic nature, but at an early date he became the personification of the dead monarch and a symbol of his rebirth in the next world. According to the myth, Osiris and his sister-wife Isis ruled Egypt, having inherited the kingship from Geb, but Osiris was murdered by Seth, who then seized the throne. The dead Osiris miraculously impregnated Isis, who then gave birth to Horus. Horus, on attaining manhood, fought with Seth to regain the throne; the mythic accounts of the struggle probably reflect the wars of the Predynastic and Early Dynastic periods. Eventually the Heliopolitan Ennead confirmed Horus in his claim to the throne. Horus, in conjunction with Isis, Nephthys, Thoth, and several of the other gods, restored Osiris to life in the underworld, where he reigned as judge and king of the dead. Owing to his connection with the earth, Osiris also took on fertility functions and was responsible for the annual rebirth of the grain. Even the Nile was sometimes considered to be his gift to Egypt, being called "the great efflux of Osiris." Alternatively, the Nile was said to result from the tears of Isis mourning the dead Osiris.

Although the afterlife promised by Osiris was originally reserved for the king and his nobility, evidence from the end of the Old Kingdom suggests that the afterlife was becoming accessible to certain members of the elite, and by the Middle Kingdom to any individual able to provide for himself the proper burial rites. The one who had received proper burial was guided by Anubis to the underworld, where his or her heart was weighed against the Feather of Maat to determine innocence or guilt, and he or she was, it was hoped, adjudged righteous by Osiris and admitted to everlasting life. Because of the ability of Osiris to grant immortality, he attained extreme popularity, and his shrine at Abydos, the site of the celebration of his mysteries, became one of the greatest places of pilgrimage in Egypt. Eventually his worship spread beyond Egypt and became known throughout the Roman Empire.

The role of Osiris made him popular as a god who fulfilled a certain need of the individual, but the function of a state deity was more readily fulfilled by the more universal sun god. The sun god was one of the most ancient of the Egyptian deities, and his influence was felt from the very beginnings of Egyptian religion and myth. His earliest form was Re, the sun god of Heliopolis, and in this name he continued to be central in myth throughout the entire history of ancient Egypt. He was often syncretized with other gods, producing such deities as Re-Horakhty, Re-Atum, Amun-Re, and Khnum-Re. Even during the reign of Akhenaten, the so-called Amarna period, Re did not disappear in favor of the Aten; the designation of the sun god as Re-Horakhty was used during the first half of Akhenaten's reign, and even after that the name Re endured in the Amarna system. When universalism arose in Egyptian thought during the New Kingdom, it was with the sun god that this universalism was associated. The importance of the sun god was a natural development in Egypt because of his prominent visibility and his obvious ability to create and sustain life.

There were various myths associated with the sun god, but these were less important than his daily cycle. The emergence of this cycle was given expression in the myth of his departure from the earth where he had originally lived, specifically at Heliopolis. During his stay on earth, a period that was a type of golden age when humans and gods lived together, Re had been required to put down several rebellions against his authority. Eventually, weary of such problems, he decided to move to the heavens, where each day he crossed the sky in his solar bark; he journeyed through the underworld at night and was reborn on the eastern horizon each morning. His journey was not without danger, for the solar bark was constantly threatened by the monstrous Apep serpent which attempted to disrupt Re's journey. In one tradition, the god Seth had the duty of standing in the prow of the bark and defending Re from his chief enemy. Despite temporary victories by the Apep serpent, apparent in such phenomena as storms and eclipses, the solar bark was always victorious, and cosmic order was constantly maintained.

As with all myth, the importance of such symbols lay not in their details but in their significance. The significance of the Re myth is well expressed in the fact that his chief symbol was the scarab beetle, from which he derived the title Khepri ("the One Who Becomes"). For the Egyptian, the universe was not a static entity, but a living force in a constant state of movement. As Khepri, the sun god was the ideal symbol of this vitality: he was Khepri, the one who comes into being, in the morning at the time of his birth; he was Re, the developed sun god, at noon; and he was Atum, the completed one, in the evening as he descended to rest on the western horizon. The simplicity and beauty of such a mythic expression underlines the Egyptian concept of the unending pattern of light and darkness, the eternal motion, through which the universe and all life moved. The sun hymns in the Theban necropolis and the worship of Re as expressed even in the funerary *Book of Going Forth by Day* (the *Book of the Dead*) give ample indication of the central importance of the solar cycle in all aspects of Egyptian life.

The pharaoh was also an essential element in the Egyptian mythic system. His mythologization was to some extent a political move, and his position was closely woven into the wider fabric of Egyptian myth in order to give the earthly political order a more cosmic and stable position. From earliest times the king was the earthly incarnation of the heavenly Horus, and it is possible that the earthly monarch may have been the actual source of the celestial Horus. In the developed form of the royal myth, the pharaoh was the physical offspring of the sun god, begotten by that deity from his actual body. Pharaoh and sun god ruled Egypt in a partnership, the sun god being the *ntr ˁ3* ("great god"), and the pharaoh the *ntr nfr* ("good god"). The term *nfr* can also be translated as "youthful," and hence the pharaoh could be seen as a "junior" sun god, the lesser member of a political-cosmic partnership. Because of his relationship to the sun god, the pharaoh was the chief priest of all the gods and the chief cultic officer of their rituals, but the priestly power was relegated to the temple clergy. Through this myth of kingship, state and religion were inseparably intertwined, each supporting and validating the other. This theory made the monarch into a sacral figure whose existence was a guarantee of the continuance of cosmic, social, and moral order, and imparted to the Egyptian political order a divine right and character. The Egyptian hegemony was thus truly a "kingdom of God" in a terrestrial setting.

In certain mythological systems, particularly those of late antiquity, eschatological thinking eventually became fairly central. It is sometimes thought that Egyptian myth was free from eschatology, and that to the Egyptian mind all things would endure eternally. For the most part, the Egyptians were not concerned with eschatology, but nevertheless it seems to have been understood that the created universe was not totally eternal, and a few texts speak of the ultimate disappearance of everything, even of the gods. Such texts are few in number, but a Coffin Text (Spell 1130) seems to predict a time when only Osiris and Atum will remain, while chapter 175 of the *Book of Going Forth by Day* states that eventually all things will return to the primeval waters, whence they came. Texts of this nature indicate that there was some awareness of the possibility of the eventual dissolution of the universe, but such negative thinking leads back to a more positive aspect of Egyptian myth: the concept of *maat*. Personified as the goddess Maat, it ensured that this dissolution would not take place or would be postponed, and that the world would continue to exist for "millions of years." In brief, eschatology was not a major element in Egyptian myth, although there were a few traces of it.

In the history of Egyptian myth, the Amarna period is frequently regarded as myth-free. It did, however, have its mythic system—a reaction against traditional myth—and even the visibility of the deity in the Aten, the sun disk, was a form of mythic expression. Unlike traditional myth, Amarna myth did not personify nature but was centered on the Aten; and Akhenaten attempted a demythologization of religion. The Amarna belief system derived from an observance of nature, and its myth was centered on the ontology of the Aten and of the king, not on the natural world. The Aten was almost myth-free but retained a modicum of mythic expression. For example, he was said to beget himself, to be born in the morning, and to rest on the western horizon at evening. The Amarna doctrine of creation was expressed in the mythic symbol of the spoken word, a more sophisticated symbol than that of procreation known in other mythic systems. The Aten was also designated as "father and mother" of everything created, a formula that in virtue of its symbolic nature was a mythical one. The most significant Amarna use of myth, however, is in statements concerning the nature of the monarch. Akhenaten was presented as the physical son of the deity, the one who had "pro-

ceeded" from and was eternally "begotten" by the Aten. The ultimate result of Amarna royal myth was a virtual identification between Akhenaten and the Aten, the king being only slightly below the Aten in stature. Some scholars have seen various expressions of trinitarian myth in the Amarna system, but there is no agreement on any one official Amarna trinity. Mention should also be made of the city of Akhetaten, a mythic expression of the divine presence on earth. This concept of a sacred city constituted what could almost be regarded as a type of realized eschatology. Amarna teachings were not myth-free dogmatic assertions, but rather statements that used a modified form of myth to create an intellectual and abstract religious system.

In the wide variety of Egyptian myth, it is possible to see a logical system wherein the themes reflect a high degree of optimism. Egyptian myth shows a strong affinity for systematization, a search for order that is evident in the traditions of creation: out of chaos comes a comprehensible and organized unity. To articulate this unity, the Egyptian myth-makers did not follow abstract philosophical reasoning but instead relied on observation of the natural world. The continuance of life through procreation provided a natural symbol for the order of the universe, and the symbol of the creative word reveals the Egyptian realization that beyond the natural world there is a divine mind. In this divine mind the Egyptians saw the ultimate reason for the ongoing cycle of the natural world. They could depend on the sun to rise each morning because it was the birth of the sun god and because behind it there lay a supreme intellect. The annual Nile flood occurred because of the cyclical nature of the creation process. The recurring theme of a trinitarian arrangement (in threes) for many of the gods further emphasizes the Egyptian awareness of the natural process of procreation.

This optimism, however, did not blind the Egyptians to the negative forces in the universe. Myths that reflect struggle and tension reveal the awareness of the danger that chaos might erupt. Order was constantly in conflict with disorder, but *maat* was a mythic expression of the confidence that order would prevail. The struggle of Horus and Seth provided an example of this victory of order in both the natural and the political spheres. It was at this point that the divine, natural, and political orders met in the pharaoh. As the offspring of the sun god and himself a god incarnate, the pharaoh was a visible guarantee of stability. When one adds to this the symbol of the sun god, one can appreciate the Egyptian awareness of the existence of a supreme deity and the universalism this deity implies.

Finally, one must take note of the stress that Egyptian myth placed on the theme of eternal life. It was, of course, Osiris who was responsible for granting this boon, but Egyptian mythological and theological thought gradually developed and the sun god increased in prominence—particularly in his manifestation as Amun-Re—to the point that even the *Book of Going Forth by Day* could open with an adoration of the sun god, an acknowledgment of his power even in the realm of the dead.

The Egyptians, as is testified by their myths, held a very positive outlook on their personal existence and on the stability of their environment. Dogmatic orthodoxy was of relatively little importance, and the variations in mythic expression indicate that they were not bound by the demands of a strict doctrinal system. What was important was the recognition of the reality of the di-

vine world, the assurance that the power of *maat* would sustain the cosmic and political orders, and that the life of the individual would continue even after death. The understanding of existence presented by Egyptian myth must therefore have been a highly satisfying spiritual experience.

Egypt has left behind a wide variety of mythic material. Iconography in tombs and temples contains extensive portraiture of the gods, their cults, and many events of myth. Decorated coffins and elaborate copies of the *Book of Going Forth by Day* can also be useful for gaining an impression of the elaborate Egyptian concept of the divine world. Iconography is of little value without the written text to give it meaning, but the available textual material is sufficient to provide an extensive account of Egyptian myth. The Old Kingdom Pyramid Texts, the Middle Kingdom Coffin Texts, and the New Kingdom *Book of Going Forth by Day* contain an abundance of material on all aspects of Egyptian myth; and although such materials are not systematically arranged, they provide the modern reader with mythic texts as they would have been known to the Egyptians. The tale of the *Contendings of Horus and Seth* contains a New Kingdom fictionalized and even humorous account of this important tradition. Also from the New Kingdom comes the text of the *Destruction of Mankind*, preserved on the walls of several royal tombs. The ancient Greek writer Plutarch provided a complete account of the myth of Isis and Osiris, although one wonders how much of Plutarch's narrative is truly Egyptian and how much has been recast in the form of a Greek myth. A more authentically Egyptian account of the Osiris myth can be found in the *Great Hymn to Osiris*, although the latter text is less a systematic narrative and more a part of liturgy. Finally, the wide variety of hymns and liturgical texts from temples and tombs can add a great deal to an understanding of Egyptian myth as it was used in actual cultic practice.

Vincent Arieh Tobin

Creation Myths

Creation myths in any culture are not intended as scientific explications of the way in which the universe came into being; rather, they are symbolic articulations of the meaning and significance of the realm of created being. Such myths are to an extent explanatory, but their "explanations" lie in the realm of metaphysics rather than in the realms of science or history. Creation mythology arises primarily out of human curiosity and the experience of the world, and even the most rudimentary culture will have its tradition of creation, whether that creation be spontaneous or the purposeful act of a divine will.

One of the most distinctively Egyptian articulations of creation mythology was the tradition now known as the Heliopolitan cosmogony, which was developed by the priesthood of Heliopolis (Egyptian On), the sacred city of the sun god, situated not far from the ancient capital, Memphis. This mythic system was the product of the Old Kingdom at a time when Egypt had only recently been unified. The Egyptians were aware of the fact that there had been a time when nothing was in existence, for, according to the Heliopolitan tradition, there had been a time when "the sky had not yet come into being; the earth had not yet come into being; humanity had not yet come into being; the gods had not yet been born; death had not yet come into being" (Pyramid Texts, 1466). In this realm of nothingness, a source of creation was necessary. One of the characteristic features of Egyptian creationism is the fact that creation was essentially an act of generation, and for that act a specific generative principle was needed. This generative principle was evident to the Egyptian mind in the yearly flooding of the Nile River, and the procreative powers of the waters suggested the ultimate source of all created being, the "primeval waters." These primeval waters of Egyptian thought were both a negative and a positive entity: negative in that they were boundless, shapeless, infinite and chaotic—all ominous concepts to the Egyptian mentality; but positive in that they contained within themselves a certain potential for being. The creative potential of the primeval waters is evident in their personification as the self-generated god Nun, as expressed in chapter 17 of the *Book of Going Forth by Day* (the *Book of the Dead*): "I am the great god who came into existence by himself, Nun who created his own name as a god in the primeval time of the gods." Thus, for the mythopoeic mentality of Heliopolis, in the beginning there was chaos, but that chaos already contained within itself the potential for order.

That potential was realized when out of the primeval waters there emerged, like the rising sun, the god Atum, the source of all created and generated being. The name Atum bears the double meaning of "totality" and "not to be." Atum was thus at once absolute being and absolute nonbeing, combining within himself these contrasting opposites. This newly emerged deity, sitting on the primeval mound in his form as Re-Atum, the Creator sun god, was frequently depicted as wearing the royal Double Crown of Egypt, symbolic of the fact that with him there came into being the kingship of the Two Lands. The Heliopolitan creation tradition, possibly for strong political reasons, thus combined within itself the created universe and the political order as two inseparable entities. From the political point of view, the Heliopolitan system attempted to create the concept of a sacral kingship, a means of justifying mythologically the newly established monarchy.

The creative power of Re-Atum is brought into action at this point with the generation of the twin couple Shu and Tefnut through Atum's act of masturbation, as is stated in the Pyramid Texts, 1248: "He is Atum, the one who came into being and who masturbated in On. He placed his penis in his fist so that he might have sexual pleasure thereby, so that the twins, Shu and Tefnut, might be born." (According to Spell 76 of the Coffin Texts, Shu and Tefnut were produced by Atum's act of spitting, and probably the two symbols, masturbation and spitting, should be combined in any full account of the myth.) With the birth of the male Shu and the female Tefnut, the Heliopolitan creation tradition moves to the point of differentiating between male and female as the two complementary sources of generation, thus making possible the continuing process of generative creation.

From the union of Shu and Tefnut were born the male Geb and the female Nut, the deities who personified the earth and the sky respectively. Thus, it is at this point in the myth that the universe comes into being, but earth and sky are not simply created things; they are generated divine beings, the source of all else to come. The frequent iconography that portrays Nut as arched over Geb points to the role of these deities as mythic symbols of the continuing generative power of life and creation. The next generation in this creative cycle proceeds to articulate the created universe even further and to admit the reality of the two opposing forces of or-

der and disorder. From Geb and Nut there sprang Osiris and Seth, Osiris embodying within himself the principle of order and Seth representing disorder. With these two were associated their sisters, Isis who became the wife of Osiris, and Nephthys who became the wife of Seth. These nine deities formed the original mythic group of the gods known as the Heliopolitan Ennead. The admission into this group of Seth, the god of confusion and chaos, is highly significant, because it articulates the Egyptian realization of the continual struggle between good and evil, order and disorder, within both the created and the political realms.

The place of humanity within this created order was not the exalted one given to it by Hebrew creationism. According to tradition, Shu and Tefnut once became separated from Atum and lost in the primeval waters. Atum sent out his Eye to look for them, and on their return he wept tears of joy, from which sprang humanity. The Heliopolitan creation myth thus assigns to humanity a certain divine origin, but at the same time the creation of humanity does not appear as a purposeful act. Human beings were little more than the accidental product of a specific emotion of the creator deity, and hence their place within the created order was certainly not intended to be the "crown of creation" one sees in, for example, the Old Testament account of creation.

It is highly significant that the Heliopolitan creation tradition is inseparably connected to the sun god, for each day was in effect a renewal and a repetition of the creation. In the rising of the sun, the Egyptian had the assurance that the created order and the life and sustenance of humanity were eternal and ongoing: the rising of the sun was in essence a sacramental symbol that gave assurance of the stability of the created universe and of the royal political system that governed it.

Hermopolis *(Khmnw)* in Upper Egypt had a cosmogony that was claimed to be the oldest of all the Egyptian creation traditions. The nearby Middle Kingdom necropolis has yielded a number of interesting coffin texts illustrating various aspects of the Hermopolitan creation myth. Like certain other cult centers, Hermopolis was said to be the site of the original primeval mound which emerged from the waters. Like the Heliopolitan myth, the Hermopolitan tradition started with the primeval waters, but within those waters were the eight Heh gods, the Ogdoad, as opposed to the Heliopolitan Ennead. These deities formed four divine couples—Nun and Naunet, Amun and Amaunet, Huh and Hauhet, Kuk and Kauket, names that reflected the basic negative characteristics of the primeval waters: boundlessness, mystery, chaos, darkness, infinity. The Hermopolitan deities were almost always nonanthropomorphic (see, however, the human forms of Amun and Amaunet in the Karnak temple), the males being depicted as having the heads of frogs, and the females, those of serpents. In later traditions concerning the Ogdoad, the specific deities were said to be the offspring of Amun, Shu, or Thoth. Though devoid of specific mythic connotations, the Hermopolitan Ogdoad was expressive of the numinous and mysterious force of the divine creative power. These eight deities created the world together, but eventually they died and took up their abode in the underworld. Even from here, however, they continued to exercise their power, causing the sun to rise each day and the Nile to flow. The Heliopolitan Ennead was the divine group that sustained the world and its political system, but the Hermopolitan

Ogdoad appears as a more basic and rudimentary system wherein the gods were the sustainers of the natural order, powers concerned less with politics and more with the essential structure of the created world.

The Hermopolitan myth had several variations—not an infrequent characteristic of myth, which is able to admit the existence of different and even seemingly contradictory symbols within itself. One significant symbol that stands out in two of these variations is the Cosmic Egg, the source from which the world emerged. According to one tradition, this Cosmic Egg was laid by the "Great Cackler," the celestial goose, while another tradition claims that it was laid by an ibis, the bird identified with Thoth. The connection of Thoth with the Ogdoad of Hermopolis developed when the Hermopolitan priesthood adopted that deity and wove him into the fabric of Hermopolitan myth. Thoth thus became yet another symbol of the supreme creator, being himself self-begotten and the source of the Heh gods.

Two other versions of the Hermopolitan myth laid a greater stress on the primeval waters. In one version, a lotus emerged from the waters and opened to reveal the sun god Re in the form of a child. Another variant states that from the lotus there emerged a scarab beetle, symbolic of the sun, and that the scarab beetle then became a male child from whose tears sprang humanity. In this lotus symbolism, it is interesting to note the attempt to graft the creator sun god onto the older symbol of the primeval waters, an example of the syncretizing skill of the Egyptian myth-makers.

From the city of Memphis in the Nile Delta came another of the chief Egyptian cosmogonies, a creation tradition that centered on the god Ptah. Ptah was a very early deity associated with the earth and was frequently portrayed wrapped in the bandaging of a mummy. The chief source for the content of the Memphite cosmogony is the Shabaka stone, erected under the pharaoh Shabaka during the twenty-fifth (Nubian) dynasty. This text, known as the Memphite Theology, claims to be a copy of an archaic scroll, and for a long time it was assumed to reflect the most ancient traditions of Memphis. However, general opinion now tends to date its composition to the time of the twenty-fifth dynasty, and it thus appears to have been one of the latest Egyptian attempts to articulate the creation of the universe. It is certainly one of the most sophisticated and abstract of the Egyptian cosmogonies, expressing creation as an act of the divine will, intellect, and word.

The Memphite tradition does not attempt to set forth a mythological narrative of creation, but rather presents a theological statement of the nature of Ptah, his relationship to the other gods, and his role as supreme deity and creator. Ptah Tatenen ("Ptah of the primeval mound") was both the source and ruler of all the gods. He was Nun, the father of Atum; he was Naunet, the female counterpart of Nun and mother of Atum; he was the heart (intelligence) and the tongue (creative power) of the Heliopolitan Ennead. The creative process was brought about through the agency of the heart and the tongue, not through physical action and reproduction as in the older Heliopolitan system: "Every word of the god came into being through what the heart mediated and the tongue commanded," as the Memphite Theology puts it. The heart and tongue of Ptah, according to the Memphite tradition, were Atum, and thus Atum was seen as a manifestation of these specific aspects of Ptah. Atum was, in effect, the instrument of the divine will of Ptah.

Ptah, therefore, was said to be "the one who had made all things and who had created the gods. He is Tatenen, the one who begat the gods and from whom all things proceeded . . . he is the most powerful of the gods."

All things, according to the Memphite tradition, were the direct creation of Ptah, and the text stresses the fact that he established the cities of Egypt, set up the nomes, appointed the gods to their shrines, and established their offerings. Ptah was thus the creator not only of the universe and its natural order, but also of the social, religious, and political order. In the absence of any real narrative myth in the text, the Memphite tradition takes on a serious theological and philosophical aspect, combined with a political aspect. Horus, in the Memphite Theology, is also an aspect of Ptah, and is moreover personified in the ruling pharaoh. Thus, the Memphite Theology, like the Heliopolitan tradition, combines the world of nature and the world of politics into a single unity—one which, moreover, also has a distinct ethical and moral quality.

The Memphite tradition must be regarded as one of the more important products of the Egyptian mind, because it brings Egyptian thinking about creation beyond the mythological and into the theological realm. The highly abstract nature of the text gives distinct evidence that the Egyptian intellect was capable of dealing with material that would later form the subject of philosophical and theological speculation in the Jewish and Christian worlds. Moreover, one may see an important political aim in this particular cosmogony. Assuming that the text was originally composed during the twenty-fifth dynasty, one might suggest that it was intended as an integral element (i.e., propaganda) in the attempt of the Nubian rulers to revitalize the Egyptian empire and nation.

The traditions outlined above do not exhaust the scope of Egyptian creation mythology. Other centers had their creator deities and myths, some of them at least as ancient as the traditions of Heliopolis and Hermopolis. At Coptos, for example, it was the archaic deity Min who was regarded as creator, and at Elephantine the potter god Khnum was given this position. With the rise of Thebes to prominence during the early Middle Kingdom, Amun (later Amun-Re) of Thebes also took on the position of creator in the Theban mythological tradition. It should also be mentioned that during the reign of Akhenaten, the "heretic" pharaoh of the eighteenth dynasty, the sole deity, the Aten, became the creator and source of all things that exist, although the articulation of the Aten's creative power was expressed in terms that were more theological than mythological.

Egyptian creation mythology is important for its variety of symbolism and for the distinct manner in which the Egyptians were able to integrate and combine different and even seemingly contradictory symbols in their articulation of the emergence and structure of the universe. This peculiar use of mythic traditions gives ample evidence of the fact that the Egyptians themselves must have seen their myths for exactly what myths are intended to be: symbolic statements about phenomena that cannot be fully comprehended by the human intellect. Thus, while the myths expressed and articulated certain concepts about the created order, they did not exhaust that order, and they were able to preserve the sense of awe and mystery that the Egyptians must have felt when contemplating the surrounding world. The Egyptian cosmogonies did not attempt to be dogmatic about the created universe; rather, they encouraged the human personality to experience and marvel at that universe with both the intellect and the spirit.

When the Egyptians contemplated the created universe through their myths and rituals, they would have been aware that the world around them was not simply a collection of material things. The universe was for them an awesome system of living divine beings. The earth, the sky, and the Nile were all entities that had a distinct lifeforce and personality and drew their life from the original creative power, no matter what name that power may have borne. These living beings were arranged and ordered in a definite system, purposely conceived as in the Memphite tradition, and naturally produced through the process of regeneration as was stressed by the Heliopolitan system. Egyptian creation myth emphasized the fact that there was order and continuity in all things and thus gave the optimistic assurance that the natural, social, and political order would remain stable and secure. The Egyptians were perceptive enough to realize that at times disorder and chaos could become evident in human life and in their environment, but their cosmogonies gave the assurance that such disorder would eventually be overcome by the power of *maat* (*m3't*), that peculiarly Egyptian concept that deified and personified the principle of order (as the goddess Maat) and made it an integral part of the cosmological system.

The concept of creation, for the Egyptians, was not an abstract theory but a reality that gave meaning and significance to their experience of life and of the universe. Behind all created entities, the Egyptians clearly sensed the presence of a divine creative force that not only had acted in the beginning of all things but also continued to act and renew the creation that had originally been brought

into being by the divine action and will. Finally, it must also be noted that for the Egyptian mind the divine creative force was primarily neither masculine nor feminine; it was rather a complex and integrated combination of both, for the creative force could be active only when both masculine and feminine were able to act in concert to realize the potential of regeneration. In the final analysis, one might say that the Egyptian creation myths bore witness to the unity, harmony, and singleness of everything that exists.
                                Vincent Arieh Tobin

Osiris Cycle

The invention of writing, in Sumeria and then independently in Egypt, enabled myths first to be recorded, probably toward the end of the fourth millennium BCE (von Soden 1994, p. 31.ff.). By the

Triad of Osorkon (Isis, Osiris, and Horus). Gold and lapis lazuli figures. 22nd dynasty, 945–745 BCE. (Scala/Art Resource, NY)

middle of the third millennium, the names of hundreds of gods and goddesses had been recorded by the Sumerians; soon afterward, the Pyramid Texts were being inscribed by the Egyptians. In both Sumeria and Egypt, a long period of oral transmission must have preceded these writings. In Egypt, the earliest funerary preparations point to a belief in an afterlife, but details of doctrine or a mythical framework are inevitably lacking in such evidence.

The phase preceding the emergence of writing stretches by mere definition into the prehistoric era, but its duration is a matter of surmise. In a well-known essay, Frankfort et al. (1946, pp. 19ff.) designate this phase as that of "mythopoeic thought," a phase with its own logic rather than a "prelogical mentality"; they aver that "it is essential that true myth be distinguished from legend, saga, fable, and fairy tale," although "all these may retain elements of the myth" (p. 15). "Legend" and "saga" share a historical substratum; otherwise, the dictum is acceptable, provided that the possibility of mixed forms is granted. It is more difficult to accept that myth "is nothing less than a carefully chosen cloak for abstract thought" (p. 15). Imagery, though, is rightly stressed; and the symbols are often part of a narrative that is, however piecemeal in its presentation, concerned with "how the world came into being."

Osiris and Heliopolis. The early sources place Osiris in the Great Ennead of Heliopolis and a doctrinal cosmogony can be inferred from the many allusions to this important group. At its head is Atum, the creator god, who appears variously as a scarab beetle, primitive mound, and serpent, but is more commonly figured as anthropomorphic. He has close affinities to the sun god Re and at times appears in the double, syncretized name, Re-Atum. In the Ennead, he is the father of Shu (air) and Tefnut (moisture), who in turn procreate Geb (earth) and Nut (sky). The separation of earth and sky was ascribed to their father Shu. Geb and Nut are the parents of two marital pairs: Osiris and Isis, and Seth and Nephthys; this arrangement gives the Ennead a total of four marital pairs, leaving Atum at the head in a status of marked isolation. He is the father of the twins Shu and Tefnut but has no wife or consort. He is said to produce his progeny by an act of masturbation or expectoration. This leads to the idea that he is a bisexual being: in the Coffin Texts, he is mentioned with the double pronoun "he-she." Moreover, the masturbating hand was worshiped as the goddess Iusaas, to whom a shrine was devoted in Heliopolis (see Rundle Clark 1959, pp. 41 ff., who believes that the myths about masturbation and spitting are "complementary, not alternative"). Perhaps the idea is that Atum swallows his own sperm and eventually spits it out in the form of developed offspring. There is clear emphasis on Atum's ontological independence; he is apparently self-begotten and needs no female aid in the process of procreation (see Griffiths 1980, p. 186). Should he therefore be regarded as an androgynous deity in the strict sense? Zandee's admirable study (1988) posits this view forcefully, and he adduces many Gnostic parallels. God as mother-father or father-mother is often present in varied periods of Egypt's literature (see Assmann 1983, pp. 119–121, and for iconography, Baines 1985, p. 120). It was especially evident in Amarna and pre-Amarna hymns (see Lichtheim 1976, vol. 2, pp. 86 ff., esp. 91). In Elaine Pagels's The Gnostic Gospels (1982, pp. 71–88), there is an eloquent chapter on "God the Father/God the Mother," but with no mention of the strong Egyptian background. In consid-

ering the idea in connection with the creator god Atum, one has to face the fact that no semblance of physical bisexuality is present; there is no parallel to Greek hermaphroditism or the Orphic Phanes, where male and female features are combined in one body. Rather, in a process akin to metaphor or allegory, the physical processes described are paradoxical fantasies; they suggest an urge to imagine a bisexual divine being who initiates the whole movement of creation, but who yet remains a totally male figure.

A firmly patriarchal society is reflected, and the same emphasis is seen in the early attitude to fertility in nature, insofar as Osiris embodies this. In contrast to Sumer, where the fertile earth is represented by the mother goddess Ninhursag, Egypt insists on a male deity of earth, Geb; and Osiris, as a figure endowed with chthonic power, also points to male precedence. It is true that after the passage of almost three millennia his sister-wife Isis takes over several of these affinities, thus bringing Egypt more into line with the earth goddesses Demeter, Gaia, Ishtar, and Astarte. In the cultures of those goddesses the sky deities are male, but for Osiris and Egypt the sovereign of the sky is his mother Nut, and her funerary role is quite dominating, although in a wider context the sun god is the lord of heaven. Immortality as a star implied that the deceased, in his identity with Osiris, was welcomed and protected by his mother Nut; and this meant that the figure of Nut often depicted on the underside of the lid of the sarcophagus was particularly fitting. Her cosmic role in the separation of sky and earth is also depicted frequently in the New Kingdom and later; here she is shown bending over her husband Geb, while Shu separates the two deities cosmically, but thus also prevents their sexual union (see Silverman 1991, p. 24, fig. 13; te Velde 1977, pp. 427–429; and te Velde 1979). This phase of cosmic separation is presented, as in several other mythologies, as a prerequisite of effective life on earth. In a mortuary context, it must mean, as te Velde shows, that rebirth in an afterlife is the analogue suggested. In the early phases of Egypt's development, Geb is viewed as the sovereign whose legacy is bound up with the historical kingship that implicates the rivalry of Horus and Seth. As a representative of the earth, he naturally figures in the ceremony of hacking the earth in Heliopolis (cf. Griffiths 1960, p. 61ff.). In chapter 18 of the *Book of Going Forth by Day*, this rite is connected with the tribunal in which Osiris triumphs over his Sethian enemies, who appear as goats and are slaughtered; their blood is mixed with the earth—a rite the translator, T. G. Allen, renders as "earthfertilizing." Horus, in one allusion, is vindicated as the successor of Osiris.

Nut, by contrast, is more constantly associated with the afterworld. An interesting suggestion has been made about the "map of heaven" given in a group of early texts: place names ascribed to various parts of the sky (the Winding Waterway, Nurse Canal, Field of Reeds, and Doors Thrown Open) refer to Nut, it is suggested, and "may even have related to her female anatomy" (Lesko 1991, p. 119). Since Nut often personified the coffin, Lesko notes, it is cogent to describe it as "the womb containing the one to be reborn."

The Osirian Group. In the Heliopolitan Ennead, Isis and Nephthys are very close to Osiris. Isis is given some cosmological affinities, especially with heaven and earth; whether she is also a goddess of rain is more doubtful (Münster 1968, p. 198ff.).

At first it seems surprising that Horus, the son of Osiris, is not named as a member of the Ennead. The basic reason was probably the fact of his identification with the living king, who was also the leader of the funerary rites for his father, now equated with Osiris. From this point of view, the deities of the Ennead might be regarded as the ancestors of Horus (cf. Barta 1973, p. 25). With time, many changes and extensions were made and, during the New Kingdom and later, Seth was often displaced by Horus (Hornung 1983, p. 222). In early dynastic history, however, these two rival gods appear together as partners in the divine tutelage of a united monarchy. The queen's title in the first dynasty, according to sealings found by W. M. Flinders Petrie, was "She who sees Horus and Seth." At the end of the second dynasty, King Peribsen opted for a Sethname, while both deities are associated with the name of Khasekhemwy. A dual god, Horus-Seth, occurs occasionally, doubtless a projection of the dual divinity envisaged in the king (see Griffiths 1960, p. 121ff.; cf. Redford 1992, pp. 36–37). Seth's part in this concept is not maintained except in certain periods, such as under the Hyksos, Ramessids, and Libyans. Thus, a granite group in the Cairo Museum shows Horus and Seth crowning Ramesses III. Seth suffers a process of degradation, although he maintains a radiantly virtuous role as defender of the sun god Re against the attacks of his enemy Apophis. Only in the Greco-Roman period does he achieve in Seth-Typhon a kind of Satanic persona in the Greek papyri; and even then it is not Satanism in the full Iranian sense of a creator of evil beings. In spite of his book's one-sided title, *Seth: God of Confusion*, te Velde (1967/1976) pays a good deal of attention to this god's multivalent nature, including its favorable facets. He was not able to take account of Leclant's discovery in that the Pyramid Text version of the homosexual episode between the two gods shows them as equally active sexually; indeed, he finds the essential antithesis of the two gods to be one relating to sexuality (Seth) and light (Horus), a rare opposition for which he finds a parallel in Tibet.

Osiris figures in a celebrated creation text, the Memphite Theology, but he is brought into it for the greater glory of Ptah, the god of Memphis, who is lauded in the text as a creator who achieves his task by the force of his divine word. According to this text, in the Nile River, near Memphis, Osiris was drowned (the most likely rendering); he was seen and taken from the river by Isis, Nephthys, and Horus, and received a stately burial in Memphis, a city that housed the royal Residence from the third dynasty onward. Since Osiris makes his first appearance toward the end of the fifth dynasty, a date at the end of the fifth dynasty would suit the origin of the Memphite Theology, but its only source is an inscription dated to 710 BCE, which claims to be a copy of a much earlier original text (see Redford 1992, pp. 399–400, with a searching analysis of the possible results on questions with impact on other cultures). An early origin, however, does not preclude the possibility of later interpolations. Creation by the divine word is a doctrine well known from the Hebrew *Genesis*, as is creation out of nothing; much later, it was found in Gnostic writings and in the *logos* of Stoicism and the New Testament. The Egyptian sources provide at least one antecedent—a fairly neutral word that leaves open the question of precise influence.

The cosmogony of Hermopolis involves four pairs of creator gods, referred to as the Eight, or Ogdoad. Each pair comprises a male and a female deity, and together they are associated with a particular concept—for example Kuk and Kuket with darkness. An urge toward abstract thinking can be discerned here, recalling the early Greek desire to define the basic elements. Nun and Naunet, the primal watery abyss, correspond to a more general Egyptian concept of the origin of things, and the creative egg has several parallels elsewhere, for example, in Orphic thought. The affinities of the Osirian religion, by contrast, are more concerned with the human predicament in its encounter with decay and death. In view of the prominence of Osiris in the concept of the afterlife, any discussion of the cosmology of the Pyramid Texts is bound to offer a cosmology of the afterlife, and this is effectively outlined by James P. Allen (1988, 1989), who states that "although gods may belong to the earth, sky is their domain *par excellence*" (1989, p. 3). Among the gods who enjoy celestial bliss are not only Osiris, the god of chthonic fertility, but also Geb, the actual deity of earth. Osiris is especially associated with the Duat (or Dat), a watery celestial region where he consorts with Orion and Sothis (Sirius), heralds of inundation and fertility. Osiris is lord of the Duat; he is also "Lord of Eternity," and in the Late period the second words of these titles probably sounded alike. In a Theban cosmogony of Ptolemaic date, the Memphite god Ptah is said to travel to Thebes in his form of Khonsu the Great and to create there the divine Ogdoad (whose origin was in Hermopolis). Khonsu, a moon god, had an early cult in Karnak, and in a section of this text devoted to Osiris he is called Khonsu-Osiris. Thoth is also named in this context; he is a god whom the early myth portrays as friendly to both Horus and Osiris, and in the judgment before Osiris he is shown recording the evidence. (For the Khonsu cosmogony, see Lesko and Parker 1988; also Lesko 1991, pp. 105–107.)

Expanding Functions. A feature of the religion of Osiris was its steadily increasing popularity, with a concomitant tendency to add to the functions ascribed to myth, cult, and symbolism. In addition to the name Khonsu-Osiris, there are many similar combined or sycretized forms; a basic prototype is seen in Osiris-Unas, with the god's name prefixed to the king's, implying identity in the full sense of religious sanction. This formula was eventually applied to every deceased person. Other couplings, such as Osiris-Andjety, point to more specific impacts, possibly including the borrowing of political symbols. Osiris-Apis was a particularly potent fusion in that the early Memphite bull cult conferred on Osiris, albeit in a posthumous context, the stamp of strong physical fertility. Only the dead Apis bull was thus named (the order Apis-Osiris was also used), and Isis was given the title "Mother of the Apis." It was the form Osiris-Apis in Memphis that gave rise to the name Sarapis, a god who became popular under the Ptolemies; it is ironic that this god displaced Osiris to some extent, especially in Egypt itself.

The union of Osiris and Re, exemplified in one notable figure and text (noted above), had a strong doctrinal significance; it alluded to the sun god's nocturnal visit to the Osirian realm of the dead and to the hope of new life symbolized by the arrival of dawn. This concept of enduring force persisted even in the Isiac rite described in the second century CE by Apuleius (*Meta.* 11.23), with its vision of the midnight sun.

Triadic formulations with Osiris were also found, and of these, one of the most influential as attested from the Middle Kingdom onward, was Ptah-Sokar-Osiris. The first two names designate

gods of Memphis, and the inclusion of Osiris fortified their funerary appeal. Osirian triads were also commonly formed that do not conjoin the names but mention them in texts or figure the gods sculpturally. The most popular group involves Osiris, Isis (or Nephthys), and Horus, with several forms of Horus being deployed. In the early Christian centuries such family groups sanctioned by religion must have been very familiar, particularly to the theologians of Alexandria (cf. Griffiths 1996, p. 302ff.).

A feature of the great Osirian festival in the month of Khoiak was a rite called the "Raising of the *Djed*-Pillar," which was interpreted as a mark of the new life warranted by the god. The pillar varied somewhat in form, but basically it was a stylized sprouting tree, a part of the lush display of vegetative renewal in the festival itself and also in burial ceremonies. It seems, however, that in origin the pillar had nothing to do with Osiris; its early connections were with Ptah in Memphis, and sometimes it was associated with Re and Khonsu. The priestly leaders of the Osirian faith were clearly very ready to take over attractive elements from other cults.

J. Gwyn Griffiths

Solar Cycle

That the Sun and other heavenly objects should have universally affected human thought is a natural result of life on Earth; and the frequent evidence of their impact on religious thought is also beyond question. A clear example occurs in the *Deuteronomy* warning (perhaps of the seventh century BCE) against the worship of the Sun, Moon, and stars (4.19). Since a prohibition presupposes a practice, we may assume that some Israelites knew of or even indulged in such worship, as did several neighboring peoples.

Physical Effects. If we consider the biological importance for Egypt of various natural phenomena, it is clearly evident that it was not the Sun or any other celestial phenomenon that counted most in physical terms. Rather, it was the Nile River, the great provider of fertility and growth. When the Greek historian Herodotus referred to Egypt as "a gift of the river," he had in mind only the part of Lower Egypt to Lake Moeris, which he regarded as formed by sedimentation through the action of the Nile. Popular misinterpretation has often applied this remark to the whole of Egypt, in a wider sense, and this view is not intrinsically wide of the mark. Yet in the background of religious thought, the import of celestial phenomena is often more dominant. It was the annual inundation of the Nile that ensured fertility, and the worship of Hapy (god of the inundation) specifically honored his blessings. The cult of Osiris also achieved a strong link with water and vegetation, though not in its early phases. A clean cut between the terrestrial and celestial worlds is not a feature of this manner of thinking; what is apparent, rather, is a constant urge to integrate the two aspects and to suggest their interdependence. Thus, the inundation of the Nile was often connected by the Egyptians with the heliacal rising of the star Sothis (the Dog Star, Sirius), seen in the constellation of Orion. A first dynasty ivory tablet from Abydos refers to Sothis as "Bringer of the New Year and of the Inundation." In Pyramid Text 965, Sothis is said to be the daughter of Osiris. In the Pyramid Texts, the nature of the afterworld is often glimpsed, that which the deceased king (identified with Osiris) is said to have experienced. It is situated in the heavens, and yet it contains fields, in particular the Field of Offerings and the Field of Reeds. Water, however, is the chief feature of the sky, and navigation on this water is the method of movement, suggesting that conditions in the terrestrial Egypt are being transferred to the heavens, with a celestial Nile affording the means of transport (see Allen 1989, p. 7).

The Basic Creator-God. The sun god Re is, however, the basic creator god of all, and among his creations are the Nile and even the primal water of Nun from which the earth itself emerged. The Hymns to Re in Spell 15 of the *Book of Going Forth by Day* (*Book of the Dead*) enlarge on the sun god's sovereignty over heaven and earth. In those hymns, Re is often lauded in his form at sunrise and also at sunset, Atum being the name given to him at the latter stage. Elsewhere three stages are assigned to him—sunrise, noon, and sunset—the names being often designated as Khepri, Re, and Atum. Khepri is a name well suited to denote the arrival of dawn because it implies the process of coming into being. Depicted sometimes as a scarab beetle, the god was regarded as a self-procreated being. A text of the Ramessid era (Pleyte-Rossi, Turin Papyrus 133, 10) refers to the triple positions of these gods during the course of the day: "I am Khepri in the morning, Re in the afternoon, Atum in the evening." Three forms or modes of the sun god are implied—an example, thus, of a modalistic trinity, comparable to the later Christian concept (Griffiths 1996). A liturgical meaning is probably embedded in the Egyptian forms, with allusions to services at morning, noon, and evening; one may also discern references to the divisions of age (child, man, and old man) and to the phases of life (birth, maturity, and death).

The *Book of That Which Is in the Underworld* (*Amduat*), the *Book of Gates*, and related writings which are profusely illustrated present the nocturnal voyage of the sun god in graphic detail. *Amduat* is concerned with the underworld which Re now enters; it adorns the New Kingdom tombs of kings in twelve sections related to the hours of the night. The sun god is provided with two boats, assigned respectively to the morning and evening. The night journey is by no means plain sailing, for Re is now threatened by demonic forces of darkness led by the serpent Apophis. In this perilous strait, Re's principal defender is none other than the god Seth, whose role in the defeat of Apophis is a far cry from that of a "god of confusion," which te Velde regards as his characteristic activity. The rebuttal of the powers of darkness culminates in the coming of dawn, and the sun god's victory is at the same time interpreted as a celebration of life over death. A natural concomitant of this concept is that a dominant desire of the deceased is to join the boat of Re and thus to share in his defeat of darkness and death. In the Roman era, Apuleius portrays the Isiac initiate as witnessing the Sun at midnight; the line of symbolism points to a clear connection. (On *Amduat*, see Hornung 1963–1967 and 1984.)

Problems of Cult and Myth. Palpable evidence for the cult of Re is most clearly present in Old Kingdom remains of the sun-sanctuaries of several kings of the fifth dynasty. The best known is that of Newoserre at Abu Gurob near Abusir, which features a high obelisk and an altar in the open air, while slaughtering places were provided for the offering of animals; the *sed*-festival of the king is also represented. More intriguing is the evidence for the cult of the solar boats, which begins with the first dynasty boat found at Helwan. An impressive example is the solar boat discovered in 1954 near the pyramid of Khufu (Cheops), which his son Djedefra (Ra-djedef) provided in an adjacent rocky cleft. What is intriguing

about this boat and similar ones is the definition of its precise purpose in relation to ritual or myth.

To some extent, a similar problem arises with regard to the several other instances of funerary boat-pits; some have proved to be empty; in others, the boats are extant, but they vary considerably in size. Some are full-size realistic objects while others are small enough to be regarded as mere models. The comparative poverty of the owner might explain the choice of the miniature mode, and a magical empowering in favor of a divinely ordained use after death could well be indicated. Even within that purpose, several options suggest themselves. One is the idea that the nocturnal voyage of Re may be imitated, to be followed by his emergence at dawn after the journey through the Osirian underworld where the union of Osiris and Re is achieved. Other ritual journeys might be envisaged, since an early tradition sanctioned visits to the hallowed precincts of Buto, Sais, Heliopolis, and especially Abydos. A kind of second burial at Abydos was the most elaborate option, but the provision of a model boat might suggest an attenuated magical substitute. A sanction for sacral use is indicated by the ancient papyriform design. The empty twin-pit raises the question of the double purpose: eastern and western voyaging was suggested, with northern and southern journeys reserved for the boats in the twin-pits on the eastern face of the pyramid. A total of five boats is attested—a supply sufficient to enable transport in both the funeral and the afterworld. Khufu's extant boat is capacious—43.4 meters (130 feet) long. This seems to favor the least transcendental of the possible explanations: that it was one of the actual boats used in the burial rites (see Jenkins 1980, pp. 160ff.; and Jones 1995, pp. 12–25, 76–78).

Other Divine Roles. Among the celestial phenomena that support the deceased's welfare, special prominence is given to the circumpolar stars. In Egyptian they are called "the never-setting stars," and the term itself points to the enduring nature of their existence; association with them clearly suggests a warrant of immortality. According to Joseph Bradshaw (1990, 1997), there are as many as fifty mentions of these stars in the Pyramid Texts. He shows that Osiris is closely associated with them, taking his throne as king of the dead in the region of the North Pole. He goes on to argue, however, that even Re was not basically a sun god, but a being dominated by circumpolar ideas, a claim rejected by several reviewers of his book.

The sky goddess Nut displays some attributes that are to be expected, but others verging on the bizarre. Her close connection with Nun, god of the primeval waters from which the earth's primal mound is said to have emerged, is in accord with the fact that she is concerned with the basic entities of earth, sky, sun, moon, and stars. The astral beings are often depicted on her body, which figures regularly on the lid of the sarcophagus and on the walls of the sarcophagus chamber. In Pyramid Text 1688, Re is said to come forth from Nut, who bears him daily; and in the New Kingdom papyrus of the priestess Anhai, the god Nun is shown lifting up the boat of Re in his sunrise, in which the sun god is depicted as a scarab beetle. Nut is also credited with a remarkable feat of astral productivity; at sunset she swallows the stars through her mouth, but with the dawn she gives birth to them anew from her vagina. Her swallowing of her star-children leads to her being compared with a sow. A text from the cenotaph of Sety I at Abydos refers to her as "the mother of swine who eats

her little pigs." Moreover, the Sun itself, as well as the stars, was a part of Nut's cosmic fertility: according to *Amduat*, at the Twelfth Hour, the Sun appears in the morning "between the thighs of Nut."

The Celestial Cow. A celebrated text found in a number of New Kingdom tombs describes how Re threatened to destroy mankind because of their rebellion against him but eventually decided to deliver them from this fate. The celestial cow is depicted with the various texts, and those texts include instructions for the painting. (The example in Shrine I of Tutankhamun appears in A. Piankoff and N. Rambova, *The Shrines of Tut-Ankh-Amon* [Princeton, 1977], p. 142, fig. 46; a translation of the text accompanies it.)

If we ask who exactly was this cow of heaven, the answer must be Mehetweret, the divine cow, whose name means "the great flood." The name is written before the cow in the text of Tutankhamun (Hornung, p. 31) and seems to be equated with the heavens in the Pyramid Texts (289c). Yet in Pyramid Text 1344, as Hornung points out, it is Nut that appears as a heavenly cow; and a third cow goddess linked to the heavens is Hathor. Both Nut and Hathor figure several times in the text.

Of much greater import is the interpretation of the myth. Here Re has the leading role, but Hathor is also a key figure, being crucially implicated in the reversal of the story. As the ruling sun god of Heliopolis, Re was regarded as king of the gods; and as the father of Maat, the all-pervading concept of truth, justice, and order (both domestic and cosmic), he was assigned a dominant judicial role—for example, as president of the tribunal of the dead, although Osiris eventually tends to take over this role. In the myth of the Celestial Cow, Re is first presented as old and decrepit, worrying that men are plotting against him; he decides to destroy them, using his fiery Eye in the form of Hathor his daughter. She duly returns to him after slaying men in the desert. For this she is praised by Re, but Hathor's relish for blood induces Re to hit on an astonishing stratagem. He produces beer on a large scale—seven thousand jars—mixed with red ocher to make the beer look like blood. Hathor partakes so avidly of this that in a drunken state she forgets her desire to kill more men. At the same time, Re has evidently changed his mind: instead of destroying mankind, he now wants to save them. In a later section, however, he declares that he is too tired to deal further with them; he withdraws from the earth as the heaven is lifted up. Now the celestial cow is identified with Nut, and Re rides on her back. After this, men on earth resort to strife and warfare, an activity condemned by Re even though they are fighting against his enemies. We are then told "and thus originated slaughter among men"—an example of the etiological urge that marks this myth. The whole affair of the seven thousand jugs of beer is another instance, since it is clearly concerned with a festival of Hathor, a goddess who was known, *inter alia*, as "Mistress of Drunkenness."

The idea of a divine decision to destroy mankind is found in several other ancient cultures. From Babylon, Israel, and Greece come myths that describe the gods as using a catastrophic flood as the medium of destruction. The difference in Egypt is due to the fact that there the annual inundation of the Nile was seen as a boon rather than a bane; the destroying medium is now the fiery eye of the sun god, suggesting the burning heat of the desert. The saving of a remnant is found in all the myths, but unlike the Egyptian example, the others accord this privilege to favored human beings—Utnapishtim in Babylon, Noah in Israel, and the pair Deucalion and Pyrrha in Greece. If we look at the moral issues, we find that Utnapishtim and Noah are excepted from doom because of their piety. But as for the human transgressions that have aroused the anger of the gods, it seems that only the Hebraic myth gives them a clearly moral emphasis. This is absent from the early Greek accounts, which may reflect the influence of Babylon, where Enlil, the ruling deity, is merely disturbed by the noise made by men; and the Egyptian tale does not go beyond an emphasis on the rebellious mutiny of man against Re (see Griffiths 1991, p. 14).

Other Solar Myths. The falcon god Horus, whose name probably means "he who is on high," is naturally, as a god of heaven, intimately connected with solar manifestations. In the earliest corpus of literary import, the Pyramid Texts, the legend of his feud with his brother Seth is given primary force; although incorporated into the Osiris myth, it is of earlier origin. In the feud Seth is said to have injured and removed one of the eyes of Horus; in reply, Horus deprives Seth of his testicles. The intervention of Thoth leads to the restoration of the mutilated parts and to a reconciliation of the warring brothers. In the integrated Osiris myth, Seth becomes the slayer of his brother Osiris, and as a result Horus becomes, by adjustment, the nephew of Seth and also the avenger of Osiris. A trial at Heliopolis is also portrayed, but in two forms: one relates to Horus and Seth concerning the eye that was stolen; the other shows Seth being tried for his violence to Osiris. In each case Seth is defeated, and it becomes clear that the real issue is the inheritance of Geb—that is, the sovereignty of Egypt. Re is often the judge, or Geb himself. The theme persists in an extensive literature that includes the Memphite Theology (where the first verdict is a division between the two, but then the whole kingdom to Horus), the *Contendings of Horus and Seth*, and several texts in the Ptolemaic temples. There are suggestions in many texts that the eyes of Horus were associated with the crowns, as symbols of sovereignty (Griffiths 1960, pp. 120–122). That Seth was yet regarded in the early dynasties as sharing in a pan-Egyptian sovereignty is evident in the first dynasty queen's title, "She who Sees Horus and Seth," found with other early queens. It is reasonable to see here clear evidence of the evolution of a united nation and kingdom. The theology of kingship is a vital element here, the living king often being identified with Horus and also called "the son of Re." A statue of King Khafre in the fourth dynasty shows the Horus falcon spreading his wings behind the pharaoh's head, suggesting close protection if not identity. Note the suggestion of Z. Hawass that the Sphinx of Giza "represents Khafre, as Horus" giving offerings to Khufu "as the sun-god" (1995, p. 227).

Various astral elements enter into the exegesis of the myth, especially in late texts that explain the right eye of Horus as being the Sun and his left eye as the Moon. Other cosmic aspects can be rightly evoked. Seth is often portrayed as a storm god, or as a deity connected with the desert or with foreign lands. The *Contendings of Horus and Seth* ends with his defeat by Horus in regard to the succession; yet he is allowed to go free and join the sun god in the sky to renew his thundering. If the court has decreed that Horus is to succeed Osiris, yet a perennial cosmic role is conceded to Seth, suggesting the doctrine that "opposing forces were in equilibrium in the universe" (Frankfort 1948, p. 129). Admit-

tedly, this is from a text tinted with a touch of the burlesque. The opposing forces ranged in the myth are differently defined in an impressive study by Herman te Velde, *Seth, God of Confusion* (1967; 2nd ed., 1977). He discounts the impress of the early historical and political background and locates the essence of the myth in the opposing forces of light (Horus) and sexuality (Seth). The universal antonym of light is of course darkness, but an opposition found in sexuality is supplied by a parallel in Tibet discovered in a work by Mircea Eliade (te Velde, p. 51). In support of this unexpected outcome, we find much emphasis on the homosexual episode in the myth, with Seth as the aggressive partner, although Horus in fact shares that role.

Egypt's solar cult reached its acme, in one sense, when Akhenaten elevated the sun disk, the Aten, to be the sole and sovereign object of worship. From the point of view of mythology, however, it was not an acme but a nadir: the solar myths were abandoned, as indeed was the mythology of other cults, including that of Osiris. Theologically, the status of "King" borrows from tradition: he is the son of the Aten, just as the pharaoh was from early times the son of Re. A triad of the Aten, King Akhenaten, and Queen Nefertiti suggests a claim that worship should include the king and his queen (see Griffiths 1996, pp. 57–59). Yet the Aten's primacy is beyond question. He is the creator and sustainer of the whole earth, including Syria and Kush; an imposing universalism is presented and also a compassionate ethic, symbolized by sun-rays seen as helping hands; but mythic details about the process of creation are missing (see Redford 1984, pp. 169, 177f.).

A feature of texts from the Greco-Roman era is their expansive treatment of mythological themes. Two solar myths are here conspicuous. One concerns the fiery raging eye of Re, identified with his daughter Tefnut or Hathor-Tefnut, who went to Nubia in the form of a lioness; the sun god sent Thoth to mollify her wrath, inducing her to return to Egypt by telling her a number of animal fables. The *Legend of the Winged Disk* and the *Triumph of Horus* come from the temple of Edfu, and their main protagonist is Re or Re-Harakhty. Although he is assisted by three Horuses—Horus of Beh. det, Horus the son of Isis, and Horus the Elder—Re himself is the theological mainspring and the leader of massive campaigns against Seth and his followers. If the general impression is given of a rehash of the Horus-Seth myth, important differences emerge. The status of Seth is much degraded as compared with the parity often granted to him in the early myth. He is now denigrated within Egypt by a series of attacks on the crocodiles and hippopotami associated with him, often culminating in a vengeful sacrificial meal. In these sections, the essence of the struggle is a cult feud in defined localities. In other sections, a wider political conflict is denoted, which seems to reflect the expulsion of the Hyksos. Seth is now the foreigner who must be driven from Egypt into the sea; the struggle between Re and Seth echoes the tension relating to the Hyksos as people who "ruled without Re." The emblematic great Winged Disk is the sun disk fitted with a falcon's wings; it is the form assumed by Horus of Beh. det in the bark of Re.

J. Gwyn Griffiths

Lunar Cycle

The Moon was considered by the Egyptians to be the nightly replacement of the Sun, yet its mythology was never as important as that involving the Sun. In the known creation accounts, the role of the Sun is always paramount. The relationship between the Moon and the stars is more important, because the lunar god can be designated as "ruler of the stars."

The Sun and Moon were commonly referred to together by Egyptians as "the two lights." The weaker light of the Moon is compared to the evening Sun. The most common theological interpretation of the lights declares them to be the eyes of Re or of the sky god Horus, whose left eye was the Moon and whose right eye was the Sun; the left eye was weaker than the right because it had been damaged. This myth was elaborated in many religious centers, giving rise to specialized forms of Horus such as Khenty-Khety of Letopolis and the later Hor-Merty of Horbeit. The mythology surrounding the eyes of the sky god was extensive, and variants abounded. Four different myths may be distinguished surrounding the divine eyes: that of the eyes of the sky god; the injured eye of Horus; the solar eye; and the distant goddess who is brought back. Often, elements of these different myths are found mixed or interchanged.

The Moon is most often depicted as a combination of the full-moon disk with the crescent moon. The lunar gods nearly always have this symbol on their heads. The full-moon disk may have the *wedjat* (*wḏ3t*) eye inside it—either the left or the right eye—or the image of a lunar divinity. The Moon, like the Sun and the stars, is represented traversing the sky in a boat. The most complete extant depiction of the entire lunar cycle is found inside the *pronaos* of the Edfu temple.

The starting point of the lunar cycle is the new moon, and its culminating point is the moment of full moon. The Moon thus becomes visible only on the second day of the lunar month. The lunar cycle is represented either as a six-day evolution up to the sixth day, or as a fifteen-day evolution up to the ideal day of full moon. The importance of the sixth day is probably explained by the increasing intensity of moonlight at this stage of the cycle. Sometimes, the seventh day is mentioned in its stead.

A Symbol of Renewal. The moon became used as a symbol of rejuvenation; in late texts it is called "the one that repeats its form." Lunar gods may be represented as youths, while the entire lunar cycle may be compared to the life cycle of a man, with the moon being the "old man who becomes a child." A New Kingdom pharaoh may be declared "young as the moon," and Amenhotpe III identifies himself fully with the moon in his temple at Soleb.

An important political application of lunar mythology followed from the identification of the moon with the god Horus. The birth of Horus (or Harsiese) was celebrated on the second lunar day in the month Pharmuthi. The full moon could then be equated with the adult Horus as in Edfu: "When he completes the half month, he assumes control of the sky rejuvenated." At the moment of full moon, Horus was declared "true of voice" and "joyful," because of his victory over Seth in the divine tribunal of Heliopolis. The lunar cycle was linked to the renewal of royal powers, and temple rituals based on this theme are known from Karnak.

Likewise, in mortuary beliefs the lunar cycle was a beloved image of cyclical renewal. The feast of the sixth day counted as the day of the victory of Osiris, and even though the moment of full moon could have the same significance, the sixth day became of particular importance in funerary rituals. Already in the Pyramid Texts, the deceased is sometimes identified with the moon. According to evidence from Middle Kingdom coffins, the funerary religion was particularly concerned with the night sky. Nevertheless, lunar associations were not common in the Middle Kingdom, but the Coffin Texts from Deir el-Bersheh accord an equal place in the afterworld to the lunar god Thoth, next to Osiris and Re. In the New Kingdom and later, the role of the moon in the afterlife remains minimal, but it is found, for instance, in chapter 131 of the *Book of Going Forth by Day.*

A Symbol of Fecundity. The moon is compared to a bull on account of the similarity in shape of the crescent moon and a bull's horns. Lunar gods may be characterized as "with sharp horns." In texts from the Ptolemaic period in Edfu and Karnak, this metaphor is developed in calling the crescent moon the "rutting bull" and the waning moon the "ox." The moon is "the rutting bull who inseminates the cows," but it is also said: "You unite with young women, you are an inseminating bull who fertilizes the girls" (Edfu VII, 116, 2–3), indicating a perceived relationship between female fertility and the moon.

The Egyptians understood that a relationship existed between the Moon and the growth of plants and that sowing was best done at the time of a full moon. Similarly, the minerals in the desert were thought to come into being under the Moon's influence.

Interruptions in the usual cycle were feared. A lunar eclipse was considered a bad omen, as is evident from some Late period texts describing the sky swallowing the moon. It was also felt to influence daily life, and the Egyptians dedicated stelae to it at Deir el-Medina, and formed personal names with the element *iˁḥ* ("moon"). On the stelae, the moon god *Iˁḥ*-Thoth may be called "the merciful," which may refer to another aspect of the lunar god, "reckoner of the lifespan."

Myth of Horus and Seth. By far the predominant myth concerning the moon relates its cycle to the battle between Horus and Seth. During this famous battle over the inheritance of Osiris, Seth steals the eye of Horus, damages it, and divides it into six parts. Thoth later restores it "with his fingers," or by spitting on it. In the temple of Kom-Ombo (scene 950) a series of medical instruments is depicted being used in the healing of the eye by the god Haroeris. The restored eye is called *wedjat* (*wḏȝt*) from the New Kingdom onward, but the myth in question is much older and was found in the Coffin Texts, as in Spell 335. Onuris, Thoth, or Osiris as moon returns the complete eye to Horus. Thoth may also be said to catch the lunar eye in a net, acting together with the god Shu.

"Filling the *wedjat* eye," "entering into the left eye," or "joining the left eye" also means restoring the eye. It was performed on the sixth lunar day. The eye is said to be filled with specific minerals and plants. Thoth, together with a specific group of fourteen gods, principally performed this act. In Greco-Roman temple reliefs from the region between Dendera and Esna, this group is the Ennead of Hermopolis. Together with Thoth, these gods represent the fifteen days leading up to the full moon, and again the days of the waning moon. As representing the latter, they are said to exit from the eye. In Edfu and Philae, the gods Tanenent and Iunyt of the Hermopolitan Ennead are replaced by the pair Hekes and Hepuy.

An iconographic variant of this theme occurs in the temples at Edfu and Dendera in the form of a staircase with fourteen steps that support the fourteen gods of the waxing moon. Reliefs in Edfu, Dendera, and Ismant el-Kharab (Dakhleh oasis) list a different group of thirty mostly male deities associated with the days of the lunar month. In the legends inscribed with these gods at Ismant el-

Kharab, the first fifteen are said to fill the *wedjat* eye with a fraction each day, after which the moon's reduction is recorded up to the twenty-fourth day, when the intensity of the moonlight has all but disappeared.

Other Myths. The opposition of Sun and Moon in the sky on the fifteenth or sixteenth day of the month was the most important moment of the lunar cycle. Its importance appears from inscriptions at temples in Edfu, Dendera, and Karnak. This moment was designated as *snsn kȝwy*, "the uniting of the two bulls," and a description of this moment was known from the New Kingdom Osireion at Abydos. In the later temples, this moment could be ritually celebrated by the offering of two mirrors, symbolizing the two lights, at this precise moment. In Thebes and in the Dakhleh oasis, the moment symbolized the rejuvenation of the sun god Amun-Re, when his son and successor, the moon god Khonsu, received his heritage of cosmic rule.

Osiris was an important lunar god. Griffiths (1969, pp. 239–240) has argued that Osiris became identified with the moon only in the New Kingdom (*The Origins of Osiris*, Münchner Ägyptologische Studien 9 Munich 1969, 239–40). At an uncertain time, the murder of the god and his resurrection were recognized in the lunar cycle, and the body of Osiris was equated with the moon. Seth cut his body into fourteen parts, which were later reassembled and restored to life. The number of parts corresponds to the days of the waning or waxing moon.

Elsewhere, the entire life cycle of Osiris related to the lunar cycle, with the god's conception on the first day and his birth on the second lunar day. The temple of Opet in Karnak was dedicated to this event. Osiris' murder and subsequent dismemberment were associated with the time following the full moon. The second day of the month then saw the reassembly of the god's members and his "entering into the moon" on the sixth day. The rejuvenation and the defeat of the god's enemies were placed on the day of full moon, when Osiris was declared victorious in the tribunal, and when Horus was awarded his heritage.

The name of the lunar god Khonsu relates to the verb "moving in various directions," which characterizes the lunar orbit. Especially in the earlier sources, Khonsu is ascribed an aggressive nature. According to later Theban sources, Khonsu traveled every day from the east (his temple at Karnak) to the west (the temple of Djeme) to revitalize his deceased father, Amun. It is especially the Theban theology that declares the moon god to be the son of the sun god.

Apart from Thoth, there were a few more gods with specific links to the moon, such as Min and the Hellenistic form of Isis. In general, goddesses were associated with the moon only when they were identified with the eye of Re, as were Tefnut and Hathor. The annual journey from Dendera to Edfu by Hathor was timed in accordance with the phases of the Moon.

Olaf E. Kaper

N

NECROPOLIS. As early as the Neolithic period, the ancient Egyptians buried their dead in cemeteries, and eventually an elaborate funerary cult developed around the tombs. Necropolises therefore emerged as privileged areas of monumental and artistic display, and consequently they are among the most prominent, archaeological sites of pharaonic Egypt.

Role in Archaeological Research. Attracted by the richness of these sites, Egyptological research has tended to concentrate on tombs and cemeteries, while neglecting other aspects of the archaeological record, the settlements in particular. The deficits in our knowledge that resulted from this attitude are being felt more and more acutely, and it is certainly advisable to strive for a more balanced appreciation of the available evidence. The prominence of the funerary sector, however, is an inherent trait of pharaonic culture.

The prosopographical and historical information derived from inscriptions in the tombs of kings and the elite is crucial to an understanding of the composition of the aristocracy, the organization of the administration, and many other aspects of the workings of society. The buildings and their decoration stand out as the finest examples of pharaonic art; scenes of daily activities on the walls provide lively (though heavily biased) views of life in ancient Egypt. Recovering and record-ing these monuments was always a priority of archaeology in Egypt. The necropolises of the elite are vast sites, and individual tombs are often quite complex, so their exploration is still far from complete. Even the site of Giza, which was excavated systematically during the early decades of the twentieth century, is still far from exhausted. Sites like Saqqara or the Theban necropolis are even less systematically explored.

The cemeteries of the ordinary people held rather less appeal to artistically and epigraphically minded archaeologists. Their scientific potential became evident when the whole epoch of Egyptian prehistory became known through W.M. Flinders Petrie's 1895 excavations in the cemeteries of Naqada and Ballas, and when George Reisner's 1910 excavations in the cemeteries of Shellal near Aswan revealed the existence of several indigenous Nubian cultures. In fact, the material from cemeteries is particularly suited to define archaeological cultures and their chronological subphases. The principle of chronological seriation, ingeniously discovered by Petrie, provided the methodological key to make the best use of this potential. Petrie also realized that it was no less necessary to describe the material culture of the historical phases of pharaonic Egypt, and the excavation of cemeteries was the ideal way to fill in the corpora of artifact types that were to embody his fascinating vision of

Representation of tombs in a necropolis, from a stele at Giza.

a "systematic archaeology" of ancient Egypt. Consequently Petrie and his co-workers spent considerable effort on systematically exploring the cemeteries situated on the desert margins during the decades before World War II. Brunton's extensive work in the area between Qau and Matmar south of Asyut (1922–1931), where he uncovered more than five thousand burials ranging from the early Neolithic until Coptic times, marks the climax of this strain in Egyptian archaeology. Deriving the definition of archaeological phases from cemetery data has come under criticism in recent years. This seems only partly justified, however. In fact, the information derived from the excavation of cemeteries is still fundamental to our knowledge of the material culture of ancient Egypt. The appreciation of many of these excavations, however, is seriously hampered by incomplete publication; in many cases, it would be both possible and worthwhile to supplement the printed volumes on the basis of the original documentation and the finds kept in museum collections.

Although a great deal of archaeological work has been done on ancient Egyptian cemetery sites, most of this work focused on individual tombs or on classes of objects and their chronology. It has been less common to study cemeteries as coherent entities playing a part in the cultural life of a community, and to address their significance within an anthropological framework. Reisner, however, grasped the importance of this aspect already in his pioneering analysis of an Old Kingdom cemetery at Naga ed-Deir (opposite Abydos), excavated in 1901–1902. In his publication, Reisner attempts to reconstruct the social composition of a provincial community on the basis of its cemetery, contrasting the cultural situation at this remote site in Upper Egypt with the contemporary necropolises of the elite. This great work well exemplifies the potential of cemetery data to elucidate the internal differentiation of pharaonic culture along both social and geographical lines. More recent studies address their value for the reconstruction of settlement patterns and demographic development as well. This new anthropological perspective can be applied to the analysis of the great wealth of cemetery data that are already available, and it should influence the research design of new excavations. A site should be excavated completely enough to enable population estimates; the excavated human remains should be analyzed by an expert biologist; close attention should be given to complex patterns of use and reuse and of cult activities; and an attempt should be made to establish the relationship between a cemetery and the settlement to which it belongs.

Necropolises and Settlements.
Egyptian cemeteries lie outside the settlements they served. Only burials of babies and very small children (often deposited in large jars) are regularly encountered within settlements, and special beliefs were probably associated with this custom; W. Blackman in *The Fellahin of Upper Egypt* (London, 1927, p. 101) reports that babies were buried within houses in modern Egypt to make sure that the mother would have another child. Otherwise, burial within the settlement is irregular; rarely, bodies of low-ranking persons are found interred in abandoned building plots. Burials in the Neolithic settlement of Merimda Beni Salama, which gave rise to the interpretation that house burial was a regular trait of the prehistoric cultures of Lower Egypt, have been shown by subsequent excavations not to have been strictly contemporary with the settlement remains. The custom of house burial, securely attested at Tell ed-Dabʿa during the Second Intermediate Period, resulted from the influence of the Syrian-Palestinian Middle Bronze II culture in the eastern Delta during that time.

The Egyptian ideal held that a cemetery should be situated on the Western Desert margin, and terms like "The Beautiful West" are used frequently as synonyms for "necropolis." Many necropolises—and, in fact, all royal necropolises—conform to this ideal, but just as many do not. Cemeteries are found on the eastern and western banks of the valley, naturally confined to sites not reached by the annual inundation. Cemeteries were preferably located immediately outside or rather close to a settlement. A greater distance between settlement and necropolis (up to a few kilometers) was accepted only if the site had to satisfy specific technical or locational demands. For the rock-cut tombs of the elite from the late Old Kingdom onward, for example, sites in the flanks of the desert mountains had to be chosen, preferably at places that overlooked the territory formerly governed by the tomb owner. For the pyramid cemeteries of the Old Kingdom, sites were selected that afforded easy access to quarries and occupied commanding positions, like the desert plateaus of Giza or Abu Rowash. Such cemeteries were at a considerable distance from residences, and therefore settlements were founded to house the people associated with the necropolis in an administrative, construction, or maintenance capacity.

The distribution pattern of cemeteries in the country, as revealed by archaeological excavation, is severely distorted by unequal preservation. Because of the rise of the alluvial land over the course of time, most of the cemeteries that originally lay in the plain of the valley and in the Delta are now buried under several meters of Nile mud, creating the false impression that cemeteries lay exclusively on the desert margins. Even here, however, preservation is rather unequal in the different sections of the valley. In Middle Egypt, for instance, the western desert margin, which was very low, was also covered by the rise of the alluvium. If the hazards of preservation and recovery are carefully taken into account, cemeteries provide the most valuable information on the structure of settlement available from ancient Egypt, and in particular on the distribution of social groups across the country.

The close relationship between settlement and cemetery does not imply, however, that the group buried in a cemetery is identical with the population of a nearby settlement. Rather, it is obvious that access to a cemetery could depend on status and social affiliation.

Cemeteries of the elite were normally inaccessible to burials of ordinary people; on the other hand, there are cemeteries where only children were interred. The unequal representation of the sexes, a very common feature in Egyptian cemeteries, equally attests to selective processes.

Types and Layouts. Ancient Egyptian cemeteries were not fenced in, and there was no communal cult site nor, as a rule, a temple attached to them. From an archaeological point of view, cemetery sites may be classified according to their geographical situation and according to the types of tombs that occupy them. In addition, the size of the group buried in a cemetery and its social structure are to be considered.

In prehistoric times, cemeteries were laid out on flat ground where strata of soft rock, compacted gravel, or sand offered little resistance to the excavation of graves. The tombs are scattered informally over the available space and were probably marked on the surface by small tumuli. Today, however, most of the surface layer has been eroded away.

A special type of elite cemetery appeared in the second half of the fourth millennium BCE near emerging Upper Egyptian cities such as Hierakonpolis, Naqada, and Abydos. These cemeteries were reserved for members of the uppermost level of local society. The first dynasty royal cemetery at Abydos also belongs to this class of necropolis.

During the Old Kingdom and in subsequent periods, the layout pattern of village cemeteries remained basically similar (though all other aspects of funerary culture underwent profound changes). Tomb shafts became deeper, and the tombs were covered by small *mastabas*. The cemeteries of important provincial towns are considerably larger, and the presence of a local elite makes

itself felt. In the Old Kingdom, these people were buried in large *mastaba* tombs, and places like Edfu, Naga ed-Deir, and Qau illustrate well how these important buildings preferably formed a continuous row occupying the most conspicuous part of the cemetery, while the lesser tombs were scattered in front of or behind this line. The layout of these cemeteries served to emphasize the dominant role of the elite within local society.

A specific type of necropolis developed during the Old Kingdom in the cemeteries of the royal court near the capital. Here the tombs of the most important officials were concentrated, and these sites abound in monuments of high artistic and epigraphic importance. Court cemeteries in the strict sense appear at the beginning of the fourth dynasty at Meidum, Dahshur, and Giza, where the royal mortuary complexes—the tombs of the members of the royal family and the important officials—were laid out (at least in part) according to a common master plan. The individual *mastabas* were arranged on a regular grid and built in standard sizes and shapes. The general principle of uniting the ruling elite in a monumental necropolis centered around the mortuary complex of the reigning king remained in effect throughout pharaonic history and characterizes, to a greater or lesser degree, the structure of the cemeteries of the Egyptian capitals.

The invention of rock-cut tombs during the latter part of the fourth dynasty had a considerable impact on the appearance of Egyptian necropolises. Already during the fifth dynasty, a type of tomb adapted to the geological conditions of Upper Egypt was developed, and it rapidly established itself there as the standard model for monumental tombs. The forecourts and the façades of these tombs are cut into the slope of the hillside, while the chapels and the burial apartments are excavated from the living rock. From this time, the flanks of the desert mountains approaching the Nile Valley became the preferred sites for the tombs of the provincial elite, which are usually laid out in several horizontal rows halfway up the hillside, so as to overlook the valley. Depending on the conditions at an individual site, cemeteries of shaft tombs of the lesser inhabitants of the town may be excavated on the hill slope or on the plain below the file of rock-cut tombs.

During the Middle Kingdom, the layouts developed during the late Old Kingdom largely remained in effect throughout Upper Egypt. Here the archaeological record is characterized by rock-cut tomb necropolises of the local elite near important provincial towns, and by cemeteries of simple shaft tombs, originally covered by small chapels, for the ordinary inhabitants. The court cemeteries near the royal residence reverted to Old Kingdom patterns as well, though on a less grandiose scale. Here the most important officials of the administration were buried in tombs, often archaistic *mastabas*, attached to the pyramid complexes of the kings. A special role was played by the necropolis of Abydos during the Middle Kingdom. Its importance as the principal center of the cult of Osiris attracted many people who were eager to participate in its festivals. Numerous mortuary chapels, including cenotaphs, therefore cluster near the processional routes used during these occasions.

During the New Kingdom, the Theban necropolis gained supreme importance. Starting in the early eighteenth dynasty, the kings and their family members were buried in the Valley of the Kings and Valley of the Queens, two strictly exclusive areas, sheltered from sight from the valley by the first range of the desert mountains. Lined up along the margin of the valley, the mortuary temples of the kings were, at the same time, shrines devoted to the cult of the god Amun, and they played an important part in the festivals of the Theban necropolis. The sites of these temples and the processional routes used during these festivals had an important impact on the location of the tombs of private individuals in the necropolis. These were mainly rock-cut tombs, some of them decorated with the finest paintings that have survived from ancient Egypt. In their location, a ranking according to status can often be discerned.

A necropolis duplicating the basic layout of that at Thebes was begun at Tell el-Amarna during the reign of Akhenaten. A second important necropolis, mainly of the later New Kingdom, is situated at Saqqara, where the officials associated with Egypt's northern capital at Memphis were buried in sumptuous tombs of temple-like appearance. In Upper Egypt, small groups of decorated rock-cut tombs have been found at a few sites. In addition, there is a series of town cemeteries in Egypt, and, in particular, in Nubia. At these sites, the tombs of lesser provincial officials and townspeople are well attested.

During the Late Period, the necropolises of the important political centers of the country, Thebes and the Memphite region, continue to flourish. Cemeteries of ordinary people as well as individual decorated tombs are attested throughout the country. Very exceptional as a type of cemetery, however, are the burials of members of the ruling house within temple precincts during the Third Intermediate Period and the Late Period. Archaeologically attested examples of this custom are the burials of the kings of the twenty-first to twenty-third dynasties at Tanis, and the Third Intermediate Period and Late Period tombs in front of the temple of Medinet Habu in Western Thebes—in particular, those of the "divine consorts of Amun," dating from the twenty-fifth and twenty-sixth dynasties. Similarly, the scions of the twenty-ninth dynasty are buried within the great Temenos of Ba-neb-djed at Mendes. A similar situation is described by Herodotus for the temple of Sais.

Patterns of Use through Time. Necropolises were often used for a considerable span of time, especially if they served large, permanent communities and if important elite tombs were present on the site. Because of the accumulation of tombs over the course of time, the center of occupation often shifted gradually from one location to another. Sometimes clear patterns of growth emerge from this process and can provide important information for establishing the archaeological chronology of a cemetery. Yet it can sometimes be shown that family members wished to be buried in close proximity to their ancestors; there are several cases in which sons had their tombs built next to those of their fathers or even chose to be buried in their fathers' tombs; in a few cases, groups of tombs spanning several generations of a single family can be discerned. Reisner grounded his interpretation of the structure of the fourth dynasty cemetery at Giza and of an Old Kingdom provincial cemetery at Naga ed-Deir mainly on hypothetical family groups, but he overemphasized the importance of this principle. In fact, there are no cemeteries that show an overall segmentary structure that could reflect long-term family groups among the occupants.

The gradual shift of a cemetery from one site to another is often associated with a shift in the social level of its occupants. Areas that had been reserved for elite tombs came to be occupied by lesser burials after the cult activities at the large tombs had ceased. Then the spaces available between the earlier buildings, in their courts and even in their chapels, were densely filled in with small tombs; in rock-cut tombs, intrusive shafts were added to receive humble burials. This sequence of reuse often followed the original occupation directly, and the personnel associated with the cults of the larger tombs even played an important part in it.

Necropolises in Social Life. Ancient Egyptian necropolises were complex social institutions, but evidence to elucidate this is sparse and unevenly distributed. The extant documents refer mainly to the elite level of society and to the necropolises of important centers. Any attempt to generalize from this evidence should take into account the differences among individual places and among social strata.

The right to receive a burial and a mortuary cult depended, in theory, on the king. In practice, however, this claim represented a reality, to a certain degree, only for the elite and the necropolises of the royal residence; after all, the sixth dynasty nomarch Djau at Deir el-Gebrawi refers in his inscriptions to a document testifying to his right to build a tomb for himself. In general, however, both burial and mortuary cult depended on the status and means of the deceased and their families.

The texts state that tombs should be built in "a pure place in which no tomb had been before." In fact, archaeological observations tend to confirm that people were careful, as far as possible, not to infringe on earlier tombs, at least not on those still in use for burials. From the late Old Kingdom onward it became more and more the rule that a single tomb served for burials of the members of an extended family over several generations, and ownership of the tomb was passed on through inheritance. There is one instance on record in which a tomb in the Theban necropolis that had become vacant was assigned to a new owner by a state official at the end of the eighteenth dynasty.

Sometimes elite tombs were built by the king and assigned to his officials, or individual items of the furnishings of the tomb—like false door stelae or costly sarcophagi—were presented by the king to his followers. Similarly, great officials sometimes cared for the burials of their attendants. In most cases, however, tombs were built from private means, and, during the Old Kingdom, tomb inscriptions frequently assert that the tomb was built from the rightful possessions of the tomb-owner and that the craftsmen who built and decorated it had received fair payment.

Apart from building the tomb, steps to secure its mortuary cult had to be taken. The cult at the tomb usually depended on the family of the deceased, ideally the eldest son. In the elite level of society, however, it was common to set up a special foundation to guarantee regular offerings in the future. A certain amount of property was set apart and assigned, on a hereditary basis, to a group of mortuary priests who in return were to conduct the cult for the deceased. Among Old Kingdom tomb inscriptions there are several documents concerned with regulations of this type. A series of contracts in the tomb of the twelfth Dynasty nomarch Djefaihapy at Asyut attest to complex legal arrangements regarding his mortuary cult between the tomb owner, the priesthoods of the temples of Asyut, and several necropolis officials.

Both through the resources regularly spent on tomb construction and through the endowments for the mortuary cults, considerable wealth was concentrated in the necropolis, providing a living for a considerable number of people. First, specialist workmen were needed to excavate and eventually decorate tombs on demand, as well as workshops to provide stelae, coffins, and other tomb equipment. A special class of stonemasons even took their title from this business. During the Middle Kingdom in particular there is a series of titles attesting to a complex organization of these gangs. During the New Kingdom, they are also found to be associated with various temples and the state administration. In fact, necropolis workmen are also listed as members of expeditions to quarries, and their title was understood to denote their special range of skills. Nevertheless, necropolis workmen are regularly found in various forms of employment in necropolises. The best-known community of workmen attached to a necropolis is the village of Deir el-Medina in western Thebes during the New Kingdom. Their main task was to excavate and decorate the royal tombs in the Valley of the Kings and the Valley of the Queens, but it is well attested that they also manufactured tomb furnishings on demand. Although this special group of workmen was housed in a separate village in the Theban cemetery, other necropolis workers, as well as the priests serving the mortuary cults, probably lived in the villages or towns near the necopolises, or, in the case of the royal necropolises of the Old and Middle Kingdoms, in the pyramid towns.

The necropolises were under the civil administration. The Theban necropolis was supervised during the New Kingdom by a "mayor for the western side of Thebes" who was also the chief of the necropolis police. In the Middle Kingdom contracts of Djefaihapy, mentioned above, there is a possible reference to an "overseer of the necropolis," and, in the same texts, an "officer of the desert" (i.e., of the necropolis) is mentioned. This person was probably in charge of security in the necropolis; during the Middle Kingdom, the title "Guard of the Necropolis" is attested as well.

In the performance of the mortuary cult, festivals were of particular importance. During the Old Kingdom (and, in a modified form, also in later periods) a standard list of festivals is attested, which features, among others, New Year's Day, various dates in the lunar month, and the festivals of the gods Thoth, Sokar, and Min. With the probable exception of the *wag*-festival, these occasions were not festivals for the dead in a restricted sense. Rather, the mortuary cults were eager to participate in these wider communal celebrations.

From the Middle Kingdom onward it is evident from the documents that mortuary cults became linked more and more with the cults and festivals of local gods and their temples. Statues for private individuals were set up in the temples to participate ideally in the daily offerings of the gods. From the contracts for the mortuary cult of Djefaihapy, it emerges that offerings were to be presented to his statues during the processional festivals of Wepwawet and Anubis, the local gods of his hometown, Asyut.

Among the known "festivals of the necropolis," the most comprehensive documentation is available for the Valley Festival, which was celebrated in the Theban necropolis at least from the twelfth dynasty onward. Its ceremonies are depicted in the wall decorations of Theban tombs, especially during the eighteenth dynasty. During this festival, the image of the god Amun from the Karnak temple was carried in festive

procession to the west bank to visit the gods of the Theban necropolis and the mortuary temples of the kings. On this occasion, cultic activities at the tombs reached their climax; families gathered at the tombs of their ancestors to celebrate the festival with joyful banquets.

Linking the cult of the dead to the great festivals of a town did not merely take advantage of the stability of the cults of the gods. Rather, it was central to the symbolic meaning of these festivals to display the sense of community and collective identity uniting the population of a town or a region. Therefore, it was perfectly logical to express the community between the dead and the living within the same symbolic framework.

A consideration of events in a necropolis cannot overlook tomb robbery and the destruction of tombs. The liveliest relevant account is provided by a series of official documents from the twentieth dynasty that pertain to investigations into several cases of royal tombs reported to have been violated by thieves. It emerges clearly from these texts that tomb robbery was a common feature in the necropolis of western Thebes at this time. Archaeological data confirm that this was not at all unusual; in many cemeteries, most tombs had been violated, in particular the better equipped ones. It seems significant that in most cases the robbers were evidently well informed about the layout and content of the burials. Evidently, most tomb robberies took place not long after the original burial. In a few cases, there is even clear evidence that a burial was partly robbed before it was complete. There are also many cases in which, after a few generations, later tombs intruded on earlier ones, obstructing their cult places and even damaging them severely.

From the available documentation, it emerges that tomb robbery, while clearly considered a criminal act, was in fact a regular phenomenon, and so it seems that religious fears did not trouble the minds of the ancient Egyptians as overwhelmingly as is sometimes supposed. On the other hand, it appears that the protection of the tombs depended mainly on the continuing interest of the living in their cults and on the continuity of the surviving group's claim to ownership. As soon as a tomb dropped out of the network of social processes within the community, it was bound to face rapid destruction.

The Necropolis in Egyptian Thought. The principal Egyptian word for "necropolis" is ḥr.t-nṯr ("the property of the god"). The word "god" in this term probably referred originally to the king who bestowed the right of burial on members of the elite. Later, however, it was probably understood with reference to other gods who were regarded as "lords of the necropolis," like Osiris. As synonyms, "the West," "the Beautiful West," and "the Western Desert" are particularly common. In addition, there exists a great wealth of expressions used for the necropolises of individual places or those bound to specific contexts, like t3-dsr ("the sacred [secluded] land"), the domain of the god Anubis, or r3-st3.w ("the beginning of the corridors"), associated in particular with the god Sokar and the Memphis necropolis.

The necropolis is the place in the real world where the tombs are. At the same time, however, the necropolis is the metaphysical realm where the destiny of the dead is carried out. Both aspects are inseparable in Egyptian thought. Necropolises as sites and as social institutions were the places at which the imaginary concepts of funerary religion were anchored to physical and social reality. The necropolis forms part of a tripartite model of a world that comprises heaven, earth, and necropolis; in its sense of "netherworld" and "hereafter," it is contrasted to the realm of the living (t3-pn "this land;" tp-t3 "[being] upon earth"). The necropolis is the realm where the dead "live" (as a class of beings, along with gods and men). In that sense, the cemetery (as a site) is just the entrance to a netherworld realm of cosmic dimensions.

The dead do not pass the threshold to the netherworld once and for all. In some sense, they continue to dwell in the tomb as the living dwell in their houses. Therefore, the dead can be approached ritually at their tombs. Yet mobility is a prime concern to the spirits of the dead: they wish to move about freely in the netherworld, and they wish to be able to exit from it to see the light of the sun and to revisit the "places of yesterday." The necropolis is thus a place of transition in both directions and of continuous contact between this world and the world beyond.

The living and the dead are engaged in a network of mutual relationships that were conceptualized in highly ambivalent, even contradictory terms. For the dead, death could be a state of ultimate weakness. The dead depended on being cared for by the surviving group, both through ritually correct burial and through regular offerings. Otherwise, they would not be able to face the many hazards of their netherworld existence. The dead therefore need to muster the solidarity of the living, and they need to be remembered. One important argument in this context is to recall the moral integrity and the achievements of the deceased person during life, which entitles her or him to claim the support of her or his group in return. The same idea is expressed in a mythological guise in the concept of a universal judgment of the dead by the divine court of Osiris. At the same time, however, the dead could be powerful beings. For the surviving group, the dead did not lose their identity nor their status as social persons. Having access to the world of gods and spirits, they could lend magical support to their families. If offended by impious behavior, the spirits of the dead could prove fearful enemies; in fact, they are cited as a frequent cause of illness. For the living, interaction with the dead therefore could be risky and highly ambivalent. The necropolis was a place to seek support from them, to conciliate them, and even to combat them with magical means.

Very much as a necropolis appears, to the archaeologist, as the counterpart to a settlement, the community of the dead appeared, in Egyptian thought, as a counterpart to the society of the living, mirroring both its structure and its norms, raised to a metaphysical level.

Stephan J. Seidlmayer

NEFERTUM. The god Nefertum was primarily a solar deity who was linked to several Egyptian creation myths. His name, *Nfr-tm,* means "Amun is good" or "he who has newly appeared is perfect," and his primary symbol was the blue lotus blossom. He is most often depicted in Egyptian art as a human male wearing a headdress composed of a lotus blossom flanked by two tall plumes. Many times, the symbols are accompanied by *menat*-necklace counterpoises, emphasizing his youthful nature. He also carries a sickle-shaped object in his left hand.

Nefertum's connection to the solar realm is made known in Spell 266 of the Pyramid Texts, in which he is referred to as "the lotus blossom at the nose" of the sun god Re. He eventually unites with Re to form a single deity. One of his other representations is a man with a lion's head or a man standing on the back

of a lion, a solar animal. His appearance in the Pyramid Texts also illustrates his connection with the Egyptian kingship; in Spell 249, he is described as "the king as a flower in the hand of the sun god."

In the Coffin Texts, Nefertum is described as a childgod. He is the son of the leonine goddess, Sekhmet, and, beginning in the New Kingdom, he fills a new role as the child-member of the Memphite triad, along with his mother, Sekhmet, and the Memphite creator god, Ptah. Because of the close connection between the aggressive lioness goddess, Sekhmet, and her more peaceful feline counterpart, Bastet, Nefertum is sometimes described as the child of Bastet. As the son of the fierce goddess, Sekhmet, Nefertum sometimes takes on a warlike role and, in that form, he can be associated with other warlike gods such as Montu, Sopdu, and Hormenty, as well as with several other leonine goddesses in whose cults he was thought to participate. Nefertum also acts together with his mother, Sekhmet, as an apotropaic deity who could be called upon for protection from illness and plague. There is a chapel of Nefertum in the temple of Sety I at Abydos, where he is accompanied by Ptah-Sokar and other Memphite deities.

Nefertum plays a role in one of the ancient Egyptian creation myths. It was believed that the lotus blossom was the first living thing to appear out of the water of chaos at the beginning of time. When the petals of this blue lotus opened, the sun god appeared for the first time. This creation image is nicely illustrated in a wooden statue of King Tutankhamun that shows the head of the youthful king appearing atop a lotus blossom.

Nefertum is also associated with funerary religion in his form as the deity Sokar-Henu-Nefertum. He appears in the *Book of Going Forth by Day* (*Book of the Dead*) as the one who brings the unfortunate evildoers to the slaughter block and as a member of the council of gods who judge the dead (chapter 125 of the *Book of Going Forth by Day*).

Because of his associations with the fragrant blue lotus flower, Nefertum is also thought of as a god of perfume. Some of his divine epithets include "Protector of the Two Lands" and "Lord of Provisions." *Jennifer Houser-Wegner*

NEITH. The goddess Neith, who occupies an important place in the Egyptian pantheon, served in a number of different capacities. She was the fierce goddess of war and hunting. Her symbols, known as early as the first dynasty in a tomb in Abydos, are a shield and two crossed arrows. The deity is frequently depicted holding these weapons; she is also crowned with these attributes.

Neith has certain domestic characteristics. She is the patron of weaving. The hieroglyph for her name is a loom, which is sometimes illustrated above her head. In addition, she is involved in funerary rituals: with Isis and other deities, she watches over the coffin of Osiris; as the goddess of weaving, she bestows mummy shrouds upon the deceased.

Neith is associated with Lower Egypt. She is worshiped as the goddess of this region, and in some of her representations she wears the Red Crown. In fact, one of her names is "she of the Lower Egyptian crown."

She is identified as the mother of all, "creating the seed of gods and men." During the New Kingdom, she is known as the mother of the sun god, Re. At this time, she is also regarded as the primeval goddess who produced the world. Neith also gave birth to Sobek, the crocodile god of Lower Egypt, who became a popular figure during the

twelfth dynasty, when the rulers enjoyed hunting in the marshes.

Neith plays a pivotal role in Egyptian myth. When Osiris is murdered by Seth and a successor must be found, it is the wise and powerful Neith to whom the other deities turn for guidance. In a letter that she writes to the gods, she states authoritatively, "Give the office of Osiris to his son Horus! Do not go on committing these great wrongs, which are not in place, or I will get angry and the sky will topple to the ground. But also tell the Lord of All, the Bull who lives in Heliopolis, to double Seth's property. Give him Anathe and Astarte, your two daughters, and put Horus in the place of his father."

Neith's roots are very ancient; in the earliest dynasties, several queens bore her name. However, it was in the Late period that she gained the greatest prominence. She was venerated by the twenty-sixth dynasty pharaohs at their capital, Sais, in the Nile Delta, where she served as protector for the fifth nome of Lower Egypt. It has been suggested that Neith was of Libyan descent; this may in part explain the Saite rulers' fondness for her, because they too were of Libyan ancestry.

A great temple was built in Neith's name at Sais. According to Plutarch, an inscription in this impressive structure read: "I am all that has been, that is, and that will be. No mortal has yet been able to lift the veil that covers me."

Catherine Simon

NEPHTHYS. Although she appears frequently in Egyptian sources, the deity Nephthys apparently did not have her own body of myth independent of the Osiris legend. Her role is primarily funerary, as the counterpart of her sister Isis, in mourning and protecting the dead. Nephthys is usually portrayed as a woman with her name, *Nb-ḥwt*, "mistress of the mansion," on her head. Sometimes she is shown with outstretched wings; more rarely she is depicted in the form of a bird.

Nephthys' character was established by the time of the Pyramid Texts (c.2400 BCE). According to the texts, she is one of the Ennead of Heliopolis, the daughter of Geb and Nut, and the sister of Osiris, Isis and Seth. Although she is Seth's consort, she supports Osiris, and is closely associated with Isis. When Osiris dies, Isis and Nephthys transform themselves into kites, lament his death, and restore his body, thus protecting it from decay. Together, they guard the young Horus and the deceased king. Isis and Nephthys are typically paired, and while both are essentially beneficent, Nephthys can be associated with darkness, as when Isis represents the ascending day bark and Nephthys the descending night bark.

The Pyramid Texts refer to Nephthys as the mother and nurse of the king, suggesting an association with divine birth, and the Westcar Papyrus portrays her aiding the birth of future kings. In solar religion, Isis and Nephthys assist Re, indicating a possible origin as sky goddesses.

Most representations of Nephthys occur in funerary contexts. She protects the canopic jars; her association is with Hapy as the guardian of the lungs. Isis and Nephthys are depicted behind the throne of Osiris in the *Book of Going Forth by Day* (*Book of the Dead*), occupying the solar bark in the *Book of Gates*, and beside the tomb of Osiris in the *Book of That Which Is in the Underworld* (*Amduat*). They adorn the exteriors of New Kingdom royal sarcophagi; the feather patterns on Theban *rishi*-coffins represent their outstretched wings, and they figure prominently in the vignettes on cartonnage coffins of the New Kingdom

and later. Funerary scenes in nineteenth dynasty private tombs show Nephthys at the head of the coffin, Isis at the foot, and Anubis administering to the deceased.

From the fifth dynasty onward, female *dryt* mourners are shown portraying Isis and Nephthys in funerary scenes. Two Graco-Roman versions of the *Lamentations of Isis and Nephthys* were intended to be performed by women impersonating the goddesses in temples and funerals respectively. There is little evidence for an individual cult of Nephthys, although three twentieth dynasty priests of her cult, and one from the Late Period, are attested. The birthday of Nephthys was celebrated on the last epagomenal day. Nephthys is usually portrayed as childless, although in some Greco-Roman versions of the Osiris legend, Anubis is the child of Nephthys by Osiris. Other sources list her as the mother of a son by Re and a daughter by Hemen. Although rarely associated with deities other than Isis, she is occasionally identified with Seshat or Anuket. In the Ptolemaic Period, Nephthys attends the Apis bull, and the Greeks sometimes identified her with Aphrodite or Nike.   *Denise M. Doxey*

NUN. For the ancient Egyptian, the sphere of life floated as a bubble, surrounded by the limitless dark waters of the inert god Nun. This oceanic abyss, while giving rise to and sustaining the cosmogony, also concealed the threat of disorder in its chaotic depths. It is the supreme mystery in the Egyptian cosmology.

The concept of the primeval waters is common to all Egyptian creation models. When the king sets sail into the realm of the afterlife, it is to Nun that he appeals. When the Egyptians dug down for water, it was in search of Nun. This presence was actively sought in temple and field as the basis for life, religious and secular. Nun, as a principle of the void mysteriously merging towards creation, is the progenitor of all differentiation, divine and earthly, and the image of water, manifesting both form and formlessness simultaneously, perfectly contains this idea in itself. One can see a poetic and sensuous appreciation of this in a text from the time of Amenhotpe III (c.1410–1372 BCE) near Luxor: "How beautiful is Nun in his pool in every season, more is he like wine than water, a full Nile, born of the Lord of Eternity."

The typical Egyptian Ennead (group of nine gods) reveals Nun as a sort of translucent entity at the point of origin alongside the actual creator-god Atum.

NUN
ATUM
SHU——TEFNUT
GEB——NUT
OSIRIS——ISIS SETH
NEPHTHYS

Nun is ubiquitous in all phases of Egyptian religious history; indeed, he is depicted on the walls of all the Ptolemaic temples in the Greco-Roman period in his usual form, and is well represented in the larger Ptolemaic temples of the South, often presented in fusion with Ptah (Kalabasha, Philae, Edfu), Sobek (Kom Ombo), Hapy (Opet temple, Karnak), Horus (Opet temple, Dendera), and Khnum-Amun (Esna).

From the Middle Kingdom onward, Nun is described as "the Father of the Gods," and this is perhaps his enduring legacy. That the Greeks derived this idea from the Egyptians is likely, and philosophy, proper, has had recourse to deal with the perennial issue of form appearing out of formlessness. One can see the conundrums of Nun permeating the writings of the third-century CE Neoplatonist Plotinus, for example, the seventeenth-century mystic Jakob Böhme, and the nineteenth-century F. W. Schelling's "will of the depths," as well as, perhaps, Arthur Schopenhauer's writings on "the will."

In Coptic Christian writings, Nun (ⲚⲨⲚ, in Coptic) came to the mean "abyss of hell." The debasement of this once-majestic creator-god was facilitated by the ambiguity of the word as it was used in Gnostic and magical texts, although the Gnostics continued to view Nun as the very wellspring of divinity. In any event, the association of the word with a pagan deity and developing heresies were the determining factors in the eventual demise of Nun. Although venerated for millennia, Nun eventually came to be exclusively associated with chaos and disorder, forces that were conceptually, as well as politically, set loose upon occupied Egypt in the Late Period.

Daniel R. Mcbride

NUT. The sky goddess Nut was probably one of the oldest deities in the Egyptian pantheon. She was incorporated into the Heliopolitan Ennead in

Detail from a coffin depicting the goddess Nut spreading her wings in protection over the deceased (Werner Forman Archive, British Museum, London/Art Resource, NY)

the Old Kingdom Pyramid Texts, the earliest surviving corpus of religious texts. In this source she is a central figure as the granddaughter of the creator-god Atum, the daughter of Shu and Tefnut (air and moisture), the sister and wife of Geb (earth), the mother of Osiris, Isis, Seth, and Nephthys, and the grand-mother of Horus. In Spell 548 of the Pyramid Texts, Nut the Great is de-scribed as a long-horned celestial cow who suckles the king and takes him to herself in the sky. This imagery recurs much later in the shrines of Tutankha-mun (r. 1355–1346 BCE), in which it is greatly elaborated, and again in the Ptol-emaic Period (305–31 BCE) in association with the goddess Hathor at her temple in Dendera.

In the Pyramid Texts and Coffin Texts there are series of Nut spells. On the sarcophagus of Teti (first king of the sixth dynasty, ruled c. 2374–2354) there are a number of recitations by Nut (Spells 1 ff.), and in the later sixth dy-nasty pyramids there are a number of ad-dresses (Spells 427 ff.) asking the sky goddess to conceal her son Osiris from Seth, to take possession of the earth, and to install every god who has a bark as an imperishable star in the sky—that is, in Nut herself.

In the Middle Kingdom Coffin Texts, Spell 77 describes Nut as "she who bore the gods," and Spell 864 calls her "mother of the gods." She enfolds and protects the sun god Re, as well as re-creating him daily. Although she is given the epithet "Mother of Seth" numerous times in the Ramessid story of the *Con-*

tendings of Horus and Seth, her role as mother of Osiris, and by extension of Horus, is much more significant in the New Kingdom.

Unlike many other great deities, Nut had no particular cult center. This situation may have resulted from her originally chthonic rather than anthro-pomorphic nature. In spite of the fact that in some texts she is associated with the cow goddess, she was also depicted very early in the history of the pantheon as a human female figure whose nude body arched over the Earth, sustained the stars, gave birth to the Sun every day, and swallowed it at dusk so that it could pass through her body. In Spell 306 of the Coffin Texts, Nut per-forms the same remaking for the de-ceased, identified with Re. This rebirth of the sun god, together with the res-urrection of her son, Osiris, gave her a very important role in the two major Egyptian cults centered on the afterlife. Coffins and burial chambers of tombs are both personified as Nut, who is frequently depicted on their lids and ceilings, for example, in the beautiful representation found in the tomb of Sety I in the Valley of the Kings.

In the Ptolemaic temples at the great cult sites of Edfu and Esna, there are sep-arate chapels to Nut near their main sanctuaries, which depict her body bent around the chapel ceilings. At Dendera, the ceiling of the first hypostyle hall prominently features the goddess Nut in what must be one of the largest repre-sentations of any deity in Egypt.

Leonard H. Lesko

O

OFFERINGS.

An Overview

Offerings to the dead have become known from prehistoric times through finds in ancient Egyptian graves. Special offering places have also been found in relation to graves throughout Egypt's historical period; the earliest were placed outside the superstructures of the tombs and the later inside. Most likely, offerings were also made in the shrines depicted on prehistoric material, since offerings were well documented in textual material and, from the New Kingdom onward, also in temple reliefs.

The Ideology of Offerings. Two concepts are linked to the notion of offerings that cover all kinds of offerings and explain the meaning of offerings in the Egyptian worldview. One concept is "the Eye of Horus" (*irt Ḥr*), one of the most important symbols of ancient Egypt and used about all kinds of gifts. The other concept is *maat*, which means "order, structure, justice, truth, and harmony."

Horus, the god who represented all that is good and all constructive forces in the universe, was once, according to a myth, deprived of one of his eyes while fighting with his eternal enemy Seth, the god of confusion, of violence, and of all destructive forces of the cosmos. Seth managed to capture the eye of Horus, demolished it, and threw it away. Thoth, the god of knowledge and magic skill, found the parts and put them together so that the injured eye was healed again. The healed eye was then called the *wedjat*-eye (*wḏȝt*), the "sound eye," and it became the symbol for the reestablishment of ordered conditions after disturbance. The eye is important in the myths, as for example in the myth of Osiris. Horus is said to have brought his eye to his dead father Osiris who devoured it as an offering meal and by means of it was recalled to life; it thus became the guarantee of life and of the regeneration of life. The fact that offerings are called "the Eye of Horus" indicates that they are considered participants in the preservation of life. This designation also characterizes the offerings as divine substance and even allows for discussions about the transsubstantiation of the material of the offerings. The Eye of Horus is the greatest gift of all, and it constitutes the quintessence of gifts.

The concept of *maat*, also used to designate offerings of all kinds, supports the idea that the gifts to the gods were meant to strengthen the established order and to help preserve it. The goddess Maat, the daughter of the creator, represented the order and structure of the creation on all levels: on the cosmic level, in the form of the right and orderly rising and setting of the Sun,

Moon, and stars; on the earth, in the form of the right and just functioning of society, its laws and rules; and in the personal human sphere, in the form of righteous and truthful lives. Maat, like the Eye of Horus, represented what was sound and perfect.

Offerings were, above all, a means to maintain the order of the world so that evil forces were checked and not allowed to prevail. They were a way to show that people put all their efforts on the side of good. Further, they were a symbol of gratitude offered by those living on earth to the divine, given in the hope of gifts in return, indicating an exchange of gifts to maintain the order of the world. At the same time they were a means of communication between the two worlds—the everyday world and the supreme reality beyond the everyday world.

The temple offerings to the gods intended for the preservation of life were actually of two different kinds. First, the offerings consisted of "all good and pure things on which the god lives." The recipient was regarded as the father or the lord of the offerings, as was often attested in the texts "to give X to its father or its lord," and supposedly the things brought back to their rightful owner were considered to strengthen the recipient so that he was able and willing to give in his turn. That process of offering was *do ut des,* which means "I give in order that you give." Second, there were offerings that represented the destructive forces, such as animals attached to the god of confusion, Seth—the ass, hippopotamus, crocodile, gazelle, and geese. They symbolize the chaotic forces threatening the created ordered cosmos.

The offerings to the dead were intended for the restoration of life. The dead were momentarily in an inert state, according to the Egyptian way of thinking, and to bring them out of that state and back to life they were given "all good and pure things on which the god lives," which was the appropriate offering for those who entered the divine world.

The Daily Temple Cult. Offerings were given to the gods during the daily temple cult. The daily ritual is known from several sources that were dated from the New Kingdom to Greco-Roman times. There are papyri, now in Berlin, dating from the twenty-second dynasty, that describe sixty-six scenes of the ritual for Amun and Mut in Karnak. Scenes of the daily cult were also depicted on temple walls, where single scenes often represented the whole ritual. The most comprehensive were found in the temple of Sety I at Abydos (thirty-six scenes), in the Edfu temple (nineteen scenes), and in the temple of Dendera (six scenes). The king was the "Lord of ritual" (*nb irt ḫt*). In all reliefs, the reigning king was always depicted officiating before a statue of god, although the duty was, in reality, delegated to the head priest of each temple.

The morning cult was the most important; the offerings were prepared in the offering room, consecrated through libations and censing, then brought into the sanctuary to be presented to the statue of the god. At noon and in the evening, a shorter ritual took place. Possibly, during some periods and in certain temples, Edfu for example, an hourly ritual was celebrated throughout the day and night.

Although many depictions and descriptions of the daily cult are known, there is no consensus about its ritual order. The cult seems to be based on human morning ritual: washing, dressing, and eating. Since the status of the cult statue was one of a mighty god, it was treated like a king and offered royal insignia. All the ritual acts were accompanied by libations and censing.

The cult was a means of entering into contact with the powers that governed the world, as well as a means of maintaining communication with the divine world. In pictured scenes, there are indications of what is being recited during the rites—what the priest says and what the god answers. Giving implied a gift in return; inherent in the nature of a gift. The very acts of the cult were, in themselves, offerings to the gods. As the priest approached the sanctuary with the intention of executing the cult ritual and bringing the offerings, the flow of gifts started in return. In response to the cult actions and the material offerings—such as food, clothes, and other objects—the god bestowed life on the king-priest who acted as a mediator, allowing all the country and its inhabitants to benefit. Linked with the gift of life were the gifts of stability, prosperity, and other beneficial states, such as health and joy. With reciprocal giving, the god also bestowed power on the king-priest to maintain the realm and to be victorious over the country's foes. The divine gifts were also intended to confirm the king's divine status; thus he was offered the rank and function of the great gods like Atum and Geb as well as the kingship of the gods Re and Horus.

Festival Cults. Numerous festivals marked the annual seasons and months. Each temple had its own calendar of festivals, which were celebrated with cultic activities within the temples and processions outside them. The daily cult as well as the festival activities within the temple were enacted in the privacy of the sanctuary, without the participation of the public. Only the processions took place in public. The lists of food deliveries for the festivals show that large amounts were brought in for those occasions and offered to the gods. During the processions, there were music, dancing, and singing; according to the Wisdom Literature (Ani), the gods also considered such activities as offerings.

The Offering Cult for the Dead. The dead were given offerings on the occasion of the burial, and their offerings were to be renewed forever, on principle, at certain named festivals during the year: the new year festival, the Thoth festival, the Wag festival, the Sokar festival, and others, according to a lengthy list. In reality there were probably not so many days celebrated with a meal at the tomb, during which members of the family came together (as was the custom in Thebes, for example, at the Valley Festival, from the Middle Kingdom to Greco-Roman times).

Food offerings had been given to the dead in prehistoric times, and this custom continued throughout historical times. As early as the first dynasties, the deceased was depicted before an offering table, beside which there was an inscription enumerating all that was offered. In the tombs in the Theban necropolis in the latter part of the eighteenth dynasty, this rather simple though copious meal was changed into a banquet with many participants, servants, and entertaining musicians, that resembled the family meal in front of the tomb during the Valley Festival.

The king presented the offerings to the gods in the temples, and the idea of the king as the giver of offerings was also maintained in the tombs. The offering formula used in the tombs says "an offering that the king gives;" this was actually true, owing to a peculiarity of the Egyptian offering system called reversion of offerings.

Reverted Offerings. The reversion of offerings implied that offerings went from the temple out to the necropolis.

Offerings presented to the main god of the temple were carried out of the sanctuary, were presented to gods having subsidiary cults in the temple, then to statues of kings and private persons placed in the temple courts, and finally to the necropolis. After all those symbolic presentations, the offerings were distributed to the priests and all the staff involved in the rituals as a reward, or salary, for their work. This custom of reverted offerings was established as early as the Old Kingdom and was continued.

The custom of reverted offerings was not only a salary system for priests and temple staff in a nonmonetary society, it also offered a possibility for old age insurance and tax planning, since fewer taxes were paid for fields belonging to the temples than for privately owned fields. From the Ramessid era onward, it was customary for higher officials to donate a statue of the king to the king and the temple, as well as the means to furnish it with offerings (i.e., fields). The king then put the donator in charge of the statue with the usufruct of the attached income. When the official retired, and thus lost the income of his former office, he kept charge of the statue and the usufruct of its income. The gifts to the gods thus had economic as well as religious implications.

Contracts of Offering. Tomb owners and the priesthood of their hometown temple contracted to ensure future offerings during the generations to come. The most well known are the ten contracts of Hapidjefa at Asyut, an important official of the Middle Kingdom; they were established between him and the *wab*-priests, the hourpriests, and some specialist priests of both Wepwat and Anubis, as well as with the overseer of the necropolis and his staff. Hapidjefa stipulated what was going to be offered to him: bread and beer. On some occa-

sions he requested provisions in very large quantities: twenty-two jars of beer and 2,255 pieces of bread of two different types, a roast of meat, wicks for the torches used during nocturnal processions, and the participation of some priests in those processions. In return for such services, bread, beer, land, and part of the temple income were given to them. On the occasion of the Wag festival, he gave in return exactly the same large amount as they offered to him on that day—an example of reverted offerings. Most of what Hapidjefa gave away came from his own inherited property ("of the house of his father," according to the Egyptian term) or property from his own special funerary foundation. He also stipulated rewards originating from income that came from his office as a nomarch, which, however, was a less secure asset (the succeeding nomarch might disapprove of the arrangement and cancel it). His stipulations primarily concerned two important moments of the year: (1) the end of the year—the first epagomenal day and the fifth—which equals new year's eve and new year's day; (2) the Wag festival, eighteen days later. The end of the year was equated with death and burial, and the new year was equated with resurrection. The Wag festival was the great festival of the dead. On those occasions, ceremonies and processions took place in the temples and in the necropolis. It was important that Hapidjefa's statue was present, as it was for all dead persons.

Ancient Egyptian Terms for Offerings. The specialized words for the verb "to offer" expressed, through their associative field, the different aspects of offerings. The word most frequently used was *hotep* (*ḥtp*), written with the hieroglyph representing the offering slab (a loaf of bread), and it has also been determined with the offering table. *Ḥtp* was the word used in the offering formula, "an offering that the king gives" (ḥtp ḏi nsw) also has the following meanings "to be pleased, happy, gracious;" "to be peaceful;" "to become calm;" "to satisfy;" "to pacify;" and their corresponding nouns. Ḥtp had to do with gifts in a holistic perspective of communication between the worlds, given in gratitude, received in happiness and grace, and leading to contentment, graciousness, mercy, and peace.

"To present" and "to hand over" the offerings were expressed by ḥnk; in hieroglyphic script, it is followed by the determinative of an outstretched arm holding a small offering bowl.

When the offerings had been carried in they had to be consecrated, and several words were used in that context. There is kherep (ḥrp), which has to do with the provenence of the offerings and which covers a large associative field. The offerings came from special districts and estates (ḥrp) that were administered (ḥrp) by the temples, and they had to pay taxes (ḥrpwt) in the form of their produce to the temple to which they belonged. So they brought in (ḥrp) their produce and provided (ḥrp) the temple with the necessities "to make offerings" (ḥrp). The products then had to be consecrated (ḥrp) and dedicated to the gods. (ḥrp) The word ḥrp has as its determinating sign an arm that holds a baton of office—very appropriate for all those different meanings. A similar determining sign, an arm with a stick, is also used in drp, with the meaning "to offer," or "to present and make offerings." So the word drp might also have to do with the consecration. That was probably also the case with skr, determined with a mace and with the general meaning of "to strike," but it was also used in the sense of "to offer" and "to present offerings." Other words for "to offer" are linked

to the things offered and to their treatment. Animals and birds were often offered, but first they had to be slaughtered. There is the word i₃m, "to offer," written with the baton of office; it also meant "to bind the sacrifice," then written with a rope as the determining sign or with a knife to indicate the next step of the process. As to birds, they were killed by wringing the neck, wšn, which besides this meaning also meant "to make an offering." Another word for "to offer" and "offering" is wdn, which has a flower on a long stalk as a determining sign. Since flowers and vegetables were an important part of the offerings, this word is probably related to such offerings.

During the offering ritual, the offering had to be purified. A purified offering was called wdḥw. The word is determined by the sign of water flowing out of a recipient, as well as with the signs of bread and beer. It is related to a word of the same stem with the meaning "to pour out" and to one of the words for "offering table."

A word that has to do with offerings and at the same time with purification and purity is abu(ʿbw). What is offered to the gods must first be pure and sanctified, and that was done by a libation poured out from special libation vessels. Abu also means "impurity," thus including the two opposites of the notion of cleanliness; so the word comprises the meaning of the impurity that has to be eliminated to make the gift suitable for the gods. The removal of what is impure and evil leads us to the word sfḫ, which means "lose," "loosen," "release," "purify," "remove evil," "to separate fighting animals," "offer to god," and "offerings." So an offering is likened to the parting of fighting animals and removing evil, thus releasing forces, or freeing from bonding. It was not only what was good and pure that was offered to god but also what was bad that had been removed and laid aside, so that energies that were blocked by evil and by fighting were released and got a chance. Among the offering animals were also animals that symbolized the bad, the Seth side of existence. Those were offered so that the bad could not spread and defile the totality. In Ptolemaic times, bound victims were occasionally seen on the offering tables, symbolizing the menacing disordered forces that had to be defeated.

Types of Offerings. In prehistoric and in early dynastic times, the offerings to the dead mostly consisted of vessels, incense, oil, cosmetics, fruit, and meat. At first, there were real food and drink offerings. Next, the real offerings were supplemented with a list of the items and the amount of each offering, as were found on early dynastic stelae. Eventually, the offering lists and an offering formula could replace the gift of the material offering.

According to Winfried Barta in *Die altägyptische Opferliste* (Berlin, 1963), at first no established custom existed as to what offerings should be presented nor was there an order for appearance in the lists. The early period enumerations included both the offerings of objects that were part of the tomb equipment plus all that was needed for the burial, the commemorative ritual, and the meal. During the Old Kingdom, those two types of offerings were gradually separated into different lists. From the fifth dynasty onward, there are great offering lists of as many as ninety items for the ritual meal.

As for the temple offerings, the temple reliefs abound in offering scenes that refer to the daily temple cult. All over the walls, the richly furnished offering tables are laden with choice meat, fruit, vegetables, and so on. The scenes are often accompanied by offering lists that enumerate the items brought to the gods; such lists contain up to forty entries: bread of different kinds; several qualities of beer with different strengths; meat from cattle and wild desert animals, such as oxen and cows, sheep and goats, gazelles and antelopes; birds of different species, such as geese and water fowl; fruits, such as dates, grapes, figs, and pomegranates; vegetables, especially onions, garlic, and leeks; honey; milk and wine; grease, oil, perfumes, and incense; lamps and wicks; wax; salt; natron; cloth; jewelry; and royal insignia.

According to Barta, the offering lists for the deceased and for the gods should be distinguished from the various other offering lists, those related to the festivals and to supplying the statues and the other foundations (which had the secular aim of nourishing the priests and attending staffs and probably also festival participants). The temple and tomb offerings had, rather, a sacred function, to contribute primarily to the preservation and restoration of life; although they, too, through the practice of reversion, secondarily entered the secular domain. Thus offerings were intended for the maintenance of life and of the living. Whether offerings were burned in a regular manner remains an open question. New Kingdom scenes sometimes show offerings surrounded by flames, and these have been interpreted as gifts to a god that no one else was to share. In the Late Period, the destruction of offerings by fire came to symbolize offerings that represented hostile powers needing annihilation.

Human sacrifices were not part of ancient Egyptian religious rites (yet a few prehistoric and early dynastic finds have been interpreted in that way by some scholars).

Substitute Offerings. Despite the

superabundance of offerings, the material offering was not the essential thing. The act of devotion was more important than the material gift, as was attested by substitute offerings. Reciting the offering formula was an adequate substitute for the actual offering. This is particularly well attested where tomb owners address themselves to passersby, demanding that the offering formula be read on their behalf. It takes no effort to read it, and it does not take long, they say, but for the grave owner, it is of great importance. As the owner's name is mentioned in the formula, reading it out makes the owner live on, in the memory of posterity. Further evidence for substitutes of the actual offerings are the figures of wax or incense and the replicas made of cake that replace material offerings.

Sculptural Offerings. As mentioned above, the offering of a sculpture with attached fields for sustenance was a means to secure an income after retiring from official service, and it belongs to the secular sphere. There were also sculptural offerings belonging to the sacral sphere. Among them were the offering of a statuette of Maat. Well aware of the fragile state of equilibrium and harmony, Egyptians saw it as the main task of the pharaoh to strengthen that state, to work for *maat*. That is why the king-priest is often shown offering a small statue of Maat. In so doing, he shows that he acknowledges the principle of *maat* and tries to keep the world in the order in which it was created.

A variant of the *maat* offering is found in cases where the king, as the officiating priest, offers his name to the god. This variant is particularly found with names of Ramessid kings that contain the word *maat*. Ramses II is on many occasions seen offering his name Weser-Maat-Re to Amun, to Re-Horakhty, or to some other god, a name that means "Re's

maat-order is powerful" or "may Re's *maat*-order be powerful." There is also the possibility of interpreting the gift of the name as an offering of the self, the name being one of the expressions of the individual.

Another gift that might be interpreted as a gift of the self is a statue of the offering king—kneeling, prostrated, or in some other posture—presented to the god by the offering king himself. It could mean that the king offers himself, his action, and his power for the maintenance of life and order. Yet there are texts, such as the Harris Papyrus, which concern such statuettes and indicate that they are made and placed in the temple "in order to give thee [the god in question] daily offerings." That is, they are meant to make the king and his gift a permanent presence in the temple. Not only the living king but also dead kings were thus permanently present in the temples by means of such statuettes piously preserved.

Priestly Personnel Connected with Offerings. Given the extensive offerings in temples and tombs, many people were involved in the handling of the offering material and of the connected rituals.

In tomb service. Usually the oldest son took the responsibility for the care of the burial, the offerings, and the subsequent rituals, but this charge could also, if necessary, be given to another individual. In the Old Kingdom, the priest in charge of the private tomb had the titles *sekhen-akh* (*sḫn-ꜣḫ*), *hem-sekhen-akh* (*ḥ-sḫn-ꜣḫ*), or *hem-sekhen-per-djet* (*ḥm-sḫn-pr-dt*) *Shn* means either "embrace," "seek," or "meet," and *akh* (*ꜣḫ*) is the designation of the deceased, so the title indicates the one who is in contact with the deceased. The word *ḥm* means "servant" and *pr-dt* is the designation of the foundation furnishing the funeral offerings of food, which the priest will eventually receive in return for his services. In the Middle Kingdom, a new title appeared, ḥm-kȝ, which means "the servant of the Ka," with the Ka being one of the designations of the immaterial, psycho-spiritual aspects of a human being. From the New Kingdom onward, the most frequent title was wȝḥ-mw, meaning "the offerer of the water," who, however, also took care of the food offerings.

In temples. The person responsible for the offerings and the reversion of offerings was entitled "Overseer of the god's offerings" (imy-r ḥtpt-nṯr) or "Scribe of the god's offerings" (sš ḥtpt-nṯr). These were the main officials but, ś ḥ given the enormous responsibilities, there were many other titles for those who handled specialized tasks.

Offerings According to the Egyptian Worldview. How did the ancient Egyptians look upon such extensive offerings? It seems that the material offerings were not the most important, and there are a few indications of this in texts from differents periods. In the *Instructions for Merikare* (lines 128–129) it is said "the good qualities of the straightforward person are preferred to the ox of the evil-doer." The same attitude toward substantial gifts was also reflected in the story of "The Shipwrecked Sailor" (line 159). When the shipwrecked Egyptian was going back home to Egypt, he took leave of the owner of the island, the divine serpent, who was a representation of the creator god, and he offered to send all the riches of Egypt to the serpent once he had reached home. The divine serpent, however, laughed at him and at his proposals and said that he had plenty of all that, since he was the rightful owner of all good things and there was nothing that did not exist in excess on his island. There was, however, one

thing that he wished, that the sailor should make his name renowned in his home town. "Lo, that is my due from you." So the inner attitude of thankfulness, remembrance, and testimony about the divine were more important than the actual gifts. Most important of all was *maat*, the righteousness, justice, truth, harmony, and balance as a gift in the temples, as that which accompanies the deceased into the netherworld.

According to Marcel Mauss in his *Essai sur le don. Forme et raison de l'échange dans les sociéte's archaïques* (Année Sociologique, II série, I, 1923–24, pp. 30–186), gifts are charged with the essence of the giver and imply that the receiver is obliged to give a gift in return. This is exactly what happened in the Egyptian offerings system. Humanity made offerings to the gods in order to urge the gods to give in turn. What was given was what had been received. Offerings were part of a continuous exchange of energies that corresponded to the Egyptian holistic worldview—where everything in the universe was ecologically linked in a network of energies. The human being had to take an active part in this network and contribute to its perfect functioning, so it is with this perspective that the offerings are to be understood.

Gertie Englund

Offering Formulas and Lists

One of the most ubiquitous classes of texts found in ancient Egypt, offering formulas have their origins in the cult of the dead. Since to ancient Egyptians death was simply a continuation—albeit on a different plane—of the life they had known, shelter and material goods were considered necessary for the deceased's well-being. A tomb equipped with clothing and everyday utensils supplied their needs, along with the appropriate food and drink. Nourishment was supplied through an elaborate set of legal transactions between an individual and the funerary priests, whereby the priests contracted to furnish a specified amount of sustenance to the individual's *ka* after that person had died. The food was brought into the tomb-chapel, where it was offered to the deceased at his false door, from which his *ka* would emerge to partake of the items spiritually. To safeguard against the cessation of sustenance within the tomb, the magical power of the written and spoken word was employed, to ensure a continual supply of offerings. This took the form of an offering formula, a genre first known from the fourth dynasty. On the false door inside the tomb-chapel a prayer was carved, requesting that offerings be given to the deceased. If the actual food offerings stopped, the offering formula would magically guarantee an eternal supply of food and enable the deceased to dispense with the assistance of the funerary priests for his continued sustenance.

The offering formula operated on another symbolic level, which related to the role of the king in granting offerings. This aspect of the offering formula had its origins in the daily offerings in the divine temples, where the king ensured the well-being of the country by presenting offerings to the gods. The essential role of the king as intermediary between the gods and mankind was central to the phrasing of the offering formula. Just as the king had struck a bargain with the gods, whereby he offered goods to them in exchange for prosperity and harmony in the land, so would the king intercede on behalf of the dead to ensure them a prosperous afterlife. On a more practical level, the offering formula grew out of the fact that the divine offerings—the actual foods—were distributed to the temple employees after the gods had spiritually satisfied themselves. Egyptologists refer to this practice as "the reversion of offerings." In this way, what the king offered to the gods could subsequently be enjoyed by the population.

Given the importance of the offering formula, it is not surprising to see it on so many objects from ancient Egypt. First appearing on the architrave of the false door, the formula was also used as a descriptive title accompanying funerary scenes. It was later written on offering tables, coffins, and statues, and eventually became the standard inscription engraved on funerary and commemorative stelae.

Composition. A typical offering formula from the Middle Kingdom demonstrates the sentiments expressed in the prayer. "An offering that the king gives (to) Osiris, lord of Busiris, the great god and lord of Abydos, that he [i.e., Osiris] may give invocation offerings consisting of bread and beer, (cuts of) oxen and fowl, alabaster ([calcite] vessels) and clothing, (in fact) all good and pure things on which a god lives, for the *ka*-spirit of N."

The offering formula always begins with the phrase "An offering that the king gives" (*ḥtp-dỉ-nsw* in ancient Egyptian). The word "offering" here was mostly meant to signify food offerings, such as the bread, beer, meat, and poultry mentioned in the prayer, but other boons were also prayed for that would guarantee success in this life and the next. Although the word *ḥtp* is rendered generically as "offering" in this phrase, the basic root meaning of the noun is "satisfaction" or "contentment," which refers to the feelings of the deceased upon the presentation of the offerings. The fact that the king (*nsw*) himself is said to "give" (*dỉ*) the offerings shows not only the symbolic role of the king, but also the fact that the king was regarded as the source of all goods in ancient Egypt. The source of the offerings was always understood to be the "reversion of offerings" as shown by one of the items requested; this was said to be "food-offerings that have gone up before the great god."

The "great god" mentioned in the example is Osiris, the preeminent god of the dead in ancient Egypt. Osiris was the god most often invoked in the offering formulas throughout the length of Egyptian history, although other divinities could be mentioned. In the Old Kingdom, for example, the god Anubis is found in all examples that predate the fifth dynasty, at which time Osiris and Geb first appear. It is noteworthy that the god Amun-Re is first mentioned sporadically in offering formulas of the twelfth dynasty but becomes popular in the eighteenth dynasty, reflecting the historical development of this divinity. Short epithets describing the god's nature and attributes were added after the divine name (". . . Osiris, lord of Busiris, the great god and lord of Abydos").

The next expression in the prayer, "invocation-offerings" (prt-hrw), literally means "the going forth of the voice" and shows the importance of the oral component of the ritual. That the offering formula was meant to be recited out loud by the dedicant is shown by the phrase itself as well as by representations that accompanied the formula. Such scenes occasionally have a caption, "Performing (the ritual of) an Offering-that-the-king-gives," and show the officiant standing with one arm raised in a gesture of invocation, reciting the offering formula aloud.

Offerings of food are the most common requests in prayer, but additional phrases such as "that which heaven gives, the earth creates, and the Nile

brings" can be added before "all things good and pure on which a god lives." Lists of funerary and calendrical festivals, specifying the time at which the offerings were meant to be given, sometimes followed this request. The requests in offering formulas are too numerous to detail here, but these can be grouped into a few categories. One set deals with wishes for a prosperous career during the owner's life. This includes petitions for a long life, especially the traditional wish for a lifetime of 110 years, as well as honor and respect in one's lifetime, participation in various religious festivals, and so forth. A second group consists of requests for a successful transitional period between life and death. The most common of these is a plea for a "fine burial in the necropolis of the Western Desert," but they also include wishes for the performance of the proper rites at the tomb, the reassurance of an unimpeded way to the tomb, and the proper placement of the mummy in the grave. The third group is concerned with wishes for a happy sojourn in the hereafter. These deal with matters as disparate as the preservation of the body, the granting of proper funerary gifts for eternity, and requests for a successful outcome of the final judgment, for freedom of movement in the underworld, and so forth. Wishes for the hereafter are noteworthy, especially when found in inscriptions from the Old Kingdom. These texts contradict an older theory that only royalty could achieve a beatific state in the hereafter during the Old Kingdom, because the only sizable body of funerary literature from that period—the Pyramid Texts—was reserved for the use of kings and queens. In fact, many of the wishes for the hereafter encountered in the offering formulas from the Old Kingdom were repeated in later funerary collections such as the Coffin Texts and the *Book of the Going Forth by Day* (*Book of the Dead*), which date to the Middle and New Kingdoms respectively. The offering formula shows that all people had access to a felicitous hereafter from the beginning of Egyptian history.

Appeal to the Living. The paramount importance given to the oral component of ritual in ancient Egypt, where the spoken word was charged with such potency, is emphasized by a development in the offering formula known as the "Appeal to the Living." If actual offerings were not forthcoming, the deceased could appeal to passersby to recite the formula for him. A typical example of such an appeal reads: "O you who (still) live upon the earth, who shall pass by this tomb of mine, whether going northward or southward, who love life and hate death, and who shall say 'A thousand loaves of bread and jugs of beer for the owner of this tomb,' I shall watch over them in the necropolis, for I am an excellent equipped *akh* spirit."

A further development of the Appeal to the Living is the "Breath of the Mouth" formula. In this formula, the deceased assures the living that nothing more than a spoken prayer is requested of them, and that giving is better than receiving. After the initial phrases of the Appeal to the Living, a typical example of this new formula adds: "Please offer to me from what is in your hands. But if (perchance) there is nothing in your hands, you need only say with your mouths. 'A thousand of bread and beer, of oxen and fowl, of alabaster (calcite vessels) and linen, (in fact) a thousand of all pure things for the owner of this tomb.' It is (after all) only the breath of the mouth. This is not something of which one ever wearies, and is more profitable to the one who does it than to

the one who receives it." Such eloquent pleas on the part of the deceased show the need for continued sustenance and the fear of not receiving it.

Offering List. On the walls of Old Kingdom tomb-chapels, in close connection with the false door, the offering formula is often accompanied by a fuller menu of the items requested by the deceased, the offering list. With its origins in the royal offering lists found in the Pyramid Texts (for example, Spells 23 to 57 and 72 to 171), the full offering list, as it had developed by the time of the fifth dynasty, consisted of more than ninety items, engraved within little rectangles neatly laid out in rows and columns, with each rectangle giving the name and a pictorial representation of the article desired, as well as the stipulated amount to be offered. A typical examples lists "Water libation, (pour) one; Incense, (burn) one; green eyepaint, one (bag); cloth, two (strips)."

Most of the items in the list are food or drink, from the standard bread and beer to cool water and five varieties of wine, and from cuts of meat to various kinds of pastries and cakes. Also mentioned are cultic items, such as pellets of natron and incense and the traditional seven sacred oils. The list usually ends with a series of ritual acts such as "assigning the offering," "presenting cool water," "breaking the red pottery," "purification," "hand-washing," and so forth. This bill of fare is sometimes accompanied by a scene of priests performing the offering ritual before the deceased, who is seated before a table laden with the traditional half-loaves of bread and reaches with one hand for the loaves. Like the offering formula, the offering list was meant to be read out loud, with the recitation enabling the items magically to come alive for the deceased.

Changes in the Offering Formula. Although there is scholarly debate over the interpretation of the offering formula, the fact that the writing of this prayer—in terms of paleographic variations and the actual words used—changed from one period to another suggests that, over time, some innovations occurred in its interpretation. For example, the opening phrases of a typical offering formula from the Old Kingdom read, "An offering that the king gives, (and) an offering that Osiris gives, (namely) invocation-offerings consisting of bread and beer, etc.," with the word "offering" repeated. This parallel construction introduces the king and the god as equal donors of the offering. By the First Intermediate Period, this introductory phrase has been reformulated with the god introduced by a preposition, although this preposition is not always written. The formula now reads, "An offering that the king gives (to) Osiris." This change suggests that the king was still considered the original donor of the offerings, but that he now gave them to the god, who then passed the offerings on to the recipient. To clarify this new interpretation, the theologians of the twelfth dynasty added the phrase "that he may give" before the expression "invocation-offerings." That "he" in the phrase refers to the divinity and not the king is substantiated by the fact that when a goddess is mentioned—for example, Maat or Hathor—the feminine form "she" is used. Thus, the beginning of a traditional offering formula from the Middle Kingdom reads: "An offering that the king gives (to) Osiris, lord of Busiris, that he [i.e., Osiris] may, in turn, give invocation-offerings."

In the system of writing devised by the ancient Egyptians, honorific consideration made it necessary to write the word "king" before the noun "offering"

and the verb "to give" (*nsw-ḥtp-dỉ*) in the writing of the introductory phrase "An offering that the king gives," even though the syntactic relationship among the three words should have demanded that "king" be written last (*ḥtp-dỉ-nsw*). This satisfied a calligraphic rule that divine or royal names, as well as the word for "king" and "god," should precede any other word in the sentence, regardless of their syntactic function. The beginning of the Second Intermediate Period in the late thirteenth dynasty saw a change in the order of these words (although a few earlier examples are known). From the earlier *nsw-ḥtp-dỉ*, the order was now *nsw-dỉ-ḥtp*, a rewriting influenced by a less formal tradition of writing, such as the bureaucracy's. Although a definitive explanation of this calligraphic change eludes us, the actual interpretation of the prayer was not changed, as far as can be ascertained. Other significant changes in the offering formula from the New Kingdom onward were the use of new divinities invoked and a proliferation of wishes.

Such variations in the offering formula are useful to modern scholars as dating criteria, since they help to determine fairly precise dates for many monuments found outside their original context. Other variations in the prayer, such as the addition during the Middle Kingdom of the "Abydos Formula," which requests participation in the great festival of the god Osiris at the city of Abydos, also help to date and localize certain types of objects, such as commemorative stelae.   *Ronald J. Leprohon*

Offering Tables

The bringing of offerings was the focal element of ancient Egyptian tomb and temple cults; thus, the offering table was one of the main features of cult monuments. As yet, Egyptologists have formulated no satisfactory definition of "offering tables." This term may designate any object on which offerings were placed, regardless of its place within a tomb, even though there are obvious functional dissimilarities between cult rooms and burial chambers and their respective equipment. At the same time, although temple offering tables are typologically very similar to those in tombs, they are often called "altars," which is confusing from the standpoint of nomenclature. Strictly speaking, only objects from cult chambers that are equipment for the perpetual cult should be regarded as offering tables; artifacts from burial chambers must be otherwise designated.

In Predynastic times, bread was put on a mat spread in front of the grave; the memory of this most ancient offering furniture survived in the shape of the hieroglyph ḥtp, used to spell the words belonging to the root with the general meaning "to be satiated," which becomes "to be satisfied, peaceful, etc.;" hence ḥtp denotes "offering" (the interpretation in Mostafa 1982, pp. 81–91 is hardly plausible).

All the basic types of offering stones had assumed their forms during the Old Kingdom, although afterward they changed noticeably. They were placed in front of the tomb's false door; inscriptions and representations on them were usually oriented in a manner to make it convenient for the tomb owner, who was meant to face out toward the opening of the tomb, or, as Egyptian texts say, "going forth."

As far back as the Predynastic period, there appeared a type of little one-legged round table (ḥꜣw.t), commonly made of calcite (alabaster) or limestone, or rarely of harder stone. Its leg is often separate from the top, suggesting that it originated from a plate on a stand. The tomb owner is represented at such a gueridon in endless table scenes, from the mid-first dynasty. Judging from these scenes, the ḥꜣw.t was used in life and was included among the tomb furniture as an article of daily necessity. The earliest ḥꜣw.wt belonged to the goods of the burial chamber, and as such they were meant to be used by the deceased; in one case, real food was found on the table, but models were also provided. These ḥꜣw.wt cannot be considered offering tables because they had nothing to do with the funerary cult. However, during the fourth dynasty they were also placed in front of the false doors and for some time even became the most common type of offering stone. Thus, in different contexts, the same object could have different functions, the meaning of the artifact being obscure if isolated from its context.

The tables with thin pedestal legs were too unsubstantial and vulnerable to serve as the main site for cult offerings. Eventually this form was replaced by a round slab without protruding parts. Such round offering tables imitating ḥꜣw.t are not among the most widespread types. Much more common were offering tables with one, two, or several rectangular depressions for libations of water, beer, or wine. These basins could be stepped, with one or several steps. Some of them had a spout to let water spurt out, but these were rare in the Old Kingdom. The original name of this type of offering stone was š, a word that could designate any reservoir, lake, or pond; in the Middle Kingdom it was replaced by the rather indefinite terms mꜥḥꜥ.t and jꜥ.

The most important type of offering table prevailing after the middle of the Old Kingdom imitates in stone the ancient mat for a loaf. In its simplest form, this is a rectangular slab with the ḥtp sign occupying its entire upper surface. The name for these offering tables was also *ḥtp*. Rarer are large *mastaba*-shaped structures, usually monolithic. Because of their considerable size (primarily their height), they could not stand in front of the false doors, and so they were placed to the side (e.g., in the Saqqara chapel of Khentika Ikhekhi). To all appearances, they were used to put out food and equipment before priestly services, and thus they cannot be considered offering tables proper. Four-legged tables (*wdḥw*) are known principally as models found in burial chambers. They were manufactured of copper or later also of bronze, or of wood. They were so light and perishable that no trace of them remains in the chapels. It is interesting that later the hieroglyph depicting *wdḥw* became a common determinative to various words for offering tables (e.g., *ḥtp*).

All the above types are extremely rare in their pure form; much more often, heterogeneous elements are combined in a single object. The upper surface may bear both the *ḥtp* sign with one or several libation basins or basins together with a circle representing the *ḥ3w.t*. Often we also see an ewer in high relief, with its spout turned to the basin, which increases the number of possible combinations. Circular offering stones may also bear the *ḥtp* sign and/or basin and ewer. The top of the *wdḥw* table may be shaped like the *ḥtp*, while the *mastaba*-form tables may have low legs, thus merging with the *wdḥw*. Numerous offering tables are covered with representations of food.

The earliest temple offering tables come from Old Kingdom pyramid complexes (starting with Djoser) and from solar temples of the fifth dynasty. These may be either monolithic or brick, and they differ from the private ones in their monumentality. Another contrasting characteristic is a generalization of form and an austerity in decoration.

At the early stage of development, offering tables may seem to have been regarded solely as receptacles for real food and drink, which would conform well to Old Kingdom realism in all spheres of ideology; however, this statement would be wide of the truth. The presence of pictorial decoration means that besides their functions in the ritual feeding of the deceased, the offering tables had to generate eternally the *ka*-doubles of the depicted food. Moreover, the imitation ewers prove that the offering stones were used also in rituals of purification. Even more telling are the steps in the basins, which show that the latter were associated with sacred lakes that had the same stepped sides (the earliest known example is in the valley temple of Menkaure). Most interesting in this regard is offering table CG 1330, on which each of the three steps of the basin bears a low, mean, and high water mark, referring to the respective seasons. Thus, the basin represents a reservoir filled with the Nile flood. Representations of boats with the tomb owner are seen on the sides of one offering table (Louvre E.25369), while on CG 1353, the same boats are arranged around the basin; in accordance with Egyptian artistic conventions, this means that they are shown navigating on it.

The Middle Kingdom followed some of the old traditions (see, e.g., the *ḥtp*-shaped offering table CG 23008), but serious changes are also obvious. The most significant innovation is the spread of offering tables with numerous basins arranged at different levels and joined by channels. Liquid poured into the upper basin, flowed down to the lower levels, and often drained from the offering stone through a spout. Usually very shallow basins occupy the whole surface of the offering table. At the same time, the number of representations of food increases; they often cover the bottom of the largest flat basin, so that water was poured onto them. Thus, the function of the offering tables shifted from the Old Kingdom practice, and henceforth they were used mainly for libations and purification rites.

Widespread are offering tables with two symmetrical deep basins which are also frequent from Old Kingdom tombs. Middle Kingdom materials explicate the meaning of this form. Often two deep grooves go out to the basins and join before the spout. Sometimes the basins are replaced by representations of two libation vessels that may have water emerging, the spurts crossing as the grooves do. These two givers of water may be identified with the two sources of the Nile, very important in the Egyptian mythological picture of the world.

The New Kingdom did not contribute greatly to the development of offering tables. Its innovations include cartouche-shaped basins, appearing as a result of the proliferation of ritual libation vessels, and pictorial compositions with two vessels flanking the ḥꜣwt table and effusing water both onto the table and into the spout.

Most unusual among New Kingdom offering tables are those from the Amarna temples. For the first time since the solar temples of the fifth dynasty, the cult was transferred from dark sanctuaries to open courts, where it was celebrated on a scale incomparable with anything else in the history of Egypt. The temple courts are packed with rows of hundreds of similar brick offering tables; the most important of them, probably the place where the king served, is distinguished only by its size. Murals depicting the temples of Akhetaten (Tell-el-Amarna) with these countless offering tables are known in the Amarna tombs of Meryre I and Panehsy.

The archaizing tendencies of the Saite Period, which followed the Old Kingdom tradition, affected offering tables as well as other items of tomb and temple furniture. In some cases, this resulted only in a general simplification in appearance, but careful reproductions were made of Old Kingdom forms. Archaization can be observed in some later monuments as well. [See Archaism.]

In the final stages of Egyptian history, the repertory of representations extended, especially as concerns the mythological significance of the offering tables. Of special note are images of the *ba*-drinking water and of the owner receiving water from the goddess of the tree. Also widespread are symbols with generally positive connotations—ʿnḥ hieroglyphs, lotus flowers, and so on. Coexisting with this tendency is one toward simplification in the form and decoration of the offering tables. Basins become optional, and the offering table often becomes only a flat slab with representations of two vessels and food. In Roman times, the exact meaning of the decoration of the offering tables was lost, and although traditional motifs survived, they no longer formed meaningful compositions; then offering tables with purely ornamental decoration were used.

Andrey O. Bolshakov

OPENING OF THE MOUTH. The Opening of the Mouth ceremony is arguably the most important ancient Egyptian ritual. It was performed on cult statues of gods, kings, and private individuals, as well as on the mummies of humans and Apis bulls; it could even be performed on entire temples. The effect of the ritual was to animate its recipient, or, in the case of the dead, to reanimate it. It allowed the mummy, statue, or temple to eat, breathe, see, hear, and otherwise enjoy the provisions offered by the cult. (It was sometimes accompanied by secondary ritual gestures said to open the eyes.) The ritual could be performed with various implements (most commonly a woodcarving adze), which were touched to the lips by a cult functionary.

The Egyptian terms for the ritual are *wpt-r* and *wn-r*, both of which translate literally as "opening of the mouth." The verb *wpi* seems to predominate, although *wn* often occurs in parallel with it. The two verbs are not exact synonyms. The verb *wpi* seems to connote an opening that entails splitting, dividing, or separating; it can be used, for example, to describe the separation of two combatants, the dividing of time, or even an analysis or determination of the truth. The verb *wn* seems to give more emphasis to accessibility and exposure and is used in contexts such as *wn-ḥr*, literally "open the face," but in fact meaning "see or be seen." It has been suggested that the use of the verb *wpi* points to the ritual's origin in statue carving, because the wood-carver's adze is more likely to split than to open up, and because the verb implies greater force. However, other uses of *wpi* are nonviolent, and the adze is normally used not to cleave but to shave wood. *Wpi* is probably favored because the opening of the mouth entails the parting of the lips.

The ritual clearly changed and evolved over the centuries of its use. The principal study on the subject is that of Otto (1960), who published an extensive translation, commentary, and analysis of the New Kingdom version of the ritual. He argues that the Opening of the Mouth was a confused amalgamation of many different rituals, some originally unrelated, and that the cult functionaries who performed it were often entirely ignorant of the origins and meanings of the implements and words they employed.

In the New Kingdom redaction of the ritual, he sees traces of a statue ritual, an offering ritual, an embalming ritual, a burial ritual, a butchering ritual, and a temple ritual. Because of the centrality of the adze in the New Kingdom depictions of the ritual, he argues that the preparation of cult statues was the earliest context in which the ritual was used, and in which it developed.

A different reconstruction of the ritual's origins has been proposed by Roth (1993), based on her analysis of its Old Kingdom version. She argues that it was not until the sixth dynasty that the statue ritual was incorporated into an Opening of the Mouth ceremony that had already developed independently as part of the funerary ritual. Based on the fact that the earliest funerary implements seem to have been the little fingers of the priest (later supplanted by finger-shaped blades of meteoric iron), and on the context in which the earliest redaction of the Opening of the Mouth occurs, she proposes that the funerary ritual was a metaphorical reenactment of the clearing of a baby's mouth at birth, and that the statue ritual may have developed independently from the same metaphor. She concludes that the New Kingdom redaction was an intentionally complex and redundant combination of new forms with the old.

Old Kingdom. The earliest Old Kingdom textual references to the Opening of the Mouth (*pace* Brovarski, *Serapis* 4[1977–1978], pp. 1–2) date to the early fourth dynasty, when references to the statue ritual can be found both in the Palermo stone and in the decoration of the tomb of the royal official Metjen. The Palermo stone tells us that the ritual takes place in the *ḥwt nbw*, the quarter of the goldsmiths (or possibly the similarly written quarry of Hatnub). The Palermo stone and similar historical notations use the formula [*god X*] *mst wpt-r m ḥwt-nbw*, "the fashioning (literally, the birth) and opening of the mouth of (a statue of) god X in the goldsmiths' quarter/Hatnub." Examples of this formula prior to the fourth dynasty use only the form [*god X*] *mst*, "the fashioning of god X," which suggests that the Opening of the Mouths of statues was introduced only in the fourth dynasty. The captions of the Metjen scenes mention that the ritual is performed four times, and a fourfold repetition may also be mentioned in a fragment from the mortuary temple of Sneferu. Metjen's Opening of the Mouth ritual occurs in conjunction with censing and the ritual of transforming the deceased into a *ȝḥ* (or *sȝḥt*). In none of these references to the ritual is the ritual action represented.

The next clear textual mention of the ritual is in the Pyramid Texts of Unas, dating to the end of the fifth dynasty. On the north wall of Unas's burial chamber is inscribed an offering ritual in which two blades of meteoric iron, called the *nṯrwy*, are said to open the mouth (Spell 30b). One blade is described as Lower Egyptian and the other as Upper Egyptian. Van Walsem (1978) argues that the ritual sequence preserved in this part of the offering ritual was already badly confused, and in fact represented a ritual of embalming entirely unrelated to the ritual of the Opening of the Mouth. Opposing this, Roth (1993) observes that this entire ritual sequence mimics the birth and maturation of a child, and that the *nṯrwy* blades represent the pair of little fingers that would have cleared a newborn baby's mouth. In later collections of Pyramid Texts, there are references to Horus's opening the mouth of Osiris with his little fingers (in Spells 1329–1330) and to the sons of Horus opening the mouth with little fingers of meteoric iron (in Spells 1983). Other el-

ements in the sequence following the *nṯrwy* blades are milk jars (one empty, one holding milk), described as the breasts of Isis and Horus, and five cloves of garlic described as teeth. The implement preceding the *nṯrwy* blades was the *psš-kf* knife, which Roth believes was used to cut the umbilical cord.

Actual *nṯrwy* blades are not preserved archaeologically; however, models are occasionally found in "*psš-kf* sets," limestone platters with recesses that hold (usually) the two *nṯrwy* blades, a blunt *psš-kf* knife, two tiny bottles, and four tiny cups. The bottles and cups are half of light-colored stone and half of black stone. These implements represent all the nonperishable requirements for the first row of the offering ritual given in the Pyramid Texts of Unas, and are therefore also known as "Opening of the Mouth sets." The same set of implements is listed together in the inventories of temple equipment found at the mortuary temple of Neferirkare at Abusir.

This ritual may be older than its earliest surviving appearance, at the end of the fifth dynasty. Elements of the same sequence of implements and offerings listed in the Pyramid Texts occur in royal offering lists as early as the reign of Sahure, the second king of the fifth dynasty. The *psš-kf* knife is attested archaeologically even earlier; it was buried in prehistoric tombs as early as the Naqada I period. Since this knife is otherwise known only in connection with the Opening of the Mouth ritual, its presence suggests that some form of the ritual dates back to prehistoric times.

Only in the sixth dynasty was a second new sequence added to the beginning of the Pyramid Text ritual (Spells 11–15). These new spells describe the Opening of the Mouth using the foreleg of a bull and an iron woodworking adze, both of which can be related to the constellation Ursa Major. These spells are clearly related to the statue ritual, since the foreleg is said to be offered four times. In addition to the little fingers and the little fingers of meteoric iron, the other implements mentioned in these later Pyramid Texts include the *dw3-wr*, probably a chisel (Spell 1329c), and the *sš3*, a mysterious implement not attested elsewhere (Spell 1329b). The rite with the *dw3-wr* was again said to occur in the *ḥwt-nbw*, so it is clearly part of the statue ritual. That these are later additions to the mortuary ritual can also be demonstrated by the fact that no adzes or chisels seem to be mentioned in the inventories of temple equipment from the mortuary temple of Neferirkare at Abusir.

Middle Kingdom. The implements used in both the original and the later redactions of the Opening of the Mouth ritual in the Pyramid Texts continue to appear in private tombs of the Middle Kingdom, in both offering lists and friezes of objects. A rather different version of the ritual also appears in the Coffin Texts (*CT I, 65*), in which Horus and Ptah open the mouth of the deceased, Ptah and Thoth do the ritual of transfiguration, and Thoth replaces the heart in the body "so that you remember what you have forgotten, and can eat bread as you desire." The importance of Ptah and Thoth points to new developments, since neither is mentioned in earlier versions; however, there is little further evidence for the development of the ritual during the Middle Kingdom period.

New Kingdom. The New Kingdom Opening of the Mouth ritual shows two different traditions. The tradition of the Coffin Text spell has developed into chapter 23 of the *Book of Going Forth by Day* (the *Book of the Dead*). In this chapter, the mouth is opened by Ptah and the local god of the deceased, while Thoth

stands by, equipped with magic. The bonds that had been obstructing the mouth and preventing it from functioning are associated with the god Seth. The mouth is also said to be opened by the god Shu with a harpoon of iron, and the deceased is identified with the goddess Sakhmet and the constellation Orion. The conclusion of the spell invokes the entire Ennead of gods to protect the deceased from any negative spell.

This tradition is clearly different from the conception of the Opening of the Mouth developed in the Pyramid Texts ritual and the related offering list sequence. Not only are different gods involved (Ptah is mentioned in only three spells altogether in the Pyramid Texts, none of them connected with opening the mouth); in addition, the protective purpose seems entirely different. The identification of Seth with the bonds restricting the mouth is in direct contradiction to Pyramid Texts Spell 14, in which the iron of the adze that opens the mouth is said to have come forth from Seth. The second New Kingdom version of the Opening of the Mouth is, however, clearly descended from the Old Kingdom version. The adze, the *dw3-wr*, the fingers, and the *psš-kf* are all included, together with several other elements.

Otto (1960) distinguishes seventy-five scenes in the New Kingdom version of the ritual. In most cases the ritual is given a title, normally "the Performance of the Opening of the Mouth for the Statue in the *Ḥwt-nbw.*" In the first scene, the mummy is placed on the sand, naked, with his face to the south, his clothes (wrappings?) behind him. In scenes 2 through 7, he is purified with poured libations, incense, and natron. These scenes are reminiscent of the first spells in the earliest Pyramid Text sequence (Spells 16–29). The similarities include not only the offerings but also the repetition of purification spells four times—once for each of four gods (Horus, Seth, Thoth, and Dewen-ʿanwy), each of whom represents one of the cardinal directions.

Scenes 8 through 22 are the scenes that are most clearly associated with the statue ritual, involving as they do craftsmen as well as priests. In scene 8, the lectorpriest and the *imy-ḫnt*-priests go to the workshop (*is*); in scene 9 they wake the *stm*-priest, who is sleeping there; and in scene 10 they converse with him about a dream or vision he has had regarding the statue. The *stm*-priest dresses (scene 11) and instructs the craftsmen about the statue (scene 12), with special instructions for the specialized workers (scene 13). In scene 14, however, the mouth of the statue is opened with the little fingers by the *stm* priest, who identifies himself as Horus. This use of the fingers, rather than the more usual wood carving tool, may be intended to emphasize the humanity of the statue. In scene 15 the workers are instructed to continue their work, while in scene 16 the priest denies Seth's ability to whiten the head of the statue. Scenes 17 and 18 are interpreted by Otto as the completion and delivery of the statue. The texts make reference to Horus's search for his father. In scenes 19 through 21, the apparel of the *stm* priest is augmented, and scene 22 is a procession of priests to the next group of rituals.

Scenes 23 through 27 involve the butchering of a bull and the presentation of its heart and foreleg, followed by Opening of the Mouth rituals using other implements—in scene 26, the *ntrty*, here pictured as an adze. In scene 27, another adze called the *wr-ḥkꜣw* ("great of magic") opens the eyes, and

the statue is delivered to the *iry-pʿt* in scene 28. Scenes 29 and 30 are repetitions of scenes 17 and 16 from the statue ritual, with some variations in the latter.

Scene 31 introduces the "son whom he loves," a priest who will carry out the next series of mouth-opening rituals. This series again includes several elements of the Old Kingdom sequence, interspersed with newer implements. In scene 32 the "son whom he loves" opens the mouth with the ebony *mḏdft*-tool and a finger of gold, while in scene 33 the little finger is again used. In scene 34 the *nms* is offered in a jar, and in scenes 35 and 36 the four *ʿbt* are offered; neither of these offerings has been identified. Scene 37 shows the offering of the *pssḳf*, with the same accompanying speech that was used in the Pyramid Texts. In scene 38 grapes are offered, and in scene 39, an ostrich feather. Scene 39 is derived from Pyramid Texts Spell 32b, where an empty *mnsꜣ* jar is offered; the feather used to write *šw*, "empty," has mistakenly been read as a separate offering. Scene 40 is a repetition of scenes 20/21 and scene 36. In scene 41 a basin of water is offered, and in scene 42 the "son whom he loves" departs, marking the end of the sequence.

Scenes 43, 44, and 45 repeat the butchering of a bull and the offering of its heart and foreleg. In scene 45, the mouth is opened with a chisel, and in scene 46, incense is burnt. In scenes 48 through 54, a sequence of cloth strips and clothing is presented (perhaps derived from the cloth offerings in Pyramid Texts Spells 60–61 and 81). Scene 55 depicts the anointing of the statue, in some examples with the seven sacred oils known from the Old Kingdom ritual (Spells 72–78), where they appear immediately after the "B sequence." As in the Pyramid Texts (Spells 79–80), the anointing is directly followed by the offering of green and black eye paint in scene 56. Scene 57 shows the presentation of scepters (perhaps a distillation of the weapons and scepters presented in Pyramid Texts Spells 57–59 and 62–71), while scenes 58 through 61 describe censing the statue in various ways.

Scene 62 begins a sequence that may have had its origin in temple rituals. It depicts an act of homage with *nmst* jars. It is followed by libation (scene 63) and censing (scene 64). Scenes 65–72 deal with the preparation and presentation of the food offering, interspersed with censing and libation. The *ḥtp-dì-nswt* offering formula is recited and the footprints of the priests are wiped away in scene 70. After an offering of incense to Re-Harakhti (scene 71), the offering concludes (scene 72).

The last three scenes deal with the final placement of the statue or the mummy, and the conclusion of the ceremony. While it is clear that many elements have been added to the Old Kingdom version of the ritual as given in the Pyramid Texts of Unas and later kings, many of the basic elements remain, in an order surprisingly close to the original sequence.

Late Period. The Late Period redactions of the Opening of the Mouth ritual continue the traditions of the earlier periods. A group of mortuary rituals in this tradition from as late as the first century CE are known (Smith 1993). These late rituals retain many elements of the New Kingdom ritual, including the variety of officiants. The later texts, however, are specifically said to allow the dead person to breathe, and as such they seem to have taken on some of the characteristics of the "letters of breathing" known from this period. In addition to being performed as part of the funeral, it is possible that, like the letters of breathing,

they were placed in the tomb for the use of the deceased. This development illustrates again the tendency of this ritual to incorporate new elements with the passage of time.

Peculiar to this period is the depiction of the ritual in temple dedication ceremonies. (The rituals may have been performed on temples from a much earlier period, of course.) The dedication ceremonies at the Ptolemaic temple of Edfu seem to combine elements of the tradition from the Coffin Texts and the *Book of Going Forth by Day* with the separate New Kingdom ritual derived from the Pyramid Texts. As summarized by Blackman (1946), the ritual contains many elements of the New Kingdom mortuary rite—for example, the use of multiple tools (an adze, a chisel, and a finger of gold) and the butchering of offerings. Yet several of the acts are said to be performed by Ptah, and Thoth is also involved; such an involvement of the gods is more typical of the Coffin Texts tradition. Like the mortuary tradition, the temple ritual would have been a complex series of actions selected from several different traditions.

Ann Macy Roth

ORACLES. To distinguish them from individual magical practices, such as oneiromancy or recourse to seers, the Egyptian consultation of oracles may be described as requesting a deity to answer some practical question through the agency of its public image. The evidence for such oracles before the Ptolemaic period comprises four sources: the many oracular decrees, either engraved on the outer walls of temples or delivered on papyrus to private persons to use as amulets; references to particular oracular processes found in administrative or private records; a few original petitions on papyrus or ostraca laid before the god;

and statues and reliefs clearly associated with oracles.

Origins and Development. A few three-dimensional artifacts have been thought to constitute archeological evidence of early oracles, but, for lack of any explicit text that supports this opinion, it is impossible to decide whether the "rocking" falcon of Predynastic date in the Brooklyn Museum was a cult statue of Horus capable of delivering oracles by nodding, or a simple ex-voto.

Actual documents concerning oracles do not predate the New Kingdom, and most come from the Ramessid or Third Intermediate Period. Recently, however, bi3yt (strictly speaking, "omen"), translated as "oracle," has been documented in the king's address engraved in the tombs of some early eighteenth dynasty viziers, in a provision pertaining to disputes about field boundaries and forbidding the settlement of such problems through "any bi3t." The date of composition of this text is much debated, however. According to van den Boorn, it is not earlier than the second part of Ahmose's reign; but the more traditional late Middle Kingdom date may be better, since titles attested before the seventeenth dynasty and already out of use at the very beginning of the eighteenth occur in it (BiOr, 48, 5/6, 821–831).

Such an early date is not surprising, since Egyptian oracles probably developed from the use of processional statues during the yearly festivals. Before Amenhotpe I, there is no figure of the dummy bark of Amun and its booth enclosing the oracular image of the god of Karnak, but the existence of this most often reproduced of all oracular statues can easily be traced much earlier through appearances of its name in texts. In New Kingdom dedications of temples visited by processions as well as in oracular documents, the idiom referring to the portable statues that were to utter public oracular sentences was "this august god." Obviously a colloquial expression, this phrase is to be distinguished from "image," the term used for the hidden cult statues. The processional Amun of Karnak, carried in his bark during the Opet and Valley festivals, was the most prominent of all such oracular gods from the Theban area. "Lord of Gods" (Nb-ntrw) his epithet in documents, stresses his supremacy over his many lesser oracular gods of the region, such as those listed in Papyrus BM 10335 dating from the reign of Ramesses IV ("Amun of Pe Khenty," "Amun of Te Shenyt," "Amun of Bukenen"). The term "Lord of Gods" for a portable image is encountered as early as the beginning of the twelfth dynasty (Stela Louvre C 200, graffito from Deir el-Bahri), suggesting that processions around Thebes were a well-established practice by then. This would explain the provision not much later in the *Duties of the Vizier* to prevent people from interrogating the portable gods about such important matters as field boundaries.

Nonetheless, we have to wait until the time of Thutmose III for details about the oracular process. In a biographical inscription engraved at Karnak, the king tells how he was chosen as the next pharaoh. During the morning, the god in his bark "perambulated" the northern hypostyle hall and, before the eyes of the gathered courtiers, eventually "settled" in front of the young prince. Thutmose III prostrated himself on the ground, and the god led him to the place reserved for the king (a procedure that was repeated by the Nb-ntrw to "enthrone" Ramesses IV some 330 years later, according to Papyrus Turin 1882). Other instances of "advice" asked by pharaohs of the "Lord of Gods" are reported during the eighteenth dynasty. To know the best route to Punt, Queen Hatshepsut herself questioned the Nb-ntnw This oracle was not sought during a procession, when the statue could move as a way to answer questions; rather, she "heard" the divine "order" "at the Lord of Gods' stairway"—a reference to his bark shrine at Karnak, where the bark rested on its altar. This may hint at a speaking oracle, or at a revelation obtained while sleeping inside this "Great Seat."

During the Ramessid Period, evidence about oracles grows more abundant. Many ostraca and papyri have been found at Deir el-Medina, where the development of the judicial powers of oracles came as a response to the collapse of the pharaonic court system (a fact emphasized by the literary topic of Amun "the vizier of the feeble," met from Merenptah on). Thus, we have information about lesser oracles of the Theban area, particularly those involving the processional statues of the deified Amenhotpe I, worshipped by the workmen of the necropolis. Through many short and often elliptical questions on ostraca found in the garbage pit near their village, we get a glimpse of what the workmen used to ask their gods: whether they would retrieve something lost or stolen; whether the object was in the hands of a neighbor; whether the questioner would be promoted. All these questions could be answered by nodding. Ramessid oracles on papyrus or stelae gives a more accurate picture of the practical way the "god" transmitted his advice to the gathered people.

Oracular Proceedings. Oracles could be uttered by any processional image. This is the reason that so many oracular gods are attested, not only at Thebes but all through the country: Horus of the Camp and Horus-khau at el-Hiba, Sutekh at Dakhla, Isis at Coptos, the de-ified Ahmose at Abydos, and others. The statues were either hidden in a tabernacle, fastened to a portable bark or mounted directly on poles, or they were unveiled and visible to the public. Thus, the statue of the deified Amenhotpe I of the west bank sat in an open palanquin. The Lord of Gods, however, always remained inside the booth of his bark, except in an oracle scene dating from 651 BCE that represents him in a portable shrine (Papyrus Brooklyn 47–218–3). Oracles took place during a public appearance of the statue carried on its priests' shoulders. The "putting down" of the tabernacle on its "Great Seat" (a station built on the processional way or a temple bark shrine, such as the granite sanctuary of Karnak) signified the end of the oracular session: from that point on, the god could no longer be approached by anyone except his priests (Papyrus Nevill, late twentieth dynasty).

Barks, shrines, or palanquins were carried around by w'b-priests, as opposed to the higher-ranking "prophets," who were the only ones admitted into the presence of the nonremovable cult statues. Of course, the Egyptians were aware that the porters, especially those who led the march, could interfere in the oracular process. That is probably why the "w'b of the front (of the bark)" and "procession master" of the Lord of Gods Pameshemu was forbidden to introduce his own petition during the oracles held under Pinudjem II to punish the scribes of the temple found guilty of embezzlement (inscription of the steward of Amun Thutmose, near the tenth pylon of Karnak).

In theory, to be successful, the oracular process had to be carried out without any influence along the route. Therefore, the path had to be carefully prepared and protected, so as to be pure. Some of the precautions include the arrangement of processional sphinx-lined avenues to connect Karnak and Luxor; the use, during the twenty-first dynasty, of a "soil of silver" (owing to its color, the purest existing material), where oracles of the Lord-of-Gods could be held safely; fan-bearers and censer-bearers all around the tabernacle to ward off flies; and the fixing of the time of the session (during the "morning," whenever stated). In all likelihood, the oracular process itself, or at least the procession during which it took place, began with an Opening of the Mouth rite carried out on the god as well as on the prow and stern figureheads of his bark, since "prophets" garbed in the leopardskin of the funerary priest associated with this ritual are always figured walking alongside the tabernacle.

Perambulating and nodding. Oracles could identify an evildoer as well as an individual worthy of appointment to an office (not just kingship). The bark was carried around before the likely persons; then it "stopped" supposedly of its own accord, in front of the appropriate person. In this way, a "chief of *mdзy*-policemen" was appointed by the bark of Isis at Abydos under Ramesses II (Stela Oxford 1894/106), and the evil scribes of Amun were identified under Pinudjem II. When it was impossible to summon all the candidates, their names could be read aloud, and the "god" likewise "stopped" at one of them. Such were the cases of the cultivator Pethauemdiamun, who stole garments (Papyrus BM 10335), or of the official Nesamun, who was promoted to the rank of "scribe of the storehouse" instead of his father (Karnak, relief dating from Ramesses XI). Usually, however, the god was only asked an oral question by the "prophet" who led the session. The god answered by "nodding" in approval or by "walking backward" as a way to

say no (tomb of Amenmose, the "first prophet" of Amenhotpe of the Forecourt under Ramesses II; Ostraca Petrie 21, Year 27 of Ramesses III; etc.).

Drawing from a pair of petitions. Sometimes, a set of two documents, one with a statement and the other with its contrary, was put before the portable statue, and the god "took" one of them. That *tзy* meant in practice some process of drawing lots is clear in Ostr. Gardiner 103 (Ramesses III's reign). According to this report of a dispute over inheritance, the contradictory documents put before the deified Amenhotpe I were "cast" twice. The most complete account of this procedure is found in the aforementioned inscription of Thutmose. These documents were also put before the god twice, and the Lord of Gods "took" twice the one that said, "one says that there is nothing to investigate against Thutmose," discarding that which said, "one says that there is something to investigate against Thutmose."

Only one original pair of documents has survived: Papyrus Boston a.b, a petition relating to a dispute over a cow dating from the early twenty-first dynasty; it is addressed to Horus of the Camp, the god of el-Hiba. But we possess examples of the documents "taken" by the god written in Demotic, Greek, or Coptic from Oxyrhynchus, Tebtunis, and Antinoe. These examples are good evidence that the oracular process by drawing of lots continued to be used well into the Greco-Roman and even Islamic Period, in spite of the disappearance of the old gods.

Speaking statues and other procedures. In many cases, however, the mechanical process employed to obtain oracular utterances remains obscure. All the amuletic decrees on papyrus protecting the carrier against a long list of diseases and dangers, delivered during the twenty-first to twenty-third dynasties, begin with the word "said" written in a darker ink before the name of the oracular god. Such an opening, also met in the Stela of Apanage from the twenty-second dynasty, does not help us to understand how these oracles were pronounced. It is likely that in addition to the moving of the statue or the drawing of lots used during the New Kingdom, other methods developed until the Late period, and that these involved some device to let people hear the voice of the god. Such speaking oracles took place in a special room, before a statue of the god or in front of a relief representing his bark facing and resting on a pedestal (Coptite chapel of Cleopatra VII). At Kom el-Wist in the Delta, a bronze tube concealed in the pedestal of a Ptolemaic statue of a bull and connected to a small chamber in which a priest could be hidden was discovered in 1941. It is recorded that Hatshepsut was told the route to Punt, and Alexander the Great was spoken to by Zeus-Ammon when alone in the temple of Siwah. This development may explain Herodotus's statement (400 BCE) that the way of issuing oracles varied from temple to temple.

Theban Theocracy and *Nb-ntrw*. Most of the Theban oracular decrees from Ramesses VI onward were issued by "this august god Lord of Gods Amun-Re," often also referred to as "the great god first to come into existence," an epithet stressing the demiurgic powers originally held by the *Nb-ntrw*, which was later taken over by lesser processional images. Many of these texts, sometimes accompanied by reliefs of the oracular setting, are engraved along the processional route of the bark, leading from the tenth pylon to the granite sanctuary, where the *Nb-ntrw* "who pronounces oracles" and "announces what comes before it exists" (Taharka's hymn

to the Lord of Gods), was stored between festivals. It is likely that this area also held the "soil of silver" of Karnak mentioned by the inscriptions of Henttawy and Thutmose as the place of the "god's approach." Such "beautiful feasts(s) of the *ph-ntr*" were sophisticated forms of oracular sessions, which could be held alongside the yearly festivals. They often included other processional images—Mut, Khons-Neferhotpe, Mentu-Re, or Thoth—with the Lord of Gods as a way of strengthening his decisions. As an image that issued decrees about such important matters as the endowment of high-ranking persons and shrines or the recall of exiles from the oases, the *Nb-ntrw* became a powerful political weapon through which his clergy ruled Upper Egypt; there are decrees concerning the properties of Henttawy, Maatkare, and the chief of Matribes Nimlot, an inscription reporting the acquittal of the steward Thutmose, and a stela from Akoris recording a donation to a temple, the socalled Stele de l'apanage and the Stele du Bannissement.

This fact perhaps explains the steady decrease in the power of the Lord of Gods after the twenty-first dynasty, when more efficient kings put an end to the independence of the Theban clergy. But in their distant capitals, the Napatan and Meroitic priests went on pulling the strings of their puppet-pharaohs through similar devices (cf. Coronation Stela of Aspelta), until their ruthless suppression by the skeptic Ergamenes around 200 BCE.   *Jean-Marie Kruchten*

OSIRIS. In origin a royal mortuary god, Osiris exemplified a cult that was begun in a fairly restricted context, but one which achieved wide popularity and a notable expansion of functions. The exclusive link with royalty was abandoned just prior to the Middle King-the flail. Elsewhere, the White Crown often became the *atef*-crown through the addition of feathers, and there were various complex versions of it. The preponderance of the White Crown in the earlier versions of Osiris suggests an Upper Egyptian origin for the god. As for the crook and the flail, they both raise questions of political and sociological import. The crook suggests a shepherd god, and Wolfgang Helck (1962) has argued that the Syrian Adonis provides the closest contemporary analogy. Marked differences existed, however, in both myths and cults; and, in fact, the concept of a sovereign god as shepherd of his people was shared by other religious ideologies of the ancient Near East, expressed both in art and literature. The function and origin of the flail are more enigmatic. Perhaps it is a fly-whisk or a shepherd's whip. It is shown sometimes with other deities, such as Min. Both flail and crook, however, appear with the god Andjety of the ninth Lower Egyptian nome, which suggests a possible source.

The constant feature of the figure of Osiris was its mummified form, with a close linkage of the legs. The funerary import was thus stressed. Whereas the Old Kingdom, by and large, has yielded no iconographic evidence, a relief on a block from the pyramid temple of the king Djedkare Izezi of the fifth dynasty presents a figure bearing the name of Osiris; it belongs to a row of divine figures, today partly damaged, and it has been dated to the closing years of that dynasty (c.2405 BCE). The lower part of the Osiris figure is missing, but the left arm hangs freely, suggesting that here the figure was not mummiform. Absent also are the flail and the crook, although the missing right arm might be grasping something; on the head is a long wig. Since the form is that of a standing anthropomorphic figure, with none of the

Bronze statuette of Osiris, from the Ptolemaic period. (Pennsylvania Museum, Philadelphia. Neg. #S8-31580)

dom; the funerary aspect, however, always persisted, and Osiris was always shown in mummy wrappings. While the funerary aspect was primarily based on the experience of death, it enabled believers, through the force of myth and ritual, to accept the conviction that life after death was warranted.

Form and Name. The representation of Osiris in its developed form shows him wearing the White Crown of Upper Egypt and carrying the crook and distinctive Osirian attributes, discussion and debate about it have emerged (see Griffiths 1980; Lorton 1985; and Eaton-Krauss 1987). Rival gods at that time were Anubis, Khentyamentiu, and Wepwawet, and all three had jackal forms; that Osiris, too, was originally imagined as a jackal has been suggested by words in the pyramid of Neferkare, that say of the dead king, "thy face is [that of] a jackal, like Osiris." Osiris' ensuing human form clearly became a vital feature of his appeal, and his identity with the dead king contributed to his popularity.

The god's name *Wsir* (in Coptic, *Oycipe* or *Oycipi*) was written at first with the sign for a throne, followed by the sign for an eye; later the order was inverted. Among the many meanings suggested is one cognate with *Ashur*, implying a Syrian origin; but also "he who takes his seat or throne;" "she or that which has sovereign power and is creative;" "the place of creation;" "seat of the Eye," with the Eye explained as the Sun; "the seat that creates;" and "the Mighty One," deriving from *usr* ("mighty"). Since the throne sign occurs also with the deity Isis, Wolfhart Westendorf tried to relate the two names, but he ended by positing an originally female Osiris, although the deity's male potency was so often emphasized. No consensus has been reached on the basic and original meaning of the name. Perhaps we must be content with the popular etymology offered in the Pyramid Texts, 2054 (PN): "The king makes his seat like Osiris;" there, elements of the name were deployed but without a valid order (Erman 1909).

Myth and Kingship. Although the Pyramid Texts do not provide a consecutive account of the Osiris myth, they abundantly supply in scattered allusions the principal details about his fate and especially about his relationship to the

deceased pharaoh. He was presented as the brother and husband of Isis and as a member of the Great Ennead of Heliopolis; and in that group, Geb and Nut were named (clearly as parents) before Osiris, Isis, Seth, and Nephthys. Osiris' brother Seth was said to have caused his death and yet there is a lack of explicit statements about the death of Osiris. Not that the death of gods was unmentionable to the Egyptian mind—even the sun god Re was depicted as suffering old age and death.

In the case of Osiris, however, despite the absence of a firm dictum that he died, a cluster of details have allowed that conclusion to be held. Above all, he was constantly represented as mummified. He was smitten by his brother Seth in a place called Nedyet or Gehestey. With that account should perhaps be connected the tradition, found in the Memphite Theology (late eighth century BCE) and elsewhere, that Osiris was drowned—a tradition that resulted in the ancient Egyptian idea that being drowned in the Nile River was a blessed death. Yet doubt has been cast on the validity of that tradition in an important study by Pascal Vernus (1991), in which he examines numerous allusions to the god's death; he concludes that the myth represents Osiris as being dead when he was hurled into the water, that it never tells of his being drowned.

In the Memphite Theology, Horus commanded Isis and Nephthys to grasp Osiris so that they might protect him from the action of *mhit*. They had been shocked when they saw him, but then they brought him to land, and the sequel implied a glorious burial in Memphis. In Egyptian, the verb *mhi* can mean "drown," but also "swim" or "drift, float," and Vernus (1991) opted for the last meaning in that and other contexts, including three references in the Pyramid Texts to "the place where you (Osiris-King) were drowned." There, "the place where you have drifted [or floated]" is not convincing, since a corpse that is drifting in the river can scarcely be attached long to a defined place. It should be added that the idea of an Osirian apotheosis by drowning has been well attested for the New Kingdom and later, when special honors in burial were accorded to the drowned.

In the earliest evidence, Osiris was given the role of sovereign ruler of the realm of the dead, and the deceased pharaoh was equated with him. Utterance 219 is the oldest Osiris litany in the Pyramid Texts, and it affirms that "he [Osiris] lives, this king lives; he [Osiris] is not dead, this king is not dead." That claim was made to Atum, then to several other deities: an analogy between Osiris and the dead king was being urged, and the claim that the king was still alive was based on the continued life of Osiris.

The argument might be made that there is a suggestion of Osiris himself being in origin a king who had died, as was the view of Plutarch and of a few modern scholars. The Turin Canon and Manetho's dynasties name several gods, with Osiris among them, as early rulers of Egypt. Yet no one has suggested that those gods—such as Re, Geb, and Horus—were originally human kings; that would imply a form of Euhemerism, with its belief that all deities were at first outstanding human beings. In the case of Osiris, it was his identification with the deceased pharaoh that furthered the idea of his historical origin as a real king. Sometimes it was by analogy (as in the example quoted above) that this equating was promoted; or a categorical claim was made, as in the Pyramid Texts (1657 a MN) "this king is Osiris." Far more often, the juxtaposition of the names occurs, as in Osiris-Unas, which means, in effect, "Unas who has now become Osiris." In the Coffin Texts, where the exclusive Osirian royal identity was relaxed, the deceased's *ba* is said to be the *ba* of Osiris; but the method of simple juxtaposition was regularly followed.

From the end of the fifth dynasty, references to Osiris occurred in private tombs, mostly in offering formulas (Begelsbacher-Fischer 1981, pp. 124–125), but with no suggestion of a special relationship to the god. A much wider area was covered by the Coffin Texts, when the "democratization of royal prerogatives" meant a more varied choice of religious themes (Silverman 1989, p. 36). Yet a steady increase in the range and appeal of Osiris was plainly attested; one reason for that was the stability of his concern with death and its sequel—his *Sitz im Tod*, if one can thus describe it. The living Horus-King, in spite of his divine theological import, has been shown of late to be subject, in facets of Egyptian literature, to the foibles of humanity. In contrast, the dead Osiris-King has escaped all that, mainly because he is rooted in the experience of death; and the same inviolate sanctity attends his identity with the multitude of non-royal believers.

Cult Centers and Ideology. Some early sources connect Osiris with the towns of Heliopolis and Busiris, both in Lower Egypt; but others connect him with Upper Egypt, especially with the town of Abydos and its nome (province), where kings of the first two dynasties were buried. Moreover, Osiris often wore the crown of Upper Egypt. Some texts link the god with both Busiris and Abydos, and David Lorton has suggested that a court at Memphis might well have planned the double emphasis, with a pan-Egyptian political purpose.

The early ritual of royal burial points to Osiris as the central ideological figure.

Mummification was the basic rite, and the deity Anubis, guide to the underworld, was considered the embalmer who rendered that service to the deceased king, just as he did to Osiris. The rites of mourning and of "Opening the Mouth" led to the idea of the mummy being endowed with renewed life. A concomitant idea was the defeat of the deity Seth, Osiris' brother and the perpetrator of his death. That was prominent in the Osirian rites portrayed in the Stela of Ikhernöfret, from the twelfth dynasty: there, Sethian enemies were said to attack the *Nšmt*-bark of Osiris, but they were repulsed, after which Osiris was glorified in Abydos.

The burial rites, including mummification, had an earlier origin than did Osiris; and probably the deity Anubis should be credited as the divine originator of the process of embalming. Perhaps Khentamentiu, the "first of the Westerners" and another jackal god at Abydos, whose identity was merged into that of Osiris, was involved. The revivified corpse, which received offerings, became the basis of belief in an afterlife; and Osiris, as the initial paradigm, received the epithet *Wn-nfr* (Gr., *Onnophris*), "He Who Is Permanently Benign and Youthful."

As the ruler of the realm of the dead, Osiris was physically associated with the earth, which embraces the dead. Yet his chthonic aspect never excluded him from generous access to the celestial world, of which the sun god Re was the chief deity. In that astral world, Osiris was especially associated with the circumpolar stars, with the constellation of Orion and with the brightest star in the sky, Sirius. During the Ramessid era, he was shown as a composite figure, united with the sun god Re, as in the tomb of Nefertiri; this striking figure was unusual, and it did not affect the figure of the god as it was regularly shown throughout most of the pharaonic era and beyond (with the exception of part of the Amarna age). Akhenaten, when king, clearly rejected Osirian myth and doctrine, promoting a form of monotheism based on Aten.

Although the mortuary role of Osiris could arouse fear and dread, his benign promise of renewed life came to be expressed through the appeal of new life, in the cycle of nature's fertility, especially with water and vegetation. Initially it was the water used in the libations for the dead, but through links with Orion, Sirius, and the new year, Osiris was associated with the Nile and its annual inundation. He was also equated with Neper, the prehistoric harvest god, and he was credited with the creation of wheat and barley. In association with this were the funerary practices of the Grain-Osiris and Osiris-Bed; for the Festival of Khoiak, a mold in the form of Osiris was filled with sprouting plants.

In the Greco-Roman era, the human appeal of the Osiris cult—which was spread to other countries—achieved emotional intensity; this direction is especially evident in the works of the ancient writers Diodorus, Plutarch, and Apuleius, who bear witness, also, to the force of Greek religion, particularly from the deities Demeter and Dionysus, and from the Eleusinian Mysteries. Isis then assumed a more prominent role and, to some extent, Osiris was replaced by the god Sarapis, also of Egyptian origin, in a combined form of Osiris and Apis. The basic elements of the myth and cult remained Egyptian.

An idea that was wrongly inferred from some of the classical and other sources was that parts of the body of Osiris were worshipped as relics in various regions. Yet the true Egyptian belief was that parts of his body were explicitly equated with the nomes of Egypt, often in relation to their standards and symbols, so that Osiris was thus identified with the whole of Egypt, but without specific cults.

The rule of Osiris over the realm of the dead led to his most important role—that of supreme arbiter in the judgment of the dead. The general concept of such a judgment appeared in the early Old Kingdom sources, but in the New Kingdom it was elaborately developed, both textually and pictorially, the *locus classicus* being Spell 125 of the *Book of Going Forth by Day* (*Book of the Dead*). There, the weighing of the heart before Osiris as the presiding judge depicts many supporting divine functionaries; among them is Thoth as "Recorder," Anubis as "Lord of the Balance," aided by Horus, and the figure of the goddess Maat, who is conceptually dominant. Magic doubtless entered into the popular idea of such a scene; a copy of the *Book of Going Forth by Day* pushed into a tomb provided all the questions and the ready-made answers (but the moral criteria expressed in the "Declarations of Innocence" point to a deep concern with humanity's final destiny). In the Roman era, an urge to intensify the deceased's identity with Osiris is seen in representations of the deceased in the form of the god, with private persons accoutred with his royal crown. The judgment before Osiris had a strong impact on other religions, particularly on the eschatology of Judaism and then Christianity—with the development of Judgment Day and the Last Judgment.

Punishments and rewards were conspicuous elements in the Egyptian doctrine, and the punishments were most often portrayed in iconography. In the Ptolemaic era, at Alexandria, Osiris was sometimes identified with Aion, the snake-clad god of time, who was much honored in Mithraism. Aion was seen as a peaceful deity, beyond the force of change; so was Osiris, "Lord of Eternity," for the most part, but it has been shown by Lázlo' Kákosy (1977) that Osiris displayed an aggressive and warlike aspect in the mythic matter relating to his feud with Seth.

J. Gwyn Griffiths

P

PARADISE. In Western culture the word "paradise" usually refers to a location: first, the Garden of Eden, where the first human beings lived in perfect harmony with their maker and with the rest of his creation, then the abode of the blessed dead where this primeval harmony has been restored and where they live forever in bliss. Comparably well-defined and more or less permanent locations did not exist in ancient Egyptian religion. This does not mean, however, that the concept of an ideal world at the beginning of time did not exist. The opening lines of the *Book of the Heavenly Cow* describe it as follows: "Once upon a time it happened that Re, the god who created himself, arose after he had held the kingship and men and gods were still united. Then mankind began to plan a rebellion against Re, for His Majesty had become old." Other texts also allude to this primeval world, the "era of Re" (*rk Rˁ*) or the "era of the god" (*rk nṯr*), and king lists often begin with a dynasty of gods, headed by either Re or Ptah, which comes before the dynasties of the human pharaohs. During this era gods and humans lived together in an undivided world, and it was humankind's fault that this harmonious situation came to an end. According to the version of the myth recorded in the *Book of the Heavenly Cow*, Re initially decided to annihilate all human beings, but after a great many of them had been killed, he

eventually took pity on them; instead of continuing the massacre, he withdrew to the back of the Heavenly Cow and retired from his duties, leaving the day-to-day running of affairs to his deputy, the god Thoth. One of the earliest references to this myth is found in the Coffin Texts (Spell 1130), where the Lord of All says, "I made everyone equal to his fellow, and I told them not to do evil, but it was their hearts which disobeyed what I had said." In chapter 175 of the *Book of Going Forth by Day* (Book of the Dead), the creator-god asks Thoth for advice after the Children of Nut—i.e., the first generation of humanity—have rebelled against him, and Thoth replies: "You should not witness evil, you should not suffer it. Let their years be shortened and their months be curtailed, for they have corrupted the hidden things in everything you have created." Human beings have destroyed the perfect order of creation; as a result, death comes into the world and "paradise" is lost.

A model of the original ideal world is found in the Egyptian temple with its perpetual cycle of rituals, the aim of which was the reigning maintenance of the perfect cosmic and social order (*maat*) established at creation. Only the reigning king, who was himself a god among men and a man among the gods and who was therefore able to act as the deputy of the gods on earth, had access to the inner temple; in everyday cultic practice, however, he was replaced by priests who acted on his behalf. Ordinary human beings had no access to the gods in the temple. Only after death were they reunited with the gods, whom they would then be able to worship directly, without a royal intermediary, as is shown by numerous representations on tomb walls and funerary objects, especially after the Amarna period.

The abode of the dead can hardly be described as Paradise, however. The spell from the *Book of Going Forth by Day* (or *Book of the Dead*) quoted above contains a dialogue between Osiris, the god of the dead with whom the deceased himself is identified, and Atum, the creator god: "O my lord Atum, why is it that I have to travel to the district of silence, where there is no water and no air, which is so deep, so dark and so impenetrable?— You will live there in peace of mind— But one cannot even have sex there!—I have given blessedness instead of water, air and sexual pleasure, and peace of mind instead of bread and beer, so says Atum." Clearly the idea of being trapped forever in the realm of the dead provoked mixed feelings in the Egyptians, and although at death everyone who successfully passed the final judgment became an Osiris, most funerary texts put emphasis on the identification of the deceased with the sun god, who is not restricted in his movements but enters the netherworld at night, only to be reborn and resurrected in the morning. The mummified body of the deceased rests in its tomb in the underworld, but his *ba*, represented as a bird with a human head, is able to move in and out of the tomb. The *ba* joins Re on his eternal journey along the sky and through the realm of the dead: at sunrise, when Re is reborn, the *ba* leaves the tomb, and at night, when Re travels through the underworld, where he temporarily unites with the body of Osiris, the *ba* returns to the mummified body in the tomb.

At first sight, the idea of a perpetual cycle would seem to be difficult to reconcile with the concept of a permanent locality such as Paradise. There is, however, a particular stretch of the daily journey of the sun god, and of the deceased with him, that has sometimes been called the Egyptian equivalent of the Greek Elysian Fields. Egyptian texts use two different names for this abode: the Field of Offerings (*sht htpw*), and the Field of Rushes (*sht i3rw*). They are mentioned together as early as the Old Kingdom Pyramid Texts, and it remains unclear whether these names refer to two different locations or whether they are two names for one and the same place; obviously, they are closely related. Although they are occasionally said to be in the northern sky, most texts agree that they are situated in the east, at the place of sunrise: "the gate . . . from which Re goes out into the east of the sky" is "in the middle of the Field of Rushes" (BD 149). In chapters 109 and 110 of the *Book of Going Forth by Day*, which describe and even depict these fields, the Field of Rushes is called "the City of the God" (i.e., Re); it is inhabited by the "Eastern Souls" and by Re-Horakhty (the rising sun) and the Morning Star (visible only in the eastern sky). Despite the term "city" used here, the Field of Rushes is really an inundated marshland divided by lakes and canals; according to the Pyramid Texts, the sun god purifies himself in the morning in the Lake of the Field of Rushes. In BD 109 and 149 it is described as follows: "Its walls are of iron, its barley stands 5 cubits high, with ears of 2 and stalks of 3 cubits, and its emmer stands 7 cubits high, with ears of 3 and stalks of 4 cubits; it is the blessed, each of them 9 cubits tall, who reap them alongside the Eastern Souls." This idealized farmland stands in stark contrast to the gloomy abode of Osiris, which is airless and without food, drink, and sexual pleasures, totally different from the picture that emerges from the opening lines of chapter 110: "Beginning of the spells of the Field of Offerings and the spells of going out into the day, entering and leaving the necropolis, attaining the Field of Rushes, dwelling in the Field of Offerings, the Great City, the Mistress of Air, being in control there, being a blessed one there, plowing and harvesting there, eating and drinking there, making love there, and doing everything that one was used to do on earth." In the vignette illustrating this chapter, the deceased, often accompanied by his wife, is shown paddling across the waterways of these fields in his boat and plowing, sowing, reaping, and threshing, often dressed in beautiful white linen garments that demonstrate that all of this hard labor should not be taken too literally: in actual fact, it is carried out by the deceased's substitutes, the *ushabti* statuettes that were an essential part of his or her funerary equipment.

The deceased spend only part of their lives after death in this place of abundance, however. When the sun goes down below the horizon and Re enters the underworld, they too return to their tombs. The next morning they will rise from the sleep of death again, bathe in the waters of the Field of Rushes, and provide for their daily sustenance there. The food offerings that they receive every day along with the daily rituals carried out by their relatives or their funerary priests, are the earthly equivalent of the products of the Field of Offerings and the Field of Rushes. One of the most common scenes in Egyptian tombs from all periods is that of the deceased seated at an offering table stacked with

tall loaves of bread. From the sixth dynasty onward, these loaves are often replaced by the reed-leaves that in the hieroglyphic script spell the word *sht* ("field"), and in later texts and representations the offering tables are expressly labeled "the Fields of Offerings."

Jacobus Van Dijk

PIETY. The concept of piety in ancient Egypt could be defined as a personal, individual expression of faith in and devotion to a deity, as opposed to institutionalized religious practice, which was traditionally the preserve of the king. The monarch was responsible for the maintenance of *maat*—the order of the universe, both cosmic and social, as established by the creator at creation— that included the maintenance of the relationship between the gods and humankind. This was achieved via the temple rituals conducted, in theory, by the king, but in practice by priests who acted for him. The ordinary person had no role in this activity.

Historical Developments. Evidence for personal religion prior to the New Kingdom is limited. Some personal names, which in ancient Egyptian are often theophoric, hint at a personal relationship between the deity and the bearer of the name. These names are particularly common in the Late Period: for example, *Padiese,* "he, whom Isis gave" (Greek, *Isidore*). Yet some are attested from earliest times: for example, *Shed-netjer,* "whom the god rescues" (from the first dynasty); from the Old Kingdom there were the names *Khui-wi-Ptah* (or *-Re,-Horus,-Khnum,* or *-Sobek*), "may Ptah (or Re, Horus, etc.) protect me." A few texts of the Middle Kingdom also make brief references to personal worship.

The paucity of evidence for personal religion prior to the New Kingdom can be explained by the limits set by what John Baines (1985) defined as "decorum," a set of rules regarding what could and could not be expressed in image and/or text in certain contexts. These guidelines can be illustrated in the way deities appeared on nonroyal monuments. Until the Middle Kingdom, decorum excluded the possibility for nonroyal persons to depict deities on their monuments; they appeared only in texts, almost exclusively of a funerary nature, or in the form of their emblems. Not until the end of the Middle Kingdom were the first representations of nonroyal persons worshiping a deity inscribed on nonroyal stelae. Even there, a barrier usually in the form of a column of inscription and/or an offering table separated the worshiper from the deity. Not until the early New Kingdom and onward did images of deities regularly appear on nonroyal monuments.

Personal religion was encouraged by New Kingdom developments that contributed to a gradual breaking down of the barriers that separated individual and deity, such as the evolution and growth of festival processions of the deities. During the New Kingdom, evidence survives for a burgeoning of such processions, when the divine images were brought out of the seclusion of their temples and carried in a portable boatshrine along a processional way. Although the images were hidden from view in the cabins of the boats (or barks, as they are often called), the ordinary person could approach them and seek the advice of the deity on all manner of personal issues, through an oracle.

Among the earliest literary evidence for personal piety in the New Kingdom are limestone *ostraca*, dated paleographically to the pre-Amarna period, which carry short prayers addressed to the god Amun. These *ostraca* may have been placed along the processional way taken by the god, and they bear some of the earliest sentiments of love and devotion to a deity: "Amun-Re, you are the beloved one, you are the only one!"

The growth of personal piety was accompanied by a diminution of the exclusive role of the king and official religion. As Jan Assmann (1984) has pointed out, one of the aims of King Akhenaten was to reverse that trend and restore to the monarch the central role in religion, as the mediator between the one god Aten and the people. His reform failed, indeed it succeeded in achieving the exact opposite—people were not prepared to abandon their old deities, and, since the official cults of the old gods were proscribed by the king, people were forced to turn to them directly. This situation probably explains the explosion of evidence for personal piety in both post-Amarna and Ramessid times, the latter dubbed by James H. Breasted in 1912 "the age of personal piety."

The trauma of the Amarna period and its aftermath doubtless also contributed to the atmosphere of uncertainty that is evident in the following historical period. That uncertainty was illustrated by theophoric names, which contain the verb *šd* ("rescue," "save"), names such as Shed-su-Amun ("may Amun save him"). Although sporadically met in earlier periods, such names were most frequently used in the New Kingdom (Ranke 1935, p. 330 f.). The letter of the scribe Butehamun to the captain of the bowmen Shed-su-Hor ("may Horus save him") also reflected this phenomenon (Wente 1990, p. 196), as did the emergence of the god Shed, the personification of the concept of the rescuing activity of a deity demonstrated in the study of Hellmut Brunner (1958, pp. 17–19). The inscriptions of Si-mut Kiki (Wilson 1970) provide a particularly good example of some of the perceived dangers and illustrate the concept of a chosen personal deity, to whom the devotee was particularly attached and from whom protection was sought, a well-attested phenomenon of piety that made its first appearance at that time.

As Assmann pointed out (1989, p. 75 ff.), a further religious development in the New Kingdom generated a change in the role of *maat*. Whereas it was previously held that one's fate depended on one's behavior (if one lived a life in accordance with the principles of *maat* then one would perforce flourish; if one transgressed against it one would be punished—the king being the one who upheld *maat* and meted out punishment), instead one came to be seen as directly responsible to the deity, who personally intervened in the individual's life and punished wrongdoing. The misfortunes from which people then needed to be saved were not only those of an impersonal kind but also included divine wrath, meted out as punishment for perceived wrongdoing.

Sources. Archaeological sources for the practice of piety have survived in the form of shrines and votive offerings, but for a proper understanding of the phenomenon we are dependent on literary sources. These are varied, including biographical inscriptions, hymns, inscriptions on scarabs, Wisdom Literature, and, in particular, the prayers (often penitential) of individuals. A very good example in a hymn may be found in those to Amun in the Leiden Papyrus (Prichard 1969, p. 369). The most important Wisdom teaching is that of Amenemope (Lichtheim 1976, pp. 146–163). The prayers of individuals, inscribed on stelae dedicated to the deity as votive offerings, are very similar to the biblical penitential psalms expressing sorrow for wrongdoing and thanks for forgiveness. The bulk

of our evidence comes from the Deir el-Medina, in Western Thebes, from the village of the workmen who built the tombs of the kings. This bias is due primarily to the chance of good preservation of the site, rather than to any unique religious development that may have taken place there, although the fact that Thebes probably suffered from the excesses of the Amarna period more than other places may also have been a factor. Ashraf Sadek (1987) presented the evidence from other locations, among which the Wepwawet sanctuary at Assyut (where more than six hundred small stelae were discovered) was particularly significant.

The Elements of the Prayers. The following themes and terminology are regularly encountered in the prayers, hymns, and votive offerings:

1. The introductory words of praise and appeal to the deity often include a description of the deity who is said to be "one who hears petitions (*nḥwt*)," "who comes at the voice of the poor (*nmḥw*) in need," "who comes at the voice of him who calls to him."

2. In the description of the transgressor, the writer claims to be a "silent one," that is, a devout person (*gr*); a poor, humble person (*nmḥw*). By way of apology, the claim is made to be ignorant and senseless (*iwty ḥȝty*), to be one who does not know good (*nfr*) from evil (*bin*).

3. The writer confesses to having committed an act of transgression (*sp n thi*), to having done what is abhorrent or "taboo" (*btȝ* or *bwt*), to having sworn falsely ('*rḳ m* '*dȝ*) by the deity.

4. The deity punishes the transgression, often with sickness; very

frequent is the expression "seeing darkness by day," an image for separation from the deity.

5. A promise is made to proclaim the might of the deity to all the world, to "son and daughter, the great and small, generations not yet born," to "the fish in the water and the birds in the air," to "the foolish and the wise."

6. An account is given of answer to prayer—the deity is said to respond to the pleas of the petitioner and "to come as a sweet breeze" to be "merciful" (*ḥtp*) to "turn" (*ʿn*) to the petitioner "in peace" (*ḥtp*).

The Deities. There was a range of deities, from the major gods and goddesses worshiped throughout Egypt (such as Amun-Re, Ptah, Hathor, Thoth, Osiris, Wepwawet, Horakhty, and Haoeris) to local deities (such as Meretseger, the personification of the western mountain, "the Peak," at Thebes). Also worshipped were deified kings, such as Amenhotpe I and less commonly, mortals, such as Amenophis, Son of Hapu, an official of Amenhotpe III. Amun was popularly worshiped in his forms *pȝ rhn nfr* ("the goodly ram") and *smn nfr n ʾImn* ("the goodly goose of Amun"). The prevalence of the former was based on his animal symbol, the ram, being the most public form of the god. It decorated the prow and stern of his portable bark, and the avenues leading to his temples in Thebes were lined with statues of rams. The god Thoth, patron of scribes, was favored by this profession, and prayers to him appear in the Ramessid schooling literature.

The Petitioners. One of the terms by which petitioners regularly referred to themselves in the penitential prayers was *nmḥw*, "a poor, humble person." This does not mean that piety was a religion of the poor, since they would not have had the means to commission the monuments that provide us with our data. The people from Deir el-Medina who called themselves *nmḥw* were relatively well-situated artisans, and most of the dedications found in the shrines around the Great Sphinx at Giza are by people of middle, lower-middle, or low rank, but even the viceroy of Nubia Huy, addressed a prayer of personal piety to his master, the king Tutankhamun. The king was also involved in this movement: Ramesses II's record of the Battle of Kadesh, inscribed on temple walls and pylons, did on a massive scale what the small votive stelae of the ordinary person did more modestly. In the prayer of Ramesses III to Amun at Karnak, sentiments and expressions are found that parallel those of the nonroyal prayers.

Other terms used to designate the ideal god-fearing pious person were *mȝʿty*, "a just one," comparable to the *sadiq*, "just," of the biblical tradition; *kbhw*, "the cool, quiet one;" and *gr* or *gr mȝʿ*, "the silent one" or "the one who is justly silent." Their antithesis is *šm* or *šm rȝ*, "the hot or hot-mouthed one." The term "the silent one" is found in prayers of personal piety but is even better known from the wisdom teachings; it refers to those who do not assert themselves but who place their trust in the divine, recognize the supreme free will of a deity, and are totally submissive to that will. That attitude is succinctly summarized in chapter 25 of the *Instructions of Amenemope*: "For man is clay and straw, God is his builder; he pulls down, he builds in a moment. He makes a thousand insignificant as he wishes, he makes a thousand people overseers when he is in his hour of life. Happy is he who reaches the West [i.e., the grave] being safe in the hand of god." There, worldly success—once seen as the result of correct behavior, of a life lived in accordance with *maat*—is held to be totally in the gift of a god; not success, then, but rather an unbroken relationship with a god, was the true mark of a successful life. The model frequently used for the relationship between the individual and a deity is that of servant (*b3k*) and master (*nb*); as does a servant his master, so the devout person "follows" (*šms*) and is "loyal" to (*šms ḥr mw/mtn*) a deity.

The confessions of fault in the penitential prayers refer to "actual sin;" the reference is always to some concrete, individual act or an inner thought or personal attitude. A concept of "general sin" is not found (i.e., the concept of the existence of a barrier between humankind and the divine that is not the result of an individual deed or thought but of the general condition of humankind—the Christian concept of "original sin"). The closest to the latter would be the statement on the stela of Nebra, that "the servant is disposed to do evil" (Lichtheim 1976, p. 106).

Locations of Cults. Ashraf Sadek (1987) has collected the evidence for the locations of cults of personal piety. They include nonofficial shrines (such as the small chapels erected by groups of individuals at Deir el-Medina or the tiny shrines set up along the path from Deir el-Medina to the Valley of the Kings), as well as places provided at official cult centers (such as the eastern temple at Karnak, dedicated to Amun and "Ramesses who hears petitions," or the monumental eastern gateway at Deir el-Medina, with its relief of "Ptah who hears petitions"). At the Tenth Pylon at Karnak, two individuals—Amenhotep, son of Hapu, and Piramesse—set up statues of themselves to act as mediators between the great god Amun and petitioners. The regular festival processions

of the deities were also important occasions for the practice of personal religion; the promise in many of the penitential prayers—to make a public proclamation of the experienced greatness and mercy of the deity—was most probably fulfilled at such processions. The stela of Pataweret (Brunner 1958, pp. 6–12) from the Wepwawet sanctuary at Asyut provides valuable data on this aspect of personal religion. Divided into three registers, the bottom one depicts Pataweret's experience of the saving intervention of Wepwawet, called "the savior," who rescued him from being taken by a crocodile. The other two registers show where he expressed his thanks to the god. In the middle one he is shown alone, praying before an image of the god at a shrine. In the top register he is shown publicly praising the god during a procession.

Although compositions comparable to those of personal piety in the Ramessid era are not known from later periods, many of the sentiments found in them appear in later biographical texts, and their formulas of piety live on in some of the Greco-Roman temple inscriptions.
Boyo Ockinga

PRIESTHOOD. For much of ancient Egyptian history, there was no class of full-time professional priests. The king served as Egypt's archetypal high priest of all divine cults, and is the only individual shown carrying out cultic activities in the temples. Until the New Kingdom, most priests served on a part-time basis while continuing to hold other administrative positions in the state or local government. Priestly service was prestigious, since the practitioner of cultic duties was filling an essentially royal role, acting as a liaison between humanity and the gods. It was also potentially lucrative, as priests on duty received a portion of the offerings presented to the gods and deceased kings in whose cults they served.

Yet there is relatively little firm evidence regarding the qualifications for priesthood. The Egyptians attributed all priestly appointments to the king himself. Private "autobiographies," such as that of the Middle Kingdom chief priest at Abydos, Wepwawet-aa, describe the official's promotion to the priesthood as taking place within the royal palace—in the case of Wepwawet-aa, this was perhaps a ceremonial palace used by the king on visits to the sanctuary of Osiris. In actual practice, highly ranked priests and officials (other than the king) must also have played an active role in selecting priests, just as they did in the performance of cult rituals in the gods' temples. In the Old and Middle Kingdoms, local officials served as priests, often apparently inheriting the role, as did the local governor (ḥ3ty-ʿ), who acted as the chief priest. In the New Kingdom, when Tutankhamun restored the temples following the Amarna period, he stated that he selected the sons of prominent dignitaries as priests. By the Late Period, according to the ancient Greek historian Herodotus, many priestly titles were inherited.

Categories of Priests. Numerous categories of priests existed in Egypt, varying with different cults, regions, and historical periods. Among the earliest documented and longest-lived categories of priest were the ḥmw-ntr (hem; "god's servants" or "prophets"), who are first attested in the first dynasty. Associated primarily with temples rather than funerary cults, these priests performed rituals, prepared offerings, and participated in the economic activities of the temples, including the maintenance of temple estates. They were among the limited number of people who had access to the innermost parts of the temple and to the hidden cult image, the tangible manifestation of the deity. In temples of local deities, particularly during the Old and Middle Kingdoms, the overseer of hem-priests (imy-r ḥmw-ntr) was almost invariably the local governor of the district.

A lower-ranked class of priests, the wʿbw (wab; "pure priests") assisted the hem-priests in the maintenance of the temple and the performance of cultic activities. Priests in this category had apparently been initiated into the priesthood, but had not yet advanced to the rank of hem-priest; biographies refer to wab-priests being promoted to the office of hem-priest later in their careers. While wab-priests were not permitted to enter the temple's innermost sanctuary, or come face-to-face with the god's image, they did handle sacred objects and cult instruments. They were therefore required to observe strict rules of purity, and they can be identified in some representations by their shaved heads. In New Kingdom temples, wab-priests are shown carrying the god's image in processions.

In temples, the ḥntiw-š, often viewed as secular officials associated with the temple, appear to have performed many of the same functions as the hem- and wab-priests, at least during the Old Kingdom, although they did not enter the sanctuary or see the god's cult statue. In ceremonies and rituals, including funerals, another priest, designated as the imy-ḥḥnt ("the one who is in front"), appears to have led the activities.

The priest who actually recited the spells and rites, both in temple ceremonies and at funerals, was a "lector-priest" (ḥry-ḥbt). Priests of this category are recognizable by their characteristic attire of a kilt and wide sash, worn diagonally over the shoulder, and they are often depicted holding or reading from a papyrus scroll. Lector-priests are first attested in the Old Kingdom cult of Re at Heliopolis. Although the earliest holders of the title were members of the royal family, by the Middle Kingdom, any literate official seems to have been able to serve in this capacity. Egyptian literature often portrays lector-priests as wise men and sages who can foresee coming events. In the *Tale of King Khufu and the Magicians*, for example, lector-priests perform miraculous feats, and are privy to secret knowledge, unknown even to the king. The Middle Kingdom prophet Neferti, who warns of disaster, followed by salvation, is also said to be a lector-priest. Owing to their knowledge of the appropriate spells, lector-priests were among the principal practitioners of magic and medicine. They also took part in funerals, reading the necessary spells and assisting in the Opening of the Mouth ceremony. The significance of chief lector-priests in researching and preserving ancient religious texts is demonstrated by evidence such as the twenty-fifth dynasty tomb of the chief lector-priest Petamenophis, who revived the long-dead Pyramid Texts, along with the Coffin Texts, the *Book of Going Forth by Day* (*Book of the Dead*), and the *Amduat* (royal Underworld Books).

From the Old Kingdom, *sem*-priests (*smw*) were associated with the Opening of the Mouth ceremony. In mortuary religion, they played the role of Horus in the funeral ceremonies, while the deceased was cast in the role of Osiris. Originally members of a high-ranking class of priests associated with the Memphite funerary deity, Ptah-Sokar, *sem*-priests came to be relatively common. From the end of the Old Kingdom onward, they are depicted in tomb scenes showing mortuary rituals. In the New Kingdom, they regularly take part in funeral ceremonies shown in the *Book of Going Forth by Day* and on tomb walls,

especially in the Ramessid period, where they can be identified by their panther-skin robes. *Sem*-priests were the first priests to wear robes of this type, although by the New Kingdom, they were worn by high-ranking priests of Amun and others as well. Another attribute sometimes associated with *sem*-priests is the sidelock, a sign of youth that identifies them with Horus.

Women in the Priesthood. During the Old Kingdom, women frequently held priestly titles, a practice that declined appreciably in the Middle Kingdom, and then reappeared later, in the Third Intermediate Period. Among the titles commonly held by elite Old Kingdom women was *ḥmt-nṯr* ("god's servant" or "priestess") of Hathor, or less often of Neith. Queens and princesses also served in this capacity in the mortuary cults of their fathers and husbands.

Although no female *wab*-priests have been identified during the Old Kingdom, the Abusir Papyri (see below) refer to women carrying out some of the duties of the *wab*-priest and receiving the same pay as their male counterparts. Two Middle Kingdom stelae identify women holding the title of *w'bt*. By the New Kingdom, when the priesthood developed into a full-time profession, women rarely played a role other than as musicians. Rare exceptions do exist, however, including a female second prophet of Amun and a female second prophet of Mut. At no period did women serve as overseers of priests (*ḥmy-r ḥmwt-nṯr*).

Upper-class women served as singers and musicians in the temple cults of a variety of deities from the Old Kingdom onward, and many of the priestesses of Hathor may have been involved in musical performances during religious festival and other rites. From the Middle Kingdom until the end of the New Kingdom, the role of singer was almost the sole priestly activity of women. The _ḥnr_ ("musical troupe") included women who danced and played music under the leadership of a woman identified as the _wrt-ḥnr_ (the "chief of the musical troupe"). Prior to the New Kingdom, the usual term for a woman serving as a singer in the temple was _ḥsyt_. The term _šmʿyt_ was first used in reference to individual singers during the New Kingdom, at which time it became one of the most frequently attested feminine titles. In addition to singing, temple chantresses apparently played a variety of musical instruments. In many instances, they are shown holding a sistrum or a _menat_ (a type of necklace sacred to the goddess Hathor), which was shaken to create music.

Three Middle Kingdom women are known to have borne the title of "god's wife" (_ḥmt-ntr_) of a deity, serving in the cults on Min, Amun, and Ptah. Although the duties associated with this title during the Middle Kingdom are unclear, by the early New Kingdom the title of "God's Wife of Amun" had taken on considerable importance, the earliest examples being associated specifically with the queen. The first queen to hold the title was Ahmose-Nefertari, the wife of Ahmose and first queen of the eighteenth dynasty. Ahmose-Nefertari had served as the second prophet of Amun, an exceptional rank for a woman, but arranged by contract to exchange the title for the position of god's wife. Following her death, she was succeeded by Hatshepsut and her daughter Neferure, and, from the reign of Thutmose III on, by a series of lesser-known women, who seem to have been related to the royal family only by marriage. New Kingdom "God's Wives" are shown taking part in temple rituals at Luxor and elsewhere, and sometimes bear the additional titles of "Divine Adoratrix" (_dwȝt-ntr_) and

"Hand of the God" (_drt-ntr_). In the Late period, "God's Wives" rose in significance to become the principal priests of the cult of Amun at Thebes (see below).

Temple Priests. Temple reliefs typically portray the king as the sole practitioner of all divine cults, the quintessential high priest of every god's temple. Although the king presumably performed cultic activities on special occasions at major temples, a hierarchy of local priests was responsible for performing the daily cultic rituals in temples throughout Egypt. These rituals, recorded in scenes from a number of temples (notably the temple of Sety I at Abydos), were performed three times per day in major temples. These ceremonies involved: the ceremonial breaking of the sanctuaries' seals; the recitation of prayers and offering of incense; the awakening of the cult statue and its removal from the shrine by the _hem_-priest; the undressing, cleansing, anointing, and reclothing of the cult image; the performance of the Opening of the Mouth to revivify the deity; the offering of food and other gifts; and, ultimately, the return of the cult statue, wrapped in clean linen, to its shrine. The Opening of the Mouth was perhaps the most vital element of the ritual, since it enabled the deity to act through his or her statue. Priests utilized a number of implements in this ceremony, one of the most characteristic being the _psškf_, a blade with which the officiating priest touched the mouth of a statue or of the mummy, thereby animating it. Finally, the priest backed out of the sanctuary, sweeping away his footprints behind him, and the shrine was resealed.

During festivals, the priests at major temples were responsible for carrying the cult statue from the temple in a bark or palanquin and bringing it into public view. Because the priests themselves are rarely labeled in scenes of these activities, it is not clear whether those who conducted the divine image were particularly important members of the priesthood or the priests who happened to be on duty at the time. From the New Kingdom onward, chief priests were also instrumental in interpreting oracles—when asked a question, the god would answer by directing his portable bark, carried by priests, in the direction of the written response it chose.

At least three institutions associated with the temple were devoted to storing and disseminating information and skills required for specialized categories of priests. In the "House of Gold" (*hwt nbw*), master craftsmen put the finishing touches on cult statues, which were then transformed into suitable residences for the deity by ceremonies, including the Opening of the Mouth. The "House of Books" (*pr mḏ3t*) housed the manuscripts of sacred texts, such as transfiguration spells, litanies of gods' names, religious treatises, and instructions for rituals. The "House of Life" (*pr ˁnḫ*) not only housed the texts of rituals, including those for crowning the king and mummifying the dead, but also served as a point of reference for both priests and royalty, thus preserving ancient ceremonies and cult practices for future generations of priests.

Funerary and Mortuary Cult Priests. Although stelae and tomb scenes usually show burial offerings being brought by family members, professional mortuary priests are documented serving in private memorial cults as early as the first dynasty. A class of specifically funerary priests included the servants of the *ka* (*ḥmw-k3*), who provided for the immortal life force of the deceased person. Scenes in tombs from the Old Kingdom onward show priests participating in the funeral—*wab*-priests pour libation offerings, while lector-priests

read aloud the funerary texts critical to transforming the deceased person into an immortal being. Lector-priests also perform the *int-rd* ceremony, sweeping away the footprints of the celebrants after the ceremony has been completed.

Mortuary literature, from the Pyramid Texts on, provides evidence that the funeral ceremony included not only the reading of religious texts, but also the performance of acts such as playing the role of deities associated with the myth of Osiris. The Coffin Texts, for example, include directions for those taking part in the ceremony, along with texts that must have been spoken aloud, presumably by a lector-priest. Women, who had served as funerary priests (*ḥmwt-k3*) during the Old Kingdom, thereafter acted as *dry*-mourners, impersonating the grieving Isis and Nephthys.

Sem-priests are identifiable by the end of the Old Kingdom, after which they are shown offering incense and performing the Opening of the Mouth ceremony on the mummy of the deceased. Beginning in the New Kingdom, scenes of the funeral accompany several chapters of the *Book of Going Forth by Day*, and form an increasingly significant part of tomb decoration. A priest wearing a mask of the god Anubis is shown preparing the mummy for burial, and supporting the upright coffin in front of the tomb entrance, while the Opening of the Mouth takes place. The heir of the deceased is typically shown performing this ritual, touching the mouth with a ceremonial implement, such as an adze tipped with iron or flint.

Wealthy and influential officials established mortuary endowments in the same way as kings, to perpetuate their memorial cults and to provide for mortuary priests. Several Abydene stelae refer to contractual arrangements with mortuary priests, and the twelfth dynasty tomb of the vizier Djefai-hapi I at Asyiut preserves the complete text of his mortuary contracts. According to the contracts, the priests are responsible for delivering offerings of bread and other items to the vizier's statues in the local temple, in exchange for being paid a portion of the offerings dedicated in the temple.

Domestic Cult and Magic Priests. Many domestic cults, aimed in large part on protecting the home and its inhabitants from harm, required literate or learned individuals to perform the appropriate rites. Hence, priests were often called upon to serve in this capacity. Lector-priests, with their specialized knowledge of religious texts, were the principal practitioners of apotropaic magic. They also appear to have been consulted in times of medical emergencies, as the Old Kingdom biography of Washptah attests. A group of men identified as $ḥk3w$ ("magicians") appears in association with the House of Life. Both lector-priests and physicians ($swnw$) also held specialized titles associated with specific types of magic, such as "Scorpion Charmer." Along with written and spoken prayers, these priests were familiar with, and able to produce, the correct amulets for protection and talismans for blessing.

Organization. Among the best preserved evidence for the organization of the priesthood during the Old Kingdom are the archives of the royal cult temples of the fifth-dynasty king, Neferirkare Kakai, at Abusir. According to the carefully recorded temple accounts, the priests and other temple staff worked on a rotating basis, serving full-time in the temple for one month in every five-month period. Some staff members were employed on the temple estates in other capacities during the remainder of the year. The priests on duty were organized into workgroups, or "phyles." Each phyle was in turn subdivided into two subgroups, each headed by a $šḏ$, ("inspector"). The temple's inventory, income, and expenditures were meticulously registered at the end of each watch.

During the Old Kingdom, while local rulers headed the temples of their own provinces, the chief priests of the state-sponsored temples of major deities were often members of the royal family, sons, or sons-in-law of the king. This pattern suggests a strong degree of royal control over the temples during this period. Certain deities and cult centers had specific titles for their chief priests: at Heliopolis, the chief priest of Ra was known as the "Greatest of Seers," while the chief priest of Ptah at Memphis was the "Greatest of Directors of Craftsmen," in recognition of Ptah's role as the god of craftsmen. The chief priest of Thoth at Hermopolis was the "Great One of the Five," referring to the creator god and the four pairs of deities that made up the Hermopolitan Ogdoad.

In the Middle Kingdom, the local governor continued to serve as the chief priest of the local temple, although in many cases these men were now appointed by the king. The excavations at Illahun, the town built for the priests maintaining the mortuary cult of King Senwosret II, produced a series of papyri, including the archives of the temple scribe, Horemsaf, who recorded both the temple's accounts and the correspondence of the chief priest. As in the Old Kingdom, priests served in rotating watches, but the number of watches was now reduced to four. The records document the distribution of offerings to several categories of priests, indicating their relative rank. The chief priest ($ỉmy-r$ $ḥmw-nṯr$) was the highest paid, followed by the chief lector-priest ($ḥry-ḥbt$

ḥry-tp), the lector-priests, the phyle reg-ulator (mty m s3), the wab-priests and other priests associated with offerings and cult maintenance, and finally the temple scribe. The homes of the priests, and the layout of the town itself, cor-roborate the written evidence of the or-ganization of the priestly community and relative status of the priests. At Abydos, the state constructed a town of similar structures to house the priests associated with the cult of Senwosret III, whose temple and cenotaph lie nearby.

No temple archives of the New Kingdom has survived to provide evi-dence similar to that of the Abusir or Illahun material. Nevertheless, the priesthood is reasonably well docu-mented, owing to the better overall preservation of temples and private tombs. Although secular administrators continued to serve as priests of many cults (at least early in the period), the priesthood emerged during the New Kingdom as a full-time profession. Dur-ing the first half of the eighteenth dy-nasty, the old title for the chief hem-priest was replaced by a new one, the "first prophet" (ḥm-nṯr tpí). At first, this new, full-time position was held exclusively by members of the royal family, but soon thereafter by other officials appointed di-rectly by the king. The first prophet en-joyed considerable authority in the ma-jor divine cults, particularly that of Amun at Thebes, and his wife typically served as the leader of temple musicians and dancers. In the largest cult centers, such as Thebes, a series of full-time sec-ond, third, and occasionally fourth prophets assisted with the running of the temple.

The first prophet of Amun at Karnak, responsible for the cult and revenues of Egypt's largest temple complex, was one of New Kingdom Egypt's most impor-tant officials. A pair of inscriptions ded-icated by the priest Bakenkhons record the progress of his career, stating that fourteen years of schooling and public service preceded his appointment to the rank of wab-priest. Thereafter, he served as "god's father," third prophet, and sec-ond prophet—a process that took nearly four decades—before he received the ti-tle of first prophet. In the early part of the eighteenth dynasty, the first prophet at Karnak also held the title of chief prophet of Upper and Lower Egypt, and with it the duty of supervising, on the king's behalf, the affairs of all the temples in Egypt. During the reign of Thutmose IV, this office was transferred to another official, often the chief priest of Ptah, serving in Memphis. The first prophet of Amun became extraordinarily influential by the end of the New Kingdom, by which time the office had come to be hereditary.

Also serving a crucial role in New Kingdom temple rituals was the chief lector-priest (ḥry-ḥbt ḥry-tp), who, as in ḫt h previous periods, oversaw the pres-ervation and recitation of the texts, prayers, and rituals. In the larger temples, he was now assisted by a second, third, and sometimes fourth lector-priest. Lector-priests are also documented an-nouncing the verdicts of the oracles that took place at festivals. Wab-priests con-tinued to function on a rotating basis as earlier, with four phyles of priests serving a one-month term. The "God's Father" (ít-nṯr), occasionally attested in the Old Kingdom, became a regular priestly title in the New Kingdom. Among other re-sponsibilities, "God's Fathers" led the processions held at festivals. The wives of priests, organized into phyles as were their husbands, served as temple musi-cians.

Although the classes of priests contin-ued essentially unchanged into the Third Intermediate Period and the Late period, the status of the priesthood of Amun skyrocketed. At the end of the twentieth dynasty, generals used the title of first prophet to take actual political control over southern Egypt, contributing to the disintegration of Egypt's central government. Some additional changes in the temple administration also took place during this time. The full-time priests were now assisted by part-time *hem*-priests, arranged in phyles and serving on a rotating basis, resuming a priestly title that had gone out of use early in the New Kingdom. Most priestly offices by this period had become hereditary.

When Egypt was reunited under the Saite and Kushite dynasties, the volatile office of first prophet of Amun was eliminated, and the "God's Wife of Amun" became the highest priestly title in Thebes. Although earlier "God's Wives" had clearly married and had children, those of the Late Period were celibate, unmarried daughters of the ruler or a powerful priest, who adopted their successors. Their chosen successors eventually came to be known as the first prophets of Amun. In the twenty-fifth dynasty, the Kushite ruler Kashta enlisted the "God's Wife of Amun," Shepenwepet I, to adopt his daughter Amenirdis as her successor, thus solidifying his own claim to power in Thebes. Amenirdis was in turn followed by Shepenwepet II and Amenirdis II, during whose term of office Psamtik I expelled the Kushites to found the twenty-sixth dynasty. In order to establish his own rule, Psamtik, with the aid of the "Overseer of Upper Egypt," Montuemhat, arranged for his own daughter, Nitocris, to be adopted as heiress. The stela recording her installment as god's wife describes the elaborate ceremony involved, and lists the enormous endowment allotted to the office during this period. The invasion of Cambyses and the Persians brought the

significance of the "God's Wives" to an end; although the title continued to exist in later times, it never regained its political importance.

During the Greco-Roman period, the full-time clergy of major cults continued to be assisted by part-time priests, divided into four phyles; until 238 BCE, when Ptolemy III reorganized the system, adding a fifth phyle. Virtually all offices were hereditary. The highest-ranking member of the priesthood in this period was the high priest of Ptah at Memphis, although the priests of Amun at Thebes retained significant status. Several categories of priest below the rank of prophet included (among others): the sacred scribes known as *hierogrammates* (of which Manetho was one); the *hierostolistes*, who tended the cult statue; the *horologoi*, astronomers who maintained the calendar of festivals; and the *pastophoroi*, who carried the gods' shrines in processions. "God's Wives" continue to function, albeit in a reduced role, and female *wab*-priests and *hem*-priests are also documented.   *Denise M. Doxey*

PTAH. The god Ptah was one of the major deities of Egypt, yet surprisingly little is known about his early history. With few exceptions, the major textual sources date from the New Kingdom or later, when Egyptian religion had long been shaped according to the dominating theology of Heliopolis. Nevertheless, Ptah is known to have been worshiped as early as the Early Dynastic period, the date of his image on a stone vessel found at Tarkhan, south of el-Lisht. There is shown in his usual anthropoid form without indication of limbs—a form that he shares with some other ancient gods such as Min and Osiris—that was later interpreted as the form of a mummy. Wearing a tight-fitting skullcap, he stands on a pedestal in an open shrine,

A detail of a wall painting in the tomb of Amen-hor-khepeshef. Ptah, the god of creation shrouded in mummy wrappings and wearing the menat collar stands within a sarcophagus. (Werner Forman Archive/E. Strouhal/Art Resource, NY)

holding a scepter. Later representations usually show him with a straight beard; the scepter is almost invariably a *was*-scepter, which from the New Kingdom on is often combined with *ankh* and *djed* symbols. Occasionally the god is shown seated.

The evidence from the Old Kingdom is sparse and consists mainly of personal names and a few titles. Theophoric names composed with the name of Ptah appear at the end of the fourth dynasty and seem to have suddenly become very popular during the fifth, suggesting that the god had begun to play an important role on the level of personal piety. By contrast, royal names of the same period ignore Ptah, and he is virtually absent from royal inscriptions. In the Pyramid Texts, Ptah occurs only two or three times, always in connection with the provision of food for the deceased king. From the end of the fourth dynasty, titles referring to the priesthood of Ptah confirm the existence of a temple in the

capital city, Memphis. Most of the holders of these titles are also connected with the royal workshops, particularly with the making of jewelry. Some of them also bear the title "Chief Controller of Craftsmen" *(wr ḥrp ḥmwt)*, which soon becomes the title of the high priest of Ptah in Memphis. Clearly Ptah was associated early on with arts and crafts. Perhaps he was originally a local god who assumed the role of divine craftsman and patron deity of artists, craftsmen, and builders when Memphis became the capital of Egypt and, therefore, the location of the royal workshops. It is equally possible that he had been associated with the royal workshops even before these were transferred to Memphis. In any case, Ptah was the chief god of Memphis throughout Egyptian history, and the name of his temple—*Ḥwt-k₃-Ptḥ* ("Temple of the *ka* of Ptah")—became the name of the city of Memphis and ultimately of the whole country (*Hikuptah.* Gr. *Aigyptos,* "Egypt"). Little remains of this temple, but it is thought to have been even larger than the vast complex of Amun-Re at Karnak. Some of the god's epithets also refer to Memphis: "South of his Wall" means "having a temple south of the (White) Wall" (i.e., Memphis), or perhaps "whose (enclosure) wall is in the south (of Memphis);" "who is upon the Great Throne" refers to the Great Temple in Memphis; and "Lord of Ankhtawy" probably refers to the area on the west bank of the Nile between the city and the necropolis in the desert. Other common epithets of the god include "Lord of *Maat*" (the principle of world order), "Great of Strength," and "Benevolent of Face," an epithet that is often wrongly said to be restricted to gods depicted in human form.

At an early date, Ptah was linked with Sokar, another Memphite god, who was chiefly a god of the dead; as Ptah-Sokar (later Ptah-Sokar-Osiris), he plays a role in many funerary texts. Other deities worshiped in Memphis were the lion goddess Sekhmet and the lotus god Nefertum, with whom Ptah forms a triad (father-mother-child) from the New Kingdom on. He is also associated with the Memphite form of Hathor, the "Lady of the Southern Sycamore," who had a temple in the southern part of the city. From the eighteenth dynasty on, the sacred Apis bull of Memphis, originally an independent god, was viewed as the living manifestation of Ptah. In the Late Period, the deified mortal Imhotep was regarded as his son. According to the ancient Greek historian Herodotus, the temple of Memphis also contained a statue of Ptah as a dwarf (Gr., *pataikos*), and images of Ptah in this form have been found.

The meaning of the name *Ptah* is not known. An etymology found in the Coffin Texts (Spell 647) connects it with a verb *pth* ("to fashion"), but although this would obviously agree well with his role of divine craftsman, it is also possible that the verb is actually derived from the god's name rather than the other way round. The same spell also contains the first allusions to Ptah as a creator god, but these are already cast in Heliopolitan terms. Texts from the New Kingdom further expand this idea, in particular the Memphite Theology—long thought to date back to the Old Kingdom, now shown to be much later, probably the Ramessid period of the New Kingdom—and a series of hymns to Ptah in a papyrus in Berlin. These texts equate him with the primeval god Atum, who created the world at the beginning of time through his "heart" (thought) and "tongue" (word); this god manifests himself as the earth god Tatenen, the Primeval Mound, who is embodied in Ptah, the divine sculptor who forms a concept of creation in his mind and then realizes it materially. As primeval creator god, Ptah, or Ptah-Tatenen, as he is often called, he becomes one of the three state gods of Egypt, along with Amun of Thebes and Re of Heliopolis. One famous text says that all the gods are forms of this trinity: "Three are all the gods: Amun, Re, and Ptah, there is none like them. Hidden is his identity as Amun. He is visible as Re. His body is Ptah." In another text, the sun god Re is said to be his own Ptah or "fashioner" who casts his body of gold. In late texts Ptah is even depicted as the father of the Ogdoad of Hermopolis, the primeval elements from which the ordered universe developed. As primeval god he encompasses the whole world: his feet are on the earth, his head is in the sky, his eyes are sun and moon, his breath is the air, and the liquid of his body is the water. Images of Ptah as a sky god show him with a blue skullcap and a body covered in feathers. This universal god is also a god of destiny, who decides between life and death and determines the length of the king's reign and of every individual's lifetime. As "Ptah who hears prayers," he played an important role in the personal religion of many ordinary Egyptians.

Outside Memphis, Ptah was worshiped in many places where artists and craftsmen were active, such as Deir el-Medina and the Sinai. He had cults in all of Egypt's important temples, including those of Karnak, Western Thebes, Abydos, Piramesse, and Nubia.

Jacobus Van Dijk

R

RE AND RE-HORAKHTY. Re is the sun god. His Egyptian name, *r*, is usually written with the sun disk. He is often called "Re-Horakhty" ("Re [is] Horus of the Horizon"); this should be understood as a surname describing the character of the god. Re was the most important god of the Egyptian pantheon because he created the world. The awe of him was based on the fact that the cosmic dimension of the sun surpasses the comprehension of man. An Old Kingdom text describes him as "glorious, shining, besouled, strong, mighty, far-reaching, farstriding."

For the Egyptians, the course of the sun was the measurement of time. After its nightly absence, it rose again on the horizon with absolute regularity. The rising sun was the symbol for the creation of the world, and the daily course of the sun the symbol of the world's cyclical renewal; hence the paramount importance of Re as creator and master of life.

The second factor in Re's importance was his unbreakable link with the king. The master of earth and the master of the universe were of the same nature; one was a mirror image of the other. In ancient Egypt, theology and political theory were interdependent: the figure of the king was always the center of attention, and the status of a god or of a mortal was measured by his or her proximity to the king.

The sun god is an interesting case in the history of religion because he is absent from the early historical sources. Between the late second dynasty and the fifth, we can observe the way his image developed as an analogy of that of the king. From the beginning, the king appeared as a god and a human at once. His divine aspect was embodied in a falcon named Horus. In the fourth dynasty the reigning king was called "the son of Re," thus defining the relationship between pharoah and sun god. A relationship was also established between the royal falcon and Re, by uniting both in the symbol of the winged sun disk, an image that remained a constant in temples and religious monuments as the omnipresent complement of the king, until the end of Egyptian history. The earliest depictions of the sun god as a man with a falcon's head and with a sun disk are preserved in the royal pyramid temples.

The kings of the fifth dynasty erected solar temples next to their pyramids in the necropolis of Abusir, and these structures differ from other temples of the time in that they feature a large, open courtyard at the center of which rises an obelisk on top of a tall pedestal; in front of this is a large offering altar. Unlike other deities, Re never has a sanctuary with a cult statue; his image is the sun itself, which rises daily over the tip of the obelisk. The pyramidion and several types of pillars also appear as symbols of Re. The most significant solar temple, that at Heliopolis (now completely destroyed), was probably erected during this period. The hieroglyph for that city's Egyptian name, Iwn, contains a pillar resembling an obelisk.

The most important early source for the sun god is the Pyramid Texts of the Old Kingdom, a collection of spells describing the fate of the deceased king in the underworld which are carved on the walls of royal tombs of the late fifth and sixth dynasties. The protagonist is once again the king, who in death has become one with his heavenly father, Re. The texts witness a highly developed theology. The sun god is not a clearly defined individual, but instead has several names and images. His multiplicity is a reflection of his many capabilities. The Pyramid Texts describe Re as the sun that rises on the eastern horizon in the morning in the shape of a scarab beetle whose name is Khepri ("the Emerging One"). The scarab in his bark is lifted by the personified primordial waters, or Nun. During the day Re traverses the sky in the bark, accompanied by a large entourage of gods; at sunset he becomes Atum, the "All-Lord." No one can halt his course. Every evening he is swallowed by the sky goddess Nut, who gives birth to him anew each morning, and thus the cycle continues. Crowns and the throne associate Re with kingship.

Creative force is the sun god's central characteristic. Although the Pyramid Texts do not relate extensive myths, they contain mythic elements, referring to the creation of the world. In the beginning there was Re under his name Atum, who came into being. He rose in the shape of a *benben* stone, or obelisk-like pillar, in the temple of the Benu-Phoenix in Heliopolis, city of the pillar. Then he spit forth Shu and Tefnut, the first divine couple, personifying air and

moisture. They begot Geb and Nut (earth and sky), and the latter in turn bore two divine couples—Osiris and Isis, and Seth and Nephthys. This completed the Ennead of gods, and the world was able to function.

Re, as creator, is in dialogue with his opposite, death, from the very beginning. In the Pyramid Texts we read that death is not the end of life, but rather its original source. Death is personified by Osiris who is murdered by his brother, Seth, and subsequently resurrected by Re to rule over the dead. The link between Re and Osiris is the deceased king who, in the afterlife identifies with both gods. Unlike most other deities, Re does not have a family; however, he has his eye, the sun disk, to give birth to other creatures. These offspring include (among others) his son, the king, and the goddess Hathor, who embodies the feminine creative principle, giving birth to her creatures and nourishing them with milk; as a sign of her connection with Re, she bears the sun disk on her head. Re's closest ally is the goddess Maat, the embodiment of order and truth; she represents the unimpeachable principle of his rule.

In the Middle Kingdom we encounter a new image of Re. Several hymns to the sun god tell how he created the world solely for humankind. Human beings are made in his image, and he provides them with everything they need for life. Evil, however, does not come from the god but from mortals' own rebellious hearts, and for this they are judged in the underworld. With his rays, that penetrate each body, Re supervises and controls human beings, rewarding the obedient and destroying the disobedient. On earth, the king does this in his stead.

The relationship between Re and Osiris is newly defined at this time. All mortals now change into Osiris in death, a concept already discernible by the end of the Old Kingdom. Re gives Osiris his power by bestowing on him his crown, and he also guards him while he travels through the underworld at night. The phase of the daily rebirth of the sun in the form of a scarab is now symbolized by an amulet in that form, which soon becomes the most popular and widespread symbol of good fortune. In an expanded political theology, the names of several other deities with roles as creator or ruler are combined with that of Re, especially as Amun-Re; in this composite form, Re expands his own potential through the incorporation of other deities into his own being.

Re worship reaches its height in the New Kingdom. The walls of its royal tombs are decorated with images of the Underworld Books that describe the nightly journey of the sun. The nocturnal Re in his bark is depicted as a human with a ram's head. In the fifth hour, the god is united with his corpse, which at this time is Osiris. This is the moment when the sun suffers death, which at the same time generates new life. In the sixth hour, Apophis, a serpent embodying evil, is killed. Then in the twelfth hour, Re is newly born as a scarab. Among the new texts is The Litany of Re, which describes how the king identifies with the seventy-five nocturnal figures of Re, and how Re and Osiris become one in the depth of night.

In the tombs of officials, Re appears in very different form. At the entrance are inscriptions of the solar hymns describing Re's creation deeds. The deceased wants to be free to leave the tomb during the day to see the sun, for gazing on Re will rejuvenate him daily through eternity. However, there is also a perception that the sun god could destroy his creation at the end of eternity; this aspect adds a philosophical dimension to the theology.

Papyri recounting Re myths exist primarily from the New Kingdom. They focus on two themes. In one, Re becomes elderly and tired, and therefore organizes the world in a way that it no longer requires his personal intervention; he transfers his power to Horus or to the king. In the other, Re conceives the heir to the throne as his physical son.

Some New Kingdom temples feature an open courtyard with an altar to Re. There a specific sun cult was celebrated: at the turn of each hour, a priest—ideally, the king—recited one of twelve poetic hymns predicting the victorious course of the sun. On the temple walls, the newborn sun is now sometimes depicted as a crouching infant, and the adult sun god in human form. In the time of Amenhotpe III, the reigning king is not merely the son of Re, but identifies so strongly with Re that he calls himself "the dazzling sun." Amenhotpe IV, also called Akhenaten, even instituted a monotheistic religion centered on the sun. He declared the physical embodiment of the sun, the solar disk or Aten, to be the only existing god. After Akhenaten's death, his idea was abandoned, and the theologians restored the traditional beliefs. Thereafter, however, Amun-Re was a "universal god," all-encompassing, who maintained life for sky, earth, gods, and humans.

From the end of the New Kingdom, the royal Underworld Books were democratized, and excerpts appear as late as the early Ptolemaic period in tombs, on papyri, and on sarcophagi. Now anyone could take the journey in Re's nocturnal bark. In addition, a new image of the king emerges: on painted coffins of the Third Intermediate Period, Re-Horakhty-Atum appears in the mummiform shape of Osiris, and the owner of the tomb worships him as the ruler of the underworld. This is the merger of Re and Osiris recognized by ordinary mortals; in the royal funerary belief it already had been accomplished in the New Kingdom in a mummiform image of the god with a ram's head. The magical-mythical papyri, intended to protect both living and dead, rely heavily on solar symbolism: they often depict the sun's course in a single image that combines the travel of Re by day and by night, with his rebirth in the morning. Thus the believers ensure their own regeneration. The Litany of Re is further developed by adding new, often grotesque figures to the existing figures of Re. Also new are lists describing the twelve images of Re for the hours of the day.

Among the amulets placed on the mummy to protect the dead, we now find several solar symbols: the sun in the horizon, the sun disk, the celestial bark, the double lion, and the obelisk. The Egyptians also used the hypocephalus, a disk depicting Re's nocturnal form with four ram's heads. Taking many shapes and possessing several heads increased the power of the god. Eventually, however, Re became less important over the course of the first millennium, as the kingship was weakened under a succession of foreign rulers.

Even in the Greco-Roman period, however, new magical-mythical papyri were created, offering a new interpretation of the sun's path. The *Book of Faiyum* tells how Re enters the body of Sobek, the crocodile god, and swims across the Faiyum lake during the twelve hours of the night. In the magical texts, Re continues to be the highest power, upon whom a magician may call if he proves the depth of his knowledge. Hence, the listing of the twelve manifestations of the diurnal sun plays an important role, as does the list of the figures that issued from Re during the act of creation as Khepri, the morning sun.

Re played a dominant role in the large Horus temple at Edfu because he was identified with Horus of Edfu and with his main symbol, the winged sun. On the ceiling of a chapel are depicted the twelve figures of Re as diurnal sun and, as a new aspect, the fourteen *ka*-powers of Re. The sun god is even the protagonist of a dramatic tale about the victory of the winged sun over the enemies of creation. However, since the kings of the Greco-Roman period were foreigners, the theology of Re had become a purely academic pursuit, limited to priests and no longer part of the living faith of the people.   *Maya Müller*

S

SACRED BARKS. In antiquity, boats represented the ultimate mode of travel in the Nile Valley, and they played a crucial role in Egyptian religious practice and belief from prehistory onward. The sun god was believed to traverse the sky by day and the underworld by night in his sacred bark (*wꜣꞯ*). Paintings on Naqada II pottery depict large ceremonial boats decorated with sacred emblems and figures. In dynastic times, both full-sized navigable craft and portable models—dragged or carried by priests—featured prominently in rituals and in festivals, when they were used to transport cult statues. Although no actual examples survive, their history can be traced in reliefs and inscriptions.

Among the most ancient examples was the Memphite god Sokar's *Ḥnw*-boat. Although the earliest known representations date to the New Kingdom, its iconography suggests that it dates back to earliest times. The *Ḥnw*-boat resembles figures on Naqada II pottery, featuring a bank of oars along the front half of its impossibly curved hull. The cabin shrine has two mummiform falcons similar to the archaic gold and copper example found at Hierakonpolis, one projecting from the roof and the other from the front of the cabin. Its hull is supported by four pairs of posts attached to a sledge, with a rope secured to the front and sides of the sledge and running underneath the hull. A second rope, tied to the front of the sledge, was used to drag it in procession. Later, in Ramesses III's temple at Medinet Habu, the *Ḥnw*-boat was transported on carrying poles.

Other primitive barks, mounted on sledges with towropes, are shown in later reliefs. Some bear enthroned statues of the king or of Hathor as a cow with the king standing before her and again kneeling beneath her udders to suckle, with examples from Deir el-Bahri and Luxor and in Ramesses II's Abydos temple. These sledgemounted barks predate those carried by priests on a platform with carrying poles. In New Kingdom barks, such carrying platforms are still represented in the form of the now obsolete sledge, an anachronism that betrays the original method of locomotion.

Another early bark, the *Nšmt*-boat of Osiris, is known from the twelfth dynasty at Abydos, where certain officials oversaw its construction. These texts probably refer to a large river-going craft rather than to a processional one, but later, in the temple of Sety I, a model vessel with carrying poles is depicted. The prow is decorated with a figurehead of the god emerging from a lotus stem, while the reliquary of Osiris protrudes from the top of the cabin shrine. A number of other sacred barks, rarely seen elsewhere, grace the walls of Sety I's Abydos temple, including those of Ptah, Re-Horakhty, Isis, and Horus.

From New Kingdom times onward,

portable barks, heavily gilded and fitted at prow and stern with emblems of the gods and supported by carrying poles, became the standard form of processional shrine, the best-known example being that of Amun-Re of Thebes. From reliefs dating between the early eighteenth dynasty and the Ptolemaic era, it is possible to trace the Amun bark's iconographic development. The earliest datable representation comes from the alabaster bark chapel of Amenhotpe I at Karnak, but it is possible that this form existed earlier. A fragmentary relief from the temple of Nebhepetre-Montuhotpe II at Deir el-Bahri shows its prow, but this relief is a post-Amarna restoration dating to the Ramessid period. Still, it is most likely a replacement of an original relief depicting the bark. A pair of reused blocks from Karnak depict the craft's prow and cabin shrine. These could belong to a monument of Amenhotpe I or to the twelfth dynasty, as they are similar in style to that found on reliefs on blocks of Senwosret I. The evidence is sketchy, but it is likely that Amun's processional bark existed in the Middle Kingdom, perhaps as early as the eleventh dynasty.

Originally, the iconography of the vessel was simple; its slim hull was slightly upturned at prow and stern, each end having ram-headed figureheads with cobras emerging from their foreheads. The cabin, in the form of the Upper Egyptian *pr-wr* shrine, was decorated with a frieze of uraei along the top of its side panels, with two friezes of alternating pairs of *dd* and *tit* amulets below; the lower half was undecorated. The cabin was protected by a light canopy roof supported by poles. Otherwise, the decoration and fittings were quite sparse. A pair of oars and their steering columns had falcon-headed terminals. A sphinx on a standard was placed behind the prow.

Dozens of blocks from Hatshepsut's Red Chapel indicate that by her reign, the bark sported a veil partly shrouding the cabin shrine, to which it was attached by a large clasp in the form of a vulture with outstretched wings. The pattern of decoration on the exposed part of the cabin now consisted of two friezes of uraei supported on *nb*-baskets and wearing *3tf*-crowns; a *šn*-sign protruding from its chest separated each cobra from its neighbor. The ram figureheads fore and aft had aegises in the form of *wsh*-collars with falcon-head terminals. The deck was peopled with a number of figurines, including ones of Hathor and Maat standing near the prow; in front of the cabin shrine were a statuette of a kneeling king proffering *nw*-jars, and a royal sphinx with human arms extending a *nmst*-jar. The four poles supporting the canopy over the cabin shrine were each steadied by a kneeling king. Finally, another royal figure acting as helmsman stood behind the oarlocks, steering by means of a tiller in the form of a uraeus. Other embellishments included a *wd3t* eye near the front of the hull and two clasps on each side of the hull in the form of winged scarabs that secured it to the carrying platform. The iconography of the bark remained largely the same before the Amarna period, but under Thutmose IV, *šbyw*-collars, consisting of two strands of biconical beads, were placed on the ram figureheads.

Since the bark was perhaps the most visible avatar of Amun-Re's cult, Akhenaten's partisans systematically expunged representations of it wherever such images appeared. Doubtless the gilded icon itself was likewise destroyed, since Tutankhamun's Restoration Edict dwells at length on the replacement of this costly and prestigious cult object. He claims to have refashioned it on thirteen carrying poles (nb3w), whereas formerly it had been on eleven. This statement has been puzzling to scholars, since there is no room in the confined inner recesses of the temples to accommodate so many carrying poles and their bearers. In fact, no more than five poles could have fit, even this increase being made possible only by a widening of the doorways in various temples and shrines. Although it has been thought that the larger bark with five poles appeared under Thutmose III, it is more likely that Tutankhamun was responsible. The reference to thirteen poles is probably hyperbole.

In the wake of the Amarna heresy, embellishments to the bark became increasingly complex. The figureheads were fitted with 3tf-crowns, large floral w3ḥ-collars and triple-stranded šbyw-collars; kneeling figurines of the king and the souls of Nekhen and Pe making jubilation and standing ones of the "Mrt-goddess" were set along the runners of the carrying platform. The formerly plain veil was now encrusted with hieroglyphic appliques forming parts of the royal titulary, arranged in rebus patterns. Two Maat goddesses with interlocking wings protecting a rebus of Tutankhamun's prenomen were most prominent among these.

This practice of incorporating titulary rebuses on the veil, and later on the exposed upper part of the cabin shrine, continued well into the Ramessid period and beyond. Certain elements, such as the winged goddesses, were retained for centuries. Others, specific to an individual king's titulary, were either discarded or altered so that they no longer referred explicitly to that king. Under Sety I, for example, the winged Maat figures knelt on mnboards and had sun disks on their heads, thereby rendering his prenomen Menmaatre. In later reigns, rebuses were modified to depict the names of other

kings, but temple reliefs indicate that some of these mn-signs, distinctive of Sety's name, were retained until the reign of Ramesses III. In this way, the rich iconography of the veil and cabin shrine underwent a continuous but gradual evolution.

Amun-Re also had a huge river barge called the Amun-Userhet, or "Amen-is-Mighty-of-Prow." Under Ramesses III, it was 130 cubits long (about 70 meters/224 feet). The barge itself closely resembled the processional bark, having elaborate ram-headed aegises, huge oars and steering columns, and even large versions of the crew of statues populating its deck. Its great cabin served as a floating temple complete with flagstaves and obelisks on its façade. All these fittings were plated with gold; from Amenhotpe III's reign on, even the hull was clad to the waterline with large gold sheets embossed with ritual scenes. During Theban religious celebrations, such as Opet and the Festival of the Valley, this dazzling floating temple was towed by ships and by men pulling dozens of tow ropes from shore, along canals and up the river, along with Amun's consort Mut and their son Khonsu, who were provided with river barges of their own as early as Tutankhamun's reign. Other gods had similar barges, but none are as well known as those of the Theban triad.

Peter Brand

SETH. The god of confusion, spirit of disorder and personification of violence, and bad faith was nevertheless venerated by the Egyptians as a god with whom one had to come to terms. Disorder, at least to a certain extent, was accepted as a reality of life and as essential to the living order.

Seth was also known as the god who brought death into the world by killing Osiris. Osiris had to die, but Seth gave

Depiction of Seth at right, teaching Thutmose III to shoot with the bow. From a relief at Karnak.

him an untimely, sordid, and lamentable death.

Seth and Horus fought for the rulership of the world, the kingship of Egypt, and the function of Osiris. In this battle Horus lost the light of his eye, and Seth the semen of his testicles. Seth, god of exuberant male sexuality not yet channeled into fertility, induced Horus to take part in pederastic acts and homosexual violation. The fruit of their relationship was the moon god Thoth, the son of the two lords. This pair of gods could also be referred to as the "two combatants." When they are mentioned by name, Horus as the royal god and prototype of the Egyptian gentleman always comes first, and Seth as the spirit of disorder comes second, for Horus has the more central and Seth the more peripheral position. Although these two

gods were the mythological symbols of all strife and the primal antagonists, they were separated, reunited, and reconciled. The justification of Horus in the verdict of the gods on their case always had an exclusive tendency; in chiefly later variants of the myth, Seth is punished and driven out. But as long as Horus and Seth are reconciled, they unite the two lands of Egypt by joining the sedge and papyrus so that pharaoh can rule over a country of order and peace. The pharaoh is a Horus reconciled to Seth, or a gentleman in whom the spirit of disorder has been integrated. Together these two gods rule over the world through the pharaoh whom they purify and crown, but still each one has his special half of the world: Horus has Lower Egypt and Seth has Upper Egypt, though this bipartition may also be reversed. During the New Kingdom, Horus is lord of the Black Land, the fertile Nile Valley, and Seth is lord of the Red Land, the desert and foreign countries. Not only the bipartition of the world but also many other contrasts were connected with these gods: north and south, heaven and earth, earth and underworld, right and left, black and red, being born and being conceived, rulership and strength, life and dominion.

Seth was also famous in a third and more positive role, first noted in the Coffin Texts: standing on the prow of the boat of the sun god Re, he repelled the evil snake Apophis. This aggressive warrior god and powerful thunder god, with his mighty scepter weighing 4,500 pounds, was employed by the sun god to conquer the reptile. In the myths of many cultures worldwide, the figure of the trickster—as this Egyptian god of confusion may be called—not only tricks gods and men, but is also the slayer of monsters.

A fourth aspect of Seth is that of the divine foreigner. His identification with Baal, the god of the Semites, is connected with the vicissitudes of the history of Seth and his cult. The first certain attestation of Seth can be found on the protohistoric votive mace head of King Scorpion on which appear clear depictions of dog-, pig-, or ass-like socalled Seth animals with the typical long curved snout, truncated ears, and raised tails. In later artifacts Seth may be represented in animal form as a sitting, standing, or lying Seth-animal, but also in human form, often with the head of a Seth-animal. More than twenty different animals, and even a bird and a fish, have been suggested as the mysterious Seth-animal. It seems best to accept the old idea of Champollion that it is a fabulous animal, like the griffin, supposed to live in the desert. It is not impossible, however, that this fabulous animal had the body of a dog or ass and the head of a pig. In writing system, the Seth-animal served as a determinative classification sign for about twenty-five words denoting confusion in cosmic, social, and personal life, such as "storm," "tumult," and "illness."

The kings of the first dynasty and also of Dynasty "0" were associated with Horus-falcons, but king Peribsen of the second dynasty replaced the falcon with the Seth-animal, and King Khasekhemwy put both falcon and Seth-animal above the *serekh* in which his name was written. But whether this indicates a Seth rebellion, as Newberry suggests in *Ancient Egypt* (1922, pp. 40–46), remains to be proved. Neither can it be proved that Seth was the god of the original inhabitants of Upper Egypt, the predynastic Naqada I culture who were subjugated by the Horus worshipers. It is interesting to note that Naqada, or Ombos, was the most important cult center of Seth in later times. The belief that one religion's devil is the god of a conquered religion is not uncommon and is not to be rejected in itself, but there is not enough proof that this was the case for Seth in Egyptian religion.

Already in the Old Kingdom, but especially in the imperial Ramessid period of the nineteenth and twentieth dynasties, Seth was viewed as the lord of foreign countries. The Libyan god Ash, the Western Semites' god Baal, and the Hittite god Teshub were recognized as forms of Seth, although such identifications or even combinations with other Egyptian gods are rare. Seth remains a god apart (*wdˁ*), as he is called since the Coffin Texts. Nevertheless, he had his traditional place in the Ennead of Heliopolis up into the first millennium BCE. His marriage with Nephthys remains a rather formal affair and, atypically, does not produce a divine child. It is at least doubtful whether Seth was ever held to be the father of Anubis, the child of Nephthys. That the crocodile Maga is said to be a son of Seth accentuates its demonic nature. Seth, whose exuberant sexual activities result in his being invoked in love charms and whose testicles are a symbol as a pendant of the Eye of Horus, has relations with the goddesses Hathor and Neith, and especially with the foreign goddesses Anat and Astarte. In texts the name of Seth is often substituted by "son of Nut," as if this violent, noisy thunder god is still a big boy. He is, however, not depicted being tended by his mother, like Horus by Isis. The texts of the first millennium BCE cursing Seth do not forget to mention that his own mother has turned against him.

Special cults of Seth were established on the border of the desert and at the beginnings of caravan routes: at Ombos, Sepermeru, the oases in the Western Desert, Avaris, and Piramesse. The frontier god or disorderly foreigner became the equal of Re, Ptah, or Amun as a god of state, court, and army when the Ramessid pharaohs of the nineteenth and twentieth dynasties had their residence in Piramesse near the border in the northeastern Delta. Even pharaohs took their name from him: Sety ("man of Seth") and Sethnakht ("Seth-is-strong").

The remarkable reputation of Seth in mythology and his reputedly violent and disorderly character did not prevent some Egyptians from adopting him as their local or personal god. Personal names show that some did not hesitate to ascribe to Seth the same qualities that others assigned to more reputable gods: "Seth-is-great," "Seth-is-gracious," "Seth-is-kind," "Seth-is-content," "Seth-givessalvation," "Seth-causes-to live."

One title of a high priest of Seth was *šd-ḫrw*, which means "he who raises the voice" or "who causes commotion" or "who kicks up a row." We do not know whether this expression indicates the social position and behavior of the priesthood of Seth, or whether it is simply a nickname given by outsiders who abhorred Seth.

In the first millennium BCE the Seth-animal disappeared from art and hieroglyphic writing. As an enemy of the gods, he was represented as an ass with a knife stuck in his head. In the western oases, where he was venerated as a god until the end of Egyptian religion in the fourth century CE he was represented with a falcon's head, like Horus, his alter ego. The turning point from veneration to demonization of Seth in the Nile Valley must be dated shortly after 700 BCE, in the time of the pious Kushite pharaohs of the twenty-fifth dynasty.

Herman te Velde

SHADOW. One of the major components in the Egyptian concept of an individual was the shadow (*shut; šwt*), along with the body, the *ka* (*k3*), the *ba* (*b3*), and the name. Like the body, the shadow was seen as a physical entity, and its relationship to light was understood. The *Prophecy of Neferti*, describing the absence of sunlight, says "no one will distinguish his shadow." The term *šwt* is used not only with reference to the shadow of individuals but also for the shade cast by any object, such as trees and buildings: the Sphinx Stela of Thutmose IV describes how the king "rested in the shadow of this great god" at noon. The term is also employed as a metaphor for protection—understandable in Egypt's climate—both from the heat of the sun and in a broader sense, as that extended by a god over the king, by the king's arm over his subjects, or even by the king's sun-shade over bystanders.

In common with the other elements

of an individual, the shadow was viewed both as a component of its owner and a separate mode of existence. The image of a god carved on a temple wall could be called the god's shadow, and the temple itself was sometimes known as the shadow of its deity.

Most references to the shadow of a human being occur in funerary texts dealing with the afterlife. The earliest instances appear in the Coffin Texts of the First Intermediate Period and Middle Kingdom, where the shadow is usually mentioned together with the ba. Like the latter, it can be viewed as a mode of existence after death. In some cases, however, the ba and shadow seem to be two parts of a single entity: "Go, my ba and my shadow, that you (singular) may see the sun." Since the deceased's ba is regularly said to possess physical powers such as eating, drinking, and copulating, the shadow in such cases may have been understood as that of the ba itself.

Other passages in the Coffin Texts present the ba and shadow as distinct entities. Both are closely associated with the body in the tomb: the ba is said to be "in the earth" while the shadow is "in the inaccessible places" (the burial chamber), and the deceased states that "my ba belongs to my body, my shadow belongs to its arm." Like the ba, the shadow returned to the mummy at night: the Coffin Texts speak of "my ba and my shadow going on their feet to the place where that man [the deceased] is." In some cases, however, the shadow is more closely allied than the ba to its body. This is reflected in a passage from the Pyramid Texts and Coffin Texts that describes the deceased's consumption of the gods' bas "while their shadows remain with their owners."

Unlike the ba, the shadow was rarely depicted, but it occasionally appears in funerary literature as a human silhouette, sometimes with an eye.   *James P. Allen*

SHU. As a member of the Heliopolitan Ennead, Shu was one of the eldest deities in the Egyptian pantheon. In the Heliopolitan cosmology, the creator god Atum created Shu and his female counterpart, Tefnut. This act of creation by Atum is described variously as having been accomplished by means of masturbation, by sneezing, or by spitting out these two deities. Thus, Shu and his sisterwife were the first sexually differentiated gods in the Egyptian pantheon. As the first male god, Shu had warlike traits like Onuris and became associated with the pharaoh.

Shu was a cosmic deity whose role in Egyptian religion, while hard to describe, was nevertheless essential for the existence of human life. Shu was the god of life; he was manifest in the wind, air, light, and water that were necessary for life to function. As a force of life, he was a creator who was present at birth. The acts of hearing and speaking were both associated with him. Typically, Shu was thought of as the god of dry air and represented as a man wearing a feather on his head.

In depictions of the Egyptian cosmos, Shu was shown kneeling and lifting up the sky goddess Nut, separating her from her husband, the god of the earth, Geb. Shu's role was to support the heavens and to provide the space for life to develop on earth. It was Shu who separated darkness from light, and he was often perceived as a column of air, or as the empty space between heaven and earth. Shu's name (*šu*) meant "dryness" or "emptiness." This empty space was not considered as a void, but rather an arena for the possibility of activity. Shu might also be envisioned as the rays of the sun.

Shu was mentioned in his role as a creative life force in both the Pyramid Texts and the Coffin Texts, but is not well known outside these religious texts until after the New Kingdom, when Shu became connected with the gods Onuris, Khonsu, Horus, and Sopdu and was worshipped along with them in their local cults. He was listed in the Turin Canon of kings as one of the early divine rulers of Egypt before this role was assumed by a mortal man. A more detailed description of Shu's reign in Egypt was found on a shrine originally from Saft el-Henna that dates to the sixth to fourth centuries BCE. Shu was related to the ram-headed god of Mendes, Banebdjedet, whose identity incorporated the first four divine rulers of the world: Re, Shu, Geb, and Osiris.

The main cult center of Shu and his consort Tefnut was at Tell el-Yahudiyya. The Greek name for this city was Leontopolis (the city of the lion), and Shu and Tefnut were worshiped here in leonine form. The local version of the Heliopolitan creation myth describes Shu and Tefnut as lion cubs who, when grown, guarded the eastern and western horizons, thus protecting the rising and the setting of the sun. Shu was also thought of as the offspring of the sun god, Re.

Jennifer Houser-Wegner

SOBEK. A crocodile god representing the Nile floods and fertility, Sobek (Eg., *Sbk;* Gr., *Suchos*) was also a symbol of royal power, leading several late Middle Kingdom pharaohs to incorporate his name into their own. Sobek became a primordial deity and creator god in the New Kingdom owing to his assimilation with Re. By the Ptolemaic period, he was identified with numerous deities, taking on the aspect of a universal god.

Sobek was depicted as a crocodile wearing a tall plumed headdress, or as a human with a crocodile's head. Among his earliest portrayals is an Early Dynastic cylinder seal showing a crocodile on a standard. He also appears as a crocodile in temple reliefs, seals, royal statuary, and papyri. Beginning in the Middle King-

Amenhotep III and the god Sobek. From Dahamsha Museum, Luxor, Thebes, Egypt. (Scala/Art Resource, NY)

dom, Sobek or Sobek-Re sometimes took the form of a ram or a ram-headed human; in the New Kingdom and later, he might appear in fully human form; in the Greco-Roman period, he took many different forms.

Sobek's characteristics were already partly established by the time of the Pyramid Texts, which portray him both as a benevolent god of the Nile floods and as potentially ferocious and destructive. The Coffin Texts associate him with the Nile and its floods, the riverbanks, and fertility. Both the Coffin Texts and Middle Kingdom hymns to Sobek assimilate him into the Osirian myth and associate him with Horus. The hymns also identify him with Re, with whom he was syncretized from the Middle Kingdom onward. Epithets of Sobek in the New Kingdom describe him as a creator god. During the Ptolemaic and Roman periods, he was depicted at the bow of the solar bark, defeating the enemies of Re.

Ptolemaic hymns not only continue to demonstrate his role as a creator but also refer to him as the supreme universal deity.

The cult of Sobek originated in marshy areas where crocodiles were common and later became so widespread that evidence of it is found throughout Egypt. His most prominent and earliest documented sanctuary was at Shedet in the Faiyum, later called Krokodilopolis by the Greeks. During the twelfth dynasty, when the reigning kings focused great attention on the Faiyum, Sobek became one of Egypt's principal state gods, reaching particular prominence under Amenemhet III. Another major cult center was situated at Kom Ombo in Upper Egypt, where several New Kingdom pharaohs dedicated buildings. Sobek's cult at Gebel es-Silsila is particularly well attested during the nineteenth dynasty. In the Theban area, he was worshipped at Gebelein and Dehamsha, where the eighteenth dynasty sanctuary included a complex installation for housing and feeding sacred crocodiles. Roman sources relate accounts of priests feeding sacred crocodiles in the Faiyum, and Ptolemaic and Roman period crocodile cemeteries have been found at a number of sites.

Neith was the mother of Sobek, and his father was Senuwy (the Greek crocodile god Psosnaus). Although he was identified with a number of different deities in pharaonic times, including Hathor, Horus, Khnum, and Re, Sobek was not portrayed as having a wife or children until Greco-Roman times, when he was worshipped at Kom Ombo and Philae with Hathor as his consort and Khonsu as their child.

Denise M. Doxey

SOKAR. The name of this divinity (Eg., *skr*; Gr., Sokaris), according to a hypothetical etymology based on Coffin Text Spell 816 and a twelfth dynasty papyrus, is derived from *sk r* ("cleaning of the mouth"), a word used in the context of the Opening of the Mouth ceremony, in which Sokar plays a role. Such word play, does not, however, constitute a true etymology. Nor (*pace* Brovarski 1987) does the name appear to be related to "Saqqara," which probably comes from the name of a Berber tribe, the Beni Saqqar.

In iconography established by the Old Kingdom, Sokar is depicted as an anthropomorphic figure with the head of a falcon, evoking his earthly representation and his divine ability to fly in the underworld, on earth, and in the heavens. He is shown either standing or seated on a throne, garbed in the cloth of a funerary god. He wears a White Crown and holds a scepter and a whip, the regalia of Osiris. Sokar is also represented in predatory form, again enveloped in fabric. As a falcon, he can be related to Horus, and like him wears the Double Crown. His solar functions are indicated by the presence of the disk and the *uraeus*. When in human form, Sokar occasionally wears the *atef*-crown.

Sokar's emblems include a barge, onions, and geese. The barge, or *ḥnw*, represents solar triumphs and is set on a sledge. At its prow may be the head of an antelope or a bull, an *lnt*-fish, and birds (falcons or swallows) along the edge of the hull. The mound-shaped *štyt*-chapel at its center culminates in a falcon's head. At the stern are three or four rudder pins. On the night preceding the procession of this barge, the deceased wears an onion necklace to prepare for the solarization of Sokar-Osiris. A luminous rebirth occurs on the morning of the twenty-sixth day in the month of Khoiak in the *ḥnw*-barge, which is protected by five geese, daughters of Re, and their barges. The transport of the *ḥnw* was organized by the high priest of Ptah in Memphis.

In the Old Kingdom, the festival of Sokar was already an annual event in the fourth month of the *3ḥt* season, on the twenty-fifth and twenty-sixth days. It involved a visit to the royal necropolis and offerings to the dead. In the Middle Kingdom, it incorporated Osirian aspects of festivals in Abydos. Later it became a solemn occasion marked by a procession of Sokar's *ḥnw*-barge in the great temples of Egypt. It celebrated the continuity of the cult of the divine king linked to the resurrection of Sokar and to the revival of the great cosmic cycles.

Egyptological tradition, however, defines Sokar as an essentially chthonic deity acting in the funerary world of the Memphite necropolis. Funerary and offering formulae that mention Sokar appear only in the Middle Kingdom. The Pyramid Texts describe Sokar as a god active in the rebirth of the king and in the ceremonies of confirmation and transfer of royal power. In the Middle Kingdom, he assumes a specific role in the transfiguration at death and in the Opening of the Mouth ceremony. In his role in the rites of statues as a metallurgist, he resembles Ptah, who transforms stone and wood. The entity Ptah-Sokar associates the wealth of the soil and its power of growth. The *Book of Going Forth by Day* (*Book of the Dead*) in New Kingdom times presents Sokar as an image of the world unified in Osiris, linked to the aforementioned festivals or to foundation rituals. The terrestrial Ptah-Sokar becomes Sokar-Osiris, the nocturnal incarnation of the sun during the fourth and fifth hours of the *Book of That Which Is in the Underworld* (*Amduat*). He enables the sun to complete its course during the night and to be reborn in the morning. In the New Kingdom,

Priests of Sokar bear the same titles as the Memphite clergy of Ptah did in the Old Kingdom, but now they almost always refer to the high priests of Heliopolis. Henceforth, an entity reuniting the three divine forms, Ptah-Sokar-Osiris, expresses creation-metamorphosis-rebirth.

In the Late Period, numerous tombs are equipped with Ptah-Sokar-Osiris wood statuettes in anthropomorphic form with a falcon's head or in full animal form as a falcon. This rests on a base containing the *Book of Going Forth by Day*, or a grain mummy reminiscent of the "beds of Osiris." In the Ptolemaic period, the Osirian form of Sokar reached its zenith, becoming the focus of the Osirian festivals in the month of Khoiak.

Sokar is related two groups of deities: the Memphite group formed by Khnum, Herremenuyfy, and Chesmu, and the solar group constituted by Nefertum and the five divine daughters of Re, all present at the feast of Sokar. The "Memphite" Khnum is among the Memphite divinities listed in the Sokar chapel and the hall of Sokar and Nefertum in the temple of Sety I at Abydos. Nephthys may be Sokar's companion, or, less often, Seshat. Called "father and mother," Sokar has no family as such, even though a grammatical doublet—Sokaret—appears; Redoudja is identified as "son of Sokar" in Spell 941 of the Coffin Texts.

In the Pyramid Texts, Sokar is called a native of Rosetjau, a site near the Sphinx of Giza, but ultimately indicating any necropolis, and of Pedju(-she), the lake of Abusir. He is also master of the *štyt*, which refers to the cabin of the *ḥnw*-barge, his sandy environment mentioned in the *Book of That Which Is in the Underworld*, and a chapel dedicated to him in the temple of Horus at Edfu. Two other names for the sanctuary of Sokar

are *pr-ḥnw* ("house of *henu*") and *ḥwt-Skr*
("chapel of Sokar"), referring to the
functions of housing the divine barge
and the statue of the deity. There are also
chapels dedicated to Sokarian aspects and
integrated in a temple consecrated to a
mother major divinity. There is still no
archaeological evidence of a temple
solely dedicated to Sokar; however, the
deity is known from sites throughout
Egypt, initially through textual documentation and later, from the Middle
Kingdom onward, through iconographic
sources. In the Old Kingdom, Sokar is
present from the Memphite necropolises
to Helwan. Already well established in
the Faiyum during the Middle Kingdom, the deity appears in the tombs of
Deir el-Bahri. It reaches Thebes with the
declaration of that city as the new capital. From the beginning of the New
Kingdom, the deity is found at Karnak;
during the reign of Hatshepsut it occupies an important place in the chapel-
cavern of Anubis on the second terrace,
as well as in the Thutmose I chapel on
the third terrace at Deir el-Bahri. Thutmose III dedicated a suite of rooms to
Sokar in Akh-menu. In the tombs of
Western Thebes, Sokarian elements occur for the first time. Amenophis III
consecrated to Sokar a monumental architectural ensemble in his temple of
"millions of years" in Thebes. The well-
established Sokar cult of Western Thebes
continued to develop in the Ramessid
period, with numerous representations of
Sokarian rites in private and royal tombs.
At Gurneh, the Hall IX of the temple of
Sety I was dedicated to Sokar, who was
also given a cult site in the temple constructed by the same king at Abydos. A
group of rooms in the Ramesseum was
consecrated to him by Ramesses II, who
also had the deity represented on the peripheral wall of the temples of Amun-
Re and of Re-Horakhty at Karnak. The

most important source for the cult of Sokar exists in the second court of the temple of "millions of years" of Ramesses III
at Medinet Habu; In addition, Room 4
of this complex is a chapel for the *ḥnw-*
barge.

The *ḥnw*-barge becomes dominant in
the late Sokarian iconography. Sources
include a few Theban sarcophagi from
the twenty-first dynasty; the silver sarcophagus of Sheshonq II (twenty-second
dynasty) with falcon mask, discovered in
Tanis; statues from the twenty-second
and twenty-third dynasties; the chapel of
Osiris Heqa-Djet at Karnak (twenty-
third dynasty); Theban Tomb 32 from
the Saite period in Western Thebes; and
the temple of Hibis at Chargha (twenty-
seventh dynasty).

The sanctuary of Alexander at Karnak and Louvre Papyrus N 3176(S)
prove that Akh-menu was active until
the Ptolemaic period. Sokar and his
barge are, however, infrequently represented in Thebes during Ptolemaic
times: on the propylaeum of Khonsu at
Karnak; at the temple of Montu in
North Karnak; in the temple of Hathor
at Deir el-Medina; in the temple of Hatshepsut at Deir el-Bahri; and on the
small temple at Medinet Habu. By that
time the Sokarian cult had moved to the
temple of Horus at Edfu (Halls XIII–
XIV) and that of Hathor at Dendera
(Hall XVI and the six roof chapels), in
the context of the Osirian celebrations in
the month of Khoiak. The last representation of Osiris-Sokar with a falcon's
head was done under Emperor Caracalla
at Philae.   *Catherine Graindorge*
            Translated from French by
            Elizabeth Schwaiger

SYMBOLS. By definition, symbols
represent something other than what
they actually depict. Generally, they are
based on conventionally agreed-on

meanings; but unlike signs, which usually stand for something quite concrete (as in the case of mathematical or linguistic signs), symbols usually stand for something less visible or tangible than the symbol itself—for example, in modern American culture the dove is used as a symbol of peace, and the hawk as a symbol of war. Symbols must frequently be differentiated from what Egyptologists call "attributes," which generally represent something by the display of one of its parts (as in the use of the crown for the king, the crook and flail for Osiris)—a case of synecdoche; and from emblems, which are distinctive badges that represent an individual, group, office, or nation (as in the use of the *serekh*, representing the palace façade, to display the Egyptian king's name). Of course, attributes and emblems often exhibit some of the characteristics of symbols.

Symbolic Expression in Egyptian Culture. The civilization of ancient Egypt was symbolically oriented to a degree rarely equaled by other cultures. It was through symbols that the Egyptians represented and affirmed many of their ideas, beliefs, and attitudes regarding the nature of life and reality. Symbols often depict aspects of reality that are difficult to represent through other modes of expression, and the ancient Egyptians used them constantly in this manner.

Symbolism, in fact, has been described as a primary form of ancient Egyptian thought, and it is necessary to understand the pervasive nature of this way of thinking in order to fully grasp the role of symbols in Egyptian society. Artists, architects, and craftspeople utilized symbols in the design and construction of objects ranging from temples, tombs, and other monuments to the smallest items of everyday life. Yet this constant incorporation of symbols was

not merely a matter of decoration or playful visual punning. The use of symbolism allowed the ancient Egyptians to impose their view of life on the surface of perceived reality by incorporating or imagining symbols in the objects, forms, and activities that surrounded them.

This is not to say that symbols were employed only in the representational forms of art and architecture, for symbolism was manifested in many other areas of life, such as the practice of formal and informal magic, or religious ritual. Egyptian religion and magic both relied to a great extent on symbolism to accomplish their ends; as a result, the symbolism inherent in a given work is often an expression of underlying religious or magical beliefs that give the work life, meaning, and power.

Because symbols are different from the things they represent, some kind of association must always be present to link the symbol to its referent, the aspect of reality it represents. In Egyptian symbolism these associations are usually visual. In fact, the Egyptian language appears to have had no single word that exactly parallels our term "symbol;" the closest and most common approximation is probably *twt* ("image"), which underscores symbolism's largely visual basis. But symbols are not limited to the visual. Sounds (for example, the onomatopoeic equation of the ram's "baa" with the *ba* of the god) and perhaps even scents (incense offerings) and other sensory perceptions (perceived divine odors) could hold symbolic content for the Egyptians. But it is largely the expression of visual symbolism that has survived, and this provides the bulk of the evidence considered in this article.

In any type of symbolism, however, symbol and reality were inextricably intertwined in ancient Egypt. Thus, a person's name (both written and spoken) not only identified and represented that person as an individual but was also a veritable part of the individual's being, to the extent that to deface or destroy the name, and thus prevent its being spoken or seen, helped to destroy the existence of the person named. Once established, the symbolic aspect of an object became a part of its identity which was rarely ignored entirely, and frequently expressed to the full. Because light-reflecting mirrors shone like the sun, for example, for the Egyptians it was perhaps preferable that mirrors be circular, and that any decoration applied to them relate in some way to solar symbolism.

Not only were symbol and reality inextricably intertwined in Egyptian thought; symbols were also used to adjust perceived reality and to impose on it a meaningful and acceptable framework. This is seen especially in the fact that the Egyptian use of symbols represents a system in which the existence of conflicting facts was often successfully resolved by means of the ambivalent nature of the symbols themselves. Symbols frequently have several meanings and may openly contradict themselves in their expression, yet, in symbolic thought, the two opposing expressions may be viewed as complementary rather than contradictory. An animal such as the crocodile, for example, could symbolize not only death and destruction but also solar-oriented life and regeneration, because both appear to be true aspects of the creature's observed and mythical nature. Despite its fearsome and destructive aspects, the crocodile faces the morning sun as though in adoration and also hunts fish, the mythological enemies of the sun god. A similar polarity is seen in the Egyptian perception of many aspects of the natural world and in the character of many Egyptian gods. Osiris, for example, may be said to symbolize both death

and regenerate life. Either meaning, or both, may be implicit to the use of a given symbol, depending on context.

The manipulation of contradictory facts through the use of symbols was not always complete, however, and in some cases symbols compete or consciously stress contradictions in the same setting. For example, the Egyptian king's position vis-à-vis that of the people is one of great power, and he is their protector, yet the king is at the same time dependent on the gods and receives their protection. Both aspects of reality are true, and both factors receive independent symbolic representation, though usually in different contexts.

To a certain extent, the function of symbols in Egyptian art, life, and thought was also contradictory. The symbols may be esoteric or exoteric—they may be utilized both to reveal and to conceal: to reveal by evoking important aspects of reality, and to conceal through limiting the audience that understands their message. Both aspects are integral parts of Egyptian symbolic expression and were employed according to context and need.

Aspects of Egyptian Visual Symbolism. In Egyptian culture the more important and frequently encountered aspects of visual symbolism are form, hieroglyphs, relative size, location, material, color, number, action, and gesture. These are considered separately below.

Form. Egyptian art utilizes form symbolism at two levels, which may be designated primary and secondary, or direct and indirect types of association. At the first level, objects are shown in the forms they are meant to represent and gain symbolic significance through association and context—for example, the use of the *djed*-pillar as a symbol of support. At the secondary level, symbolic association occurs when significant forms are represented indirectly, as in the case of the clenched-hand amulets that represented sexual union.

In many cases, images that are widely disparate in form may actually relate to the same underlying symbolic theme; conversely, even small modifications of form may result in significant changes in symbolic meaning. The former may be seen in the array of symbols associated with the goddess Hathor, ranging from the papyrus plant to the cow; modification of a form is frequently seen in representations of the human figure, where different poses—kneeling, seated, standing, striding, etc.—may imply very different meanings. In formal architectural decoration, programmatic modification of forms—as in the location and color of solar disks in tombs, or the transition from plant bud to fully open capital forms of columns in temples—is frequently employed to symbolize spatial and temporal aspects of the cosmos.

Hieroglyphs. A specialized subset of form symbolism, hieroglyphic symbolism is one of the most frequent sources of symbols encountered in Egyptian art and may be expressed in several ways. In *ideographic* representation (the depiction of a figure or object in the form of a hieroglyphic sign), hieroglyphic forms may function as representations of individuals and as manifestations of the gods themselves. *Rebus* representation (the spelling out of personal names or titles by combining hieroglyphic signs with syllabic values in the composition) was also commonly used for two- and three-dimensional representations of kings, and not infrequently for others.

While visual metaphor (the use of a sign to suggest something else with which it is somehow associated) is relatively infrequent, visual analogy (the use of hieroglyphic signs for things that they resemble) is particularly common in Egyptian art. In the latter type of representation, objects are made in the form of hieroglyphic signs they resemble—a mirror case or a vase in the shape of an *ankh* sign, or a headrest in the form of the horizon hieroglyph. This type of mimicking of forms is usually being tied in some way to the meaning or significance of the object.

The forms of hieroglyphs were also "projected" by the Egyptians onto actual objects in two ways. On the one hand, hieroglyphic forms were used in the design and production of various objects; on the other, natural objects were viewed and represented in the form of hieroglyphic signs that they resembled.

Only the educated elite of Egyptian society could properly write and read, and it was for them that most artworks were produced. Nevertheless, many people probably recognized at least some of the more common hieroglyphs and could understand common examples of hieroglyphic symbolism.

Size. The stratified sizes of god and human, king and subject, tomb owner and servant, or parent and child are usually symbolic of relative status and power within Egyptian compositions. This is particularly clear in scenes recorded on temple walls and in other settings that show the Egyptian king at a much larger scale than his enemies, heightening the hierarchical effect of the representation by emphasizing the helplessness of the enemy and the king's superhuman stature. In two- and three-dimensional colossal representations of kings and gods, the stratification is actually based on the relative scale of the colossus and the viewer. In a similar manner, even fully adult children are frequently depicted standing beside their parents as tiny figures, even though their figures, hair, and clothing leave no doubt as to their actual maturity. While Egyptian artists also used reduction of scale for purely artistic, compositional reasons, such instances are usually clearly discernible from symbolic ones.

The principle of same-sizing—to suggest equality or near-equality of status—may be achieved through both isocephaly and equality of scale. Isocephaly may indicate equality between subjects by placing heads of figures at the same level, or it may maintain a hierarchical difference by ensuring that an individual of lesser importance does not look down on a more important figure. Although isocephaly is frequently the result of use of the same drafting grid for both figures in Egyptian representations, many examples exist that indicate conscious same-sizing. Equality of scale does not always imply equality of status, however, and in New Kingdom battle scenes a single enemy figure may be depicted at the same scale as the Egyptian king in order to represent the enemy as a whole.

The adjusted size of individual body parts or areas for symbolic reasons must also be considered under this heading. Bodily proportions may be adjusted or emphasized as a means of suggesting maturity or status—as in the purposefully corpulent rendering of temple statues and tomb representations of private officials, and in some cases in royal representations. Many so-called fertility figurines clearly exaggerate male or female sexual characteristics for symbolic and magical purposes.

Location. The symbolism of location may be absolute or relative, referring on the one hand to the specific location of a representation, object, building, or place (such as a sacred site), and on the other to the positioning or alignment of something in relation to some other representation, object, building, or place. From very early times, funerary scenes depicting pilgrimages to sacred sites are clear indicators of the importance of locational aspects in ancient Egyptian religion. Even when the sites were not actually visited, they maintained a symbolic role that involved the spiritual continuity of the veneration of the sacred place. While locational symbolism thus frequently applies to actual specific sites, absolute locational symbols are often paired or juxtaposed as representatives of a more abstract geographic or cosmic dichotomy, such as Upper and Lower Egypt, east and west, or heaven and earth. This type of oppositional or symmetrical pairing is often expressed, in turn, through relative locational symbolism, which may range from the careful arrangement and alignment of elements within individual compositions and funerary (tomb goods) and religious (temple furniture) assemblages, to the architectural and decorative programs of whole buildings such as temples and tombs, and even the planning of groups of buildings and cities. Sometimes the orientation is according to a simple right/left, east/west, or north/south dichotomy; in other cases, it reflects subtler divisions within the structure of the individual composition or building.

Small-scale manifestations of this kind of relative placement may be seen, for example, in the "prepositional" placement of representations of kings before the figures of protective deities such as the overshadowing Horus falcon, the Hathor cow, and the sphinx in its various forms. This orientation implies the idea of protection for the king and is reflected in the hieroglyphic formula "protection behind him," commonly written behind the king. Similarly, to be "beneath" another figure might connote inferiority or subjugation, as may be seen in the carefully controlled relative placement of figures in scenes of victory over fallen enemies, and in the depiction of captives on the bases of royal thrones and footstools.

Material. Various materials held symbolic significance for the Egyptians, and not least of these were precious metals. Gold was regarded as divine on account of its color and brightness (symbolic of the sun) and its untarnishing nature (symbolic of eternal life). The flesh of the gods descended from the sun god Re was said to be of gold, and thus many images of deities were formed from this substance or gilded. Silver also had divine associations: the bones of the gods were said to be of this substance, and it was used extensively as a symbol of the moon in mirrors and in figures of lunar gods such as Khonsu and Thoth.

Many more common materials were also symbolically important. Among stones, for example, the black coloration of basalt gave it a natural association with the underworld, and lapis lazuli was symbolic of the heavens because of its blue ground color and star-like golden specks. Similarly, materials as diverse as wood, wax, and water could suggest one or more symbolic associations; water, for example, functioned as a symbol of purification and acceptance, and also of life, renewal, and fertility. The symbolic importance of a substance was often based on its natural color, but a substance might also be important because of some unusual characteristic or through mythological associations.

Color. This was one of the most important aspects of Egyptian symbolism and is the underlying reason for the symbolic associations of many materials. Individual colors could suggest different things according to context and use, however. Red, the color of fire, the sun, and blood, could symbolize any of these things, or the more abstract concepts of life and destruction associated with

them. Blue was naturally associated with the heavens and water, and in the latter association could represent the concept of fertility. Yellow, a primary solar color, was used extensively for solar-related objects such as the scarab and the golden bodies of the gods. Black, although a color of the netherworld and its deities, could also be used in nonfunerary contexts and was symbolic of fertility through its associations with the rich black earth of the Nile Valley. Green, the color of luxuriant vegetation and thus of life itself, could signify health and vitality, and the sound or undamaged eye of Horus is often depicted in this color. White was sometimes used as a symbol of purity; but as a solar color, white could also be used as an alternative to yellow in some contexts.

The interchange of colors that exists in Egyptian art is partly a result of the somewhat different classification of colors used by the Egyptians, and partly of the principle of equivalence, whereby different colors were treated as one owing to physical similarities (for example, the white, yellow, and red appearances of the sun), or because of abstract, symbolic connections between them (e.g., black and green as colors of regeneration).

Number. Several numbers held symbolic significance for the Egyptians, especially the integers 2, 3, 4, 7, and their multiples—all of which are usually, in some way, expressions of unity in plurality. It is thus unity rather than diversity that is stressed in many of the dualities seen in Egyptian art. The phenomenon of duality pervades Egyptian culture and is at the heart of the Egyptian concept of the universe, which views the many evident dichotomies of light and dark, sun and moon, east and west, and so on, as expressions of the essential unity of existence. Similarly, while three was the number associated with the concept of plurality, three was also a number of unity inherent in plurality, as may be seen in the many divine families that Egyptian theology constructed of a god, his wife, and their child, or in the characterization of Amun, Re, and Ptah as the soul, face, and body of god. To a great extent, although they may often connote simple plurality, symbolic use of the numbers four, six, seven, nine, and twelve also follows this pattern of unity in plurality. Larger numbers, such as one thousand (as in the offering formula "a thousand loaves of bread") and greater, usually symbolize plurality alone.

Actions. Actions depicted in Egyptian art may be performed by gods, humans, or animals. They may be real, mythical, or iconographic, and may also be classed as ritual or nonritual. Any of these types of action may have symbolic significance.

Real actions are simply actions that take place in the real world. Many representations of the Egyptian king engaged in some kind of ritual activity depict real events in which the king actually participated. By contrast, images showing the king involved in mythically related activities may represent something that was acted out (as in certain temple rituals where costumed priests may have represented various deities), but these actions also appear to have been depicted largely for symbolic purposes. The motif of ritual slaying of enemies may well have been a real action at times, but it is frequently depicted in a mythical, generic manner. When actions in Egyptian art are of an apparently realistic nature but are depicted in an exaggerated or unrealistic manner for symbolic or propagandistic purposes, they may be described as *iconographic* actions.

The majority of formal actions depicted in Egyptian art are of a ritual nature; that is, most aspects of the activity—time, place, and manner—were carefully prescribed and conducted according to an established pattern or protocol. Each detail of such ritual actions may have specific symbolic significance. Nonritual actions, however, are the actions of everyday life, though these may sometimes have symbolic significance; thus, representations of pouring and throwing in some contexts may relate covertly to physical sexuality and hence to birth and the rebirth of the afterlife.

Gestures. A particular aspect of the symbolism of actions, gesture symbolism—using the positioning or movement of the body, head, arms or hands—is the most complex and least understood aspect of Egyptian visual symbolism. This is largely because Egyptian artists usually worked within established formulae for the depiction of the human body, and this conventional depiction serves both to obscure certain types of gestures and to summarize others, with gestures usually being "frozen" in the representations at a single characteristic point. Many, if not most, gestures depicted in Egyptian art functioned as nonverbal communication, however, and connoted general or specific meanings relating to themes such as greeting, asking, praising, offering, speaking, rejoicing, and so on. As a result, despite the frequent difficulty of analysis, many of these gestures may be observed in specific contexts and interpreted with some certainty.

Over all, two types of gestures can be differentiated: independent and sequential. Gestures such as that exhibited by mummiform representations of Osiris with the arms folded across the chest exist in isolation and have complete meaning in and of themselves without reference to any other gesture, action, or context, and may thus be termed "independent." More complex gesture patterns also exist, however, where a certain pose or gesture seen in representations actually occurred within a sequence of continuous action. These sequential gestures are found in contexts such as ritual funerary activities and formalized expressions of praise and offering and are understandably more difficult to reconstruct and interpret. It should also be remembered that a number of similar gestures actually represent different poses with different meanings; on the other hand, truly different gestures may sometimes function within the same range of meaning.

Interpretation of Symbols. In a given representation, artifact, or monument, one or several of the above symbolic dimensions may be present. In fact, it is rare that an Egyptian work has none of these elements; and the presence of symbolic aspects must be addressed in any thorough analysis of Egyptian artistic and architectural work.

Although different symbolic aspects may be emphasized in different settings or types of work, certain basic principles may be widely applied. Generally speaking, while a single, salient symbolic aspect is evident in a given representation or object, other aspects may reinforce this association or provide additional levels of meaning.

Once a symbolic association has been established between an object and its symbolic referent (e.g., the color red, sun), anything with the same characteristic may be said to be symbolic of that referent. Once an object or characteristic has become symbolic of a given referent, then its other characteristics may also be interpreted in terms of the same symbolic association. For example, the heron is associated with the Nile primarily because of its aquatic habits, but its blue coloration also ties into the same association. The swallow is associated with the sun primarily because it flies out from its nest in the ground at dawn and returns at dusk—and also because of its red coloring.

Interpreting the various types of symbols—discovering what they meant for the ancient Egyptians themselves—is not always a simple matter, however, and may be approached from a number of physical and psychological viewpoints. Even at a purely Egyptological level, the interpretation and understanding of symbols requires a careful approach. Primarily, we must beware of assuming that a given aspect of a two- or three-dimensional representational work or architectural structure had some symbolic significance for the Egyptians without reasonable indication that this was the case.

Because it developed in an open system of thought that allowed and encouraged the free association of ideas, Egyptian symbolism is easily misunderstood. This was as true for ancient and medieval observers as it is for us today, as we see, for example, in many of the "interpretations" of Egyptian symbols recorded by Plutarch. He tells us, for example, that the cat was regarded by the Egyptians as a symbol of the moon on account of its activity in the night and the "fact" that it produces increasing numbers of young (corresponding to the daily increase in the moon's light), and especially because its pupils expand and contract like the full and crescent moon. Yet how much, if any, of this reasoning was true for the ancient Egyptians' original association of the cat with the moon is difficult to ascertain. Even when care is taken in this regard, it must be remembered that symbols can be fluid things. Their meanings may certainly change over time, and it does not always follow that the symbolic significance of a given element in one composition will be identical in another work of earlier or later date.

The symbols utilized in Egyptian art may also exhibit different meanings in different contexts in the same period. In funerary contexts, feather patterning may be symbolic of the wings of certain protective goddesses, or of the avian aspects of the *ba* of the deceased. Textual evidence suggests even more possibilities, associating or identifying the deceased with a hawk, a swallow, or some other bird, so that in certain cases where context does not render a clear choice, it is difficult to decide on the specific significance of such a symbolic element— or if there could be some kind of generic symbolism meant to embrace many or all of these possible ideas. At the same time, many different symbols may be used for the same symbolic referent (e.g., the swallow, baboon, and *bulti*-fish, all used for the sun), but in many cases relatively little study has been devoted to the reasons for the choice of given symbols in different settings.

The Egyptians themselves were conscious of the ambiguity in their own symbolism and even seem to have encouraged it. Enigmatic statements in religious texts are not infrequently glossed with several divergent explanations, and the principle doubtless applies to representational as well as literary use of symbols. There is often a field or range of possible meanings for a given symbol, and while we may select a specific interpretation that seems most likely according to context, we must remember that other symbolic associations may also be involved.

This is not to say that ancient Egyptian symbolism is inchoate, inconsistent, or imprecise, but that a flexible approach must be maintained in attempting to understand its workings. Successful analysis must avoid unfounded speculation, yet at the same time it must attempt to incorporate the intellectual flexibility that the Egyptians themselves displayed.

Richard H. Wilkinson

T

TABOO. In Genesis 3.1–7, all creation is divided into two categories, good and evil; the fruit from the tree in the idle of the garden would, if eaten, then provide the insight and means to distinguish between the two. The Egyptians looked on their universe in terms of a similar dichotomy. The concept *bwt,* which bears a certain resemblance to some definitions of the term "taboo," was the mechanism through which the two categories were differentiated.

"Taboo" is one of the few Polynesian words to be incorporated into European language and thought. Careful distinction must be made between at least three uses of the term. First, there is the everyday, casual application to various phenomena (things, persons, notions) that should be avoided. Those subject to the violation of this form of taboo may experience emotions ranging from offense to anger, while feelings of agonizing guilt may plague the perpetrator of the violation.

A second use of the term is found in the various technical definitions that historians of religion and anthropologists have worked out, based on comparative material from a great number of cultures. Here we find numerous reports on, and analyses of, prohibitions and "taboos," and even a cursory inquiry into the material will show clearly that there is a striking uniformity as to what is declared "taboo" in the most diverse societies at the most diverse times. The key words are "impurity," "contagion," "penalties," and similar expressions. Thus, for example, menstruation taboos are among the most universal, and the Egyptian material is no exception. The fate of the laundrymen is pitied in the *Instructions of Dua-Kheti;* their position in the social hierarchy is so humble that they have to wash the clothes of menstruating women. References to menstruation seem to show that contact with women during this time might even be dangerous. This would explain why the menstruation of wives or daughters was accepted as a legitimate cause for a worker to stay at home, as is documented in the well-known absentee lists from Deir el-Medina. The phenomena that form the substance of this group are prohibitions of which we are conscious. We know when we violate these taboos, and we know that their violation will make us "taboo" as well. Depending on the specific cultural circumstance, we may also be cleaned of our impurity. What may pass for a taboo in ancient Egypt often comes under this heading.

Third, there is the mechanism— prominent among the features known from the Polynesian material—whereby taboos are used as a means of establishing and maintaining social strata. Thus, appropriation of property and power was accomplished by declaring something taboo, and the political power of a person was delimited by the taboos he could impose. Taboos could be rendered invalid only if overruled by the taboos of a superior of the original instigator of the taboo. In Egypt things were different, but the king, as god, could make something *bwt*. He could not, however, exercised this power indiscriminately or at will, but only in order to reestablish the original, primeval order of the world (*maat*).

The development of the ancient concept *bwt* can be followed for more than two millennia. At the end of this time, which coincides with the Greco-Roman period, *bwt* is often used in a sense that comes close to some of the technical definitions of taboo produced by the historians of religion, but the core meaning of *bwt* was very different, because it was an integral part of the Egyptians view of the universe as the result of a process of differentiation. In Egypt, the world was created according to, and by means of, *maat*, a word that is often rendered as "world order" or "truth," but which also implies plenty and abundance-of food, for example. Creation resulted from the transformation of a part of nonexistence, or potential existence. In the Egyptian conception of being, the continuity of existence required repeated, cyclical contact with nonexistence. Yet at the same time, the latter had to be combated, because it embraced not only potential being but also all the forces antagonistic to *maat* that were commonly part of true and immutable nonexistence. In theory, an Egyptian might commit acts that would cause him to die the "second death," which meant being forever associated with those same evil, uncreated, *maat*-antagonistic forces. Violating a *bwt* would bring this about, because *bwt* served to define all that was not of *maat*.

In order to understand better the nature of the Egyptian dichotomy between what might be labeled "good" and "evil," we must look at the earliest evidence for an expression of the opposition between *maat* and *bwt*. Here, at first it seems surprising to find hunger, thirst and feces as prototypes of things *bwt*; but on second thought, if in the earliest times the epitome of good, *maat*, was abundance of food, then lack of food would be bad. If nourishment is *maat*, then excretion becomes *bwt*. Further, these *bwt* things also applied to the realm of the dead and gods. The deceased declares in his funerary inscriptions that he has had no contact with feces, just as visitors to tombs and temples were admonished not to enter after having had contact with things that were *bwt*—not because this would be detrimental to the visitors themselves, but because of its harmful impact on the dead or the gods.

The ultimate concern of the Egyptians was salvation, which meant participation in the eternal cycle of life and death of the created world. Dying, in the normal sense of the word, led to other and more varied forms of existence. Death was an element of existence and, as such, it was within the realm of *maat*. Life emerged from death. However, in order to attain the desired state of a spirit or god in the afterworld, the deceased must have acquired a detailed knowledge of the essential properties of the hereafter. This implied a rejection of the idea of the afterworld as a reversed world—a world where, for instance, nourishment is feces and where the inhabitants move about upside down—as envisioned by demons representing the realm of nonexistence. In other words, the deceased must know the difference between what is of *maat* and the phenomena classified as *bwt*. And thus, whereas in Genesis knowledge was damning, in Egypt it was a prerequisite for salvation.

We may hypothesize that food and excrement played this role in the conception of the world because they are of such vital importance for life. These two categories further attained their status as prototypical symbols of good and evil because sharing food is the principal act of social incorporation in all societies. The dead is in a state of transition, and in that so-called liminal phase, he is subjected to a number of trials and tribulations. Interrogations are one of the ordeals that the dead must go through in order to prove himself a god. By virtue of its metonymic character, food is one of the principal means of putting his ability to the test. He is in a state of want and, still in terms of metonymy, hunger, and is therefore encouraged to eat what purports to be the lifegiving food of the afterworld. However, only by choosing the right kind of food in the afterworld could the dead become one of its blessed inhabitants.

The historical experience of the Egyptians, especially that of the painful transition between the Old and Middle Kingdoms, provoked renewed reflections on the characteristics of evil, and the time-honored categories of excreta were inadequate to articulate the complex relationship between good and evil. During the Middle Kingdom, a process of rethinking was initiated. From the standpoint of the great dichotomy, the rest of the history of Egypt was a period of intensifying preoccupation with the problem of evil, reflected in the ever-increasing number of phenomena that were classified as *bwt*.

In this process, the contact with a *bwt* became harmful also to the living. The body's orifices and their counterpart, the thresholds of buildings, retained their status as being marked by *bwt*, and eventually the concept of *bwt* gave rise to numerous injunctions and prohibitions. Thus, access to temples required abstinence from sexual activity, observance of rules of cleanliness, and avoidance of certain types of food, such as pig, fish, or honey, depending mainly on the local cosmology (customs already seen inscribed on tomb walls of the Old Kingdom). In fact, each nome had its specific *bwt*, and each god had his *bwt*. The concept of *bwt* was further used to delimit acceptable moral standards, even to the extent that the Egyptians distinguished between various forms of dying and killing: a man could be killed and still be "alive," but if he died as a result of having been *sm3*-killed, he would be annihilated—that is, die the "second death." In the Late Period there is finally some evidence that one could be cleansed of a *bwt*.   *Paul John Frandsen*

TAWERET. Depictions of the goddess Taweret depart sharply from the typically slim and beautiful female deities of ancient Egypt. In comparison with them, her image is frightful and grotesque: a composite deity with the head and body of a hippopotamus, the tail of a crocodile, and the hands and feet of a lioness. Most often she is shown standing upright on her hind legs. She usually carries or rests on the *s3* symbol, which means "protection," and she is often shown carrying a knife. The name Taweret (*T3-wrt*) means "the great one," and her frequent epithet is "Lady of Heaven."

Like those of the similarly strange-looking god Bes, images of the fearsome Taweret were used apotropaically by pregnant and nursing women, to keep evil away from their infants. Taweret has the rounded belly of a pregnant woman and the heavy breasts of a woman who is nursing. Her epithets include "Who Removes the Water," which may allude to the process of birth. Vessels from the New Kingdom in the shape of pregnant women echo the swollen form of the goddess, and there are also examples of "Taweret vessels" that have openings at the nipples, presumably for pouring milk.

From the Amarna period of the eighteenth dynasty—when worship of gods other than Aten was proscribed—there are even examples of Taweret images from the site of Tell el-Amarna, the center of the worship of the Aten. Taweret's presence emphasizes the importance of this protectress of pregnant woman in the lives of the common people, who did not cease their worship of this popular goddess.

Another epithet of Taweret is "She of the Pure Water," which may refer to her connection to the Nile River. Taweret was associated with the inundation because of her form as a riverine creature. She is called as "The One Who is in the Waters of Nun" in a shrine at Gebel es-Silsila. As a mother goddess, Taweret had associations with Hathor and Isis and was often depicted wearing the Hathor crown with a sun disk between two cow horns. Ostraca from the site of Deir el-Medina indicate that Taweret could have had a demonic aspect, and her composition from ferocious creatures may have connected her with Seth, the god of chaos.

Taweret was a popular domestic goddess, and her image appears on household items such as beds, stools, and headrests. Her likeness also appears on magical wands made of hippopotamus ivory. Amulets of the goddess were very popular and appear into the Roman period (31 BCE–395 CE). Stelae attest to her role as a healing deity. Much of her cult took place in domestic shrines, however, she may have had a sanctuary at Deir el-Medina. Apotropaic images of Bes and Taweret were placed on the outside of Ptolemaic temples to ward off evil. Taweret's popularity spread outside the borders of Egypt, and images of her have been found in Crete and at the sites of Kerma and Meroe in Nubia.

Taweret was one of several goddesses who could take the form of a hippopotamus, including Ipet ("the Nurse"), Reret ("the Sow"), and Hedjet ("the White One"). All these goddesses were associated with pregnancy and protection, and they are often difficult to distinguish from one another.

A constellation in the form of Taweret is depicted in the Theban tombs of Tharwas (tomb 353 in Western Thebes) and Senenmut (tomb 232 in Western Thebes), and in the Osiris Chapel in Medinet Habu as part of a scene showing the northern sky.

Jennifer Houser-Wegner

TEFNUT. In the tradition of the city of Heliopolis in the Nile Delta, the goddess Tefnut and her twin brother Shu were the offspring of Re-Atum and comprised the first generation of the Ennead. As a deity, Tefnut remains a vague figure and has little myth associated with her. The meaning of her name (*Tfnt*) is dubious, although there is a slight possibility that it was derived from the verb *tfn* ("to rise"). Tefnut's function is ambiguous, but as the twin of Shu she may have been a feminine deity of the air, balancing the similar masculine function of her brother and spouse and assisting him to support the sky. If this was her earliest significance, one might suggest that her function of personifying the moist air was a balance to that of Shu, who personified the dry air. Hence, Tefnut was more a mythologization of a theological concept, or a cosmic function, than a hypostatic deity.

In Heliopolitan tradition, Tefnut and Shu engendered Geb (Earth) and Nut (Sky), the two complementary elements of the cosmic structure. This relationship was more than a genealogical connection, for it meant that the abstract signification of Shu and Tefnut as the air evolved into a more concrete expression in the "tangible" deities Geb and Nut. Tefnut and Shu may thus be seen not simply as personifications of parts of the cosmos, but as integral elements upon which creation depended. In the later Memphite tradition, Tefnut was identified with the tongue of Ptah and became an instrument of divine creativity. Tefnut's association with Ptah is reflected in the temple at Hibis, where in front of the seated Ptah appear two *ba*-birds labeled Shu and Tefnut. Such a portrayal is not the iconography of popular belief but is symbolic of the theological function of the figures depicted.

Tefnut's antiquity is evident in her appearance in the Old Kingdom Pyramid Texts, but the Middle Kingdom Coffin Texts stress an important development in her signification. At an early stage she became identified with the goddess Maat, the principle of eternal order. This identification is expressed in Spell 80 of the Coffin Texts when Atum states, "Tefnut is my living daughter . . . Maat is her name." Atum is also described as kissing his daughter Maat "so that he may rise every day . . . so that the god may be born." Such a statement provides evidence of the central spiritual importance of the concept of Tefnut/Maat within the Egyptian theological synthesis.

Tefnut was frequently depicted as a lioness or a human female with the head of a lioness, sometimes wearing the solar disk and the *uraeus*. The solar function thus suggested was expressed in the myth that she and Shu received the sun god Re as he was reborn each morning. In her aspect as guardian of Re and of the pharaoh, she was also depicted as the *uraeus* alone. At times she was also said to be the wife of Thoth, a tradition connected with a legend of Tefnut's flight to Nubia, which states that she was brought back by Shu and Thoth, after which she became the wife of one of them. Although this tradition testifies to the flexibility of Egyptian myth, it appears to be a later reinterpretation of an original myth.

Vincent Arieh Tobin

THOTH. A deity with a wide range of associations, including nature, cosmology, writing, science, medicine, and the afterlife, Thoth (Eg., *Dhwty*) was worshiped throughout Egypt from the Early Dynastic period through Roman times. The meaning of his name is obscure. Because Thoth was the divine messenger, the Greeks associated him with Hermes, calling him Hermes Trismegistos ("thrice great Hermes"), a title probably derived from his Egyptian epithet *p3ʿ3ʿ3ʿ3*.

Thoth takes two major iconographic forms. As a squatting dog-headed baboon, he appears in figurines as early as the first dynasty (c.3050–2850 BCE). Early Dynastic slate palettes show ibises on standards, an image clearly associated with Thoth by the Old Kingdom. In later periods, he is frequently depicted as an ibis or ibis-headed human, often carrying the palette and pen of a scribe. His headdresses include the crescent moon and disk, the *atef*-crown, and the crowns of Upper and Lower Egypt. In both baboon and ibis forms, Thoth is portrayed overseeing and protecting scribes. In scenes from temples, he and Horus anoint the king with water. They also pour libations over the deceased on cartonnage coffins of the Third

Intermediate Period. In scenes of divine judgment, such as the vignettes accompanying chapter 125 of the *Book of Going Forth by Day (Book of the Dead)*, Thoth records and announces the verdict, typically appearing as an ibis-headed man, and sometimes as a baboon seated atop the scales of justice.

As a moon god, Thoth regulated the seasons and lunar phases and counted the stars. Hence, he was associated with astronomy, mathematics, and accounting. As the god of scribes and writing, Thoth, the "lord of the sacred word," personified divine speech. Seshat, the goddess of writing and literature, was said to be either his wife or daughter. By the Middle Kingdom Thoth, as a god of wisdom and justice, was connected with Maat, the personification of rightness and world order. The Greeks viewed him as the source of all wisdom and the creator of languages.

At Hermopolis, Thoth was worshipped as a cosmogenic deity, believed to have risen on a mound from the primeval chaos to create the Ogdoad consisting of Nun, Naunet, Heh, Heket, Kek, Keket, Amun, and Amaunet, coordinated male and female couplets representing various forces of nature. In solar religion, Thoth and Maat navigated the bark of Re. Some sources refer to him as the son of Re. The *Book of Going Forth by Day* describes him as returning Re's eye, which had wandered away. According to Plutarch, after Re had forbidden Nut from giving birth during any month of the year, Thoth tricked the moon goddess Selene into giving him some of her light, which he used to create the five epagomenal days, on which Nut gave birth to the great Ennead. Texts from the Ptolemaic temples of Edfu and Dendera credit Thoth with traveling to Nubia on behalf of Re to pacify the raging Tefnut and persuade her to return to Egypt.

Textual evidence for Thoth and his cult is found throughout Egyptian history. The Pyramid Texts portray him as the advocate and protector of the deceased king, destroying his enemies and carrying him across the river if the ferryman refuses. The dead king may be transformed into a bird with the wings of Thoth. Thoth introduces the king to Re. He also appears as a lunar god, the nightly manifestation of Re, and as a god of thunder and rain. By the Old Kingdom, the festival of Thoth is regularly mentioned in funerary offering formulas. In the Middle Kingdom, the Coffin Texts associate Thoth with divine justice, claiming that his verdict can satisfy both Horus and Seth. The *Book of Two Ways* refers to the deceased as stars that reside in the sky beside Thoth. Middle Kingdom instructions and tales regularly use Thoth as a metaphor for justice, and in funerary autobiographies, officials demonstrate their impartiality by claiming to be "truly precise like Thoth." In the New Kingdom, Thoth figures prominently in the *Book of Going Forth by Day*, of which he is said to be the author. He acts on behalf of the deceased before a series of divine tribunals, just as he had done for Osiris. He also conducts the interrogation, records the results of weighing the heart against *maat*, and announces the verdict. Hymns and prayers to Thoth, focusing on his role as patron of scribes, were used as school texts (as in Papyrus Anastasi V) and appear on statues of scribes. New Kingdom didactic literature, such as the *Instructions of Amenemope*, refers to Thoth as a symbol of justice. The *Book of Thoth*, believed to contain all knowledge of laws, magic, nature, and the afterlife, figures prominently in the Ptolemaic stories of Neferkaptah and Setna Khaemwaset, both of whom seek to appropriate the book's information, only to suffer unforeseen consequences.

Thoth plays the role of aide and mediator in the Osiris legend. He assists Horus and Anubis in reconstructing the body of Osiris and teaches Isis the spells necessary to revive him. In one version, he heals the infant Horus after Isis finds him dead of a scorpion bite. He is a staunch advocate of Horus in his battle against Seth, finding and restoring Horus's eye after Seth casts it away. He replaces the head of Isis after Horus cuts it off in a rage, and after Seth has eaten lettuce containing Horus's semen, Thoth invokes the semen to appear as a sun disk from the head of Seth. Finally, he helps to bring the proceedings to a conclusion by suggesting that the Ennead contact Osiris for his opinion.

The principal cult center of Thoth was at Hermopolis, ancient Egyptian Khemenu, near the modern town of el-Ashmunein. This was the site of a major New Kingdom temple, at which Amenhotpe III claims to have dedicated a pair of thirty-ton quartzite baboons. The biography of the fourth-century BCE high priest of Thoth, Petosiris, from his tomb at Tuna el-Gebel, recounts his renovation of the temple, said to house the egg from which Thoth had hatched, following the Persian invasion. Tuna el-Gebel was also the site of a massive fifth-century BCE cemetery of sacrificed baboons and ibises, as well as a sacred lake around which the ibises lived. Saqqara was home to a similar cemetery at which more than five hundred thousand ibises and baboons were buried in subterranean passageways; it was also the site of an oracle of Hermes Trismegistos. The Ogdoad of Hermopolis, headed by Thoth, was worshipped at Thebes because of its association with Amun. Sanctuaries of Thoth existed at a number of other sites as well.

Denise M. Doxey

TOMBS.

An Overview

Few ancient cultures have had their mortuary customs as intensively studied as ancient Egypt, but even today the origins of its remarkable dynastic burial practices are poorly understood. The earliest known burials come from the Nubian desert and date to about 12,000 to 14,000 years ago. They are simple pit graves, oval in plan, about 100 centimeters long and 50 centimeters wide, consisting of shallow depressions that were covered with large pieces of sandstone. The bodies—there could be several in a single grave—were tightly contracted and lay on the left side, head positioned to the east. There were no grave goods buried with them.

Except for these early finds, the archaeological record is virtually silent for the next seven or eight millenia, until the Neolithic period. In part, this is due to the fact that, with only localized exceptions (notably the work of Werner Kaiser in Upper Egypt and of Fred Wendorf in Nubia), no thorough or systematic archaeological surveys of Paleolithic and Epi-Paleolithic sites have yet been undertaken along the edges of the Nile Valley. Numerous Neolithic sites, however—particularly in Upper Egypt—have revealed scores of cemeteries, some of them large and used over long periods of time. They include such principal sites as Naqada, Abydos, Hierakonpolis, el-Ahaiwa, Nag el-Deir, el-Gerza, el-Amra, Mahasna, Mesaed, and many others. (I omit from lists of Neolithic cemeteries the burials at Merimda in

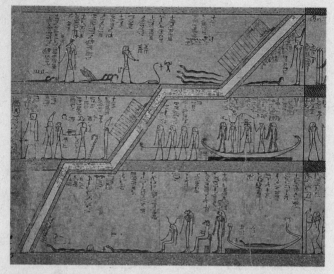

Descent of the sarcophagus into the tomb. Wallpainting, 18th dynasty. Tomb of Thutmose III, Valley of the Kings, West Thebes, Thebes. (Giraudon/Art Resource, NY)

Lower Egypt; the evidence from there of intra-village burials is now considered dubious.)

During the first millennium of the Upper Egyptian Neolithic, from roughly 5000 to 4000 BCE, graves of the Badarian culture continue to be small (c. 100–150 centimeters/3.2–4.8 feet in diameter), round or oval, shallow pits with single bodies lying in a contracted position, head to the south, face to the west. Yet there are now funerary goods in these graves—the earliest known in Egypt—and they attest to an already well-developed belief in the afterlife. Pottery is especially common, but we also find jewelry, flint tools, small slate cosmetic palettes, and ivory and bone figurines of women and animals. Bodies may be

dressed in linen kilts or robes, wrapped in skins, or placed in basketry containers. In a few cases, graves are lined with reed matting, but as yet there is no solid evidence of superstructures over the pit.

A similar pattern of burial continues into the Naqada culture, but with some elaboration. For example, tombs are now often covered with branches or reed mats over which a small mound of gravel is placed. Grave goods are more numerous and varied and include black-topped redware pottery, stone vessels, slate palettes, bone and ivory figurines, combs, and small "tags" topped with carvings of human or animal heads.

During the next stage, burial patterns show an increasing degree of sophistication and complexity. In later phases of the Naqada culture, settlement sites in both the north and the south were becoming more urbanized, and the adjacent cemeteries exhibit increasing evidence of social differentiation. Graves are larger and often have a rectangular plan instead of an oval one. The substructure of the tomb is now constructed using a series of narrow walls to divide what formerly was a single pit into a series of rectangular cells, the centermost of which serves as a burial chamber. This relatively large cell is surrounded by a number of smaller ones in which increasingly large quantities of grave goods are placed. To the extent that the number and size of cells indicate quantities of funerary equipment, it is revealing that the tomb of Khasekhemwy has a burial chamber of less than 18 square meters (193 square feet), but surrounding cells cover more than 1,000 square meters (10,720 square feet). Some cells are lined with woven reed mats or wooden planks; a few have painted walls. At the site of Hierakonpolis, the famous Painted Tomb 100 has plaster walls decorated with scenes that have been interpreted as showing hunting, boating, fighting, and perhaps ritual dancing. Such a tomb is thought to have been intended for an individual of particularly high social rank. Grave goods in Naqada II become more elaborate and numerous, and include finely painted pottery, palettes and mace heads, stone vessels, jewelry (some of the pieces in gold and silver), and elegantly worked flint tools.

In very late Neolithic and Early Dynastic times, a series of dramatic changes in mortuary architecture undoubtedly reflect significant changes in funerary customs and religious beliefs. Some may have been influenced by western Asian (Near Eastern) cultures, but it is certainly appropriate to emphasize the indigenous character of Egyptian funerary customs and their architectural manifestations. Some were perhaps tied to regional Egyptian environmental and cultural differences; others were the outgrowth of dynastic Egypt's increasingly complex culture and stratified society.

In discussing changes in the mortuary architecture, it is convenient to deal separately with the superstructure and the substructure of the Egyptian tomb, because these followed relatively independent lines of development. The first typology of tomb architecture was developed in an elaborate 1936 study by George Andrew Reisner. Only recently, thanks in part to the important excavations at Abydos, have the general patterns layed out by Reisner been significantly expanded on.

At Abydos, from a period Egyptologists now call dynasty zero, elaborate burial complexes have been found lying in the western desert. In each complex, a large, multichambered substructure, apparently based on domestic architectural plans and filled with hundreds of local and imported pottery vessels, served as the tomb of an official of high social standing, probably a king. Above this large, central tomb lay a mound of sand, surrounded by small retaining walls. The top of the mound did not extend above the surrounding desert surface and was apparently covered by thin roof. The excavator, Gunther Dreyer, believes that this mound was of magical significance and that there was a second mound built above it, with a pair of stelae standing before it that gave the name of the deceased and served as a tomb marker. Near the superstructure lay hundreds of subsidiary graves, apparently of wives, family members, and servants. Some distance away, at the edge of cultivation, a large and apparently empty mud-brick rectangle (covering as much as 5,000 square meters/53,600 square feet) was constructed, perhaps to serve as an early form of the later valley temple that formed a part of the royal funerary complex.

In the first and second dynasties, the oval gravel or sand mounds that covered the tombs were made even larger and their plan became more nearly rectangular. Such mounds are known from Abydos and Hierakonpolis, but some believe that they might originally have been associated with the so-called Sand Mound of Heliopolis, a symbol of the island in the great primeval sea on which the first creation was said to have occurred. The mound was now built of mud brick, and some superstructures, particularly at Saqqara, measured up to 25.60 meters (80.192 feet) and stood 3 to 4 meters (10 to 13 feet) high. These flat-topped structures had outer walls constructed with an elaborate pattern of niching, a device sometimes referred to as a "palace façade." Early examples of this façade are complex examples of brickwork; later examples tend to be simpler; all seem intended to imitate the wooden paneling or woven reed matting associated with shrines representing Upper and Lower Egypt. Some early niched façades, such as that of Saqqara *mastaba* 3503, had hundreds of clay ox heads with real horns placed on a narrow, low platform within and in front of the niches.

By the end of the Early Dynastic Period, the niched façade had been reduced to two simple niches, one at each end of the superstructure's eastern wall; the remainder of the exterior had smooth, sloping-sided faces, giving the structure the appearance of an inverted bread pan, or a bench of the type that sits outside many modern Egyptian village houses. Such benches are called *mastaba*s in Arabic, and that word is used to describe this type of tomb superstructure. *Mastaba*

tombs of substantial size and complexity are to be found at Saqqara, but they may never have been used for burials: many Egyptologists believe that the Saqqara structures were cenotaphs (dummy tombs), and that the actual burial place of Egypt's early royal families was Abydos.

The substructures of these tombs were also growing larger, and the number of cells a tomb might contain, their size, and their depth below ground also were increasing as offerings of food and drink, clothing, jewelry, games, and the like became more numerous. These cells were roofed with wooden boards and beams. Access to them initially was only through the top, prior to construction of the superstructure, until, in the mid-first dynasty, a staircase was added leading to the burial chamber. These tombs were surrounded by an enclosure wall and, beyond it, a series of subsidiary burials, a pit in which a model boat was placed and, in some instances, dummy buildings ("fictive architecture," it has been called) whose purpose can in most cases only be guessed.

During the Old Kingdom, *mastaba* tombs were built in great number for officials of the royal court and others of Egypt's upper class. At Giza, these *mastaba*s are laid out in large, well-ordered cemeteries that followed a carefully designed grid system. The substructures of these tombs are small because actual funerary offerings were now being replaced by representations on chapel walls. Often the substructure consists of little more than a vertical shaft leading to a single, undecorated burial chamber dug perhaps ten meters underground. The superstructure of these *mastaba*s, on the other hand, grew considerably, and often covers several hundred square meters. Instead of being solid stone structures, they now have within them numerous chambers, usually rectangular rooms laid out in a simple but seemingly meandering plan.

The southern of the two niches on the eastern wall of Early Dynastic *mastaba*s had evolved into a doorway by the late third dynasty, and it led into a chamber in which were placed decorated panels or stelae giving names and titles of the tomb owner. An early example is the tomb of Hesy-Re, in which elegantly carved wooden panels show the tomb owner and give his name and titles. During the fourth dynasty, the size and number of such chambers grew as their walls were decorated with increasingly large and elaborate scenes of offerings and rituals and long lists of names and titles. Such texts and scenes replaced actual offerings of food and drink that had formerly been placed in the substructure and the small, inscribed stelae set in niches. The types of scenes shown and their distribution apparently were subject to a number of rules that changed gradually during the Old Kingdom. Most frequently, the scenes depict activities involving the preparation of food—planting, harvesting, herding, slaughtering, cooking, storing, banqueting—and, a bit later, scenes of assorted craftsmen at work: carpenters, potters, leatherworkers, jewelers, and the like. Texts, originally little more than a name and a few titles, gradually grew to include elaborate offering lists, prayers, and autobiographies.

Two additional features also appeared within the superstructure: a *serdab* (cellar), a room in which, behind a slit window, was placed a statue of the deceased; and a "false door," through which the soul of the deceased could move between the burial chamber and the offering chapels. The earliest example of a *serdab* may be seen in the first dynasty tomb of Den at Abydos; an especially well-known example is that in Djoser's Step Pyramid complex.

The growing elaboration of both super- and substructures in Early Dynastic *mastaba* tombs laid the foundation for one of the most dramatic and sudden changes to be see in mortuary architecture: the appearance of the pyramid as the royal burial place, the earliest known example of which is the third dynasty Step Pyramid complex of Djoser (Netjerykhet) at Saqqara. Fortunately for Egyptology, for more than seventy years, since 1926, this remarkable monument has been carefully excavated and studied by an equally remarkable scholar, Jean-Philippe Lauer. It is to his work that we owe our picture of the Step Pyramid complex and the origin of Egyptian pyramids generally.

A pyramid, the elaborate complex of buildings that surrounded it, and the huge bureaucracy needed to maintain it and perform the functions it was intended to serve were of profound importance. A pyramid was intended as the burial place of the pharaoh, but the complex also served as a temple to the god Horus, with whom the pharaoh was identified in this life, and to Osiris, with whom he would be identified in the next. Thus, the pyramid was not merely a tomb; it was a physical and symbolic expression of the relationship Egyptians believed existed among ordinary humans, the pharaoh, and the gods. Its design and content were of such importance we must assume that its every aspect was the result of careful and regular deliberations about sacred beliefs and practices. Changes made in mortuary architecture or funerary cults were the result of rethinking the man-god relationship and speculating about the nature of the afterlife. Such changes would not have been made frivolously; they reflected the Egyptians constantly evolving ideas about life and death. To understand Egyptian mortuary architecture, we must therefore know as much as possible about Egyptian religious beliefs, kingship, folk traditions, and such secular matters as economics and politics. Unfortunately, we shall almost certainly never have enough data to be able to think like an ancient Egyptian or to explain fully the meaning of these monuments and their component parts. But we should remember that, for the Egyptians, there were compelling reasons for building mortuary monuments as they did. Tombs neither grew randomly nor changed form or content without reason.

The Step Pyramid changed dramatically throughout Djoser's reign. Later tradition says that it was the work of a great architect and wise man, Imhotep. If he actually existed, he is the first architect in history to whom we can give a name. In a series of six building phases, Imhotep took what had begun as a relatively small *mastaba* superstructure and changed it into a step pyramid that rose in six stages to a final height of more than 60 meters (192 feet). Its base covered over 12,000 square meters (128,640 square feet), and it contained over 330,000 cubic meters (10.6 million cubic feet) of limestone blocks. Beneath the pyramid, more than 30 meters (100 feet) below ground, workmen cut a labyrinthine series of corridors nearly 6 kilometers (4 miles) long, then filled them with more than forty thousand stone vessels and countless other funerary offerings, including objects of earlier kings, perhaps family heirlooms or historical reminders of Djoser's antecedents. A huge central shaft, measuring 7.7.28 meters (22.22.90 feet), led from the surface down to a granite burial chamber at the center of the subterranean complex.

Above ground, surrounding the pyramid, a 10-meter-high (32-foot-high) stone enclosure wall with a simple niched facade extended 1,600 meters (5,120 feet) north to south and 300 meters (960 feet) east to west. Within it lay open courtyards, dummy buildings, courts for religious festivals, and mortuary temples—structures thought necessary not only for the requisite funeral ceremonies but also for the pharaoh's activities in the afterlife.

At the southern end of the Step Pyramid enclosure, a staircase descended more than 28 meters (90 feet) below the enclosure wall into a much smaller but no less complex series of corridors and chambers. Here, too, another huge shaft led to a granite chamber. This was Djoser's so-called Southern Tomb. It has been called the cenotaph of Djoser (especially by those who argue that the Early Dynastic tombs at Abydos were cenotaphs, while those at Saqqara were true royal burials, not the other way round). Others contend that it was the burial place of Djoser's *ka*.

Only two other certain stepped pyramid complexes were built after Djoser's: one by his successor, Horus Sekhemkhet, also at Saqqara; and another by the next king, Khaba, at Zawiyet el-Aryan, halfway between Saqqara and Giza. That of Sekhemkhet was intended to be larger than Djoser's, but it was never finished and, apparently, never used. The so-called Layer Pyramid of Khaba is smaller than Djoser's, and it too was unoccupied. Both of these step pyramids show subterranean chamber plans similar to each other but significantly different from that of the Djoser complex. (Seven other stepped pyramids, none more than about 15 meters [48 feet] high, were constructed late in the third dynasty at sites as far south as Elephantine; they seem to have been purely symbolic structures, erected near sites of religious or royal significance.)

Sneferu, first king of the fourth dynasty, may be credited as Egypt's greatest builder of pyramids and as builder both of the last step pyramid and the first "true" pyramid. His pyramid at Meidum was begun as a step pyramid of seven stages, then eight, then finally changed to a true pyramid with sides that sloped upward at an angle of 51°5". A 58-meter-long (185-foot-long) passage descends through the pyramid's north face to a horizontal, subterranean corridor, then extends vertically to a small, corbelled burial chamber, the floor of which lies at ground level. This basic plan, seen here for the first time, was to be followed by most later pyramid builders. So was Sneferu's addition of a small "satellite pyramid" adjacent to the main one, and his construction of a causeway reaching from the Nile Valley westward to the enclosure wall of the pyramid complex.

For reasons that are unclear, Sneferu also built two other pyramids, each substantially larger than that at Meidum, 25 kilometers (15.6 miles) to the north at the site of Dahshur. One is called the North (or Red) Pyramid, and the other is the Bent Pyramid; each has from two to three times the volume of the pyramid at Meidum. The variations in design of Sneferu's three pyramids suggest that his reign was a period of experimentation with pyramid design, and the variations were almost certainly due as much to theological considerations as to problems of engineering and stability.

The best-known pyramids, of course, are the three built in the fourth dynasty on the Giza Plateau: the Great Pyramid of Khufu, the Pyramid and Sphinx of Khafre, and the Pyramid of Menkaure.

Between construction of the first and second of these, there also was a pyramid constructed by Djedefre, son of Khufu and his successor as pharaoh, at Abu Roash, about 10 kilometers (6.25 miles) north of Giza. The pyramids of Khufu and Khafre are the largest ever built: each contains more than 2 million cubic meters (64 million cubic feet) of stone. That of Menkaure has only a tenth as much; that of Djedefre only a twentieth.

By any standard, the Giza Pyramids are impressive, but each was just a part of what by the fourth dynasty had come to be a fairly standard complex that included the pyramid, a mortuary temple (although there is some question as to whether it was ever used as such), an enclosure wall and causeway, pits for sacred barks, smaller pyramids for principal wives, cemeteries for officials and noblemen, and extensive domestic buildings that housed the large number of priests, servants, craftsmen, and others needed to ensure the proper functioning of the royal funerary cult.

During the fifth and sixth dynasties, another dozen pyramids were constructed, but on a much smaller scale than those at Giza, and with rubble fill replacing the large cut limestone blocks used in earlier construction. The pyramid itself is of reduced size in these complexes, but there is greater emphasis on such other features as the mortuary temple. Most of these pyramids were built either at Abusir, a site just north of Saqqara, or at Saqqara itself. Thanks to the discovery of several very fragmentary papyri at Abusir, we know something about the economy and administration of such temple complexes. Pyramid complexes and their mortuary cults were enormous, expensive institutions and clearly formed very significant components of the Egyptian economy and bureaucracy. Indeed, some Egyptologists have attributed the economic and political decline of Old Kingdom Egypt in part to the expense of maintaining these funerary endowments.

With the reign of Unas at the end of the fifth dynasty, royal pyramids came to include hieroglyphic religious texts, called Pyramid Texts, on the walls of the burial chamber and its antechamber. These texts provide us with important clues to the funerary, offering, and magical rituals associated with the burial of a pharaoh and his anticipated role in the afterlife. Pyramid Texts grew increasingly elaborate during the sixth dynasty; by the First Intermediate Period, they also came to be inscribed in nonroyal tombs. They were replaced in the Middle Kingdom by Coffin Texts, and in the New Kingdom by the *Book of Going Forth by Day (Book of the Dead)*.

During the First Intermediate Period, a few small pyramids were constructed—two at Saqqara and one in Middle Egypt; several so-called *saff* tombs at Ta'arif on the western bank of the Nile at Thebes apparently had small pyramids in their entrance courtyards. But except for these few examples, most tombs during this time were small rock-cut tombs laid out in varying provincial styles. These tombs, dependent on locally available materials and labor, varied greatly in size and quality, although their basic plan was the same as rock-cut tombs of the Old Kingdom, such as those at Giza or Aswan. Among the principal sites of First Intermediate Period and Middle Kingdom rock-cut tombs, one also should note Beni Hasan, Deshasheh, Sheikh Said, Meir, Bersheh, and Qaw.

The tradition of constructing large royal pyramids was revived during the Middle Kingdom. At el-Lisht, Amenemhet I and Senwosret I each built pyramids of, respectively, 55 and 61 meters

(176 and 195 feet) in height; at Dahshur, their several successors built pyramids about 75 meters (240 feet) high. Surrounding Amenemhet I's pyramid was a series of twenty-two pit burials for royal women, and there were also small *mastabas* within the enclosure. The pyramid of Senwosret, little more than a hill of rubble today, was a large structure surrounded by nine subsidiary pyramids, apparently for wives of the pharaoh. The Dahshur pyramid of Senwosret III also had six queens' pyramids within its enclosure. But in the pyramid complex of Amenemhet III, also at Dahshur, queens' pyramids were abandoned, and two suites of rooms within the king's pyramids were set aside for his principal wives. Several Middle Kingdom pyramids (that of Amenemhet III at Haware, for example) show experimentation with ways to thwart tomb robbers by installing sliding blocks, dummy chambers, blind alleys, and other techniques, but they were not successful.

Only a few pyramids or *mastabas* were constructed after the Middle Kingdom. *Mastabas* are found at level sites where cliffs are unavailable for rock-cut tombs and/or in districts where deliberately archaizing funerary customs were in favor. There are small pyramids associated with workmen's tombs in the New Kingdom Theban village of Deir el-Medina, and rather more impressive pyramid fields at such Nubian sites as el-Kurru, Nurri, and Meroe (which date to late dynastic times and continue into the fourth century CE). But for the most part, after the Middle Kingdom, both kings and noblemen were interred in rock-cut tombs.

Rock-cut tombs, sepulchers cut horizontally into a cliff face or hillside, appeared in Egypt in the third to fourth dynasties, perhaps first in quarries on the Giza Plateau, and slightly later at sites in Upper Egypt, where they became extremely common. At first, these rock-cut tombs were similar to small *mastabas* in their interior plan, but the *serdab* was replaced by deeply cut relief figures of the deceased and his family carved in the tomb's rear wall. The burial chamber lay below, accessible down a vertical shaft. Later, the burial chamber might be found beneath the forecourt or even some distance from the tomb-chapel itself. By the fifth to sixth dynasties, the plans of rock-cut tombs were following their own line of development, a line that quickly led to more and larger chambers, a columned portico, and interior pillared halls.

By the Middle Kingdom rock-cut tombs had become common, and at several large necropolises—Beni Hasan, Nag el-Deir, Gebelein, and Asyut, for example—many superbly carved and decorated examples may be found. The tombs at these sites vary in size, chamber proportions, and plan, suggesting that different areas of Upper Egypt followed different mortuary traditions. Examples of such differences may be seen by comparing tombs at Deir Rifa, Nag el-Mashaykh, Abydos, Esna, Elkab, and Hierakonpolis.

One of the most important sites of rock-cut tombs is the Theban necropolis. Tombs may be found here from the later Old Kingdom onward, initially small and relatively isolated. Under the eleventh dynasty Inyotefs, the tombs were cut in clusters in the faces of large sunken courtyards—and hence are called "saff" or "row" tombs—and consisted of one to four small chambers in one or two of which pillars were carved. By the New Kingdom, hundreds of rock-cut tombs were carved at Thebes, occupying virtually all of the hillsides (but few of the sheer cliffs) in the Theban necropolis.

Private rock-cut Theban tombs are of three general types: those with a rectangular façade and a central entrance; those with a pyramid in a courtyard at the front of the tomb; and those with columned or pillared porticos at their entrance. Generally, beyond the courtyard and doorway, there is a long, narrow chamber at right angles to the entry axis, called the *wsht* (broad hall); beyond that lies a long hallway, its axis at right angles to that of the *wsht;* at the end of the hallway is a small shrine or *naos*. It is a simple cruciform plan. Some tombs have an additional square chamber between the *wsht* and the long hallway, and sometimes that chamber contains a varying number of pillars.

The best-known rock-cut tombs are those of the New Kingdom pharaohs in the Valley of the Kings at Thebes. Their plans are more elaborate than private tombs, and they are substantially larger. Their chambers can occupy hundreds of cubic meters, and it is clear that they were not simply repositories for foodstuffs and funerary equipment but played a significant role in the processes intended to ensure the continued functioning of kingship and the balance of *maat* after the death of a pharaoh. Such important objectives demanded that the decoration of royal tombs be more formal and more focused on religious themes than that of private tombs. Especially good examples of the various plans and decorative programs of royal tombs may be seen in the tombs of Thutmose III and IV, Horemheb, Sety I, and Ramesses III. Tomb five in the Valley of the Kings, the burial place of several sons of Ramesses II, is the largest and most unusual tomb ever found in Egypt, boasting well over a hundred chambers and corridors.

Following the New Kingdom, royal tombs were built in the Nile Delta, where environmental conditions precluded the use of features common to tombs in Upper Egypt. It was not unusual for tombs to be built in courtyards cut beneath temple compounds. At Thebes, private tombs continued to be dug, some of them among the largest complexes of chambers and corridors to be found in Egypt (e.g., tomb 33, Pedamonopet; tomb 34, Montuemhet; tomb 37, Harwa). Many contain details taken from the architecture of earlier times (e.g., the use of the niched façade).

There are numerous other necropolises in Egypt from the Late Period and from Greek and Roman times, including Coptos, Beni Hasan, el-Hiba, Giza, el-Fostat, and Alexandria. At Saqqara, the Serapeum, the burial place of sacred Apis bulls from the New Kingdom onward, must certainly rank as one of the most impressive examples of Egyptian rock-cut tombs.   *Kent R. Weeks*

Royal Tombs

The Egyptian idea of kingship attributed divine spiritual qualities to the king, in addition to his mortal nature, but this divine aspect did not keep a pharaoh's human body from dying. In order to resolve this conflict between reality and theology, an enormous mechanism was created to explain and correct this calamity. Essentially, the king's body had to be properly buried like those of everyone else, but the body was understood not to be dead, and the burial place was not a tomb in the modern sense but rather a station for transitional or spiritual events. With the help of funerary rituals, rich grave goods, the magic of spells and pictures on the tomb walls, and a powerful symbolic architectural framework, the "dead" king was revived and his eternal life and rulership established. The ideas and methods changed over the course of the millenia, and the degree of

material investment in this mechanism varied from kings of inferior status to rulers of high prestige and godlike qualities. Thus, the diminishing divine power of the king at the end of the New Kingdom is reflected in the royal tombs of the twenty-first and twenty-second dynasties at Tanis.

Burial. Several royal burials have been found intact, albeit of ephemeral kings: Tutankhamun, Amenemope, Psusennes, Sheshonq II, and Osorkon II. In several other royal tombs robbers overlooked or left parts of the burial and the grave goods. These objects, together with parallels from private tombs and representations in tomb paintings, help us to reconstruct the ideal contents of a royal funerary assemblage. The basic burial of a royal body was not much different from that of a wealthy private person, but ideally, it had to outshine private funerary equipment in both quantity and quality. The grave goods consisted of personal belongings—objects of daily use, weapons, and tools—and of the official regalia (crowns, scepters, jewelry, etc.). However, the divine aspect of the pharaoh also required magic objects that made his resurrection possible and protected him in the next life: for example, multitudes of shrines with images of deities, and huge ceremonial resurrection beds with the heads of Hathor, cheetah, and hippotamus. Vessels with food provisions, oils, and ointments, which predominated in the grave goods in early times, were gradually reduced in consequence of the development of daily offering ceremonies. The complete grave goods of one of the great kings must have been overwhelming.

During the first three dynasties, the royal body probably rested in a wooden coffin, of which no traces have survived. From Khufu on, the body was placed in

The nineteenth dynasty burial chamber of Sety I in the Valley of the Kings. (Photography by the Egyptian Expedition, The Metropolitan Museum of Art, NY)

a stone sarcophagus. During the Old Kingdom the royal sarcophagus is plain and box shaped; it may have housed one or several inner wooden coffins. In the the Middle Kingdom the royal granite sarcophagus has the symbolic shape of a Lower Egyptian reed shrine standing inside a paneled enclosure with gates. Some early New Kingdom sarcophagi are of red quartzite and are made in the shape of a royal cartouche. The corners of those of the later eighteenth dynasty are sculpted with figures of the protective goddesses Isis, Nephthys, Neith, and Selket. On the lid of the sarcophagi of Merenptah and Tawosret, the figure of the deceased is shown in the round. From the twelfth dynasty on, the royal body was enclosed in an anthropoid coffin of gilded wood. Like the bark of the gods, the sarcophagus is sheltered by a huge gilded wooden shrine. Similarly the canopic chest receives, from the twelfth dynasty, a burial of its own in a separate chamber; accordingly the shape and size of the canopic box represent a smaller version of the sarcophagus.

Architecture. The royal tombs of the Early Dynastic period are clustered around the Umm el-Qaʿab at Abydos. They apparently reflected the dwelling aspect of the eternal existence in the afterworld. A huge, cabin-like wooden chamber is sunk under the desert surface and protected by a brick retaining wall with small, niche-like side chambers. Some walls seem to have been sheathed with green faience tiles depicting an otherworldly palace. Above ground, stelae with the royal name marked a flat, *mastaba*-like platform. The main tomb is surrounded by a considerable number of smaller tombs of servants, who may have been sacrificed at the king's death. In the second dynasty, more side chambers were added for the storage of the enormous quantities of grave goods, and ac-

cess to the tombs was provided by straight staircases. Also at Abydos, but at a distance from the actual burial tombs, monumental brick enclosures (known as "forts") supply the second important aspect of the royal afterlife. Completely above ground and without underground chambers, they seem to be models of palace-fortresses or arenas for the display of royal ceremonies in the afterlife. Table 1 lists the identified royal tombs of the Early Dynastic period.

Monumental, elaborate *mastaba*s of the first dynasty at Saqqara North, excavated by Walter B. Emery beginning in 1936, are no longer believed to be the tombs of kings. At least the kings Hotepsekhemwy, Ranebi, Ninuter (and perhaps Khasekhemwy) of the second dynasty built huge underground gallery tombs at Saqqara, and in the Western Desert vast stone enclosures seem to represent the associated "forts" or "palaces." The underground apartments still represent the tomb type of a residential palace surrounded by enormous galleries filled with supplies. The aboveground structures are lost.

A new type of otherworldly residence was designed for King Djoser at Saqqara. For the first time, a huge, multilayered superstructure was built in stone, representing a full-scale palace city. The complex contains two similar underground tombs under stone *mastaba*s, the northern one probably the tomb for the royal body. Later the northern *mastaba* was transformed into a 60-meter-high (192 foot-high) step *mastaba*. The chambers are huge granite boxes surrounded by a system of corridors ornamented with a façade of reed palaces cased with green faience tiles. Enormous underground galleries were filled with pottery and stone vessels containing food.

Some ephemeral successors of Djoser began building similar complexes that were all to be provided with a step *mastaba*. They remained unfinished and display the gradual abandonment of the idea of a huge otherworldly residence.

A new building type, probably expressing a more heavenly aspect, appeared under Sneferu, culminating in the first true monumental pyramids. The burial apartments are partially elevated into the pyramid core, and the burial chambers, with the help of corbeled roof construction, achieve the enormous interior height of 15 meters (48 feet). The galleries for the grave goods have disappeared. These architectural features and the simultaneous appearance of a superstructure in pyramid shape suggest a reorientation of ideas about the royal afterlife under Sneferu, probably in consequence of the growing importance of the solar religion. The royal tombs of Khufu, Khafre, and Menkaure follow this tendency and are marked by the enormous size of their pyramids. The funerary apartments still show experimental changes and are marked by efforts to protect the roofs of the entrance passage and the crypt against structural damage. So-called air shafts in the pyramids of Khufu and Khafre were probably meant to permit communication between the royal chamber and heaven.

The long experimental period ended with Menkaure, and under Shepseskaf (in the Mastabat Fara'un), a scheme for the underground chambers emerges that would predominate in royal tombs of the Old and Middle Kingdoms. The burial crypts from Khufu on are dominated by the royal stone sarcophagus. The rectangular crypt is oriented east–west so that the sarcophagus can occupy the short western side, with its head to the north. The entrance opens opposite it from an antechamber to the east. From Khafre on, the ceiling of the chamber is usually saddle-shaped because of the efficiency

of this building form in supporting the heavy pressure of the pyramid core, and also because of the symbolic, heaven-like tent shape of the ceiling. Additional granite beams or several layers of sloping limestone beams protect the interior ceiling slabs. A narrow, shallow, sloping passage enters the antechamber from the north. After the funeral, this passage was blocked with several huge portcullises. One or three chambers—probably wrongly termed *serdab*—branch off to the east of the antechamber; these may have contained grave goods. This type of underground apartment is closely connected with the aboveground form of the pyramid. Both architectural units seem to aim at the transformation of the king, apparently through permitting his participation in the daily voyage of the sun. He would leave his tomb through the top of the pyramid in the morning in order to join Re-Horakhty in his bark and return into the tomb at sunset.

The crypts of the pyramids of the twelfth dynasty only partially follow the Old Kingdom pattern; one difference is the existence of a separate side chamber for the canopic burial. The crypt of Senwosret I, which is lost in the ground water, may have copied the Old Kingdom ground plan, as does the granite crypt of Senwosret III. However, the relatively modest tomb of Amenemhet I does not differ from contemporary private tombs. The crypts and passages in the tombs of Amenemhet II and Senwosret II develop unique plans of their own, without exact prototypes. The tomb of Amenemhet III at Dahshur has an enormous system of chambers and passages that may have housed grave goods or represented mythical localities. After structural damage, the pyramid was abandoned, and the underground apartment of Amenemhet III's second pyramid at Hawara reflects an overriding concern for basic safety principles: a monolithic crypt, and massive protective roof construction to resist pressure from above.

The tombs of the kings of the thirteenth dynasty also concentrate on the protection of the royal sarcophagus (which becomes one with the chamber) and on mechanisms for blocking the passages. The tombs of the seventeenth dynasty kings at Dra Abul Naga (Western Thebes) are relatively simple rock-cut tombs beneath a brick pyramid with a cult chapel. Their architectural remains were lost again after their discovery and robbing in 1827.

A new type of royal tomb appears only with the New Kingdom, influenced by local conditions in the Valley of the Kings at Thebes. Beneath the vertical limestone cliffs, sloping passages and staircases lead into deeply hidden crypts. These rock-cut tombs have no superstructure, but their entrance sections seem to have been partially accessible for ceremonial purposes. The sloping access corridors and staircases of the tombs down to Amenhotpe III show a 90° bend or curve (in the case of Hatshepsut) that is considered to be characteristic of the tomb of Osiris at Abydos. Each corridor branch ends in a chamber; the upper one probably marks a ceremonial tomb, and the lower one is the burial crypt with the sarcophagus. Crypts from Thutmose I to Thutmose III have rounded corners; apparently their oval shape may represent a royal cartouche, or the twelfth nocturnal hour of the *Book of That Which Is in the Underworld* (*Amduat*). From Amenhotpe II on, the sarcophagus stands in the rear part of a huge pillared burial hall, and from Thutmose IV on, in a deeply recessed basin. A deep shaft, considered to be dedicated to Sokar, separates the sloping entrance passage from the interior of the tomb.

From Horemheb on, the axis of the tomb (except in the tomb of Ramesses II) is straight but splits into a second parallel section that leads to the actual lower crypt. The upper section is considered to be a secondary, symbolic tomb for the king as a personification of Osiris. The lower burial hall develops into an impressive architectural space. The roof of the crypt is slightly vaulted and supported by two rows of four pillars. The area between the pillars is lowered and contains the prominent sarcophagus. Here the Osiris king was thought to unite with the sun god. The crypt is surrounded by a number of side chapels, some for storage and some dedicated to deities of the underworld. During the Ramessid period, the entrance shaft and the steep staircases disappear and the originally considerable slope of the passages is flattened out, assimilating the tomb to the form of a rock-cut temple. An unusual feature is the very slight increase in the dimensions of the doors, passages, number of pillars, and size of the sarcophagus. The royal tombs in the main valley are as follows:

Thutmose I and Hatshepsut KV 20
   (KV Valley of the Kings)
Thutmose II KV 42
Thutmose III KV 34
Amenhotpe II KV 35
Thutmose IV KV 43
Tutankhamun KV 62
Ramesses I KV 16
Sety I KV 17
Ramesses II KV 7
Sons of Ramesses II KV 5
Merenptah KV 8
Sety II KV 15
Amenmesse KV 10
Siptah KV 47
Horemheb KV 57
Twosret and Sethnakhte KV 14

Ramesses III KV 11
Ramesses IV KV 2
Ramesses V and VI KV 9
Ramesses VII KV 1
Ramesses IX KV 6
Ramesses XI KV 4
Amenhotpe III WV 22 (WV Western Valley)
Ay WV 23

The tombs of the kings of later periods were built as temple tombs in the residence cities of the Delta. Some of the royal tombs of the twenty-first and twenty-second dynasties were found by Pierre Montet in 1939 at Tanis. The 50 × 60-meter complex contains the tombs of Psusennes I, Amenemope, Osorkon II, Sheshonq III, and some other high-ranking persons. They stand in the forecourt of the temple of Amun. Because of the level of ground water, the chambers are situated close beneath the surface. They are massive stone constructions with a small antechamber and a niche for the sarcophagus. As an exception, the kings of the Kushite twenty-fifth dynasty were again buried in plain rock-cut chamber tombs beneath small, steep pyramids in the cemeteries of el-Kurru and Nuri at Napata. The tombs of the twenty-sixth dynasty (Apries, Amasis) in the temple of Neith at Sais are lost, but from descriptions by Herodotus (II.169), it is known that the sarcophagus stood in an aboveground shrine surrounded by palm columns. Some tombs of the twenty-ninth and thirtieth dynasties were situated in Mendes; they were destroyed by the Persians in 343 BCE. Remains of the tomb of Nepherites are preserved. The sarcophagus of Nektanebo II was found dislocated in Alexandria (Brit. Mus. EA 10).

The tombs of Alexander the Great and the Ptolemies were separate mausoleum buildings, probably in a mixed classical and pharaonic style, some topped with pyramids. They stood in the Sêma (Sôma) of the royal palace at Alexandria. Ptolemy VI built a common mausoleum for Alexander and the early Ptolemies; the precise location of the cemetery is unknown but is supposed to be in the quarter of the Nabi Danial mosque.

Decoration. The oldest example of decoration in a royal tomb is the depiction of the starry sky on the ceiling of Djoser's burial chamber. Tomb walls were inscribed from the time of King Unas on with the Pyramid Texts, covering the walls of the entrance passage, antechamber, and burial chamber (tombs of Unas, Tety, Pepy I, Merenre, Pepy II, and Ibi). The royal tombs of the Middle Kingdom all seem to be uninscribed; the texts may have been transferred onto the wooden coffins.

When decoration reappears in the eighteenth dynasty, the program has changed. All tombs from Thutmose I to Ramesses XI are decorated with religious texts and scenes, at first only painted, but from Horemheb on in relief. The decoration and text mainly address the extension of the king's life and rule in the netherworld. From relatively simple inscriptions in tombs from Thutmose I to III, which are restricted to the *Book of That Which Is in The Underworld,* more complicated textual programs develop, including the *Book of Gates* and *Book of Caverns.* The old motive of ensuring the king's participation in the daily journey of the sun is further developed, culminating in the hope that the king might not only travel through the realm of the underworld but also rise with the sun (the Solar Litany near the tomb entrance). Impressive are the huge astronomical representations in the vaults of Ramessid sarcophagus halls. The increasing decorative program of the New Kingdom seems to be one reason for the extension of the tomb chambers and walls.

Spiritual Tombs or Cenotaphs. The more spiritual, otherworldly aspects of the king also needed an architectural stage, and this was provided in the form of an empty tomb, or cenotaph. Such secondary royal tombs are known from all periods, but we do not understand with which property of the king they were associated, mainly because they are not inscribed or decorated. The difficulty is exacerbated by the fact that some kings have not just one but several cenotaphs. Were they meant for the *ka*, or for the official aspect of kingship, or were they intended as a god's tomb—perhaps Osiris or Sokar? Some are probably canopic burials; others may simply be abandoned tomb projects. Because the cenotaph is associated with the divine aspects of the king, it has almost no parallel in private tomb architecture. Following is a list of known cenotaphs of the Old Kingdom:

Djoser
1. Stepped Mastaba at Saqqara
2. South tomb at Saqqara

Sneferu
1. Pyramid of Meidum
2. Secondary Pyramid of Meidum
3. Bent Pyramid of Dahshur north tomb
4. Bent Pyramid at Dahshur western tomb
5. Secondary pyramid at Bent Pyramid
6. Pyramid of Seila

Khufu
1. Lower chamber of Giza Pyramid (?)

2. Middle chamber of Giza Pyramid (?)
3. Secondary pyramid at Giza

Khafre
1. Lower chamber of Giza Pyramid (?)
2. Secondary pyramid south of Giza Pyramid

Menkaure
1. Upper chamber of Giza Pyramid (?)
2. Secondary pyramid south of Giza Pyramid

All succeeding kings of the Old Kingdom have only one burial crypt and a smaller, secondary pyramid at the southeastern corner of the main pyramid, which certainly are symbolic tombs, because their chambers are too small for a regular coffin or burial. The last secondary pyramid is that of Senwosret I at el-Lisht.

Some royal tombs of the Middle Kingdom also show other installations for symbolic burials of unknown purpose. In the chamber of the Bab el-Hosan of Nebhepetre Mentuhotep at Deir el-Bahri, an empty coffin and a seated statue of the king colored black (as Osiris?) and wearing *sed*-festival dress were found (Egyptian Museum, Cairo, JE 36195). Senwosret III built a subsidiary tomb in the northeast of his pyramid at Dahshur. His main achievement was, however, his cenotaph at Abydos, comprising four different tomb sections. Finally, Amenemhet III apparently had a "south tomb" inside his Dahshur pyramid, in addition to numerous other chambers of unknown purpose.

Cenotaphs were not necessarily empty. They might incorporate a sarcophagus, as well as grave goods or a statue of the king (e.g., Mentuhotep), or perhaps a royal *ka*-statue (as for King Hor at Dahshur; Egyptian Museum, Cairo, JE 30948).

The royal tombs of the New Kingdom seem to have contained installations for a subsidiary burial. From Thutmose III on, an upper antechamber of the burial crypt develops into a separate tomb. During the nineteenth dynasty, royal tombs clearly show an independent upper tomb with a pillared chamber that did not, however, have a sarcophagus of its own. A staircase at its side leads into the real crypt at a lower level. Kings Ahmose and Sety I, following the prototype of Senwosret III, built enormous cenotaphs—or rather, Osiris tombs—at Abydos. The royal tombs of later periods no longer contain cenotaph-like features.

Cult Installations at Royal Tombs. The double nature of the king is also reflected in the two different types of postmortem ceremonies carried out at the royal tombs relating to pyramid temples. From Sneferu on, buildings for these cults were erected in the pyramid enclosure, starting with modest stone buildings set against the east side of the pyramid (Meidum, Dahshur) and later developing into huge temples (Giza, Abusir, Saqqara). The divine aspect of the king is treated in the same way as that of the "real" gods. The king receives a statue cult similar to that of the gods; the earliest identifiable is located in the so-called valley temple of the Bent Pyramid. A much larger valley and pyramid temple was built for Khafre, dominated by huge installations for a royal statue cult. Simpler versions of this statue temple developed into the front part of the standard pyramid temples of the later Old Kingdom.

The second, inner part of the pyramid temple derives from a different source. With the gradual diminishing of

divine powers and qualities at the end of the fourth dynasty, the dead king became a more human entity in need of the assistance of his surviving subjects. This resulted in a royal mortuary cult with features similar to those of private practice. From the time of Shepseskaf and Userkaf, offering halls for this mortuary cult were included in the pyramid temples of the fifth and sixth dynasties, and later in those of the twelfth. The last examples of this type of pyramid temple were built for Senwosret I at el-Lisht and Amenemhet II at Dahshur. A smaller secondary offering chapel was built in the center of the north side of the pyramids, covering the pyramid entrance. It might have originated in the secondary false door niche at the northern end of private *mastabas* of the fourth dynasty.

During the Middle Kingdom the old forms were soon emptied of their original significance, and the new situation was met by the creation of a new type of royal cult temple that was separate from the pyramid and its cult. In these sanctuaries, cults of gods probably played a more significant role and served as a kind of support system for the cult of the king. The prototypes of this new cult form are the huge temple south of the pyramid of Senwosret III, and the so-called Labyrinth at the pyramid of Amenemhet III at Hawara.

These royal cult temples of the late twelfth dynasty seem to have developed into the so-called mortuary temples for the kings of the New Kingdom, most of which are situated on the western bank of the Nile at Thebes and are designated "mansions of millions of years." The main cultic feature seems to have been the linking of the cult of Amun-Re with that of the dead king. The temples are marked by a specific architectural program.

The royal tombs of the New Kingdom seem to have been accessible for some cultic activities even after the funeral but do not display specific installations for that purpose. The cult chapels of the kings of the Late Period have disappeared but certainly included provisions for a funerary cult.   *Dieter Arnold*

Private Tombs

Both royal and private tombs in ancient Egypt shared the ideal prototype of a sepulchre with two distinct elements, the below ground closed burial chamber (the substructure) and the above ground offering place (the superstructure). Yet only private individuals of the very highest status could afford fully fledged examples of both. For most of Egyptian history, the execution of both elements differed between those provided for kings and those for others. Behind that

A Ptolemaic "temple-tomb" at Tuna el-Gebel (Courtesy Aidan Dodson)

division was the divine status of the king, one who was regarded as taking his place alongside his fellow deities in death, in contrast to the private person, who would in some form continue to enjoy in the afterlife his or her mode of life on earth.

Thus, while the offering places (mortuary temples) of the pharaohs closely followed in decoration and function the cult-places of the gods, those attached to private tombs were usually adorned with scenes of life on earth, with a view to magically re-creating the terrestrial environment in the hereafter. Some scholars argue that many such vignettes actually hold some ritual significance, particularly those with a view to the rebirth of the dead in the next world though an erotic subtext. Although such implications are quite possible, one should probably see them as secondary developments, during the New Kingdom, overlain on the basic re-creation of the earthly environment and its food-production potentialities. That would also seem to lie behind the models of daily life scenes that are found within the burial chambers of First Intermediate Period and Middle Kingdom tombs.

Apart from the agricultural food-production category of depictions (together with the production of clothing and other items of personal adornment), a number of others were found fairly consistently through time, although there were changes in emphasis during the different historical periods. First, there was the motif of the tomb owner and his family, in particular his wife, who usually shared her spouse's tomb. Sepulchres belonging to nonroyal women were probably those of the unmarried or divorced.

In addition to simple scenes of the owner and family as recipients of offerings, there were sometimes scenes relating to the owner's role in relation to the king, the fundamental relationship in determining a person's status in ancient Egypt. For that reason, in a number of eighteenth-dynasty chapels, relevant office-bearers preserved copies of the statement of "Duties of the Vizier." Officials who had served as tutors of royal children are shown with their charges upon their laps; when viewing such scenes it is important to realize that they may relate to periods of service that were far in their past at the time when the tomb was being decorated: an infant prince, in some cases, was actually the reigning sovereign by the time his image was inscribed upon a wall.

Hunting depictions are frequent from the Old through New Kingdoms, and they fall into four basic types. Three feature the tomb owner: fowling in the marshes on a light papyrus boat; hunting hippopotami in a similar manner; and hunting desert animals. The fourth comprises fishing or fowling by professionals, perhaps under the watchful gaze of the tomb owner. Sports and recreation were also shown; singing and dancing, perhaps in the context of a banquet, were most common, but there are Middle Kingdom examples of wrestling scenes, and others of board gaming, although the popular *senet* (*snt*) certainly had a significance in the struggle to pass to the afterlife.

The appearance of funerary rites in a tomb chapel is not surprising, although in general these avoid the mythological elements, the main motif being the procession of the body and its funerary equipment to the tomb, accompanied by wailing mourners; to this, the ceremony of Opening the Mouth was added in New Kingdom times.

Superstructures. A number of different forms were used in private tombs to incorporate the tomb chapel. All share

the feature of an offering place, centered on a stela, that often took the form of a false door, which acted as the interface between this world and the next. The simplest examples have no more than this, but the most elaborate have whole series of vestibules, corridors, and chambers, often extensively decorated in relief and/or paint with the kinds of vignettes described above.

The offering place and any associated rooms could generally be housed according to one of three basic modes. The first mode is against, or within, a low, rectangular structure of brick or stone, known as a *mastaba;* while regarded as most characteristic of the Archaic Period and Old Kingdom, *mastaba*s are found throughout Egyptian history. The second mode is for rooms to be carved out of the rock, without any appreciable built element (known as a rock-cut tomb); such tombs began in the Old Kingdom, and they are then ubiquitous. The third mode is for the structure to be entirely free-standing, with particularly elaborate examples known as temple-tombs; this approach seems to begin in the Middle Kingdom and became much more frequent in the New Kingdom and later, when it was more widely used in locations that would have previously used the *mastaba* (i.e., in flat areas of desert without significant rock escarpments).

There are, of course, anomalous examples that combined features of more than one of those basic types, while each may be further subdivided into subcategories, which will be described below, where appropriate. The choice of chapel type seems usually to have been determined by the topography or geology of the chosen site.

Tomb Chambers. The actual burial place, or substructure, is always distinct from the chapel, although frequently closely associated with it. Many lower status burials are without any kind of offering place, or they may have a stela built into the entrance to the substructure.

In private tombs, the burial chamber itself is very seldom decorated and, with a handful of exceptions, any adornment is usually restricted to offering lists and/or to extracts from the various funerary books—the collections called the Pyramid Texts, Coffin Texts, *Book of Going Forth by Day* (*Book of the Dead*), *Book of That Which Is in the Underworld* (*Amduat*), and others. (Among the most elaborately decorated of all private burial chambers are those of the nineteenth dynasty necropolis workmen at Deir el-Medina. Tellingly, those were the very men who spent their time preparing the intricately decorated royal places in the Valley of the Kings.) The burial chamber's architecture was generally simple, as was that of any antechambers, although some very elaborate examples are known, particularly in the New Kingdom and Saite period, when a series of galleries and pillared halls could be used.

In parts of Lower Egypt, especially in the Nile Delta, owing to the proximity of groundwater, or in locations elsewhere in which the cutting of deep shafts was otherwise impracticable, substructures were constructed of stone or brick in large but shallow cuttings in the ground surface. Within such, one or more rooms could be constructed of stone or brick, and then covered over with soil. In the former case, flat stone roofs could be employed, but in most brick structures a vaulted roof was frequently used (known as a vaulted tomb).

The ideal form of substructure, however, was cut into the rock (rock-cut), approached by either a vertical shaft (a pit-tomb) or a sloping gallery (a corridor-tomb). In most private tombs, the substructure lay below, or in close

association with, the chapel. In certain cases, however, it could be separated from it by some very considerable distance, good examples existing in the New Kingdom, when a very favored individual could be granted burial near the king's tomb, in the Valley of the Kings. In such an event, the chapel continued to be located on the other side of the Theban cliffs, alongside those of the owner's peers.

Early Dynastic Period. The first tombs differed little from those of late Predynastic times, being brick-lined cuttings in the desert gravel, roofed in wood and topped by little more than a sandy mound. During the first dynasty, however, substructures become more elaborate, more deeply cut, with greater subdivision and the addition of an access stairway. *Mastaba* superstructures, initially containing store-chambers, and with elaborately paneled outer surfaces, are found from the very beginning of the dynasty. Very large examples, excavated between 1935 and 1956 by W. B. Emery, are known at Saqqara and were formerly regarded as belonging to kings; however, their private nature was clearly demonstrated by Barry Kemp in the mid-1960s ("The First Dynasty Royal Cemetery" *Antiquity* 41 [1967], 22–32), although the debate continues in some circles.

During the second dynasty, *mastabas* became solid, sometimes losing their paneling decoration to more closely resemble the plain brick benches that gave such tombs that Arabic appellation. Belowground, tomb chambers are frequently to be found tunnelled deeply into the bedrock, approached by stairways, rather than being built in open cuttings. Such substructures are sometimes quite elaborate. Chapels, where identifiable, seem restricted to stelae inserted in the back of a niche at the southern end of the eastern wall of the *mastaba*, opposite the break in any enclosure wall.

Old Kingdom. Third-dynasty tombs represented a further development of the immediately preceding types. Most notable was the expansion of the chapel, which was cut into the core of the *mastaba* and was frequently in cruciform shape. It may also be more intimately connected with the adjacent enclosure wall, producing a corridor parallel to the face of the *mastaba*. In the tomb of Hesyre at Saqqara, the chapel was decorated both in paint and by the insertion of relief-carved wooden panels.

During the fourth dynasty, the first stone-built *mastabas* appeared. Paneling was by then restricted to the chapel areas. The principal offering place continued to be at the southern end of the eastern wall, but a second one, generally belonging to the wife, was sometimes made at the northern end. As time went by, the size and decoration of the offering place increased in size, penetrating deeper into the core of the *mastaba*, in some cases incorporating an open courtyard. The most elaborate of all *mastaba* chapels is that of Mereruka (c.2360 BCE) at Saqqara, which has nearly thirty rooms that occupy most of the *mastaba*'s ground area.

An important element of most chapels was the *serdab*, a term derived from the Arabic word for "cellar." This was a room, usually near the stela, in which lay one or more statues of the deceased and his family—in some cases running into the tens. The only communication between the *serdab* and the outside world was one or two small apertures, through which the statues could "see" out or be reached by incense burned outside in the chapel.

From the fourth dynasty onward, most substructures were approached by vertical shafts beginning on the roof of the *mastaba* and penetrating deep into the bedrock, although in some (e.g., the tombs of Tiye at Saqqara and Ptahshepses at Abusir) the burial chamber was directly below the chapel floor, with access via a shallow sloping ramp. A number of tombs of the sixth dynasty had their burial chambers decorated with offering lists, arranged in the same way that such catalogs were placed on the interior of contemporary coffins and sarcophagi. A number of similarly decorated chambers have been found at Delta sites, for example at Tell Basta, where they were constructed in pits excavated only a little way below the surface. Stone sarcophagi are found in very many of the private tombs of the Old Kingdom, and in the succeeding Middle Kingdom, but the use of stone for the outer mortuary container was less frequent in other periods. The entrance to fourth dynasty burial chambers sometimes accommodated a so-called reserve head, a stone portrait of the deceased that seems to have been intended to replace the real head if it was damaged or destroyed.

While the *mastaba* remained the standard for cemeteries lying on the desert plain, such as Giza and Saqqara, rock-cut chapels were employed on the edge of escarpments at both sites, their form and decoration similar to what may be seen within contemporary *mastabas*. Farther south, in the Nile Valley, the number of major private tombs increased as the period continued and were often built at sites unsuitable for *mastabas*. The rock-cut chapels in those areas tended to use plans symmetrical about their main axis and, as such, provide prototypes for examples in later periods.

First Intermediate Period and Middle Kingdom. Around the royal cemeteries of Lower Egypt, principally at el-Lisht and Dahshur, most private tombs took the form of *mastabas*. Others were built at Abydos and at other Middle Egyptian sites. As is the case with most Middle Kingdom sepulchres, their substructure designs varied considerably, with both shaft and corridor entries. Certain tombs incorporated features aimed at improving the security of the substructure, including large sliding portcullisblocks and shafts arranged above corridors to shower a plunderer with large volumes of sand. The *mastaba* of Senwosret-ankh at el-Lisht had its substructure decorated with extracts from Old Kingdom Pyramid Texts.

At Western Thebes, beginning with the eleventh dynasty, the *saff*-type of rock-cut chapel is first found, with a very wide portico supported by rock-cut pillars, behind which a passage leads toward the offering place. Early examples open off the sunken courtyards of the tombs of kings Antef I, II, and III at el-Tarif; the later ones occupy high locations on the Sheikh Abd el-Qurna hill.

In the late First Intermediate Period/early Middle Kingdom a considerable devolution of power occurred for the provinces; hence there were built a number of very rich necropolises. The rock-cut tomb chapels had fairly standardized plans, although some had added structures on their exteriors (for example, at Qau el-Kebir, where some of the largest of all were created). Those high-status sepulchres were accompanied by large fields of middle-status burials, usually comprising simple shaft tombs without superstructures. The best recorded such site is Beni Hasan, where more than four hundred shafts, containing some one thousand burials, were opened by John Garstang from 1902 to 1904.

A series of governmental reforms carried out by Senwosret III, which concentrated far more power—and hence high-status individuals—at the national capital, resulted in a major reduction in the number of large private tombs built away from the royal necropolis after his reign. Aside from those directly adjacent to the royal pyramids, few significant private tombs of the late twelfth and thirteenth dynasties have been recorded.

Second Intermediate Period. Very few tombs of the end of the thirteenth and the seventeenth dynasties have been properly excavated, but those known at Thebes seem to have comprised little more than a small cavity in the rock, into which the coffin and a small quantity of funerary equipment were inserted. More substantial tombs may begin again in the late seventeenth dynasty, but are difficult to distinguish from those of the early eighteenth.

New Kingdom. Until the middle of the eighteenth dynasty, almost all known high-status tombs were rock-cut chapels at Western Thebes, with the exception of a few at Elkab and certain other southern locations. Earlier Theban chapels may have been reused Middle Kingdom structures; most follow the same T-shaped pattern, with a wide, but shallow, forehall or portico, and a passage leading back to the offering place. Most early tombs were placed high up on the cliffs of the Sheikh Abd el-Qurna hill, to provide an imposing site. Since the rock at that elevation is fairly poor in quality, nearly all such chapels were decorated in paint only.

Access to the substructure was usually by means of a vertical shaft within the chapel or just outside, although some of the larger tombs had a ramp approach. Certain Sheikh Abd el-Qurna chapel owners, however, had their burial chambers some distance away. For example, Senenmut (c.1482 BCE) had his at Deir el-Bahri, and the vizier Amenemopet (c.1430 BCE) was interred over a kilometer (almost a mile) away in the Valley of the Kings. Some other nobles with Valley of the Kings burial chambers have not yet had their chapels identified (e.g., Yuya and Tjuiu, parents-in-law of Amenhotpe III).

Elaborations of the basic chapel and substructure plans are frequent in the later eighteenth dynasty, principally through the addition of one or more pillared halls. This is particularly the case during the reign of Amenhotpe III, the chapel of Amenemhat-Surero having no fewer than seventy columns supporting its roof. Some of the later tombs were constructed at a very low level on the Theban hillside, to allow access to rock suitable for relief decoration. Only a few burial chambers were decorated, usually with cursive renderings of the *Book of That Which Is in the Underworld (Amduat)*, but that of the mayor Sennefer was given anomalous scenes and a roof painted with grapevines. Very few private tombs of the New Kingdom were equipped with stone sarcophagi, wooden examples being standard. Only under Amenhotpe III was stone once more used with any frequency for private mortuary containers, but then only for anthropoid (human-shaped) coffins, not normally rectangular sarcophagi. The stone anthropoid coffins are particularly characteristic of the first half of the Ramessid period.

During the Amarna period there was a major upheaval in tomb decoration. The private tombs at Amarna itself, together with a handful at Thebes, abandoned the scenes of daily life that were used in private tombs since Old Kingdom times. They were replaced with a decoration centered on the doings of the royal family, who became regarded as the sole interface between this world and that of the divine. In these chapels, the tomb owner was relegated to a subsidiary role; his main substantive depiction

was on the jambs of the outermost doorway. Otherwise, he might be included as a minor figure in some scene or he might be receiving a reward from his monarch. Yet the plans of the tombs remained very similar to earlier tombs.

In the period immediately preceding the accession of Amenhotpe IV, major tombs can once more be easily identified away from Thebes, particularly at Saqqara, where was buried the vizier Aperel. His tomb was built on the escarpment at the edge of the plateau and is a conventional rock-cut chapel, with a fairly elaborate substruc ture reached via shafts. As of 1999, much of the escarpment was still covered by debris to the depth of tens of meters, and a very extensive necropolis may lie farther down, probably including earlier tombs; excavations there are under the direction of Alain Zivie and may yet reveal a hillside of tomb chapels akin to those seen at Thebes.

Following the return to orthodoxy, there was a major use of another area of Saqqara for private tombs, in that case an area of flat desert south of the causeway of Unas, unsuitable for rock-cut chapels. Instead, temple-tombs were constructed, the larger examples fronted by pylons and closely resembling the sanctuaries of gods. Complex substructures were approached by shafts, one example, belonging to the treasurer Maya (c. 1340 BCE), being decorated with painted relief. The superstructures were elaborately decorated with scenes that were geared rather more toward ritual and the career of the deceased than in earlier private tombs. The finest example of all is the tomb of General Horemheb, who later became king. Much smaller freestanding chapels were also built in the area, sometimes comprising but one room. Similar structures were also built at Saqqara near the pyramid of Teti.

A similar shift in decorative themes in the post-Amarna era was noted in the rock-cut tombs at Thebes, and the chapels of the Ramessid period are distinctly different from those of the earlier eighteenth dynasty, with an almost total loss of daily-life depictions. Instead, the deceased were shown adoring deities, while elements of funerary books creep up from the burial chamber to take their place upon the chapel wall. Ground plans, however, continued to follow earlier norms in most cases.

An interesting group of tombs were those built for and by the Royal Necropolis workmen at Deir el-Medina, which have small decorated rock-cut chapels and substructures. They were adorned with small pyramids, which are also a feature of many Ramessid private tombs, in particular those on the Dra Abul Naga hill at Thebes. Pyramids had ceased to be used by kings at the end of the Second Intermediate Period, but were adopted by private individuals during the eighteenth dynasty.

In addition to the cemeteries at Thebes and Saqqara, high-status tombs were found at a variety of sites throughout Egypt, and even in Nubia, between the Amarna period and the end of the New Kingdom. Most are conventional rock-cut tomb chapels, or freestanding chapels, but in the Delta they are brick-vaulted built structures that were erected in cuttings within or near temple precincts; the superstructures are almost universally lost, but they may have been small brick chapels directly above the burial chambers. Good examples are known at Tell Basta, including the tombs of the viceroys of Kush, Hori II and III (c.1200 and c.1160 BCE). Examples of such vaulted tombs are well known at Abydos, where the earliest specimens were dated to the first part of the eigh-teenth dynasty; they can be seen to have been surmounted by *mastaba*s.

Third Intermediate Period. Following the end of the New Kingdom, there were radical changes in private burial practice. Almost all recorded private burials of the period seem to come from Thebes, and tomb chapels of any sort seem to have disappeared altogether, with the exception of one or two usurpations of earlier monuments. Instead, single or multiple burials were placed in superstructureless subterranean chambers, often appropriated from earlier owners in the area of the Asasif. In these, coffins were set without sarcophagi and with the most abbreviated of funerary equipment—occasionally a box of *shawabtis* and, even less regularly, a set of (empty) canopic jars.

The first part of the twenty-second dynasty continued late-twenty-first-dynasty norms. Under Osorkon I, however, there were changes in the forms of coffins and mummy adornment that seem to be coeval (at Thebes) with the center of burial being moved down to the locale of the Ramesseum. Small brick chapels, sometimes lined with sandstone reliefs, were built to surmount tombs in shallow shafts, giving access to chambers little larger than the contained coffin(s). Such coffins were accompanied by limited quantities of funerary equipment, principally dummy canopics and wooden funerary figures. Other twenty-second/third-dynasty burials, under the eighteenth-dynasty temple at Deir el-Bahri, featured the reintroduction of wooden sarcophagi into the private funerary record. Monumental private tombs were reintroduced at Thebes during the twenty-fifth dynasty, but their substantive development occurred in the first part of the next (Saite) dynasty.

In the north of Egypt, the built tomb that was sunk in the ground adjoining a major sanctuary continued in use, although only a few nonroyal Third Intermediate Period examples are known. In particular, a series belonging to high priests of Ptah under Osorkon II and Sheshonq III were found at Memphis by Ahmad Badawi in 1942, stone built and enclosing in one case a silver coffin.

Something akin to the New Kingdom temple tombs were built during the Third Intermediate Period at Abydos, although these examples show a blurring between this type and the ancient *mastaba*. High-status examples are that of Pasebakhanut, son of the twenty-first dynasty high priest of Amun, Menkheperre, and a whole series of those of female members of the twenty-fifth-dynasty royal family. Substructures were often vaulted, directly supporting the superstructure, and were completely integrated with it during the twenty-fifth dynasty, when such tombs were often given multiple chambers and a superstructure with a circular, corbelled chamber, although the exact form of the exterior remains a matter for debate.

Saite Period. While the small-scale burials used at Thebes since the early years of the Third Intermediate Period persisted during the new period, huge rock-cut tombs and tomb chapels were constructed once again both there and in northern cemeteries. The monumental Theban tombs were all set in the area of the Asasif; aboveground, they comprise mud-brick enclosures, fronted by large pylons of the same material. They were centered on a large courtyard, sunk into bedrock, and approached by a sloping passage and vestibule. Chambers and chapels opened from the courtyard, while inner parts of the main chapel were cut in the rock behind it. The con-cealed substructure led on, deep into the rock, and in some cases continued for hundreds of feet before reaching the burial chamber, perhaps ultimately approached by shafts. In the largest of all, that of the lector-priest Petamenophis, the burial chamber was the twenty-second chamber or gallery beyond the courtyard, every room being decorated with funerary texts. [*See* Petamenophis.]

A very similar sepulchre was built at Saqqara for the vizier Bakenrenef, but most of the remainder of the Saite tombs at the site (and also at Abusir) apparently lacked superstructures other than walls; they also incorporated stelae, surrounding an extremely wide, deep, open shaft in the bedrock. The kernel of the tomb was a stone or brick-built burial chamber, in the form of a contemporary wooden sarcophagus, constructed at the bottom of the shaft. Such tombs were designed to be entirely filled with sand after the burial; temporarily closed holes in the chamber roof were opened after the funeral to allow sand in from the main shaft, to engulf the sarcophagus and also to fill a parallel access shaft and connecting vestibules. Access to the burial was thereby impossible, unless almost every grain of sand had been removed from the tomb first (thousands of cubic meters). Certain tombs added to the effect by arranging a series of concentric sand-filled shafts around the perimeter of the tomb. The success of the design has been shown by the number that survived intact; another example, datable to the early twenty-seventh dynasty, was found by Ladislaw Beres at Abusir in 1995 and proved to contain the undisturbed burial of the priest Iufaa.

Other tombs of the period adopted the *mastaba* form. An example would be that of Tjery at Giza, where a symmetrical arrangement of rooms was enclosed.

Late Period. Very little is known of burials of the Persian twenty-seventh dynasty. Some of the shaft tombs at Saqqara and Abusir overlap the dynasty, but otherwise almost nothing can be attributed to the time. A funerary stela of an Egyptian-Persian was found at Saqqara in 1994 but in a reused context that tells little about its place of origin.

To the Egyptian twenty-eighth to thirtieth dynasties may be attributed a quantity of stone and wood coffins and sarcophagi, but only a handful of the tombs from which they come have been studied or published. They include free-standing chapels and *mastaba*s at Abydos, as well as various types of communal burial.

Ptolemaic Period. In early Ptolemaic times, in certain areas, the New Kingdom tradition of having the superstructure in the external form of a miniature contemporary temple was reintroduced; for example, the tomb of Petosiris at Tuna el-Gebel (c.300 BCE). Its inner room was decorated after the manner of a Ramessid royal tomb; burial chambers led off a shaft in the center of the chamber. The outer part was adorned with daily-life scenes, in an unusual composite Egyptian/Greek style. Other tombs at the same site are more akin to houses, with doors, windows, and drain spouts carved onto the exterior. Yet the majority of burials seem to have been in communal tombs, as seems to have been the case for most interments of the Third Intermediate Period.

Besides these Egyptian-derived tombs, purely classical sepulchres were constructed in some areas, in particular at Alexandria and in other then-newly founded cities. A good range of specimens have been excavated since 1987 at Marina el-Alamein, including column tombs of a type well known from Asia Minor, and elaborate hypogea, incorporating a banqueting hall, and burials within loculi and/or communal side chambers. While architectural detail was usually classical, quasi-Hellenized representations of Egyptian deities were sometimes used.

Roman Period. Hellenistic-style tombs were continued after the Roman occupation of the country, as well as more traditional types, with body treatments ranging from purely Egyptian to those with heavy Hellenistic influence. The major innovation of Roman times was the introduction of painted portraits into the mummy wrappings, particularly in the Faiyum region, while three-dimensional heads and hands became far less traditionally Egyptian in appearance.

In some regions, rather than being immediately buried, mummies apparently remained for considerable periods among the living, at home and/or in a public repository, in which homage could be offered to them, perhaps housed in some kind of wooden shrine. Many very finely adorned mummies, with painted portraits or gilded stucco masks, show signs of rough handling over a considerable period of time, and it has been noted that the foot and shin portions of some of them had scribbles and knocks that might be acquired by being left in an accessible place. Many also show weakness in the bandaging around the ankles that could have been caused by years of being propped upright. Groups of bodies would periodically be removed from homes or repositories to the cemetery, where they would be placed in mass burial pits, piled one atop another, presumably reflecting the need to make way for more recent dead among the living.   *Aidan Dodson*

W

WEPWAWET was one of several ancient Egyptian deities who appeared in canine form. Usually depicted as a dog-like creature with a gray or white head, Wepwawet is often incorrectly identified as a wolf, but the animal sacred to Wepwawet was most probably the jackal. The jackal was an appropriate representation for a funerary deity since the ancient Egyptians had no doubt observed the jackal's nocturnal activities in the desert areas used for cemeteries.

Like another jackal god, Anubis, Wepwawet was a funerary deity. He was one of the earliest deities worshiped at the cemetery site of Abydos in southern Egypt. The worship of Wepwawet at Abydos paralleled that of Khentyamentiu, yet another jackal god. When Osiris absorbed the characteristics of Khentyamentiu, Khentyamentiu's role as the lord of the cemetery at Abydos was filled by Anubis. With the rise of solar religion at the beginning of the twelfth dynasty, Osiris's role was limited to the underworld, and the position of local god and lord of the cemetery was in turn filled by Wepwawet, who bears the epithets "Lord of Abydos" and "Lord of the Necropolis." Wepwawet was also the local deity of the thirteenth nome of Upper Egypt, modern Asyut. The ancient Greeks called the town Lycopolis ("Town of the Wolf"), indicating early confusion about the original form of this god. Other cult centers of Wepwawet included Quban, el-Hargarsa, Memphis, and Sais.

Wepwawet's name (*Wp-w3.wt*) means "the opener of the ways" and refers to his role in leading the deceased through the paths of the underworld. In the funerary texts of the New Kingdom, such as the *Book of Going Forth by Day (Book of the Dead)* and the *Book of That Which Is in the Underworld (Amduat)*, Wepwawet's role is that of a protective deity. In royal mythology, the king was accompanied by a fast, dog-like creature while hunting, and the animal was referred to as the "the one with the sharp arrow who is more powerful than the gods." These arrows also "opened the way," and may be connected to the name of this deity.

Wepwawet is often depicted atop a standard. His image is accompanied by a *uraeus* and an enigmatic hieroglyph, which has been described as a representation of the placenta of the king. The standard of Wepwawet was carried preceding the king, and, in the Middle Kingdom, preceding Osiris in processions from the palace or temple. The Narmer mace head shows such a standard in use as early as the first dynasty. This use of the god's image on a standard may indicate his early role as a warlike deity. The jackal god Wepwawet symbolized Upper Egypt in royal processions, while Lower Egypt was represented by the Apis bull of Memphis.

Wepwawet was thought of as the messenger and the champion of royalty. He is called the son of Isis and has close connections with the deities Harendotes and Herishef. Like the god Shu, Wepwawet is referred to as "the one who has separated the sky from the earth."

Jennifer Houser-Wegner

WORKS CITED

Allen James P. "The Cosmology of the Pyramid Texts." In *Religion and Philosophy in Ancient Egypt*, edited by W. K. Simpson, pp. 1–28. Yale Egyptological Studies, 3. New Haven, 1989.

Allen, James P. *Genesis in Egypt: The Philosophy of Ancient Egyptian Creation Accounts*. Yale Egyptological Studies, 2. New Haven, 1988.

Assmann, Jan. *Ägyptische Hymnen und Gebete*. Zurich, 1975.

Assmann, Jan. "Aton." In *Lexikon der Ägyptologie*, 1:526–540. Wiesbaden, 1975.

Assmann, Jan. *Re und Amun*. Freiburg, 1983.

Assmann, Jan. "State and Religion in the New Kingdom." In *Religion and Philosophy in Ancient Egypt*, edited by James P. Allen, et al., pp. 55–88. Yale Egyptological Studies, 3. New Haven, 1989.

Baines, John. *Fecundity Figures*. Warminster, 1985.

Baines, John. "Practical Religion and Piety." *Journal of Egyptian Archaeology* 73 (1987), 79–98.

Barta, Winfried. *Aufbau und Bedeutung der altägyptischen Opferformel*. Münchener Ägyptologische Studien, 3. Munich, 1963.

Barta, Winfried. *Untersuchungen zum Götterkreis der Neunheit*. Münchner Ägyptologische Studien, 28. Munich, 1973.

Begelsbacher-Fischer, Barbara. *Untersuchungen zur Götterwelt des Alten Reiches im Spiegel der Privatgräber der IV. und V. Dynastie*. Orbis biblicus orientalis, 37. Freiburg, 1981.

Bell, Lanny. "Luxor Temple and the Cult of the Royal *Ka*." *Journal of Near Eastern Studies* 44 (1985), 251–294.

Bell, Lanny. "The New Kingdom 'Divine' Temple: The Example of Luxor." In *Temples of Ancient Egypt*, edited by Byron Shafer. Ithaca, 1997.

Blackman, A. M., and H. W. Fairman. "The Consecration of an Egyptian Temple According to the Use of Edfu," *Journal of Egyptian Archaeology* 32 (1946), 75–91.

Borghouts, J.-F. "Magical Texts." In *Textes et langages de l'Egypte pharaonique*, vol. 3, pp. 7–19. Bibliotheque d'Étude, 64 3. Cairo, 1974.

Bradshaw, Joseph. *The Night Sky in Egyptian Mythology*. London, 1997.

Breasted, James H. *The Development of Religion and Thought in Ancient Egypt*. New York, 1912.

Breasted, James H. *The Edwin Smith Surgical Papyrus*. Chicago, 1930.

Brunner, Hellmut. "Eine Dankstele an Upuaut." *Mitteilungen des Deutschen Archäologischen Instituts, Abteilung Kairo* 16 (1958), 5–19; reprinted in Hellmut Brunner, *Das Hörende Herz*, pp. 173–188. Orbis biblicus et orientalis, 80. Freiburg and Göttingen, 1988.

Buck, Adriaan de. *The Egyptian Coffin Texts*. 7 vols. Oriental Institute Publications, 34, 49, 64, 67, 73, 81, and 87. Chicago, 1935–1961.

Derchain, Philippe. "Divinité: Le probleme du divin et des dieux dans l'Egypte ancienne." In *Dictionnaire des mythologies*, edited by Y. Bonnefoy, pp. 324–330. Paris, 1981.

384 Works Cited

Eaton-Krauss, Marianne. "The Earliest Representation of Osiris." *Varia Aegyptiaca* 3 (1987), 233–236.

Englund, Gertie. *Akh—une notion religieuse dans l'Égypte pharaonique.* Uppsala, 1978.

Erman, Adolf. "Zum Namen des Osiris," *Zeitschrift für Ägyptische Sprache und Altertumskunde* 46 (1909), 92–95.

Faulkner, Raymond O. *The Ancient Egyptian Pyramid Texts.* Oxford, 1969. Translation of Sethe's edition.

Fischer, H. G. "The Cult and Nome of the Goddess Bat." *Journal of the American Research Center in Egypt* 1 (1962), 7 ff.

Frankfort, Henri. *Ancient Egyptian Religion.* New York, 1948.

Frankfort, Henri, H. A. Frankfort, John A. Wilson, and Thorkild Jacobsen. *Before Philosophy: The Intellectual Adventure of Ancient Man.* Harmondsworth, 1949; reprint, Chicago, 1977.

Griffiths, J. Gwyn. *Apuleius, Isis-book.* Leiden, 1975.

Griffiths, John Gwyn. *The Conflict of Horus and Seth.* Liverpool, 1960.

Griffiths, J. Gwyn. *The Divine Verdict.* Leiden, 1991.

Griffiths, John Gwyn. *The Origins of Osiris and His Cult.* Studies in the History of Religions, 40. Leiden, 1980.

Griffiths, John Gwyn. *Triads and Trinity.* Cardiff, 1996.

Hawass, Z. "On Royal Funerary Complexes of the Fourth Dynasty." In *Ancient Egyptian Kingship,* edited by D. O'Connor and D. P. Silverman, pp. 221–262. Leiden, 1995.

Helck, Wolfgang. "Osiris." *Paulys Realencyclopä die der Classischen Altertumswissenschaften,* edited by George Wissowa, suppl. 9: 469–514. Stuttgart, 1962.

Helck, Wolfgang. *Untersuchungen zur Thinitenzeit.* Ägyptologische Abhandlungen, 45. Wiesbaden, 1987.

Hornung, Erik. *Ägyptische Unterweltsbücher.* 2d ed. Zürich and Munich, 1984.

Hornung, Erik. *Conceptions of God in Ancient Egypt: The One and the Many.* Translated by John Baines. Ithaca, 1982.

Hornung, Erik. *Das Amduat.* 3 vols. Wiesbaden, 1963–1967.

Hornung, Erik. *Les dieux de l'Égypte: Le Un et le Multiple.* Monaco, 1986.

Jacobssohn, Helmut. *Die dogmatische Stellung des Königs in der Theologie der alten Ägypter.* Ägyptologische Forschungen, 8. Glückstadt, Hamburg, and New York, 1939, 1955. See in particular pages 18 ff.

Jansen-Winkeln, Karl. " 'Horizont' und 'Verklärtheit': Zur Bedeutung der Wurzel *Ꜣḥ.*" *Studien zur Altägyptischen Kultur* 23 (1996), 201–215.

Jenkins, Nancy. *The Boat beneath the Pyramid: King Cheops' Royal Ship.* London, 1980.

Jones, Dilwyn. *Boats.* London, 1995.

Kàkosy, Làzlo'. "Osiris als Gott des Kampfes und der Rache." In *Fragen an die altägyptische Literatur: Studien zum Gedenken an Eberhard Otto,* edited by Jan Assmann, et al., pp. 285–288. Wiesbaden, 1977.

Leclant, Jean. *Histoire de la diffusion des cultes Égptians.* Paris, 1981-1988.

Lesko, Leonard H. "Ancient Egyptian Cosmogonies and Cosmology." In *Religion in Ancient Egypt,* edited by Byron E. Shafer, pp. 88–122. Cornell, 1991.

Lesko, Leonard H., and R. A. Parker. "The Khonsu Cosmogony." In *Pyramid Studies and other essays presented to I. E. S. Edwards,* edited by John Baines, pp. 168–175, pls. 33–37. London, 1988.

Lichtheim, Miriam. *Ancient Egyptian Literature.* 2 vols. Berkeley, 1975, 1976.

Lorton, David. "Considerations on the Origin and Name of Osiris." *Varia Aegyptiaca* 1 (1985), 113–126.

Meeks, D., and C. Favard-Meeks. *Daily Life of the Egyptian Gods.* London, 1997.

Miosi, F. T. "God, Fate and Free Will in Egyptian Wisdom Literature." In *Studies in Honour of Ronald J. Williams,* pp. 69–111. Toronto, 1982.

Mostafa, Maha M. F. *Untersuchungen zu Opfertafeln im Alten Reich.* Hildesheimer ägyptologische Beiträ ge, 17. Hildesheim, 1982.

Münster, Maria. *Untersuchungen zur Göttin Isis vom Alten Reich bis zum Ende des Neuen Reiches.* Münchner Ägyptologische Studien, 11. Berlin, 1968.

Newberry, Percy E. and H. R. Hall. *Catalogue of an Exhibition of Ancient Egyptian art.* London, 1922.

Otto, Eberhard. *Das Ägyptische Mundöffnungsritual.* Ägyptologische Abhandlungen, 3. Wiesbaden, 1960.

Otto, Eberhard. *Beiträge zur Geschichte der Stierkulte in Agypten.* Leipzig, 1923.

Otto, E. *Egyptian Art and the Cults of Osiris and Amon.* London, 1968.

Petrie, W. M. Flinders. *Amulets.* London, 1914.

Prichard, J. B., ed. *Ancient Near Eastern Texts Relating to the Old Testament.* Princeton, 1979.

Ranke, Hermann. *Die Ägyptischen Personennamen.* Vols. 1–2. Glückstadt, 1935 and 1952.

Redford, Donald B. *Akhenaten, the Heretic King.* Princeton, 1984; reprinted, 1987.

Redford, Donald B. *Egypt, Canaan, and Israel in Ancient Times.* Princeton, 1992.

Ricke, Herbert. *Das Kamutef-heiligtum in Karnak.* Beiträge zur ägyptischen Bayforschung und Altertumskunde, 3. Cairo, 1954.

Ritner, Robert K. *The Mechanics of Ancient Egyptian Magical Practice.* Studies in Ancient Oriental Civilizations, 54. Chicago, 1993.

Roth, Ann Macy. "Fingers, Stars, and the Opening of the Mouth: The Nature and Function of the *Nt. rwj* Blades." *Journal of Egyptian Archaeology* 79 (1993), 57–79.

Rundle Clark, R. T. *Myth and Symbol.* London, 1959.

Sadek, Ashraf Iskander. *Popular Religion in Egypt during the New Kingdom.* Hildesheim, 1987.

Sandman, M. *Texts from the Time of Akhenaten.* Brussels, 1938.

Sethe, Kurt, *Altägyptischen Pyramidentexte.* 4 vols. Hildesheim, 1960. (Orig., Leipzig, 1908–1922.)

Sethe, Kurt. *Urgeschichte und älteste Religion der Agypter.* Leipzig, 1930.

Silverman, David P. "Divinity and Deities in Ancient Egypt." In *Religion in Ancient Egypt,* edited by Byron E. Shafer, pp. 7–87. Cornell, 1991.

Silverman, David P. "The Nature of Egyptian Kingship." In *Ancient Egyptian Kingship,* edited by David O'Connor and David Silverman, pp. 79–92. Leiden, 1995.

Silverman, David P. "Textual Criticism in the Coffin Texts." In *Religion and Philosophy in Ancient Egypt,* by James Allen, et al., pp. 29–53. Yale Egyptological Studies, 3. New Haven, 1989.

Smith, Mark. *The Liturgy of Opening the Mouth for Breathing.* Oxford, 1993.

Soden, Wolfram von. *The Ancient Orient.* Translated from the German by D. G. Schley. Grand Rapids, Michigan, 1994.

van den Boorn, G. P. F. *The Duties of the vizier: civil administration in the Early New Kingdom.* London, 1988.

van der Plaas, Dirk. "Voir Dieu: Quelques observations au sujet de la fonction des sens dans le culte et la dévotion de l'Egypte ancienne." *Bulletin de la Société Française d'Égyptologie* 115 (1989), 4–35.

van Walsem, Rene. "The *Pssj-kf:* An investigation of an ancient Egyptian funerary instrument." *Oudheidkundige Mededelingen uit het Rijksmuseum van Oudheden te Leiden* 59 (1978), 193–249.

Velde, Herman te. *Seth, God of Confusion.* 2d ed. Leiden, 1977.

Velde, Herman te. "The Theme of the Separation of Heaven and Earth in Egyptian Mythology." *Studia Aegyptiaca* 3 (1979), 161–167.

Vernus, Pascal. "Le Mythe d'une Mythe: le prétendue noyade d'Osiris." *Studi di Egittologia e di antichita' Puniche* 9 (1991), 19–32.

Wente, Edward F. *Letters from Ancient Egypt.* Society of Biblical Literature Writings from the Ancient World, 1. Atlanta, 1990.

Wilson, John A. "Akh-en-Aton and Nefert-iti." *Journal of Near Eastern Studies* 32 (1973), 235–241.

Wilson, John A. "A Note on the Edwin Smith Surgical Papyrus." *Journal of Near Eastern Studies* 11 (1952), 76–80.

Wilson, John A. "The Theban Tomb (No. 49) of Si-Mut, Called Kiki," *Journal of Near Eastern Studies* 29 (1970), 187–192.

Witt, Reginald Eldred. *Isis in the Graeco-Roman World.* London, 1971; reprint, Baltimore, 1997.

Yoyotte, Jean. "Héra d'Heliopolis et le sacrifice humain." *Annales "d'École*

Pratique des Hautes Etudes, sec. 5, 89 (1980–1981), 29–102.

Zandee, Jan. "Der androgyne Gott in Agypten: Ein Erscheinungsbild des Weltschopfers." *Agypten und Altes Testament* 14 (1988), 240– 278.

Žakbar, Louis V. "The Theocracy of Amarna and the Doctrine of the Ba." *Journal of Near Eastern Studies* 13 (1954), 87–101.

Žakbar, Louis V. *Hymns to Isis in Her Temple at Philae.* Hanover and London, 1988.

FURTHER READING

The following works are suggested to assist the interested reader in furthering his study of Ancient Egyptian Religion. In a field in which archaeological and textual discoveries are ongoing, it is difficult to amass a roster of books that will defy change. The present list has been drawn up with an eye to the most definitive and/or recent treatments of the various areas into which the general topic is broken down. To accomodate the expected new discoveries the reader is advised to make use of such Egyptological journals as KEMET or the JOURNAL OF EGYPTIAN ARCHAEOLOGY.

One further caveat: the list has been shaped in the interests of an English-speaking readership, but this fact should not be misinterpreted. A vast amount of "cutting-edge" research is being done in Europe and the Middle East and reported in French, German, Italian, Spanish, and Arabic. Most of these books and articles are never translated into English.

1. General Works

Assmann, J. *The Search for God in Ancient Egypt*. Cornell University Press, Ithaca, 2001.

Englund, G. (ed) *The Religion of the Ancient Egyptians: Cognitive Structures and Popular Expressions*. Uppsala University, Sweden, 1989.

Frankfort, H. *Kingship and the Gods*. University of Chicago Press, Chicago, 1948.

Hornung, E., *Conceptions of God in Ancient Egypt*. Cornell University Press, Ithaca, 1982.

Hornung, E. *Idea into Image: Essays on Ancient Egyptian Thought*. Princeton University Press, 1992

Morenz, S. *Egyptian Religion*. Cornell University Press, Ithaca, 1973.

Quirke, S. *Ancient Egyptian Religion*. British Museum, London, 1992.

Sadek, A.I. *Popular Religion in Egypt during the New Kingdom*. Hildesheim, Gerstenberg 1987.

Shafer, B. (Ed.). *Religion in Ancient Egypt*. Cornell University Press, Ithaca, 1991.

Trauneckar, C. *The Gods of Ancient Egypt*. Cornell University Press, Ithaca, 2001.

2. Temples and Cult

Arnold, D. *Temples of the Last Pharaohs*. Oxford University Press, New York 1999.

Meeks, D. & C.F. *Daily Life of the Egyptian Gods*. Cornell University Press, Ithaca, 1996.

Quirke, S. (Ed). *The Temple in Ancient Egypt*. British Museum, London, 1997.

Shafer, B. (Ed.) *Temples of Ancient Egypt*. Cornell University Press, Ithaca, 1991.

Wilkinson, R.H. *The Complete Temples of Ancient Egypt*. Thames & Hudson, London, 2000.

3. Concepts of the Afterlife

Andrews, C. *Egyptian Mummies*. British Museum, London, 1988.

D'Auria, S. and others. *Mummies and Magic: The Funerary Arts of Ancient Egypt*. Museum of Fine Arts, Boston, 1993.

Faulkner, R.O. *The Ancient Egyptian Pyramid Texts*. Clarendon Press, Oxford 1969.

Faulkner, R.O. *The Ancient Egyptian Coffin Texts* (3 vols.). Aris & Phillips, Warminster, 1973.

Faulkner, R.O. *The Ancient Egyptian Book of the Dead*. British Museum, London, 1985.

Griffiths, J.G. *The Origins of Osiris and his Cult*. E.J. Brill, Leiden, 1980.

Hornung, E. *The Valley of the Kings: Horizon of Eternity*. Timken, New York, 1990.

Hornung, E. *The Ancient Egyptian Books of the Afterlife*. Cornell University Press, Ithaca, 1999.

Ikram, S., and A. Dodson, *Royal Mummies in the Egyptian Museum*. American University, Cairo, 1997.

Lehner, M. *The Complete Pyramids: Solving the Ancient Mysteries*. Thames & Hudson, London, 1997.

Reeves, N., and R.H. Wilkinson, *The Complete Valley of the Kings: Tombs and Treasures of Egypt's Greatest Pharaohs*. Thames & Hudson, London, 1996.

Spencer, A.J. *Death in Ancient Egypt*. Penguin, Harmondsworth, 1982.

Taylor, J.H. *Death and the Afterlife in Ancient Egypt*. British Museum, London, 2001.

Wilkinson, R.H. *Valley of the Sun Kings*. University of Arizona, Tucson, 1995.

4. Mythology

Allen, J.P. *Genesis in Egypt: The Philosophy of Ancient Egyptian Creation Accounts*. Yale University Press, New Haven, 1988.

Assmann, J. *Egyptian Solar Religion in the New Kingdom*. Kegan Paul, London, 1995.

David, R. *Cult of the Sun: Myth and Magic in Ancient Egypt*. J. M. Dent, London, 1980.

El-Mahdy, C. *Mummies, Myth and Magic*. Thames & Hudson, London, 1989.

Kramer, S.N. (Ed), *Mythologies of the Ancient World*. Doubleday, New York, 1961.

Griffiths, J.G. *Triads and Trinity*. University of Wales Press, Cardiff, 1996.

Lichtheim, M. *Ancient Egyptian Literature*, 3 vols. Berkeley, 1975–80.

Rundle-Clark, R.T. *Myth and Symbol in Ancient Egypt*. Thames & Hudson, London, 1959.

Thomas, A.P. *Egyptian Gods and Myths*. Aylesbury, 1986.

5. Magic

Borghouts, J.F. *Ancient Egyptian Magical Texts*. E.J. Brill, Leiden, 1973.

Pinch, G. *Magic in Ancient Egypt*, University of Texas Press, Austin, 1994.

Ritner, R.K. *The Mechanics of Ancient Egyptian Magical Practice*, University of Chicago Press, Chicago, 1993.

Wilkinson, R.H. *Symbol and Magic in Egyptian Art*. Thames & Hudson, London, 1994.

6. Amulets

Andrews, C. *Amulets of Ancient Egypt*. University of Texas Press, Austin, 1994.

Petrie, W.M.F. *Amulets*. Legan Paul, London, 1914.

7. Monotheism

Hornung, E. *Akhenaten and the Religion of Light*. Cornell University Press, Ithaca, 1999.

Porter, D.N. (Ed). *One God or Many? Concepts of Divinity in the Ancient World*. Casco Bay Assyriological Institute, 2000.

Redford, D.B. *Akhenaten, the Heretic King*. Princeton University Press, 1986.

Shanks, H. *Aspects of Monotheism: How God Is One*. Biblical Archaeological Society, Washington, 1997.

8. Egyptian Religion in the Greco-Roman Period

Bowman, A.K. *Egypt after the Pharaohs*. University of California Press, Berkeley, 1986.

Frankfurter, D. *Religion in Roman Egypt*. Princeton University Press, 1998.

Griffiths, J.G. *Plutarch: De Iside et Osiride*, University of Wales Press, Cardiff, 1970.

Griffiths, J.G. *Apuleius. The Isis Book*, E.J. Brill, Leiden, 1975.

Witt. R.E. *Isis in the Ancient World*. Johns Hopkins University Press, Baltimore, 1997.

9. Historical Orientation

Dodson, A. *Monarchs of the Nile*. Rubicon Press, London, 1995.

Donadoni, S. *The Egyptians*. The University of Chicago Press, 1997.

Grimal, N. *A History of Ancient Egypt*. Blackwells, Oxford, 1992.

Iversen, E. *The Myth of Egypt and Its Hieroglyphs in European Tradition*. Princeton University Press, 1993.

Kemp, B.J. *Ancient Egypt: Anatomy of a Civilization*. Routledge, London, 1989.

Shaw, I. (Ed). *The Oxford History of Ancient Egypt*. Oxford University Press, 2000.

Vercoutter, J. *The Search for Ancient Egypt*. Abrams, New York, 1992.

Index

Contendings of Horus and Seth, 110, 159, 160, 167, 245, 260
Coptic (Christian) era, 28, 164, 192, 218, 229, 277
Corcoran, Lorelei H., 218
coronation, 68. *See also* royal festivals
cosmic egg, 21, 53, 240, 248. *See also* creation myths
cosmogony. *See* Heliopolitan; Hermopolitan cosmogony; Memphite theology
cow goddess. *See* Hathor
craftsmen and god Ptah, 80, 323, 324
creation myths, xi–xii, 98–99, 160, 246–51, 326; cosmic egg, 21, 53, 240, 248; Heliopolitan, 98, 112, 240, 250; Hermopolitan, 98, 240–41, 248, 254; and Khonsu, 186; and kingship, 3; lotus blossom in, 99, 240, 248, 274; and monotheism, 227, 229; word and, 106, 244
creator god: *See* Amun; Atum
crocodiles, 41, 122, 166, 206, 334, 341; and Sobek, 12, 187, 275, 328, 336–37
cult centers, 126, 230, 315, 355; of Horus, 164–65; of Isis, 170, 171; of Maat, 190–91; Osirian, 305; priests in, 320–21; at royal tombs, 371–72; of Seth, 333, 334; for Shu, 336; of Sobek, 337. *See also specific centers*
cult rituals: and Amun-Re, 20–21; daily temple, 20, 64–65, 284, 318; funerary cults, 39–41
cults, 61–91; and deification of mortals, 79, 85–86, 101–2; divine, 81–86; funerary, 8–9, 68–70, 71–73, 76–77; mortuary, 76, 270–71, 272, 319–20; and myth, 239–40; and oracles, 79–80; private, 67, 76–81, 131, 208; and ritual, 63. *See also* animal cults; royal cults
cult statues, 60–61, 294, 318–19; of gods, 161, 196–97, 218–19, 231; and healing, 203, 208; of king, 75, 83, 85, 285, 371; as offerings, 280, 285; as oracles, 79–80, 299–302; in sacred barks, 130, 205, 329–31; and temple ritual, 64–65, 84
curses, 91–93, 193, 212–13. *See also* execration rituals

dance and music, 64, 77, 160, 318
David, Ann Rosalie, 237
dead: and *akh,* 8–9; as demons, 104–5; interactions with, 80, 208, 213–14, 273–74; masks to cover, 216; offerings to, 280, 281. *See also* funerary ritual; judgment of the dead
dead, preservation of. *See* mummification
death: and afterlife, 1, 7, 173; and curse, 91; and fate, 121, 122; in-life, x, xii, xv–xvi; and salvation, 350–51
death cult. *See* mortuary cults
Decan stars, 105
decoration: coffin, 49–51, 56; symbolism of, 342; tomb, 34, 37, 181–82, 210, 369–70, 372–73, 377–78. *See also* iconography
deification, 79, 101–2; of kings, x, 4, 5, 71, 85–86, 98, 102, 108–9
Deir el-Bahri (cult center), 60, 79, 84, 159, 218, 330, 339
Deir el-Medina, 102, 194, 204, 300, 313; personal piety in, 67, 314, 315; tombs at, 36, 80, 135–36, 374, 378
De Iside et Osiride (Plutarch), 167, 170
deities (gods), 95–102; and afterlife, 2; *ba* of, 27; bark shrines of, 66–67; categories of, 99–102; cults of, 81–86; and divinity, 106–12; environment and, 96, 97; human origins of, 305; identity of, 106, 109; kings as, x, 4, 5, 71, 85–86, 98, 102, 108–9; local, ix–x, 80, 99, 100, 109–10, 334; and man, xi, 287; mortals as, 79, 85–86, 101–2; multiplicity of, 106, 108–10, 112, 225, 326; and piety, 311–15; and ritual, 63; skin color of, 60–61; social needs and, 95, 96, 98; unions of, 19, 99; unity of, 227, 344–45. *See also* animal cults; Ennead; Ogdoad; monotheism *and specific god*
De Jong, Aleid, 124
demons, 40, 102–6, 118, 350; and afterlife, 4, 6, 163; of fate, 103–4, 121, 122; and magic, 104, 105; protection from, 92, 102, 207; in underworld, 100, 105–6. *See also* fantastic animals
Dendera (cult center), 159
Derchain, Philippe, 107
desert, ix, 59
Destruction of Humanity, 159
Destruction of Mankind, 245
Dialogue of a Man with His Ba, 28
Die altägyptische Opferliste (Barta), 284
Diodorus Siculus, 235, 236, 306
disorder. *See* chaos (disorder)
divine cults, 81–86. *See also* deities *and specific gods and goddesses*
divine judgment. *See* judgment of the dead
divine plan, 121. *See also* fate
divine power, 19, 103, 192–93, 241, 248
divine unions, 19, 99, 107
divinity, 106–12; concept of, 106–8; and identity, 106, 109; of kings, 108–9; multiplicity of, 106, 108–10, 112, 225, 227, 326; non-transcendence of, 110–11. *See also* deities
Djedefre, king, 361

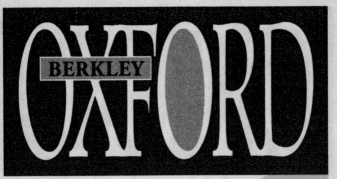